Dictionary of Literary Biography

Dictionary of Literary Biography Documentary Series

1 *Sherwood Anderson, Willa Cather, John Dos Passos, Theodore Dreiser, F. Scott Fitzgerald, Ernest Hemingway, Sinclair Lewis,* edited by Margaret A. Van Antwerp (1982)

2 *James Gould Cozzens, James T. Farrell, William Faulkner, John O'Hara, John Steinbeck, Thomas Wolfe, Richard Wright,* edited by Margaret A. Van Antwerp (1982)

3 *Saul Bellow, Jack Kerouac, Norman Mailer, Vladimir Nabokov, John Updike, Kurt Vonnegut,* edited by Mary Bruccoli (1983)

4 *Tennessee Williams,* edited by Margaret A. Van Antwerp and Sally Johns (1984)

5 *American Transcendentalists,* edited by Joel Myerson (1988)

6 *Hardboiled Mystery Writers: Raymond Chandler, Dashiell Hammett, Ross Mac-* donald, edited by Matthew J. Bruccoli and Richard Layman (1989)

7 *Modern American Poets: James Dickey, Robert Frost, Marianne Moore,* edited by Karen L. Rood (1989)

8 *The Black Aesthetic Movement,* edited by Jeffrey Louis Decker (1991)

9 *American Writers of the Vietnam War: W. D. Ehrhart, Larry Heinemann, Tim O'Brien, Walter McDonald, John M. Del Vecchio,* edited by Ronald Baughman (1991)

10 *The Bloomsbury Group,* edited by Edward L. Bishop (1992)

11 *American Proletarian Culture: The Twenties and The Thirties,* edited by Jon Christian Suggs (1993)

12 *Southern Women Writers: Flannery O'Connor, Katherine Anne Porter, Eudora Welty,* edited by Mary Ann Wimsatt and Karen L. Rood (1994)

13 *The House of Scribner, 1846–1904,* edited by John Delaney (1996)

14 *Four Women Writers for Children, 1868–1918,* edited by Caroline C. Hunt (1996)

15 *American Expatriate Writers: Paris in the Twenties,* edited by Matthew J. Bruccoli and Robert W. Trogdon (1997)

16 *The House of Scribner, 1905–1930,* edited by John Delaney (1997)

17 *The House of Scribner, 1931–1984,* edited by John Delaney (1998)

18 *British Poets of The Great War: Sassoon, Graves, Owen,* edited by Patrick Quinn (1999)

19 *James Dickey,* edited by Judith S. Baughman (1999)

See also DLB 210, 216, 219, 222, 224, 229, 237, 247, 253, 254, 263, 269, 273, 274, 280, 284, 288, 291

Dictionary of Literary Biography Yearbooks

1980 edited by Karen L. Rood, Jean W. Ross, and Richard Ziegfeld (1981)

1981 edited by Karen L. Rood, Jean W. Ross, and Richard Ziegfeld (1982)

1982 edited by Richard Ziegfeld; associate editors: Jean W. Ross and Lynne C. Zeigler (1983)

1983 edited by Mary Bruccoli and Jean W. Ross; associate editor Richard Ziegfeld (1984)

1984 edited by Jean W. Ross (1985)

1985 edited by Jean W. Ross (1986)

1986 edited by J. M. Brook (1987)

1987 edited by J. M. Brook (1988)

1988 edited by J. M. Brook (1989)

1989 edited by J. M. Brook (1990)

1990 edited by James W. Hipp (1991)

1991 edited by James W. Hipp (1992)

1992 edited by James W. Hipp (1993)

1993 edited by James W. Hipp, contributing editor George Garrett (1994)

1994 edited by James W. Hipp, contributing editor George Garrett (1995)

1995 edited by James W. Hipp, contributing editor George Garrett (1996)

1996 edited by Samuel W. Bruce and L. Kay Webster, contributing editor George Garrett (1997)

1997 edited by Matthew J. Bruccoli and George Garrett, with the assistance of L. Kay Webster (1998)

1998 edited by Matthew J. Bruccoli, contributing editor George Garrett, with the assistance of D. W. Thomas (1999)

1999 edited by Matthew J. Bruccoli, contributing editor George Garrett, with the assistance of D. W. Thomas (2000)

2000 edited by Matthew J. Bruccoli, contributing editor George Garrett, with the assistance of George Parker Anderson (2001)

2001 edited by Matthew J. Bruccoli, contributing editor George Garrett, with the assistance of George Parker Anderson (2002)

2002 edited by Matthew J. Bruccoli and George Garrett; George Parker Anderson, Assistant Editor (2003)

Concise Series

Concise Dictionary of American Literary Biography, 7 volumes (1988–1999): *The New Consciousness, 1941–1968; Colonization to the American Renaissance, 1640–1865; Realism, Naturalism, and Local Color, 1865–1917; The Twenties, 1917–1929; The Age of Maturity, 1929–1941; Broadening Views, 1968–1988; Supplement: Modern Writers, 1900–1998.*

Concise Dictionary of British Literary Biography, 8 volumes (1991–1992): *Writers of the Middle Ages and Renaissance Before 1660; Writers of the Restoration and Eighteenth Century, 1660–1789; Writers of the Romantic Period, 1789–1832; Victorian Writers, 1832–1890; Late-Victorian and Edwardian Writers, 1890–1914; Modern Writers, 1914–1945; Writers After World War II, 1945–1960; Contemporary Writers, 1960 to Present.*

Concise Dictionary of World Literary Biography, 4 volumes (1999–2000): *Ancient Greek and Roman Writers; German Writers; African, Caribbean, and Latin American Writers; South Slavic and Eastern European Writers.*

Twenty-First-Century American Novelists

Dictionary of Literary Biography® • Volume Two Hundred Ninety-Two

Twenty-First-Century American Novelists

Edited by
Lisa Abney
Northwestern State University
and
Suzanne Disheroon-Green
Northwestern State University

A Bruccoli Clark Layman Book

GALE®

THOMSON

GALE

Detroit • New York • San Diego • San Francisco • Cleveland • New Haven, Conn. • Waterville, Maine • London • Munich

Dictionary of Literary Biography
Volume 292: Twenty-First-Century American Novelists
Lisa Abney
Suzanne Disheroon-Green

© 2004 by Gale. Gale is an imprint of
The Gale Group, Inc., a division of
Thomson Learning, Inc.

Gale and Design™ and Thomson Learning™
are trademarks used herein under license.

For more information, contact
The Gale Group, Inc.
27500 Drake Rd.
Farmington Hills, MI 48331-3535
Or you can visit our Internet site at
http://www.gale.com

LIBRARY OF CONGRESS CATALOGING-IN-PUBLICATION DATA

Twenty-first-century American novelists / edited by Lisa Abney and Suzanne Disheroon-
    Green.
    p. cm. — (Dictionary of literary biography ; v. 292)
"A Bruccoli Clark Layman Book."
Includes bibliographical references and index.
        ISBN 0-7876-6829-X (hardcover)
        1. American fiction—21st century—Bio-bibliography—Dictionaries.
        2. Novelists, American—21st century—Biography—Dictionaries.
        I. Abney, Lisa, 1964– II. Green, Suzanne Disheroon, 1963– III. Series.

PS380.T89 2004
813'.609'03—dc22   2004000219

Printed in the United States of America
10 9 8 7 6 5 4 3 2 1

Contents

Contents

Plan of the Series

. . . Almost the most prodigious asset of a country, and perhaps its most precious possession, is its native literary product—when that product is fine and noble and enduring.

Mark Twain*

The advisory board, the editors, and the publisher of the *Dictionary of Literary Biography* are joined in endorsing Mark Twain's declaration. The literature of a nation provides an inexhaustible resource of permanent worth. Our purpose is to make literature and its creators better understood and more accessible to students and the reading public, while satisfying the needs of teachers and researchers.

To meet these requirements, *literary biography* has been construed in terms of the author's achievement. The most important thing about a writer is his writing. Accordingly, the entries in *DLB* are career biographies, tracing the development of the author's canon and the evolution of his reputation.

The purpose of *DLB* is not only to provide reliable information in a usable format but also to place the figures in the larger perspective of literary history and to offer appraisals of their accomplishments by qualified scholars.

The publication plan for *DLB* resulted from two years of preparation. The project was proposed to Bruccoli Clark by Frederick G. Ruffner, president of the Gale Research Company, in November 1975. After specimen entries were prepared and typeset, an advisory board was formed to refine the entry format and develop the series rationale. In meetings held during 1976, the publisher, series editors, and advisory board approved the scheme for a comprehensive biographical dictionary of persons who contributed to literature. Editorial work on the first volume began in January 1977, and it was published in 1978. In order to make *DLB* more than a dictionary and to compile volumes that individually have claim to status as literary history, it was decided to organize volumes by topic, period, or

*From an unpublished section of Mark Twain's autobiography, copyright by the Mark Twain Company

genre. Each of these freestanding volumes provides a biographical-bibliographical guide and overview for a particular area of literature. We are convinced that this organization—as opposed to a single alphabet method—constitutes a valuable innovation in the presentation of reference material. The volume plan necessarily requires many decisions for the placement and treatment of authors. Certain figures will be included in separate volumes, but with different entries emphasizing the aspect of his career appropriate to each volume. Ernest Hemingway, for example, is represented in *American Writers in Paris, 1920–1939* by an entry focusing on his expatriate apprenticeship; he is also in *American Novelists, 1910–1945* with an entry surveying his entire career, as well as in *American Short-Story Writers, 1910–1945, Second Series* with an entry concentrating on his short fiction. Each volume includes a cumulative index of the subject authors and articles.

Since 1981 the series has been further augmented by the *DLB Yearbooks*, which update published entries, add new entries to keep the *DLB* current with contemporary activity, and provide articles on literary history. There have also been nineteen *DLB Documentary Series* volumes, which provide illustrations, facsimiles, and biographical and critical source materials for figures, works, or groups judged to have particular interest for students. In 1999 the *Documentary Series* was incorporated into the *DLB* volume numbering system beginning with *DLB 210: Ernest Hemingway.*

We define literature as the *intellectual commerce of a nation:* not merely as belles lettres but as that ample and complex process by which ideas are generated, shaped, and transmitted. *DLB* entries are not limited to "creative writers" but extend to other figures who in their time and in their way influenced the mind of a people. Thus the series encompasses historians, journalists, publishers, book collectors, and screenwriters. By this means readers of *DLB* may be aided to perceive literature not as cult scripture in the keeping of intellectual high priests but firmly positioned at the center of a nation's life.

DLB includes the major writers appropriate to each volume and those standing in the ranks behind them. Scholarly and critical counsel has been sought in deciding which minor figures to include and how full their entries should be. Wherever possible, useful references are made to figures who do not warrant separate entries.

Each *DLB* volume has an expert volume editor responsible for planning the volume, selecting the figures for inclusion, and assigning the entries. Volume editors are also responsible for preparing, where appropriate, appendices surveying the major periodicals and literary and intellectual movements for their volumes, as well as lists of further readings. Work on the series as a whole is coordinated at the Bruccoli Clark Layman editorial center in Columbia, South Carolina, where the editorial staff is responsible for accuracy and utility of the published volumes.

One feature that distinguishes *DLB* is the illustration policy—its concern with the iconography of literature. Just as an author is influenced by his surroundings, so is the reader's understanding of the author enhanced by a knowledge of his environment. Therefore *DLB* volumes include not only drawings, paintings, and photographs of authors, often depicting them at various stages in their careers, but also illustrations of their families and places where they lived. Title pages are regularly reproduced in facsimile along with dust jackets for modern authors. The dust jackets are a special feature of *DLB* because they often document better than anything else the way in which an author's work was perceived in its own time. Specimens of the writers' manuscripts and letters are included when feasible.

Samuel Johnson rightly decreed that "The chief glory of every people arises from its authors." The purpose of the *Dictionary of Literary Biography* is to compile literary history in the surest way available to us—by accurate and comprehensive treatment of the lives and work of those who contributed to it.

The *DLB* Advisory Board

Introduction

As the twentieth century in America drew to a close, a vast array of subjects provided fodder for the literary imagination as readers grew increasingly disenchanted with postmodernist literary techniques. Fin de siècle authors at the dawn of the twenty-first century focus, predictably, on topics that influence their society. Recurring with notable frequency in the writing of contemporary American authors are issues such as the environment, gender roles, terrorism and ecoterrorism, domestic abuse, religion and spirituality, technology, sexual and racial identities, the economy, the family and its construction, drug use and its social ramifications, and a resurgence in regionalism.

Critic Cornel West suggested in *The Columbia History of the American Novel* (1991) that postmodernism encompasses the years between 1945 and 1989. The period following postmodernism demonstrates similarities to previous literary cycles as well as some marked differences; critics have thus far not arrived at a consensus about a proper name for this period, which occupies an important, yet evolving, position in literary history. Regardless of the name applied to this period, American readers in the new millennium have witnessed a proliferation of literary works by marginalized and previously underrepresented voices.

Social critics and academics in the closing years of the twentieth century pondered the nature of writing in the electronic age. Sven Birkerts wrote in *The Gutenberg Elegies* (1994):

> Over the past few decades, in the blink of the eye of history, our culture has begun to go through what promises to be a total metamorphosis. The influx of electronic communications and information processing technologies, abetted by the steady improvement of the microprocessor, has rapidly brought on a condition of critical mass. Suddenly it feels like everything is poised for change; the slower world that many of us grew up with dwindles in the rearview mirror. The stable hierarchies of the printed page—one of the defining norms of that world—are being superseded by the rush of impulses through freshly minted circuits. The displacement of the page by the screen is not yet total (as evidenced by the book you are holding)—it may never be total—but the large-scale tendency in that direction has to be obvious to anyone who looks. The shift is, of course, only part of a larger transformation that embraces whole economies and affects people at every level. But, living as we do in the midst of innumerable affiliated webs, we can say that changes in the immediate sphere of print refer outward to the totality; they map on a smaller scale the riot of societal forces.

Social commentators have uttered concerns similar to those of Birkerts in every generation since the invention of the television and the beginning of the space race. The technologies that have emerged in the years since the dawn of the television age—computers, video games, DVD players, and most notably, the Internet—have given many American citizens and social critics pause. Researchers have documented a gradual decrease in reading skills and literacy rates. Perhaps the most alarming trend of all is the public perception that reading and writing are not necessary nor even desirable skills for well-rounded, educated individuals.

The increase in technology and the decline in public literacy, when coupled with the rise of postmodernist writing in America, led critics and readers to ponder the question of writing and the viability of the publishing industry, since reading as a pastime appeared to be declining. Although readers of the 1970s and 1980s enjoyed the light fare of mysteries and romance novels, book sales indicated that Americans generally did not enjoy postmodernist narrative regardless of scholarly evaluations praising the literary value of these works. As Jean Baudrillard asserted in *The Concise Oxford Dictionary of Literary Terms* (1990), "postmodernity is said to be a culture of fragmentary sensations, eclectic nostalgia, disposable simulacra and promiscuous superficiality, in which the traditionally valued qualities of depth, coherence, meaning, originality, and authenticity are evacuated or dissolved amid the random swirl of empty signals." While mysteries and romance novels captured the attention of popular readers, literary artists and academics alike openly criticized these forms, preferring instead nonlinear narratives, imagistic fiction, intertextuality, and other forms of narrative innovation that became synonymous with postmodernism. The American reading public, however, maintained its allegiance to believable characters in interesting stories and plots, some of which integrated a gritty realism that addressed collective cultural experiences. Such works allowed readers a glimpse into subcultural groups whose voices had hitherto spoken too softly for the general public to hear.

As children who had never been without television came of age, literacy rates in America fell steadily, especially among younger readers. The tendency to prefer the visual image over the printed page was exacerbated by the proliferation of television channels, program choices, and unstructured, unsupervised time available to children. Reading skills became a major social issue in the late 1980s, when First Lady Barbara Bush championed the cause. In response to the growing national awareness of literacy problems, talk-show host Oprah Winfrey began a series of televised reading groups, which met at regular intervals for the sole purpose of discussing current novels. "Oprah's Book Club" drew many Americans back into bookstores and libraries; yet, the literature that they enjoyed was largely determined for them by the media. Any book chosen as an "Oprah book" was guaranteed to become a best-seller, nearly overnight; and while many of the books chosen were worthy examples of literary writing, the American public unquestioningly accepted Winfrey's seal of approval as the mark of good literature. Meanwhile, writers whose subject matter fell outside of the concerns of the daytime viewing public went largely unnoticed, regardless of the quality and value of their works. American readers, to a large extent, allowed their literary tastes to be dictated, reinforcing the influence of television on the literary community and the reading public.

During this period of televised reading lists, and in part because of them, the writing style of American authors shifted away from the postmodern techniques that had alienated many readers. Many contemporary American writers returned to traditional, linear narrative techniques and explored universal themes such as love, community, family, and identity formation. Novels depicting regional life gained popularity, in much the same way as they had at the turn of the nineteenth century. Contemporary readers easily identify with the reemerging tendency toward realism. In some measure, television has influenced this trend through the many reality-based programs. Twenty-first-century "dirty realists" often relate sordid tales based on the everyday lives of ordinary Americans, and their stories cut across all social classes, racial groups, and sexual identities. American fiction has regained its former popularity, in part because it often titillates a public jaded by graphic visual images, and in part because narrative strategies focus upon clearly delineated plots and vividly portrayed characters. Across the United States, the reading-group movement has grown, becoming such a significant phenomenon that publishers such as Ballantine, HarperCollins, and Simon and Schuster regularly include reading-group guides in their popular novels. Because of the popularity of both local and televised reading groups and a greater awareness of literacy in general, reading as a hobby has resurged, as evidenced by the proliferation of megabookstore chains and Internet booksellers. Bookstores have become sprawling establishments featuring physical amenities and cultural events that encourage readers not to conduct business and depart, but to remain, enjoy the environment, and delve into books in a leisurely atmosphere.

Within the context of what is arguably an American reading renaissance, publishers see an increased interest in literary works, especially those of fiction writers, and accordingly have sought to publish such works. The lives and writing of such authors provide the focus of this volume. This book has posed some intriguing challenges in its compilation, for a solid definition of twenty-first-century writing is still in flux, especially given the evolving debate among critics and readers concerning the defining characteristics of the era. The reemerging interests in new treatments of realism and regionalism are indicative of trends in the literary community; yet, the ways in which these interests, which are common to writers and readers alike, will develop is still to be seen. Given the absence of a clear canon of authors who exemplify trends and techniques of twenty-first-century novelists, the editors were faced with the challenge of identifying writers whose body of work provides insight into the novel form as it is evolving. Authors with a solid publication record of work that represents the wide diversity that typifies the American experience provide the foundation for this volume.

Twenty-first-century novelists challenge the limits of what constitutes acceptable topics for public view, describing acts of incest, violence, and selfishness. It is misleading to suggest, however, that contemporary writers are obsessed with the horrifying, for they also demonstrate a sustained interest in the everyday, the ordinary, and the mundane, often raising such occurrences to the level of artistry. Contemporary writers attend to the inner workings of relationships but frequently shift their focus to love that exists outside of the traditional marriage paradigm. Familial relationships provide the basis for a great deal of contemporary fiction, but the focus of such fiction is just as likely to be a single mother with children, or a homosexual in search of a life partner, or urban singles seeking a connection that extends beyond a single night. Writers explore growth, destruction, and blending within families as well as the negotiation that occurs on a daily basis between generations, between members of communities, and between subcultures within the larger framework of the United States.

American readers have continued to maintain an interest in peering into the fictional lives of groups whose experiences they perceive as radically different from their own, as well as in reading stories in which they can mentally point to characters, thinking "I know that person." Works such as those by Andre Dubus III and David Guterson illustrate the American readers' passion for a neorealism that shares similarities with the realism of authors such as Edith Wharton, Henry James, and W. D. Howells. Most contemporary American readers praise the return to linear narrative, expressing their approval with their wallets and their comments, which many freely share in cyberspace and reading groups.

While many readers eschew postmodern techniques, narrative experimentation does occur with some regularity in the works of twenty-first-century writers. The novels of Carl Hiaasen, Mark Leyner, and Jayne Anne Phillips, for example, demonstrate a nihilism and an alienation reminiscent of the modernists as well as an interest in preserving narrative integrity through the use of multiple narrators to describe one event. The American literary community has embraced a diverse group of writers who have been influenced by traditional and popular culture, native culture, historical events of the 1990s and early 2000s, and political ideologies that dominate contemporary discourse in nearly every discipline.

Americans continue to be fascinated with emerging voices. The concerns of twenty-first-century authors transcend class, gender, and ethnic boundaries in order to incorporate the experiences of individuals living in poverty, of individuals living in homes governed by non-Judeo-Christian ideologies, or of individuals who inhabit nontraditional homes. The experiences of all these writers are transformed onto the printed page. Additionally, the subject matter of contemporary American writers crosses hemispheric and continental lines, giving voice to writers from a variety of cultural backgrounds. One defining characteristic of the twenty-first-century American novel is that many writers from other cultures, who just a few generations ago would have been considered foreign writers, are now considered American writers. They relate their experiences in acculturating American life and negotiating the difficult line between the native and adopted lands. Many writers from other cultures write their narratives in English, leaving them to be translated into the author's first language at a later date, as is the case of writers such as Cristina García, Ha Jin, and Sandra Benítez. These first- and second-generation Americans address the

experiences of many Americans whose ancestors were immigrants as well.

The turn of a century has historically fostered paradoxes in behaviors and values, and the impending new millennium intensified these reactions. Some segments of American society publicly endorsed conservative religious, social, and fiscal values while privately engaging in sexual, financial, and political escapades that they would go to extreme measures to conceal. While this type of dissembling is not uncommon in any age, the tendency to cultivate a moral and upright public image at all costs tends to become more widespread near the turn of a century. Perhaps this driving need to give the appearance of moral purity comes from what Elaine Showalter terms the "end of the century disease"; as she explains in her book *Sexual Anarchy* (1990), "the terminal decades of a century suggest to many minds the death throes of a diseased society and the winding down of an exhausted culture." During the 1990s, groups with opposing political and moral ideologies clashed over significant American issues such as the economy, gun control, freedom of speech, racial injustices, abortion rights, education, family values, gay rights, the AIDS crisis, and technology. These issues influenced American artists across the gamut of creative venues, providing an abundance of source material for creative expression. In the visual arts, both avant-garde and traditional exhibits found audiences, and in literature, writing ranged from serious to humorous, macabre to mainstream.

The historical and economic events of the 1990s led to a great many dichotomies. Within the art world, artists struggled to overcome the rising tide of conservatism of the late 1980s and early 1990s. When Robert Mapplethorpe introduced his series of homosexual and erotic photographs, controversy about the exhibit became heated. When the news was released that the exhibit had been funded in part by the National Endowment for the Arts, Americans were drawn into the discussion of what constitutes art and who the arbiters of artistic merit should be. Such battles between liberal artists and conservative social commentators continued intermittently for several years, and in 2001, New York mayor Rudolph Giuliani openly condemned an exhibit at the Brooklyn Museum of Art and formed the Cultural Affairs Advisory Commission to determine the appropriateness of exhibits in city-funded museums. Similarly, Jonathan Larson's play *Rent* (1996), a modern version of *La Bohème* (1896), found loyal audiences despite detractors who claimed that the subjects of drug abuse, homelessness, and AIDS were not suitable for musical theater. Novelists also found themselves in the center of controversy. Bret Easton Ellis's *American Psycho* (1991) was condemned by women's rights organizations for its extreme and shocking depictions of the torture of women; conversely, Alice Hoffman, who presented a young female AIDS victim in *At Risk* (1988), was chided for soft-pedaling the AIDS crisis.

The 1990s were marked by violent episodes on United States soil and overseas that changed the face of American society and the literature that captured that society in print. Challenges to the limits of religious freedom were personified by David Koresh and his followers in Waco, Texas, in 1993. The 1995 bombing of the Oklahoma City Federal Building caused many Americans to reconsider their views on the ways in which the Constitution is interpreted and enforced, as well as what it means to be an American, especially since the terrorist behind the attack was an American. Further violent acts ranged from the Olympic Park bombing in Atlanta in 1996 and the bombings of several abortion clinics to the 2000 attack on the USS *Cole* by Middle Eastern terrorists and the destruction of several United States embassies. These acts of violence led American readers to learn more about other cultures and to embrace the positive qualities of their own culture more overtly. America had only begun to understand the effects of such mass violence; these few isolated incidents did not prepare Americans for the kind of terrorism that occurred on 11 September 2001 with the destruction of the World Trade Center. The swell of patriotism that began with the events of 11 September and the righteous fury that they elicited have only begun to influence the American literary scene. The aftershock of these events will undoubtedly ripple through the literary world for many years into the new century.

These seemingly isolated incidents, prior to 11 September 2001, influenced the American economy only marginally; during the 1990s, the stock market flourished, and the economy thrived. Consumers possessed substantial purchasing power, and American culture reflected this golden age of materialism. Urban writers drew from this prosperity and conspicuous consumerism, a social pattern that also mirrored attitudes and behaviors of the turn of the previous century. Social theorist Thorstein Veblen documented a similar proclivity among newly wealthy Americans on the eve of the twentieth century, and the literary works of the era reflected these excesses. Writers such as Wharton, Edward Bellamy, and Kate Chopin depicted extravagant lifestyles, offering cultural critiques from subtle to comedic to satiric. The other side of this conspicuous consumption, the have-nots who had to toil so that the wealthy might have leisure, was aptly demonstrated by writers such as Frank Norris and Theodore Dreiser. At the dawn of the twenty-first century, writers such as

"brat-packers" Tama Janowitz and Jay McInerney focus upon the "live fast, die young, leave a beautiful corpse" urban lifestyle. Indeed, urban angst plays a role in these novels as the characters struggle to find meaning in an existence filled with endless shiny toys but no substance. Similar stories come from African American writers such as Eric Jerome Dickey, Terry McMillan, and Omar Tyree, who offer an insider's look at upwardly mobile urban life in African American communities.

While such writers as Janowitz, Tyree, and Dickey focus upon the wealthy and upwardly mobile sectors of American society, other contemporary novelists examine the lives of those less fortunate. Despite a thriving 1990s national economy, the 1990s and early 2000s offered little relief to the many Americans still living in poverty. For them, tough choices about whether to buy medicine or food were a part of daily life. Middle-class Americans fared only slightly better, as taxes and insurance costs were high. Average Americans generally did not find themselves with much time to examine their situations; many worked long hours. Literary works reflective of these economic and social elements of American culture include Dubus's *House of Sand and Fog* (1999) and Guterson's *Snow Falling on Cedars* (1994). The works of women writers such as Lorna Landvik, Jodi Picoult, and Connie May Fowler demonstrate the effects of these economic hardships—often induced by bad relationships and unplanned pregnancies—on women of the lower classes.

Along with their depictions of the American economy and its effects on average Americans and their relationships, writers such as Randall Kenan, Christopher Rice, and Michael Cunningham profile gay lifestyles and have garnered acclaim from gay-rights activists for their realistic and honest portrayals. "Queer theory" has become an increasingly influential approach to reading literature, based in part on the more open acceptance of alternate sexual identities, leading to critical and popular discussions about the ways in which such lifestyles are represented in fiction. For the most part, conservative groups in America have ignored this writing, instead condemning the gay lifestyle as a whole. However, the rising popularity of this fictional subgenre is indicative of a shift in American social attitudes and is reflective of an increasing acceptance of difference.

African American writers, too, proliferated during this period. Writers in this tradition frequently demonstrate the double bind that may occur when an individual identifies with more than one region, race, religion, or other characteristic. For example, Kenan, a self-identified gay author, also writes of the African American experience in the South. Gender and class issues temper the works of Tyree, Dickey, and McMillan as well. Their urban novels stand in sharp contrast to predecessors such as Richard Wright's *Native Son* (1940) and Ralph Ellison's *Invisible Man* (1952). These contemporary writers focus less vociferously upon racial and economic rights, though these issues are still present in their texts; instead, they examine personal and familial relationships. Contemporary urban novels trace their origins to the intermediary generation of writers such as Alice Walker and Toni Morrison. The novels of contemporary African American writers incorporate elements of police brutality, the drug culture, and the continuing conflicts between middle-class African Americans, lower-class African Americans, and middle-class whites.

While the genre of the African American urban novel has been expanding, the genre of regional writing has reemerged. David Holman writes in *A Certain Slant of Light: Regionalism and the Form of Southern and Midwestern Fiction* (1995):

> I am interested here in literary and cultural regionalism rather than in the statistical studies of geographers and social scientists. Such studies are concerned with facts; I am concerned with fictions, but only insofar as they help to explain the truths and the fictive nature of regional mythologies. I would maintain that what is not factual, but rather what is believed without prior regard for any facts, is at the core of what informs regional mythologies and the literature of the region.

The works of Michael Lee West, Mark Childress, Rebecca Wells, and Mary McGarry Morris illustrate Holman's belief about regionalism. These authors demonstrate a commitment to the realistic depiction of the many regions of America. The characters that these writers create become entirely identifiable with the region in which they are placed, and the landscapes and cultures are depicted vividly. These writers' diligence in emphasizing the defining characteristics of varied American regional experiences suggests that what was once an American melting pot has perhaps simmered into regions that may share homogeneous characteristics inside their loosely defined borders but in fact highlight the differences.

Regional writing is further distinguished by the issues that residents of particular regions find significant. These variables include social conventions, economic considerations, geography, and racial and ethnic diversity. For example, several contemporary Florida writers have concerned themselves with ecological matters. While Fowler favors writing about relationships, poverty, and domestic violence, her work, like that of Hiaasen, maintains an ecological focus. Hiaasen's *Sick Puppy* (2000) and Fowler's *River of Hidden Dreams* (1994) deal with the ecology of Florida and a variety of envi-

ronmental factors. Louisiana writers such as West and John Dufresne, who maintains close emotional ties to the state despite his residence in Florida, demonstrate the quirky brand of Southernness that exemplifies the Bayou State, focusing on accurate depictions of characteristics such as dialect, social class, and the influence of religion—especially Catholicism—on the residents of the region. Landvik offers a similarly detailed view of the women's subculture found in the Upper Midwest, and despite the apparent similarities between her novel *Patty Jane's House of Curl* (1995) and Robert Harling's drama *Steel Magnolias* (1987)—both works are set in beauty shops and focus on a strong and closely knit cast of women—the regional differences serve to make these two narratives seem as if they derive from divergent literary traditions.

Public interest in women's writing grew steadily throughout the twentieth century, leading women writers to command as much shelf space in bookstores as their male counterparts. Women's novels often chronicle the diverse lifestyles of American women, most often providing realistic representations of their relationships as well as characterizing the ways in which women mentor each other through coming-of-age experiences such as puberty, childbirth, aging, and death. Not all women's fiction focuses exclusively on the more difficult aspects of life, nor do these authors write only about women; Morris, Picoult, and Anita Shreve chronicle distinctive characters in their fiction. The rise of female novelists can be credited to a greater acceptance of women's strength and value as individuals, as Carolyn Heilbrun describes in *Reinventing Womanhood* (1979):

> "Now and then it is possible to observe the moral life in the process of revising itself." The words are Lionel Trilling's; he taught me the process, and its recognition, but would have despaired at the direction I perceived culture to be taking. He understood that what he called the "bitter line of hostility to civilization" runs through modern literature, but he was constitutionally incapable of perceiving the source of that hostility: the revolution of the feminine in life. No more profound revision of the modern life can be contemplated than from this source.

Best-seller lists, book-review sources, and scholarly articles since the 1980s show the ascendancy of female writers.

Along with America's homegrown writers, a variety of international expatriate writers have emerged. Jin and García are examples of writers who focus upon their former countries and the ways in which America functions as a backdrop to their expatriate experiences. In the works of these authors, their native land becomes an important narrative element, often rising to the status of a character in the novel, as do the political climates of their home cultures. In Jin's and García's works, the influence of communism is apparent, leading each author to voice criticism of the communist system. These writers illustrate the conflicts and difficulties inherent in living as expatriate and first-generation American writers.

American novelists will continue to examine social issues with a special interest in the ways in which lifestyles are governed by place, whether regional, urban, or rural, or whether determined by race, class, or gender. The writers covered in this volume focus upon relationships between men and women; the fragmentation and loss of community; the displacement, disenfranchisement, and alienation of individuals and groups; the failure of the American Dream; the loss of humanity; and the rise of a reinvigorated patriotism that has lain dormant since the end of World War II. In many ways, the themes of twenty-first-century American novels reflect those of the modernist period in theme, content, and style more closely than those of the postmodern period, despite the divergence of characterization and plot from modernist techniques. The neorealism that emerges in twenty-first-century novels indicates a general rejection of the postmodernist narrative style in favor of approaches that exhibit greater levels of verisimilitude.

To view contemporary literature as little more than a summary of the issues haunting writers from the early 1900s, however, is to minimize the accomplishments of writers recording the dawning of the twenty-first century. New voices emerged, sometimes gently and sometimes stridently, at the turn of the twentieth century. In the contemporary era, these voices are truly polyphonous, as Mikhail Bakhtin has said in *The Dialogic Imagination* (1981), leading to a more diverse, and paradoxically universal, depiction of the experience of being an American in the twenty-first century.

–Lisa Abney and Suzanne Disheroon-Green

This book was produced by Bruccoli Clark Layman, Inc. Tracy Simmons Bitonti was the in-house editor.

Production manager is Philip B. Dematteis.

Administrative support was provided by Ann M. Cheschi and Carol A. Cheschi.

Accountant is Ann-Marie Holland.

Copyediting supervisor is Sally R. Evans. The copyediting staff includes Phyllis A. Avant, Caryl Brown, Melissa D. Hinton, Philip I. Jones, Rebecca Mayo, Nadirah Rahimah Shabazz, and Nancy E. Smith.

Editorial associates are Jessica Goudeau, Joshua M. Robinson, and William Mathes Straney.

In-house prevetting is by Catherine M. Polit.

Permissions editor and database manager is Amber L. Coker.

Layout and graphics supervisor is Janet E. Hill. The graphics staff includes Zoe R. Cook and Sydney E. Hammock.

Office manager is Kathy Lawler Merlette.

Photography supervisor is Paul Talbot. Photography editor is Scott Nemzek.

Digital photographic copy work was performed by Joseph M. Bruccoli.

Systems manager is Donald Kevin Starling.

Typesetting supervisor is Kathleen M. Flanagan. The typesetting staff includes Patricia Marie Flanagan, Mark J. McEwan, and Pamela D. Norton.

Walter W. Ross is library researcher. He was assisted by the following librarians at the Thomas Cooper Library of the University of South Carolina: Jo Cottingham, interlibrary loan department; circulation department head Tucker Taylor; reference department head Virginia W. Weathers; reference department staff Laurel Baker, Marilee Birchfield, Kate Boyd, Paul Cammarata, Joshua Garris, Gary Geer, Tom Marcil, Rose Marshall, and Sharon Verba; interlibrary loan department head Marna Hostetler; and interlibrary loan staff Bill Fetty, Nelson Rivera, and Cedric Rose.

Twenty-First-Century American Novelists

Dictionary of Literary Biography

Sandra Benítez

(26 March 1941 –)

Suzanne Disheroon-Green
Northwestern State University

BOOKS: *A Place Where the Sea Remembers* (Minneapolis: Coffee House Press, 1993);
Bitter Grounds (New York: Hyperion, 1997);
The Weight of All Things (New York: Hyperion, 2000);
Night of the Radishes (New York: Hyperion, 2004).

The years that novelist Sandra Benítez spent in El Salvador, where her father served as the commercial attaché for the American embassy, shaped her developing social consciousness in ways that she continues to explore in her fiction. Since the appearance of her first book, Benítez has enjoyed sustained critical and popular success because of her lyrical prose, the sweeping nature of her narratives, and her ability to create sympathetic characters. Readers find themselves identifying equally with the idealistic rebel and the idle rich, with the adulteress and the people whom the adulteress betrays. Her unemotional narratives of violence, poverty, and loss transfix audiences, taking them to places that do not exist outside of the television screen in their Westernized reality.

Benítez was born Sandra Jeanette Ables in Washington, D.C., on 26 March 1941. Her parents, James Q. Ables and Marta Benítez Ables, moved often as a result of her father's diplomatic work, living for periods of time in Mexico, El Salvador, and Missouri. She has a sister, Anita. Witnessing the disparity between the privileged and the poverty-stricken as well as the social unrest in El Salvador that ultimately resulted in civil war, Benítez observed firsthand the realities of life on each side of the great financial divide. Her brother-in-law, a surgeon in El Salvador, was kidnapped by guerilla forces during the civil war and was released only after his family paid what Benítez calls a "war tax." She was also privy to the personal, and often

Sandra Benítez (photograph © by Ann Marsden; from the dust jacket for Bitter Grounds, *1997; Richland County Public Library)*

tragic, stories of the women who worked for her family. Poor, illiterate, and separated from their families by their efforts to earn a living, these women would ask Benítez to read and write letters to their families. She internalized their deeply troubling stories, using the lessons of El Salvador's people, culture, and volatile social history to create her fiction.

After returning to the United States permanently as a young adult, Benítez enrolled in college courses at Truman State University, where she earned both a bachelor's degree in education in 1962 and a master's degree in comparative literature in 1974. She married James Kondrick in 1980. Benítez has two sons from a previous marriage: Christopher Title, born in 1963, and Jon Title, born in 1965. Following the completion of her education, Benítez worked at a variety of jobs, including stints as a teacher, Spanish-language translator, and marketing liaison.

Benítez has remarked that she "came to writing late." She published her first novel, *A Place Where the Sea Remembers* (1993), when she was fifty-two years old. Speaking with the writer who prepared an on-line reading guide for her second novel, *Bitter Grounds* (1997), Benítez described the circumstances of her decision to become a writer:

> When I was 39, almost as a lark, I took a class in writing and all the stories that had impressed my heart began to bubble up. I was hooked and began to think of being a writer. I quit my job and began writing full time. It was an especially big risk, I think, because I was writing stories about "the other America," Latino stories that had not yet found a place in mainstream American literature. It took me 13 years to get my first book published.

Benítez left her job translating management-training manuals to begin writing her first novel, a mystery set in Missouri that she has not published because of the harsh rejections it received—a novel that she reports remains hidden under her bed: "a book too dreadful to submit, but a book that taught me the discipline needed to rise and face the page each day. . . . That first book taught me that writing is an act of faith: We must keep faith each day with our writing if we want to call ourselves writers." After the rejections of the first book, she decided to revisit her early years; and after adopting her mother's maiden name as her own surname, Benítez began writing on Latin American themes.

Set in the small village of Santiago, Mexico, *A Place Where the Sea Remembers* is a circular narrative that relates the story of Candelario and Chayo and their wish to have a child. When it appears that their wish will finally come to pass, many lives are affected. The character who unifies the novel is Remedios, the *curandera* (healer), who listens to the secrets that the sea whispers to those who would hear them. Making use of the techniques of fantastical realism that often influence the texts of Hispanic writers, Benítez provides vignettes of the lives of the ordinary folk of Santiago, illuminating what *Kirkus Reviews* (1 July 1993) described as the "lives that tourists glimpse from the outside." The primary narrative, however, focuses on the attempts of Marta, Chayo's sister, to gain supernatural revenge on Candelario and Chayo. After learning that Marta has become pregnant because of a rape, the couple offers to raise Marta's child, believing that they cannot have a baby of their own. When Chayo becomes pregnant unexpectedly, they rescind their offer to Marta, who, by then, is too far into her pregnancy to terminate it, which she had been planning to do before the couple intervened. This sequence of decisions impacts the entire village in various ways, culminating as it begins, with Remedios waiting calmly by the sea to hear its most recent tale—and to recover the body whose life the sea has claimed.

A Place Where the Sea Remembers received warm literary reviews. The winner of the Minnesota Book Award and the Barnes and Noble Discover Award, and a finalist for the *Los Angeles Times* Book Award, Benítez's first novel has been called a "universal tragedy which resounds with a sense of hope" by well-regarded Latino writer Rudolfo Anaya. Cristina Garcia, writing for the *Washington Post Book World* (5 September 1993), praised the book as "profound in its simplicity and rhythm" and described it as "a quietly stunning work." From the beginning, Benítez has been highly regarded for her adept and poetic use of language, leading novelist Chris Bohjalian to remark in *The New York Times Book Review* (31 October 1993) that her "descriptions of people and places are crisp, and the staccato rhythms of her prose are just right for this dark fable of a story."

In her next book, *Bitter Grounds,* Benítez weaves a story of the plantation coffee culture in El Salvador. The novel is set in the context of frequent civil revolts resulting from the dramatic differences in standards of living between the plantation owners, or *patrónes,* and the campesinos, workers whose lives are roughly parallel to those of American sharecroppers. Benítez depicts the oppression of governmental forces, demonstrating the ruthless violence that the landowners use to maintain order.

Bitter Grounds tells the stories of three generations of the upper-class de Contreras family—the wives, daughters, and friends of the owners of Finca La Abundancia—and of the Prieto women who serve them. The story begins with the matriarch, Elena de Contreras, and her best friend, Cecelia de Aragón, who grew up together, married men of similar stature, and lived near each other after their marriages; their friendship is "legendary," leading their parents to describe each as "the

Dust jacket for Benítez's first novel (1993), about a couple in Santiago, Mexico, who rescind their offer to raise the baby that results from the rape of the wife's sister (Richland County Public Library)

shadow of the other" and their husbands to understand that "the bond the women shared was one they must never attempt to weaken." Their relationship is irreparably rent, however, when Elena's wedding ring, a one-of-a-kind bejeweled symbol of her marriage with a man she adores, becomes bewitched. The ring begins to collapse on her finger while she is wearing it, painfully cutting off her circulation. Troubled by the frequent recurrence of this event, seemingly without cause, Elena visits the *curandera* La Verídica—a local woman who is "part healer, part witch"—to find a solution. She hesitatingly follows the directions given to her by the *curandera,* a course of action that leads her to discover that Cecelia, a recent widow, has been engaging in an affair with Elena's husband. Elena cuts Cecelia out of her life from the moment that she discovers the betrayal, although after a time she forgives her husband. Only when Cecelia lies on her deathbed does Elena read the letter that she received from her former

friend after discovering the affair, in which Cecelia begs for Elena to banish her only for a while, and after a set period of time, to forgive her. The women reconcile as Cecelia lies dying of a stroke, ruefully realizing that their friendship was of equal value to Elena's marriage, and that they have wasted nearly half of their lives as a result of Elena's bitterness and anger.

The destruction of Elena and Cecelia's relationship ripples through both of their families. At the time that the betrayal comes to light, Elena's daughter, Magda, is making final preparations for her wedding, and Cecelia's daughter is to be her maid of honor. The wedding plans are abruptly changed, leading to tongue-wagging among the townspeople because of the highly public nature of the marriage of the only daughter of the wealthiest plantation owner in the region. An independent woman, Magda marries Alvaro, a man who is as traditional as he is dominant, but who is also highly sexual and adores her. The couple endures tumultuous periods in their marriage, often as a result of Alvaro's unwillingness to accept Magda's multiple roles as successful businesswoman, wife, and mother.

Alongside the elite planter class are the coffee pickers who live in poverty and find themselves always in danger from the roaming bands of state-sanctioned *Guardias* who question, torture, or kill peasants for suspected communist ties. Many of the poor characters are killed violently—without provocation in some cases, and in others because of their militant ties to the rebellion. Many are pressed into military service by a government that does not protect or respect them. Benítez depicts the campesinos as virtual slaves; even those with the best positions, such as the house workers who are well trusted by the families they serve, are paid barely a living wage and are allowed afternoons off about once per month. Benítez illustrates the familial and romantic relationships that develop among the members of the working class, taking care not to gloss over the oppression and abuse that they tolerate as a way of life.

As each generation unfolds, the dissatisfaction with the class and economic inequities becomes more apparent. The first generation, that which chronologically parallels Elena and Cecelia's peer group, consists of faithful servants who are thankful for their positions in the households of the wealthy because of the relative advantages that they enjoy in such privileged environments. The second generation presents something of a dichotomy, showing the children named after the *patrónes* in some instances, yet striving to attain the same level of social and financial success that they are immersed in as they grow up. The third generation of children, who have witnessed or heard stories of their relatives being brutally murdered in the name of quashing political dissension, seek empowerment and liberation from the oppressive economic situation, resorting to membership in radical rebel groups that espouse violence as the only realistic means of upsetting the rigid class system that reduces them to poverty. The granddaughter of Elena's beloved servant Mercedes—whose husband was killed by the *Guardia* before she went to work for Elena, and who herself is killed by accident when her daughter and her daughter's lover are identified as communist sympathizers—is instrumental in the kidnapping and murder of Magda's husband.

The epic quality of Benítez's narrative derives from the telling of a multigenerational, multiclass story that transcends the mundane illustration of romantic liaisons or fortunes gained and lost. Not only are many of Benítez's characters—on either side of the financial divide—highly sympathetic to the reader, but they demonstrate great courage in the face of danger, harsh working conditions, separation from family members and communities, and the constant threat of civil war. Coexisting with the epic qualities of Benítez's narrative is a natural storytelling voice that is reminiscent of the narrations of Hispanic writers such as Anaya and Julia Alvarez.

Critics were expansive in their praise of *Bitter Grounds,* and, notably, Benítez received accolades from Hispanic writers such as Isabel Allende, who described the book in a dust-jacket blurb as "A story of passion, politics, death, and love. . . . This is the kind of book that fills your dreams for weeks." The winner of the 1998 American Book Award, *Bitter Grounds* was described as "addictive" with "elegant prose" that is "mesmerizing in its simplicity and frankness" (*Publishers Weekly,* 11 August 1997). *Kirkus Reviews* (1 August 1997) called the novel "luminously rendered. . . . A vivid chronicle of strong women facing the challenges of living in sad and violent times."

The Weight of All Things (2000), Benítez's third novel, returns to war-torn El Salvador during the civil war that left more than seventy-five thousand citizens dead and many others destitute, homeless, and oppressed. Told from the perspective of a nine-year-old boy, *The Weight of All Things* begins with a literal weight descending on young Nicolás when his mother, Lety, takes him to the funeral of the slain Archbishop Oscar Romero, whom she and many other believers revere as a saint. A massacre ensues during the funeral services; Lety throws herself on top of her son, using her body as a human shield, and is killed. Nicolás is unable to grasp the reality of his beloved mother's death, and as the mayhem begins to settle, he tries to follow the soldiers who drag her limp body into the cathedral where the funeral was to be held. He finds her shoe after she is dragged away and holds on to it. The shoe comes to symbolize his hope that he will find Lety alive and well.

Benítez shows the civilians of El Salvador suffering mightily during the war, for if they are forced to harbor or assist guerillas and are apprehended by the *Guardia,* they are executed brutally and immediately as communist conspirators. Yet, signing up to serve in the army offers little protection—although soldiers in the *Guardia* do not go hungry, at least—because of the violent and unpredictable attacks continually launched by the rebels. The poor, living in small villages or on privately owned *ranchos,* find themselves caught in the middle, never knowing when their homes will be appropriated by one side or the other, when they will be accused of sympathizing with the wrong element, or when they will be brutally murdered because of the clothing they are wearing or merely because they are in the wrong place at the wrong time.

The boy draws a great deal of strength from his mother's belief in *La Virgen,* the Virgin Mother. She taught Nicolás to believe that *La Virgen* is a second mother to him, and when he finds himself fearful or unsure of what course of action he should take, he has guiding visions of the Blessed Mother. He draws comfort from his visions, in part because the insight that he gains from them consistently saves him from danger and in part because his belief represents a strong connection to his mother.

Nicolás gradually realizes that his mother has indeed been killed, but not until he has experienced the oppression of the civil war firsthand. When he is unable to locate his mother and realizes that he does not know where she works, he decides to return to his family home, where he lives with his grandfather, so that he can find a letter that his mother had sent to him with the address of her employer. In the process of traveling to the *rancho,* he is nearly apprehended by the *Guardia,* finds that the nearby town of El Retorno has been raided and largely destroyed, and discovers that his grandfather has been forced to hide out in a nearby cave on their property to ensure his safety. Tata, as Nicolás calls him, soon finds his *rancho* inundated by members of the resistance, who appropriate it for a field hospital. Nicolás undertakes several journeys to nearby towns with the rebels, and the associations that he builds within their network of supporters later on allow him to escape from captivity and certain death in a military garrison. During this time, he comes to the stark realization that his mother did in fact die in the massacre at the cathedral.

While he is held at the garrison, Nicolás is outwardly docile and hardworking, but he rapidly devises a plan to escape and rejoin Tata, whom he misses terribly. A rebel attack allows him the opportunity to escape just in the nick of time, as the cook has begun to accuse him of giving information to the rebels, which undoubtedly would have led to the boy's immediate execution once the assault on the garrison ended. Nicolás finally finds his way back to Tata, but not before he is shot during his escape. After securing medical attention from a rebel friend, he arrives in El Retorno and reunites with his grandfather. The few remaining members of the small community realize that because the *Guardia* is once again sweeping the area for communist sympathizers, they must flee from their town and devise a plan to sneak across the Honduran border at dawn. Thousands of refugees line the border, and at first light, they are massacred as they attempt to cross the Sumpul River into Honduras; some are killed by Salvadoran *Guardia* troops, and others are shot by Honduran soldiers whose mission is to keep the refugees from flooding into the country with whom El Salvador had only recently been at war.

Nicolás and his grandfather are among the few who escape death in the crossfire from two well-trained

Dust jacket for Benítez's 1997 novel, about conflicts between coffee-plantation owners and impoverished migrant workers in El Salvador (Richland County Public Library)

armies. As the novel ends, Nicolás and Tata find themselves under the protection of his mother's former employer, who cares for the dead woman's family members and sees that Nicolás is well educated. The epilogue of the novel reveals to the reader that Nicolás has gone on to become a well-respected, award-winning doctor, that he has married well and built a safe and satisfying life for himself. Nicolás de la Virgen Veras rises out of the ashes of brutal civil war to become a success, in large part because of his unflinching belief that he is protected by *La Virgen.*

Like her first two novels, *The Weight of All Things* was hailed by critics as another excellent offering from Benítez. One reviewer for *The New York Times* (25 March 2001) called the book a "graceful and unabashedly tender hearted novel" in which "the politics behind the fighting is almost beside the point." A critic for the *Chicago Tribune* (18 March 2001) pointed out that *The Weight of All Things* "ably conveys that intimate texture and an authentic sense of the personal experience of living through war. . . . And Benítez can move easily and flu-

Note: change to new title
the Weight of ALL Things SB.

Basilio, a .38 caliber Smith and Wesson revolver. ~~Amazingly,~~ They seemed to be alone.

But they took no chances. They communicated only by a wave of a hand or the tilting of

a
the head. Their ears strained to catch the sound of a bootfall or the racheting click of a

at each
rifle ~~clip being loaded;~~ their eyes sharpened ~~toward a~~ subtle change of light, an

the clips would already be loaded

a. non sequitur after the preceding phrase

unexpected movement.

Though it was surely close to noon, ~~the day was cloudy and so~~ it was not as
because of the cloud cover.
sweltering as it might have ~~been~~ The sun poked weakly through the trees creating spare

and scattered shadows. Birds flitted about, and a few times their scuttlings caused the
the three   stare   looked directly ahead
~~trio to stop abruptly and look hard.~~ As they walked, Nicolás ~~trained his gaze in front of~~
and   He did not want to see it
~~him,~~ away from ~~the pull of~~ the river flowing at the foot of the hill to his left. ~~He kept his~~
He did not want to see   there
~~gaze from~~ the human cargo its swift waters carried: here an old man or a woman, ~~then~~
and
a child, ~~then,~~ perhaps, its mother floating by.

They had been walking for an hour ~~or so~~ when the ridge turned to the right and
down
dropped ~~down~~ gradually to the river. Nicolás hiked up the backpack resting between his

shoulders. Our Lady at his back was a firm hand keeping him upright. His wound

burned and now he feared that it was bleeding. He could feel the moisture soaking

through his shirt and around the side of his jeans.

asked
"Can we stop for a moment?" he ~~said,~~ breaking the silence they had maintained.

"I think it's safe," Tata said. As he had done many times during the flight, he

passed a hand over his head, then let it drop. He had left his hat behind (as Basilio had),
disturbed
and he was obviously ~~perplexed~~ by its absence.

"Tata, see if I'm bleeding." Nicolás lifted his shirt. He did not look down. His

used often

Corrected typescript page for Benítez's 2000 novel under its original title. The notes are by Benítez's husband, James Kondrick, and Hyperion editor Leslie Wells (courtesy of the author).

idly from a graphic description of a field amputation to a sensual tribute to the joy of eating a tangerine." *Book Magazine* critic Mimi O'Connor (January 2001) remarked that "While on one level the book traces the brave Nicolas' tragically premature coming-of-age, the novel also delivers, with straightforward and evocative prose, a deeply affecting and startling portrait of a country ravaged by warring factions, and the innocent people caught, quite literally, in the crossfire." Benítez's metaphoric return to El Salvador once again rewarded the author with critical and popular success.

Benítez's fourth novel, *Night of the Radishes* (2004), draws upon the Midwestern side of her bicultural background as well as her family history. The protagonist, Annie Rush, is a thirty-four-year-old Minnesota woman who is happily married with two sons, but who is haunted by loss. Her identical twin sister was killed in an accident when the girls were nine years old; her guilt-ridden father subsequently committed suicide; and her older brother, Hub, ran away. Now, decades later, Annie honors her mother's dying wish and sets out to find Hub. She traces him as far as Oaxaca, Mexico, during the Christmas festivities, which include the Night of the Radishes—an annual competition in which local artisans carve tableaux from giant nonedible radishes. In Oaxaca, Annie is attracted to Joe Cruz, a Berkeley anthology professor dealing with his own losses, who helps her find her brother and come to terms with her past.

In "The Saving Grace of Story," an essay on her official website (http://www.sandrabenitez.com), Benítez reveals that she is also a "twinless-twin": her identical twin sister, Susana, lived only thirty-seven days after their birth. Writing the novel became "a healing journey" for her as she explored issues of survivor's guilt and putting the past to rest. She also discusses on her website how this novel allowed her to bring to her work not only her mother's Latino heritage, which shaped her first three novels, but also her father's Mid-western heritage. She adds, "For as many years as I have left to write, I hope to continue to dip my pen into this bilateral reality."

Initial critical response to *Night of the Radishes* was generally positive. In *Booklist,* GraceAnne A. DeCandido commented, "As comforting and predictable as a box of caramels, Benítez's gentle romance is all about reassurance and wish fulfillment," and she praised the vivid depiction of Oaxaca. A critic for *Kirkus Reviews* called the novel "a nice mix of family drama, exotic settings, mystery, and psychology," while Joanna M. Burkhardt in *Library Journal* considered it "a moving story about loss, guilt, anger, and forgiveness," one that addresses "the human need to tell one's story."

Sandra Benítez represents one of an emerging group of Hispanic American writers who gives voice to the experiences of those who have endured the political struggles and warfare of Central and South America. In the context of family sagas such as she creates in *Bitter Grounds,* Benítez does not stray far from the wrenching political realities of life in Central America. The stories of extended families, as well as the individuals who work for them, are melded to demonstrate the benefits and disadvantages of plantation culture as well as small-town life and the poverty associated with it.

Interview:

"Author Interview: Sandra Benítez, in Her Own Words," *ReadingGroupGuides.com* (2000) <http://www.readinggroupguides.com/guides/bitter_grounds-author.asp#interview>.

References:

Kevin Baxter, "Sandra Benítez: Rediscovering Roots Through her Writing," *Las Mujeres* (28 November 2002) <http://www.lasmujeres.com/sandraBenitez>;

John Habich, "Mother Country," *Las Mujeres* (28 November 2002) <http://www.lasmujeres.com/sandraBenitez>.

Elizabeth Berg

(2 December 1948 –   )

Heather Salter
Northwestern State University

BOOKS: *Family Traditions: Celebrations for Holidays and Everyday* (Pleasantville, N.Y.: Reader's Digest Association, 1992);

Durable Goods (New York: Random House, 1993);

Talk Before Sleep (New York: Random House, 1994);

Range of Motion (New York: Random House, 1995);

The Pull of the Moon (New York: Random House, 1996);

Joy School (New York: Random House, 1997);

What We Keep (New York: Random House, 1998);

Escaping into the Open: The Art of Writing True (New York: HarperCollins, 1999);

Until the Real Thing Comes Along (New York: Random House, 1999);

Open House (New York: Random House, 2000);

Never Change (New York: Pocket Books, 2001);

Ordinary Life (New York: Random House, 2002);

True to Form (New York: Atria, 2002);

Say When (New York: Atria, 2003);

The Art of Mending (New York: Random House, 2004).

SELECTED PERIODICAL PUBLICATIONS–
UNCOLLECTED: "In Praise of the Imperfect Body," *Good Housekeeping,* 225 (July 1997): 58;

"The Late Blooming Gardener," *Good Housekeeping,* 226 (March 1998): 104–105;

"My Mother's Private World," *McCall's,* 125 (June 1998): 100;

"12 Easy Ways to Give Your Kid a Happy Childhood and to Make the Good Times Last," *Parents,* 74 (April 1999): 62;

"What I Never Told My Father," *McCall's,* 126 (June 1999): 116;

"Confessions of a Barbie Lover," *Parents,* 74 (September 1999): 140–142;

"Getting it Write," *Health,* 15 (January/February 2001): 82–89.

Elizabeth Berg writes about the tragedies, joys, and disappointments that women and men endure in their relationships, marriages, and friendships. Her main characters often learn to rely on the strengths of others while discovering their own hidden strengths as they cope with death, loss, betrayal, and heartbreak. Critics agree that Berg deals with these themes in a fresh and realistic manner. While writing her novels, Berg often draws from her own personal struggles.

Berg was born Elizabeth Hoff on 2 December 1948 in St. Paul, Minnesota, to Jeanne and Arthur Hoff. Since her father was a colonel in the U.S. Army, the family moved to an army base in a new city every two to three years. Hoff later returned to St. Paul to attend college at the University of Minnesota after graduating from high school around 1966. She majored in English during her first semester at the university and later switched to the humanities. Then after working as a waitress, a receptionist, an actress, and a singer in a rock-and-roll band, Hoff enrolled at St. Mary's Junior College in Minneapolis. She earned an A.A.S. degree in 1970 and became a critical-care nurse. On 30 March 1974 she married marketing director Howard Berg; the couple moved to Boston and had two children, Julie and Jennifer. (The couple later divorced.) In 1985 Berg resigned from her nursing position to stay home with her young daughters. She wrote an essay about her decision to stay home and entered it in a contest in *Parents* magazine, where it won first place.

Around the same time, she was diagnosed with mycosis fungoids, a rare and often fatal T-cell lymphoma. Berg refused to let the news of her illness put an end to her desire to start a writing career, however. After winning the essay contest, Berg went on to write other articles for *Parents* and similar magazines, including *Family Circle, Redbook,* and *Ladies' Home Journal.* Then in 1992 Berg wrote her first book, *Family Traditions: Celebrations for Holidays and Everyday,* on a work-for-hire basis. The book is a nonfiction work that discusses ways for families to celebrate special occasions.

A year later, Berg published her first novel, *Durable Goods* (1993), which traces the coming of age of the twelve-year-old narrator, Katie, and her fourteen-year-old sister, Diane. The novel is set on an army base in

Elizabeth Berg (photograph by Marion Ettlinger; from the dust jacket for
Say When, *2003; Richland County Public Library)*

Texas during a summer in the 1960s. As the novel opens, the girls have recently lost their mother to cancer. They live with their abusive father, an army officer who treats them as if they were boot-camp recruits. Katie copes with the loss of her mother and the brutality of her father by indulging in her active fantasy life and by writing poetry. She also confides in her best friend, Cherylanne. Berg admits that she drew on her own childhood experiences while writing the novel and that there are some similarities between her father and Katie's. Berg told Don O'Briant in an interview in *The Atlanta Journal-Constitution* (17 April 1997): "My father wasn't as bad as my character, but he was a scary guy. A real disciplinarian."

Durable Goods received largely positive reviews. Critics applauded Berg for evoking strong emotions, for focusing on humor and significant details, and for creating natural dialogues. Diane Seaman in *Booklist* (15 April 1993) remarked that *Durable Goods* is "suffused with humor and admiration for youth's great capacity for love and instinct for truth." The only major problem that reviewers had with the novel is its abruptness. Renee Loth in *The Boston Globe* (14 June 1993) claimed that Berg does not fully develop some of the minor subplots in the novel.

Berg's second novel, *Talk Before Sleep,* published in 1994, is dedicated to women with cancer and focuses on the friendship between Ann, a nurse, and Ruth, who is dying. Berg wrote *Talk Before Sleep* after losing a close friend to breast cancer. In a preface Berg explains that the purpose of her novel is "to demonstrate the strength and salvation of women's friendships" and "to personalize the devastating effects of losing someone to the disease." The novel is also a way for Berg to deal with her own illness. Berg told O'Briant, "All that talk between Ann and Ruth is my dialogue with myself." Throughout most of the novel, Ann looks back on her friendship with Ruth, remembering the ways in which her friend has touched her life. In addition to Ann, three other of Ruth's closest friends surround her to comfort her and give her strength. The friends come to realize that they cannot save her from death, and the novel ends with Ruth's funeral.

Talk Before Sleep is considered Berg's best work. Critics praised Berg's ability to balance humor with painful, sad events. Meg Meir in *The Star Tribune* (18 June 1994) remarked that the novel is "wickedly funny" as well as sad and that the dialogue is "incredibly accurate in revealing what women talk about when they know each other well and are running out of time." For the most part, reviewers were generally positive in their estimations of the work; however, some complained that the tone of the novel is overly sentimental.

Nevertheless, Berg continued her sentimental tone in her next novel, *Range of Motion* (1995), which also deals with personal tragedy and the power of women's friendships. Before the opening of the novel, Lainey's husband, Jay, suffered an accident that left him in a coma: a huge chunk of ice fell from a rooftop and struck him while he was walking down the street. The novel follows Lainey's faithful vigilance at her husband's bedside in a nursing home and back in her own home. Lainey fights for Jay's recovery, copes with her daughters' fears and anxieties, and tries hard to be optimistic. In times of need, she draws her strength from a compassionate nurse named Wanda and from her neighbor Alice. Lainey talks to Jay, and Berg provides Jay's answers, which Lainey cannot hear, in dream-like poetic language. The themes of the novel include coping with unpredictable tragedies, keeping faith, appreciating normal life, and cherishing everyday events.

Range of Motion received mixed and often contradictory reviews. Strong points of the novel are Berg's focus on Lainey's conflicting emotions and her convincing interpretation of family life. Alix Madrigal in *The San Francisco Chronicle* (17 September 1995) called the novel a "luminous, bittersweet, almost mystical meditation on the unexpected, often hidden joys found in the least likely of places." Other critics have claimed that Lainey's attitude is unrealistic at times. Diane Cole in *Newsday* (24 September 1995) noted that "there are times when Lainey's optimism, as admirable as it is, can seem sentimental, if not downright cloying." In spite of the mixed reviews, in 2000 a movie version of *Range of Motion,* with screenplay by Grace McKeaney and starring Rebecca de Mornay, appeared on the Lifetime television network.

Berg's fourth novel, *The Pull of the Moon* (1996), is different from her previous novels because it does not involve a character coping with the loss of a loved one. In this novel, fifty-year-old Nan leaves her husband, Martin, and their eighteen-year-old daughter to reexamine her life, traveling west from her Boston home in her Mercedes. On her journey, Nan picks up hitchhikers and stops to talk to women on their porches, and then writes about her experiences in her letters home to Martin and in her journal entries.

While reviewers agreed that Berg presented a common theme—the unhappy menopausal woman—in a refreshing and interesting way, they disliked Berg's writing strategy. The major complaint was that the letters and journal entries that compose much of the narrative do not fully develop Nan's character. Heller McAlpin suggested in *Newsday* (28 April 1996) that Berg should have overlapped information in the letters and journal entries to present "different angles on the same events." Other critics pointed out that Berg could have made Nan more interesting and recognizable by revealing her ulterior motives.

Joy School (1997) is a sequel to *Durable Goods* and resumes Katie's story a year after the end of that novel. Katie's sister has eloped and is living in Mexico, and Katie and her father are living in Missouri. *Joy School* explores Katie's relationship with her father, her adjustment to a new school, and her obsession with a married man. Katie's father is less harsh in *Joy School,* and he no longer practices corporal punishment, but he is still terrifying. Katie still corresponds with Cherylanne in Texas while also finding new friendships in Missouri: faithful and boring Cynthia; pretty and popular Taylor; heroic Jimmy; and a wise Catholic priest, Father Compton. Katie's most valuable friend is Father Compton; she confides in him, and he tells her that she must be schooled in sorrow before she can fully learn to appreciate joy.

Critics have praised Berg for her insights into the hardships of adolescence in *Joy School*. Comparing the novel to *Talk Before Sleep,* Carole Goldberg in *The Houston Chronicle* (4 May 1997) called the novel a "milder, more minor achievement" and said that "nothing truly dramatic happens" and that the characters sometimes "border on caricature"; yet, Goldberg also admitted that Berg provided accurate and insightful details of teen experiences in the 1960s. Sara Isaac in *The Baltimore Sun* (4 May 1997) said, "Growing up is hurtful, humorous, petty, and very, very serious. Berg has beautifully wrought this stage of life in her witty, warm way." Critics also praised *Joy School* for having a tightly constructed plot, which made the novel both a good sequel and a compelling story, even without the background provided by *Durable Goods.*

What We Keep (1998) continues Berg's theme of familial discord and explores the relationship between a mother and her daughters. In *What We Keep,* Ginny and Sharla's mother deserted them early in their childhoods, and they have not seen her in thirty-five years. Sharla has recently been diagnosed with a potentially fatal illness and wants to meet with her mother. She convinces Ginny to meet with her, too, so Ginny flies from Boston to California to see her mother. While en route to California, Ginny remembers the summer when her mother left and ponders the events leading up to her mother's departure. During the flight, Ginny comes to accept events in her past. The book ends when Ginny meets with her mother and they begin to reach an understanding.

Critics praised Berg's suspense, crisp imagery, and graceful shifts from present to past in *What We Keep*. Susan Kelly in *USA Today* (25 June 1998) remarked that "Berg's tender depiction of a young girl's view of the world is uncanny and gives the story its heart. She captures perfectly what it was like to grow up in the 1950s, presenting it like a long forgotten, but still sharp photograph." Nevertheless, a strong beginning could not save the disappointing conclusion of the novel, according to critics. The reunion is criticized as unrealistic, causing the novel to seem half-finished. Tricia Springstubb in *The Cleveland Plain Dealer* (26 April 1998) stated that "Berg is so good at evoking the innocent idyll of their childhood, she fails to elicit much sympathy for a mother who would willfully destroy it." Reviewers agreed that if Berg had explained the mother's actions more thoroughly, the ending would have seemed more satisfying.

Patty Murphy, the main character of Berg's seventh novel, *Until the Real Thing Comes Along* (1999), desperately wants children but is unable to find a mate because she is in love with her gay best friend, Ethan. During the course of the novel, she gives up on Ethan for a while, accepting a blind date with Ethan's co-worker Mark. However, Patty's affair with Mark is short-lived. After Mark marries her close friend Elaine, Patty convinces Ethan to sire her son and move with her to a different city. At the close of the novel, Patty's mother's illness brings them back to their hometown, and Patty learns to accept Ethan's homosexuality.

While reviewers criticized Berg for developing a plot based on the postfeminist cliché of the ticking biological clock, many also praised her for developing an accurate cast of characters. Nancy Connors in *The Plain Dealer* (25 July 1999) called the characters "well-meaning people trying hard to do right by each other while remaining true to themselves and life with all the sadness and humor that such a struggle entails." However, in addition to the plot cliché, reviewers also criticized the tone of the novel. In the *Chicago Sun-Times* (15 August 1999) Jonathan Yardley described Patty as unsympathetic and selfish, pointing out that "what's meant to come across as her self-mocking humor looks for all the world like sniveling." Several critics concurred that the main character seems pathetic instead of humorous.

Dust jacket for Berg's debut novel (1993), the first in her trilogy about the adolescent Katie Nash (Richland County Public Library)

Berg returned to writing nonfiction in her next book, *Escaping into the Open: The Art of Writing True* (1999). This work is a guide to writing fiction and nonfiction and includes helpful exercises, reviews of workshops and various writers' aids, and interviews with writing instructors, editors, and agents. GraceAnne A. DeCandido in *Booklist* (1 June 1999) said that "Anyone who ever needs to write anything will find bright shards of useful stuff here." Berg has also put her teaching skills to work in a writing workshop at Radcliffe College.

After *Escaping into the Open*, Berg continued writing about painful emotion in *Open House* (2000), a novel about divorce. Samantha's husband, David, has just walked out of their marriage as *Open House* begins. The novel follows Samantha's struggle with loneliness, her determination to survive on her own, and her search for true love. Although her husband suggests that they sell their house and vows that he will help support her and their child, Samantha becomes determined to keep her house and to accept as little as possible from him. She recruits a series of boarders to provide income, and she meets a temporary furniture mover named King when her first boarder moves into her guest room. King, who possesses a degree in astrophysics, convinces Samantha to sign up as a temporary worker. She takes King's advice and finds unexpected satisfaction in handing out quarters at a coin-operated laundry, pulling nails at a construction site, and walking dogs. Samantha and King fall in love, and she becomes comfortable with her new life. At the end of the novel, David decides to come back to her, but she tells him that their relationship is completely over.

Reviewers praised Berg's ability to portray the despair and loneliness of divorce. Rochelle O'Gorman in the *Los Angeles Times* (11 February 2001) reported that "Berg captures the insanity that divorce brings on, balancing the hurt with a wry humor that makes it extremely accessible." In spite of Berg's accuracy and tenderness, critics had a problem with unnecessary events in the story. Margaret Quamme in *The Columbus Dispatch* (17 September 2001) argued that Samantha's decision to take in boarders and perform menial jobs to survive seems highly unlikely since her husband comes from a wealthy family.

Never Change (2001) tells the story of a middle-aged woman named Myra Lipinsky. When the book opens, Myra is a lonely visiting nurse with few close friends. Myra's life changes when she learns that her newest patient is Chip Reardon, her unrequited love from high school. Although she knows that Chip has terminal cancer, Myra tries desperately to nurse him back to health and falls in love with him again in the process. During the course of the novel Chip must accept the fact that he is dying, while Myra struggles with the realization that she cannot rescue him.

Reviewers of *Never Change* noted that Berg's minor characters, especially Myra's patients, are captivating and intriguing. Greg Johnson in the *Atlanta Journal-Constitution* (3 June 2001) elaborated: "Rather than distractions from the main plot, these ancillary characters help to develop the predominate themes of love and loss, dependency and abandonment." However, some reviewers had problems with Myra. Ann Hood, in *The Washington Post* (19 August 2001), claimed that Myra's bizarre personality traits ruin the credibility of her character and the balance of the novel: "for example when we learn that Myra keeps a scrapbook for her dog, it's hard to believe that this is the same articulate, interesting character." Most critics agreed that while the characters are interesting, they sometimes appear to be unrealistic.

Ordinary Life (2002) is a collection of fifteen stories that explore themes of marital malaise, isolation, familial discord, morality, and relationships. In "White Dwarf" Phyllis hopes to reconnect with her husband during a marital retreat. In "Martin's Letter to Nan" Martin from Berg's novel *The Pull of the Moon* responds to his wife's letters. "Catering" consists of a daughter's meditations on her relationship with her sick mother. Critics praised Berg's stories for being sensitive, introspective, and subtle. Karen Campbell in *The Boston Globe* (7 June 2002) said, "Berg's gift as a storyteller lies most powerfully in her ability to find the extraordinary in the ordinary, the remarkable in the everyday." Critics agreed that Berg's stories capture related issues and lessons, but Karen Dukess in *USA Today* (14 March 2002) claimed that presenting similar themes is a shortcoming of the anthology.

In *True to Form* (2002) Berg revisits Katie Nash. Katie has a stepmother now and is looking for summer employment. She secures a job working for the Randolphs, a kind, elderly couple. When she wins a free plane ticket in a radio contest, she flies back to Fort Hood, Texas, and visits her friend Cherylanne, but she soon realizes that they no longer have anything in common. Back in Missouri, Katie attends an upscale school on a scholarship. She learns about betrayal and friendship when she rejects her best friend Cynthia so the girls at her new school will accept her.

True to Form, like the other two Katie novels, was well received by critics. Rosemary Herbert in *The Boston Herald* (24 May 2002) stated that "Katie's commentary—on other teens, adults and about everything from getting sunburned to facing an important betrayal—provides a convincing teen's eye view on growing up in the summer of 1961." The Katie trilogy was on the American Library Association list of the best books of the year.

Berg's thirteenth novel, *Say When* (2003), explores two of her most common themes: adultery and marital discontent. However, this novel differs from most of Berg's previous works because she tells the story from the husband's perspective. Frank Griffin's shy, eccentric wife, Ellen, informs him that she has been having an affair with an auto mechanic and wants a divorce. Hurt and confused, Griffin refuses to move out of the house and makes life unbearable for both of them. During the course of the novel, Griffin engages in a massive amount of soul-searching, survives the terror of midlife dating, finds positive outlets for his emotions, and develops a closer bond with his eight-year-old daughter, Zoe. The turning point of the story occurs when Griffin finally realizes that his indifference toward his wife has made her feel worthless and rejected.

*Dust jacket for Berg's 2000 novel, in which a woman facing divorce finds
both new love and job satisfaction (Richland County Public Library)*

Although a few critics have been disappointed in Ellen's character development, the book has received mostly good reviews. Some critics have even compared the novel to Berg's early successful works, such as *Durable Goods* and *Talk Before Sleep*. Sue Piperman in the *Milwaukee Journal Sentinel* (1 June 2003) called *Say When* "vintage Berg, enlivened with a new twist." Critics also agree that Berg has successfully created a believable, sympathetic male narrator and that her examination of a man's emotions and resolutions is the strongest feature of the novel. Elizabeth Leisure in the *London Free Press* (5 July 2003) asserted, "The book's most tender moments come when Griffin's emotions are bared, as he realizes the ways that he has neglected Ellen's fragile spirit and tries, clumsily and uncertainly, to change." Critics and readers alike have appreciated Berg's efforts in this work to explore and explain the mysteries of the male psyche while presenting themes familiar to her audience.

Berg has received other awards for her novels, including the New England Book Award for fiction in 1997, and several of her works have appeared in Oprah Winfrey's book club. Critics often call Berg the master of soft focus, applauding her ability to present heartbreaking events with tenderness and understanding. She is also able to avoid overwhelming readers with sentimentality. Reviewers and readers often agree that while the main characters of Berg's novels and stories are primarily women, Berg's works have universal appeal.

Interviews:

Michael Harris, "In Brief: Fiction," *Los Angeles Times,* 16 May 1993, p. 6;

Gerald Wade, "Emotions Spur Writer," *Omaha World Herald,* 23 October 1995, p. 31SF;

Don O'Briant, "Literary Therapy," *Atlanta Journal-Constitution,* 17 April 1997, p. E1;

Susan Larson, "Comfort and Joy," *New Orleans Times-Picayune,* 11 May 1997, p. 1;

Gail Cook, "Author, Author, Author!: Berg No Tortured Writer, Finds Her Vocation a Great Joy," *Milwaukee Journal Sentinel,* 4 November 1998, p. 7;

Nancy Gilson, "In Touch: Author's Introspective Tales Often Focus on Relationships," *Columbus Dispatch,* 10 June 2002, p. 8.

Chris Bohjalian

(12 August 1960 –)

Austin Booth
SUNY Buffalo

BOOKS: *A Killing in the Real World* (New York: St. Martin's Press, 1988);

Hangman (New York: Carroll & Graf, 1991);

Past the Bleachers (New York: Carroll & Graf, 1992);

Water Witches (Hanover, N.H.: University Press of New England, 1995);

Midwives (New York: Harmony Books, 1997);

The Law of Similars (New York: Harmony Books, 1999);

Trans-Sister Radio (New York: Harmony Books, 2000);

The Buffalo Soldier (New York: Shaye Areheart Books, 2002);

Idyll Banter: Weekly Excursions to a Very Small Town (New York: Harmony Books, 2003).

Chris Bohjalian characterizes his writing as "domestic dramas. . . . Sometimes that term sounds pejorative, but that's not how I mean it. I write about ordinary people in what I hope are extraordinary circumstances." The people in Bohjalian's novels are confronted with domestic tragedies and professional crises; many of his works focus on the aftermath of dramatic loss. Bohjalian's works explore the ways in which social controversies play themselves out in the domestic arena. His writing covers such controversial topics as midwifery, dowsing (the practice of locating and redirecting underground water sources), homeopathy, and transsexual surgery, and the ways that these topics lead to personal, moral, and ethical dilemmas. Many of the situations in which Bohjalian's characters find themselves are too complex to be easily resolved by the law, professional ethics, or medical protocols—let alone small-town mores. Bohjalian describes his works as "fictional memoirs." His narratives are typically related in the first person (often female) and center around epiphanies and moments of crisis in ordinary lives.

Christopher Aram Bohjalian was born on 12 August 1960 in White Plains, New York, to advertising executive Aram Bohjalian and Annalee Nelson Bohjalian. He has an older brother, Andrew. He studied at Amherst College, was elected to Phi Beta Kappa, and graduated summa cum laude with a B.A. in 1982.

Chris Bohjalian (photograph by Victoria Blewer; from the dust jacket for Water Witches, *1995; Richland County Public Library)*

He married Victoria Blewer, a photographer, on 13 October 1984, and throughout the 1980s he worked as an advertising executive while producing weekly humor columns and book reviews for the *Burlington Free Press* after he and his wife moved from Brooklyn to Vermont. He also contributed fiction and essays to several magazines, including *Reader's Digest, Cosmopolitan,* and *The Boston Globe Magazine.* Bohjalian continues to write a weekly column for the *Sunday Burlington Free Press,* in addition to magazine articles and book reviews. He lives in Lincoln, Vermont, with Blewer and their daughter, Grace.

Bohjalian's first two novels—*A Killing in the Real World* (1988), a mystery, and *Hangman* (1991), a ghost story—are what he calls "apprentice fiction." Although both *A Killing in the Real World* and *Hangman* deal peripherally with families, his third novel, *Past the Bleachers* (1992), establishes domestic fiction as his genre.

Past the Bleachers tells the story of Bill and Harper Parish, who have lost their eight-year-old son to leukemia. Despite his son's death, Bill coaches the local Little League team, and soon he encounters a mysterious, mute boy named Lucky Diamond who appears on his roster. Bill works out his grief over the death of his son through coaching Lucky, and he comes to self-understanding through the discovery of the hidden stories of those around him. As a reviewer for *Publishers Weekly* (23 March 1992) pointed out, Bohjalian does not muddy genuine insights into the intricacies of grief with melodrama; instead, he carefully explicates complex, even contradictory emotions. In *Past the Bleachers* Bohjalian establishes a narrative pattern that runs throughout his fiction: the revelation of stories that lie beneath the apparently docile facade of both small-town and domestic life.

With his fourth novel, *Water Witches* (1995), Bohjalian begins to experiment with descriptions of alternative social practices and the ways in which small communities react to transforming events (in this novel, drought and tensions between environmentalists and ski-resort developers). Janet St. John, in *Booklist* (1 March 1995), applauded Bohjalian's "detailed descriptions of New England settings" and his ability to personalize the conflict between capitalist and environmental agendas. The protagonist, Scottie Winston, is a lawyer who represents the ski-resort industry, which is embroiled in ongoing battles with environmentalists. At the same time, he is surrounded by environmentalists at home. Scottie represents both points of view in the conflict between development and environmental protectionists. When he and his young daughter see three endangered catamounts in an area targeted for ski-resort expansion, Scottie testifies against the ski-resort company for whom he works.

The story of a ski industry in trouble, rampant unemployment, and fragile environmental systems runs parallel with a story of drought and Scottie's family's relation to water. Scottie has married into a family of dowsers, or water witches, who are able to locate and even shift the physical location of underground springs with the use of divining rods. In *Water Witches* dowsing stands for more than the ability to find water: it represents the ability to see what others cannot see, and further, to have faith in the visions or perceptions of others. To be a successful dowser requires faith in the unseen and in the possibility of change. Like his family, Scottie has seen the impossible—a family of catamounts—and, like them, he is redeemed through his

Dust jacket for Bohjalian's 1995 novel, about a lawyer involved in a struggle between the ski-resort industry and environmentalists (Richland County Public Library)

ability to believe in what others see that he cannot. The narrative is a testimony to Scottie's faith in the visions and dowsing abilities of his daughter, Miranda.

Water Witches ends with a postscript by Miranda that testifies to her father's belief in her. *Midwives* (1997) is also a novel about faith in family members, in this case the faith of a daughter in her mother. Like many of Bohjalian's novels, *Midwives* describes a world populated by women. The men in his novels are outnumbered by strong women filling a wide variety of roles: mothers, sisters, daughters, coworkers, in-laws. Bohjalian is well known for his ability to capture female voices in a believable way; in fact, he recalls with pride that more than one reviewer has assumed he is a female writer. (He began publishing as Chris Bohjalian with *Water Witches*, after publishing his first three books as Christopher A. Bohjalian.)

Midwives opens with a memory of Connie, midwife Sibyl Danforth's daughter: "I used the word *vulva*

Dust jacket for Bohjalian's 1997 novel, in which a midwife is accused of involuntary manslaughter when a mother dies during a home birth (Richland County Public Library)

Then as she told me little bits about her life—the sensations of delivering (or "catching") a baby in a bedroom, the wonderful drama that seems to attend almost any birth—I became hooked. Sitting beside me, I realized, was a woman who saw more sobbing men than any other professional I was likely to meet. After all, she was there from the moment a labor began until the baby arrived. She witnessed the absolutely momentous roller-coaster of emotion that seems to accompany every birth.

As Bohjalian investigated the phrase "catching a baby," he interviewed more than sixty midwives, nurse-midwives, and parents, all of whose stories influenced the birth stories related in the novel.

Midwives raises many questions, not only about home birth versus hospital birth but also about institutional authority and professional ethics. The novel is also about a community's need for ethics in general, its need to hold someone, anyone, accountable in the face of the inexplicable. *Midwives* does not, finally, resolve the question of whether Sibyl is responsible for Charlotte Bedford's death; rather, the novel emphasizes the importance of coming to terms with the ambiguities and complexities of assigning responsibility. Indeed, as the reviewer for *Publishers Weekly* (20 January 1997) commented, the novel "manages to present all the participants in this drama . . . as complex, fully realized individuals," without reducing them to simplistic, opposing camps of villains and heroes. Sibyl's final diary entry (which Connie discovers) indicates her own lack of confidence in her judgment the night of Charlotte Bedford's death. Similarly, Connie's choice to become an obstetrician "was neither an indictment of my mother's profession nor a slap at her persecutors." Connie is able to atone for her mother's actions without, finally, pronouncing her guilty.

Sibyl's final diary entry reveals that despite the series of provocative questions the novel raises about home birth and alternative medical practices, the primary focus of *Midwives* is the effects of these controversies on Sibyl, Connie, and their relationship. As Suzanne Berne remarked in *The New York Times Book Review* (4 May 1997), "Connie's story is a coming-of-age tale, in which disturbing incidents awaken a child to the world's complexity and unpredictability." *Midwives* became a best-seller after it was chosen as an Oprah Winfrey book club selection and introduced many new readers to his fiction. Like Bohjalian's other works, *Midwives* is literary fiction that is popular.

The Law of Similars (1999) also tells the story of a strong woman who practices alternative medicine and is surrounded by controversy. Both narratives focus on tragedies that lead the protagonists to self-examination and raise ethical questions about alternative medicine as

as a child the way some kids said butt or penis or puke. It wasn't a swear exactly, but I knew it had an edge to it that could stop adults cold in their tracks." Connie is a typical Bohjalian protagonist: independent, strong willed, on the boundary between the world of conventions and the world of alternatives.

Midwives tells the story of a night in 1981 when Sibyl is trapped by extreme weather at a home birth gone wrong. Believing the mother, Charlotte Bedford, has died of a stroke during labor, Sibyl performs an emergency cesarean to save the baby. Later, the status of the mother at the time of the cesarean is called into question, and Sibyl is accused of involuntary manslaughter. The idea for *Midwives* originated from a comment a midwife made to Bohjalian at a dinner party—she told him that if he and his wife had had their baby at home, he could have "caught" his daughter at her birth. As he recounts in an interview for Random House, the term captured the writer's imagination:

CHAPTER 1

Carly

I was eight when my parents separated, and nine when they actually divorced. That means that for a little more than a decade, I've watched my mom get ready for dates. Sometimes, until I started ninth grade, I'd even keep her company on Saturday afternoons, while she'd take these long, luxurious bubble baths. I'd put the lid down on the toilet and sit there, and we'd talk about school or boys or the guy she was dating.

I stopped joining her in the bathroom in ninth grade for a lot of reasons, but mostly because it had started to seem a little weird ~~to me~~ to be hanging out with her when I was fourteen and she was naked.

But she has always been very comfortable with bodies and sex, and for all I know she wouldn't mind my joining her in the bathroom even now when I'm home from college. For better or worse – and, usually, for better – my mom has always been very comfortable with subjects that give most parents the shivers. ~~really rocks when it comes to bodies and sex.~~ A couple of days before my fifteenth birthday, she took me to the ob to get me fitted for a diaphragm, and told me where in her bedroom she kept the spermicidally lubricated condoms.

8

Corrected typescript page for Bohjalian's novel Trans-Sister Radio *(2000), about a woman who falls in love with a man shortly before his sex-change operation (courtesy of the author)*

well as professional and personal ethics. Both novels, too, are about redemption, not only of the women who practice alternative medicine but also of the narrators who work to protect them. *The Law of Similars,* however, is a distinctive work that creates new narrative energy. *The Law of Similars* depicts the romantic relationship between Leland Fowler, a widowed attorney with a small daughter, and Carissa Lake, a homeopath and psychologist. Carissa treats Leland for a cold that resists traditional prescriptions. She helps Leland to recognize his lack of emotional well-being by making him tell his story; this narrative act may have more to do with his recovery than the remedy she prescribes him. Leland not only is physically cured but also falls in love with Carissa. At the same time, another of Carissa's patients, Richard Emmons, dies while under her care. Carissa is investigated for Richard's death, and Leland helps to protect her from a legal system that would condemn her.

Leland's decision to be, as he puts it, "a full-fledged justice obstructer" in order to save Carissa is finally what emotionally cures him. As a reviewer for *Publishers Weekly* (5 October 1998) pointed out, the focus on Leland's fallibility makes the novel function on a more complex level than a courtroom thriller. Leland's feelings for Carissa and Richard's feelings about his body have been linked since Christmas Eve, when Leland and Carissa first make love at the same time that Richard decides to self-medicate. The "law of similars" is a central dictum of homeopathy: like cures like. Rather than traditional prescriptions that counteract symptoms, homeopathy relies on remedies that cause symptoms in a healthy person; taken in infinitesimal doses, the remedy stimulates the body's own healing processes. Both Richard and Leland respond to the curing power of homeopathy by taking matters into their own hands and self-medicating. For both men, self-medicating represents what they are looking for: a sense that they, rather than forces beyond their control, can dictate their circumstances. Both men are taking risks, extending themselves beyond their comfort zones and taking charge of their environments in attempts to create fuller lives. The dictum of like cures like, then, comes to stand for much more than the body's healing process. It also stands for a more complex result: for Leland, the loss of one woman, Carissa, cures his grief for the loss of another woman, his wife. Leland and Carissa save each other through unexpected means: Leland by breaking his professional ethics, and Carissa by leaving him. Like Bohjalian's other novels, *The Law of Similars* is about characters dealing with the aftermath of tragedy. With this second dose, Leland is cured, enabling him to attempt the salvation of someone he loves.

Bohjalian's next novel, *Trans-Sister Radio* (2000), also examines the effects of a socially controversial topic—transsexuality—on a family. The idea for the book came out of the experience of a friend of Bohjalian's, a woman who fell in love with a man who was planning to have a sex change. That relationship did not last because of the complex issues that were brought up about sex, gender, and sexual preference. In *Trans-Sister Radio* Bohjalian tells the story of a sixth-grade teacher, Allison Banks, who falls in love with a man, Dana Stevens, who is about to undergo sex-reassignment surgery. *Trans-Sister Radio* describes their relationship before, during, and after the surgery, as well as the relationships among Allison, Dana, Allison's former husband (Will), and Allison's teenage daughter (Carly). In preparing to write the novel, Bohjalian undertook a great deal of research, including extensive interviews with pre- and postoperative transsexuals as well as surgeons and other hospital staff who are involved in sexual-reassignment procedures.

Transsexualism draws attention to the socially constructed nature of gender. Bohjalian's novel suggests that gender and sexuality matter more than sex—that masculinity and femininity, heterosexuality and homosexuality, are more important than biological sex. In *Trans-Sister Radio,* however, Bohjalian is not necessarily interested in theories of sex, gender, and sexuality, nor even in the strained relationships between homosexual and transgendered communities. Rather, he is interested in asking what happens to people when transsexualism is introduced into their lives and how a small community reacts to difference. As Bohjalian says in a 2000 interview with Jana Siciliano, "I live in a small town, and one of the dynamics that fascinates me is that they engender both great comfort and great paranoia." The townspeople's understanding of difference allows Bohjalian to explore the before and after, the ways in which knowledge and perception, so much a part of transsexual experience, are crucial to the experience of sex/gender and sexuality for all people.

Like his other books, *Trans-Sister Radio* can be called a fictional memoir, with a first-person narrator telling the story of the moment or event when his or her life changed. In *Trans-Sister Radio* Bohjalian presents four such intersecting stories—the stories of Allison, Dana, Will, and Carly. Surprisingly, however, other than Dana, the characters do not spend much time investigating their own sense of gender, but rather, investigating the nature of love and its relationship to sexuality. Dana comes to represent a love that can transcend sex. *Trans-Sister Radio* asks whether society can get beyond sexual stereotyping and homophobia but does not explore the inevitability of gender as a social category. As Louis Bayard stated in *The New*

York Times Book Review (4 June 2000), "the honest, messy pain of gender dysphoria would be too unsettling for this book, with its cutesy title and perky prose. And a more nuanced heroine might not comport so easily with the countercultural sympathy that, in novels like *Midwives* and *The Law of Similars*, Bohjalian lavishes on people who do things differently from everyone else." Difference in this novel is more than difference in points of view: the novel does expose gender difference as central to one's understanding of the world, yet does not fully explore the effects of calling gender difference into question.

The Buffalo Soldier (2002) also focuses on difference within a small community. Bohjalian states in a 2002 interview with Alden Mudge that originally he had considered writing about a flood that had nearly wiped out his town a few months before, but when he looked at a picture of his daughter's kindergarten class, he changed the focus of the story:

> There were 16 adorable white kids and not a single African American, not a single Asian American, not a single Latino child. There are many things I cherish about Vermont, but its homogeneity is not among them. . . . I thought to myself . . . what must it be like to be different in this environment? That led to the creation of Alfred Benoit, the 10-year-old African-American foster child who is part of the ensemble cast of this novel.

In *The Buffalo Soldier* these two stories—the experience of being different and the cataclysmic effects of nature—come together in a story of tragedy and redemption. Two years after their twin nine-year-old daughters drown in a flood, Laura and Terry Sheldon decide to foster Alfred. As Laura develops a maternal relationship with Alfred, Terry begins a romance with another woman, Phoebe, and the Sheldon family begins to disintegrate. Meanwhile, Alfred develops an extremely close relationship with the Sheldons' neighbors, who have given him a book about Buffalo Soldiers—the U.S. Army's all-black Ninth and Tenth Cavalry units who served on the American frontier in the second half of the nineteenth century. To Alfred, the Buffalo Soldiers come to represent not only heroes within a racist community but also alternative family and community arrangements.

The Buffalo Soldier describes an array of families: the original Sheldon family, Alfred's large number of foster homes, the families of Laura, Terry, and Phoebe, and two potential families: Alfred, Laura, and Terry; and Terry and Phoebe. The novel continuously asks what a family is and what it should be. Each chapter begins with a quotation associated with another family: that of George Rowe, a Buffalo Soldier, a mixed-race (Comanche and African American) family of the early

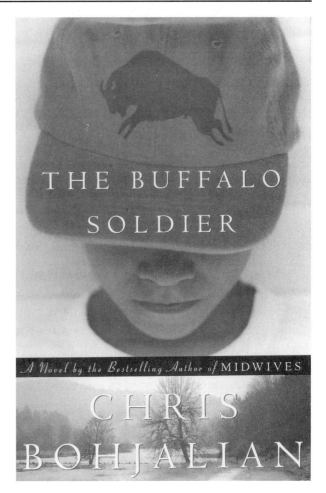

Dust jacket for Bohjalian's 2002 novel, about a white couple whose failing marriage is saved by their black foster son (Richland County Public Library)

twentieth century. Rowe's story of a family forming against all odds is told in contrast to the impending destruction of the Sheldon family. Despite the descriptions of multiple arrangements, however, the novel does not pay the same degree of attention to the complexity of definitions of family (especially mixed-race families) as Bohjalian's earlier works did to definitions of medicine or professional ethics. The novel does not ask how race or family change historically, or how changes in concepts of both race and family are defined or experienced. As Philip Herter commented in *The Boston Herald* (24 March 2002), *The Buffalo Soldier* "raises more questions about race in America than it attempts to answer. . . . the novel ducks the real social issues that give it weight." The fact that Alfred is black is not explored in the novel; that is, the novel does not examine the importance of race as the mark that makes Alfred an outsider.

and Willow attributed the girl's longing to be of assistance to the reality that before yesterday she hadn't seen her parents in almost two weeks.

"Sure there is," John ~~Seton~~ told his niece. "Replant the garden and turn the property into a petting zoo. If you can't beat 'em, feed 'em."

Willow knew it was a family secret that her father had taken up hunting ~~and would have been all too happy to have blasted a buck back in November if he'd had the chance.~~ When he'd started to speak, for a brief second Willow had presumed with no small amount of astonishment that he ~~has~~ was about to admit to the McCulloughs that he owned a gun and bullets and those water-repellent army fatigues. The whole deal. ~~Among the presents Mom had given him for his birthday in May had been a seat pad with these strange pellets inside it that gave off heat when they were compressed. It was supposed to help keep him warm when he sat down on boulders or logs while hunting.~~

She had never told Evelyn about her father's new hobby, and a couple of times when deer had come up in the last twenty-four hours, her mother had looked at her with raised eyebrows, a gentle reminder that Uncle Spencer and his family did not need to know that Dad now owned a gun.

"Anyway, I think we should all have dinner tomorrow night at Gerta's," her father was saying. "See if the busboys are still wearing lederhosen and the waitresses still have to wear those bib-things with the push-up bras. You just loved that costume, didn't you, Sis?"

"We did not wear push-up bras," her Aunt Catherine said.

Corrected typescript page for Bohjalian's forthcoming novel "Before You Know Kindness" (courtesy of the author)

Like the father in *Past the Bleachers,* Terry Sheldon is redeemed by a silent child. The novel ends with Terry and Laura, reconciled, watching Alfred achieve confidence and freedom of movement as he rides a horse: "His whole body starting forward with the big animal in two-point and then–the horse's legs extended before and behind him, a carousel pony but real, the immense thrust invisible to anyone but the boy on the creature's back–he was rising, rising, rising. . . . And aloft." Alfred has saved Terry, as Terry's interest in the boy will allow him back into Laura's life, and through this act, both have committed themselves to each other as family members. Yet, the question of Terry's feelings for both his wife and Phoebe remain unresolved, as do his feelings about Alfred. In *The Buffalo Soldier* the third-person narration also serves to distance the reader rather than help to manage the multiple perspectives that Bohjalian achieved in *Trans-Sister Radio.* According to a reviewer for *The New York Times,* 31 March 2002 "The novel's resolution is puzzling, involving even more piling on of coincidence in a book already overloaded with strange turns of fate." Terry's redemption, finally, is not narrated with the detail that is lavished on his fall from the grace of his family.

In 2003 Bohjalian published *Idyll Banter: Weekly Excursions to a Very Small Town,* a collection of columns from his twelve years of writing for the *Burlington Free Press.* In these pieces he vividly depicts rural life and occupations such as dairy farming and maple sugaring. Although a reviewer for *Publishers Weekly* noted that Bohjalian "occasionally sounds too Pollyannaish as he gushes about smalltown New England life," the critic also added that the author "writes movingly about serious, intimate moments."

Chris Bohjalian is an adept chronicler of married life; of the details of married sex, work, and domestic routines; and of the secrets within relationships that unfold over long periods of time. His characters are not simply affected by the events that surround them; they are transformed by their tenacious perseverance in attempting to decipher the extraordinary circumstances in which they find themselves. Readers are prompted to seek answers beyond simple explanations, with narrative as the means to laying out the ambiguities and complexities of their everyday lives.

Interviews:

Jana Siciliano, *Bookreporter.com* (26 May 2000) <http://www.bookreporter.com/authors/au-bohjalian-christopher.asp>;

Alden Mudge, "Exploring the Trials and Triumphs of an All-American Family," *BookPage.com* (March 2002) <http://www.bookpage.com/0203bp/chris_bohjalian.html>;

A Q & A with Chris Bohjalian <http://www.random-house.com/features/midwives/author.html>.

Larry Brown

(9 July 1951 –)

Jean W. Cash
James Madison University

See also the Brown entry in *DLB 234: American Short-Story Writers Since World War II, Third Series.*

BOOKS: *Facing the Music* (Chapel Hill, N.C.: Algonquin, 1988);

Dirty Work (Chapel Hill, N.C.: Algonquin, 1989);

A Late Start (Chapel Hill, N.C.: Algonquin, 1989);

Big Bad Love (Chapel Hill, N.C.: Algonquin, 1990);

Joe (Chapel Hill, N.C.: Algonquin, 1991; London: Hodder & Stoughton, 1992);

On Fire (Chapel Hill, N.C.: Algonquin, 1993);

Father and Son (Chapel Hill, N.C.: Algonquin, 1996; Ansley, Leicestershire, U.K.: F. A. Thorpe, 1997);

Fay (Chapel Hill, N.C.: Algonquin, 2000; London: Black Swan, 2001);

Billy Ray's Farm: Essays from a Place Called Tula (Chapel Hill, N.C.: Algonquin, 2001);

The Rabbit Factory (New York: Free Press, 2003).

PLAY PRODUCTION: *Dirty Work,* Washington, D.C., Arena Stage, January 1993.

SELECTED PERIODICAL PUBLICATION–
UNCOLLECTED: "Faulkner's Legacy in Oxford, MS," *Algonkian* (June 1996).

Larry Brown (photograph by Joe Osgoode; from the dust jacket for Fay, *2000; Richland County Public Library)*

After Mississippi writer Larry Brown published *Facing the Music* (1988), his first collection of short stories, Harry Crews, whose work Brown had read and admired for years, wrote a cover blurb for a 1996 edition announcing that "talent has struck." Since this propitious beginning Brown has emerged as one of the leading new talents in Southern fiction. His success seems even more remarkable because he is a self-taught literary artist, one who barely graduated from high school. Hard-packed, realistic, and heavily fraught with emotion, his work has drawn readers not only in the South but also throughout the rest of the country.

William Larry Brown was born on 9 July 1951 in Oxford, Mississippi; in an interview with Kay Bonetti, he said he arrived "at the old hospital up the street from the courthouse, but we lived twelve miles out in the country." The family on both sides were country people who worked hard, hunted the land, and fished the waters for both food and pleasure. At that time his father, Knox Brown, was a sharecropper "in a small creek bottom" at Potlockney, about eight or nine miles south of where Brown and his family live in Yocona (pronounced "Yocknee"); Potlockney is also south of Tula, where the family lived after their return to the Oxford area in 1964 and where Brown still owns land. Knox Brown, a veteran of World War II, had been wounded at the Battle of the Bulge. In *A Late Start* (1989) Brown writes that his father's war experience left emotional scars on him that were never to heal. He would never mention the war when he was sober, but when he was drinking, which was frequent in the years of my growing up, he would begin to talk about it and about the horrors he had seen, and he would eventually break down.

Brown's mother, Leona Barlow Brown, was a homemaker and later postmaster and storekeeper. Brown has two brothers and a sister who also still live in northern Mississippi.

When Brown was three years old, the family moved to Memphis, Tennessee, where Knox Brown took a job at the Fruehauf Trailer Company; his heavy drinking, however, kept him from remaining employed for any length of time. In an interview with Judith Weinraub, Larry Brown termed his family life "troubled . . . but through it all, I loved my father as children will, no matter what happens." In Memphis the Brown family lived in a series of rented houses, which Brown describes in *Billy Ray's Farm: Essays from a Place Called Tula* (2001) as "stacked tightly side by side behind their tiny yards." In the same collection, he remembers not having room for a dog and no place to fish or roam: "It's one thing to have a life in a place and to be happy in it is quite another."

In 1964, before Brown finished eighth grade in Memphis, the family returned to Mississippi. His father worked in the Chambers stove factory in Oxford, where Brown himself later worked briefly. Their lives continued to be plagued by his father's drinking and the consequent lack of money. Brown told Weinraub, "Let's just say I got an early education in trouble. And a childhood that had some hard times." In 1968, when Brown was sixteen, his father, who had finally conquered his drinking problem, died.

Though as a youngster Brown had no dreams of becoming a writer (he told interviewer Dorie LaRue, "It never crossed my mind"), he was an inveterate reader. In his interview with Bonetti, Brown said that his love of books and reading came "Mainly from my mother. One of my earliest memories is of seeing her reading. There were always books in our house. I just grew to love it real early, I guess—escaping into stories and discovering other worlds." His mother had bought the family a set of encyclopedias; a bonus was the ten "classics" that came with it: works by Edgar Allan Poe, Mark Twain, Zane Grey, Herman Melville, and Jack London, as well as *Grimm's Fairy Tales* (1812–1815), a collection of Greek mythology, and the *Iliad* and the *Odyssey*. Brown told Susan Ketchin, "When I read the *Iliad* and the *Odyssey* when I was little, on my own, it got me thinking in terms of myths and dreams; I was really

into Greek mythology, all the battles and gods. . . . They formed the core of my belief about storytelling."

On the other hand, Brown was not interested in school texts, though he read books from the school library on hunting, fishing, and cowboys. In an interview with Bob Summer, he elaborated, "nothing you would call literature. It took me a long time even to learn what literature was." Brown had no aspirations beyond completing high school–his mother's wish for him. Brown's earliest enthusiasms were for hunting and fishing; as he writes in *Billy Ray's Farm,* "When I was sixteen that's what I wanted to do. I wanted to stay in the woods with my gun and hunt every day and half the night sometimes, too." This outdoor enthusiasm interfered with his scholastic life. Telling LaRue he was a "terrible student," Brown admitted that he failed English in the twelfth grade and did not graduate with the rest of his class because he made an F on his term paper on deer hunting. After attending summer school, however, Brown graduated from Lafayette High School in August 1969.

After working a few months at the Chambers stove factory, Brown joined the U.S. Marine Corps in 1970 instead of waiting to be drafted by the army. He trained at Camp Lejeune in North Carolina, but instead of being sent to Vietnam, he spent two years at the marine barracks in Philadelphia. For his later writing, as he told Bonetti, the most relevant experience Brown had there was interaction at a veterans' hospital with "disabled Marines . . . guys who were in wheelchairs, who had lost their arms and legs and had made that great sacrifice, too."

Upon his discharge from the marines in 1972, Brown returned to Lafayette County and renewed his acquaintance with Mary Annie Coleman, whom he had first met there in 1969 when she was just fourteen years old. They married in 1974; she was nineteen and he was twenty-two. Of their marriage, which has endured almost thirty years, Brown told Weinraub, "I've got a happy marriage and I'm crazy about the girl I'm married to. I couldn't ask for anybody better." The marriage produced four children, including a daughter, Delinah, who died in infancy in 1977. Brown's other children are Billy Ray, Shane, and LeAnne; in the essays in *On Fire* (1993) and *Billy Ray's Farm* Brown makes clear his love and concern for them.

In 1973 Brown became a paid fireman for the Oxford Fire Department. He was unable to support his growing family with the money he made there, however, so for six years he held a wide variety of part-time jobs: bagging groceries, working with molds in a local pottery, setting out pine trees, helping to build houses, cleaning carpets, cutting pulpwood and deadening timber, building chain-link fences for Sears and Roebuck,

Dust jacket for Brown's first novel (1989), about a day in the lives of two severely wounded
Vietnam veterans (Richland County Public Library)

painting houses, and hauling hay. In *A Late Start* Brown writes, "When I was twenty-nine, I stopped and looked at my life and wondered if I was ever going to do anything with it." Because he had long been an inveterate reader of popular fiction (Stephen King and John D. MacDonald were among his favorites), he decided that he could teach himself to write salable fiction in the same way that he had learned other skills such as carpentry and fire fighting. His chief early aim was financial: he writes in *A Late Start* that he wanted to make sure that his three young children would not have to start their adult lives "working in a factory." In *On Fire* Brown recalls that in 1982 he told a friend of his about his decision to become a writer: "he didn't laugh. . . . He just listened to me seriously and nodded his head."

Using his wife's "old portable Smith-Corona electric" typewriter, he set out to write a novel "about a man-eating bear in Yellowstone National Park, a place I'd never been to, and it had a lot of sex in it." Working steadily around his other jobs, Brown finished the

novel in five months and immediately sent it to New York publishers. Brown admitted to Summer, "Of course, I didn't know what I was doing. I didn't even know about double-spacing. I typed that whole novel single-spaced, 327 pages." Publishers immediately rejected the novel and a few stories that Brown in *A Late Start* describes as horrible. In an interview with Jean Ross for *Contemporary Authors* Brown said, "I didn't have any idea about how much work was involved. I surely didn't think it would take seven years before my first book was published." But, as he writes in *On Fire,* "I had one burning thought that I believed was true. If I wrote long enough and hard enough, I'd eventually learn how."

Brown visited the local library in Oxford, seeking books on writing. He also began to read books by serious writers, whose fiction made him realize how bad his own efforts were but also increased his determination. In *A Late Start* he recalls that he also found "tremendously heartening" essays by successful writers, especially those who had succeeded after long struggles. Around 1980, Brown also became a patron of the newly opened Oxford Square Books, which provided him with books by contemporary writers such as Crews and Raymond Carver.

By 1982 Brown had been writing for two years and had produced three unpublished novels and about ninety stories. Besides the novel about the grizzly bear, he had written a second novel, with characters who are marijuana growers in Tennessee, and a third that was a tale of the supernatural. Everything he sent out came back, usually rejected without comment. In *On Fire* Brown describes how discouraged he began to feel; he decided that he needed to study writing in a more formal way.

In the fall of 1982 Mississippi novelist Ellen Douglas was teaching creative writing at the University of Mississippi, and Brown enrolled as a special student in her graduate class. After reading some of his fiction, Douglas told him that she had no problems with his sentence structure, just his subject matter, which she felt was too extreme, too violent. He began to moderate his topics beginning with his fourth novel. Brown credits Douglas with pointing him to the work of writers such as Joseph Conrad, Fyodor Dostoevsky, Ambrose Bierce, Katherine Anne Porter, and Flannery O'Connor, whose fiction he had not previously read.

In 1982 Brown received his first acceptance when *Easyriders,* a motorcycle magazine, took one of his early stories, but after that he published nothing else for two more years. By 1985, Brown had published just three stories: the one in *Easyriders,* a second in *Fiction International,* and a third in *Twilight Zone,* a magazine no longer in print. In 1987, however, Frederic Barthelme at the *Mississippi Review* accepted Brown's short story "Facing the Music." Shannon Ravenel, senior editor of Algonquin Press, contacted Brown after reading this story about the aftermath of a mastectomy. Brown told Weinraub, "She called me, saying she wanted to recommend it for the Best American Short Stories. And she asked me if I had enough stories for a collection. I wrote back and said, 'I've got a hundred. How many would you like to see?'" A year later, Algonquin Press published *Facing the Music.*

Brown's first public appearance as a published writer came in April 1989 when he participated in the Fifth Biennial Conference on Southern Literature in Chattanooga, Tennessee. On 8 April, Brown gave his talk "A Late Start" and read from his novel *Dirty Work* (1989). In "Chattanooga Nights," one of the essays in *Billy Ray's Farm,* Brown recalls his reactions to being there and meeting other writers: "it was pretty stunning to me to see Ernest Gaines and Louis [Rubin] going down the street just talking like regular people.

My eyes got big seeing William Styron and Andrew Lytle and Horton Foote in the flesh." In 1995 Brown returned to Chattanooga; this time, feeling confident, he became friends with Madison Smartt Bell. By then, Brown felt accepted as a member of the writing community and enjoyed being "able to sit back and relax [in the evenings] with some of the people who do what you do for a living, who stay alone in rooms by themselves for large portions of their lives and craft stories and novels."

When Brown published *Facing the Music* in 1988, his ten stories had immediate impact. Dedicated to his wife, Mary Annie, the original hardback version sold between three and four thousand copies. The best of these stories, including "Facing the Music," "Kubuku Rides (This Is It)," "Samaritans," "Old Frank and Jesus," and "Night Life," force middle-class readers to accept the essential humanity of people they might ordinarily ignore. In this collection he introduces the theme that permeates many of his later short stories: the difficulty of maintaining permanent love in relationships that have passed through the physical thrills of youth and raising children, to the threat of old age and the abandonment of dreams. Of the people of *Facing the Music,* Ketchin wrote: "Brown introduces us to people who seem to be paralyzed by calamity, and who eventually must learn, often with only the slightest glimmer of understanding, how to deal with it—through resignation, denial, or a wan faith."

Brown says that he worked on his novel *Dirty Work* for two and a half years after he fastened onto the idea in the mid 1980s when he was building his house. In his interview with Bonetti, he says, "The idea had grown and festered in those months and I just had to get it down. It turned out that I had to write it five different times and throw out six hundred pages. It went through five complete revisions." Brown described in detail the two soldiers he met in the Philadelphia veterans' hospital who became prototypes for the main characters, Braiden Chaney and Walter James:

> There were two guys I was most impressed by. One of them didn't have any legs at all, but he had a pair of artificial legs, with pants on and tennis shoes on the bottom. . . . The other guy had the kind of injury that Walter has. He had been shot all the way through the base of his skull. To look at him, he didn't have any kind of disfiguring wound. . . . But he had blackouts, seizures.

Dirty Work deals with the aftermath of war, through Brown's depiction of two permanently scarred veterans. Brown dedicated the novel to the memory of his father: "For Daddy who knew what war does to men." Covering only about a day in their lives, Brown alternates the narrative perspectives of his protagonists. To disclose the misery of both characters, Brown uses mainly stream-of-consciousness narration, limiting actual conversation between Braiden and Walter. Having lost both his arms and legs in Vietnam, Braiden Chaney has spent seventeen years in the VA hospital; Walter, who has no face and suffers from seizures and blackouts, has tried to live in the "outside" world. Both suffer dramatically from a lack of human connection. Once the two soldiers begin to communicate, Braiden asks Walter to help him commit suicide.

Suzanne Jones identified the "bonding" that occurs between the two veterans, one black and one white, as a later version of the relationships that William Faulkner created between young males of both races, such as Bayard Sartoris and Ringo in *The Unvanquished* (1938); Faulkner's friendships, however, end when the young men mature. In *Dirty Work* a friendship develops between the two adult men as they focus on their similar "war experiences, but more immediately on coping with their debilitating injuries and their frustrated desires for more normal lives."

In a review of *Dirty Work* in the *Atlanta Journal-Constitution* (3 September 1989) Greg Johnson asserted that Brown's first novel "unquestionably puts him into the front ranks of the South's contemporary writers," a view supported by most other critics. *Dirty Work* forced Brown to make his first connections with the literary world outside Oxford. Though he hated traveling to New York City, he even promoted the novel in an interview with Jane Pauley on *The Today Show*. Brown said that the interview was not as daunting as he had expected, for at that point he was still living in two worlds: he told Harry Levins that the night after the interview, he was back "pulling down the ceiling in a burning bait shop in Oxford." In *On Fire,* however, Brown admits that the appearance altered his life: "that television show has changed something, the shape and order and regularity my world once had. People know where I am now." Brown also wrote a theatrical version of *Dirty Work* that became a three-week workshop production at the Arena Stage in Washington, D.C., in January and February 1993.

Brown published his second collection of short stories, *Big Bad Love,* in 1990. These stores received strong critical praise, including that of Crews, who in the *Los Angeles Times,* asserted "In 25 years of writing it was the first time I picked up the phone and tried to call the author." As the title reveals, most of the stories deal with the problems inherent in love relationships gone sour. Written almost completely from the masculine point of view, the stories feature the sexual frustrations of men whose wives or lovers have abandoned them; however, Brown uses trenchant humor to undercut any

hint of sentimentality. For example, in "Falling Out of Love," his cynical narrator says:

> It looked like when you first met somebody everything was just hunky-dory, and then you got to know each other. You found out that in spite of all her apparent beauty she had a little nasty-looking wart on her ass or she'd had six toes when she was born and they'd just clipped it off and then you got to wondering about genetics and progeny.

Two of the most interesting stories in the collection are clearly autobiographical. In "The Apprentice" the male narrator has an uneducated wife, Judy, who decides to become a writer. In creating her, Brown is clearly enjoying himself as he retrospectively satirizes his own early attempts to produce salable fiction. Virtually without talent when she begins, Judy becomes obsessed but has almost no success. Her first novel is the same as Brown's, the tale of the grizzly bear in Yellowstone National Park. The other story that documents Brown's early difficulties is the novella "92 Days." The major difference between reality and fiction, however, is that protagonist Leon Barlow's wife, Marilyn, is not a Mary Annie, who has consistently supported Brown's efforts to succeed as a writer. Disgusted with her husband's dedication, Marilyn has taken their two children and left him. Leon works to make only enough money to keep him alive as he writes, but he spends as much of it on beer and cigarettes as he does on food. Leon is where Brown was just before Barthelme accepted "Facing the Music." Readers at magazines tell Leon that his stories are good enough for publication, yet they continue to refuse them. As another autobiographical element in the story, Brown includes the death of Leon's young daughter.

Selling approximately twenty thousand copies in its first printing, Brown's novel *Joe,* published in 1991, achieved major success. In his review for the *Washington Post* (20 November 1991) Daniel Woodrell said that in "this brilliant novel of down home grit, tragedy, and redemption, Larry Brown has slapped his own fresh tattoo on the big right arm of Southern Lit." Brown told Alexander Parsons that he began to write the novel in the mid 1980s after he "originally had an idea about a family of people who were homeless, just traveling around without any solid roots or any home, who made their way around working wherever they could. I started with them. The idea of Joe as a protagonist came along a little later." Joe is an appealing human being, in spite of his penchant for violence. Rebellion against law-enforcement officers has sent him to jail and cost him his family. Still, as Brown told Bonetti, Joe possesses a work ethic: "He believes that a man ought to get up and go to work every morning." Erik Bledsoe called Joe the "moral center of the book. He is another in the long line of American rebels whose behavior often runs afoul of the law but whose ethical values are generally superior to the society to which he does not conform." Joe's interaction with the "white trash" family of patriarch Wade Jones redeems Joe from his own excesses but sends him back to jail.

If Joe is one of Brown's most sympathetic characters, Wade Jones emerges as one of his most revolting. Congenitally evil, Wade will do anything for the money he needs to satisfy his lust for alcohol. He trades his son Calvin for an automobile and prostitutes his twelve-year-old daughter, Dorothy; however, his son Gary, a fifteen-year-old, has, like Faulkner's Sarty Snopes, abjured the hopelessness of his heritage. Gary provides the link between Joe and Wade. In his interview with Bonetti, Brown said that he invented Joe Ransom to "take care of him [Gary] for a little while. . . . I wanted him to have a chance."

The novel also allowed Brown to write about the glory of the Mississippi countryside as he revealed to Bonetti:

> *Joe* gave me a great opportunity to show the landscape, and to set my characters against it. And to have this larger thing, even larger than the lives that are going on, which is the land. The ground is so ancient. It's the oldest thing we've got. I like to have people picture what it looks like—that distant watershed where all the lines of trees fade into this little blue line that's the end of the horizon. That's what I love. This is my country, and I love this place. I try to recreate it on the page.

Brown also says that most of the places in the novel are real but that he shifted them around to suit the needs of his novel: the old log house in which the Jones family squats, the store owned by Joe's friend John Coleman, and the springhouse all are places Brown knew as a young man growing up in north Mississippi.

Algonquin published *On Fire,* Brown's first collection of essays, in 1993. He based some of the material in this volume on a journal he kept while working at the Oxford Fire Department, which he left in early January 1990 with the rank of captain. During his seventeen years as a fireman, Brown participated in dramatic events, many of which he vividly describes in *On Fire.* Through the clarity of his descriptions, Brown depicts the realities of major fires, such as the one at the University of Mississippi Law School in the late 1980s, and those in private homes, as in one instance when a fire blazed only twenty feet away from a gas tank and it was Brown's job to prevent an explosion. His talent for suspenseful narrative is most gripping in stories of disastrous automobile crashes. Sometimes Brown and the other firefighters were able to save these victims; some-

Dust jacket for Brown's 1996 novel, about a young man whose evil behavior has been caused by a lack of parental love (Richland County Public Library)

times they were helpless to rescue them or alleviate their suffering.

As striking as the descriptions of a firefighter's work are, the book is also important for what Brown tells about his family life and about becoming a writer in a world where most of his companions spent their time playing poker, washing trucks, telling stories, watching television, or pitching horseshoes. Brown appreciated the companionship of the other men, but he spent some of his "off" time on duty reading. His aim through the last ten years of his employment was to transcend what he continues to call the noble work of the firefighter in order to follow, as Michael Pearson wrote in the *New Orleans Times-Picayune* (27 March 1994), the "more alluring voice of the creator of Yoknapatawpha."

Five years elapsed between Brown's publication of *Joe* in 1991 and his next novel, *Father and Son* (1996). This novel is arguably his best; in the *Boston Globe* (20

October 1996) fellow novelist Rick Bass praised *Father and Son* for the grace with which Brown wrote it and the richness of its themes:

> The entire novel . . . is a metaphor for the loss of cultural diversity, independent thinking and a certain unnameable fierceness of spirit. . . . The oldest themes in literature are illuminated sharply. . . . The poisons of anger and violence, and an inability to forgive become the stew of tragedy, and the characters' struggles against these lines of fate become the story.

Written with taut structure, effective characterization, clarity of language, and strength of theme, *Father and Son* covers the last few days in the life of Glen Davis, an angry, misguided young man who has just been released from prison after serving three years for vehicular homicide. Glen is viciously cruel, unrepentant, and unable to accept any responsibility for his evil actions; however, as Brown slowly unfolds his protagonist's history, the reader learns that Glen is the victim of a ruinous family. Because his parents failed to love each other, they could never give their sons the quality of love essential to normal survival. Brown said in an interview with Susan Larson that the genesis of the novel was a story he had heard "about an old man who died. And he'd accidentally killed his brother, and his parents kept catching him up on the barn about to jump off." Brown transformed this real-life anecdote into just one of the horrors that haunt Glen. In the *Atlanta Journal-Constitution* (29 September 1996) reviewer Johnson called the novel "a surprisingly affirmative, human book, offering the reader a guided tour of hell without neglecting the possibility of redemption."

As in his other fiction Brown in *Father and Son* draws on the history of his own life in Oxford. He sets the novel in the Oxford area of the late 1960s; in *Billy Ray's Farm* he recalls that he visualized the famous Oxford Square as it was then with its simple stores and restaurants and its local truck farmers selling "watermelons and roasting ears and purple hull peas. . . . I saw all that and I knew that they [Glen and his brother Randolph] had driven in one hot Saturday afternoon during my childhood, and I remember the way things are." Glen's father, Virgil, shares some of Knox Brown's history as a veteran of World War II, deeply scarred by the physical and psychological damage that participation in war incurs. Mary Blanchard, a genuinely nurturing mother, possesses qualities of Brown's own mother. The long-suffering Jewel Coleman, who cares deeply for David, the son she and Glen had out of wedlock, reflects the loyalty of Mary Annie Coleman Brown.

Characterization contributes most to the success of the novel. Brown's female characters in this novel, in the richness of their development, foreshadow his use of the female perspective in his next novel. Mary Blanchard and Jewel Coleman are believable as women from their time and place. Both manage to become self-supporting financially when their relationships with men deteriorate, and Brown presents their powers as nurturers with sympathy and realism. Good cooks, they take pride in feeding their families, literally and figuratively. In an interview with Suzanne Mantell, Brown described how the characters in his novel evolved:

> The characters kind of took over, as they usually do, and do things you didn't know. That's the most fascinating thing about writing. The discovery of a story day by day is what keeps me going. That's what's going to happen to the reader later on, but in a more compressed time.

Father and Son, like *Big Bad Love* and *Joe,* attracted Hollywood moviemakers. Brown has said that scriptwriters have prepared a version of the book, considerably different from the novel, but it has yet to reach the stage of filming.

Brown published his fourth novel, *Fay,* in the spring of 2000. At nearly five hundred pages, *Fay* is his longest work of fiction and arguably his most ambitious. In *Fay* Brown maintains his focus on the lives of lower-class Southerners. Writing in the *St. Louis Post-Dispatch* (16 April 2000), Harry Levins asserted, "you'll find yourself liking a lot of people of the sort you may have ignored for most of your life." In this novel, however, Brown has replaced his primarily male protagonists with a seventeen-year-old girl–Fay, whom he first introduced in *Joe* as Gary's runaway sister. As early as 1995, Brown told Bonetti that he wanted to write from the female perspective: "I would be happier with myself if I was able to write a whole novel from a woman's point of view. If I was able to pull that off I'd probably be pretty happy with my abilities." Although he writes the novel from a third-person limited perspective and in the last part of the novel shifts back and forth between Fay and Mississippi state trooper Sam Harris, the character with whom he makes the reader identify throughout the novel is Fay. Of his continued interest in her, Brown told Joe Hartlaub, "I always wondered what happened to Fay. She was a character that lived on in my mind and her fate was unsettled and I knew that I had another story to tell, one about her. As soon as I finished *Father and Son,* I sat down and started on *Fay.*"

Brown has written a female picaresque with Fay as a contemporary version of Daniel Defoe's *Moll Flanders* (1721); he sets his young protagonist on a road that leads to sexual initiation, violence (her own and that of others), and, for her, a conclusion of qualified hope. When she takes to the road, Fay has no sense of how alluring she is, but under the influence of her first "savior," Sam Harris, she achieves a sexual awakening that allows her to be, in the words of Rodney Welch in a review for the Columbia, South Carolina, *Free Times* (12–18 April 2000), "at least the equal of the men in her life when it comes to exerting her own sexual power."

Brown claims that writing from the female perspective was difficult; in an interview with Charles Robinson, he said, "I had to rely on women to find out some of the things I needed to know." Applauding Brown's success, George R. Pelacanos, writing in the *Washington Post Book World* (18 June 2000), asserted that Fay's creator "gets into the head of his female, teenage protagonist cleanly and completely." James L. Dickerson was even more enthusiastic: "Probably not since F. Scott Fitzgerald's incursions into the female sensibilities of the 1920s and 1930s has a writer been so successful crossing that literary minefield. . . . Fay is as complicated and beguiling as any real-life woman who ever walked the planet."

Other reviewers placed the novel in the pantheon of classic works. In the *Boston Review* (Summer 2000) Roger Boylan compared Brown with European naturalists, particularly Guy de Maupassant and Thomas Hardy. He called Fay a modern version of Hardy's Tess. The novel, Boylan asserted, "carries the same sense of inexorability, it reflects the same resignation to fate." Welch praised the realistic detail of the novel and noted Brown's "camera eye, which closely observes everything–from the way people fish to the way they smoke their cigarettes–with an interest and sympathy that is warm and forgiving, but also detached." With its compelling central character and highly dramatic plot, *Fay* seems almost certain to become a movie. Brown also told Hartlaub that he expects to write a third novel about the Jones family: "At this point I plan to make a trilogy. The last book will probably focus on Gary as well as answer the question of what happened to Calvin, the little brother of Fay and Gary who was traded for a car in *Joe*."

In the fall of 2000 a crew from Sun, Moon and Stars Productions came to Mississippi and produced a full-length motion picture based on Brown's novella "92 Days" and titled *Big Bad Love*. Jim Howard wrote the script, and Arliss Howard directed and played Leon Barlow; Debra Winger (Arliss Howard's wife) played Leon's former wife. Others in the cast included Paul LeMat, Rosanna Arquette, Michael Parks, and Angie Dickinson; Brown himself had a minor role in the movie, which received favorable reaction at the Cannes Film Festival in May 2001.

Billy Ray's Farm is a compilation of articles Brown originally published in journals and magazines as diverse as *The Southern Quarterly*, *The Chattahoochee Review*, *The Oxford American*, *Glamour*, *Men's Journal*, and *AOL*, *The Book Report*. By content, the essays fall into several categories: stories of family and personal adventures; writing and his relationships with other artists; and appreciation for a life lived close to nature. Because of the variety of subjects and experiences Brown records in the essays, their overall quality is a bit uneven, though each of them has its own appeal.

"Billy Ray's Farm" is the most dramatic and the most detailed of the personal essays. Anyone with rural or farm experience can immediately identify with the woeful story of Brown's son Billy Ray's desire to continue the farming tradition of his family and raise a herd of cattle. Rural readers will not shudder at his tales of calves too large for their young mothers to bear or the futility of trying to treat a cow that has "gone down," becoming too weak to survive. This narrative, however, can be read as more than a tale of agrarian drudgery. As Billy Ray loses cow after cow but does not relinquish his dream, his efforts recall Brown's own struggle to give birth to the writer he is today.

"So Much Fish, So Close to Home, *An Improv*" is another narrative that reads more like fiction than personal narrative. Brown details his all-night partying with friends at a local club, futile attempts to recapture Billy Ray's bull that has strayed onto a neighbor's property, and later his attempt to participate in a county-wide fish grab. Authorities have drained Enid Lake for cleaning and allowed a more-than-willing public to wade through the mud to capture and carry off hordes of fish in their coolers. An almost surreal atmosphere surrounds Brown's actions during these episodes. In "Shack," in which Brown proudly (and fully) reports his attempts to build a writing cabin for himself on the land he owns near Tula, he admits:

> The truth is that if I hadn't gotten sober for a long time the year before [he began to build the cabin], none of it would have happened. The idea of building it had always been in my head. It had probably been in my head for ten years. I work hard and I play too hard all the time. But I get sober for a while, and I look around, and I see what all is possible. It's always a revelation.

By the time he finished *Billy Ray's Farm*, the cabin had a roof; Brown leaves no doubt that he will complete the project.

Many of the essays include statements that reveal Brown's philosophy of writing: producing genuine work is demanding; the writer must always base his fiction on what he knows; and he must present that knowledge using concrete, realistic detail. Citing himself as proof, Brown asserts that perseverance can pay off. Brown's tributes to other artists highlight the collection. His praise for Crews is unqualified; Jonathan Yardley, in his 29 March 2001 review in the *Washington Post*, called that

Dust jacket for Brown's picaresque tale of the adventures of seventeen-year-old Fay Jones, whom he introduced in his 1991 novel, Joe *(Richland County Public Library)*

already disclosed his plans to complete his trilogy of the Jones family; other novels and more nonfiction will certainly follow. He may even publish poetry, having told Dorie LaRue in 1992, "I've written a lot of poetry. I just have not tried to publish any of it." He told Don O'Briant that, at his current level of success, he is "doing pretty much what I want to be doing. What would I do if I got a lot more money? I don't think I'd do anything much different. I guess I would like to get my little writing cabin finished."

Since 1992 Brown has also spent time teaching. In 1992 he was an instructor at the famous Bread Loaf Writers' Conference. LaRue describes his success: "He was a popular teacher, accessible, funny, totally committed to his students. He was known to leave functions early or refuse late socializing so that he could mark short stories." He later taught briefly at Bowling Green State University in Ohio and Lynchburg College in Virginia. In the spring semester of 1998 Brown taught creative writing at the University of Mississippi while Barry Hannah was on leave teaching at Iowa. He had established an earlier permanent connection with the university in 1996 when he sold his collection of more than one hundred manuscripts to their Department of Archives and Special Collections. In the fall semester of 1999 Brown became the inaugural Kittredge Writer-in-Residence at the University of Montana.

Brown has also established several connections with Hollywood. In the 1997 release of Jeremy Horton's *100 Proof,* Brown played the role of a dope dealer. In 2002, Blue Moon Filmed Productions released *The Rough South of Larry Brown;* directed by Gary Hawkins, the documentary examines Brown's life and work. In addition to appearing in interview footage, Brown also has a cameo role as the fire chief in a dramatization of one of his stories.

Brown's next novel, *The Rabbit Factory,* was released in September 2003 by The Free Press, a division of Simon and Schuster. It traces the intersecting lives of several down-and-out characters, including a rich, impotent man and his much younger, restless wife; a former convict and marijuana dealer; an abused teenager whose father runs a rabbit factory (which, as the reviewer for *Publishers Weekly* pointed out, is "a metaphor for the uncaring world in which these people exist") and a pit bull named Jada Pinkett. Reviews of the novel varied from enthusiastic to lukewarm. Writing in *The Miami Herald,* Fred Grimm said:

essay "the best piece in the book." Brown's comments on Madison Jones are equally laudatory; he also pays a heartfelt tribute to his friend, musician Charlic Jacobs, who died of a drug overdose in April 1997.

Brown turned fifty in July 2001; although he got off to "a late start" as a writer, he has made an extraordinary effort to "catch up" during the 1990s and into the new century. Despite the celebrity he has achieved, Brown remains rooted in north Mississippi, saying in a *Time* review of *Fay* in May 2000: "I've been to a lot of places, and I've never found any one I like as much as this one." He continues to live outside Oxford in Yocona in the house he and his wife built in the 1980s. Owning sixty acres allows him the freedom of a rural existence: he can watch the pecans, soybeans, and cotton grow, and enjoy the animals, both domestic and wild. He spends many hours writing, but he also reads, fishes, works on his house, and continues to share his son's struggle with farming. After years of using typewriters Brown switched to a computer in 2000. He writes every day until he gets tired—usually five to ten hours. Brown has

> Brown's novel is populated by characters who grasp the flimsiest hopes to pull themselves out of despair, their prospects stunted by daunting circumstance. None of them can quite see the way out of their respective doldrums. All of them, even the dogs, are damaged goods.

As Brown himself has said, this novel is quite different from those that preceded it. It is far more comic–many episodes in the novel, especially those involving animals, are genuinely funny. Grimm observed, "A strange savage humor streams through *The Rabbit Factory.* The reader confronts all manner of pathos while struggling not to laugh aloud." With its broad spectrum of characters, the novel seems almost like a comic version of Victor Hugo's *Les Misérables* (1862).

Brown has also shifted the setting of the novel: this one takes place in Memphis in the immediate present, though most of the characters have roots in northern Mississippi. In flashbacks throughout the novel, Brown returns to the rough, country setting of *Joe, Father and Son,* and *Fay.* The theme that connects this novel with the earlier ones is the essential humanity Brown imbeds in his characters, all of whom seek vital human connections in a world that offers too much sex and violence and too little genuine sympathy.

Larry Brown writes fiction that shows his allegiance to his native north Mississippi and his dedication to the people he knows best. He concentrates on accuracy of detail and language, sympathy for his suffering characters, and dedication to the basic themes of the human condition. He has achieved his aim to become a writer and, in the process, attracted many readers. Brown received the Mississippi Institute of Arts and Letters Award in 1989 for *Dirty Work* and has twice won the Southern Book Critics Award for fiction (for *Joe* in 1992 and *Father and Son* in 1997). In 1998 Brown also received the Lila Wallace-Reader's Digest Fund Writers' Award. In his review of *Billy Ray's Farm* Yardley evaluated Brown's current status: "Brown is the real thing: a self-taught country boy who may now make the rounds of the writing conferences but whose heart is obviously, and wholly, in the country he loves."

Interviews:

Judith Weinraub, "The Back-Roads Blue-Collar Artiste," *Washington Post,* 9 December 1990, pp. F1, F4;

Bob Summer, "Author's Popularity Is Poised to Expand," *Richmond Times-Dispatch,* 3 November 1991, p. F4;

Dorie LaRue, "Interview with Larry Brown: Bread Loaf 1992," *Chattahoochee Review,* 13 (April 1993): 39–56;

Susan Ketchin, "Interview with Larry Brown," in her *The Christ-Haunted Landscape, Faith and Doubt in Southern Fiction* (Jackson: University Press of Mississippi, 1994), pp. 126–127;

Kay Bonetti, *A Conversation with Larry Brown* (Columbia, Mo.: America Audio Prose Library, 1995);

Susan Larson, "Keeper of the Flame," *New Orleans Times-Picayune,* 2 October 1996, pp. E1–E2;

Suzanne Mantell, "Larry Brown, Son of the Literary South," *Publishers Weekly,* 2 June 1997;

Harry Levins, "Novel Provides an Interesting Look at Working-Class White Southerners," *St. Louis Post-Dispatch,* 16 April 2000, p. F10;

James L. Dickerson, "America's 'Bad Boy Novelist' Enters Virgin Territory with *Fay,*" *BookPage* (18 April 2000) <http://www.bookpage.com/0004bp/larry_brown.html>;

Joe Hartlaub, "Interview," *Bookreporter.com* (28 April 2000) <http://www.bookreporter.com/authors/au-brown-larry.asp>;

Charles Robinson, "A Biography of Larry Brown," *The Mississippi Writers and Musicians Project of Starkville High School* (May 2001) <http://www.shs.starkville.k12.ms.us/mswm/MSWritersAndMusicians/writers/LarryBrown/larrybrown.html>;

Alexander Parsons, "Waiting in the Gloam: An Interview with Author Larry Brown," *UNo MAS Magazine* <http://www.unomas.com/features/larrybrown.html>.

References:

Erik Bledsoe, "The Rise of the Southern Redneck and White Trash Writers," *Southern Cultures,* 6 (Spring 2000): 68–90;

Suzanne Jones, "Refighting Old Wars: Race Relations and Masculine Conventions in Fiction by Larry Brown and Madison Smartt Bell," in *The Southern State of Mind,* edited by Jan Nordy Gretland (Columbia: University of South Carolina Press, 1999), pp. 107–120;

Susan Ketchin, "Larry Brown, Proceeding Out from Calamity," in her *The Christ-Haunted Landscape, Faith and Doubt in Southern Fiction* (Jackson: University Press of Mississippi, 1994), pp. 100–101;

Don O'Briant, "Writer Larry Brown, In Faulkner's Footsteps," *Atlanta Journal-Constitution,* 9 April 2000, pp. L1, L6;

"Ole Miss Archives Acquire Larry Brown Manuscripts," *Foundation News,* 18 July 1996.

Papers:

Larry Brown's papers are at the Department of Archives and Special Collections at the University of Mississippi.

Mark Childress
(21 September 1957 –   )

Jennifer Vance

BOOKS: *A World Made of Fire* (New York: Knopf, 1984);
V for Victor (New York: Knopf, 1988);
Tender (New York: Harmony Books, 1990);
Joshua and Bigtooth (Boston: Little, Brown, 1992);
Crazy in Alabama (New York: Putnam, 1993);
Joshua and the Big Bad Blue Crabs (Boston: Little, Brown, 1996);
Henry Bobbity Is Missing and It Is All Billy Bobbity's Fault! (Birmingham, Ala.: Crane Hill, 1996);
Gone for Good (New York: Knopf, 1998).

PRODUCED SCRIPT: *Crazy in Alabama,* motion picture, Columbia TriStar, 1999.

RECORDINGS: *Tender,* read by Childress, Harper, 1990;
Crazy in Alabama, read by Childress, Harper, 1993;
"At the Pond with Grandmother," *In Southern Words: A Collection of Southern Stories and Reminiscences Written and Read by Some of the Region's Most Renowned Authors,* read by Childress and others, Southern Living, 1995.

OTHER: Hubert Shuptrine, *Home to Jericho,* edited by Childress and Cecilia C. Robinson (Birmingham, Ala.: Oxmoor House, 1987).

Mark Childress (photograph by Tony Metaxas; from the dust jacket for Gone for Good, *1998; Richland County Public Library)*

SELECTED PERIODICAL PUBLICATIONS–UNCOLLECTED: "A Life in Wood: Work of G. McKoy," *Southern Living,* 18 (February 1983): 85;
"Polishing a Reputation in Glass: J. A. Janick and A. Janick," *Southern Living,* 18 (March 1983): 106+;
"The Dark Riddle of Jorge Luis Borges," by Childress and Charles McNair, *Saturday Review,* 9 (March/April 1983): 32–34;
"Jimmy Faulkner Remembers Brother Will," *Southern Living,* 18 (April 1983): 176+;
"Talk about Good! The Cajun Kind of Cooking," *Southern Living,* 18 (April 1983): 166–173+;
"Collecting for Art's Sake," *Southern Living,* 18 (May 1983);

"A Once-in-10-Lifetimes Discovery," *Southern Living,* 18 (July 1983): 106+;
"A Time for the Magic of Stories," *Southern Living,* 18 (September 1983): 164+;
"A Gift of Hope to Texas Towns: Work of A. Read," *Southern Living,* 18 (November 1983): 130+;
"The Airport Lady," *Southern Living,* 18 (November 1983): 206;
"Heir to a Century of Georgia Clay," *Southern Living,* 18 (December 1983): 132+;
"The Missions of San Antonio," *Southern Living,* 18 (December 1983): 126–131;
"Quackery Is What Ails Him: Views of J. H. Young," *Southern Living,* 19 (January 1984): 86;

"A Tree Fanatic in Memphis," *Southern Living*, 19 (March 1984): 132;

"Places of the Man: R. E. Lee," *Southern Living*, 19 (April 1984): 162–173;

"At the Pond with Grandmother: Fishing," *Southern Living*, 20 (April 1985): 144;

"Sounds of the South," *Southern Living*, 21 (June 1986): 131–134+;

"I Am Having an Adventure," *New York Times Book Review*, 91 (13 July 1986): 12;

"Simple Gifts," *New York Times Book Review*, 92 (12 October 1986): 38;

"A Boat Off the Coast," *New York Times Book Review*, 92 (6 December 1987): 30;

"Whoever Finds This," *New York Times Book Review*, 93 (21 August 1988): 12;

"Useful Gifts," *New York Times Book Review*, 94 (21 May 1989): 21;

"The Wild Life," *Southern Living*, 24 (July 1989): 104;

"Power Lines and Other Stories," *New York Times Book Review*, 94 (24 September 1989): 38;

"Springs of Living Water," *New York Times Book Review*, 95 (25 March 1990): 19;

"Farlanburg Stories," *New York Times Book Review*, 95 (19 August 1990): 16;

"The Road to Salvation Never Did Run Smooth," *New York Times Book Review*, 97 (9 August 1992): 6;

"Our Traveling Christmas," *Southern Living*, 27 (December 1992): 84;

"Dangerous Love," *New York Times Book Review*, 98 (26 September 1993): 23;

"American Anomie," *TLS: The Times Literary Supplement*, 4756 (27 May 1994): 20;

"A Man of Good Character Disappears," *TLS: The Times Literary Supplement*, 4471 (9 September 1994): 21;

"The Witches of Magnolia Street," *New York Times Book Review*, 100 (25 June 1995): 25;

"Tom and the Blue Devils," *TLS: The Times Literary Supplement*, 4840 (5 January 1996): 5–6;

"Bob Stoller's Black Mark," *TLS: The Times Literary Supplement*, 4851 (22 March 1996): 30;

"A Gathering of Widows," *New York Times Book Review*, 101 (12 May 1996): 10–11;

"Looking for Harper Lee," *Southern Living*, 32 (May 1997): 148–150;

"Kwaku," *New York Times Book Review*, 102 (11 May 1997): 33;

"No Ordinary Idiot," *New York Times Book Review*, 102 (11 May 1997): 33;

"Up to No Good," *New York Times Book Review*, 102 (28 September 1997): 19;

"Southern Comfort," *New York Times Book Review*, 103 (4 January 1998): 26;

"Family History," *New York Times Book Review*, 103 (22 February 1998): 16.

Mark Childress is the author of five novels and three children's books as well as many journalistic pieces. All of his novels have a distinctively Southern flair that reflects Childress's Alabama roots. Since the appearance of his first novel, *A World Made of Fire*, in 1984, Childress has grown in both popularity and importance as a Southern author.

Born in Harper Lee's hometown of Monroeville, Alabama, on 21 September 1957, Mark Gillion Childress absorbed the rich literary history surrounding him. His father, Roy Childress, was a sales manager for Ralston-Purina; his mother, Mary Helen Gillion Childress, was a homemaker. Childress has two brothers. His parents encouraged him to read from an early age, and the influences of his favorite books have remained visible throughout his literary career. Though his family moved from Alabama to Ohio and later to Indiana when he was still quite young, he returned to the place of his birth to visit friends and family almost every summer during his formative years.

During one such trip to Monroeville, Childress read Lee's classic novel, *To Kill a Mockingbird* (1960). In his 1997 essay "Looking for Harper Lee" he describes this experience as life-changing, because through it he found his inspiration to become an author. Lee's book continues to hold a special place in Childress's heart as the "first adult book I ever read." Not only is it set in a fictionalized Monroeville, a town he knew well, but also he actually knew some of the same people as Lee. The importance of Lee's novel to Childress is made clear in the essay as Childress discusses receiving a letter from her after she read *A World Made of Fire*.

Childress graduated from the University of Alabama in 1978 with a B.A. in English and journalism and a minor in creative writing. In 1977, while still in school, he began a short career with the *Birmingham News* as a reporter. In 1980, John Logue, then the editor of *Southern Living* magazine, noticed Childress's potential as a reporter and contacted him to interview for the magazine. Though Childress had already been offered a position with *The Charlotte Observer*, he accepted Logue's offer and shortly thereafter began his four-year career as a feature writer for *Southern Living*. Childress wrote some of his most memorable pieces for that magazine, including "Looking for Harper Lee," "At the Pond with Grandmother: Fishing" (1985), and "Our Traveling Christmas" (1992) as well as those discussed in Logue and Gary McCalla's *Life at Southern Living: A Sort of Memoir* (2000), such as "Talk about Good! The Cajun Kind of Cooking" (1983), a story that brought chef Paul Prudhomme to the attention of the nation.

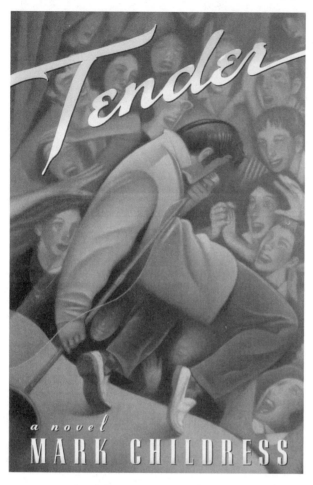

Dust jacket for Childress's 1990 novel, about a singer based on Elvis Presley (Richland County Public Library)

In 1984 Childress began a three-year stint as national editor of the *Atlanta Journal-Constitution* and published his first novel. *A World Made of Fire* is a coming-of-age story set in the early 1900s in Camellia, Alabama. The narrative is set between 1909 and 1918. While the novel encompasses the lives of Callie Bates and all of her children, the main characters are Stella and Jacko Bates (two of Callie's children) and Brown Mary (an old "witchy woman" and midwife). *A World Made of Fire* uses cyclical time, fire, serpents, and magic as its primary themes while Stella and Jacko attempt to discover their personal destinies. As the novel concludes, Stella and Jacko each come to terms with their past as they find their inner strength and magic.

A World Made of Fire received positive reviews, such as that written by Valerie Miner in *The New York Times Book Review* (16 December 1984): Miner stated that "Stella's coming of age in grief and loneliness is drawn with graceful authenticity," and she touted Childress as "an author of imagination." To date, *A World Made of Fire* is the only one of Childress's novels to draw

scholarly attention; the Winter 1988/1989 issue of *The Mississippi Quarterly* includes Marian Motley-Carache's "Magic Realism in Mark Childress's *A World Made of Fire*." While magical realism traditionally refers to a type of literature largely derived from South America and Mexico, Motley-Carache defines its characteristics as "juxtaposition of the real and the magical," "distortion or suspension of the concept of spatial and temporal reality," and "preoccupation with style and form." *A World Made of Fire* exhibits all of these characteristics.

Childress's next novel, *V for Victor* (1988), is also a coming-of-age tale; however, it lacks the supernatural elements and magical-realistic elements so key to *A World Made of Fire*. While the action of *V for Victor* also takes place before Childress's birth, its 1942 setting is more modern than that of *A World Made of Fire*. In this novel sixteen-year-old Victor is sent to take care of his ailing grandmother, who lives on an island in Mobile Bay near the Gulf of Mexico in southern Alabama. While there, he envisions himself fighting the Germans in World War II and becoming a hero like his older brother. The action rises as Victor discovers a Nazi submarine in the waters of Mobile Bay near his grandmother's island and must generate a plan to stop it from reaching Gulf waters. Through his adventures, Victor learns things about himself and his family for which he is not always prepared.

V for Victor received largely positive reviews. In the *Los Angeles Times* (14 May 1989) Douglas Unger criticized the novel for romanticizing World War II: "It's unfortunate that Childress, in trying to exploit World War II for so much unbelievable action and melodrama, didn't concentrate more on what is truthful, penetrating, and honest about his landscape and people." Heather Vogel Frederick sharply contrasted this opinion with her review in the *Christian Science Monitor* (22 May 1989): "*V for Victor* is a rich, compelling story: funny, suspenseful, tender, and thoroughly enjoyable. Best of all, in the wonderfully engaging character of Victor, Childress shows boyhood in all its endearing awkwardness, fervency, and fire in a boy eager to cast off the traces of childhood and become a man."

Childress's next work, *Tender* (1990), became an immediate success in Germany but was not as popular in the United States. *Tender* relates the story of Leroy Kirby, who overcomes his impoverished background to become a successful singer during the 1950s. The novel closely parallels biographical details of Elvis Presley's life and reintroduces the presence of the supernatural, as Kirby talks through mirrors to a being with a silvery voice. *Tender* received mainly favorable reviews from critics such as Vicki Brown of the Associated Press, who wrote on 4 December 1990: "The clean, crisp prose of Childress re-creates the poverty-stricken childhood that forged the ambition and drive the real Elvis Presley had to have to become an American icon." Other reactions were less enthusiastic. Ken Tucker wrote in *The New York Times* (23 September 1990) that Childress "is no hack writer, and his novel is not pulp junk churned out as the umpteenth exploitation of the Elvis myth. 'Tender' is an exceptionally well-written, deeply sympathetic, kind of boring fictional retelling of Presley's life." Jay Cocks wrote in the 24 September 1990 issue of *Time:* "*Tender* is meant to be a biographical novel, but it reads more like an overextended vamp on a folk hero."

After *Tender,* Childress took a short leave from novel writing to produce his first children's book, *Joshua and Bigtooth,* which was published in 1992. Joshua goes fishing on the Magnolia River but catches more than he planned when a baby alligator attaches himself to the line. Mesmerized by the alligator's smile, Joshua decides to make a pet out of him and names him Bigtooth. Though many adults disagree with keeping a baby alligator as a pet, since "baby alligators grow up to be big alligators," no one is able to resist Bigtooth's wonderful smile. The book teaches children not to fear difference and not to make judgments based on appearances or stereotypes alone.

Childress's next novel, *Crazy in Alabama* (1993), became his most popular. The novel, published in nine countries including the United States, appeared on several Top Ten lists for 1993, winning awards and acclaim for Childress. It was named "Book of the Year" by *The Spectator* and a "Notable Book of the Year" by *The New York Times.* Childress also won the 1994 Alabama Library Association's Writer of the Year for his efforts. The popularity of *Crazy in Alabama* only increased after Antonio Banderas directed the 1999 movie based on Childress's original screenplay.

Crazy in Alabama takes place amid the tumultuous events during the summer of 1965 in rural southern Alabama. The novel tells two parallel stories. The main character of the first story line, Lucille Vinson, is on the road to Hollywood, fulfilling her lifelong dream of stardom. In the second story line, Peejoe Bullis, Vinson's nephew, battles racial injustices in segregated Industry, Alabama. The two stories ultimately converge when Lucille is brought back to Industry to stand trial for her husband's murder. Despite its serious themes, *Crazy in Alabama* is fraught with humor; its success is a direct result of this combination of humor, absurdity, and darkness.

Crazy in Alabama is by far Childress's best-received novel. Laurence O'Toole wrote in the *New Statesman and Society* (19 November 1993): "This is fine, old-style entertainment; fast, comic and a pleasure to read. But it's sheer comfort." Pam Lambert of *People Weekly* (27 September 1993) commented, "By turns comic, tragic,

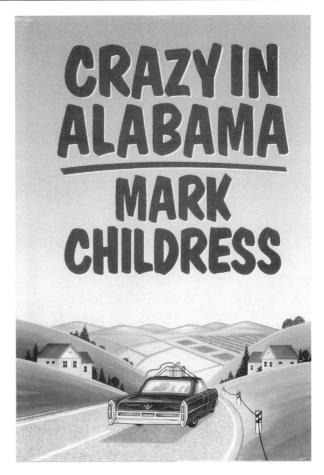

Dust jacket for Childress's 1993 novel, his most popular and acclaimed work to date, about a woman who cuts off her husband's head and goes to Hollywood to become a movie star, while her twelve-year-old nephew witnesses racial strife in 1965 Alabama (Richland County Public Library)

and, most of all, moving, *Crazy in Alabama* is a heartfelt original that cuts to the quick." In *Entertainment Weekly* (6 August 1993) Rhonda Johnson stated, "Writing with dark humor and finely wielded detail in his fourth book, Mark Childress establishes himself as a flamboyant master of the comic grotesque." Rosellen Brewer of *Library Journal* (1 June 1993) called the novel "a funny, insightful, and poignant tale with full-bodied, passionate characters who capture the essence of our memories of the middle Sixties."

In 1996 Childress returned to the children's book genre with *Joshua and the Big Bad Blue Crabs.* The lessons children learn from this book remain the same as in *Joshua and Bigtooth.* An older Joshua faces torment from a large group of blue crabs who repeatedly steal his favorite sweets, leaving Joshua to take the blame for their disappearance. Eventually the boy learns that the crabs are not as angry or bad as he originally sees them.

1 | Superman Considers His Obligations | 1972

Superman ambled onstage in his flip-flops, old holey jeans, the tattered sky-blue

work shirt. He squinted into the blaze of lights with an uncertain grin, like a stagehand

who has wandered past the wrong curtain to find ten thousand people standing and

cheering for him. Superman Willis was famous, and so was that shirt. He had worn it

for years, at every concert, in every album-cover photo. It was part of his image,

indelible as the inkstains under the breast pocket.

His fans thought he must have a whole closet full of sky-blue shirts, identically

tattered and stained, but in fact he had just that one. He never took it off unless his wife

made him wash it, then he'd hang around bare-chested in the laundry room waiting for

it to dry.

One time after a show in Milwaukee, a moon-eyed young girl offered him five

hundred bucks for the shirt. "Sorry, darlin'," he said, "Superman's got no powers

without his shirt," but when he saw her little-rich-girl disappointment he put on his

most charming smile. "Tell you what, though, I believe we could make a deal on these

pants."

He was part of the folk-rocker wave that rolled over America in the years just

after the Beatles, when rock-and-roll wore itself out and people started buying the

1

Typescript page for Childress's novel Gone for Good, *in which a singer crash-lands his plane on a tropical island inhabited by such figures as Amelia Earhart, Marilyn Monroe, and Jimmy Hoffa (courtesy of the author)*

As both Joshua and the crabs make sacrifices, they learn to coexist harmoniously.

Childress also published another children's book in 1996, *Henry Bobbity Is Missing and It Is All Billy Bobbity's Fault!* It is a vivid, imaginative fantasy, set to rhyme, about sibling rivalry. While the book has been hailed for its creativity, Childress's story line is often overshadowed by Ernie Eldredge's colorful illustrations.

Childress visited and subsequently moved to Manuel Antonio, Costa Rica, in 1993. In *Fighting Words: Words on Writing from 21 of the Heart of Dixie's Best Contemporary Authors* (1995) Bill Caton quotes Childress's reasons for moving to "Costa Rica, which he calls 'the far, deep South. I couldn't afford property in the states. I went there on vacation and loved it. . . . I don't consider myself in exile. Going different places keeps you fresh.'" In Costa Rica, Childress was able to look out over the Pacific Ocean and concentrate on writing fiction.

In an interview with Steven Guiterrez, Childress described his next novel, *Gone for Good* (1998), as "Latin American magical realism meets Southern Gothic." Through *Gone for Good,* Childress explores the same elements of magical realism as he does in *A World Made of Fire.* Unlike Childress's earlier novels, *Gone for Good* bears Costa Rican influences; it is set on an island closely resembling Manuel Antonio. The novel relates the errant adventures of folk-rock star Superman Willis, who in his subconscious desire for freedom from fame crashes his plane on La Isla del Mago off the coasts of Costa Rica and Panama instead of landing it in Phoenix, Arizona, the site of his scheduled concert.

A reviewer in the 13 April 1998 issue of *Publishers Weekly* described *Gone for Good* as "A disappointing allegory from a proven talent about wealth, fame and wisdom" and added that the novel "begins with some effective hooks but bogs down in silly subplots." A *Kirkus Reviews* critic (15 April 1998) claimed, "This one never takes off. Childress isn't doing much more than taxiing, in what is pretty clearly his weakest book yet." Most agree that his other works better represent his talents as a writer.

Mark Childress returned to New York in 2000, and he has plans for a sixth novel. The author's official website, <http://www.markchildress.com>, features an excerpt from a work titled "One Mississipi," which Childress says is "All about high school." He continues to write occasional book reviews for *The New York Times Book Review* and *TLS: The Times Literary Supplement* as he works on the new novel and a movie project with Columbia Pictures. While he continues to write thought-provoking and entertaining novels, Childress's ultimate contribution to the literary canon remains to be seen.

Interviews:

Steven Guiterrez, "A Conversation with Mark Childress," in *Gone for Good,* by Childress (New York: Ballantine, 1998);

"Mark Childress," *Page ONE Literary Newsletter Web Site* (15 February 2001) <http://www.pageonelit.com/interviews/Childress.html>.

References:

Bill Caton, "Mark Childress," in *Fighting Words: Words on Writing from 21 of the Heart of Dixie's Best Contemporary Authors,* edited by Caton (Montgomery, Ala.: Black Belt, 1995), pp. 34–41;

John Logue and Gary McCalla, *Life at Southern Living: A Sort of Memoir* (Baton Rouge: Louisiana State University Press, 2000);

Marian Motley-Carache, "Magic Realism in Mark Childress's *A World Made of Fire,*" *Mississippi Quarterly,* 42 (Winter 1988/1989): 57–67;

Dianne Young, "Books about the South for Children," *Southern Living,* 31 (December 1996): 58.

Michael Crichton
(John Lange, Jeffrey Hudson, Michael Douglas)
(23 October 1942 –   )

Lisa A. Kirkpatrick Lundy
University of North Texas

See also the Crichton entry in *DLB Yearbook: 1981*.

BOOKS: *Odds On,* as John Lange (New York: Signet, 1966);

Scratch One, as Lange (New York: Signet, 1967);

Easy Go, as Lange (New York: Signet, 1968); republished as *The Last Tomb,* as Lange (New York: Bantam, 1974);

A Case of Need, as Jeffrey Hudson (New York: World, 1968; London: Heinemann, 1968);

Zero Cool, as Lange (New York: Signet, 1969; London: Sphere, 1972);

The Andromeda Strain (New York: Knopf, 1969; London: Cape, 1969);

The Venom Business, as Lange (New York: World, 1969);

Drug of Choice, as Lange (New York: Signet, 1970); republished as *Overkill,* as Lange (London: Sphere, 1972);

Five Patients: The Hospital Explained (New York: Knopf, 1970; London: Cape, 1971);

Grave Descend, as Lange (New York: Signet, 1970);

Dealing; or, The Berkeley-to-Boston Forty-Brick Lost-Bag Blues, by Crichton and Douglas Crichton, as Michael Douglas (New York: Knopf, 1971; London: Talmy, 1971);

Binary, as Lange (New York: Knopf, 1972; London: Heinemann, 1972);

The Terminal Man (New York: Knopf, 1972; London: Cape, 1972);

The Great Train Robbery (New York: Knopf, 1975; London: Cape, 1975);

Eaters of the Dead (New York: Knopf, 1976; London: Cape, 1976);

Jasper Johns (New York: Abrams, 1977; London: Thames & Hudson, 1977; revised and expanded edition, New York: Abrams, 1994);

Congo (Franklin Center, Pa.: Franklin Library, 1980; New York: Knopf, 1980; London: Allen Lane, 1981);

Michael Crichton (photograph by Jonathan Exley; from the dust jacket for The Lost World, *1995; Richland County Public Library)*

Electronic Life: How to Think about Computers (New York: Knopf, 1983; London: Heinemann, 1983);

Sphere (New York: Knopf, 1987; London: Macmillan, 1987);

Travels (Franklin Center, Pa.: Franklin Library, 1988; New York: Knopf, 1988; London: Macmillan, 1988);

Jurassic Park (New York: Knopf, 1990; London: Century, 1991);

Rising Sun (Franklin Center, Pa.: Franklin Library, 1992; New York: Knopf, 1992; London: Century, 1992);

Disclosure (Franklin Center, Pa.: Franklin Library, 1993; New York: Knopf, 1994; London: Century, 1994);

The Lost World (New York: Knopf, 1995; London: Century, 1995);

Airframe (Franklin Center, Pa.: Franklin Library, 1996; New York: Knopf, 1996; London: Century, 1996);

Twister: The Original Screenplay, by Crichton and Anne-Marie Martin (New York: Ballantine, 1996);

Timeline (New York: Knopf, 1999; London: Century, 1999);

Prey (New York: HarperCollins, 2002; London: HarperCollins, 2002).

PRODUCED SCRIPTS: *Westworld,* motion picture, M-G-M, 1973;

Extreme Close-Up, motion picture, National General Pictures, 1973;

Coma, motion picture, M-G-M, 1978;

The Great Train Robbery, motion picture, United Artists, 1979;

Looker, motion picture, Warner Bros., 1981;

Runaway, motion picture, Columbia TriStar, 1984;

Jurassic Park, by Crichton and David Koepp, motion picture, Universal, 1993;

Rising Sun, by Crichton, Philip Kaufman, and Michael Backes, motion picture, 20th Century-Fox, 1993;

Twister, by Crichton and Anne-Marie Martin, motion picture, Warner Bros., 1996.

OTHER: Harlan Ellison, *Approaching Oblivion: Road Signs on the Treadmill Toward Tomorrow,* foreword by Crichton (New York: Walker, 1974);

Mathea Falco, *The Making of a Drug-Free America: Programs that Work,* foreword by Crichton (New York: Times Books, 1994);

Carl Jensen, *Censored: The News that Didn't Make the News and Why: The 1996 Project Censored Yearbook,* foreword by Crichton (New York: Four Walls Eight Windows, 1995);

Richard Farson, *Management of the Absurd: Paradoxes in Leadership,* foreword by Crichton (New York: Simon & Schuster, 1996);

Kevin Padian and Philip J. Currie, eds., *Encyclopedia of Dinosaurs,* foreword by Crichton (New York: Academic Press, 1997);

"Johnny at 8:30," "Untitled," "Life Goes to a Party," and "The Most Important Part of the Lab," in *First Words: Early Writings from Twenty-Two Favorite Contemporary Authors,* edited by Paul Mandelbaum (Chapel Hill, N.C.: Algonquin Books, 2000), pp. 47–65.

SELECTED PERIODICAL PUBLICATIONS—
UNCOLLECTED: "Predicting the Future," *Creative Computing,* 9 (March 1983): 188–203;

"Computers and Human Evolution," *Creative Computing,* 10 (November 1984): 189–190;

"Art a la Albers," *Creative Computing,* 11 (February 1985): 126–129;

"Travels with My Karma," *Esquire,* 109 (May 1988): 94–102;

"Greater Expectations," *Newsweek,* 116 (24 September 1990): 58;

"Is Biotechnology Creating a Monster?" *Business and Society Review,* 81 (1992): 43–46;

"Time for Tough Talk in the Land of the Setting Sun," *New York Times,* 10 August 1992, p. A17;

"Installer Hell," *Byte,* 18 (September 1993): 294;

"Mediasaurus," *Wired,* 1.04 (September/October 1993): 1–5;

"Looking at the Sun," *Washington Monthly,* 26 (April 1994): 54–57;

"Ritual Abuse, Hot Air, and Missed Opportunities," *Science,* 283 (5 March 1999): 1461–1463.

Michael Crichton has been called a "megastar" who has made a resounding impression on the literary world. Critics applaud him as a writer who is entertaining to read and who can "elaborate a gripping high concept into a crackerjack tale" (*Publishers Weekly,* 1 November 1999). Often referred to as elusive or "an enigma," Crichton is a graduate of Harvard Medical School; a noted critic of contemporary social issues, including science and new art; a screenwriter, director, and producer; the executive producer for the popular television program *ER;* and the writer of more than twenty-five books that range in style, structure, technique, and topic from adventure, drama, mystery, and science fiction to nonfiction reporting. Crichton is credited with inventing the "techno-thriller," a work that combines technology, suspense, and contemporary social issues.

In his autobiography, *Travels* (1988), Crichton claims, "Writing is how you make the experience your own, how you explore what it means to you, how you come to possess it, and ultimately release it." While his literature is, to him, self-expression, it is also a craft—one of which critics and scholars have taken note. His style and technique have been compared to literary predecessors from Gothic Victorianism (Mary Shelley's *Frankenstein* [1818]), detective fiction (the popular narrative style of Edgar Allan Poe in "The Purloined Letter" [1845] and "The Murders in the Rue Morgue" [1841] and Arthur Conan Doyle in the Sherlock Holmes series), adventure fiction (H. Rider Haggard's *King Solomon's Mines* [1886]), and science fiction (Jules Verne's *20,000 Leagues Under the Sea* [1869]). Crichton acknowledged to Andrea Chambers for a

THE
ANDROMEDA
STRAIN
A NOVEL
MICHAEL CRICHTON

Dust jacket for the first novel Crichton published under his own name: a 1969 medical thriller about scientists fighting to control a deadly microorganism brought back from space by a satellite (Bruccoli Clark Layman Archives)

1981 article, "All the books I've written play with preexisting literary forms."

Critics generally agree on three aspects of Crichton's work: their realism comes from great attention to detail; the creation of suspense relies on short, episodic plot structures and overlapping story lines that draw readers into the conflicts; and finally, their weak character development leads to the common observation that his fiction gives more life to the story and to the technical details than to humans. As Elizabeth A. Trembley notes about Crichton's science fiction, "readers remember the diseases, the computer implants, and the horrifying monsters in detail. But most cannot name even one of Crichton's major characters." Crichton's work brings forth the concern that the human obsession with power, and the resultant pride and greed that accompany that obsession, robs people of long-term foresight and results in failure to ever reach natural potentials.

John Michael Crichton was born in Chicago, Illinois, on 23 October 1942, to John Henderson and Zula (Miller) Crichton. The oldest of four children, Crichton grew up in Roslyn, New York. Because of his height (6'7" by the time he was sixteen) and his self-proclaimed need for acceptance by his peers, Crichton played basketball at Roslyn High School. In addition to his achievements in this sport, Crichton also enjoyed academic success. Influenced by his father, a journalist and the president of the American Association of Advertising Agencies, he discovered a proclivity for writing. At age fourteen he published a travel article about Sunset Crater Monument, Arizona, in *The New York Times*. He wrote several pieces that were praised by his teachers and his parents. "Johnny at 8:30," "Untitled" (a short play), and "Life Goes to a Party" are just three of the works he wrote in high school. Following these and subsequent writing successes, Crichton decided he would attend Harvard to become a professional writer.

The English department at Harvard, however, was unreceptive to Crichton's chosen writing style. After receiving several Cs for his work, Crichton decided to assess whether he was being misjudged: he plagiarized a little-known essay by George Orwell and submitted it to his professor for a grade. When the Orwell essay—undetected as borrowed—received a B-, Crichton abandoned his pursuit of an English degree and devoted his undergraduate work to anthropology. Crichton received his A.B. in 1964, graduating summa cum laude. He worked as a visiting lecturer at Cambridge University and won a Henry Russell Shaw Fellowship, which allowed him to travel in Europe and Africa on anthropological excursions for a year following graduation. He recounts many of these experiences in *Travels*.

Upon his return in 1965, Crichton married his high-school sweetheart, Joan Radam, and began medical training at Harvard. In order to pay his medical-school tuition, Crichton began writing novels under various pseudonyms. In an 8 June 1969 interview in *The New York Times*, Crichton revealed that the pseudonym John Lange arose as a result of his knowledge of a fairy-tale writer named Andrew Lang. He added an "e" to Lang and substituted his rarely used first name for Andrew. His second pen name was Jeffrey Hudson; he discussed its origin in the same interview as having been borrowed from a dwarf in the court of Charles I. His last pen name was Michael Douglas; this name was simply a combination of his and his brother's first names for the book they wrote together in 1971. Crichton had several reasons for writing under pseudonyms. He did not want to be treated differently by his peers in medical school, and he also wanted to protect his grades. In *Travels* Crichton reports, "At Har-

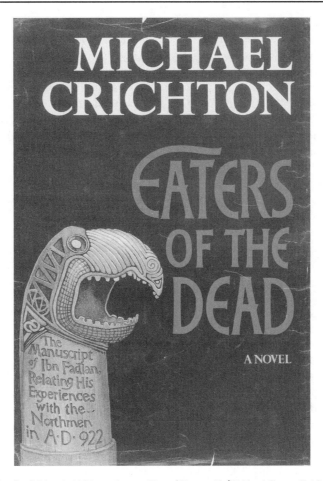

Dust jacket for Crichton's 1976 novel, a retelling of Beowulf *(Richland County Public Library)*

vard, in your clinical years, you were given grades according to the informal opinion of the people you worked with. If these people found out I was writing books, my grades would fall precipitously." Additionally, Crichton did not want his patients to think their health problems would become material for his next writing project (although he admits in *Travels* that he often asked himself upon hearing a patient's symptoms, "How can I use this in a book?").

Crichton's career as a novelist began in 1966 with the publication of his first book, *Odds On*. Crichton wrote this book and his subsequent medical-school writings with the intent of competing with in-flight movies: in order to sell (and pay the bills), they had to be attention-getting and "fast reads." Critics refer to *Odds On* and the other Lange works as super-suspense thrillers. Set in Spain, *Odds On* presents three men driven by greed to rob a hotel through the manipulation of information gained from a computer. Crichton employs technology with criminal schemes and varied romance to entice his readers. Although critics commented on the shallow, stereotypical characters, they uniformly applauded the building of suspense through multiple scenes of mystery, combining to form an irresistible plot. The books written as John Lange earned Crichton $2,000 each—and consequently served their purpose of paying his bills while providing entertainment for the flying public.

Crichton's next book, *Scratch One* (1967), was influenced by his European travels as well as his medical-school experiences. In this thriller Roger Carr gets caught up in an international scheme concerning the shipment of weapons from the United States to Saudi Arabia. Calling this book "wonderful escape reading" (*The New York Times*, 10 February 1974), critics and scholars compared it to James Bond–type adventures; however, like most of Crichton's books, it was criticized for its lack of character development. *Scratch One*, while intriguing, presents some characters in rather glib fashion: Dr. George Liseau, the mastermind in the thieves' circle, enjoys his surgical instruments as toys and has named his estate Le Scalpel. Ernst Brauer, reflective of World War II stereotypes, is a German hit man. As in *Odds On*, the main character seems autobiographical in his observant yet bumbling mannerisms. Also, as Crichton admits, the main characters are all a bit promiscuous and somewhat sexist. This book was also largely criticized for its confusing beginning–a series of murders with a glaring lack of explanation.

Crichton's third book written as Lange, *Easy Go* (1968), is set in Egypt and follows the adventures of five men–again driven by their greed–in an effort to discover hidden treasures of the pharaohs. Critics argue that this work may have provided the groundwork for *The Great Train Robbery* (1975). However, the same critics fault the ending as rather uneventful and not at all characteristic of the super-suspense thriller author John Lange. These first three novels led Crichton to consider writing a more provocative career than medicine.

Also in 1968, Crichton's third year in medical school, he wrote a new book–this time as Jeffrey Hudson–that won him dangerous recognition. In *A Case of Need* Crichton explores a surgical procedure gone wrong, resulting in a female patient's death. In this work Crichton reveals fairly detailed knowledge of Harvard's Medical School and the faculty and students employed within. When the novel received the Edgar Award from the Mystery Writers of America, Crichton figured he had been unmasked for certain; however, his luck held, and he accepted the award without his medical-school colleagues discovering his identity.

A Case of Need was a pivotal piece for Crichton because of its controversial subject matter: the surgical procedure in question was a then-illegal abortion. Listing the novel in a column on "The Year's Best Chillers," Allen J. Hubin of *The New York Times* (18 August 1968) stated that this work "demonstrates . . . the ability of detective fiction to treat contemporary social problems in a meaningful fashion."

Crichton, in his last year of medical school and during his postdoctoral fellowship at the Salk Institute for Biological Studies (1969–1970), produced three more novels. *Zero Cool* (1969) is another novel set in Europe that explores greed as it drives the main character to perform a surgical procedure on a corpse or die. Called a "bizarre mystery," this novel presents layers of intrigue that accumulate to an elaborate ending.

Having decided that writing was more interesting as a profession than medicine, Crichton published *The Andromeda Strain* (1969) under his real name, launching his publicly known literary career. This work earned him immediate recognition and set the pattern for his future success; it also, as he had anticipated, caused his medical-school colleagues and teachers to view him differently in his newfound fame. *The Andromeda Strain* quickly became a best-seller, made the Book-of-the-Month Club, and sold to Universal Studios for $250,000. (The movie version, with screenplay by Nel-son Gidding, appeared in 1971; Crichton even had an uncredited cameo role as "Bearded Surgeon.") Realistically written, *The Andromeda Strain* received high praise from critics. Referred to in a 10 June 1969 *Pittsburgh Press* review as "relentlessly suspenseful," *The Andromeda Strain* follows five biophysicists as they battle a deadly virus rapidly spread on Earth by a contaminated satellite, which has just crashed in an Arizona town. The virus, the "Andromeda strain," soon kills all humans in the vicinity of the crash site. Crichton builds the highly applauded suspense of the work through detailed descriptions, a race against a fast-moving, dangerous microorganism, and the drama of allowing the reader to possess more information than the characters do. The primary conflict, of course, is between humans and the unknown virus; however, secondary conflicts exist as well. Crichton points out that, while the scientists are battling time in their war against the virus, they are also fighting off the government, which is at cross-purposes with the scientists. *The Andromeda Strain* features characters who are not memorable as individuals; it is enough to refer to them–the scientists–as a group. The focus of the work is the interaction of the team against the virus. However, critics also recognize a theme emerging: that neither the government nor scientists should be allowed to work unmonitored by the public. While the majority of critics call the work science fiction, former Knopf editor in chief Bob Gottlieb evaluated the text as "a documentary, and its strengths were in that–not in its characterizations" (*Publishers Weekly,* 1 November 1999). Webster Schott of *The New York Times* (8 June 1969) said, "As art, *The Andromeda Strain* lacks human heat. As craft, it's pure stainless steel."

Also in 1969, Crichton–again as Lange–published *The Venom Business.* This work reveals contemporary concerns and stereotypes of the era. The main character, Charles Raynaud, visits Paris with preconceived notions of France: "fast cars, exotic food, and erotic women." Crichton perpetuates the American stereotype of France when a secondary character refers to the French: "Incompetent frogs. The only decent thing about the country was the women. Without the women, France would be a desert. Just a few crappy cathedrals." The content shows influences from Crichton's travels in Venezuela and his experience with snakes as well as his knowledge of medicine. In the novel, the primary villain, Jonathan Black, is a researcher into the science of anger. He experiments with cats and, conclusively, on humans with drug therapy that kills the part of the brain that controls anger. In this way, he is able to manipulate an inheritance through multiple murders.

Having graduated from Harvard Medical School in 1969, Crichton decided not to seek his medical

Poster for the 1973 science-fiction movie written and directed by Crichton, about out-of-control androids at a futuristic amusement park (Collection of Paul Talbot)

license but to become a professional writer. His seventh Lange novel, *Drug of Choice* (1970), published in Britain as *Overkill* (1972), delves further into chemical mind control. Dr. Roger Clark assumes the role of a scientific detective who explores a company's production of a drug that controls one's mental state. Claiming that the public is already subject to mind manipulation by mass media, antagonist Harvey Blood claims, "Already you are manipulated . . . by your world. Do you think a car is beautiful? If you do, it is only because somebody paid millions in advertising to make you think so." As in several of his early works, Crichton reveals juvenile humor typical to college students. At a party Clark attends, his hostess comments, "I'm glad you decided to come.' 'Anytime,' he said. 'Well, later then,' she said. 'Ladies first,' he said." Crichton shows literary humor as well when he titles one chapter "Olive or Twist." Critics agreed that this work is completely involving.

Grave Descend (1970) is another super-suspense thriller, which explores the manipulation of a diver to find sunken treasure in the Caribbean. Crichton reveals techniques for diving and methods of swimming in and around shark-infested waters, knowledge gained from travels in the Virgin Islands in 1968. The text also includes several quotations from Samuel Johnson, revealing Crichton's familiarity with his works. The antagonist in the story is an avid student of Johnson, and the name of the ship–the *Grave Descend*–comes from a Johnson poem, which describes an earnest scientist as he falls to death.

Also during 1970 Crichton published his first nonfiction work under his own name: *Five Patients: The Hospital Explained*. This text presents health-care issues of the late 1960s. In a note added to a later reprinting of the text, Crichton claims, "When I reread the book . . . I was struck by how much medicine has changed–and also, by how much has not changed." The work explores the training of doctors and the ongoing job of adapting to new technologies and surgical techniques. The stories of five patients (Ralph Orlando, John O'Connor, Peter Luchesi, Sylvia Thompson, and Edith Murphy) are told from the point of view of a fourth-year medical student. Crichton accurately presents issues that hospitals and health care providers face: rising costs, new drugs and techniques, the role of technology in clinical decision making, insurance issues, and quality patient care. Several critics claim this work to be the genesis of the television series *ER*. In a *New York Times* review (2 August 1970) F. C. Redlick called this work "a guide to the modern teaching hospital written for intelligent readers." The text is written in rather candid language; while they were somewhat shocked at its blatancy, critics agreed with Redlick that "such language helped to recreate the world of the teaching hospital, where

death and agony are routine and where a certain professional detachment is required." *Five Patients* was so well received that Crichton won the title of Writer of the Year (1970) from the Association of American Medical Writers. Also in 1970 he and Radam divorced.

In January 1971 Crichton and his brother Douglas Crichton published a combined effort: *Dealing; or, The Berkeley-to-Boston Forty-Brick Lost-Bag Blues*. Written to "the lawmakers of our great land," this work is a first-person narrative that features stereotypical characters, such as college kids who use drugs; exchanges between those who buy and sell drugs; and the obligatory boy/girl scenarios. Critics received this book as a public commentary that narcotics laws in the United States are not strong enough. Beyond that, the work received little more than passing notice. Christopher Lehmann-Haupt wrote in *The New York Times* (3 February 1971), "admittedly, it is entertaining–slick and cool and savvy. . . . So 'Dealing' was only meant to be fun– Heads and Narcs instead of Cops and Robbers. Let's just not pretend it's anything more."

Crichton produced two novels in 1972. Because techno-thrillers were now associated with his pen name rather than with his own, Crichton published *Binary* under the name John Lange. It presents a crazed millionaire who plans to exterminate the San Diego populace with a deadly nerve gas during a Republican convention. John Graves, government agent, must thwart the criminal's plans. The time span of the work is only twelve hours–the shortest of any of Crichton's works. This novel earned reviews similar to those of his other med-school thrillers; in a *New York Times* book review (3 December 1972) Newgate Callendar called *Binary* "a down-to-the-wire thriller, with God and Satan in thrust and counterthrust." Others praised the suspenseful ending. Crichton was able to use this book as his initiation into the world of movie directing. In addition to *The Andromeda Strain*, Crichton had seen two of his early works made into movies, with screenplays by other writers. *A Case of Need* was produced as *The Carey Treatment*, directed by Blake Edwards, in 1972. The novel Crichton wrote with his brother, *Dealing*, was also made into a 1972 movie directed by Paul Williams. (Neither of these movies won much recognition, however.) In 1972 Crichton directed the made-for-television movie version of *Binary*, renamed *Pursuit* (screenplay by Robert Dozier), starring Ben Gazzara and Martin Sheen.

Critics claim the early works written by Crichton as John Lange serve the reader "as entertainment and diversion of the purest sort." While these super-suspense thrillers were never considered "high art," they did what was intended: paid the medical-school bills and at the same time served to launch a profitable writing career for Crichton.

Also in 1972 Crichton published *The Terminal Man,* under his own name. In this work the author combines mind control, neurological disorders with resultant anger, and computer programming. The main character, Harry Benson, undergoes an experimental procedure: electrodes are implanted in his brain that, when triggered, will control the anger and violent tendencies caused by brain damage from an auto accident. As in *Frankenstein,* a figurative monster develops from this experimentation. Also considered science fiction, *The Terminal Man* follows the pattern created in earlier works. Scientists in this novel aim to create a smarter human, a superhuman. But the scientists, like Victor Frankenstein, fail to see the possibility of something going wrong with the outcome of their experiment. As in most science fiction, the focus is on the action; as Trembley notes, "The characters often seem stereotypical . . . used only to advance the exciting plot." Again in this work Crichton reminds the public to be aware of what researchers are doing. The 1974 movie version of *The Terminal Man,* with screenplay by Mike Hodges, starred George Segal as Benson.

In 1973 Crichton wrote his first screenplay, titled *Westworld.* The story is set in a futuristic amusement park, a complex that includes the set of an 1880s frontier village populated by androids. When the computer system fails, the androids become dangerous. This work reveals Crichton's continued concern with technology. Critics compare this movie to Crichton's later work *Jurassic Park* (1990), another story of an amusement park gone out of control. Crichton also directed *Westworld,* which was released on 21 November 1973. In 1980 six episodes of a television series based on the movie and titled *Beyond Westworld* were produced, but only four were aired before the show was canceled.

Crichton points out on his website, <http://www.crichton-official.com>, that in an effort to present an android's point of view in one sequence, "*Westworld* was the first feature film to process imagery by computer." While *Westworld* had been somewhat forgotten, its remaking with newly digitized images resulted in Crichton's achievement of another award. In 1994 he won an Oscar for Technical Achievement for his part in the new technology. Crichton produced another original screenplay in 1973, *Extreme Close-Up;* however, little information exists concerning this work about a television reporter involved in a story on voyeurism.

The first of Crichton's novels that does not focus on technology and its impact on society appeared in 1975. *The Great Train Robbery,* set in 1855 London, depicts the brilliant plan of a roguish thief, Edward Pierce, to steal a large amount of gold bullion from a

Dust jacket for the first trade edition of Crichton's 1992 novel, about the investigation of the murder of a call girl at a Japanese company party (Richland County Public Library)

strongly guarded train bound for Russia to replenish the British Army. Considered by critics to be an adventure novel, the story actually presents a reenactment of a real crime. Drawing from fact and using the technique of the picaresque novel, *The Great Train Robbery* presents several of Pierce's escapades that all come together to define him. Trembley calls Pierce "the perfect criminal hero for a society that admires independence and wealth." Critics applauded the verisimilitude of the work and the unusually three-dimensional qualities of the characters, who are (somewhat uncharacteristically for Crichton) entertaining and interesting. As Trembley notes, "Crichton's ability to use historical material gathered from government documents to make characters come alive is extraordinary."

In 1976 Crichton published *Eaters of the Dead,* a retelling of *Beowulf,* also dubbed Crichton's "sword and sorcery" novel. In an essay published with the paperback edition of the novel, Crichton explains its genesis and his creation of academic footnotes and references to his supposed source, a tenth-century nonfiction Arab

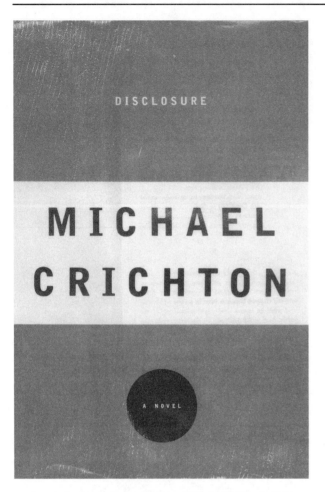

Dust jacket for the first trade edition (1994) of Crichton's 1993 novel, about a businessman who is sexually harassed by his female boss (Richland County Public Library)

travelogue by Ibn Fadlan. The story depicts Ibn's kidnapping by Vikings and his role in their battle against the Wendol, black fiends who murder and eat humans. As Trembley comments,

> This use of fictionalized scholarship is a unique example of Crichton's usual attention to detail. In other novels he produces computer printouts, maps, and coded messages to add to the scientific realism of his story. However, in this story, set in a pretechnological era, Crichton had to produce pretechnological "documentation" to create that same realism.

While the novel was applauded by Crichton fans for its Gothic conventions, some critics found the scholarship to be somewhat cumbersome to the story. In *The New York Times* (25 April 1976) Jack Sullivan stated that the "densely footnoted apparatus of anthropological and literary scholarship" creates verisimilitude that "becomes a pedantic mannerism, a puzzle that the reader wearies

piecing together." Eden Ross Lipson agreed in another *New York Times* review (3 April 1977) for the paperback version of the novel that the "modern commentary that is supposed to authenticate the document" simply muddles the work and tires the reader. Also, comparing the tale to *Beowulf,* critics were disappointed with the exacting descriptions of the Wendol. Whereas in *Beowulf* Grendel and his dam are somewhat amorphous and mysterious, in Crichton's novel so much detail is given that the element of terror is somewhat removed. In 1999 *Eaters of the Dead* was made into a movie titled *The 13th Warrior,* with screenplay by William Wisher and Warren Lewis; Antonio Banderas starred, and Crichton was a producer.

In 1977 Crichton published a second nonfiction work, *Jasper Johns,* a catalogue to accompany a retrospective of the artist's works at the Whitney Museum. Written much like a literary biography, the work offers quotations from Johns's friends and family to illuminate his personality, then presents his life history through the chronology of his works. The catalogue includes 186 illustrations and 231 reproductions of Johns's paintings, prints, sculptures, and drawings in a thorough, all-encompassing collection. Critics praised the work for its accurate scholarship and exhaustive presentation. Mary Ann Tighe, evaluating the book for *The New York Times* (4 December 1977), called it "refreshingly unorthodox in approach," adding that it is "the most charming and readable art book in recent years."

Crichton took a break from novel writing between 1977 and 1980 and channeled his energies into screenplays and movie production. In 1978 he married Kathleen St. Johns; the couple divorced in 1980. (A third marriage, to Suzanne Childs, also ended.) Also in 1978 he wrote and directed the motion picture *Coma,* a medical suspense thriller based on the 1977 novel by Robin Cook. When a young doctor begins an unofficial investigation into the details of the failed surgery that resulted in her friend's terminal coma, she uncovers a conspiracy to harvest organs from comatose patients for profit. *Coma* allowed Crichton—despite his timidity—to succeed in the direction of some (as he terms them in *Travels*) "big stars," including Geneviève Bujold, Michael Douglas, Rip Torn, and Richard Widmark. When the cast of Crichton's next movie, his 1979 adaptation of *The Great Train Robbery,* expressed doubts about his ability to direct, they viewed a copy of *Coma.* The effect was immediate, and the rest of the shoot progressed smoothly. Starring Sean Connery (as Edward Pierce), Lesley-Anne Down, and Donald Sutherland, *The Great Train Robbery* was received by critics as entertaining, suspenseful, and "delightfully engaging."

Crichton's next novel, *Congo,* came out in 1980. In this novel Crichton explores a mythological story of the Lost City of Zinj–supposedly home to vast treasures, including large raw diamonds. When the heroine, Karen Ross, discovers through video footage that scientists from her company on a dig in Africa have had their heads crushed, she begins a rescue mission both to save a former boyfriend and to solve the mystery of the scientists' deaths. Most critics recognized the pattern of adventure fiction inspired by Haggard's *King Solomon's Mines,* including an engaging search for treasure (diamonds) and a hero who conquers all obstacles. Although the characters of this tale do not encounter natives, they do have run-ins with extraordinary, trained gray gorillas, allowing Crichton to incorporate knowledge he had gained on travels in Rwanda. The critics noted Crichton's tendency to update the adventure genre by working technology into the tale. A reviewer for the *Des Moines Sunday Register* (7 December 1980) commented, "*Congo* is jam-packed with facts and knowledge about computers, technology, the jungle and 'talking' apes." While many reviews were favorable, a few critics were not so admiring. Cary Wolfe complains, "Crichton's novel is a beguiling jumble of factoids . . . and it is made all the more inscrutable by its affective flatness, its characteristic postmodern depthlessness." However, Wolfe does acknowledge the questioning of nonhuman intelligence and culture, racial stereotyping, and the "immense technoscientific apparatus driven to dizzying accomplishments . . . under the spur of free market global capitalism." The director of the 1995 movie version, Frank Marshall, looked at the movie as a challenge, applauding Crichton's combination of technology and nature.

In 1981 Crichton continued his movie direction with *Looker,* for which he also wrote the screenplay. This work is about the conversion of women from nearly perfect models to perfect simulations of women. Following plastic surgeries, several fashion models–whose likenesses have been technologically copied–are murdered. Their "copies" then replace them as controllable, perfect workers who advertise and sell at the whim of the market. This movie relies on the audience's astonishment at the blatant objectivity of women. The audience, however, was less than receptive. Most critics reported that the only memorable assets of the movie were nudity and "cool cars."

Crichton's third nonfiction work, *Electronic Life: How to Think about Computers,* was published in 1983. Linda Robinson of *The New York Times* (6 November 1983) evaluated this "dictionary of computer subjects" as a "lucid explanation" and "a light and chatty primer on computers intended to reduce our fears of the new

machines." The text was generally approved by critics as encouraging and informative.

His next endeavor as both screenwriter and director came in 1984 with the movie *Runaway.* Starring Tom Selleck, Gene Simmons, and Cynthia Rhodes, this work depicts a criminal who manipulates robotics to steal computer chips that will give him power in the technologies industries. The movie, however, did not earn the recognition for which Crichton had hoped.

After many travels and years of frequent exploration into the realm of psychic abilities, Crichton published *Sphere* (1987). This novel presents an investigation of an alien spacecraft; inside is a large, metal sphere into which one can only go through psychic means. In *Travels* Crichton relates one experience that helped to inspire the novel. On a trip to Singapore, he stayed at a hotel in which the carpeting in the elevators was changed every day to match the day of the week: "Today is Saturday–Have a nice day." He describes a similar experience inside the spacecraft. During the same trip, extended to New Guinea, Crichton went diving to see a B-24 bomber from World War II. He recalls, "When I got to the surface, I asked about the plane. Did anyone know its history, how it got there, why it had crashed? No one did. There were only stories, and theories, and possibilities." Applauded for its incredible suspense, *Sphere* gained recognition for Crichton's attention to detail. Critics also commented on the technique by which Crichton builds the suspense through limited omniscient point of view, through which the reader empathizes with one usually likable, average character. In this work the feelings of team psychologist Norman Johnson affect the reader as if he or she is standing in Norman's place, as Trembley observes: "Events that terrify or surprise him have the same effect on audiences." In this novel, Crichton lauds the imagination: those who can transcend ordinary processes can enter the sphere.

Edward A. Kopper Jr. notes that the many literary allusions in *Sphere* are lost on readers, particularly the connections to Joseph Conrad's *Lord Jim* (1900). However, Kopper acknowledges only the influence; he credits Crichton's characters as being more original, selfless, and realistic than Conrad's narcissistic, romantic Jim. Recalling Crichton's early goal to compete with in-flight movies, critic Robin McKinley applauded this novel for occupying her as she sat in a grounded plane: "*Sphere* continued to keep me happy. . . . No one can ask more of a thriller, except maybe that it be a little longer" (*The New York Times,* 12 July 1987). While the novel is fairly predictable in its plotline, critics agreed that it is both riveting and interesting. Crichton was also a producer of the 1998 movie

Dust jacket for Crichton's sequel to Jurassic Park, *his 1990 novel about cloned dinosaurs
and the dangers of biotechnology (Richland County Public Library)*

version, which starred Dustin Hoffman, Sharon Stone, and Samuel L. Jackson.

While working as a visiting writer at the Massachusetts Institute of Technology in 1988, Crichton published his autobiography, *Travels.* This book reveals Crichton's search for knowledge–of almost everything–throughout his childhood on Long Island, and it chronicles his first writing efforts and his lifelong travels. The text is divided into two parts. The first is a relatively short section devoted to his medical-school experiences between 1965 and 1969 and his emerging participation in the field of novel writing. Included in this part are chapters titled "A Good Story," "The Gourd Ward," and "The Girl Who Seduced Everybody," titles that reflect Crichton's talent at drawing reader interest. The second, longer section of his autobiography is devoted to his travels, including his participation in workshops and conventions devoted to extrasensory perception. This work was generally well received for its superb writing style and honesty. One critic for *The New York Times Book Review* (10 September 1989) referred to Crichton as a "richly informed mind" with a "driving curiosity," adding that "he seems bound . . . to explore every single mystery in the universe."

In 1990 Crichton published *Jurassic Park,* which *The New York Times* (15 November 1990) called "easily the best of Mr. Crichton's novels to date." In this novel, entrepreneur John Hammond capitalizes on the revolutionary discovery of scientific abilities to recover and clone dinosaur DNA. He manufactures dinosaurs with the hopes of creating the world's greatest theme park. However, as eccentric mathematician Ian Malcolm reminds him, life cannot be controlled; it "finds a way." When security measures fail, the park becomes a nightmare.

Reviewers commented consistently on Crichton's narrative technique, observing that telling this story from different points of view is an effective means for a realistic view of both plot and characters. Further, they complimented the educational aspect of the work, and, as with almost all of Crichton's works, they applauded the thorough research done regarding the history and the ever-advancing work in science. Scholars and critics almost unanimously commented on the verisimilitude of both *Jurassic Park* and its sequel, *The Lost World* (1995); as Warren Buckland observes, "Michael Crichton's novels . . . do not open in the realm of pure fantasy . . . but present a possible world, by drawing out extreme consequences from a non-fictional state of affairs in the actual world."

As G. Thomas Goodnight notes, Crichton is "famous for doing his homework, for introducing popular audiences to complex concepts. . . . His character Ian Malcolm presents us with Chaos Theory, often taken for granted, and this view represents the postmodernist, skeptical view of life as we know it." Other critics see Crichton's main theme as one of techno-dystopia, a warning against technology out of control. The New Historicists claim that Hammond's "re-creation" of dinosaurs is not reality; it is a new reality with an unknown outcome, and scientists in their greed for fame and fortune fail to recognize this unpredictability. Evan Watkins views *Jurassic Park* as a retelling of the creation story, with Hammond as God of a creation that fails to behave as he wants—and in which the tenets of Chaos Theory interfere. Whether Crichton imbues his scientific characters with a God complex or some other motivation, critics recognize Crichton's tendency to portray scientists with flaws: overwhelming pride, greed, and lust for control.

Jurassic Park presents a cautionary stance toward biotechnology and computerization. As Nigel Clark notes, Crichton offers a morality tale that teaches that artificial life—cloning through DNA restructuring—through biotechnology will result only in an unknown outcome: "simple entities might evolve their own more complex successors." This novel, according to Evans Watkins, is a postmodern reminder that creation in an ever-changing environment will result in ever-changing outcomes. As recognized by the majority of critics, Crichton possesses and expresses a naturalist point of view—that "if we are gone tomorrow, the earth will not miss us" (*The New York Times,* 15 November 1990).

Crichton released his next novel, *Rising Sun,* in 1992. It depicts the murder of a high-priced call girl during a Japanese company party. The leaders of the company try to avoid the possibility of publicity. However, when Peter Smith and John Connor begin their investigation of the crime, they discover a web of technological cover-ups, political deviations, and unusual kowtowing to the Japanese executives, all of which require a closer look. Reflective of the 1980s attempt of a Japanese company to purchase American Fairchild Semiconductor, *Rising Sun* presents a metaphor for the United States in dire jeopardy, a metaphor of America as the dying prostitute. A reviewer for *The New York Times* (9 February 1992) applauded Crichton's "gifts" but called his work polemic in entertainment form, "witty and erudite." The reviewer noted Crichton's thorough research into the tensions that exist between America and Japan and the complex tale that Crichton realistically weaves in and around the rather tenuous intercontinental relationship. Critics agreed that the work is more than a mystery and that Crichton is again commenting on controversial issues through detective fiction: this time, overly ambitious American capitalism as it blindly causes Americans to sell their country and culture piece by piece to other countries.

Floyd D. Cheung examines *Rising Sun* as "postcolonial discourse." *Rising Sun* presents the United States under attack by the Japanese, who strive to conquer it as an economic colony. Both Cheung and the *New York Times* reviewer concur that the character John Connor is the voice of Crichton and that his message is a postmodern concern "to reevaluate whether United States cultural and economic borders are as intact as they once seemed." Cheung, however, criticizes Crichton's view of American women as "constructed as beings interested only in physical pleasure and monetary reward."

Fred G. See and Jacob Raz and Aviad E. Raz caution that the work is an "unmasking" of Japan; and while the research is thorough and well documented, it "actively promotes certain normatively held xenophobic and racist attitudes." Of the 1993 movie version of the novel (with screenplay by Crichton, Michael Backes, and director Philip Kaufman), critics agree that the relationships in the movie are reflective of "a lasting condition of alienation from which the personalities and cultures in the film never recover." Commentators point out that in both novel and movie, the Japanese mimic Americans to achieve economic, social, and political goals. One critic mentioned that even though Peter Smith is an African American in the movie rather than Caucasian, and even though Kaufman has changed the murderer from Japanese to white, he fails to acknowledge the Asian American views. The tone of the movie still paints Japan as an evil machine. Japanese activist Guy Aoki commented in a 1996 interview with Robert M. Payne, "We were concerned that the film's portrayal of the Japanese would play into all the evil stereotypes that had gone before." Most critics agree that both the novel and the movie perpetuate a racist view of Japan and its citizens.

While writing *Rising Sun,* Crichton was also involved in the making of the movie version of *Jurassic Park,* directed by Steven Spielberg. Crichton wrote the screenplay with David Koepp. The movie, which starred Sam Neill, Laura Dern, Jeff Goldblum, and Richard Attenborough, was released in 1993 and achieved worldwide success.

Crichton's next novel, *Disclosure* (1993), was soon followed by the movie version, of which he was executive producer. In this work Crichton explores sexual harassment from an interesting perspective. Having lost a promotion to a female colleague, Tom Sanders falls

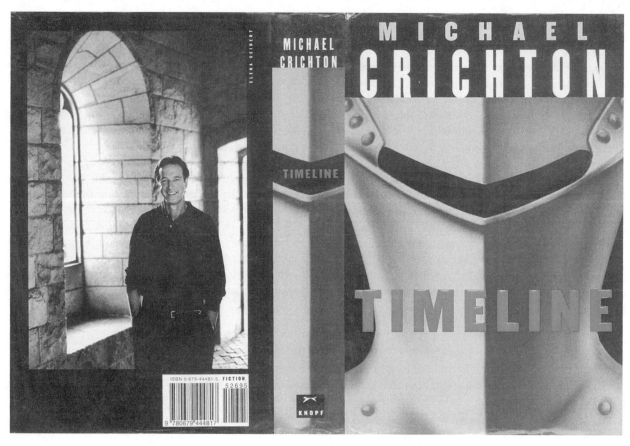

*Dust jacket for Crichton's 1999 novel, in which a Yale history professor time-travels back to medieval
France and is retrieved by his students (Richland County Public Library)*

victim to her advances as she attempts to reignite their previous love affair. A reviewer for *The New York Times* (6 January 1994) applauded this work for its research: "While only 5 percent of sexual harassment suits are brought by men against women, only 5 percent of corporate supervisors are women." Not only is this fact a relevant observation of the corporate status quo but also a contribution to the awareness of how little the equal rights movement has actually affected big business.

Disclosure, the subject of which Nancy Collins describes as "more prickly than Japanese-American tensions," is based on a true story. The work, according to critics, should be considered a document of the 1990s, particularly of women in the 1990s. According to Carol Watts, "Women are figured here as a source of practical knowledge . . . adaptable pragmatists" whose "flexibility is at once a strength and a perceived threat" to males. Feminists such as Watts present the work as reflective of the definition of "disclosure" that is exactly what women experienced in the 1990s—self-clarification: "If sex equals power . . . it is women who are the prime movers." Most critics, however, including Trembley, noticed Crichton's insistence that "males and females are no different in their tendency to abuse . . . power." In *Travels* he states his belief that "The best way to think about men and women is to assume there are no differences between them." While largely applauded, *Disclosure* also found criticism. Maureen Dowd, in "Women Who Harass Too Much" (*The New York Times,* 23 January 1994), claimed that Crichton "lurches between slow-paced didactic lecturing and fast-paced thriller plotting."

In 1994 a project that Crichton had nurtured for a long time came to fruition. He explains on his official website that after finishing *Westworld* in 1974,

I wrote a documentary-style movie about what happened during 24 hours in an emergency room. I thought the screenplay was terrific, but nobody would make the movie, finding it too technical, too chaotic and too fast-moving. It sat on the shelf for the next nineteen years—brought out every five or ten years, for updating, and for the studios and networks to look at, and reject yet again.

Finally NBC made it as a TV pilot. And then it became a series.

That series, *ER,* was hugely successful, applauded for its detail, accuracy, and realism. In 1995 the series won eight Emmy Awards, and executive producer Crichton also personally won two awards for the show, the George Foster Peabody Award and one from the Producers Guild of America.

The Lost World, the sequel to *Jurassic Park,* presents a world of surviving dinosaurs six years after the deaths of both John Hammond and his creation, Jurassic Park. This work has been among Crichton's least praised, and indeed lambasted by many; Ursula K. Le Guin gives a scathing critique in her 1996 article "Concerning Dinosaurs." She claims Crichton plays on the general public's fear of science and their ignorance of it: "he mixes science fiction lingo and tropes into a pseudo-fantasy that degrades narrative coherence to formulaic action-horror plotting." Mark Annichiarico wrote in *Library Journal* (15 September 1995) that while it follows the pattern of adventure and science fiction, *The Lost World* is so "bereft of plot and characterization in deference to action" that it barely resembles "the entertaining and educational novel that preceded it." Executive producer Spielberg made a third *Jurassic Park* movie in 2001, based on Crichton's characters, but that was the extent of the author's involvement.

In 1996 Crichton produced the movie *Twister* and published a new novel, *Airframe.* Crichton wrote *Twister* with his fourth wife, Anne-Marie Martin, whom he married in 1987 and with whom he has a daughter, Taylor. The movie, filled with special effects, follows a group of "storm chasers," meteorologists researching tornadoes. Helen Hunt and Bill Paxton starred.

Airframe, about a woman investigating an airline disaster, received applause for Crichton's thorough research and cataloguing of airplanes and mechanical parts. However, the critics agreed that the protagonist, Casey, is somewhat incredible; one reviewer for *The New York Times* (15 December 1996) stated that Casey sounds like "Mr. Crichton in drag." This book, like *The Lost World,* was criticized for its slower pace and called "an anti-Crichton novel–an anti-thriller." The *New York Times* review further stated that the novel is a "book about air disasters that you could quite happily pick up at the airport and read in the plane, before slipping into deep, dreamless sleep." However, other critics such as Jill M. Smith in *Romantic Times Magazine* posited that this work is a marvel in suspenseful technique, an "intense, chilling new thriller, which is also a stinging indictment of both the media and airline industries."

His next novel, *Timeline,* was published in 1999. This novel received the usual responses to a Crichton work: praise for his accurate details and criticism for the thin characterization. The story involves Yale students and their time travel back to 1357 France to rescue their history professor. *Publishers Weekly* (1 November 1999) called the novel "vintage Crichton, a slick, immensely involving blend of science fiction and fantasy that's reminiscent in tone of *Jurassic Park* and could be his most popular novel since that juggernaut." Although one critic called the work "*Jurassic Park* in drag" (*The New York Times,* 21 November 1999), the combination of the quantum technology used for time travel and a complex medieval past won praise from the majority of critics.

Also in 1999 Crichton announced his intention of entering into the field of interactive software. He formed a computer gaming company called Timeline Studios. In *Publishers Weekly* (24 May 1999) Karen Jones reported that, like Tom Clancy and Red Storm Entertainment, Crichton intends to "create worlds" by "crossing media."

Crichton's fiction and nonfiction made him the "most lucrative author" at Knopf publishers. In February 2001 Crichton signed a two-book contract with HarperCollins, a contract speculated as being worth at least seven figures. According to *Forbes* magazine (March 2000), Crichton earns in the neighborhood of $65 million a year, "more than any other writer in the world." His 2002 novel, *Prey,* earned him accolades again for his plot development. Focusing on current unknowns in nanotechnology, Crichton explores the chaos of creating life through scientific means and the dangers of its developing its own survivalist methods.

Because of a chronic battle with depression, Crichton tries to stay busy. His many hobbies, work interests, and family life continue to occupy him in addition to his literature, movies, television dramas, and computer software production. By all indications, Michael Crichton will continue to affect not only the world of media but also the literary world as he pursues a lifelong exploration of meanings.

References:

Peter S. Alterman, "Neuron and Junction: Patterns of Thought in *The Andromeda Strain,*" in *The Mechanical God: Machines in Science Fiction,* edited by Thomas P. Dunn and Richard D. Erlich (Westport, Conn.: Greenwood Press, 1982), pp. 109–116;

Jeff Azleski, "The High Concept of Michael Crichton," *Publishers Weekly* (1 November 1999);

Sharon Begley, "Here Come the DNAsaurs," *Newsweek* (14 June 1993): 56–61;

Janet Bergstrom, "Androids and Androgyny," *Camera Obscura: A Journal of Feminism, Culture, and Media Studies,* 15 (1986): 36–65;

Warren Buckland, "Between Science Fact and Science Fiction: Spielberg's Digital Dinosaurs, Possible Worlds, and the New Aesthetic Realism," *Screen,* 40, no. 2 (1999): 177–192;

Andrea Chambers, "Author-Director Michael Crichton Is a Master of Multimedia Monkey Business," *People Weekly* (16 February 1981): 94–98;

Floyd D. Cheung, "Imagining Danger, Imagining Nation: Postcolonial Discourse in *Rising Sun* and *Stargate,*" *Jouvert: A Journal of Postcolonial Studies,* 2, no. 2 (1998);

Nigel Clark, "Panic Ecology: Nature in the Age of Superconductivity," *Theory, Culture & Society,* 14, no. 1 (1997): 77–96;

Nancy Collins, "The Androgen Strain," *Mirabella,* 56 (1994): 65–67;

Brendan Darrach, "Andromeda's Author Casts Long Shadow," *Life* (3 March 1972): 65;

Dan Donlan, "Experiencing the *Andromeda Strain,*" *English Journal* (September 1974): 72–73;

Dennis Fischer, "Congo: Director Frank Marshall on Filming the Bestseller," *Cinefantastique,* 26, no. 5 (1995): 56–57;

Fischer, "Congo: Filming Michael Crichton's Long-Shelved Epic Adventure," *Cinefantastique,* 26, no. 4 (1995): 12–13;

G. Thomas Goodnight, "The Firm, the Park and the University: Fear and Trembling on the Postmodern Trail," *Quarterly Journal of Speech,* 81, no. 3 (1995): 267–290;

Harriett Hawkins, "Paradigms Lost: Chaos, Milton and Jurassic Park," *Textual Practice,* 8, no. 2 (1994): 255–267;

Zoe Heller, "The Admirable Crichton," *Vanity Fair* (January 1994): 32–49;

Geoffrey James, "Five Personal Odysseys," *Maclean's* (15 August 1988): 50–51;

Edward A. Kopper Jr., "Conrad in Michael Crichton's *Sphere,*" *Notes on Contemporary Literature,* 19, no. 4 (1989): 11–12;

Ursula K. Le Guin, "Concerning Dinosaurs," *Paradoxa: Studies in World Literary Genres,* 2 (1996): 531–533;

Allen Michie, "New Historicism and Jurassic Park," *NOTE: Notes on Teaching English,* 25, no. 1 (1997): 15–22;

Robert M. Payne, "Total Eclipse of the Sun: *Rising Sun:* Interview with Activist Guy Aoki," *Jump Cut: A Review of Contemporary Media,* 40 (1996): 29–37;

Jacob Raz and Aviad E. Raz, "'America' Meets 'Japan': A Journey for Real between Two Imaginaries," *Theory, Culture & Society,* 13, no. 3 (1996): 153–178;

Eric Sauter, "A Tall Storyteller," *Saturday Review* (November/December 1984): 20–25;

Fred G. See, "'Something Reflective': Technology and Visual Pleasure," *Journal of Popular Film and Television,* 22, no. 4 (1995): 162–171;

Elizabeth A. Trembley, *Michael Crichton: A Critical Companion* (Westport, Conn.: Greenwood Press, 1996);

Evan Watkins, "The Dinosaurics of Size: Economic Narrative and Postmodern Culture," *Centennial Review,* 39, no. 2 (1995): 189–211;

Carol Watts, "Thinking Disclosure: Or, the Structure of Post-Feminist Cynicism," *Women: A Cultural Review,* 6, no. 3 (1995): 275–286;

Cary Wolfe, "Faux Post-Humanism: Or, Animal Rights, Neocolonialism, and Michael Crichton's *Congo,*" *Arizona Quarterly: A Journal of American Literature, Culture, and Theory,* 55, no. 2 (1999): 115–153.

Michael Cunningham

(6 November 1952 –   )

Paul Christian Jones
Ohio University

BOOKS: *Golden States* (New York: Crown, 1984);
A Home at the End of the World (New York: Farrar, Straus & Giroux, 1990);
Flesh and Blood (New York: Farrar, Straus & Giroux, 1995);
The Hours (New York: Farrar, Straus & Giroux, 1998);
Land's End: A Walk Through Provincetown (New York: Crown, 2002).

OTHER: "Ignorant Armies," in *Penguin Book of Gay Short Stories,* edited by David Leavitt and Mark Mitchell (New York: Viking, 1994), pp. 481–495;
Virginia Woolf, *The Voyage Out,* introduction by Cunningham (New York: Modern Library, 2000).

SELECTED PERIODICAL PUBLICATIONS-
UNCOLLECTED:
FICTION
"Cleaving," *Atlantic Monthly,* 247 (January 1981): 60–66;
"Bedrock," *Redbook,* 156 (April 1981): 92–93, 146–155;
"Pearls," *Paris Review,* 24 (Winter 1982): 202–209;
"White Angel," *New Yorker,* 64 (25 July 1988): 25–33;
"Ghost Night," *New Yorker,* 65 (24 July 1989): 30–40;
"Clean Dreams," *WigWag* (August 1990): 53–58;
"Grave," *Blind Spot,* 10 (Spring/Summer 1997): 52–53;
"Mister Brother," *DoubleTake* (Fall 1998): 92–94;
"A Room at the Normandy," *New Yorker,* 74 (21 September 1998): 120–131.

NONFICTION
"After AIDS, Gay Art Aims for a New Reality," *New York Times,* 26 April 1992, pp. H1, H16–17;
"If You're Queer and You're Not Angry in 1992, You're Not Paying Attention; If You're Straight It May Be Hard to Figure Out What All the Shouting's About," *Mother Jones,* 17 (May/June 1992): 61–68.

Throughout the 1980s and most of the 1990s, critics usually considered Michael Cunningham to be just another of the growing number of novelists chronicling the experience of gay Americans in the age of

Michael Cunningham (photograph by Sigrid Estrada; from the dust jacket for Flesh and Blood, *1995; Richland County Public Library)*

AIDS. These novelists included David Leavitt, Edmund White, Robert Ferro, Stephen McCauley, Lev Raphael, Paul Monette, and Armistead Maupin, all writers who challenged the rhetoric of American family values by illustrating that the idea of "family" had grown beyond the traditional nuclear unit of married heterosexual parents and their children. Cunningham's early fiction was a part of this revisionist project. Additionally, Cunningham was involved in activist politics ranging from publishing confrontational pieces in *The New York Times* and *Mother Jones* to participating in radical political demonstrations arguing for more government funding for AIDS research, organized by the gay activist group ACT UP. He chained himself to a White House gate and later was arrested for interrupting a speech by President George Bush. He helped to engineer an on-air disturbance of the *MacNeil/Lehrer News Hour* in 1991. Both the gay content of his work and his personal activism overshadowed Cunningham's carefully crafted novels and delicate prose, and he rarely transcended this designation as a gay writer.

However, during the mid 1990s Cunningham's reception began to change. For example, in the *Los Angeles Times* (9 April 1995) Richard Eder called Cunningham "perhaps the most brilliant of the many novelists who have dealt with gay themes over the past dozen years, and one of our very best writers, in any case, on any theme." When Cunningham won the 1999 Pulitzer Prize in fiction for *The Hours* (1998), his homage to Virginia Woolf's *Mrs. Dalloway* (1925), Eder's evaluation seemed to be confirmed; Cunningham is now considered one of the best prose writers of his generation, gay or straight.

Cunningham was born on 6 November 1952 in Cincinnati, Ohio, to Don and Dorothy Cunningham. Don Cunningham's advertising career led the family to make several moves, including a four-year residence in Germany, before they ultimately settled in Pasadena, California, when Cunningham was ten. In his teenage years Cunningham began to develop an interest in serious literature, reading works by Woolf and T. S. Eliot. In 1972 he entered Stanford University, intending to study painting but eventually focusing on literature courses. He graduated from Stanford in 1976 with a degree in English. Two years later he entered the University of Iowa Writer's Workshop, graduating with a master of fine arts degree in 1980. At the University of Iowa, Cunningham was able to study with talented writers and teachers, including novelist Hilma Wolitzer, and to work at refining his style. While in the program, he began to submit stories and quickly had several accepted for publication in periodicals such as *Atlantic Monthly, Paris Review,* and *Redbook.*

The beginnings of Cunningham's central literary concerns can be seen in these early stories. His first published story, "Cleaving" (1981), tells the story of Bobby, a gay man who has just ended a relationship with a married doctor in San Francisco and who has traveled to Cincinnati to introduce himself to his twelve-year-old son, whom he has never met. When he arrives, the child's mother refuses to let Bobby see the boy. Hence, Bobby has to be content with watching his son playing in the school yard during recess. In "Bedrock" (1981) Jerry, a recently divorced man, quits his job and retreats to the home of his parents in Pasadena. Jerry treats this time as a vacation, lying by the pool and reading mysteries while obsessively thinking about his former wife. His parents, Fred and Wilma, try to push Jerry back into life, and by the end of the story they appear to have succeeded in convincing him to go out on a date. In each of these early stories the importance of family to individuals serves as the focal point.

After leaving the University of Iowa in 1980, Cunningham accepted a one-year residency at the Provincetown Fine Arts Work Center; after this residency he began working in New York City for the Carnegie Corporation, where he wrote annual reports and press releases. During the early 1980s he became frustrated because his initial success had not endured, and finding publishers for his material was no longer as easy as it had been a few years before. Intent upon finishing a novel before he reached the age of thirty, Cunningham wrote his first novel, *Golden States,* a work that he has referred to as "a journeyman effort."

Published in 1984, *Golden States* is the story of the Stark family, living in southern California in the early days of Ronald Reagan's presidency. The mother, Beverly, has been widowed by her first husband and divorced by her second. Her oldest daughter, Janet, has recently returned home, leaving her fiancé in San Francisco after deciding to pursue her medical studies. The youngest daughter, Lizzie, has become increasingly eccentric and suffers great anxiety about visiting her father in Spokane. The central character, twelve-year-old David, is the only male in the household, and he finds himself filling the role of the protector of the women in his family. He is convinced that only he can shelter them from the threats coming from outside of the household—the pack of coyotes that has invaded the neighborhood and the Peeping Tom that he spies prowling around at night.

Golden States is a coming-of-age novel, wherein the central character is concerned with asserting his manhood. At the same time that David watches his body transform through puberty, he faces a challenge to his protection of his family when Janet's fiancé appears at the house and eventually convinces her to return with him to San Francisco. In response to this threat to his family's unity, David sets out in the middle of the night on a quest to travel to San Francisco and bring his sister back with him. Armed with his mother's gun, he crosses the freeway and buys a bus ticket. On the way to San Francisco he encounters many obstacles, including being nearly seduced by a man who gives him a lift, and eventually being taken into police custody as a runaway. Though he is unsuccessful in retrieving his sister, he does triumph in chasing one of the coyotes away from the yard. This achievement, it appears, is a small victory.

Like most of Cunningham's subsequent work, *Golden States* focuses on the precipitous status of American families. The final image in the novel reveals Cunningham's vision of the challenge of family life. As David holds up an umbrella he found on his journey, he envisions himself as a tightrope walker standing in the spotlight, perfectly balanced:

> He held the umbrella over Mom's head and then over Lizzie's. They were circus performers too, a family of acrobats who walked blindfolded from one spangled crow's nest to another on a silver wire. The blindfolds kept them from knowing how high up they were. . . . He held the umbrella over her [Lizzie's] head. For the first time in memory, his arm felt strong. "Okay," he said. He waited for them to open their eyes.

This closing image of the book completes David's transition, and he now sees himself as strong enough to look after his family. Additionally, this image serves as a fitting segue into Cunningham's future work, representing his view of family as a delicate balancing act, with everyone perched upon the same wire. While most of the members are unaware of how close they are to disaster, David sees that the slightest act of any member of the family will have direct consequences upon each of them. Living as a family thus becomes an impressive and beautiful achievement.

Golden States received little critical attention. One of the more enthusiastic reviews, by Ruth Doan Mac-Dougall in *Christian Science Monitor* (4 May 1984), offered qualified praise: "However much one might object to the theme of protection of women, one cannot help savoring every moment of this novel." MacDougall called the novel "a joy to read." In the years following the publication of this first novel, Cunningham had little success publishing his fiction. In an attempt to illustrate to his partner, psychologist Ken Corbett, how little interest there was in his work, he submitted a chapter from a novel in progress to *The New Yorker,* expecting a quick rejection letter. To his surprise, the magazine instead accepted the chapter, and it was published under the title "White Angel" in 1988. The story describes the experiences of Bobby, the youngest son of a hippie family, who idolizes his older teenage brother, Carlton. Bobby follows his brother around as Carlton smokes pot, has sex in a cemetery, and listens to the latest rock songs. During a family party, a freak accident occurs: Carlton runs through a plate-glass door and is killed, leaving Bobby without his hero. Cunningham gained much attention from this story. It was included in *Best American Short Stories, 1989* and

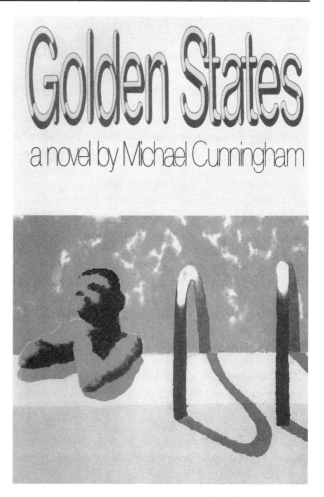

Dust jacket for Cunningham's first book (1984), about a twelve-year-old boy who takes it upon himself to become the protector of his mother and older sister (Richland County Public Library)

subsequently has been anthologized in several collections. Most significantly, the story sparked the interest of book publishers in the work from which it came, *A Home at the End of the World.*

Published in 1990, *A Home at the End of the World* begins as the story of two Cleveland boys—Bobby Morrow, the character from "White Angel," and Jonathan Glover, a gay youth who acts as his young mother's confidant, plays with dolls against the wishes of his father, and admires his father's beauty. The boys meet in seventh grade and become instantly inseparable. Bobby, still suffering the grief of his brother's death, craves the seeming normalcy of the Glover household. He begins to eat his meals and spend the night with the Glovers and to wear Jonathan's clothes. While Bobby is drawn to the simple middle-class life of this family, Jonathan seems attracted to Bobby as a way out of his safe and dull existence. Jonathan's mother calls Bobby a "refugee from some distant place." Bobby introduces

Jonathan to the latest music, to drugs, and to a sense of rebelliousness in life. He also provides Jonathan with an erotic focus to his developing sexuality. Jonathan finds himself drawn to his new friend, and the two soon become involved sexually. After high school, the boys separate. Jonathan heads off to New York to attend college. Following the deaths of his own parents, Bobby moves in with the Glovers and attempts to play the role of the perfect son. He begins cooking their meals and cleaning their house, and he even opens a restaurant in honor of Alice, Jonathan's mother. Both young men get what they want: Bobby finds a place inside a family, and Jonathan achieves freedom from it.

In the second section of the novel, Jonathan, now age twenty-five, has graduated from college and is writing a restaurant-review column for a New York City paper. He maintains a relationship with a lover, Erich, with whom he shares no intimacy beyond sex. He lives with a thirty-six-year-old woman, Clare, with whom he shares every intimacy except sex. He and Clare even discuss having a child together. When Jonathan's parents move from Cleveland to Arizona, Bobby heads to New York to live with Jonathan, invading his friend's "family" yet again. Bobby and Clare soon become lovers, and the trio lives out their version of the typical family. Calling themselves "the Hendersons," the friends parody a traditional family. Though this arrangement initially seems like a joke to them and the world around them, they eventually grow to see themselves as "a new kind of family." As such, the three attend the funeral of Jonathan's father in Arizona, and during the cross-country drive back home, Clare discovers that she is pregnant with Bobby's child.

The final section of the novel details the life the three establish in Woodstock, New York, after the birth of their daughter, Rebecca. With Clare's inheritance, they buy a house and start a restaurant, which Bobby and Jonathan run together. They settle into a routine similar to the one they had previously mocked: "We don't talk about the Hendersons anymore, maybe because the difference between our actual lives and their hypothetical ones has shrunk below the measuring point." While Clare still questions the nature of their bond, Bobby defends the arrangement: "We're really, you know, not much weirder than any family. . . . At least we love each other." Upon the arrival of Jonathan's former lover Erich, who is now living with AIDS, Clare flees with Rebecca, apparently unable to handle the presence of illness in her world or perhaps the thought that Jonathan may himself become ill as well. Left alone, Jonathan and Bobby become caretakers of the ailing Erich and construct yet another family unit at the end of the novel. The final scene features Bobby and Jonathan taking a frail, barely conscious

Erich for a cold swim. Jonathan reveals that "I realized that if I died soon I would have known this, a connection with my life, its errors and cockeyed successes. The chance to be one of three naked men standing in a small body of clear water. I would not die unfulfilled because I'd been here, right here and nowhere else." As in *Golden States,* the novel ends with the small victory of establishing this delicate family, surviving with these people, helping and loving one another.

The critical response to *A Home at the End of the World* was positive. Many reviewers, such as David Kaufman in the *Nation* (1 July 1991), admired the daring of Cunningham's project, which argued for "nothing less than a new definition of the American family." Others were more impressed by the prose style than the subject matter. For example, Matthew Gilbert in the *Boston Globe* (19 November 1990) argued that "the big attraction" of the novel "is not the story, moving as it is. Really it's the writing, which is a constant pleasure, flowing and yet dense with incisive images and psychological nuance." The one recurring qualm that appears in many of the reviews was the similarity among the voices of the four first-person narrators—Bobby, Jonathan, Clare, and Alice—who, as Sybil Steinberg noted in *Publishers Weekly* (17 August 1990), "are not as different as one would expect from such fully realized characters." In an interview with Philip Gambone, Cunningham defends this lack of distinguishable voice in the four characters as "a conscious decision" inspired by his reading of Woolf's *The Waves* (1931), "in which she essentially gives one incredible voice to this whole gaggle of characters." He explains in this interview that he was trying "to speak from these people's souls, which are more articulate than their fumbling tongues."

As he moved on to his third novel, Cunningham imagined a trajectory of a broadening scope in the progression of his works. He explained in the interview with Gambone that he views *Golden States* as the story of a single character, while *A Home at the End of the World* is "a big step . . . in terms of scale" because it is "about more lives. It's a bigger picture." He called his third novel, *Flesh and Blood* (1995), "another step forward along those lines" because of its magnitude. Certainly, in its attempt to chronicle three generations of a single Greek American family over a hundred-year period, *Flesh and Blood* became Cunningham's most ambitious work and perhaps his most extensive examination of the essence of American families.

Flesh and Blood begins in 1935 with the childhood in Greece of Constantine Stassos, the youngest son of a working family who eventually immigrates to New Jersey. As an adult, Constantine weds Mary, an Italian American, and fathers three children. As they pursue the American Dream, which Constantine achieves by building cheap housing, Constantine and Mary struggle to raise their offspring: the oldest, Susan, is homecoming princess and her father's favorite; the son, Billy, upsets his father with his feminine smallness and his close attachment to his mother; and the youngest, Zoe, is oddly withdrawn. In pictures, however, the Stassos family appears to be the perfect American family thriving in the suburbs. Beneath this image lurks Constantine's raging temper, his sexual advances toward Susan, his conflict about Billy's emerging homosexuality, Mary's habit of shoplifting, and Zoe's drug use. This traditional family is slowly revealed to be living in a suburban nightmare.

As the action moves to the 1970s, Susan marries her high-school sweetheart, a law student and future politician; Billy, now using the name Will, goes off to Harvard; and Constantine's business continues to thrive. However, each member of the family searches for some means of making happiness. Bored with her marriage and unable to get pregnant, Susan begins an affair with another man and eventually conceives a child. Will becomes a teacher, transforms his small body by madly working out at a gym, and eventually meets a man with whom he will spend his life. Zoe begins a relationship with a black lover, who gets her pregnant and infects her with AIDS, and establishes a new family under the care of Cassandra, an older drag queen who is also living with the virus. After learning of Constantine's marital infidelities, Mary leaves him and struggles to make a life of her own. Constantine marries his younger secretary and builds an even bigger house for his new family than he provided for his first. All of the Stassos clan abandon the expectations of the traditional family and fashion alternative arrangements for their lives.

The next generation carries on the struggles of the generation before. Susan's son, Ben, becomes Constantine's favorite grandchild, the son he has always wanted. Ben is strong, athletic, handsome, "the perfect boy." Like his uncle Will, however, he is also gay and hides his sexuality from every member of his family, except Jamal, Zoe's biracial son, with whom he begins a sexual relationship. The climax of the novel occurs when the family has gathered at the beach for a reunion of sorts and Ben dies during a sailing accident. This death sets up Constantine's final confrontation with Will as well as his public shaming by Susan at Ben's funeral, where she exposes her father's sexual abuse in front of the gathered mourners. The conclusion of the novel quickly traces the lives of the remaining characters through 2035, when Jamal introduces his own child to the family legacy.

The critical response to *Flesh and Blood* was also generally positive, though it was dismissed by some as

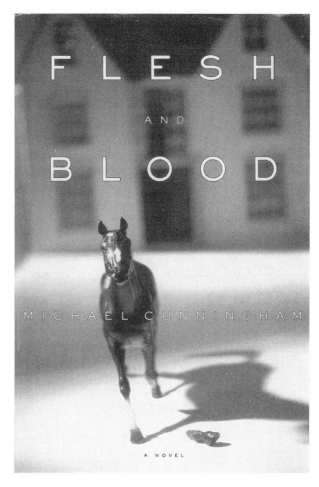

Dust jacket for Cunningham's 1995 novel, about three generations of a Greek American family (Richland County Public Library)

a thesis novel about the dark side of the American Dream. However, most critics admired Cunningham's examination of American life. Meg Wolitzer, for example, in *The New York Times* (16 April 1995), wrote that the novel "barely misses a telling detail or a larger emotional truth. . . . As Mr. Cunningham well knows, there's a great deal hidden inside those identical suburban houses. In this novel, he throws all their doors wide open."

Seeming to depart from the subject matter of his first three novels, Cunningham turned to one of his literary heroes, Woolf, for his next work. Cunningham's lifelong fascination with Woolf began as teenage admiration but eventually developed into a careful study of her work. At one point he planned to write a biography of the author, and he has written an introduction to a 2000 edition of her first novel, *The Voyage Out* (1915). His admiration most clearly reveals itself, however, in his novel *The Hours,* which was Woolf's initial title for *Mrs. Dalloway.* Cunningham's novel serves as an homage to Woolf and her famous work but also as a larger

Dust jacket for Cunningham's Pulitzer Prize–winning 1998 novel, about three women, one of whom is Virginia Woolf, who do not know each other but whose lives are connected by Woolf's 1925 work Mrs. Dalloway *(Richland County Public Library)*

meditation on suicide and living. The narrative follows three women through a single day of their lives. One of these characters is Woolf herself, depicted in the prologue to the novel on the 1941 day when she filled her pockets with stones and walked into a river, ending her life out of the dual fear of artistic failure and madness.

The main narrative focuses on Woolf on another day—in 1923, as she hosts a visit from her sister, Vanessa, and thinks through the plot of her novel in progress, *Mrs. Dalloway*. She and her husband, Leonard, have settled in the countryside for the benefit of Woolf's health. While Woolf fears the cost to her mental state, she desperately wants to return to live in London and tries to prove to her husband that she is capable of managing herself, her home, and her art without decline. As she considers the plot of her novel, Woolf initially conceives Clarissa Dalloway as a suicide who will kill herself at the end of the day being depicted. However, as Woolf herself struggles with the art of everyday life, dealing with stubborn servants, enjoying the presence of her niece and nephew, and gossiping with her sister, she realizes that Clarissa loves

life too much to ever end it. Woolf transfers the suicide plot to the mad poet Septimus and looks forward to getting back to the pleasure of life in London.

The second narrative details the life of Laura Brown, a young Los Angeles housewife in 1949, who is reading *Mrs. Dalloway* with great pleasure. Her own life is unfulfilling; she is the mother of a young son, pregnant with a second child, and planning a modest birthday dinner for her husband. Like both Woolf and Clarissa Dalloway, Laura funnels her artistic tendencies into her everyday life as she attempts to craft the perfect birthday cake and dinner, even while juggling her bothersome child, intrusive neighbors, and the overwhelming urge to spend the day reading. She does eventually succumb to this desire; after leaving her son with a sitter, she drives downtown and checks herself into a hotel for two hours of undisturbed reading time. When she considers how easy it was for her to escape from her life, she imagines that suicide "would be as simple as checking into a hotel." Despite the temptation to kill herself, Laura returns to her life, where she enjoys the success of her little party and feels the watchful eyes of her son keeping her in this life.

The third narrative takes place in New York City in the 1990s as Clarissa Vaughan, a fifty-two-year-old publisher, also spends the day planning a party, this one in honor of her gay poet friend, Richard. This section of *The Hours* is a contemporary retelling of the plot of *Mrs. Dalloway*, as Clarissa (dubbed "Mrs. Dalloway" by Richard) attempts to celebrate her friend's receiving a major award for his literary work, despite the fact that he is in the late stages of AIDS and may not even be well enough to attend the party or the award ceremony. As she buys flowers and invites party guests, Clarissa also deals with her own everyday struggles, which include her rebellious daughter's rejection of her "bourgeois" lesbian parents in favor of her radical gay activist friend. This section of the novel comes to a climax as Clarissa goes to pick up Richard for the party and finds him perched on his windowsill. Explaining that he does not think he can face "the party and the ceremony, and then the hour after that, and the hour after that," he throws himself out the window, like Septimus in Woolf's novel, unable to endure "the hours." At the funeral, Clarissa entertains Richard's mother—Laura Brown, who has continued living after all by leaving her husband for a new life in Canada.

The Hours concludes with an elaboration of the message of the novel, which ties the events of the three major characters' lives together:

> We throw our parties; we abandon our families to live alone in Canada; we struggle to write books that do not change the world, despite our gifts and our unstint-

ing efforts, our most extravagant hopes. We live our lives, do whatever we do, and then we sleep–it's as simple and ordinary as that. A few jump out of windows or drown themselves or take pills; more die by accident; and most of us, the vast majority, are slowly devoured by some disease or, if we're very fortunate, by time itself. There's just this for consolation: an hour here or there when our lives seem, against all odds and expectations, to burst open and give us everything we've ever imagined, though everyone but children (and perhaps even they) knows these hours will inevitably be followed by others, far darker and more difficult. Still, we cherish the city, the morning; we hope, more than anything, for more. Heaven only knows why we love it so.

Much like Woolf's novel, this novel about suicide is ultimately about the joys of daily existence.

Response to *The Hours* was enthusiastic. It was awarded the Pulitzer Prize and the PEN/Faulkner Award in 1999. Some reviewers even made comparisons between Cunningham and his model, Woolf; Brooke Allen in *New Criterion* (June 1999), for example, claimed that Cunningham "succeeds brilliantly, so much so that in the end" he "gives Woolf herself a run for her money." While this tribute to Woolf might appear to have taken Cunningham away from the concerns of his early work, family matters are still at the center of each of these narratives. From Virginia's realization that Vanessa's raising of her children "is the true accomplishment" that "will live after the tinselly experiments in narrative have been packed off along with the old photographs and fancy dresses," to Clarissa and Sallie's successful raising of their daughter, Julia, *The Hours* celebrates the impressive achievement of constructing

and holding together a family, in whatever shape or size it might appear. In an interview with Michael Coffey, Cunningham confessed that "I do seem to have some kind of fixation on the whole notion of family," but admitted to thinking that with *The Hours* he had put that behind him. "And guess what? As it turns out, here, once again, is the specter of the queer, extended, postnuclear family." The 2002 movie adaptation of *The Hours,* with screenplay by David Hare, starred Meryl Streep, Julianne Moore, and Nicole Kidman.

Cunningham teaches creative writing at Brooklyn College and continues to write in his studio in Greenwich Village. His publications following *The Hours,* including the 1998 short story "Mister Brother" (for which he won an O. Henry Award in 1999) and the nonfiction volume *Land's End: A Walk Through Provincetown* (2002), indicate that his future work will likely continue in the same vein, encouraging his readers to rethink American family life.

Interviews:

Michael Coffey, "Michael Cunningham: New Family Outings," *Publishers Weekly* (2 November 1998): 53;

Philip Gambone, "Michael Cunningham," in his *Something Inside: Conversations with Gay Fiction Writers* (Madison: University of Wisconsin Press, 1999), pp. 142–154;

Justin Spring, "Michael Cunningham," *BOMB,* 66 (Winter 1999): 76–80;

David Bahr, "The Difference a Day Makes: After Hours with Michael Cunningham," *Poets & Writers Magazine,* 27 (July–August 1999): 18–23.

Eric Jerome Dickey

(1961 –   )

Stephen Spencer
Wilmington College

BOOKS: *Sister, Sister* (New York: Dutton, 1996);
Friends and Lovers (New York: Dutton, 1997);
Milk in My Coffee (New York: Dutton, 1998);
Cheaters (New York: Dutton, 1999);
Liar's Game (New York: Dutton, 2001);
Between Lovers (New York: Dutton, 2001);
Thieves' Paradise (New York: Dutton, 2002);
The Other Woman (New York: Dutton, 2003);
Naughty or Nice (New York: Dutton, 2003).

PRODUCED SCRIPT: *Cappuccino,* by Dickey and Craig Ross Jr., motion picture, Urban Media, 1998.

RECORDINGS: *Milk in My Coffee,* abridged, read by Dickey and Brenda Denise Stinson (New York: Viking Penguin Audio, 1999);
Cheaters, read by Dickey, Stinson, and Steven Anthony James (New York: Viking Penguin Audio, 1999);
Liar's Game, read by Dickey and Gabriella Callender, New York, Penguin Audiobooks, 2000.

OTHER: "Thirteen," in *River Crossings: Voices of the Diaspora,* edited by C. Jerome Woods (Los Angeles: International Black Writers and Artists of Los Angeles, 1994);
"Café Piel," in *Got to Be Real: Four Original Love Stories,* by Dickey, Marcus Major, E. Lynn Harris, and Colin Channer (New York: New American Library, 2000), pp. 1–73;
"Fish Sammich with Cheese," in *Mothers & Sons: A Celebration in Memories, Stories, and Photographs,* edited by Jill M. Morgan (New York: New American Library, 2000), pp. 131–154;
"Days Gone By," in *Griots Beneath the Baobab: Tales from Los Angeles,* edited by Randy Ross and Erin Aubry Kaplan (Los Angeles: International Black Writers and Artists of Los Angeles, 2002).

In a market that has been dominated by women, Eric Jerome Dickey's best-selling novels about contem-

Eric Jerome Dickey (photograph by Jim Belfon/Photo Center of Harlem; from the dust jacket for Between Lovers, *2001; Bruccoli Clark Layman Archives)*

porary African American urban life and relationships represent a significant African American male voice. In 1987, Terry McMillan's novel *Mama* found an audience eager for portrayals of urban black characters exploring various relationships. Since then, such women writers as McMillan (*Waiting to Exhale,* 1992, and *How Stella Got Her Groove Back,* 1996), Lorene Cary (*Pride,* 1998), Delorys Welch-Tyson (*Gingersnaps,* 1998), and Renee Swindle (*Please, Please, Please,* 1999) have found a large audience. Dickey joins a growing number of African American male writers whose works have consistently made it to the best-seller lists: E. Lynn Harris (*A Love of My Own,* 2002), Colin Channer (*Satisfy My Soul,* 2002),

Marcus Major (*4 Guys and Trouble,* 2001), and Brian Peterson (*Move Over, Girl,* 2000).

Following the success of his debut novel, *Sister, Sister* (1996), Dickey's next three books—*Friends and Lovers* (1997), *Milk in My Coffee* (1998), and *Cheaters* (1999)— all went to number one on the *Blackboard* best-seller list, while *Cheaters* was named Book of the Year by *Blackboard.* Dickey's fifth novel, *Liar's Game* (2001), hit number eight on the hardcover fiction list in *Publishers Weekly* after one week on the shelves. The first printing of his *Between Lovers* (2001) was 120,000, and New American Library began publishing Dickey's backlist in trade paperback editions. Recognizing the potential appeal and talent of these emerging writers, New American Library teamed Channer, Harris, Dickey, and Major to write *Got to Be Real: Four Original Love Stories* (2000).

Critics have recognized the increasing popularity of African American writers but have not fully analyzed the reasons why these works are rising onto the best-seller lists. In a 2001 *New York Times* article by Martin Arnold, Henry Louis Gates Jr., chairman of Afro-American studies at Harvard, attributes the success of these writers to the increasing ability of American readers to identify with black characters. Although Gates recognizes that white audiences are reading more black writers, he also points out that black readers have represented a large and growing part of the market since the 1980s. Karen Angel's analysis in *Publishers Weekly* (23 February 1998) supports Gates's contention that the success of African American writers like Dickey is a result of their appeal to black readers. Angel points to Dickey's first novel, *Sister, Sister,* as an example of the success of target marketing to black readers. Tamara Henry, reviewing *Got to Be Real* for *USA Today* (21 December 2000) attributed the success of Dickey and other male African American writers to their ability to write stories with "fresh, believable characters" that struggle with common modern-day problems of love and relationships. An article in *The Detroit Free Press* (30 November 2000) also recognized the increasing popularity of African American male writers; Dickey's particular strength, according to this article, is his ability to portray women well. Dickey's primary literary device—first-person narration from the points of view of various characters, many of them women—has captured in contemporary prose the lives and romances of urban characters.

Despite such success, Dickey did not publish his first novel until he was thirty-five years old, after moving from his birthplace and home, Memphis, Tennessee, to Los Angeles, California. Growing up in Memphis, he attended Riverview Elementary and Junior High School. After graduating from Carver High School, Dickey attended Memphis State University (now the University of Memphis), where he earned a B.S. in computer systems technology. During his college years, Dickey worked at the game room on campus, at Federal Express, and at Lowenstein's, a now-defunct retail store in downtown Memphis. Dickey also earned a black belt in karate from Kang Rhee Karate Institute and pledged the fraternity Alpha Phi Alpha. After completing his college work, Dickey took a job with Rockwell, now Boeing, in Tennessee. When he was laid off from that job, he moved to Los Angeles, where he worked as a substitute teacher while waiting for acting jobs. Dickey began performing stand-up comedy in clubs in Los Angeles and eventually traveled to Seattle and San Antonio to perform.

Except for a few short stories in high school, Dickey had not previously written fiction and did not have formal academic training in creative writing, but he began writing stories based on his experiences as a comedian. With the help of an agent, he was able to secure a contract with Dutton, the publisher of all of his novels to date.

Dickey's first novel, *Sister, Sister,* tells the story of California siblings Inda and Valerie, and their search for meaningful relationships. *Sister, Sister* establishes Dickey's use of first-person narration from the points of view of various characters. Inda is independent, but she has been involved in several failed relationships with men who have mistreated her. Valerie, who is dependent compared to her sister, realizes that her six-year marriage to Walter is unfulfilling, but she cannot conceive of herself outside of marriage to a man. Their parents' divorce has added to the sisters' sense that true love and meaningful relationships are ultimately unattainable. Inda, who inherited her father's dark complexion in contrast to her sister's lighter skin, has a stable career; but her divorce from a white husband and the infidelity of her current lover, Raymond, have caused her to grow increasingly cynical about love and relationships. Inda meets Chiquita, a young, attractive flight attendant, and discovers they both have been deceived by Raymond, who is engaged to a third woman. Chiquita then falls in love with Thaddeus, Inda and Valerie's brother. In the end, all three women form lasting bonds with each other and learn that they must not define themselves in relation to either men or their parents.

Sister, Sister was well received by readers and critics alike and successfully launched Dickey's writing career. Initial reviews focused on the realistic portrayal in the novel of contemporary urban life. Sybil Steinberg, however, delivered a mixed review in *Publishers Weekly* (5 August 1996). She criticized the multiple points of view and uneven characterization while praising Dickey's humor and his sympathetic, accurate portrayal of African American urban women.

Dust jacket for Dickey's 1999 novel, about two sets of
friends—three men and three women—and their
various romantic entanglements (Bruccoli
Clark Layman Archives)

Published one year after *Sister, Sister,* Dickey's second novel, *Friends and Lovers,* portrays the lives of Debra, a quiet, introspective nurse, and Shelby, an outspoken, impulsive flight attendant, who have suffered a series of setbacks in their relationships with men. The two friends meet Leonard, an aspiring stand-up comedian, and Tyrel, his best friend, who works at the same software company where Leonard has his day job. Debra decides to wait to consummate her relationship with Leonard; when his career as a comedian blossoms, the couple buys a house and begins a satisfying marriage. Unlike Debra and Leonard, Shelby and Tyrel immediately give in to their sexual desire and begin a rocky relationship. Leonard's death in a car accident eventually brings Tyrel and Debra together, and each of the characters realizes that the most important thing in life is family.

Reviews of *Friends and Lovers,* like those of Dickey's first novel, continued to focus on the realism of Dickey's writing and generally praised the novel as a strong follow-up to *Sister, Sister.* In *Publishers Weekly* (1 September 1997) Steinberg said of *Friends and Lovers* that Dickey "offers another sexy, sophisticated portrayal of hip black L.A." This novel, according to Steinberg, has witty, fast-paced dialogue and renders the characters realistically. Ann Burns in *Library Journal* (1 November 1997) called *Friends and Lovers* "another fine novel" about characters searching for love and happiness.

In his third novel, *Milk in My Coffee,* Dickey moves from examining black romances to exploring the idea of interracial relationships. Jordan Greene, while embroiled in a troubled relationship with an African American woman, meets Kimberly Chavers, a fair-skinned, red-haired artist, when they share a cab ride. Kimberly is different from the women Jordan has been dating: she is assertive yet feminine, attentive, and independent. Jordan begins experiencing feelings of guilt over his attraction to Kimberly because she is white. However, he eventually finds out that Kimberly's father was racially mixed and that she has experienced firsthand the effects of racism. As a result, the novel ends with the hope that Jordan and Kimberly will establish an enduring relationship.

Much like its predecessors, *Milk in My Coffee* was also favorably reviewed as a realistic portrayal of urban life, and most reviews also mention Dickey's ability to address a controversial topic. Emily Jones in *Library Journal* (15 October 1998) described *Milk in My Coffee* as stronger than Dickey's first two novels, both in style and content. Despite her concern that his comparison of black and white women verges on stereotypes, she concluded that the novel is realistic and highly recommended it.

Cheaters, Dickey's fourth novel, tells the story of Stephan Mitchell, a single software designer, and his best friends—Jake, a single man, and Darnell, a married attorney and aspiring author. Stephan and Jake date many beautiful black women, while Darnell remains faithful to his faltering marriage. Chante Marie Ellis, Karen, and Tammy are African American women who have remained lifelong friends through various personal trials. Chante meets Stephan in a nightclub and thinks she has finally found the right man. As Darnell grows increasingly committed to his writing, his wife misunderstands and criticizes his commitment, calling it his "hobby." Darnell reacts by turning to another woman in search of the support and understanding he needs to sustain his passion for writing. Meanwhile, Stephan seeks a meaningful relationship in spite of the legacy of his philandering father. Each character eventually matures as he or she searches for love, understanding, and fidelity.

Cheaters was more widely reviewed than Dickey's previous three novels, and critics continued to agree that Dickey's characters are believable and his prose accurate. Lillian Lewis in *Booklist* (15 May 1999) called *Cheaters* Dickey's "most ambitious novel." Although Steinberg's review in *Publishers Weekly* (7 June 1999) pointed out the overuse of jokes about such matters as sex toys and organ size, as well as the strained denouement, she concluded that *Cheaters* is humorous and provocative. In a review in *Library Journal* (15 May 1999) Jones described the novel as sexy and humorous and Dickey's writing as witty and honest, concluding that Dickey's work improves with each novel.

Dickey's fifth novel, *Liar's Game,* continues to portray characters struggling to find meaningful relationships. *Liar's Game* tells the story of New York native Dana Ann Smith as she flees a failed relationship, leaves the East, and moves to Los Angeles to start a new life as a real-estate agent. There she meets and falls for Vincent Calvary Browne Jr. As their relationship begins, they both choose not to reveal portions of their respective pasts. Their hidden pasts eventually cause problems when both Dana's former lover and Vince's former wife suddenly reenter their lives, forcing the couple to confront painful unresolved issues. The novel includes two subplots—one involving Dana's friend Gerri and Gerri's unfaithful rap-promoter boyfriend, Jefferson, and the other involving Vincent's friend Womack, who suspects his wife of having an affair. Eventually, Vince and Dana find that together they may have a chance at forming a meaningful relationship and overcoming their past mistakes.

As with Dickey's previous works, *Liar's Game* received positive critical attention; and, for the first time, reviews addressed the substantive social issues present in the novel. Lewis in *Booklist* (15 April 2000) called *Liar's Game* "witty and engrossing," while Steinberg in *Publishers Weekly* (22 May 2000) noted that *Liar's Game* examines issues such as police brutality, justice, child custody, and conflicts between Africans and African Americans. Other reviews were less favorable, however; C. Leigh McInnis observed in *Multicultural Review* (December 2000) that *Liar's Game* seems to suggest that conflicts between African American women and men are a result of innate characteristics of African Americans, without critically examining the cultural and historical contexts that may lead to these problems. Scott Powell commented in the *Austin American Statesman* (27 August 2000), "'Sex games' might have been a more fitting title . . . because the act occurs every third page or so." Powell warned readers that the novel "sucks you into an ethnic literary soap opera overflowing with experience-sobered men and women of varying earthy

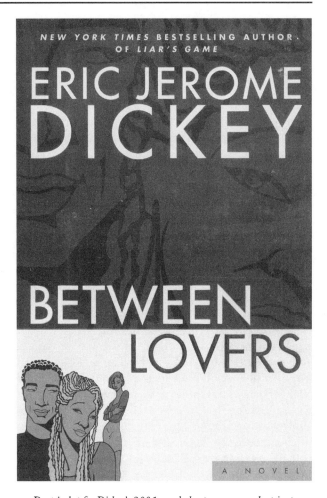

Dust jacket for Dickey's 2001 novel about a woman who tries to maintain both her renewed relationship with her former fiancé and a lesbian affair (Bruccoli Clark Layman Archives)

skin tones involved in disastrous, co-dependent relationships."

Between Lovers, Dickey's sixth novel, is set in the San Francisco area. The unnamed narrator, a successful author, renews his relationship with Nicole, the woman who left him at the altar seven years earlier. The narrator and Ayanna, Nicole's female lover, compete for Nicole, who is determined to maintain her relationships with both lovers. Reviews reflected the earlier positive reception of Dickey's work. Vanessa Bush in *Booklist* (15 June 2001) praised Dickey's ability to capture "the ambience of Oakland and the angst of three fascinating characters." Jeff Zaleski in *Publishers Weekly* (25 June 2001) called the novel "another spicy slice of African-American dramatic fiction from an author who seems only to get better."

In his next novel, *Thieves' Paradise* (2002), Dickey shifts his emphasis from professional, affluent characters to a young L.A. man who has served time in juvenile detention and has been laid off from his job in technology. A review in *Essence* (July 2002) described the novel as "a noirish tale of grifters, gamblers and gumshoes." Such a world is simply too enticing to Dante Brown, who faces mounting debt, a broken-down car, and impending eviction. Scamz, a figure from Dante's past, lures Dante into a life of crime with the promise of designer clothes, expensive cars, and a Hollywood mansion. Although Dante struggles with his conscience, he ultimately cannot seem to find a way out of this new life, especially when his friend Jackson teams up with him and when his girlfriend Pam finds his new wealth appealing. Even though *Thieves' Paradise* diverges from Dickey's previous formula, it has been as positively received as his earlier work. Ann Burns in *Library Journal* (15 September 2002) characterized the book as "a refreshingly different offering."

Dickey's subsequent works represent a return to his earlier formula of contemporary urban romance. In *The Other Woman* (2003) the unnamed narrator, a successful television producer in Los Angeles, finds out that her husband, a teacher, is having an affair. Although her husband admits the affair and claims that it is over, the narrator searches for something that will heal her pain and restore her life. A review for *Publishers Weekly* said that in this novel "Dickey offers plenty of straight-on sex and violence, but also probes questions of contemporary morals and the psychology of betrayal, writing compellingly and believably from his heroine's point of view." *Naughty or Nice* (2003), set in Los Angeles during the Christmas/Kwanzaa season, follows three sisters, Frankie, Livvy, and Tommie, as they search for love and engage in affairs with various types of men. Reviewers have commented on the explicit sexuality in these two novels. Glenn Townes in *Black Issues Book Review* (May/June 2003) called *The Other Woman* "steamy, lascivious and realistically chilling." Jeff Zaleski of *Publishers Weekly* (6 October 2003)

noted that "the real focus of the book is sex" and added that Dickey "is a master at writing about women and what they want and how they want it. There are three kinds of physical love in these pages: hot, red hot and nuclear." Lillian Lewis added in *Booklist* that the novel also "offers plenty of the laugh-out-loud humor that has made his work a staple on best-seller lists."

Dickey currently resides in Los Angeles. In addition to Memphis and Los Angeles, he has lived in Anaheim, Hawaiian Gardens, Lakewood, Downey, Pomona, and Phillips Ranch. In Los Angeles, Dickey volunteers as a mentor with the organization Project Reach, an alternative school program for at-risk students. He continues to write, to tour extensively promoting his work, and to answer e-mail from readers through his official website, <http://www.ericjerome dickey.com>.

Dickey's presence in American writing provides an interesting look into the world of the African American urban male. His work broadens the reading public's concept of African American culture and provides a greater understanding of the struggles and triumphs of the urban culture about which he writes.

Interviews:

Lee E. Meadows, *Book Beat,* radio, Detroit, WPON, 25 January 1999;

"Q & A with Eric Jerome Dickey," *chance22* (11 April 2001) <http://www.chance22.com/qa-ejd.htm>.

References:

Karen Angel, "Sister, Brother, Friend, Lover: A New African American Novel?" *Publishers Weekly* (23 February 1998): 22–23;

Martin Arnold, "Making Books," *New York Times,* 26 July 2001, p. 3.

Ellen Douglas
(Josephine Ayres Haxton)
(12 July 1921 –)

Suzanne Disheroon-Green, Barbara Ewell, and Jennifer Vance
Northwestern State University

BOOKS: *A Family's Affairs* (New York: Houghton Mifflin, 1962);

Black Cloud, White Cloud (Boston: Houghton Mifflin, 1963);

Where the Dreams Cross (Boston: Houghton Mifflin, 1968);

Apostles of Light (Boston: Houghton Mifflin, 1973);

The Rock Cried Out (New York: Harcourt Brace Jovanovich, 1979);

A Lifetime Burning (New York: Random House, 1982);

A Long Night (N.p.: Nouveau Press for Mississippi Civil Liberties Union, 1986);

The Magic Carpet and Other Tales (Jackson: University Press of Mississippi, 1987);

Can't Quit You, Baby (New York: Atheneum, 1988);

Truth: Four Stories I Am Finally Old Enough to Tell (Chapel Hill, N.C.: Algonquin, 1998).

OTHER: "On The Lake," in *Prize Stories of 1963: The O. Henry Awards,* edited by Richard Poirier (Garden City, N.Y.: Doubleday, 1963);

"Faulkner in Time," in *"A Cosmos of My Own": Faulkner and Yoknapatawpha 1980,* edited by Doreen Fowler and Ann J. Abadie (Jackson: University Press of Mississippi, 1981), p. 284; reprinted as "Reading and Writing: Beginnings," in *Mississippi Writers: Reflections of Childhood and Youth,* volume 2, edited by Dorothy Abbott (Jackson: University Press of Mississippi, 1986), p. 175;

Helen Dick Davis, ed., *Trials of the Earth: The Autobiography of Mary Hamilton,* foreword by Douglas (Jackson: University Press of Mississippi, 1992);

Shannon Ravenel, ed., *New Stories from the South: The Year's Best, 2000,* preface by Douglas (Chapel Hill, N.C.: Algonquin, 2000);

"Imaginary Countries," in *Sewanee Writers on Writing,* edited by Wyatt Prunty (Baton Rouge: Louisiana State University Press, 2000), p. 24.

Ellen Douglas (Josephine Ayres Haxton; photograph © by Emily Haxton; from the dust jacket for Can't Quit You, Baby, *1988; Richland County Public Library)*

SELECTED PERIODICAL PUBLICATIONS—
UNCOLLECTED: "Death and Homecoming," *Esquire,* 56 (December 1961): 199+;

"Fragments of Family Life," *Harper's,* 225 (November 1962): 76+;

"Provincialism in Literature," *New Republic,* 173 (5 July 1975): 23+;

Review of *Dreams of Sleep* by Josephine Humphreys, *New York Times Book Review,* 13 May 1984, p. 15;

"How Pinkney Made It," review of *Last One Home* by John Ehle, *New York Times Book Review,* 23 September 1984, p. 49;

"Leaving the Country," *Lactuca*, 8 (1987): 73+;

"Black and White Women Tell Their Tragic-Comic Tales," review of *Telling Memories Among Southern Women: Domestic Workers and Their Employers in the Segregated South* by Susan Tucker, *Chicago Tribune*, 15 January 1989, p. XIV: 6;

"There She Was When She Was Needed," review of *Mother Wit: An Alabama Midwife's Story* by Onnie Lee Logan, *Washington Post Book World*, 27 August 1989, p. 7;

"She Wrote The Book," review of *Southern Daughter: The Life of Margaret Mitchell* by Darden Ashbury Pyron, *New York Times Book Review*, 27 October 1991, p. 21;

"The Power of Sisterhood," review of *And Do Remember Me* by Marita Golden, *Washington Post Book World*, 21 June 1992, p. 3;

"I Have Found It," *Southern Quarterly*, 33, no. 4 (1995): 7;

"Proust, Ava Gardner, and the Last Frontier," *Southern Review*, 32 (Spring 1996): 310–315.

Ellen Douglas is best known for her re-creations of the small-town South and has been critically acclaimed for her efforts. She sets many of her narratives in the fictional community of Homochitto County, Mississippi, where the sensibilities of place, family, and propriety provide a foundation for stories that examine the troubled racial inheritance of the region, the ways in which family members relate among themselves and with outsiders, and the sexual roles imposed upon middle-class white women. Although critics have described Douglas's fiction in terms ranging from "old-fashioned" to "postmodern" and "avant-garde," Charline R. McCord suggests that one of the significant strengths of Douglas's writing is that "the voice is incredibly consistent throughout."

Ellen Douglas is the pseudonym of Josephine Ayres Haxton, who assumed the pen name out of respect for her maternal aunts. After completing her first novel, *A Family's Affairs* (1962), Haxton harbored concerns about the effect that the stories in her book would have on her family, especially the two aunts whose lives provide the material for many of the incidents in the volume. When Haxton asked their permission to publish the book, the women gave their blessings, on two conditions: that they never be asked to read the novel and that she publish it under an assumed name.

Haxton was born Josephine Ayres in Natchez, Mississippi, on 12 July 1921, with family connections that reach deep into the state's history. She was the second child of Richardson and Laura Davis Ayres. Because of her father's career as a civil engineer, Ayres grew up in Arkansas and Louisiana. She later transferred family characteristics, idiosyncrasies, and conversations from these formative years to the characters in her novels. Douglas attributes her love of reading and writing to the women in her family. Though Laura Davis Ayres was not an author herself, she inspired her children with a love of reading. In her interview with McCord, Douglas says of her mother's influence, "she read aloud to us every night when I was a child." Ayres's paternal grandmother (alternately dubbed Grandmother Two and Nellie in Douglas's work) was an author of children's books and also contributed greatly to Ayres's love of the written word.

Ayres attended Randolph-Macon Woman's College from 1938 to 1939 but finished her degree in 1942 at the University of Mississippi. She married composer Kenneth Haxton on 12 January 1945; shortly thereafter, the couple moved to Greenville, Mississippi. There, Haxton was soon busy raising their three sons, Richard, Ayres, and Brooks. (She and her husband ultimately divorced in 1980.) Greenville proved to be a rich resource for Haxton, whose friends there included historian Shelby Foote and the journalist Hodding Carter, whose newspaper provided a singularly liberal voice during the civil rights struggle that struck Mississippi with particular ferocity. Some of Douglas's best fiction has drawn on her experience of the racial tensions that have beset Southerners and particularly the structures of self-deception that people erect to preserve familiar notions of reality. Douglas's thoughtful and unflinching exposure of those structures, in her characters' personal lives as well as in contemporary society, has been a hallmark of her work.

Although she had made attempts at writing as early as sixth grade, Haxton began writing in earnest during the time she spent in Greenville. According to the author, she entered a wager with her husband and a mutual friend concerning who could finish a novel in the least amount of time. Haxton won the bet, but when the novel was passed from the hands of her friend Charles Bell to Craig Bell, an editor for Houghton Mifflin, Haxton was reluctant to publish it because of its autobiographical nature. She finally agreed after obtaining her aunts' permission and the name Ellen Douglas.

A Family's Affairs recounts the experiences of several generations of an upper-class Southern family that cherishes the long-held Southern values of family, propriety, and honor. The narrative begins with the core group of three sisters, Anna, Charlotte, and Sarah D., and the family matriarch, Kate Anderson. Moving forward and backward through time, Douglas weaves the stories of individual family members, showing their relationships to one another and the ways in which

Dust jacket for Douglas's 1973 novel, about mistreatment of the elderly both by their well-intentioned but thoughtless relatives and by corrupt professional caregivers (Richland County Public Library)

they resist the restrictions inherent in Southern culture. *A Family's Affairs* was immediately successful. It won the Houghton Mifflin Esquire Fellowship Award for best new novel and was named as one of the year's ten best books by *The New York Times*.

Douglas closely followed this success with her 1963 collection of short stories, *Black Cloud, White Cloud,* which, like its predecessor, was also named among the year's best fiction by *The New York Times*. One of her most recognized short stories, "I Just Love Carrie Lee," is taken from this collection, which weaves a tapestry of life in Homochitto County, the fictional equivalent of Greenville and the setting for most of Douglas's work. Linked by characters and themes, the work also displays one of Douglas's strongest gifts as a writer–her interest in stories and storytelling. Douglas's novels are often founded on the ways in which stories redefine experience, at once exposing and concealing what readers understand to be true. The narrator of "I Just Love Carrie Lee" clearly sees herself as a broad-minded white woman with a special understanding of African

Americans, especially one like Carrie Lee, with whom she has spent most of her life. Through her recollections and asides, readers are made to see a rather different picture, one shaded by guilt and narrowly framed, of an African American woman's life.

Douglas took a short break from publishing while she wrote her second novel, *Where the Dreams Cross* (1968). Though it remains true to Douglas's style, *Where the Dreams Cross* is probably one of her least commercially successful works, and as such, it has received little critical attention. Protagonist Nat Hunter Stonebridge is a newly divorced woman in her mid thirties when she returns to Philippi, the small town she once called home. As the novel opens, readers gain their first glimpse of Nat through the eyes of those who knew her, or at least her scandalous reputation, during her high-school and college years. Douglas thus reveals Nat's past, both personal and familial, by weaving backward and forward through time in the first part of the novel. Though Nat returns to Philippi to escape the nightmarish world of an abusive marriage, she finds herself crossing from one nightmare into another in both her waking and dreaming lives, to such an extent that she is constantly unsure whether she is awake or asleep. Through her desire to define her own reality, Nat finally escapes to Hollywood, where she enacts the dreams of others. In so doing, she escapes the place "where the dreams cross" and begins to truly understand herself, her family, and her past for the first time in her life.

In 1973 Douglas released her third novel, *Apostles of Light,* a moving account of the way society treats the elderly. In the opening scene Martha Clarke sits helplessly reminiscing about her former life as younger members of her well-intentioned but thoughtless family decide what is to be done not only about Martha but also about her sister, Elizabeth, who lies in a hospital bed battling the last stages of cancer; Martha's longtime love, Lucas Alexander; and all of their possessions. Throughout the course of the novel, the family invalidates the lives of these three elderly people by seizing control of them and forcing the conversion of Martha's family home into the Golden Ages Acres retirement home. Though much thought is given to the potential problems and burdens placed on the family by the failing health of all three, no thought is given to how the elderly would like to spend their remaining days. As Laurel Graeber remarked in her 28 May 1995 review in *The New York Times,* the family successfully turns "Martha's house into a nursing home and their lives into a prison." In their attempts to escape the corruption of the nursing-home custodians who neglectfully allow patients to remain in their soiled bedsheets rather than changing them because "you'll just pee again," Martha and Lucas decide on what they see as their only means of freedom: death.

In 1976 Douglas received a National Endowment for the Humanities Fellowship and began teaching as a writer-in-residence at Northeastern State University of Louisiana in Monroe (now Louisiana State University, Monroe). While there, Douglas completed work on her fourth novel, *The Rock Cried Out* (1979). Douglas stated in her interview with McCord that *The Rock Cried Out* was the most successful of all her novels upon its initial release.

In the novel, Alan McLaurin leaves college life in Boston and returns to his familial home in Homochitto County in order to overcome his frustrations with city life and get back to the natural world. While there, Alan hopes to write poetry and better understand himself. However, in his quest to find meaning in his present, Alan is soon forced to confront his and his family's pasts as he becomes increasingly enmeshed in family dramas and the struggle for civil rights. *The Rock Cried Out* marks a departure for Douglas, who intricately intertwines sex, politics, religion, and race in a novel that explores the violence of the civil rights era through the eyes of Alan, her only male narrator. Douglas later returned to this tumultuous time period in her out-of-print novella *A Long Night* (1986), which details the riotous integration of the University of Mississippi.

Between these two accounts of the civil rights movement, Douglas returned to Mississippi as a writer-in-residence at the University of Mississippi in Oxford and to her use of the female narrator. *A Lifetime Burning* (1982) is once again set in fictional Homochitto County and focuses on a woman named Corrine. However, the novel is different from other Douglas works because it is written in the form of a journal, so that the narrator's psychological state takes precedence over her external setting. Corrine is a college professor in her sixties who uses her diary as a method for communicating with herself and leaving a record of her life for her children. Throughout the course of the novel, readers deeply sympathize with Corrine as she relates her husband's suspected affair with an unattractive female neighbor whom Corrine nicknames "the Toad," his actual affair with another man, and finally, her own affair. However, as readers quickly learn, Corrine has a penchant for mendacity and is not to be trusted in all of her accounts. The novel is one of Douglas's best-known works; like its predecessor, *The Rock Cried Out,* it won the Mississippi Institute of Arts and Letters Award.

Douglas took a brief hiatus from novel writing when she followed in her grandmother's footsteps to publish a volume of children's stories, *The Magic Carpet and Other Tales* (1987). Walter Anderson illustrated Douglas's retellings of classic myths, legends, and fairy tales in this collection. Though this book is a marked departure for Douglas, her versions of such classic tales as "Cinderella," "The Three Billy Goats Gruff," "The Frog Prince," "The Birth and Coronation of Arthur," and "Sleeping Beauty" ensured the continued popularity of the volume and subsequent reprints.

Despite this short break, Douglas soon returned to her novelistic roots with the publication of her most popular novel, *Can't Quit You, Baby* (1988). An exploration of the interlocking lives of a white housewife and her black servant, *Can't Quit You, Baby* expands upon the theme of gender-specific race relations touched upon in "I Just Love Carrie Lee," *A Family's Affairs,* and *Where the Dreams Cross.* All of Douglas's fictional interests converge in this remarkable novel—the role of storytelling and stories, the struggles of Southern women, relationships and the elusiveness of truth, and the ways that social fabrications collide with people's most intimate selves. With its adroit uses of voice and perspective, *Can't Quit You, Baby* is one of the most searching novels about the intimate spaces of Southern life in this era.

Born in Natchez, Mississippi, Ellen Douglas (a pseudonym for Josephine Haxton) is the author of three
earlier novels and a book of short stories. Her first
novel, *A Family's Affairs* (1962), was selected by the
New York Times as one of the five best novels of that
year, and her most recent, *Apostles of Light* (1973),
was nominated for the National Book Award in that
year. Ellen Douglas lives in Greenville, Mississippi,
and is Writer-in-Residence for one semester each year
at Northeast Louisiana University in Monroe. She
received a grant from the National Endowment for
the Arts to complete *The Rock Cried Out.*

0-15-178322-5

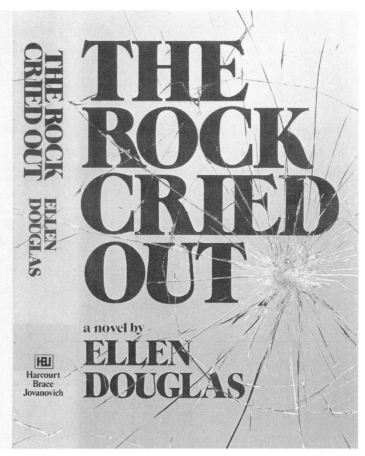

*Dust jacket for Douglas's 1979 novel, the only one to date to feature a male narrator, in which a young man
returns home to Mississippi and is confronted with his family's past and the violence
of the civil rights era (Richland County Public Library)*

In the novel, which pulls its title and major symbol from a Willie Dixon song of the same name, Cornelia, a white woman prone to creating her own
world, and her black cook, Tweet (who is known to
everyone else as Julia), must learn to overcome the stereotypical relationships in which they are immersed in
order to develop a true friendship. Tweet finds personal meaning in her family's past and relates familial
anecdotes to Cornelia as they work together in the
kitchen. Cornelia only half hears these stories with
condescension as Tweet tells them; but when the perfect world she has created for herself crumbles, and
Cornelia retreats to a small apartment in New York
City in order to end her life or find a new beginning,
Tweet's words echo in her ears and act as her salvation. Cornelia sees this realization as a basis for truly
open communication, but when she returns home, she
learns that Tweet has been rendered speechless by a
massive stroke. Cornelia nurses her friend back to
health, but only after the women confess their secret

hatred of one another can they begin to develop a true
friendship. The novel ends with the women laughing
and singing Dixon's lyrics, "Oh, I love you baby, but I
sure do hate your ways." Thus, Douglas indicates that
the necessary lines of honest communication are
finally open for Cornelia and Tweet, and though they
do not have a fully developed friendship at this point,
they have the opportunity to develop one based on
their newfound honesty.

Karen J. Jacobsen discusses the primary theme
of *Can't Quit You, Baby:* it "imagines an alternative
social order in which black and white women share
their stories, allowing them to form authentic friendships." Likewise, Ann M. Bomberger examined the
perplexing portrayal of the relationship between black
and white women in the novel, exploring the implications of race, hatred, and misconceptions in Cornelia's
and Julia's attempts to form an honest friendship. She
notes Douglas's use of a third-person female narrator
who comments on the nature of race relations without

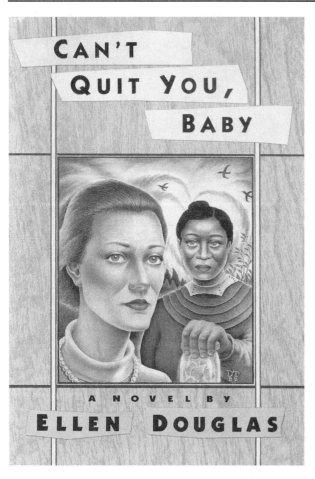

Dust jacket for Douglas's 1988 novel, in which a white Southern housewife and her black cook overcome stereotypes and prejudices to form a deep and lasting friendship (Richland County Public Library)

"expecting to come up with definitive answers, yet entering and engaging the debate over racial politics nonetheless."

The success of *Can't Quit You, Baby,* which has never been out of print, drew attention to the rest of Douglas's work, which was all soon reprinted. In 1989 Douglas received the Fellowship of Southern Writers Fiction Award for the body of her work and became a Welty Professor at Millsaps College in Jackson, Mississippi. Douglas focused on her teaching and toyed with the construction of a new novel during the following years but largely remained out of the public sphere until the publication of *Truth: Four Stories I Am Finally Old Enough to Tell* (1998).

Despite the title, Douglas's semi-autobiographical book does not always tell the whole truth but rather the truth as she remembers it or chooses to tell it. This set of tales draws on both history and family experience to explore the thin borders between fiction and nonfiction and the novelist's complicity in blurring those lines. While there are essentially four chapters corresponding to the "four stories" in Douglas's title, the book weaves pieces of varying tales from several generations in order to give the main stories a full context. In the first story, "Grant," Douglas relates the hardships of becoming the primary caregiver for her husband's uncle, Grant, when he was diagnosed with cancer. Douglas weaves her own experiences of caring for three sons and a terminally ill patient with the details of Grant's life and Southern folklore concerning death. The remaining stories in the collection follow a similar pattern. "Julia and Nellie" tells the story of Douglas's grandmother's friend, Julia, and her long-standing love affair with her distant cousin, Nellie, who "took care of the cows for her." In the third story, "Hampton," Douglas attempts to understand the life of her grandmother's gardener. "On Second Creek," the final story in the collection, details Douglas's investigation of a local historical event in which several slaves were reportedly questioned and executed in 1861 as the result of a purported plan to carry out an uprising. Through her research on the matter, Douglas must confront not only the horrors of the incident but also her own family's involvement in it and the meaning that that could have for her life.

Haxton's pseudonym offered her little anonymity after the publication of her first novel; townspeople recognized her fictionalized portraits. However, she continues to publish under the name Ellen Douglas. Despite the acclaim her novels have won and the length of her writing career, Douglas remains a relatively unknown author. In an article published in the spring 1996 edition of *The Southern Review,* "Proust, Ava Gardner, and the Last Frontier," Douglas relates her experiences during a summer trip to Las Vegas in 1946. She notes, "I continue to move through a landscape as fantastic as Las Vegas. My children's and grandchildren's lives, my friends', my students', my own, are not imaginable to me in any landscape where everyone would seem to occupy a predestined place." Just as Douglas's displacement in the world is evident in this passage, perhaps her fiction lacks the popularity offered to other writers because it too is difficult to place in any particular genre.

Josephine Haxton, otherwise known as Ellen Douglas, has produced a body of work that offers an unflinching look at some of the most troubling issues in American culture. Douglas resides in Jackson, Mississippi, where she continues to write short stories and occasionally teaches workshops in creative writing. When McCord asked if readers can expect another novel, Douglas remarked, "Well who knows? . . . If I live long enough, maybe I'll write another one."

Interviews:

Charline R. McCord, "Interview with Ellen Douglas: February 25, 1997," *Mississippi Quarterly,* 51 (Spring 1998): 291–322;

Conversations with Ellen Douglas, edited by Panthea Reid (Jackson: University Press of Mississippi, 2000).

Bibliography:

Elisabeth Lamothe, "Ellen Douglas: Bibliography," *Colloque Eudora Welty: The Poetics of the Body* (16–18 October 2002) <http://www.uhb.fr/faulkner/WF/pages/welty/biblio_douglas.htm>.

References:

Ann M. Bomberger, "The Servant and the Served: Ellen Douglas's *Can't Quit You, Baby,*" *Southern Literary Journal,* 31 (Fall 1998): 17–34;

Panthea Reid Broughton and Susan Millar Williams, "Ellen Douglas," in *Southern Women Writers: The New Generation,* edited by Tonnette Bond Inge (Tuscaloosa: University of Alabama Press, 1990), pp. 46–69;

"Ellen Douglas (Josephine Ayers Haxton)," *The Mississippi Writers Page* (May 2001) <http://www.ole miss.edu/mwp/dir/douglas_ellen/>;

Karen J. Jacobsen, "Disrupting the Legacy of Silence: Ellen Douglas's *Can't Quit You, Baby,*" *Southern Literary Journal,* 32 (Spring 2000): 27–41;

Carol Manning, "Ellen Douglas: Moralist and Realist," *Southern Quarterly,* 21 (Summer 1983): 117–134;

Panthea Reid, "Inventions and Truth, Ellen Douglas and *Truth,*" *Virginia Quarterly Review,* 75 (Summer 1999): 583–589;

Southern Quarterly, special Douglas issue, 33 (Summer 1995);

Linda Tate, *A Southern Weave of Women: Fiction of the Contemporary South* (Athens: University of Georgia Press, 1994), p. 50.

Papers:

The University of Mississippi has some of Ellen Douglas's papers.

Andre Dubus III

(11 September 1959 –   )

Lisa Abney
Northwestern State University

BOOKS: *The Cage Keeper and Other Stories* (New York: Dutton, 1989);
Bluesman (Boston: Faber & Faber, 1993);
House of Sand and Fog (New York: Norton, 1999).

RECORDING: *House of Sand and Fog,* read by Dubus and Fontaine Dollas Dubus, New York, Harper-Collins, 2001.

OTHER: Philip Zaleski, ed., *The Best Spiritual Writing 2001,* introduction by Dubus (San Francisco: HarperSanFrancisco, 2001);
Breece D'J Pancake, *The Stories of Breece D'J Pancake,* afterword by Dubus (Boston: Little, Brown, 2002).

Andre Dubus III resisted the idea of being an author for many years because his father, Andre Dubus, who died in 1999, continues to be well recognized as one of America's best short-fiction writers, and the younger Dubus simply wanted to do something different. Additionally, noted detective-fiction writer James Lee Burke is Dubus III's cousin. The younger Dubus has held a variety of jobs—bounty hunter, private investigator, carpenter, bartender, actor, and teacher—but, as he told Oprah Winfrey in a 24 January 2001 television interview, "Growing up, I never wanted to be a writer. I found that when I did start writing, I felt more like myself than I've ever felt. I had to write to be me." The Dubus stock has had a significant impact upon the writing of the late twentieth and early twenty-first centuries.

Dubus was born on 11 September 1959 in Oceanside, California, to Andre Dubus Jr. and his wife, social worker Patricia Lowe. Dubus's parents divorced when he was eleven years old, but he maintained a strong relationship with his father. As a result of his parents' divorce, however, Lowe and the children (Dubus has a brother and two sisters, as well as two half sisters from his father's remarriage) lived in poverty for many years. When Dubus completed high school, he

Andre Dubus III (photograph by Marion Ettlinger; from the dust jacket for House of Sand and Fog, *1999; Richland County Public Library)*

attended Bradford College in Massachusetts and earned an associate of arts degree in 1979, and then continued his studies at the University of Texas in Austin. Dubus was drawn to the University of Texas because of its progressive curriculum and atmosphere. He earned his B.A. in 1981 after studying sociology and political science. Shortly thereafter, he returned to Massachusetts for a year to, as he says in an interview with Robert Birnbaum, "get out of the books a bit."

In Massachusetts he worked in construction with his younger brother and boxed at the Lynn Boys Club. At the time, he was dating a girl who was one of his father's students. When she told Dubus that she had a crush on a classmate because she was impressed by his writing, Dubus read the classmate's manuscript and became inspired to write. Ultimately, he began writing a short story to impress the girlfriend, but he ended up enjoying writing so much that he continued.

Dubus initially planned to earn a Ph.D. in Marxist social science at the University of Wisconsin and then to attend law school. He went to Wisconsin and stayed four days, during which time he realized that he did not want to be a sociologist. He then returned to Texas briefly and went to Colorado for a year, where he worked in corrections and continued writing. His first published story, "Forky," appeared in *Playboy* in 1984 and won the National Magazine Award a year later. The student whose manuscript had impressed him became his friend, and when Dubus returned to Massachusetts from Colorado, his friend recommended him for a position at Emerson College, where he taught until 1999. Dubus has also taught writing at Tufts University and Harvard, although he did not give up construction work.

In 1989 Dubus married Fontaine Dollas, a dancer and choreographer. He and Dollas have three children, and Dubus devotes a significant portion of his day to being an active parent. Also in 1989 Dubus published a collection of short fiction, *The Cage Keeper and Other Stories*. Some of these stories chronicle the lives of two counselors at a halfway house and the various inmates who inhabit the facility. Doubtless, the topics of the collection were influenced by the year Dubus spent working in Colorado at such a facility in the early 1980s. The title story involves a young corrections counselor, Allen, and an escaped inmate who kidnaps him and demands to be driven to Canada. Along the way, the kidnapper, Douglas Agnes McElroy, makes a fatal mistake in attempting to rob a 7-11 store, where he is killed by a pistol-packing store clerk. After the inmate's death, Allen returns to the corrections facility for another day's work and ponders McElroy's actions. In "Duckling Girl" Dubus depicts the death of an idealistic and chivalrous cab driver who intervenes in the life of an abused young woman, Lorilee Waters. Lorilee's drug-addled cohorts, Freeze and Barry, refuse to stop pestering Lorilee, and after the cab driver attempts to make the boys leave the cab, Freeze kills him. The disturbing story catalogues a violent world and the senseless murders that have become a disturbing element of late-twentieth-century America. The volume also includes "Forky," which chronicles the experiences of an inmate as he moves from prison to civilian life and goes on a

Dust jacket for Dubus's first novel, published in 1993, about a sixteen-year-old boy's coming of age during the Vietnam War era (Richland County Public Library)

date with a woman. The final scene provides a series of brutal images that blur and ultimately leave the reader pondering the ending. Other stories involve a troubled Vietnam veteran's ill-fated relationship with a younger lover, and a camping trip undertaken by two children and their stepfather, newly estranged from their mother. Dubus's first book delves into many troubling sides of contemporary society—urban violence, decaying relationships, loss of community and family, loss of identity, and unfulfilled dreams.

While Dubus's range of character development and plotlines make this collection noteworthy, no academic articles have been written regarding the work, and it received few reviews. Starr E. Smith of the *Library Journal* (January 1989) gave the collection an A grade, while *The New York Times Book Review* critic Deborah Solomon stated that it was an average book. A review in the *The Los Angeles Times* (11 February 1990) described the collection as "Darkly powerful stories of the American underclass: drifters, bikers, ex-cons and

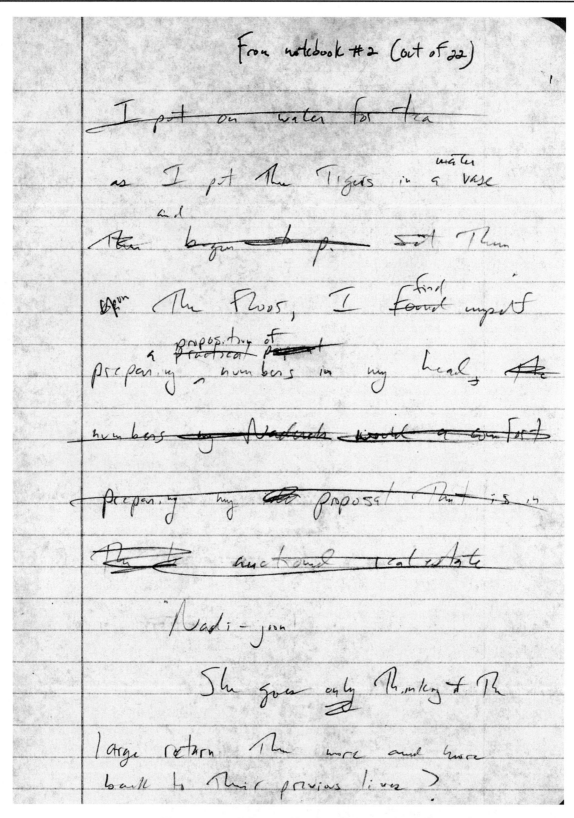

Manuscript pages for House of Sand and Fog, *Dubus's widely acclaimed novel about the battle between a woman wrongfully evicted from her home and the immigrant Iranian former army colonel who buys the house at a tax sale (courtesy of the author)*

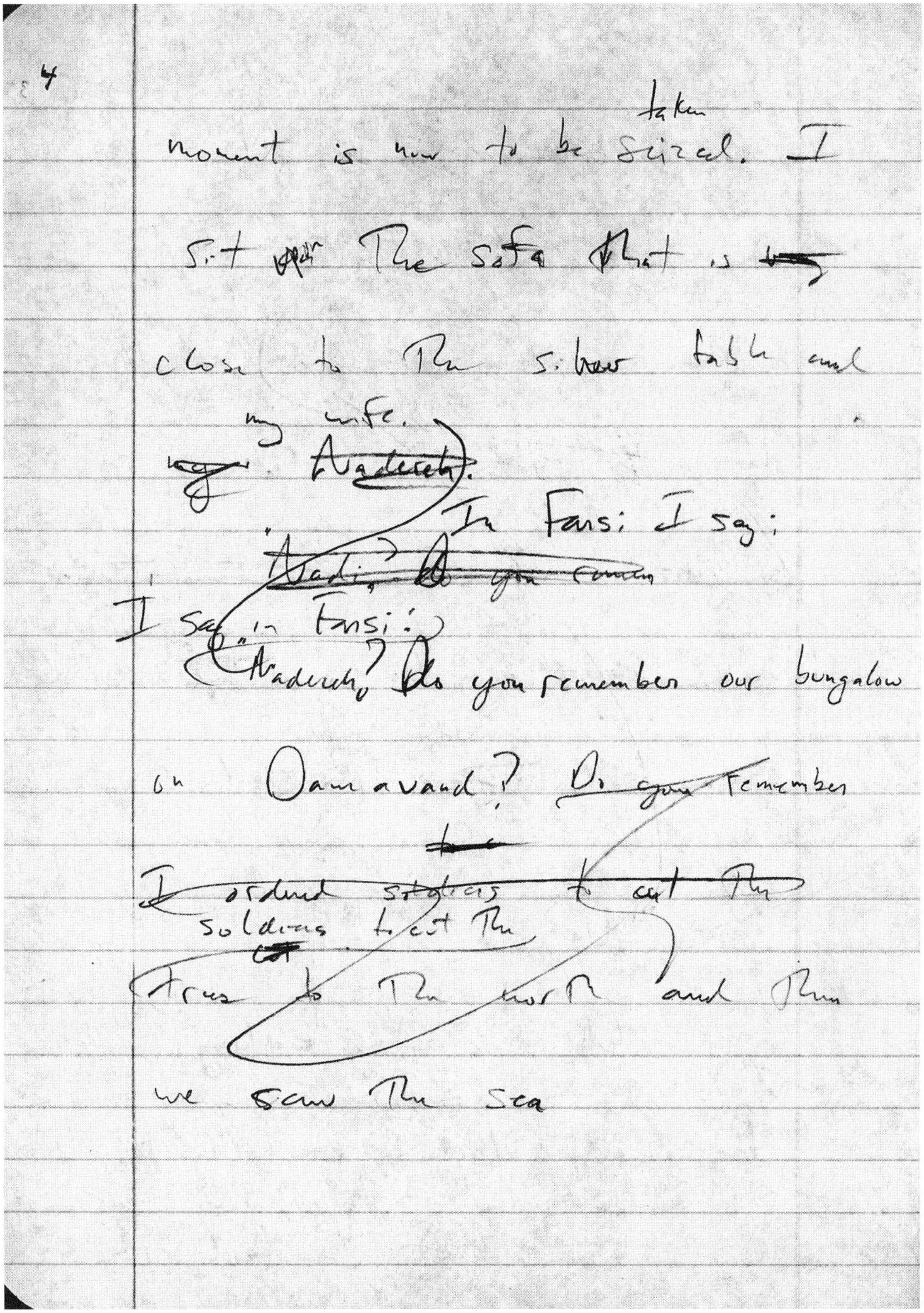

4

moment is now to be seized. I

sit on the sofa that is

close to the silver table and

my wife. Nadereh.

"In Farsi I say;

I say in Farsi:

"Nadereh? Do you remember our bungalow

on Oamavand? Do you remember

I ordered soldiers to cut the
Soldiers cut the

trees to the north and then

we saw the sea

drop-outs." The review continued: "Dubus's characters fight to keep functioning, even after their lives have ended, as far as society is concerned." A 5 March 1989 review, again from *The Los Angeles Times,* asserted that Dubus

> crafts powerful stories about people struggling to find something to affirm in the weary souls and bleak surroundings. With richly original and consistently believable sketches, Dubus carries us deep into the lives of his characters, from wardens to inmates and abused women, who live on society's edge in prisons of their own or of their state's construction.

Given Dubus's popularity following his novel *House of Sand and Fog* (1999), these stories may receive more critical attention in the future.

Dubus's second book, *Bluesman,* appeared in 1993. This novel, like his first collection, also did not garner much critical acclaim nor readership. *Bluesman* is a contemporary coming-of-age story in which sixteen-year-old Leo Sutherland learns about life, the blues, and Marxism during the late 1960s and early 1970s. His new boss for his summer construction job is his girlfriend's father, Chick Donovan. Allie, his girlfriend, is blonde and beautiful, and Leo's job with her father's company initially seems like a dream come true. However, on the first day at the job, Leo learns that Chick is a communist. As the summer passes, Leo yearns to learn more about life, about the burgeoning Vietnam War, about communists, about America, and about himself. During this summer his father gives him a collection of writings by his deceased mother. He begins to think about his mother, his father, and his place in the family and in the world. After many different discussions with people including communist Chick, Leo's father, and his friends, and after losing Allie, Leo decides, after a great deal of deliberation, to enlist in the military.

This introspective piece differs from Dubus's earlier work, which was filled with action. *Bluesman* has earned praise from some critics as an important voice in the discussion of the Vietnam War and war era. A *Publishers Weekly* (29 March 1993) review commented that "Dubus is a sympathetic and compassionate chronicler of ordinary lives. He understands the rhythms of hard labor and the needs of the people who do it; the sensitivity and decency of his working-class heroes make them genuinely compelling and likeable." Valerie Ryan, writing for the *Seattle Times* (29 August 1993), stated: "In a style as strong, sweet, and clear as the blues he writes about, Andre Dubus III has crafted a story that starts on a single theme, carries us through a series of riffs, and diminishes on a high, mournful note." Patrick Samway, in his review for *America* (28

August 1993), asserted: "Dubus deftly explores what he seems to know best: family life, music and searching for love." With the publication of the Vintage Contemporary edition, one reviewer from the *TLS: The Times Literary Supplement* (21 September 2001) stated that the novel is

> written with a thoughtful eye that marks the casual detail of important events, although it often misses the mark in its assessments of what distance to keep in relation to adolescent preoccupations. However, the book improves as it progresses, and the drama of its conclusion is restrained yet convincing.

The book also had some detractors: an anonymously written notice in *Kirkus Reviews* termed the novel "thin-blooded" and further maintained, "The narrative, fine as it is, ultimately has a rather hollow ring—and needs badly to encase something more than it has been given. Rather flat and wide of the mark: a disappointment." Dubus's next novel, however, received a solidly positive response.

House of Sand and Fog treads the same waters as *The Cage Keeper and Other Stories* in terms of themes and characterization. In many ways, the themes of the novel are close to modernist concerns—alienation, loss of community, a skewed vision of love, and plenty of angst—yet, Dubus adds a contemporary twist. Kathy Nicolo is a troubled young woman who is also a recovering drug addict, estranged from her family. All she has left is her house, which she has inherited from her father. Partially because of her own inattentiveness and partially because of faulty county record keeping, her house is mistakenly auctioned for back taxes, and Persian immigrant Colonel Behrani buys the house. Behrani, a former leader in the air force of the Shah of Iran, has been relegated to several odd and menial jobs during his time in America, and he desperately strives to maintain appearances by buying this house. Lester Burdon, a county sheriff's deputy, comes to evict Kathy from her home, but he feels sorry for her and ends up in a relationship with her. Burdon, however, is married, and a relationship with Kathy is the last thing he needs. He winds up helping Kathy by inappropriately using his credentials to attempt to scare Behrani out of the house after the colonel has made expensive improvements and repairs. Ultimately, all parties concerned are locked in a battle that ends catastrophically.

The writing of *House of Sand and Fog* took four years. The book was originally composed in longhand in pencil; Dubus wrote in his car outside a nearby cemetery because his house was small, and the sounds of his three small children playing distracted him.

Dubus told Birnbaum: "It took me three years to write the story and another year to type up twenty-two notebooks. And another six months of extensive revision after it was acquired by Norton." Dubus's desire to write about these particular characters grew from his experiences with a Persian family whose daughter he had dated for several years while pursuing his undergraduate degree and from a newspaper clipping that detailed the story of an older woman who was wrongly evicted from her home for not paying taxes (which she in fact did not owe). The man who bought her house at auction was named Mohammed, which sparked Dubus's interest in incorporating the Persian expatriate element into the novel.

House of Sand and Fog became a selection of Oprah Winfrey's book club in 2000, and sales of the novel went from 165,000 copies to more than 1,700,000. In a 13 May 2001 interview with James Macgowan, Dubus, grateful for Winfrey's help and support, said of the talk-show host: "I'll have enough money to build my home. I've never lived in my own home; I never lived in an owned home as a kid. So my wife and I are getting ready to build a house." After his appearance on her show and her on-line chat website, sales again climbed.

Even before the fanfare that comes with being named an Oprah book, critics had already heralded the novel. A review in *Publishers Weekly* (30 November 1998) declared: "Dubus writes with an authority regarding the American lower middle class that is reminiscent of Russell Banks and Richard Ford, and his limber imagination is capable of drawing the inner lives of three very different main characters with such compassion that readers will find their sympathies hopelessly divided." Larry Weissman asserted in *Bold Type Magazine* (1999) that "Though their decisions are often infuriating, these characters are as real and involving as any in contemporary literature. Told with generous empathy, *House of Sand and Fog* is a powerful modern-day Greek tragedy that marks the arrival of a true literary star." Liz Keuffer stated in a *Bookreporter.com* review in 2000 that the novel was an anomaly in terms of character and plot development:

> It is rare in contemporary literature to read a book in which the characters are naturally allowed to make the decisions that propel the plot forward. So often the people in novels are at the mercy of the story—mere puppets of clever plot twists or of writers who want to showcase their ability to wring every possible bit of suspense from a situation. Andre Dubus's second novel, *House of Sand and Fog,* is a throwback to a time when writing was more important than plot, and the characters mattered more than the cunning of the author who created them.

Keuffer's comments were echoed by other critics. Richard Eder called the novel "fine and prophetic" in his review in *Newsday* (22 February 1999); yet, he noticed two elements with which he takes issue—the "code switching" of Colonel Behrani from Persian language to English, and the "madness and violence" to which the book descends at the end. Ultimately, however, Eder praised the novel for its originality and integrity. Reba Leiding of *Library Journal* (1 March 1999) felt that the novel conveyed "a hard-edged, cinematic quality, but unlike many movies, its outcome is unexpected." (A movie version of the novel, with screenplay by director Vadim Perelman and starring Jennifer Connelly, Ben Kingsley, and Ron Eldard, was released in December 2003.) Few if any critics wrote negative reviews of the novel, and *House of Sand and Fog* was a finalist for the 1999 National Book Award in fiction.

While Andre Dubus III's career remains in its early stages, his works already in print serve as a firm foundation. Dubus continues to teach at Tufts University while maintaining a busy schedule of writing and spending time with his children. Doubtless, more of Dubus's innovative work will allow readers and critics more material for perusal and evaluation.

Interviews:

Jerome V. Kramer, "Double Dubus," *Book* (March/April 1999) <http://www.bookmagazine.com/archive/issue3/dubus.shtml>;

James Macgowan, "Oprah Helps a Son Come into His Own," *Ottawa Citizen,* 13 May 2001, p. C12;

Robert Birnbaum, "Interview: Andre Dubus III," *Identity Theory/The Narrative Thread* <http://www.identity theory.com/people/birnbaum3.html>;

Larry Weissman, "A Conversation with Andre Dubus III," *Bold Type* <http://www.randomhouse.com/boldtype/0300/dubus/interview.html>.

John Dufresne

(30 January 1948 –   )

Jeffery K. Guin

BOOKS: *The Way That Water Enters Stone* (New York: Norton, 1991);

Louisiana Power & Light (New York: Norton, 1994);

Love Warps the Mind a Little (New York: Norton, 1997);

Deep in the Shade of Paradise (New York: Norton, 2002);

The Lie That Tells a Truth: A Guide to Writing Fiction (New York: Norton, 2003).

John Dufresne's novels reflect the postmodernist themes apparent in American society at the end of the twentieth century. His works present an interesting mixture of sociological determinism combined with a distinctly regional flavor. At the same time, Dufresne's novels provide dramatic contrasts between dream-like postmodernism and the Southern literary tradition. He reconciles these contrasts through vivid descriptions of time and place, tying his characters to these elements to create worlds that are at once surreal and personally identifiable.

Born on 30 January 1948, John Dufresne was the oldest of four children of French-Canadian parents in the working-class Grafton Hill neighborhood of Worcester, Massachusetts. His upbringing was blue-collar Catholic. The foundation of his narrative craft was formed in his family home, where storytelling was a way of life–particularly at mealtimes, when stories and gossip about friends and relatives were regularly traded: "Like Uncle George, who claimed to be pals with all the Red Sox. When he drove home from Fort Devens in a jeep he said the colonel lent him because they were friends, we believed him. Until the MPs showed up," Dufresne told Eve Richardson of *Poets & Writers*.

Dufresne credits his parents–Bernard V. Dufresne, who worked at New England Power, and Doris Berard Dufresne, an office worker–with giving him the freedom to pursue his dream of writing. Dufresne stated in an unpublished June 2002 interview, "My parents have always been supportive of my writing, and have always encouraged me to go my own way. I never felt any pressure to work at something more secure." Dufresne's

John Dufresne (photograph by Cindy Chinelly; from the dust jacket for Louisiana Power & Light, *1994; Richland County Public Library)*

first attempts at creative writing came primarily in the form of poetry during his years at St. John's High School in Worcester. In a personal interview he noted, "All of my high-school compositions sounded like Holden Caulfield." His first published work was a story titled "Two Students," which was published in a Canadian magazine called *Dreamweaver*.

Even with his family's own storytelling tradition, Dufresne says his New England upbringing made it difficult to see a person's true character. In "Fiction Is My Religion: Conversations with John Dufresne" (2001) the author told interviewers Kevin Blaine Bell and David Caudle:

In New England everything was clipped–language was for information. In New England, the population was more transient. There was always an influx of immigrants. In my neighborhood there were probably nine churches, and each one for a different ethnic group. . . . People identified with that, rather than with the neighborhood. They closed themselves up; they narrowed life down a lot.

His world was broadened through stories, which, in his words, were the essence of life. While his creativity was germinating, he devoted much of his time to Catholicism, working in his early teens at a church-run nursing home and planning to become a priest. "In my mind, that was the best thing you could be, so I aspired to that," he said to Bell and Caudle. "I really was quite religious as a kid–the kind of guy who carried around a prayer book in my pocket as a good luck charm."

Dufresne drifted from the faith in high school as many of his questions went unanswered by church leaders. He remarks to Bell and Caudle that "as I became more interested in thinking, faith gave way, as a way of knowing. Thinking became more important than faith." His thinking as a young man, as well as his writing in later life, was influenced by Southern writers, as he told Richardson:

In the work of Flannery O'Connor, William Faulkner, Harper Lee, I found characters who have been held out of the mainstream or have decided to hold out. The honesty was attractive and familiar. I knew the world was a mess because I saw young men grown pale, soft, and cynical, all up and down Grafton Hill in the Diamond Café, the Cosmopolitan Club, Jack's, Uncle Charlie's Tavern, the American Legion, sitting in the dark watching TV, smoking, drinking shots and beers, reminiscing. . . . I saw friends, teenagers already alcoholics, toothless and conniving.

After parting from the church, Dufresne saw anew the potential depth and diversity of humanity. He also began to see how he could use his varied experiences in his literary career.

Dufresne earned a B.A. from Worcester State College in 1970. After graduation he first worked with troubled youth as a street social worker, then formed an alternative school and started a crisis hot line, training people in phone counseling. In 1971 he married Marilyn Virbasius; the couple divorced in 1978. During this time, he wrote, though he did not aggressively seek publication. He freelanced and did odd jobs, including housepainting with a friend. Gradually, writing began to take more of his time, and ultimately, it became his passion. He applied to writing programs and was accepted to the University of Arkansas, where he studied with John Clellon Holmes, whom he calls his hero, and Bill Harrison. He learned the mechanics of writing and also studied the Southern penchant for storytelling

and the ways in which those narrators use language like an instrument.

When he completed his master of fine arts degree in 1984, Dufresne and poet classmate Cindy Chinelly left Fayetteville to teach at Northeastern Louisiana University in Monroe, Louisiana. Bolstered by a community of writers, Dufresne's literary voice began to take shape. Dufresne and Chinelly married in May 1985; in late 1987 the couple and their son, Tristan, moved to Worcester State, then to the State University of New York at Binghamton, and finally to Augusta College in Georgia. Since 1989 Dufresne has taught creative writing at Florida International University in North Miami. During this time, Dufresne sent a manuscript to literary agent Richard McDonough, who forwarded it to Jill Bialosky, an editor at Norton. Bialosky contracted *The Way That Water Enters Stone* (1991), Dufresne's first collection of short fiction.

Dufresne's narrative voice as well as the themes that he tackles in his novels–love, death, and religion– are introduced in the thirteen stories included in *The Way That Water Enters Stone*. The title story is a first-person narrative contrasting the dysfunctional marriage of a science teacher with that of his mentally challenged neighbors, who are happy together and blissfully ignorant of the responsibilities of life and parenthood. Other stories relate the lifestyles of common people, with Dufresne's trademark attention to detail. Most significant is "The Fontana Gene," which introduces the Fontana clan and is the story that has led to two other works: *Louisiana Power & Light* (1994) and *Deep in the Shade of Paradise* (2002). "The Fontana Gene" was added at the request of Dufresne's editor after the rest of the collection had been presented for publication.

When *The Way That Water Enters Stone* was published, reviewers recognized and applauded Dufresne's efforts to present a larger view of the human condition. In a review for *Publishers Weekly* (January 1991) Sybil Steinberg remarked: "The characters in this powerful debut short story collection desperately seek a salvation that they suspect will never come and yet, in just muddling through, his drifters, fast-food clerks, farmers, innkeepers, movie addicts, loners and losers achieve a certain dignity." Especially noted was "The Fontana Gene," the story in which Dufresne is generally considered to have hit his narrative stride.

Building on positive reaction to "The Fontana Gene," Dufresne later expanded the story into his highly acclaimed first novel, *Louisiana Power & Light*. The book reprises the misfortunes of Billy Wayne Fontana, the sole survivor of the doomed Fontana line. Billy Wayne's ancestor, who is credited for starting the Fontana line, is described repeatedly as having emerged from the primordial ooze. All manner of misfortunes

Dust jacket for Dufresne's first novel, about a Southerner who tries to stop the propagation of his degenerate genes (Richland County Public Library)

(including genetic malformations) befall the Fontanas in successive generations. As one of the few Fontanas with the sensibility to recognize this fate, Billy Wayne also feels a responsibility to prevent the line from continuing. As in the earlier short story, Billy Wayne struggles to reconcile his need to love and be loved with the guilt he feels about being a Fontana.

With his first wife, Earlene, Billy Wayne is unable to overcome his feelings of guilt, unable to make love to his wife for fear of producing genetically defective children. He overcomes this feeling with his second wife, Tami Lynne, only to have his fears confirmed with the births of two physically disabled sons. The resulting plot demonstrates Dufresne's beginning mastery of Southern dialect—and the language of need. For example, in a conversation with his estranged first wife, Billy Wayne asks:

> "I need your forgiveness, Earlene."
> "I can't give you that, Billy Wayne."
> "I've sinned."
> "It would have been better if you had killed me," Earlene said. She sat on a folding chair.

Billy Wayne sat on the ottoman facing her. "Just listen to me, Earlene," he whispered. "I need to tell you."

Earlene held the roses on her lap. "Why?"

"You deserve to know."

"I don't care to know. It won't change what happened, will it?"

"I couldn't stop myself, Earlene. I knew the affair was wrong, but I couldn't stop it. I ached."

The intersection of genetic predestination and religion rivals themes of love and death in Dufresne's books. Dufresne uses religious beliefs as motivators for the actions of his characters. For example, for Billy Wayne's son Moon Pie, religion fills the void left by the disappearance of his father and brother: Billy Wayne abandoned the physically disabled Moon Pie, who was born with flippers for appendages, taking his more normal-looking son with him when he left town. In dealing with this loss, Moon Pie discovers new meaning for himself through his religious ponderings, leading to his own radio talk show.

For his own part, Dufresne eschews any kind of affiliation with organized religion. In an interview he told Susan Larson:

> Fiction is my religion. I think it has replaced going to church. You tell yourself that this is what's holy—people's lives, community, giving each other hope. That's what faith is. It's asking questions and confronting the human condition, those old questions about why we're here and what we're doing. The church used to do that for me. I was raised Catholic and you don't get away from it, you only lapse, as they say. I am that and I'm grateful that I had it. I'm not even sure that I believe in God, but I believe in people.

This belief is examined in the critical essay "Postmodernism Goes South: John Dufresne's *Louisiana Power & Light*" (2001), in which David Caudle notes the strong religious influence and symbolism in the novel and its unlikely melding of traditional religious determinism and the postmodernist view of sociological determinism. Caudle believes that by using religious symbolism such as Billy Wayne's death in a pit of snakes, Dufresne produces a postmodern book that is, at the same time, strongly Southern.

Dufresne bridges these elements in *Louisiana Power & Light* by hedging the issue of fate. In the first sentence of chapter eleven he suggests that a "degenerate gene" is the cause of the troubles of the Fontanas, then goes on to pose the question, "Or does the responsibility for tragedy rest not with fate and heredity, but with man and his fatal act of will? Perhaps, in the end, it does not matter. A choice is made, a step taken, a stone loosed, the landslide begun." Certainly, the multitude of characters in each of Dufresne's novels demonstrates a wide range of experiences, providing ample illustration of fate and the domino effect produced by the decisions of individuals.

Response to *Louisiana Power & Light* was almost uniformly positive, though its themes and characters disturbed some. A reviewer for *Publishers Weekly* (2 May 1994) described the narrative as "oddly schizophrenic, alternating abruptly between farce and elegy, with some peculiar authorial interpolations. . . . And Dufresne cannot seem to escape an unfortunate edge of condescension toward his characters from time to time. It is a skillful, often lively performance, but one that leaves a disconcerting aftertaste." The disturbing subject matter garnered interest in the book, but the presentation of the characters gave the novel its celebrated depth. *Booklist* reviewer Bill Ott remarked on the method in which Dufresne "takes this nearly surrealistic story of southern-style squalor well beyond parody, making us care about his white-trash cast even though we know our caring will lead to pain" (July 1994). Ultimately, reviewers and readers alike hailed the author as a postmodern Faulkner.

Given Dufresne's preference for writing about the South and the influence of Southern writers on his narrative style, he is often pegged with the "Southern writer" label—a label he was quick to brush off in a personal interview: "I'm a writer who lives in the South, and sometimes writes about the South. All writing is regional. All stories have to take place somewhere. The term 'Southern Writer' can often be pejorative and restrictive. It's like anyone who's not in New York is a regional writer." In a March 2002 interview with Robert Birnbaum for *IdentityTheory.com,* Dufresne discussed his views on what constitutes Southern writing:

> you'd have to ask whoever calls it Southern writing, what it is. I suppose it's meant to reflect a particular region. But I'm not even sure what the South is. I'm not sure anybody is. . . . In America there is a great tradition of Southern literature. It was the literature I loved when I was growing up. It's not why I moved to the South, but it's why I felt at home there, in a way. My imagination had been there. Certainly it had been in Yoknapatawpha County and so on. So I felt at home and intrigued by the storytelling tradition of the South. So I started writing about it. I write about the North, too.

Dufresne went north for the follow-up to his successful first novel. *Love Warps the Mind a Little,* published in 1997, takes place in Worcester, Massachusetts, and features 192 characters who are questioning themselves and their relationships. According to Dufresne, he is on the same journey as his characters. In an interview with Ellen Kanner of *BookPage.com* (January 1997) he said, "I

Dust jacket for Dufresne's 1997 novel, about a writer who is thrown out of his home by his wife and whose mistress is then stricken with cancer (Richland County Public Library)

write about what I don't understand—love and death. Everything else is extra." The character of Lafayette "Laf" Proulx, the protagonist of *Love Warps the Mind a Little,* demonstrates this lack of understanding. Laf is a writer who clings to his craft as an anchor and a security blanket as his personal life crumbles around him. Dufresne counts Laf among his favorite characters because he is "a writer like me. He thinks the way I think. He's screwed up his life at times. He perseveres."

Though tackling complex topics, *Love Warps the Mind a Little* is perhaps Dufresne's most straightforward work, using first-person narrative with a fairly linear story line while retaining some of his stream-of-consciousness method. In it, he writes:

> Love is anticipation and memory, uncertainty and longing. It's unreasonable, of course. Nothing begins with so much excitement and hope and pleasure as love, except maybe writing a story. And nothing fails as often, except writing stories. And like a story, love must be troubled to be interesting.

The world of Lafayette Proulx is certainly troubled as he is thrown out of his home by his wife, Martha, and goes to live with his mistress, Judi, who is not sure she wants him there. Shortly afterward, Judi is diagnosed with cancer, and everyone is faced with less than ideal circumstances.

Laf often recollects scenes from his youth to explain his feelings about current life. For example, in a scene where he and Judi are visiting with a healer, Dorie Marcelonis, he feels out of his element and out of control. He compares the encounter to being at his grandmother's house as a child: he says he feels "tiny." A similar feeling of helplessness pervades another of Laf's contemplations on his predicament: "While you wash chemotherapy-induced vomit from your lover's shoes, you worry that you may not have time, before work, to call your wife, pay the telephone bill, walk the dog. Why did you get in this mess?" This question serves as the basis of all of Dufresne's fiction. As he told Richardson of *Poets and Writers,* "The most important question a fiction writer can ask is, 'Why?' . . . I confront the human condition. What makes us human, what we have in common, is trouble." Trouble is also what all of Dufresne's stories have in common. Dufresne writes his characters so that their actions blend with the external forces acting on them, with extraordinary results. However, even when his characters act outrageously, they still maintain a kind of dignity and seriousness.

Love Warps the Mind a Little garnered mostly favorable reviews from critics, though inevitable comparisons were made to *Louisiana Power & Light.* As a reviewer for *Publishers Weekly* (January 1997) stated, "The novel never quite reaches the tragicomic heights of its predecessor, and in making Laf see the world through the lens of his literary ambition (or pretension), Dufresne has to ward off a certain parochial preciousness." While reviewers found the Northern characters and setting less colorful than their Southern counterparts, the work was recognized as important in its exploration of issues of purpose. Brian McCombie, reviewer for *Booklist* (15 December 1996), stated that its "breezy and egocentric narrative propels a story that's very funny, quite sad, and occasionally tragic."

The same troubled yet sympathetic treatment found in *Louisiana Power & Light* and *Love Warps the Mind a Little* is given to the characters of Dufresne's 2002 work, *Deep in the Shade of Paradise.* The interrelated struggles of Dufresne's characters are foreshadowed in his statement in the prologue: "Nothing is random. Everything connects." The plot details the encounters of dozens of characters as they prepare for the wedding of Grisham Loudermilk and Ariane Thevenot. Like *Louisiana Power & Light,* the book is focused on north

Louisiana, specifically Monroe. This time, however, the action is centered on the mythical town of Shiver-de-Freeze. Earlene Fontana is present in the book, as well as Boudou, the child she conceived with Billy Wayne shortly before his death.

Characters are introduced in rapid succession, complete with background stories that begin to make more sense as the narrative progresses. As in other works, Dufresne gives his characters free rein and writes as though he is the outlet for their experiences. For a Norton Reading Group Guide to *Deep in the Shade of Paradise* he explained the genesis of the novel:

> There was a promise at the end of *Louisiana Power & Light,* that promise being the birth of a child and the continuation of the Fontana family. So these few years later I decided to find out about that boy, what he was like, and what he was up to. Wanting to know who Boudou was led me to Shiver-de-Freeze, a town with its own time zone, a place apart, where anything, apparently, could happen. Now, you have to write about what's important to you, what you don't understand, what keeps you up at night. So I knew I'd be writing about death and love and self and identity, and then when I found out that Boudou had an eidetic memory, I realized that I'd be exploring the past and how it shapes us, and thinking about memory led me to consider imagination, and so it went. One notion leads to another.

Dufresne ties these notions together with his compelling conveyance of his character's feelings and remembrances. His characters are complex and are written with affection and care. None is portrayed in a black-and-white manner, although their motives are clearly demonstrated. Ultimately, Dufresne's portrayals of his individual characters lead back to his foundational themes—storytelling, families, and communities, and how such institutions provide meaning to one's life.

In *Deep in the Shade of Paradise* Boudou plays counterpoint to Royce, an elderly man suffering from Alzheimer's. The two characters provide an interesting exploration of the theme of memory—a theme Dufresne believes is essential in making sense of the puzzle of existence: "Memory is crucial to creation and to a sense of self. Memory is our autobiography. It's who we think we are. I think memory and imagination are the same process. One creates a past from some raw material, some history, the other creates a whole new world."

Dufresne's musical narrative style and off-beat characters have prompted many comparisons of his writing with that of John Irving. His books serve as both entertainment and food for thought. In his dual role as observer/narrator and author, Dufresne does not shy away from breaking his narrative flow to assert his

GRISHAM

He needs to suffer. Perhaps, when he learns that Arwin has gone off with Adlai (to boathouse? hotel? room?) he realizes that he loves her & needs her & both. He's frantic (perhaps she's been bold enough to leave a note and crafty enough to accidently leave clues to their destination). He goes after her, brings her back. Suddenly all his doubts about her, about them, all his petty resentments, all his irritation, all of it is washed away. It may return at the altar, but for now he is relieved, and order has been restored. Grisham likes order, resi now. Likes to know what's what. Knowledge is crystal, control is power. Disorder is for losers.

We need to experience his suffering. Even though it happens quickly — from discovery of note to discovery of A & A. So we'll need to be with him, in his POV. The resi muse, the self-loathing, the fear.

At the wedding - just before the vows, he is apprehensive once more. What would have happened if I hadn't gone after them. He also knows that he has a bullet to fire - her infidelity. (how far did they go? - no matter really) that her behavior is her Get-Out-of-Jail-Free card. And he sees his rosy future with a woman he loves, and one he can screw around on, if not with impunity, then with a bit of confidence, at least. He looks at her and smiles. She smiles back. (shift to her POV)

Manuscript page for Dufresne's 2002 novel, Deep in the Shade of Paradise, *about the son of the protagonist of* Louisiana Power & Light *and his remarkable memory (courtesy of the author)* thoughts on life and love. In *Deep in the Shade of Paradise* he gives his readers a chance to write parts of the story on their own. This approach has met with negative reactions from some critics who question the efficacy of such a method. In a 2002 personal interview Dufresne pointed out, however, that a book involves the reader as much as the author:

> I am always interested in the creative process. I'm trying to figure it out. And I think of a story as the accomplishment of both the writer and the reader. Both are creative. The writer provides the clues, the reader completes the image. And each reader brings his emotional history to the reading, and I wanted the reader to be aware of it–hence they get to write a bit about it–writing is thinking.

Jay McDonald of the *Fort Myers News-Press* (18 June 2002) noted further examples: "Here, he considerately interrupts the narrative to alert the reader not to start a particularly lengthy chapter if they don't have the time. There, he pops in to encourage the reader to write about their first love, leaves them a blank page to do so, and even offers to read it via e-mail." Dufresne's fondness for experimental narrative was likely inspired by his literary heroes, including Faulkner.

Reaction to Dufresne's digressions, narrative asides, and extensive appendix was somewhat mixed, although reviewers generally hailed Dufresne's return to his trademark Louisiana characters and setting. In *The New York Times Book Review* (16 June 2002) Robert Kelly stated: "What Dufresne gives us in *Deep in the Shade of Paradise* is a world of grotesques and exaggerations, a comic-opera vision of Cajun country. But it is comic, and it is a world. And although it has nothing to say about race and class, it has a lot to say about religion and its counterparts." A reviewer for *Publishers Weekly* (19 November 2001) commented, "The all-out quirkiness of Dufresne's sparkling second [*sic*] novel may put some readers off, but others will surely think this talented writer's time has come." *Deep in the Shade of Paradise* is a book about complex issues, and it elicited reviews that pondered the questions posed in the novel rather than simply evaluating plot and narrative style.

Dufresne tackles the intricacies of the writing process in *The Lie That Tells a Truth: A Guide to Writing Fiction* (2003). Using his skill and experience, he instructs the reader on techniques for developing characters and developing a strong sense of place, characteristics for which his own novels are recognized. Dufresne also includes activities in the book that help would-be writers develop confidence in their skills.

While sometimes exaggerations, John Dufresne's characters are nonetheless biting reflections of American values, including the dysfunctional, lonely, and self-destructive way of many modern lives. He relates the gravity of the human experience, often with exaggerated comedy, yet he sees both as part of the same thing. As he noted in *Poets & Writers,* "I'm dead serious in my books. I don't think tragedy is ever trivial. Illness and death are so serious, in fact, that we cannot bear them without relief." His characters and stories complement the intangible and universal themes of love, death, and religion; still, his books remain explorations of these themes rather than answers. Moreover, they provide opportunity for his readers to explore the same issues in their own lives.

Interviews:

Ellen Kanner, "John Dufresne on Writing, Love, and Death," *BookPage.com* (January 1997) <http://www.bookpage.com/9701bp/fiction/lovewarpsthemindalittle.html>;

Kevin Blaine Bell and David Caudle, "Fiction Is My Religion: An Interview with John Dufresne," in *Songs of the New South: Writing Contemporary Louisiana,* edited by Suzanne Disheroon-Green and Lisa Abney (New York: Greenwood Press, 2001), pp. 87–98;

Robert Birnbaum, "John Dufresne: Author of *Deep in the Shade of Paradise* Talks with Robert Birnbaum," *Identity Theory/The Narrative Thread* (21 March 2002) <http://www.identitytheory.com/people/birnbaum40.html>;

Eve Richardson, "The Tragicomic Vision of John Dufresne," *Poets & Writers,* 30 (March/April 2002) <http://www.pw.org/mag/richardson.htm>;

Susan Larson, "A Little Bit of Louisiana: John Dufresne's New Novel Puts the Imaginary Town of Shiver-de-Freeze, La., on the Map," *New Orleans Times-Picayune,* 28 June 2002.

References:

David Caudle, "Postmodernism Goes South: John Dufresne's *Louisiana Power & Light,*" in *Songs of the New South: Writing Contemporary Louisiana,* edited by Suzanne Disheroon-Green and Lisa Abney (New York: Greenwood Press, 2001), pp. 77–86;

"*Deep in the Shade of Paradise* Reading Group Guide," *W. W. Norton Online* (2002) <http://www.wwnorton. com/rgguides/deepintheshade.htm>.

Bret Easton Ellis

(7 March 1964 –   )

Roy C. Flannagan
South Carolina Governor's School for Science and Mathematics

BOOKS: *Less Than Zero* (New York: Simon & Schuster, 1985; London: Picador, 1985);

The Rules of Attraction (New York: Simon & Schuster, 1987; London: Picador, 1988);

American Psycho (New York: Vintage, 1991; London: Picador, 1991);

The Informers (New York: Knopf, 1994; London: Picador, 1994);

Glamorama (New York: Knopf, 1999; London: Picador, 1999).

SELECTED PERIODICAL PUBLICATION–
UNCOLLECTED: "The Twentysomethings: Adrift in a Pop Landscape," *New York Times,* 2 December 1990, p. H1, 37.

Frequently disliked by reviewers, faulted for his youth and apparent disregard for political correctness, Bret Easton Ellis was the enfant terrible of 1980s fiction. His first novel, *Less Than Zero* (1985), became a national best-seller when Ellis was just twenty-one years old, and he published *American Psycho* (1991) when he was only twenty-seven. Though he tends to court controversy and to polarize his critics, he has earned a more substantial critical reception than other "brat pack" writers such as Tama Janowitz and Jay McInerney, with whom he was often associated in the early 1980s. While some consider his novels to be little more than sociological documents, Ellis successfully adapts contemporary multimedia aesthetics to the novel form and, in the process, offers an unrepentant portrait of a generation that has resisted easy categorization. Dominated by popular culture, drugs, and Ronald Reagan–era materialistic excess, his work enjoys a youthful cult following, in part because it frequently violates the moral and aesthetic values of other, often older, readers.

Born on 7 March 1964 in Los Angeles, California, Ellis was the firstborn son of Robert Martin Ellis, a real-estate analyst, and homemaker Dale Ellis. While other children played with toys, Ellis began to write instead, creating stories as Christmas presents. A

Bret Easton Ellis (photograph by Ian Gittler; from the dust jacket for Glamorama, *1999; Richland County Public Library)*

self-described "valley boy," Ellis adopted the lifestyle of the wealthy and young in Los Angeles, touring the malls and spending time with his two sisters. His parents divorced during his teenage years. While attending the private Buckley School in Sherman Oaks, California, Ellis discovered Ernest Hemingway's *The Sun Also Rises*

(1926) and decided to read all of his works. Hemingway and Joan Didion, another early favorite, both supplied a visible influence on the stripped-down style of Ellis's first novel, *Less Than Zero*. Like Didion, Ellis used the techniques of new journalism, blurring traditional boundaries between fiction and nonfiction. As Ellis said during an interview in *Reasons to Believe: New Voices in American Fiction* (1988), "I like posing situations and questions, and having people react to them. I'm not a psychologist or sociologist. I feel that, in lots of ways, what I'm doing is documenting much more than answering questions or giving reasons why people misbehave in this fashion." This reportorial detachment and lack of a judgmental overview left Ellis open to critical attacks against immorality in his works.

In addition to writing, Ellis also played keyboards in a garage band before college. His main interests of the time were new-wave bands and movies, in part because many of his friends had relatives in the movie industry. Ellis later developed a cinematic style in his novels, in which the gradual accumulation of scenes and images replaces a more traditional narrative structure. As Ellis says of *Less Than Zero* in the 1988 interview, "It was really important to make the book cinematic, to integrate the language of film into the writing. I remember being heavily influenced by the films of Robert Altman—especially *Nashville*, and its powerful, wandering technique."

Even though his father wanted him to major in business, Ellis applied to Bennington College in Vermont because its emphasis on the liberal arts suited his creative inclinations. Once at Bennington, he enrolled in an upper-division creative-writing class with Joe McGinniss, the author of *Fatal Vision* (1983), who sent some of Ellis's work to Morgan Entrekin at Simon and Schuster. Entrekin met with Ellis in New York and recommended that he put together a novel; so Ellis took a "nonresident term" from Bennington, got high on methamphetamines, and sat down to write an early draft of *Less Than Zero* in eight weeks. McGinniss then helped Ellis revise this draft over a two-year period, assisting him mainly in whittling down a much longer manuscript into a more focused story.

Told in Ellis's trademark first-person present tense, *Less Than Zero* depicts the aimless experiences of Clay, a student returning home to Los Angeles for Christmas vacation from Camden, a college in New Hampshire. Given the elements of divorced parents, two sisters, and the family's level of prosperity, critics assumed the novel was autobiographical; but Ellis characterizes Clay as a "wretch," someone who is too passive in the face of evil to reflect his creator. The novel proceeds impressionistically in a deadpan, nonjudgmental style as Clay and his friends hang out at various parties and clubs in Los Angeles and snort lots of cocaine. Blond, tanned, and often stoned, the characters are frequently hard to distin-

guish from one another. Thematic phrases are repeated throughout the book, such as "Disappear Here" (first seen on a billboard), "People are afraid to merge on the freeways of Los Angeles," and "Wonder if he's for sale." Clay enjoys the trappings of wealth, but he also notices that people are too often victimized by the hedonistic, impersonal social circles in which they move. A suicidal undertow moves beneath all the glamour, and Clay is simultaneously fascinated and repelled by the hints of destruction around him.

A study in the alienation of the idle rich, *Less Than Zero* eventually develops a more delineated subplot involving the mysterious absence of Julian, one of Clay's old friends, who has allowed himself to become a male prostitute working for a loan shark named Finn. Julian borrows some money from Clay, and in order to get it paid back, Clay is obliged to watch Julian sleep with an older businessman in a hotel. Since Clay knew Julian when he was a young classmate at school, he finds the scene painful and grotesque, but he admits to himself that he wants "to see the worst." Indeed, as the novel progresses, Clay's desire is fulfilled. The latter third of the novel turns increasingly violent. Clay is a passive witness to part of a snuff movie, a friend shooting up heroin, a girl drugged and repeatedly raped on a bed, and a dead body that people visit for kicks. Such sensationalistic imagery shows the influence of punk rock on Ellis's aesthetics. *Less Than Zero* shares with the punk movement of the late 1970s a willingness to outrage the sensibility of the reader, a consistent lack of emotion, a nihilistic worldview, and a youthful experimental antiestablishmentarianism. When Clay protests the treatment of the drugged girl, Rip, a cocaine dealer, defines the morality of many of the characters in the novel when he says: "If you want something, you have the right to take it. If you want to do something, you have the right to do it." As Nicki Sahlin points out in a 1991 analysis, the reader finds a void at the heart of Ellis's rendition of the American dream, an MTV-stylized continuation of the long line of dystopian visions of the underside of Hollywood often seen in works such as Nathanael West's *Day of the Locust* (1939) and F. Scott Fitzgerald's *The Last Tycoon* (1941).

The blend of atrocity and understatement in the novel tapped into a hidden youth market, and *Less Than Zero* became a best-seller across the United States. Critical reception was mixed but often respectful of Ellis's innovative talent. Writing for *The Los Angeles Times Book Review* (26 May 1988), John Rechy proclaimed *Less Than Zero* "the first novel of MTV" while stating that "the book suggests the possibility of sensationalized distortion." A reviewer for *The New Republic* (10 June 1985) characterized the novel as being "written in the inarticulate style of a petulant suburban punk." In *The New York Times Book Review* (8 June 1985) Michiko Kakutani suggested that the novel "possesses an unnerving air of documentary reality." Several critics compared Ellis to the 1920s Lost Generation writers, not only because of his stylistic indebtedness to Hemingway but also because of the similarities between the jaded, decadent youth of that era and the young rich of the 1980s. Ellis, still living in Bennington during his sophomore year, unexpectedly found himself a literary star and was asked to appear on talk shows and at magazine photo shoots.

Written as his senior thesis at Bennington, Ellis's second novel, *The Rules of Attraction* (1987), concerns the interlocking stories of three college undergraduates—Sean, Lauren, and Paul—and takes as its main theme the nature of modern romance. The novel opens with a young woman describing the drunken loss of her virginity to two men in a dorm room. She ends her hapless story with the ironic coda: "I always knew it would be like this." *The Rules of Attraction* continually emphasizes the discrepancy between romantic expectation and haphazard, often cruel reality. The three students take turns narrating short vignettes: Lauren has an unrequited love for Victor, who tours Europe in a kind of parody of a Henry James novel; Sean and Paul share a brief liaison that involves lots of video-game playing, shoplifting, and skipping class; and a young woman writes love letters to Sean and places them in his mailbox before committing suicide during "The Dressed to Get Screwed Party." As Paul visits with his mother to discuss her impending divorce, Sean dates Lauren until she gets pregnant, after which they drive aimlessly across the New England countryside until they agree to her abortion. The story line progresses without much sense of resolution or consequence. In the end, all three principal characters still search for liaisons and attachments.

In *The Rules of Attraction* Ellis makes some technical advances in the fictional strategies he established in *Less Than Zero*. While in college, he read and admired *Ulysses* (1922) and tried to adapt some of James Joyce's techniques for this novel. For instance, *The Rules of Attraction* begins and ends in midsentence, a device reminiscent of Joyce's *Finnegans Wake* (1939). Instead of one voice, multiple voices give ambiguously different accounts of the same scene. Lauren's passive withholding of emotion in her account is an ironic contrast to Sean's deluded notion that she is in love with him. After her abortion Lauren leaves behind a blank page to express her despair. Ellis depicts his media-savvy college students as basically indifferent to everything except the pleasures of the moment, be it a video game, a sexual encounter, a bong hit, or a motorcycle ride. Since Ellis admits that he is not interested in editorializing on the passivity and fecklessness of his characters, the novel leaves it to the reader to speculate on the meaning behind their nearly indistinguishable voices. At one point, when Paul's mother is

Poster for the 2000 movie version of Ellis's controversial 1991 novel, about an image-conscious investment banker who is also a sadistic rapist and serial killer
(Collection of Chris Poggiali)

telling him about her divorce from his father, she notes his "placid, expressionless" look and declares: "My son—a cipher." But the reader knows from Paul's narrative that he is not blank, just reluctant to show himself. In this way the young narrators elude interpretation.

After all of the media attention surrounding Ellis's first novel, *The Rules of Attraction* had disappointing sales and a more muted, sometimes dismissive critical response. While Gore Vidal praised *The Rules of Attraction* as a "wonderfully comic novel," reviewers criticized its lack of craft amid heavy marketing. For instance, in *The New Yorker* (26 October 1987), Terrence Rafferty claimed:

> The only reason [Ellis's] two raw, fumbling novels have been published, is, of course, that they contain large, even toxic, doses of the elements that stimulate sales: lots of sex, brand names on every page, and a cynical tone that's perfect for readers who want to lap up the decadent behavior and then feel righteously shocked at its emptiness.

A notice in *Publishers Weekly* (7 August 1987) dismissed the novel as "the very book that countless students have dreamed of writing at their most self-absorbed and childish moments."

After graduating from Bennington, Ellis moved to New York, where he cultivated friendships with other young writing talents such as Janowitz, McInerney, and Jill Eisenstadt. He also began to associate with the stockbrokers who inspired his next novel, *American Psycho* (1991). Simon and Schuster paid Ellis a reported $300,000 advance on the novel, which his editor, Robert Asahina, scheduled for publication early in 1991. Then Simon and Schuster abruptly canceled its release, in part because advance portions of the book published in the magazines *Time* and *Spy* gained controversial publicity for their graphic depictions of serial murder. Ellis was able to keep his advance but briefly found his work without a publisher. Sonny Mehta, the chief of Vintage Books (an imprint of Random House), quickly picked it up and released it in paperback without a promotional tour or advertising. During the media storm that ensued, Ellis received fourteen anonymous death threats as well as photographs of himself with his eyes gouged out and an ax in his head, items he characterized as "a little dismaying." Even before the book was released, *The New York Times Book Review* printed a review by Roger Rosenblatt titled "Snuff This Book! Will Bret Easton Ellis Get Away with Murder?" Rosenblatt's reaction was typical of the larger critical reception:

> *American Psycho* is the journal Dorian Gray would have written had he been a high school sophomore. But that is unfair to sophomores. So pointless, so themeless, so everythingless is this novel, except in stupefying details about expensive clothing, food and bath products, that were it not the most loathsome offering of the season, it certainly would be the funniest.

Critics seemed to have difficulty responding in any kind of measured way to the novel. In reaction to the depictions of misogynistic violence, the Los Angeles chapter of the National Organization for Women called for a boycott of all of the books published by Random House. Some women even read violent passages of the novel aloud in bookstores in order to disturb the peace and get arrested. Only gradually did some critics and authors start to acknowledge in print some of the merits of the book.

American Psycho concerns a rich Manhattan investment banker, Patrick Bateman, who is also a psychotic killer. Heavily influenced by advertising copy from fashion magazines, stereo catalogues, popular-music reviews, and slasher movies, Bateman wants simultaneously to fit into upper-crust New York society and to kill people savagely. While he chops up his victims and

expresses every kind of homophobic, racist, and sexist opinion, he also suffers from the continual one-upmanship of his peers in their conspicuous consumption. He becomes perturbed when he finds he cannot get a reservation in the ultraposh, ultra-inaccessible restaurant Dorsia while his brother Sean, from *The Rules of Attraction,* gets a table effortlessly. Bateman obsesses about his body image, his hairstyle, his clothes, and the proper accessories in his apartment. Other characters' personalities often remain unclear as Bateman numbingly describes every nuance of their designer clothes. Although it is rumored that his family owns half of Wall Street, Bateman still works in a firm called Pierce and Pierce, because he says he wants "to fit in."

Bateman freely confesses his killings to various people in the course of the book; part of the comedy in the novel relates to others' inability or refusal to acknowledge his crimes. Bateman's evil tends to get lost in the larger greed and amorality of the world he moves in. As Ellis's epigraph from the rock group Talking Heads puts it, "As things fell apart, nobody paid much attention." Bateman carries the peculiar curse that no one cares what he does, and he is both lethal and pitifully ineffective, since the same nihilism that leads him to kill also makes his every action seem inconsequential. His colleagues think him incapable of committing the crimes, because of his palpably visible anxiety in trying to maintain the status quo. They call him "the boy next door."

Bateman's world consists of visits to fancy restaurants, attempts to get cocaine in nightclubs, and envious encounters over other men's embossed business cards. He studies the biographies of serial killers and imitates them by luring people into his apartment and then either quickly dispatching the men or more slowly raping, torturing, and dismembering the women. Bateman uses the same deadpan delivery, whether describing the use of a creme rinse or the severing of a head. He is never caught, nor does the novel explain his behavior in terms of his upbringing. Part of the point of the novel, as Fay Weldon points out, is that there is no justice in the nihilistic universe of the book. Critics were mostly shocked by both the lack of a humane response to the killings and the way the various body parts became indistinguishable from the consumer objects that surround Bateman.

Is *American Psycho* a satire of slasher movies for what Ellis calls an "unshockable" generation, or is it a "how-to novel on the torture and dismemberment of women," as the National Organization for Women claimed? Ellis used FBI criminology textbooks to help research the techniques of serial killers for his portrayal of Bateman, and he suspected that readers reacted as they did because of the sexual nature of Bateman's crimes. As the feminist Naomi Wolf points out, Ellis's close pairing of sexually arousing scenes with violence conditions the reader to associate the two. In his defense, Ellis claimed that critics were not sufficiently looking at the larger satire of the novel. He felt that the novel reflected the ugliness of the 1980s and that critics mistakenly confuse Bateman's perspective with Ellis's own. As he says in an interview for *Rolling Stone,* "The acts described in the book are truly, indisputably vile. The book itself is not. Patrick Bateman is a monster. I am not." At first, readers had difficulty telling the difference.

After the initial condemnatory reaction of the critics, creative writers weighed in with more careful assessments of the novel, and many of them saw morality in the satire. In her essay "Trashing Women, Trashing Books" (1990) Lorrie Moore discusses the tendency of the media to depict the dismembering and killing of women in loving detail as a new kind of pornography that can sometimes be confused with the novelist's need to head for "danger zones or forbidden psychic places." In "Children of the Pied Piper" (1991) Norman Mailer finds *American Psycho* aesthetically lacking, but he does grant Ellis the right to explore "intolerable material." As he writes, "*American Psycho* is saying that the eighties were spiritually disgusting and the author's presentation is the crystallization of such horror. . . . in effect, says Ellis, we have entered a period of absolute manipulation of humans by humans: the objective correlation of total manipulation is coldcock murder." Ultimately, Mailer finds Ellis's craft cannot live up to such an ambitious theme.

In contrast, Weldon wholeheartedly approved of the book. She claims that people objected to *American Psycho* so strongly because other books still "pay lip service to respectability" and make sure that "Justice is done." Given a culture saturated in media violence, critics hypocritically condemned a book that fails to include the usual moral responses to its depicted crimes. In this novel "nobody cares"—and that nihilism is the point. As Bateman phrases it, "Reflection is useless, the world is senseless. Evil is its only permanence. God is not alive. Love cannot be trusted. Surface, surface, surface was all that anyone found any meaning in . . . this was civilization as I saw it, colossal and jagged." Still, Weldon's sympathy for the novel was unusual. Most critics found Ellis's implication that nothing underlies the surface to be an unacceptable thesis.

By the late 1990s, *American Psycho* had garnered several scholarly critical essays. In *Modern Fiction Studies* (2000) Ruth Helyer discusses the ways in which the novel fits into the Gothic tradition. The depictions in *American Psycho* of transgressive acts, its mixing of genres, and its satire on consumerism all show the correlations between postmodern novels and Gothic excess. Helyer ultimately defends the ability of the novel to show that "Life cannot be easily contained, nor explained, and attempting as much will result in a 'bursting out' . . . of

the restrictions of his [Bateman's] class, his sexuality, and his society's moral codes." In *Southern Humanities Review* (1998) David W. Price places *American Psycho* within Mikhail Mikhailovich Bakhtin's theory of the carnivalesque and in the tradition of Rabelaisian excess. Price emphasizes that Bateman's murders turn people into consumer objects, pointing out that "In such a culture, everything is an object—our bodies, our possessions, our sex partners, even ourselves." Writing for *Diacritics* (1997), Carla Freccero examines the social and philosophical underpinnings of controversy that surround *American Psycho* in the cultural context of music and video censorship. She finds the critical response to the novel inadequate because of the critics' inability to see their own biases projected onto the surface-oriented aesthetics of Ellis's novel. Ultimately, the Ellis novel that earned the most initial scorn also received the most scholarly analysis of all his work.

After the furor over *American Psycho* died down, Ellis began the eight-year process of writing his next novel, *Glamorama* (1999). The novel took an unusually long time to complete because of the furor attending the publication of *American Psycho,* the death of Ellis's father, and the breakup of a seven-year relationship. In the meantime, Ellis put together *The Informers* (1994). A sequence of sketches that he began writing in 1983, *The Informers* was never intended for publication, but Ellis offered the stories to Knopf when he was bogged down with the writing of *Glamorama.* More isolated flashes of brilliance than a sustained narrative sweep, *The Informers* includes thirteen stories from a series of male and female narrators that include teenagers reminiscent of *Less Than Zero,* rock stars, baby-boomer parents, and vampires. Themes that characterize Ellis's longer fiction receive more focused treatment. For instance, one of the stories concerns a movie executive who decides to take his estranged, college-aged son to Hawaii for some enforced vacation. His depiction of a parent's attempts to connect with his son as he drinks cocktails and flirts with other tourists highlights the extent of the generational divide. The stories read like sketches lacking the heft of well-crafted longer fiction, but they can also be more direct and satirical, as is the case of "Discovering Japan," in which an unsavory rock star spends his time sadistically hurting groupies as his manager screens him from direct contact with the outside world. In "The Fifth Wheel" Ellis contemplates the suffering of the innocent when a gang kidnaps a child and ties him up in a bathtub for several days. The stories end up emphasizing Ellis's almost Darwinian fixation on the interaction between predator and victim that typifies his social world.

Like the reviews of *The Rules of Attraction,* the critical reception of *The Informers* was largely negative. Writing for *The New York Times* (2 August 1994), Kakutani

Dust jacket for Ellis's 1999 novel, about a hedonistic New York model and actor who is replaced by a double at the instigation of his U.S. senator father and ends up among terrorists in Europe (Richland County Public Library)

claimed that "the animating emotion of *The Informers* seems to be contempt: the author's contempt for his characters and for his readers. The result is a novel that is as cynical, shallow and stupid as the people it depicts." Although Kakutani called the work a novel, Ellis told interviewer Jaime Clarke, "It wasn't ever supposed to be a full-fledged novel, and I don't consider it a novel. It's a group of short stories and I think it's better to read it knowing that it's a group of short stories rather than approaching it as a novel. I think if you go into reading it as a novel, you're utterly confused and you'll have no idea what's going on." In *The New York Times Book Review* (18 September 1994) George Stade praised Ellis's "intelligence and craft." A reviewer for *Publishers Weekly* found the book "so inconsequential . . . it should neither vex Ellis's critics nor gratify its fans." Only generating mild controversy this time, mostly in reaction to the vampire narrators, *The Informers* falls between the larger critical receptions accorded to *American Psycho* and *Glamorama*.

Glamorama was influenced by the conspiratorial worldview of author Don DeLillo, and it is the first of

Ellis's novels to maintain a traditional plot. A character from *The Rules of Attraction,* Victor Ward, narrates the story as a semisuccessful model-actor who becomes a victim of his U.S. senator father's conspiracy to have him replaced by a double. Victor's trendy lifestyle, supported by his lascivious modeling for the popular press, jeopardizes his father's candidacy for the presidency, so his father arranges for him to leave for Europe as his double takes over his old life in the States. Victor becomes imprisoned among terrorists and eventually, it is suggested, killed. In some ways as violent as *American Psycho,* the novel differs considerably in tone from its predecessor, because Ellis shifts from the perspective of killer to victim. Victor is so wrapped up in his appearance and his ability as a seducer that at first he cannot see that he has become a pawn in a larger game.

Glamorama depicts the complete domination of the media over its characters' lives. Ellis describes a world given over to idealized photographic representations of itself; to emphasize this point, various camera crews follow Victor around during the latter half of the novel, although he is not clear what movie he is shooting, nor is the reader sure that he is not imagining the camera crews in his despair over losing his New York City paparazzi. Within this self-reflective world of photo shoots, MTV documentaries, and spokesmannequins, evil can flourish with fascistic ease. As long as a character looks good, he or she can get away with anything. For example, male supermodel Bobby Hughes runs a terrorist organization in England and France, blowing up trendy eateries in London, torturing and killing a Korean ambassador's son, and bringing down a jet full of passengers in a scene of gore and carnage. In contrast, Victor just wants to open a club and enjoy the fruits of his low-level fame as a model-actor in New York. He believes that living under the adage "The better you look, the more you see" will suffice, but the trajectory of the plot proves that he has been blinded by his vanity. Like any commodity, Victor can be discarded in favor of a newer, improved version of himself who cheerfully adopts his old girlfriends, attends law school, and does not interfere with his father's career.

While it shares with *American Psycho* a fascination with the superficiality of popular culture, *Glamorama* explores the easily manipulated nature of the image and its negative effects on American consumers. Victor notes how his arm or his leg may appear independent of the rest of him in an advertisement; this observation translates later in the novel to the fragmentation of body parts blown up by terrorist bombs. Victor's father's plot to remove his child from New York forms part of larger, sinister forces at work in American culture. Ellis describes the main point of the novel as "Be aware." Too many people allow themselves to be manipulated by the media in the name of trendiness.

Critical reactions to *Glamorama* were mixed but often respectful of its ambition. Writing for *National Review* (8 March 1999), James Panero claimed that the novel secretly pursues a conservative agenda: "*Glamorama* is a devilishly heterodox novel. Yes, maybe even a conservative novel–though one so steeped in liberal pop culture that it's easy to miss the point. What does it mean to be conservative, anyway? Well, in part, it means making fun of liberal chic, right?" Weighing in at a hefty 482 pages, *Glamorama* was called "a bloated, stultifyingly repetitive, overhyped book" by its *New York Times* reviewer Daniel Mendelsohn (24 January 1999), who added:

> Like its predecessors, *Glamorama* is meant to be a withering report on the soul-destroying emptiness of late-century American consumer culture, chichi downtown division; but the only lesson you're likely to take away from it is the even more depressing classic morality tale about how premature stardom is more of a curse than a blessing for young writers.

Critics frequently were confused by the central conceit that connects fashion models with terrorism, a connection that even Ellis acknowledges as "loopy." *Glamorama* has begun to earn sustained critical treatment: in a 2000 article, Sheli Ayers suggests that the novel can be better understood as a "system of textual effects analogous to other scripted spaces: themed architecture, animated digital games, and special-effects films." Unlike other novels, Ayers notes, *Glamorama* "was conceived from the outset as post-consumer waste." Looked upon as a deliberate reflection on media junk, *Glamorama* at least is true to its sources.

Like Mark Leyner and David Foster Wallace, Ellis has spent his career thus far depicting a landscape increasingly dominated by popular culture. In an interview with Chris Heath in *Rolling Stone* (24 December 1998), he characterizes his vision as "A kind of shallowness, vanity, narcissism, an obsession with surfaces, finding the truth in surfaces." He describes the writer as someone unafraid to state his view of things, and his writings reveal a perspective where people's identities are frequently interchangeable, where consumer objectification affects human relations in untold ways, and where the blizzard of different media enticements mask a fundamentally Darwinian world in which the image is more important than any consciousness that may underlie it. Frequently too funny and satirical to be purely moralistic, Ellis looks for new, experimental ways to make sense of contemporary experience.

Interviews:

Michael Schumacher, "Bret Easton Ellis," in his *Reasons to Believe: New Voices in American Fiction* (New York: St. Martin's Press, 1988), pp. 118–135;

Roger Cohen, "Bret Easton Ellis Answers Critics of *American Psycho*," *New York Times,* 6 March 1991, p. C13;

Robert Love, "Interview," *Rolling Stone* (4 April 1991): 45–46, 49–51;

Jaime Clarke, "An Interview with Bret Easton Ellis" (4 November 1996 & 22 October 1998) <http://www.geocities.com/Athens/Forum/8506/Ellis/clarkeint.html>;

Chris Heath, "Bret Easton Ellis," *Rolling Stone* (24 December 1998 – 7 January 1999): 114–117.

References:

Sheli Ayers, "*Glamorama* Vanitas: Bret Easton Ellis's Postmodern Allegory," *Postmodern Culture,* 11 (2000) <http://www.iath.virginia.edu/pmc/text-only/issue.900/11.1contents.html>;

Frances Fortier, "L'esthetique hyperrealiste de Bret Easton Ellis," *Tangence,* 44 (1994): 94–105;

Carla Freccero, "Historical Violence, Censorship, and the Serial Killer: The Case of *American Psycho*," *Diacritics,* 27 (1997): 44–58;

Ruth Helyer, "Parodied to Death: The Postmodern Gothic of *American Psycho*," *Modern Fiction Studies,* 46 (Fall 2000): 725–746;

Thomas Irmer, "Bret Easton Ellis's *American Psycho* and Its Submerged References to the 1960s," *Zeitshrift für Anglistik und Amerikanistik,* 41 (1993): 349–356;

Norman Mailer, "Children of the Pied Piper," *Vanity Fair,* 54 (March 1991): 154–159, 220–221;

Lorrie Moore, "Trashing Women, Trashing Books," *New York Times,* 5 December 1990, p. 27;

David W. Price, "Bakhtinian Prosaics, Grotesque Realism, and the Question of the Carnivalesque in Bret Easton Ellis's *American Psycho*," *Southern Humanities Review,* 32 (Fall 1998): 321–346;

Terrence Rafferty, "Advertisements for Themselves," *New Yorker,* 63 (26 October 1987): 142–145;

Nicki Sahlin, "'But This Road Doesn't Go Anywhere': The Existential Drama of *Less Than Zero*," *Critique: Studies in Contemporary Fiction,* 33 (Fall 1991): 23–42;

Fay Weldon, "Now You're Squeamish?" *Washington Post,* 28 April 1991, p. C1, C4;

Naomi Wolf, "The Animals Speak," *New Statesmen and Society* (12 April 1991): 33–34;

Robert Zaller, "*American Psycho,* American Censorship, and the Dahmer Case," *Revue Francaise d'Etudes Americaines,* 16 (1993): 317–325.

Connie May Fowler

(3 January 1958 –)

Lisa Abney
Northwestern State University

BOOKS: *Sugar Cage* (New York: Putnam, 1992; London: Bantam, 1992);

River of Hidden Dreams (New York: Putnam, 1994; London: Black Swan, 1994);

Before Women Had Wings (New York: Putnam, 1996; London: Black Swan, 1997);

Remembering Blue (New York: Doubleday, 2000; London: Bantam, 2000);

When Katie Wakes (New York: Doubleday, 2002; London: Virago, 2002);

The Problem with Murmur Lee (Garden City, N.Y.: Doubleday, forthcoming 2004).

PRODUCED SCRIPT: *Before Women Had Wings,* television, ABC, 2 November 1997.

RECORDINGS: *Before Women Had Wings,* abridged, read by Fowler, Audio Literature, 1997;

Remembering Blue, abridged, read by Fowler, Audio Literature, 2000.

SELECTED PERIODICAL PUBLICATION–
UNCOLLECTED: "No Snapshots in the Attic: A Granddaughter's Search for a Cherokee Past," *New York Times Book Review,* 22 May 1994, pp. 49–50.

Connie May Fowler (photograph by Mika Fowler; from the dust jacket for Remembering Blue, *2000; Richland County Public Library)*

Connie May Fowler's books present scenes of domestic abuse, portrayals of a wide variety of Florida's ethnic groups, and interesting and well-developed characters. Several themes emerge in Fowler's work, including love and the need for humans to find wholeness through a relationship, whether with parent, spouse, friend, or lover; traditional culture in conflict with the contemporary world; and the importance of the environment and ecology to humans. Fowler's novels, while set in Florida, demonstrate themes and characters that are universal in their appeal. Her work has drawn praise from both critics and the general reading public, and it has appeared on *The New York Times* best-seller lists many times. Her novel *Before Women Had Wings*

(1996) was an Oprah Winfrey book-club selection that was subsequently made into a television movie by Winfrey's production company in 1997.

Fowler's life has provided her with a wealth of experiences from which to draw her fiction. Fowler was born Connie May on 3 January 1958 in North Carolina, but she was raised in Florida, as her fiction reflects. Her parents, Lenore Monita Looney and Henry Jefferson May, had an unhappy existence together, and her family endured abuse and volatility until her father died from a heart attack when she was only six years old. Her father's death marked the start of an even more difficult time for Connie and her sister, Deidre, as their mother struggled to support the family while working as a bookkeeper and a maid in exchange for room and board in a series of motels. The family lived from paycheck to paycheck and on public assistance. Her mother often blamed their destitution upon the girls. Life for the family was dismal and poverty-stricken. Even before her father's death, Fowler remembers living in a shack infested with roaches and other vermin. She recalled in an interview with Dorothy K. Fletcher: "Some people don't believe roaches bite, but they do. I would wake up in the morning with red roach-bite welts on my legs. It was tough and horrible." Her primary means of escaping her difficult life was through reading. Among her favorites when she was a girl were the works of Lois Lenski. As she grew older, her love of reading sustained her. Despite the grinding poverty and the less-than-ideal home life of the family, Connie May maintained a high grade average in high school and earned a full scholarship from the University of Tampa.

After graduating from high school at age seventeen, May entered college at the University of Tampa. Shortly after May started college, her mother died from cirrhosis of the liver. May was devastated, for despite their rocky relationship, May loved her mother and felt a huge loss when she died. The next few years proved just as tumultuous as the earlier parts of her life had been. She entered into a relationship with a college professor who physically and emotionally abused her. During this time, she held a variety of jobs—ranging from bartender to editor—and tried to find the best way to end the relationship. About four years later, she left the abusive situation and returned to the University of Tampa, completing her B.A. in English literature with minors in French and art in 1982. From 1982 to 1987, May continued to work as an editor and to write.

In 1987 May married photographer Mika Fowler and moved to Kansas, where she entered graduate school at the University of Kansas. She earned her M.A. in English in 1990. Fowler's original intention was to study poetry, but Carolyn Doty, her professor and mentor, urged her to take a course in fiction writing. Her first efforts in short-story writing were rewarded when Doty encouraged her to develop the story into a novel, which was published by Putnam in 1992 under the title *Sugar Cage*.

Sugar Cage chronicles the lives of two Florida families through their relationships with Inez Temple, an African American domestic worker who meets the Looneys and the Jewels while both couples are honeymooning at the motel where she works. Inez is one of several narrators in the novel, and her story serves as

Dust jacket for Fowler's 1994 novel, about a mixed-race tour-boat operator in the Florida Everglades who tries to come to terms with her heritage (Richland County Public Library)

the unifying element between two generations of these families, starting in 1945 and continuing until the Vietnam War era. The novel depicts some of the distinctly Floridian cultures; the life of rural sugar-cane cutters is juxtaposed with the city life of the Looneys and Jewels. Haitian and African cultural practices overlap with those of the Anglo characters, and this complex story integrates these cultures through the experiences of the two families.

While *Sugar Cage* has received little academic attention, it garnered many favorable reviews upon publication. Fellow fiction writer Amy Tan in May 1992 called *Sugar Cage* "the genuine article," adding:

And that feeling stays with you up to the last, glorious page. . . . I'm amazed at the breadth of humanity she writes about, the uncanny ways she captures the rhythm of inner lives: a reluctant seer of future trage-

Dust jacket for Fowler's semi-autobiographical 1996 novel, about the struggle of a mother and her two daughters to survive abuse and poverty (Richland County Public Library)

text, including Inez's, could have been stronger and ultimately made the book more vivid and engaging. Elizabeth Cook-Lynn stated in a review from *The Los Angeles Times* (15 March 1992) that the "reliable narrator one expects in fiction of this sort is, instead, a meandering point of view lurching from one event and one character to the next. The reader is left confused about the naivete of these characters, both white and black." For the most part, *Sugar Cage* received positive reviews and led Fowler to write her second novel, *River of Hidden Dreams* (1994).

Set in the Florida Everglades with a spunky firebrand for a protagonist, *River of Hidden Dreams* equals its predecessor in the presentation of Florida's diverse cultural traditions. Sadie Hunter is a mixed-blood tour boat operator, and her lover, Carlos, a Cuban exile. Sadie is a tough businesswoman who suffers the foolish only in small doses and only long enough to take their money, as readers see when she takes a group of college boys through Key West on a tour. Sadie and Carlos's story is not the single most important one of this novel; the stories of a mummified infant and of Sadie's grandmother Mima and her lover, Mr. Sammy, become integral parts of Sadie and Carlos's lives as Sadie struggles to put the pieces of her past together so that she can move on with her life with Carlos. The plot includes many narrative threads that ultimately form a tightly knit story.

Like *Sugar Cage*, *River of Hidden Dreams* received positive reviews. Sue Gaisford, in the London *Independent* (16 June 1994), declared:

> There is great truth here. Even if, like Sadie, our memories of grandparents are sketchy, we know something about their memories. Not only do these linger in family lore, but they are mysteriously imprinted on us, unspoken but ineradicable. If all this sounds fey and implausible, I am not doing this book justice. Connie May Fowler is a superb craftsman, palpably unable to write less than beautifully.

A reviewer from *Booklist* (15 July 1994) stated that Fowler has, in *River of Hidden Dreams,* "established herself as a romantic dramatist of Florida's fecund cultural blend and luxurious geography and wildlife." Joanna Duckworth, in a review in the *Limited Sunday Times* (8 May 1994), noted that "it is Fowler's eye and ear for detail, however, that lifts this novel out of sombreness." George Packer, in a *Book World* review (31 July 1994), dissented: "Sadie's commitment phobias trivialize her foremothers' losses, and her transformation by storytelling into a kind and loving woman comes across as no more than conceit." Along with popular critical reviews, the book has one scholarly article devoted to it, written by Elizabeth S. Bell in 2001. This article

dies, a disappointed wife, a Haitian cane worker, an abandoned young boy, a philandering but loving husband, a dying intellectual, a grieving widow and a merry one, a soldier facing death, and a little girl who is haunted by the ghosts of her parents' past. She weaves this unlikely community of characters into a mesmerizing story.

Other critics agreed; Kathryn Mead asserted in the London *Sunday Telegraph* (14 March 1992) that "Connie May Fowler has written a first novel to send everyone else back to the pencil sharpener. . . . She writes with tenderness of eye and an ear extraordinarily attuned to the cadence of language." Roy Hoffman, in a review from *The New York Times* (9 February 1992), generally concurred but argued that some of the voices of the

points out the absence of historical documents relating to Native Americans during and before the Indian Removals of the 1800s and analyzes Fowler's use of memories and the integration of memory into the search for ancestry.

While *River of Hidden Dreams* is, perhaps, the most intricately woven of her novels, Fowler's *Before Women Had Wings* has become her most highly acclaimed novel. This loosely autobiographical piece chronicles the lives of Avocet Abigail Jackson, nicknamed Bird; her sister, Phoebe; and their mother, Glory Marie. The novel recounts the abuse, poverty, and struggle for survival of these three fragile, yet strong, characters across several years of their lives. Named a selection of Winfrey's book club shortly after its publication, the novel gained many readers and became the focus of activities in reading groups nationwide.

Critical praise for the book abounded upon publication. Maxine Chernoff in *The New York Times Book Review* (21 July 1996) stated: "*Before Women Had Wings* emerges as a vivid reminder of the ability of storytelling to restore innocence and dignity." An anonymous reviewer for the *Chicago Tribune* (May 1996) called the novel "A thing of heart-rending beauty, a moving exploration of love and loss, violence and grief, forgiveness and redemption." Along with these reviews, the novel also received the 1996 Southern Book Critics Circle Award for fiction. When Winfrey called Fowler to negotiate the television movie offer, Fowler at first thought it was a crank or threat call. Because of her environmental activism, she has become an occasional target of those who advocate development rather than conservation of Florida's tenuous wetlands and wilderness areas. As Fowler reported in an interview with Patricia Holt in the *San Francisco Chronicle* (29 October 1997), when Winfrey called saying that she was a friend of Bird, Fowler responded with "I'm sorry. I have no idea who this is." Once Winfrey announced her identity, Fowler said, "Things sort of got better from there."

Fowler's commitment to social and environmental issues becomes apparent in her next novel, *Remembering Blue* (2000). This novel presents the lives of Nick Blue, a fisherman of Greek origin off Florida's Atlantic coast, and Matilda Fiona O'Rourke (Mattie), who hails from an Irish American family in which Fowler's ubiquitous themes of alcoholism and abuse appear. Unlike the protagonists in previous novels, Mattie manages to build a happy life for herself with Nick and his Greek family. The novel vividly depicts the culture, occupational practices, and folkways of the expansive Blue clan. Mattie and Nick find themselves madly in love and embark upon a new life together. They plant a garden, repair Nick's cottage, and endure a hurricane. Just

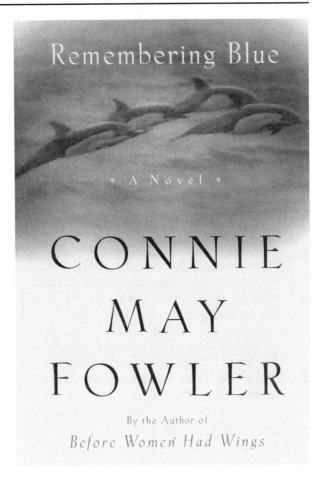

Dust jacket for Fowler's 2000 novel, about the passionate, tragically brief marriage of a Greek American commercial fisherman and an Irish American woman (Richland County Public Library)

after Nick decides to sell his boat and find a safer occupation, he sees a coworker at his new job in the timber industry get killed, and he returns to sea until he can decide upon a new occupation. During one trip, however, he meets an untimely demise while fighting the rough seas. The heartbreak Mattie experiences is overwhelming; but she soon discovers that their last night of passion has left her pregnant. Mattie stays with Nick's family on their island and raises her child with their help.

This novel is distinctive among Fowler's writing in that the narrator, Mattie, finds peace within herself much more easily and much earlier in the novel than the protagonists in her other works. Additionally, the narrative style differs: Fowler still relies upon multiple story lines, but she retains Mattie and Nick as the primary narrators in the novel instead of employing several narrators as she does in her earlier works.

Critical reviews of *Remembering Blue* were mixed. A notice in *Kirkus Reviews* (March 2000) stated:

But Mattie has dropped so many hints about Nick's demise that when this occurs, the emotional tension, even when ratcheted up by a hurricane, doesn't transform his death into a box-of-kleenex event. Luminous prose and beautifully rendered settings, but not enough to give life to this would-be fable of love, loss, and the mysterious workings of the sea and its creatures.

While this reviewer found the novel to be less interesting than Fowler's other works, another anonymous reviewer for *Publishers Weekly* (15 November 1999) asserted that "Fowler writes lyrically of the Florida coast. The love story carries strong appeal, and Fowler's tender portrayal of Nick and Mattie's idyllic relationship will please romantics everywhere." Penny Stevens, in *Library Journal* (January 2000), stated that the novel is "Full of interesting allusions to mythology and animal folklore . . . a pleasure to read even though the reader knows that a tragedy is lurking." While some critics found the plot overly contrived and obvious, the reading public received the book well, and many readers feel that the story is one of Fowler's best. Catherine Swenson in *Library Journal* (July 2000) noted of the audio version of the novel: "As a reader, Fowler aptly portrays the variety of colorful characters she has developed. Highly recommended."

Fowler's next work, *When Katie Wakes* (2002), is a nonfiction piece that focuses upon the death of her mother and the tumultuous relationship that followed her mother's death. *When Katie Wakes* illustrates the difficulty that battered women have in deciding to leave abusive relationships. In this memoir Fowler shares the part of her life in which she completed her college degree, took a variety of jobs to support the ungrateful and abusive partner, and finally gained the courage to leave the relationship. Her dog, Katie, becomes an integral element of the story as Fowler defends and protects the dog in ways that she is unable to do for herself. The memoir provides an honest and graphic depiction of domestic violence and the ways in which abusers and victims make excuses to themselves for their behavior.

Critics praised Fowler's honesty and courage in self-revelation in this memoir. Diane Roberts, in the *Atlanta Journal-Constitution* (10 March 2002), said that "Fowler's spare, elegant style and clear eyed honesty hit the heart like a dagger of ice. She skillfully alternates between narratives of her grown self and her child self . . . presenting a life that was tormented almost past bearing." Carol Hag-

gas, for *Booklist* (1 November 2001), wrote: "Fowler is mercilessly sincere about her own shortcomings and brutally honest about the torment and torture she is subjected to." She continued: "Fowler is a testament to the will of human spirit: to delude itself, certainly, but ultimately, to prevail." A critic for *Library Journal* (December 2001) asserted that "Her fans will welcome this compelling memoir." Generally, reviews of this work have been positive, and while painful to read, the work brings to light the chronic worldwide problem of domestic violence.

Fowler resides in Alligator Point, Florida, where she is a faculty member in the Brief Residency Creative Writing Program at Spaulding University. In 2003 Fowler held the Bachellor Chair in Creative Writing at Rollins College. She hopes to offer the students in her programs the kinds of opportunities that she was given when Doty assisted her in the development of her first novel, *Sugar Cage*.

Domestic violence has played such a role in Connie May Fowler's life that she maintains a strong commitment to eradicating abuse, and one way in which she does so is through the Women with Wings Foundation, a nonprofit organization that supports women and children as they attempt to leave abusive situations. In addition to drawing attention to the issue of domestic abuse, she conducts a thorough study of the native cultures about which she writes, and the detailed depictions of cultural practices and folk traditions of these disparate cultures provide a high level of verisimilitude within her novels and make Fowler's intricate story lines successful.

Interviews:

"A Conversation with Connie May Fowler," *Davis-Kidd Booksellers* <http://www.daviskidd.com/html/Fowler archive.html>;

Patricia Holt, "When Oprah Called, Author Didn't Hang Up: TV Star Liked Novel, Made It Into a Movie," *San Francisco Chronicle,* 19 October 1997, p. E1.

Reference:

Elizabeth S. Bell, "'And She Begins to Speak': Life History, Biography, and Fiction in Connie May Fowler's *River of Hidden Dreams*," *Critique: Studies in Contemporary Fiction,* 43 (Spring 2001): 327–335.

Charles Frazier

(4 November 1950 –)

Joseph Schaub
Newberry College

BOOKS: *Developing Communications Skills for the Accounting Profession,* by Frazier and Robert W. Ingram (Sarasota, Fla.: American Accounting Association, 1980);

Adventuring in the Andes: The Sierra Club Travel Guide to Ecuador, Peru, Bolivia, the Amazon Basin, and the Galapagos Islands, by Frazier and Donald Secreast (San Francisco: Sierra Club Books, 1985);

Cold Mountain (New York: Atlantic Monthly Press, 1997; London: Sceptre, 1997).

OTHER: "Licit Pursuits," in *The Best of the West 2: New Short Stories from the Wide Side of the Missouri,* edited by James and Denise Thomas (Salt Lake City: Peregrine Smith, 1989), pp. 213–222;

The Pocket Canons: Job, introduction by Frazier (New York: Grove, 1999).

SELECTED PERIODICAL PUBLICATIONS–
UNCOLLECTED: "An Analysis of Hopkins' 'Andromeda,'" *Language of Poems,* 8 (1979): 5–9;

"Cold Mountain Diary," *Salon Magazine* (9 July 1997) <http://archive.salon.com/july97/colddiary970709. html>;

"Cold Mountain Diary: Road Miles," *Salon Magazine* (23 July 1997) <http://www.salon.com/july97/ colddiary970723.html>;

"Cold Mountain Diary: Part Three," *Salon Magazine* (6 August 1997) <http://www.salon.com/aug97/ colddiary970806.html>;

"Cold Mountain Diary: Part Four," *Salon Magazine* (21 August 1997) <http://www.salon.com/aug97/ colddiary970821.html>.

Charles Frazier (photograph by Katherine Frazier; from the dust jacket for Cold Mountain, *1997; Richland County Public Library)*

Charles Frazier's *Cold Mountain* became a phenomenon when it was released in 1997, producing massive sales for its publisher, Atlantic Monthly Press, and eventually garnering Frazier the National Book Award for fiction. In achieving this honor, Frazier surpassed such well-established literary figures as Don DeLillo and Thomas Pynchon, who had also published novels in the same year. Though not as reclusive as the mysterious Pynchon, Frazier is an intensely private man who has imparted little of his own personal history, preferring to avoid answering questions about himself and his family and deflecting inquiry toward his work. From the evidence available about him there emerges a quiet, meticulously slow, and detailed writer who has the luxury of time, and the novel clearly shows the great amount of time invested in its writing. *Cold Mountain* has its detractors, but the general critical reception has been favorable, especially for its attention to detail and its evocation of a lost time and place.

Charles Robinson Frazier was born on 4 November 1950 in Asheville, North Carolina. The oldest of three children, Frazier grew up in nearby small towns, including Franklin and Andrews. In Franklin his father, Charles O. Frazier, was the high-school principal, while his mother, Betty, was employed as a school librarian and administrator. Frazier has described himself as a moderately good student, but his interest in literature seems not to have been an early passion; in his 6 August 1997 entry for *Salon Magazine* he admits to having been during his high-school years "a great reader of junk." Frazier graduated from Franklin High School in 1969; of his aspirations at that time, he was later quoted in Michelle Green's 23 February 1998 interview as saying "I thought I wanted to teach literature, probably, if I thought about it much at all." Bolstering Frazier's interest, a high-school friend encouraged him to venture further into the discipline, recommending Edith Wharton's *Ethan Frome* (1911), Ernest Hemingway's *The Sun Also Rises* (1926), and works by Edgar Allan Poe. Frazier took the advice to heart.

Following this direction, Frazier pursued his undergraduate education at the University of North Carolina, Chapel Hill, where he received his B.A. degree in 1973. He entered the M.A. program at Appalachian State University in Boone, North Carolina, the next year and graduated in 1975. There he met his future wife, Katherine Beal, who was an accounting student. The two were married in 1976, and she became an instrumental factor in his writing career. During his twenties Frazier attempted to write fiction but was disappointed with the results of his work and abandoned it. After earning his M.A., Frazier entered the Ph.D. program at the University of South Carolina in Columbia, specializing in twentieth-century American literature. He is remembered by one of his professors, Donald J. Greiner, as a quiet, polite, and courteous student whose written assignments revealed an engaging prose style. In class he typically did not volunteer his opinions but when called upon was always prepared and gave insightful and extensive answers to direct questions. These classes also revealed that by this time he was more broadly read than most of his fellow students. While at the University of South Carolina, Frazier made the necessary contacts to produce his first significant published work, *Developing Communications Skills for the Accounting Profession* (1980), a practical manual written with Professor Robert W. Ingram in the College of Business Administration. The previous year,

in 1979, Frazier had contributed an essay—a structural and linguistic analysis of a Gerard Manley Hopkins poem—to a small journal locally published by the English department at South Carolina.

Upon completing course work at the University of South Carolina, Frazier and his wife moved to Boulder, Colorado, where he spent the next several years teaching at the University of Colorado, a job that he did not particularly enjoy. During this time he also traveled extensively in western South America and used these experiences to write a travel guide to Peru with Donald Secreast, titled *Adventuring in the Andes: The Sierra Club Travel Guide to Ecuador, Peru, Bolivia, the Amazon Basin, and the Galapagos Islands,* which was published in 1985. Written for a variety of travelers, the guide discusses hiking trails and cuisine found in the regions described, along with practical tips on where to stay and how to avoid the common regional maladies. Reviews of the guide were generally favorable. The Fraziers' daughter, Annie, was also born during this period. Since Katherine Frazier was the major wage earner of the family, Charles Frazier became their daughter's at-home parent.

In 1986 Frazier reached two important milestones in his life: earning his Ph.D. in English from the University of South Carolina and moving back to his home state, where Katherine Frazier became an accounting professor at North Carolina State University in Raleigh. Though he had not cared for his job in Colorado, his time in the West and his travels seem to have affected him profoundly; his dissertation, "The Geography of Possibility: Man in the Landscape in Recent Western Fiction," was devoted to the writings of several Western authors: Edward Abbey, Thomas McGuane, James Crumley, Barry Holstun Lopez, Elizabeth Tallent, and Donald Unger. The dissertation discusses the writers' evocation of the spiritual aspects of the Western landscape and their creation of a relatively new regional American literature that eschews much of the myth of the old West in favor of the West as it is today. Frazier's concurrent work on the travel guide and his dissertation indicates his interest in the role of landscape in written works, which became a theme he later explored in *Cold Mountain*. Frazier also uses Western imagery in a short story titled "Licit Pursuits," originally published in *Kansas Quarterly* (1987). In it, a lone nineteenth-century lawman, who serves as the narrator, rides across the "blue mountains" in pursuit of a murderer. The lawman eventually captures the fugitive at his wedding and hangs him from a tree outside the church. The story was later collected in the second volume of the anthology series *The Best of the West: New Short Stories from the Wide Side of the Missouri* (1989). Strangely enough, though, no conclusive evidence exists within the story placing it in the West; instead, the narrator makes reference to North Carolina place names such as Toxaway and Keowee. The Western designation probably arises from Frazier's prose style, which evokes Western writers such as those examined in his dissertation.

The move to Raleigh was the more consequential of the two major events in Frazier's life during 1986. Though employed as an English instructor at North Carolina State University, he spent much of his time doing independent research. Deeply affected by his experience at a bluegrass festival the summer he returned from Colorado, he began to seek a connection to the Appalachian culture that should have been his birthright but was quickly disappearing. He therefore sought to write, though he did not know what form his project would take: fiction or nonfiction. The copious research that he conducted eventually led to the writing of *Cold Mountain*. During this period he was absorbed in the work of old-time musicians, field guides to the Appalachian and Blue Ridge Mountains, the diaries of farm women of the previous century, and the accounts of travelers and naturalists such as Frederick Law Olmsted and the man whose work plays a prominent role in *Cold Mountain*, William Bartram. Intent on writing, but without a clear initial vision of what form or direction the writing would take, Frazier also studied and took notes on the music, natural history, and folklore of the region, as well as the history of white settlers and Indian residents of the southern Appalachians. Guided by stories of explorer Hernando de Soto's possible routes through the mountains, Frazier also hiked the region extensively, attempting to learn its topography, flora, and fauna, as well as its culture. Frazier admitted that he had difficulty reaching the actual writing stage of the project because he was so heavily involved in researching the mountains and nineteenth-century lifestyle. He was especially interested in the area around Cold Mountain, where he visited his grandparents.

Frazier found the focus for his writing project when his father, who had been conducting research into the family's history, told him the story of W. P. Inman, the younger Frazier's great-great-uncle. Inman, a Confederate soldier during the Civil War, had deserted after being wounded in battle and returned on foot to his home at Cold Mountain. Frazier also found supplementary plot material in the stories of two double graves from the time of the Civil War. One held the remains of two civilian men killed by federal troops and buried in a single grave. The other purportedly contained the bones of a fiddler and a mentally handicapped man shot by the Confederate Home Guard, a localized group of armed men whose job was to apprehend deserters and who often dispensed ready justice.

These stories would eventually be incorporated into the characters Stobrod and Pangle, no-account outliers, or deserters, who also are gifted musicians. The nebulous writing project began taking shape as a novel. Frazier focused his research further; among the authors and sources he consulted were Daniel Ellis's *Thrilling Adventures of Daniel Ellis Written by Himself* (1867), Phillip Shaw Paludan's *Victims: A True Story of the Civil War* (1981), Richard Chase's *Jack Tales* (1943) and *Grandfather Tales* (1948), and Walter Clark's *Histories of the Several Regiments and Battalions from North Carolina, in the Great War 1861–'65* (1901). Frazier's wife soon persuaded him to quit his teaching position at North Carolina State in order to devote more time to the novel. Since he was only teaching part-time and the family's finances allowed this change, he left his job at North Carolina State in 1990 and immersed himself in his research and writing. While his daughter was at school he wrote—somewhat irregularly—and devoted time to the family's horse farm.

The novel took the better part of seven years to complete; obsessed with details and authenticity, Frazier says that, for him, a page per day is "a very good day's work." Annie Frazier would read aloud her father's daily output so that Frazier could hear afresh the language that he was trying to make as musical as possible, emulating the rhythms and cadences of the old people he had known. He ended up writing a large portion of the novel at an authors' retreat in the North Carolina mountains. During the long period he was writing, the Fraziers met novelist Kaye Gibbons through a carpool for their children's Montessori school. In 1993 Katherine Frazier gave Gibbons a hundred pages of the novel; Gibbons was impressed and quickly helped Frazier find an agent. Just before Christmas 1995, Atlantic Monthly Press bought the unfinished manuscript, and the completed novel was published in June 1997.

Cold Mountain takes as its central plot the family story of W. P. Inman, though in the novel the fictionalized character is referred to simply as Inman. He is one of the many men from the Blue Ridge Mountains who volunteered for service in the Confederate army in the early days of the war, only to question that involvement later. In the opening pages of the novel, the veteran soldier Inman recuperates in a Raleigh hospital, having recently received a neck wound at Petersburg. Exhausted, sickened, and disillusioned by the war, as were many of his fellow volunteers, he turns his back on the war and sets out on the western path to his home beneath Cold Mountain. As Frazier has no interest in generals and battles, the war as it relates to troop movements and large-scale engagements lies in the background. The greater part of *Cold Mountain* instead

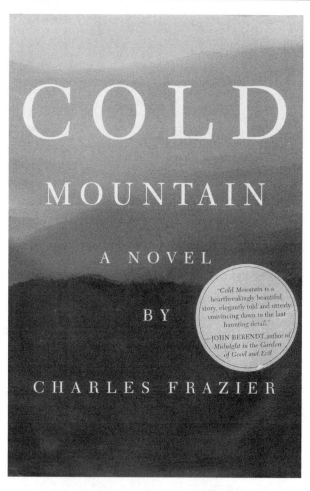

*Dust jacket for Frazier's National Book Award–winning novel
about the homeward odyssey of a Confederate deserter in
the Civil War and the woman who waits for him
(Richland County Public Library)*

concerns Inman's journey homeward and the forces that work against his homecoming. Paralleling Inman's story is that of his prewar sweetheart, Ada Monroe, a Charleston-bred daughter of an intellectual, minister father whose death has forced Ada to confront her helplessness. While Inman's struggle is in the journey, Ada's is in survival at home, turning the deteriorating farm into a working enterprise. Along Inman's way, he meets several distinctive characters who either hinder or help him in his travels, while Ada finds challenges in the landscape itself and invaluable assistance in the dauntless young drifter Ruby. Stobrod, Ruby's father, is a recurring secondary character who imposes himself on the lives of Ada and Ruby.

Inman's chapters are filled with conflicts on a smaller scale than that of the Civil War battles, which makes them all the more real to the protagonist. Whereas in his large-scale battlefield experiences Inman could feel detached from events, he cannot do so when

a direct attempt is made upon his life or when he is offered help on his journey home. He is attacked outside a small village store because the perpetrators do not like his looks. Hardened by war, Inman defeats them, but the men show up later when Inman is crossing the Cape Fear River, where a teenage girl tries to keep her family solvent by operating her father's ferry service in his absence. The two are shot at and pursued by the former assailants but escape harm. Later, Inman interrupts a preacher on the verge of tossing his pregnant and drugged paramour to her death; Inman saves the young woman and leaves the preacher tied up, forcing him to confess to the inhabitants of the village. Despite his treatment, the preacher, named Veasey, later joins Inman in his westward trip. After they help a man known as "Junior" move a dead bull from his feeder creek, Junior takes the two travelers into his home, where he drugs them and turns them over to the Home Guard. The forced march of prisoners ends when they are all shot and thrown into a mass grave; Inman, only wounded, escapes when feral hogs uncover the bodies. After Inman has his revenge on Junior, a young war widow takes him in. She takes Inman into her bed, but only for the security of his sleeping next to her in her husband's place. The next day he saves her and her child from Union scavengers. Later, arguably the most intriguing character in the novel, a goat-herding old mountain woman, heals Inman of his wounds and provides for the final leg of his journey. Behind every one of his adventures is the threat of the band of Home Guard led by the sinister Teague. Through all his travels, Inman emerges as a laconic, introspective loner with a sensitivity that war has not taken away. He is always ready to help another in trouble and has finely honed survival skills that see him through many near-fatal scrapes. He might be a one-dimensional hero except for the despair, longing, and self-doubt that bring more roundness to his character. Still, of all the major players, he seems less interesting than the others.

Inman's story is a kind of picaresque, an episodic series of adventures dealing with his survival on the road home. Ada's alternating chapters, on the other hand, explore her psychological development and demonstrate her true character growth. With the help of Ruby, Ada undergoes a transformation from helpless Charleston belle to self-sufficient farm woman. Her travails are less spectacular than Inman's but no less intriguing, as the reader sees her grow from a dependent naïf who is afraid of her own rooster to a woman in communion with the land who is skilled in both production and barter. This development of character makes Ada a somewhat more engaging character than Inman. Ruby, perhaps even better drawn than both

Inman and Ada, helps Ada to become attuned to the seasons of nature and to recognize her place within it. Critics remark that Ada's journey within herself is a richer and more fulfilling one than Inman's physical journey across the miles. The character of Stobrod adds another human dimension to the Ada chapters and the whole novel. Once a worthless layabout, Stobrod has been changed by the war, but not through battle, as in Inman's case. When asked to play music on his fiddle to soothe a dying girl's passage, Stobrod is transformed from a dabbler with a repertoire of six copied tunes to an original composer of soulful and varied melodies. Both Inman's and Ada's chapters include prewar flashbacks about Ada's coming to Cold Mountain, the lovers' courtship, and Inman's friendship with a Cherokee Indian, Swimmer. The flashbacks ground the characters in the region and establish the tender relationship of the lovers, providing the sense of urgency in Inman's journey home, not only to the woman he loves but also to the mountains he loves equally well.

The parallels to Homer's *Odyssey* are noted in nearly all reviews of the book. Like the travels of Odysseus, Inman's journey homeward from war to Ada–his Penelope–often takes a circuitous route as he takes back roads, tries to avoid the Home Guard, and runs into situations that take him out of his way, experiences likened to those that angry Poseidon inflicted on Odysseus as punishment. Other aspects of the novel come straight from Homer: the episode with the goat-woman, for instance, recalls Circe's animal necromancy; Junior's wife and sisters-in-law are Siren-like; the Cape Fear River is described in Stygian terms; the burial of prisoners is a direct parallel to the descent into the underworld. This evocation of Homer is intentional but not derivative. Frazier even mentions the work specifically during one of Ada's chapters. When the daily work is done, Ruby and Ada often exchange knowledge: Ruby's folk wisdom for Ada's stories from written sources. During one of these instances Ada reads *The Odyssey* to Ruby, causing her to enjoy and laugh at Odysseus's travails while becoming exasperated with Penelope.

Though *Cold Mountain* draws on the epic source, Frazier's main concerns are not epic; he does not involve himself in showing the effects of the war on troops, generals, and politicians. Rather, he is concerned with the everyday folk who are experiencing their own brand of suffering and personal triumphs. The characters Inman encounters are involved in their individual daily struggles, being deeply affected by the degradation of war but maintaining their insularity. They are, in Frazier's words, a people "caught in the crossfire of two incompatible economies," unconnected to the slave trade, large-scale agrarianism, or industrial capitalism. The lives of those insular, agrarian, non-slaveholding characters like Inman who leave their homes to fight in the war contrast the mythical concept of war as a noble enterprise to which all Southerners were committed. Instead, Frazier shows the characters as pawns in a larger game who, upon the subsiding of the prewar hysteria, realize that the real tragedy of war is not the passing of the plantation South but their own loss of life for a cause that had little or nothing to do with them. The epigraph to the novel, taken from Charles Darwin, attests to Frazier's concern with the small conflicts amid the larger struggle in the world: "It is difficult to believe in the dreadful but quiet war of organic beings, going on in the peaceful woods, & smiling fields." *Cold Mountain* therefore is less a Civil War novel and more a novel enlightening the reader about a Southern Appalachian culture that has all but vanished.

Frazier's strict attention to detail creates a nineteenth-century otherworldliness that testifies to the loss of American Appalachian culture. Responding to what he feels is his audience's desire to be transported to another time and place, Frazier makes his reader go slowly through the details of books, implements, and other aspects of another era, uncovering a mostly buried past. For instance, though some names are recognizable (references are made to George Eliot, Nathaniel Hawthorne, and William Gilmore Simms, writers with whom general readers are still familiar), probably not many readers were familiar with Bartram or G. A. Lawrence before reading *Cold Mountain*. To further stress that the reader is encountering a different world, Frazier also evokes a lost language, compiled from his written sources and from older generations of mountain folk, mostly dead now. The diction of the characters and even the narrator is often unfamiliar, though readers can typically discern the meaning of an outdated word from its context. Writing a list of chores, Ada wonders if they have the necessary implements to repair the barn roof, a "maul and froe." Other obsolete words–such as spurtle, fleam, hinnies, spavins, taliped, harls, keeler, and snath–appear throughout.

One of the two more remarkable contemporary items upon which Inman most relies is his pistol, a Lemat's–a strange and deadly weapon. With a revolving cylinder that holds nine .40-caliber rounds and turns around a shotgun barrel, it is a curious firearm even to the nineteenth-century characters of the novel. The other is a coverless copy of Bartram's *Travels*. Originally published in 1791, *Travels* is the account of a naturalist called Flower-Gatherer by the Cherokee for his collections of plants and his interest in the living, growing things of America. While the Lemat's protects Inman's body, the reverence for nature exhibited in the Bartram book protects his soul, easing his mind and keeping it in tune with the nature of his home in the mountains. During pauses in his journey, Inman often opens the book to random passages and reads, as many people do with the Bible; unfailingly, the passage relates to his life at the time and his longing for home. These two items represent the major concerns for the protagonists: survival of the body and prosperity of the spirit.

For the most part, reviewers praised *Cold Mountain,* though they were critical of certain elements of the novel. Mary Carroll, in *Booklist* (1–15 June 1997), believed readers would find certain elements anachronistic, and Claire Messud, in *The Washington Post Book World* (6 July 1997), called the ending of the novel too "cinematic" and reliant upon standard romance. Both reviewers praise other aspects of the novel, however. James Polk's evaluation in *The New York Times Book Review* (13 July 1997) cited the supporting characters as a major strength. Malcolm Jones Jr.'s *Newsweek* review (23 June 1997) represented the general critical consensus, applauding the rich language and calling it "forceful and perfectly cadenced to capture the flavor of a long-gone era." Frazier's skill with the antiquated diction also encourages a better understanding of the story; rather than alienating readers, the language forces them to slow their reading and appreciate every passage. Still, Jones calls the language "merely a side dish" to the evocation of the natural world in the novel. Many critics—including David Heddendorf in *The Southern Review* (2000) and Bill McCarron and Paul Knoke in *Mississippi Quarterly* (1999)—have made studies of the theme in *Cold Mountain* of man's relationship to the natural world and have lauded Frazier's ability to capture the natural history of North Carolina, especially its mountain region. Both Inman and Ada thrive as they learn more about their surroundings and how to work with them. As Inman finds inspiration and spiritual sustenance from Bartram's *Travels* and from his progression toward home, Ada finds that the area around Cold Mountain continues to bring her comfort. From Ruby she learns stewardship for the land that in turn gives to her. The landscape thus becomes the most enduring factor of the novel.

Critical praise of the novel has been matched by its commercial success. In its first nine months of publication *Cold Mountain* sold 1.6 million copies and spent eighteen weeks at the top of the *New York Times* bestseller list. Frazier sold the movie rights soon after the novel became a phenomenon and has stated that he has done so well with the book that his family need not ever worry about money. The highest honor received was the 1997 National Book Award for fiction. The award came as a great surprise to everyone, since competing in the same category was DeLillo's *Underworld.* Pynchon's *Mason and Dixon* had been a favorite to be nominated but was passed over. Most people, Frazier included, expected DeLillo to win, and the upset caused a stir, eliciting some ire among attendees at the ceremony and among literary critics, though DeLillo was magnanimous.

In the year following the publication of *Cold Mountain,* Frazier spent most of his time on book tours and in granting interviews. The double-edged sword of success took away much of his free time and compounded Frazier's already slow writing pace. In interviews conducted between 1997 and 2000 he said that he was working on a novel about the stark contrast between the wealthy residents of North Carolina mountain resorts and the surrounding native population of mostly poor working farmers and daily wage earners. In April 2002 Frazier revealed that instead he was writing about an historical North Carolina man, Will Thomas, who grew up among the Cherokee and led a group of Native Americans in the Civil War. Whatever the subject of Frazier's next novel, or even if he does not publish again, he has probably changed the landscape of Civil War fiction, bringing to light the lives of the men and women who lived day-to-day on their farms and in their small towns, working to survive another day and unknowingly struggling to maintain a culture.

Interviews:

Polly Paddock Gossett, "From Family Roots a Best-Seller Grew," *Charlotte Observer,* 27 July 1997, p. C5;

Elizabeth Farnsworth, "Cold Mountain," television, *Newshour,* PBS, 20 November 1997.

References:

Michelle Green, "Peak Performance: A Hot First Novel, *Cold Mountain,* Brings Charles Frazier Literary Stardom," *People* (23 February 1998): 107–109;

David Heddendorf, "Closing the Distance to Cold Mountain," *Southern Review,* 36, no. 1 (2000): 188–195;

John Inscoe, "Appalachian Odysseus," *Appalachian Journal,* 25 (1998): 330–337;

Malcolm Jones Jr., "The Pinnacle of Success," *Newsweek* (6 April 1998): 62–65;

Bill McCarron and Paul Knoke, "Images of War and Peace: Parallelism and Antithesis in the Beginning and Ending of *Cold Mountain*," *Mississippi Quarterly,* 52 (1999): 273–285.

Kinky Friedman

(1 November 1944 –   )

Lori Rowlett
University of Wisconsin–Eau Claire

BOOKS: *Greenwich Killing Time* (New York: Beech Tree Books, 1986);

A Case of Lone Star (New York: Beech Tree Books, 1987);

When the Cat's Away (New York: Beech Tree Books, 1988);

Frequent Flyer (New York: Morrow, 1989);

Musical Chairs (New York: Morrow, 1991);

The Kinky Friedman Crime Club (London & Boston: Faber & Faber, 1992)–comprises *Greenwich Killing Time, A Case of Lone Star,* and *When the Cat's Away;*

Elvis, Jesus and Coca-Cola (New York: Simon & Schuster, 1993);

More Kinky Friedman (London: Faber & Faber, 1993)–comprises *Frequent Flyer, Musical Chairs,* and *Elvis, Jesus and Coca-Cola;*

Three Complete Mysteries (New York: Wings Books, 1993)–comprises *Greenwich Killing Time, A Case of Lone Star,* and *When the Cat's Away;*

Armadillos and Old Lace (New York: Simon & Schuster, 1994);

God Bless John Wayne (New York: Simon & Schuster, 1995);

The Love Song of J. Edgar Hoover (New York: Simon & Schuster, 1996);

Roadkill (New York: Simon & Schuster, 1997);

Blast from the Past (New York: Simon & Schuster, 1998; London: Faber & Faber, 1998);

Spanking Watson (New York: Simon & Schuster, 1999; London: Faber & Faber, 1999);

Even More Kinky Friedman (London: Faber & Faber, 2000)–comprises *Armadillos and Old Lace, God Bless John Wayne,* and *The Love Song of J. Edgar Hoover;*

The Mile High Club (New York: Simon & Schuster, 2000; London: Faber & Faber, 2000);

Steppin' on a Rainbow (New York: Simon & Schuster, 2001; London: Faber & Faber, 2001);

Kinky Friedman's Guide to Texas Etiquette; or, How to Get to Heaven or Hell Without Going Through Dallas–Fort Worth (New York: Cliff Street Books, 2001);

Kinky Friedman (photograph by Briana Voelkel; from the dust jacket for Kill Two Birds & Get Stoned, *2003; Richland County Public Library)*

Meanwhile Back at the Ranch (New York: Simon & Schuster, 2002; London: Faber & Faber, 2002);

Kill Two Birds & Get Stoned (New York: Morrow, 2003);

Curse of the Missing Puppet Head (Brooklyn: Vandam Press, forthcoming 2004);

The Prisoner of Vandam Street (New York: Simon & Schuster, forthcoming 2004);

The Great Psychedelic Armadillo Picnic: A Walk Through Austin (New York: Crown, forthcoming 2004);

My Willie, Your Bush: Country Singers, Presidents and Other Troublemakers (New York: Morrow, forthcoming 2004).

RECORDINGS: *Sold American,* New York, Vanguard VSD 79333, 1973;

Kinky Friedman, ABC ABCD-829, 1974;

Lasso From El Paso, New York, Epic, PE 34303, 1976;

Live From the Lone Star Café, Bruno-Dean Enterprises BD-349, 1982;

Under the Double Ego, Austin, Texas, Sunrise Records 41200, 1983;

Old Testaments and New Revelations, Fruit of the Tune 777, 1992;

From One Good American to Another, Fruit of the Tune 1111, 1995;

Roadkill, read by Friedman, Los Angeles, Audio Renaissance, 1997;

Pearls in the Snow, Nashville, Kinkajou 669291181821, 1998;

Classic Snatches From Europe, Houston, Sphincter Records 001120D, 2000;

Kinky Friedman: Proud to be an A**hole from El Paso, Kultur, 2003.

Kinky Friedman is a mystery novelist from the "baby boom" generation known for his wry wit and irreverent approach to issues of political correctness. Prior to becoming an author, he had a cult following as a country singer. Although no scholarly criticism of his novels has yet been written, there is one academic article that deals with the cultural significance of his song lyrics, many of which have to do with being both Jewish and a Texan. His mystery novels have reached a broad audience, however, and are popular not only in the United States but also in England, Australia, and New Zealand.

Richard Samet Friedman was born in Chicago on 1 November 1944. He was raised in Texas, where his father, Tom Friedman (who had been a navigator during World War II), was a psychology professor at the University of Texas. His mother, Min Samet Friedman, was a teacher and speech therapist with a background in summer-camp administration. In 1953 his parents opened a summer camp of their own called Echo Hill Ranch in the Texas hill country outside of Kerrville, between San Antonio and Austin. Friedman has a brother, Roger, and a sister, Marcie.

Friedman graduated in 1965 from a highly selective honors program called "Plan II" at the University of Texas at Austin. The demanding program focused on the liberal arts, an emphasis that is evident in the allusions in his writing, from the myths of Ariadne and Arachne to literary references to William Shakespeare,

Ernest Hemingway, F. Scott Fitzgerald, and Dylan Thomas. According to legend, Friedman's nickname, Kinky, comes from a hair-straightening incident in his college days. The attempt was unsuccessful—his hair remained kinky, and the name stuck. Contrary to popular belief, the name has nothing to do with any unusual sexual proclivities.

After college Friedman served with the Peace Corps in Borneo, where he began to write the irreverent, witty songs that he later performed in Austin, New York, and around the world. The wry humor applied to grim subject matter, which became a Friedman hallmark, was evident even in those early songs from his Peace Corps stint. "The Ballad of Charles Whitman," for example, concerns the unhinged student-turned-mass-murderer who climbed up the University of Texas Tower and fired randomly at passers-by in 1966. It includes the refrain, "there was a rumor of a tumor nestled at the base of his brain." While such songs did not earn Friedman mainstream fame, other songs were later recorded by artists such as Willie Nelson, whose rendition of a sad song about the Holocaust, "Ride 'em Jewboy," enabled Friedman's music to reach a broader audience.

Friedman did, however, accumulate a cult following in Austin during the 1970s along with his band, the Texas Jewboys. Austin, at the time, was the birthplace of a musical movement called progressive country. The primary venue was a large hall called the Armadillo World Headquarters, where Friedman often performed. The Austin sound included more than country music: it was a multicultural amalgam of folk, rock, bluegrass, Tejano, and blues. Country singers who later became known as the "outlaws" in Nashville lived in Austin at the time, the most famous of whom is Nelson, who became a good friend of Friedman's and subject of one of his mysteries. Out of this milieu emerged Kinky Friedman and his Texas Jewboys, with their sardonic, folk-tinged country ballads on unlikely subjects.

Following the "urban cowboy" craze, which takes its name from the 1980 John Travolta movie set in Houston, Friedman took his act to New York City, where clubs such as the Lone Star, Max's Kansas City, and the Bottom Line were cashing in on the Texas mystique. Friedman's music made the transition, but some Jewish-owned record stores refused to carry his records. The store owners did not understand his typically Austinite self-mocking irony, and they thought the band's name was intended as an anti-Semitic slur.

After the urban cowboy craze died out in the 1980s, Friedman began to find his niche as a mystery writer. His books read like parodies of hard-boiled detective fiction. On the surface level they might recall the works of Raymond Chandler or Dashiell Hammett,

*Dust jacket for Friedman's first book (1986), in which a New York City private detective
named Kinky Friedman solves a murder (Richland County Public Library)*

but with an undercurrent of humaneness, literacy, and perverse charm. They are also, at another level, a self-parody: the books feature a protagonist named Kinky Friedman, who is a Jewish former country singer from Texas, living in Greenwich Village, just as Friedman did at the time. The character, just like the real Friedman, smokes cigars and has a cat.

Each of the early mysteries, up through *Elvis, Jesus and Coca-Cola* (1993), is set in New York. *Armadillos and Old Lace* (1994), which is set in Texas and draws upon Friedman's hill-country years, marks a turning point. Subsequent novels show the protagonist traveling extensively. The supporting characters are based on real people in Friedman's world. Cleve Hattersley, the night manager of the Lone Star, plays a role in the plot of the early novel *A Case of Lone Star* (1987), which is set in and around the club where Friedman used to perform. Sammy Allred, a musician from Friedman's Austin days, makes an appearance in *Roadkill* (1997) under his own name. His friend Willis Hoover appears as a murder suspect in *Armadillos and Old Lace*. The character of police sergeant Marc Cooperman was in real life not a policeman but a former owner of the Lone Star. The Big Wong, a Chinese eatery, existed in real life as well

as in Friedman's fiction. The cat, made famous by the recurring Friedman line "The cat, of course, said nothing," was based on Cuddles, a New York stray he adopted.

The first of Friedman's mysteries, *Greenwich Killing Time,* which debuted in 1986, is about a murder for which Friedman's journalist friend McGovern has been framed. Kinky, the character, has to solve the crime and clear his friend's name. The cat is introduced as a character: "I rarely meddled in the cat's personal life and she rarely meddled in mine. Neither of us was foolish enough to attribute human emotions to our pets." This statement reflects Friedman's typical humor.

Although Friedman prides himself on being "politically incorrect," the ethnic stereotypes he employs tend to have an ironic twist that undermines the offensive potential, similar to his self-mockery of being Jewish. For example, McGovern is described as half-Irish and half-Indian, both ethnic groups often stereotyped as hard drinkers. Friedman, however, says that, "like every journalist I ever knew, he would take a drink." He makes the drinking a trait typical of the profession, not the ethnic identities, of the character. In later novels, McGovern is described simply as Irish and does not drink any more than the other "Village Irregulars," Friedman's band of shady but helpful crime-solving friends. They all imbibe various substances to excess on a regular basis.

In *Greenwich Killing Time* he tacitly employs a structure that he later discusses explicitly in *Roadkill*. A character named Adrian is at the center of the mystery in *Greenwich Killing Time*. Friedman uses spider imagery to describe Adrian as she sits at the center of a web: all of the threads of the plot lead back to her. She is not the murderer, however. Like Ariadne, she is a helper who hands Kinky the threads he needs to find his way through the labyrinth. In *Roadkill* the modern-day New York Ariadne, like the Adrian of the early novel, is also a cocaine dealer and stained-glass artist. In *Roadkill* he discusses the myth of Ariadne, linking her imaginatively to Arachne, the mythic spider. He uses both as metaphors for solving a mystery, which involves following the threads to unravel the plot.

The second mystery novel, *A Case of Lone Star,* includes multiple meanings in the title. Lone Star refers to the now-defunct club in Manhattan but is also the name of a Texas beer. The word "case" thus refers to a case of beer as well as to the murder cases. In the novel, country singers who perform at the Lone Star begin vanishing. Someone has sent each of the disappearing singers a note that includes Hank Williams song lyrics—a plot device that exemplifies Friedman's nostalgic interest in classic country music.

The next novel, *When the Cat's Away,* published in 1988, concerns a case of petnapping that Kinky is called upon to solve. The purloined pet is not his own cat but one that belongs to a friend. While his two previous novels took an ironic look at the New York country-music scene, his third turned his sardonic gaze on the New York publishing world. In it, he begins his musings on place, a theme that recurs in the later novels:

> The road could've ended anywhere but it didn't. So you keep on driving life's lonely DeSoto, looking ahead in the rain and darkness with the windshield wipers coming down like reaper's blades just missing your dreams. And you don't stop until you're damn well ready. Till you come to the right place. Till you come to the right face. The place may be New York or Texas or it may be somewhere painted with the colors Negroes use in their neon lights.

The word "Negro" was already an anachronism, probably intended to enhance the Chandleresque tone of the passage and add an element of ironic distance. The passage assumes a melancholy flavor that still comes through, however.

Both groups that compose Friedman's ethnic identity, Jews and Texans, are famous for a well-developed sense of place. No one is more loyal to a particular state, with its distinct culture and mythos, than a Texan. Although Friedman pokes gentle fun at some aspects of the culture, he returns seasonally, both literally and in his fiction, to the Texas hill country. Jews, even more than Texans, have strong religious beliefs about a promised land as home, beliefs that extend thousands of years into the past. As Seth L. Wolitz says in the only extant academic article on Friedman: "The entire history of Texas Jews fits the experience of a diasporic culture. There is a desire for fixity after nomadism, continuity after displacement." For Friedman, a tension always exists between the desire for fixity and the desire to be somewhere else. Jewish identity and Texan identity are always at play in this tension. New York is, for American Jews, a homeland of sorts, a center for Jewish culture in a way that other major cities, even Los Angeles or Chicago, never are. Given this aspect of New York as a cultural Mecca, this city provides one of the geographical poles for Friedman's axis, with Texas as the other.

Not surprisingly, Wolitz explores the Friedman "bifocality" in some of his song lyrics, especially the cult favorite "They Ain't Making Jews Like Jesus Anymore." In the song a Texas redneck picks a fight in a public beer hall by taunting a Jew with anti-Semitic slurs, including the accusation as Christ-killers. The Jewish Texan, "one little hebe from the heart of Texas," as the song says, responds at first with verbal wit, saying "We Jews believe it was Santa Claus killed Jesus Christ," a reference to the commercialism that has edged genuine Christianity out of Christmas. After enduring further racist invective from the other, the Jew hits him "right square between the eyes," saying "They ain't making Jews like Jesus anymore / They don't turn the other cheek the way they done before." The observers cheer as the Jew leaves the beer hall in the last verse of the song. As Wolitz points out, the rhetorical strategy of the song sets stereotype against its mirror image: "the populist Texas Bubba anti-ethnic against the meanest, toughest Texas Jew in the Texas public space of a beer hall. The song celebrates Jewish muscle and Jewish rights to win the day in a mythic Texas fashion: a brawl." The Texas Jew is, therefore, confirmed as being just as Texan as the redneck through the mythic Texas tradition where "muscular performance carries truth and right." At the end, the redneck is called a "honky," which reintegrates him into the Texas economy of ethnic slurs in the song. Although Wolitz's article does not address the novels, only the songs, his observations could apply to the Kinky hard-boiled persona of the mysteries as well.

Friedman's fourth novel, *Frequent Flyer,* published in 1989, deals more overtly with Jewish themes. A

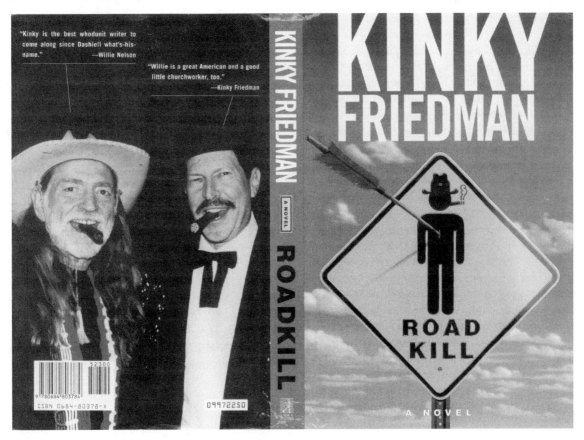

Dust jacket for Friedman's 1997 novel, in which Friedman rescues the singer Willie Nelson from a Hopi shaman's curse (Richland County Public Library)

female character leads Kinky and his friend Ratso, one of the Village Irregulars, to the den of a notorious Nazi living in Manhattan. Once again Friedman returns to his signature playful breaking down of dichotomies:

> There's a little bit of Nazi, I thought, and a little bit of Jew in all of us. How we deal with these diverse parts of our being will have a lot to do with what kind of lives we will eventually lead and what kind of world we'll be able to make for our children and our kittens.

Friedman refers to the struggle between good and evil, cruelty and kindness, but in a distinctively Jewish framework. His use of Jewish images, ideas, and themes, as exemplified here, tends to be more cultural than overtly spiritual in a traditional sense, but he does occasionally touch on the religious aspects. "Even with the excess baggage that Judaism sometimes brings," Kinky says, "I was suddenly very glad that I wasn't a Christian Fundamentalist," referring to the plethora of guilt-inducing rules in some religions.

In *Frequent Flyer* the battle between good and evil is played out as a cat-and-mouse game between the Nazi

and Kinky, who takes on the role of Jewish Nazi-hunter, one of the most macho of the modern Jewish male types. In contrast to the "nebbish" or "schlemiel" type common in Yiddish folklore (the Jewish version of the ninety-eight-pound weakling or the nerd with a book under his arm and tape on his glasses), the relentless, fearless Nazi-hunter is the avenger of the oppressed. Although Kinky falls into the role by accident in the novel, it is another example of Friedman's rewriting of Jewish identity in keeping with the Texas-tough mythos: his Nazi-hunter wears a cowboy hat.

His next novel, *Musical Chairs*, appeared in 1991. The familiar theme of lost people and places returns when Kinky's former guitarist, Tequila (Kinky claims never to have known his real name), calls with the alarming news that someone is trying to kill him. Kinky allows him to visit as a houseguest, a "housepest," as Kinky puts it, but Tequila ends up murdered anyway, right in the shower of Kinky's loft apartment. Someone then systematically begins killing off all the former members of Kinky's defunct band, the Texas Jewboys, one by one.

The longing for people, times, and places that can never be recovered dominates the novel. It begins with a scene on Christmas Eve in which "ghosts of Christmases past" appear mysteriously through the window of a diner, including another friend who had been dead for a year and long-dead politician Adlai Stevenson, remembered fondly by many as a classic liberal from an illiberal era, the 1950s. In a metonymic analogy, Kinky also waxes bitter about the illiberal "Young Republicans" of the 1980s, anathema to many who, like Friedman, have positive views of 1960s and 1970s idealism. Other signs of the times include a Mercedes that drives by bearing a license plate that says "Greed," and a skinhead that walks by kicking at pigeons. Kinky calls himself "married to the wind" and expresses longing for a "dead Dixieland of the spirit . . . that will sometimes rise again," but only as a phantom place.

References to a nostalgic past also appear in *Elvis, Jesus and Coca-Cola,* published in 1993. It concerns the death in 1982 of Friedman's friend, Tom Baker, "the Bakerman," an actor who appeared in several of Andy Warhol's movies but was otherwise fairly obscure. The plot of the mystery involves the disappearance of a movie that Tom had been working on at the time of his death, a documentary about Elvis impersonators. The novel opens with the funeral scene, featuring Kinky singing "Ride 'em Jewboy." Although primarily about the Holocaust, the song's lyrics are a melancholy paean to diasporic people everywhere:

> How long will you be driven
> Relentless around the world . . .
> Your dreams were broken,
> Rounded up and made to move along
> The loneliness which can't be spoken
> Just swings a rope
> And rides inside a song . . .
> So ride, ride, ride 'em Jewboy
> Ride 'em all around the old corral
> . . . I'm with you boy if I got to ride six million miles.

Tom's ethnicity is Irish, which Friedman sees as similar to Jewishness. "As Brendan Behan said: The Irish and the Jews do not share a nation; they share a psychosis," he remarks on the first page of the novel. The sad song lyrics show once again the typical Friedman connection between Western or Texan imagery and the longing for a homeland to which one could truly belong.

In *Armadillos and Old Lace* Kinky finds himself back in the Texas hill country, working for the summer at his parents' camp and living in a green trailer, the inside of which is decorated like a watermelon. The walls are adorned with pictures of Hank Williams and Gandhi. This detail not only reflects the personality of the Kinky character but also sheds some light on the values that shape Friedman the author.

In the plot someone is killing elderly women, all of whom had been at the same San Antonio cotillion in the 1930s. The perpetrator turns out to be the illegitimate son of a disgraced member of their social set, but the pretext of the novel gives its author the chance to use his Texas background to humorous effect. Cotillions are not unique to Texas, nor even to the South, but they are a quaint feature of Texas culture, even in the present day. Other examples of Texas womanhood appear in the novel, including a large and fierce female sheriff and a formidable, highly intelligent justice of the peace.

Friedman gleefully repeats the name of the local library—the Butt-Holdsworth Memorial Library—throughout the novel, as Kinky does research to help solve the mystery. The name connotes something authentically small-townish, and Kinky also takes an adolescent delight in references to certain parts of the anatomy and the fact that the words Butt-Holdsworth are vaguely reminiscent of anal retentiveness. (The philanthropic Butt family is real: H. E. Butt's is a grocery-store chain in south-central Texas.) Friedman includes other pieces of Texas nostalgia, such as a reference to the old opera house where Jimmie Rodgers, the "singing brakeman," used to perform.

Although his descriptions of the Texas hill country are beautiful, Friedman touches on the problem of trying to "go home again" several times in the novel: "Kerrville wasn't quite my hometown, I reflected, but neither was New York. My hometown was probably spiritually somewhere between the two, very far away, its longitude and latitude lost in a lullaby. Its citizens were smoke." At another point Kinky refers to himself as a "jet-set gypsy" who has no real home to return to. As his character Kinky becomes increasingly peripatetic, the author Friedman reflects more often on the themes of belonging and rootlessness.

In his next novel, *God Bless John Wayne* (1995), Friedman again makes reference to this theme by quoting one of his own songs, as he did in *Elvis, Jesus and Coca-Cola.* This time he quotes from his lyrics to "People Who Read People Magazine" in an epigraph at the beginning of *God Bless John Wayne:*

> And to tell you the truth this telephone booth gets lonesome in the rain,
>
> But, son, I'm 21 in Nashville and I'm 43 in Maine.
>
> And when your mama gets home would you tell her I phoned—it'd take a lifetime to explain
>
> That I'm a country picker with a bumper sticker that says: "God Bless John Wayne."

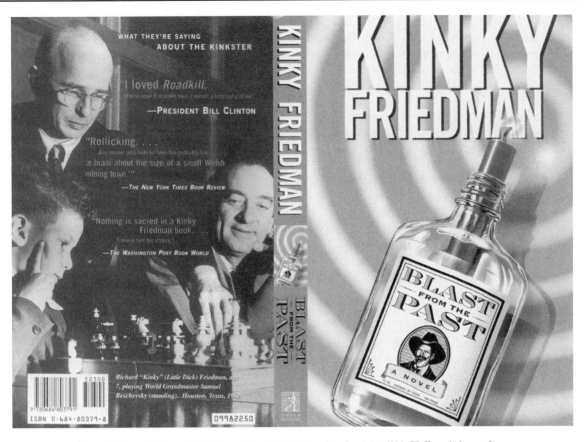

Dust jacket for Friedman's 1998 novel, in which 1970s political activist Abbie Hoffman hides out from the authorities in Friedman's Greenwich Village apartment (Richland County Public Library)

As the song lyrics hint, the subject matter is also mothers and uncertain parentage. Kinky is called upon to help his friend Ratso, an adoptee, search for his birth mother. The novel ends, however, in true Friedman fashion, not with the search for a person but with the wistful search for a place seen only in a dream, the "Road of the Loving Hearts."

In *The Love Song of J. Edgar Hoover* (1996) Kinky takes on the FBI. Despite the title, the novel has little to do with Hoover's secret personal life, although the oddness of it is mentioned in passing. Hoover spied on gay groups, and also on Jewish organizations and civil rights leaders, publicly proclaiming his suspicions that they were subversive and "Un-American"; meanwhile, Hoover himself was a closeted gay man. The novel, however, is not concerned with Hoover's love life but is instead a story of subterfuge and surveillance. Kinky's friend McGovern is once again involved. A man named Leaning Jesus has given him a chicken recipe in which the directions to the hidden treasure of Al Capone are encoded. The FBI realizes the importance of the map before McGovern does, and tries to find it. Eventually, when Kinky discovers

the code in the recipe by accident, the object of his affection, Stephanie, goes to Florida in search of the treasure. Naturally, the treasure proves to be elusive in the end.

Friedman deals with yet another theme in *Roadkill:* the identity of Native Americans. He repeatedly says that "Every Indian is not a drunk," a counterpoint to Village Irregular Rambam's statement in the same novel that "Every drunk is not a poet, Kinky." His statement harks back to the earlier use of the stereotype of the half-Indian McGovern in his first novel, for which he had undoubtedly been criticized. *Roadkill* is surprisingly reverent in its use of Native American religious elements.

The plot centers on Friedman's real-life friend Willie Nelson, who is himself part Native American. In the novel, after Willie's tour bus inadvertently hits an elderly shaman of the Hopi people in Arizona, Willie receives a medicine bundle that has negative power. After calling on some of his Native American friends, who purify his New York apartment with a smudge stick, Kinky is able to solve the mystery of Willie's disappearance and free him from a possible curse.

Blast from the Past, published in 1998, is an imaginative reconstruction of the 1970s. Political activist Abbie Hoffman, a.k.a. Barry Freed, is a houseguest of the character Kinky in Greenwich Village, hiding from the police and the FBI. Although the real Friedman was living in Texas at the time, performing around Austin with the Texas Jewboys, the novel gave him an opportunity to imagine what life in New York might have been like when Hoffman was on the run, if he had had the chance to know him. Friedman evokes the paranoia as well as the exhilaration of life on the run. As the title suggests, he also taps into the nostalgia that members of the "baby boom" generation often have for the radical politics that seemed to hold so much hope for a more just future but which soured so quickly in the 1970s. Hoffman functions in the novel (as often in life) as an embodiment of both youthful idealism and its loss.

Spanking Watson (1999) concerns Kinky's neighbor, lesbian dance instructor Winnie Katz. She appears in nearly every novel, usually as an irritant, with her noisy dancing upstairs. After Kinky writes a threatening note to create a false mystery, someone else actually begins menacing Winnie. At one point Kinky impersonates one of the dancers by wearing a woman's wig, posing as a decoy in silhouette to fool the stalkers. He solves the case with the help of the Village Irregulars. As a result, although Winnie is a lesbian, her gratitude almost leads her into Kinky's bed. Once again the author is playing with opposites, having the character Kinky find some sort of rapprochement, even mutual attraction, with Winnie.

Throughout the novel Friedman links Winnie with Emily Dickinson: both of these women lived alone without apparent need for male company. Oscar Wilde is also frequently mentioned and quoted in many of the novels, usually in connection with gay sexuality. Although Friedman identifies himself as a heterosexual, many of his books make reference to the continuum of sexual orientations. In *Greenwich Killing Time* he says that at the subconscious level, "you'd find that every homosexual was a heterosexual and every heterosexual was a homosexual. You'd probably also find that neither group was too fond of Sigmund Freud." In the later books he returns to the same theme, that an individual's sexuality is not necessarily at one pole or the other. At the end of *Spanking Watson* the note written by Kinky has been supposedly analyzed by a graphologist: "He says that the shaky, poorly defined crossings of the T's indicate a confused sexual identity." Sexual fluidity returns as a theme in *Roadkill* as well: "There's probably a lot less difference than we think between homosexuals and heterosexuals. . . . Whether we like it or not,

we're all part of one big soul." At another point Kinky and Willie Nelson discuss the possibility of recording a duet of a song written by Ned Sublett called "Cowboys are Frequently Secretly Fond of Each Other."

The Mile High Club appeared in 2000. In this novel Kinky meets a mysterious woman on an airplane between Dallas and New York. Her name is Khadija, a name Kinky does not immediately recognize as Arab. It is actually the name of the prophet Muhammad's first wife, something the real Friedman would know. She disappears, leaving him with her bag, which she had asked him to hold. He is pursued by various frightening and threatening people, including men from the State Department and later the woman's irate brother. In the meantime, a dead Israeli agent is found on the toilet in Kinky's loft apartment. Dying on the toilet is a common theme repeated by Friedman: he mentions in several of his novels that Elvis Presley and Judy Garland both died in this fashion. *The Mile High Club* marks his first foray into international affairs. Other than the theme of airline terrorism, though, he does not discuss the Palestinian-Israeli conflict in a political way. He never takes a stand, for example, on the issue of Zionism. He never even mentions the details of the various territorial solutions proposed in the political arena to the Middle East conflict. Instead, the book uses the Middle Eastern troubles as mere background for the unfolding of the mystery.

Steppin' on a Rainbow, which appeared in 2001, takes place primarily in Hawaii. After the disappearance of McGovern, Kinky and friends follow his convoluted trail to the islands. Although Kinky thinks McGovern may have stepped on a rainbow—a Kinky euphemism for "died"—his friend turns up alive and well. (In all of the novels, Kinky is fond of distinctive euphemisms and colloquialisms: anything wonderful is "killer bee," a yarmulke is a "yamaha," hair is "moss," the cash register is a "Jewish piano," and to defecate is to "take a Nixon.") Like the Native American spirituality in *Roadkill,* the native Hawaiian religious tradition is referred to respectfully throughout the novel. Its lore provides most of the clues that solve the mystery and help to restore McGovern to his circle of friends.

In 2001 Friedman also wrote a book of etiquette, actually a humorous look at Texas customs and foibles. *Kinky Friedman's Guide to Texas Etiquette; or, How to Get to Heaven or Hell Without Going Through Dallas–Fort Worth* includes a list of things a "real Texan" would never say, such as: "The tires on that truck are too big." A quiz asking "Redneck, Good Old Boy, or Oilman: What Kind of Texan Are You?"

is also included, along with an entire chapter on Aggie jokes and a tongue-in-cheek explanation of Texas lore, such as the Alamo and the song "The Yellow Rose of Texas."

Although technically retired from being a country musician, Friedman still performs his music occasionally. He recorded a live album from a European tour, *Classic Snatches from Europe* (2000) on his new label, Sphincter Records, with his new band, Little Jewford. Inspired by Cuddles the cat, Friedman also created the Utopia Animal Rescue Ranch, whose board of directors includes Willie Nelson and former Texas governor Ann Richards. It was featured in the March 2001 issue of *Southern Living* magazine. Beginning in April 2001, he started writing a column for *Texas Monthly Magazine*.

Never one to take himself too seriously, Kinky Friedman would probably be amused to know that academics are beginning to write articles about him.

As he himself quipped, "People seem to be getting a lot more out of my books than I'm putting into them." Meanwhile, Friedman continues to produce a new book approximately every year, to the delight of a broad, international audience.

Biography:

M. Allen Swafford, *The Kinky File: Investigating the Mystery of Richard "Kinky" Friedman* (Brooklyn: Vandam Press, 2003).

References:

The Official Kinky Friedman Web Site <http://www.kinky friedman.com>;

Seth L. Wolitz, "Bifocality in Jewish Identity in the Texas-Jewish Experience," in *Jewries at the Frontier: Accommodation, Identity, Conflict,* edited by Sander L. Gilman and Milton Shain (Urbana: University of Illinois Press, 1999), pp. 185–208.

Cristina García

(4 July 1958 –)

Persis M. Karim
San José State University

BOOKS: *Dreaming in Cuban* (New York: Knopf, 1992);
Cars of Cuba, text by García, photographs by Joshua Greene (New York: H. N. Abrams, 1995);
The Agüero Sisters (New York: Knopf, 1997);
Monkey Hunting (New York: Knopf, 2003).

OTHER: *Cubanísimo!: The Vintage Book of Contemporary Cuban Literature,* edited by García (New York: Vintage, 2003).

Cristina García is one of several late-twentieth-century Cuban American writers whose work represents the experiences and issues of a generation of Cuban-born children who immigrated with their families to the United States after the Cuban Revolution in the early 1960s. Her novels contribute to a body of writing that has been considered the literary "coming of age" for Cuban American literature. García's first novel, *Dreaming in Cuban* (1992), received widespread acclaim and has exerted a tremendous influence on the ways that American readers understand the complexity of the Cuban American immigrant and exile experience. Reviewers from publications such as *Time* and *Publishers Weekly* praised the novel as a literary tour de force for its ability to capture the experience of "living between two cultures." For García, *Dreaming in Cuban* established her writing career and marked her entry into the American multicultural literary scene.

García was born on 4 July 1958 in Havana, Cuba, to Francisco M. García, a cattle rancher, and his wife, Esperanza Lois García. Like many members of Cuba's middle and upper classes, after the establishment of Fidel Castro's government and the experience of confiscation of private property and vilification by the new regime, the García family left Cuba in 1960 for a life of exile in the United States. The family settled in New York City, where they had relatives, and established a small restaurant. García grew up in the Brooklyn Heights neighborhood, where she attended the Dominican Academy. She graduated from Barnard College at Columbia Uni-

Cristina García (photograph by Norma I. Quintana; from the dust jacket for The Agüero Sisters, *1997; Richland County Public Library)*

versity in 1979 with a bachelor's degree in political science. While studying at Barnard, she continued working in her parents' restaurant. García later entered the School of Advanced International Studies at Johns Hopkins University in Baltimore with the goal of working in the Foreign Service.

Although García earned a master's degree in European and Latin American studies, a strong interest in writing led her to a career in journalism. In the early 1980s García worked for several prominent publications. She began her journalistic career as an intern at the *Boston Globe* and later worked for United Press International, *The Knoxville Journal,* and the Washington, D.C., bureau of *The New York Times.* During the 1980s and early 1990s García worked as a correspondent at *Time* magazine in New York City, San Francisco, and Los Angeles. In 1990 García married Scott Brown, with whom she has a daughter, Pilar García-Brown. A one-year position as the *Time* bureau chief in Miami (1987–1988), reporting news and features on Florida and the Caribbean, nurtured her burgeoning interest in writing about her family and their heritage. Journalistic writing, however, proved to be too restrictive for García. She then turned to fiction as a venue to bring the images and memories of her childhood and the stories of Cuban immigrants to life.

The populous and vibrant Cuban American population of Miami had a strong impact on García, reawakening her interest in Cuban culture and reconnecting her to memories of her family on the island. In 1984 García returned to Cuba to confront these memories and to meet many of her relatives for the first time. Five years later, the trip still haunted García. She equated meeting her family members to "finding a missing link in my own identity." Early in 1989 García set out to write *Dreaming in Cuban.* The publication of the novel three years later initiated her into a group of writers and artists of Cuban origin that Gustavo Perez-Firmat, a scholar of Cuban American culture, has called "one-and-a-halfers"—those Cuban Americans born in Cuba but who have lived a majority of their lives in the United States and are, to some extent, marginal to both Cuban and American culture.

Some critics have referred to *Dreaming in Cuban* as a feminist novel, despite the fact that García does not view herself as a feminist writer. The novel chronicles aspects of the Cuban diaspora from the point of view of three generations of women who experience their national and cultural status as Cubans through the periods of revolution and exile. The novel begins with an image that stayed with García long after her trip: a woman sitting on her porch by the sea, scanning the Cuban coast for invaders. In the novel, members of the extended del Piño family struggle to make sense of their personal, historical, and political circumstances as a result of the Cuban Revolution. Moving between Cuba and New York, the novel focuses on Celia del Piño, the matriarch of the family, who stays behind in Cuba; her

vehemently anticommunist, procapitalist daughter Lourdes, who runs the Yankee Doodle Bakery in Brooklyn; and Pilar, Lourdes's daughter, who has assimilated into American culture and rebels against her parents and their rigid political and largely anti-Castro views. As she comes of age, Pilar experiences a longing to know Cuba firsthand. Based loosely on García's life, the novel depicts the strong emotions evoked by exile, nationalist disillusionment, and alienation with which many Cubans, both in the United States and in Cuba, have had to deal. As Ibis Gomez-Vega asserts:

> The only one of Celia's descendants who shares Celia's generosity is Pilar, who makes the journey home to Cuba and to Celia only to find out that she cannot live in Cuba. Life in the United States has made her less a Cuban than a New Yorker, and she chooses to leave Cuba all over again although she realizes that she may never see her grandmother again. The journey home is often as disturbing as the life lived in exile, for one risks finding out that the dream of going home can never be made real.

The characters in *Dreaming in Cuban* struggle to maintain their connections to family, culture, and nation, despite the ideological rhetoric that has divided Cuban families on both sides of the Straits of Florida.

Dreaming in Cuban challenges readers to understand the Cuban American experience not only as a single event of a national migration but also as an attempt to grapple with the historical disruptions of the revolution and the ensuing American blockade of the country. The novel also suggests the deeply scarring events of the Cold War and the impact of anticommunist fervor on populations whose nations were affected by policies of this period. *Dreaming in Cuban* demonstrates the ways that families can be divided politically and geographically yet still remain united. The novel highlights strong nationalist sympathies, which were evoked by the ideological fallout from the 1959 revolution that eventually changed the nature of Cuban life. García's narrative voices have drawn readers in part because of the style in which they are written. Rather than featuring a single narrator, *Dreaming in Cuban* is written through a polyphonic, multivocal narrative that suggests the impossibility of representing a single truth about the Cubans and their experiences with revolution and emigration, which are two of the single most important historical events for Cuba in the twentieth century. The novel also highlights Cuba's interesting cultural mix of Catholicism and Santeria, a religion that was brought to the island by African slaves centuries earlier and that features magic spells, incantations, and sacrifice as elements of ritualistic practice.

Dust jacket for García's first book, a 1992 novel about three generations of female Cuban exiles; it was a National Book Award finalist (Richland County Public Library)

Dreaming in Cuban received favorable reviews and was hailed as an accomplished first novel. Several reviewers found García's attempt to consider several generations of Cubans an innovative and important literary device that diffused the inflammatory political rhetoric surrounding Cuba. Laura Cumming commented in *The Guardian* (19 November 1992): "For humility aside, this fervent tale of patriotism, voodoo, reincarnation and passion has a sophisticated politeness about it, a tactfulness that diminishes unpleasantness in favor of delicate poetry." Cumming observed that the intertwined narratives of grandmother, daughter, and granddaughter complicates the singular image of Cuba as either island paradise or communist bastion by creating a narrative that offers a "dutiful pluralism in which Garcia makes no judgements." While some reviewers praised García's fragmented style and the use of diverse female voices to narrate the story of Cuba and its complex and painful history for Cubans both at home and abroad, other reviewers found this polymorphous

prose difficult to follow. The reviewer for *Kirkus Reviews* (1 January 1992) called the novel a "patchwork of incident, memory, letters, dreams and visions."

While García's work shows the influence of other Latin American writers and the stylistic qualities of magical realism embodied by an earlier generation of writers such as Gabriel García Marquez and Mario Vargas Llosa, it moves beyond these forms to tackle the difficult social and political issues that are characteristic of the Cuban American experience. When asked by an interviewer whether she considered herself a magical realist writer, she answered that indeed she was "influenced by magical realism as it exists in contemporary Latin American fiction and elsewhere."

García's first novel was instrumental in breaking into a new niche within the Latino literary world: her novel, unlike those of an earlier generation of Cuban American writers, is written in English and translated into Spanish. García, who grew up speaking and reading Spanish at home but English at school, is acutely aware of the changing demographics in the United States that indicate by the year 2010 Hispanic Americans will become the largest minority group in the nation. Her commitment to writing in English also stems from her desire to convey the Cuban American experience to an English-speaking audience. In a *Newsweek* article on Latino writers, she expressed her growing sense that as Latino immigrants make their way in the United States and become better educated, "there is going to be more good writing [in English] surfacing" (April 1992).

Dreaming in Cuban was a finalist for the National Book Award, and an excerpt was anthologized in *Iguana Dreams,* a volume of Latino fiction, that same year. García's success as a writer of fiction won her the 1992–1993 Hodder Fellowship at Princeton University and the Cintas Fellowship from the Institute of International Education. From 1992 until 1995 García taught courses in creative writing at the Los Angeles and Santa Barbara campuses of the University of California. Since 1995 García has been teaching in the English department at the University of Southern California, near the home she shares with her daughter. With the success of *Dreaming in Cuban,* García set out to write a second novel, which she later shelved, and instead began writing *The Agüero Sisters* (1997). A 1994–1995 Guggenheim Fellowship augmented her ability to work on the novel.

Like its predecessor, *The Agüero Sisters* is set in Cuba, New York, and Florida and also features female protagonists. Constancia and Reina Agüero are half sisters who struggle with their relationships to their past, their culture, and their society. Constancia and Reina share the same mother, whose cause of death remains a mystery to everyone but Constancia's

Dust jacket for García's 1997 novel, about the reunion of two Cuban half sisters in Miami
(Richland County Public Library)

father, Ignacio, who killed himself shortly after his wife's death. This novel delves into García's concern with the deep divides between Cuban immigrants and those who remained behind on the island and their attempts to reconcile both personal and national history with memory. Constancia leaves Cuba to go to the United States, where her husband, Heberto, is working as a cigar salesman in New York; he reserves the finest (albeit illegal) Cuban cigars for his best customers. They have two children and eventually retire to Florida to join fellow Cuban expatriates. Shunning "their habit of fierce nostalgia, their trafficking in the past like exaggerating peddlers," Constancia dislikes the Key Biscayne Cubanas.

Reina lives in Cuba, where she works as a talented electrician and remains fiercely loyal to her mother and stepfather's memories. When a lightning strike unsettles Reina's life, she decides to go to Miami to see her estranged half sister. Their meeting ignites a series of divisions that are reflected in their attempts to find meaning and to reconcile their memories with their current circumstances. García presents Cuba's history in what is portrayed as the waning years of Fidel Castro's power. These historical and political events form the backdrop for these characters and their attempts to

come to terms with their place in Cuban history, culture, and national memory. Like other novels by Latina authors, *The Agüero Sisters* deploys magical realism; it includes the mystical elements of Santeria and its impact on Cuban culture. Although García was not exposed to Santeria when she was growing up, her travels to Cuba led her to seek out more information about the religion and its practices. García has a cousin in Cuba who is a *santera* from whom she has learned a great deal and who has offered her the privilege of witnessing the rituals and practices firsthand.

The Agüero Sisters was praised for its refined evocations of homeland and exile. Again, García employs the same shifting narrative, whereby the complex web of events and people reveals the history not just of the two sisters but of Cuba and immigration itself. As in her previous novel, García shows the intransigence of politics that keep families apart and distant, focusing on the human costs that prevent these two sisters from knowing each other. Alejandra Bronfman in *The Washington Times* (25 May 1997) commented: "The story of the convergence of all these characters, as they zero in on Miami and on their shared past, is told in many registers, and the novelist's deft maneuvers through them reveal a brilliant send of narrative. She moves seamlessly from the subtle ambiguities of emotion to Miami's raucous absurdity and overabundance, surprising us with lively satire." Other critics, however, found García's second novel more elusive and difficult than the first. Several reviewers criticized her overly wrought use of magical realism. Overall, the critical reception for *The Agüero Sisters* was positive, but the novel did not quite make the same impression as *Dreaming in Cuban*.

García's next novel, *Monkey Hunting* (2003), charts the history of Chinese immigration to Cuba and the cultural influences and contributions of the Chinese community to Cuban society and culture. Protagonist Chen Pan unwittingly signs a contract as an indentured servant and is sent to Cuba in 1857, but eventually he becomes a prosperous businessman in Havana. The multigenerational story also traces the lives of Chen Pan's granddaughter Chen Fang, back in China, who disguises herself as a boy to gain an education and become a teacher but who dies in one of Mao Tse-Tung's prisons, and great-great-grandson Domingo Chen, who immigrates to the United States after Fidel Castro gains power and is then traumatized by his experiences in the Vietnam War. Reviews of *Monkey Hunting* were positive; one critic for *Publishers Weekly* wrote: "Though García ranges farther afield here than in previous works, her prose is as tight and polished as ever." Donna Seaman of *Booklist* called the novel "Gorgeously detailed and entrancingly told, erotic, mystical, and wise."

García's novels situate family loyalties as the ultimate casualty of history—showing the divisions between those who have lived with the aftermath of the revolution and those who have left and found a second home in places like New York and Florida. In both of her novels, families are divided geographically and politically, and it is left to various narrators and voices to suggest the incongruity and irreconcilability of each of these narratives. With these multiple narratives and voices, García suggests that there is more than one truth and more than one way of experiencing the ruptures that have become so central to Cuban American existence and identity.

The success of Cristina García's novels has not occurred in a vacuum. Like other Latino writers of her generation, García has found a niche and audience for her work. While her novels are heavily influenced by the history of Cuban Americans and reflect the complexity of exile and immigration, her work has attained widespread appeal in part because she cuts across geographical and cultural boundaries. Unlike the writings of an earlier generation of Latino writers, García's work appeals to Anglos as well as Latinos. Her work draws on a continuing theme of American life: the need to participate in and acknowledge the multicultural texture of American society.

Interview:

Allan Vorda, "A Fish Swims in My Lung: An Interview with Cristina García," in *Face to Face: Interviews with Contemporary Novelists,* edited by Vorda (Houston: Rice University Press, 1993), pp. 61–76.

References:

Katherine-Gyekenyesi Gatto, "Mambo, Merengue, Salsa: The Dynamics of Self-Construction in Latina Autobiographical Narrative," *West Virginia University Philological Papers,* 46 (2000): 84–90;

Ibis Gomez-Vega, "The Journey Home: Defining Identity in Cristina García's *Dreaming in Cuban,*" *Voces: A Journal of Chicana Latina Studies,* 1 (Summer 1997): 71–100;

Gustavo Perez-Firmat, *Life on the Hyphen: The Cuban-American Way* (Austin: University of Texas Press, 1994).

Tim Gautreaux

(19 October 1947 –)

Julie Kane
Northwestern State University

BOOKS: *Same Place, Same Things* (New York: St. Martin's Press, 1996);
The Next Step in the Dance (New York: Picador USA, 1998);
Welding with Children (New York: Picador USA, 1999);
The Clearing (New York: Knopf, 2003).

OTHER: "Left-Handed Love," in *A Few Thousand Words About Love,* edited by Mickey Pearlman (New York: St. Martin's Press, 1998), pp. 127–142.

SELECTED PERIODICAL PUBLICATIONS–UNCOLLECTED:
FICTION
"Just Turn Like a Gear," *Massachusetts Review,* 27 (Spring 1986): 5–32.
NONFICTION
"Behind the Great Stories There Are Great Sentences," *Boston Globe,* 19 October 1997, Books: P4;
"Perfect Strangers on a Train," *Oxford American,* 32 (March/April 2000): 26–36.

Tim Gautreaux (photograph by Winborne Gautreaux; from the dust jacket for Welding with Children, *1999; Richland County Public Library)*

Tim Gautreaux was forty-nine years old and had been honing his craft for almost two decades when his first book of fiction was published in 1996. The acclaim for his character-driven narratives about Louisiana blue-collar workers wrestling with moral dilemmas was immediate, as reviewers from *The Arkansas Gazette* to *Commonweal* and *Kirkus Reviews* compared his talent to that of Flannery O'Connor. Over the next four years, Gautreaux delivered on the promise of that debut performance by publishing a novel and a second short-story collection to equally strong reviews. Though he objects to being labeled a "Cajun" or "Southern" writer, insisting that his themes are universal and that he just writes about the environment he knows best, Gautreaux continues to demonstrate that the Southern literary hallmarks of regionalism, storytelling, and concern with moral issues are time-less in their appeal and are capable of reinvigorating the postmodern novel and short story.

Timothy Martin Gautreaux was born in the rough, blue-collar, oil-industry town of Morgan City, Louisiana, on 19 October 1947, to Florence Ella Gautreaux, née Adoue, and Minos Lee Gautreaux. One grandfather was a steamboat chief engineer; his father was a tugboat captain; and other male relatives worked in the railroad industry or on offshore oil rigs. The men in his family delighted in trading outlandish stories about their jobs and their machines; this type of storytelling became the motivating force behind Gautreaux's mature fiction. Gautreaux is a collector of antique machines and their repair manuals, and machines almost always figure prominently in his plots.

"My wife says that the only reason I write fiction is that it gives me the chance to describe big machines," he said in a 1998 *New Delta Review* interview.

To Morgan City, as well, can be traced the germ of many of Gautreaux's female characters, who are almost always tougher and less sentimental than the males. He stated in an interview for *Voices of the Americas* (2004) that "a lot of the rural women that I grew up with had to be pretty tough, intellectually and physically and emotionally, to survive the poverty and the rough men they'd married." That, he explained, was why "some of the women in my stories are a little rough around the edges, a little hardhearted."

Morgan City lies on the edge of the "Cajun country" of southwest Louisiana, a region settled by French Acadians who were driven out of Nova Scotia by the British in the eighteenth century after refusing to sign a loyalty oath. The elderly members of Gautreaux's family spoke Cajun French, a language distinct from the French spoken in Europe, and one with no dictionary nor written literature at the time; Gautreaux's father spoke Cajun French to converse with them. However, Louisiana families as well as government-run schools considered the language to be a source of shame, and young people were discouraged from learning it. Along with the English-language storytelling of the Gautreaux family males, the oral, Cajun French linguistic culture of the Gautreaux family elders can be seen as a direct influence on Gautreaux's oral narrative techniques of dramatic monologue, idiosyncratic dialogue, and action-laden plots. Gautreaux himself spoke English with a Cajun accent until he went away to college.

Gautreaux received his early education in parochial schools run by nuns of the Marionite order. Morgan City in the 1950s, he said in the *New Delta Review,* was so Catholic that even the waitresses would remind you of what day it was if you forgot and ordered a hamburger on a Friday. Lapsed or practicing Roman Catholics, priests, and themes of sin and confession and redemption appear frequently in his fiction, linking his work to that of two of his most admired Southern literary mentors, O'Connor and Walker Percy. He does not hesitate to identify himself as a Catholic writer.

After graduating in 1969 from Nicholls State University in Thibodaux, Louisiana, Gautreaux might well have gone on to teach high-school English or to open a machine shop or used-car lot, as he mused in *Voices of the Americas.* However, one of his Nicholls State English professors, impressed with the poems that Gautreaux had written in a creative-writing class, entered them in a contest sponsored by the Southern Literary Festival. Poet James Dickey was the keynote speaker at the con-

ference that summer in Knoxville, Tennessee, and when he read the prizewinning poems in the festival magazine, he offered Gautreaux a teaching assistantship to the Ph.D. program in English at the University of South Carolina. There Gautreaux met and married Winborne Howell, a master's degree student in American literature, whom he acknowledges to be the best critic of his draft writing. His 1972 dissertation was a volume of poetry titled "Night-Wide River."

Gautreaux's early training in poetry can be seen not only in the precision of his metaphors but also in his concentration on the line, and not the paragraph or scene, as the fundamental unit of his fiction. He makes up to five "passes" in revising his writing drafts, with each pass focusing on a single area such as word choice, imagery, or punctuation. As with the parts of a well-built machine, he is fond of stating, each line in a fictional work must contribute to the functioning of the whole narrative, and whatever seems extraneous gets cut. Not only must each line have a definable function, but—as with poetry—"every sentence becomes about capturing and holding attention," as he told the *New Delta Review* interviewer.

In 1972 Gautreaux and his wife moved to Hammond, Louisiana, where he was hired to teach English at Southeastern Louisiana University (SLU). Hammond lies about sixty miles north of New Orleans—significantly, for Gautreaux's fiction, well outside of the boundaries of "Cajun country," although the population there is also predominantly rural and working-class. Reviewers from outside of Louisiana tend to conflate the stories set in Acadiana (southwest and south-central Louisiana) with those set farther north, which is akin to believing that residents of Buffalo, New York, must speak with Brooklyn accents.

Teaching a heavy course load at an open-admissions state university in a state with notoriously high poverty and low literacy rates, Gautreaux had little time to write poetry during the next five years; he and his wife were also raising two sons, Robert and Thomas. Then, in 1977, Gautreaux learned that Percy was handpicking students for a novel-writing course to be taught at Loyola University in New Orleans. Gautreaux applied and was accepted; among his eight or nine classmates were Valerie Martin, who went on to achieve success as a novelist, and Walter Isaacson, the future managing editor of *Time* magazine. Percy's treatment of moral issues in his novels, Gautreaux has acknowledged, encouraged him to take up the same concerns in his own fiction, however unfashionable they might have seemed at the time. Prior to taking Percy's course, Gautreaux thought of himself as a poet, but afterward he set about honing his craft as a writer of fiction.

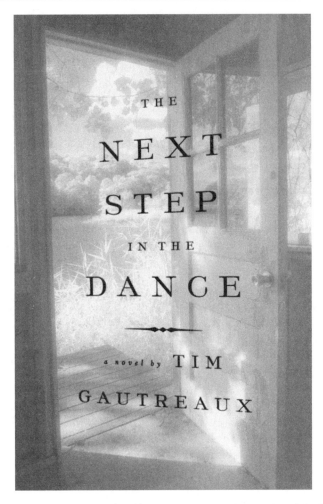

Dust jacket for Gautreaux's first novel (1998), about a small-town Cajun mechanic who follows his wife
to California to try to win her back (Richland County Public Library)

During the 1980s, Gautreaux wrote two "busted novels" that are now "sealed in Tupperware in the attic," as he proclaimed in private correspondence. He also published two short stories in *Kansas Quarterly* and *The Massachusetts Review*. During this time, Gautreaux was moonlighting from his teaching as a player-piano repairman, which took time away from his writing but, unlike writing, produced both income and acknowledgment of his craftsmanship. In the early 1990s he drafted a literary detective novel titled "Black Bayou," but he did not complete it. Its plot of an unscrupulous industry baron polluting the Louisiana landscape with toxic chemicals did, however, become a subplot of his first published novel, *The Next Step in the Dance* (1998).

While Gautreaux was struggling with the manuscript of "Black Bayou," his first short story broke through to a national audience. "Same Place, Same Things" appeared in *The Atlantic Monthly* in 1991 and

was collected in *Best American Short Stories of 1992* the following year. That little ripple of literary success was followed by a steady tide of accomplishments beginning three years later. "Waiting for the Evening News," a short story published in *Story,* won the 1995 National Magazine Award for fiction, and that same year "The Bug Man," originally published in *Gentleman's Quarterly,* was selected for *New Stories from the South: The Year's Best 1995.* Both stories were concerned with blue-collar Louisiana workers faced with difficult moral decisions. In "Waiting for the Evening News" a drunken train engineer flees the scene of a derailment he may or may not have caused, holing up in a New Orleans motel room to contemplate the inferno of the wreck and the manhunt for him on network TV news. Conversations with a low-key French Quarter priest ultimately convince him to take responsibility for the consequences of his actions and turn himself in: "When you throw a rock in a pond, you make ripples," the priest tells him.

In "The Bug Man" a Cajun pest-control man, who is witness to the literal and figurative messes that people and insect parasites make, cannot stop meddling in his clients' lives. He plays matchmaker to a lonely single man and single woman who rank far above him in social class, then tries to stop the woman from aborting the child of the failed relationship.

The following year St. Martin's Press brought out Gautreaux's first collection of short fiction, *Same Place, Same Things.* Among its twelve stories were the two that had won awards in 1995 and a third, "Little Frogs in a Ditch," that was included in both *New Stories from the South: The Year's Best 1997* and *Best American Short Stories 1997,* the latter guest-edited by E. Annie Proulx, one of the contemporary fiction writers Gautreaux most admires.

The qualities that characterize Gautreaux's first novel are evident, in miniature, in his debut collection. Reviewers praised his regional Louisiana details, his ear for dialogue, his swiftly rendered characterizations, his depictions of machines and their blue-collar operators, his humor and irony, his intricate plotting, and above all, his concern with morality, hope, and redemption. One critic for *Kirkus Reviews* (15 July 1996) called *Same Place, Same Things* "A terrific debut collection from a Louisiana writer whose stylish, sympathetic understanding of working-class sensibilities and Cajun culture gives his work a flavor and universality unique among contemporary writers."

Perhaps the story most reminiscent of O'Connor is the title piece. Set during the Depression years, it concerns a mysterious, itinerant pump repairman from Missouri who arrives at a drought-stricken Louisiana strawberry farm to fix a broken pump, only to find the farmer dead of electrocution in his field. Over the next few days the farmer's widow, hoping for a ticket out of the town and her dreary life, turns seductive, and the repairman nearly takes her up on it—until he discovers that her husband's death was not accidental. When he attempts to leave town without her, the widow stows away under the tarp of his truck, hits him over the head with his own wrench, and steals the truck and all of his tools. Although she has stolen the sources of his livelihood, she has not been able to steal the repairman's memories of his late wife and of their good marriage; in his capacity to love, not to earn a living, lies the hope of his redemption.

Typical of O'Connor, of course, are the 1930s Southern rural setting, the attractive traveling "mystery man," the sudden turn toward violence, and the hope of grace and transcendence. All Gautreaux's own, however, are the sharply etched Louisiana landscape, the natural dialogue ("'My McCormick won't throw no spark,' he said"), the female character who seems the embodiment of the word "toughness," the male character faced with a difficult moral decision, and the machines that seem to exude the presence and dignity of human characters: "He heard an International hit-and-miss engine fire once and then coast slower and slower through several cycles before firing again. . . . Across the road, a little McCormick muttered in a ditch. In the quiet night the engines fought the drought, popping like the musketry of a losing army." As Rand Richards Cooper put it in his 1996 review of the book for *Commonweal,* although Gautreaux shows traces of O'Connor's influence, his work is "a little less mordant, his humor more doleful than baleful."

In the fall of 1996 Gautreaux was appointed to the John and Renée Grisham Southern writer-in-residence position at the University of Mississippi. Although the appointment was for one semester only, it had the beneficial effect of frightening SLU officials into thinking that they might lose Gautreaux to another institution after twenty-five years of employment. Upon his return to Hammond, he was named writer-in-residence at SLU, and his teaching load was cut in half, from twelve hours to six. From that point forward, both his fictional output and his fame have accelerated markedly.

The Next Step in the Dance, Gautreaux's first novel, was published in 1998 by Picador USA, a division of St. Martin's Press. Although Gautreaux maintains that his work is not autobiographical and that each of his characters is normally a combination of traits from many different "real people," with fictional elements blended in, he has also admitted in *Voices of the Americas* that Paul Thibodeaux, the main character of his novel, is "the closest to how I feel about certain things." Paul, like Gautreaux, is a Cajun French Roman Catholic from a small Louisiana "oilpatch" town who is an expert dancer and mechanic.

Distressingly for Paul, his childhood sweetheart and now wife, Colette, has dreams of escaping the swamps of Louisiana for the lights of Los Angeles. Paul's great sin, in Colette's eyes, is that he is content with his simple life of fixing things and jitterbugging. "You work on those machines like they were people. You shoulda been a doctor," she tells him. In the *New Delta Review* interview, Gautreaux mused that "when men can't understand people, they relate to things they can understand, like mechanical devices. Maybe that's one of the reasons some men are so mechanical; other parts of life mystify them so much." Indeed, Paul's only insights into his wife's motives and behavior seem to come when he can compare her to a machine. Machines, in Gautreaux's writing, can stand for human beings at their most material, as mere

dark, smelling the enamel and tobacco latent in the air. A steam whistle shouted in mid-river as a steamer passed; he felt the amniotic movement of the *Newman* as the water sucked her away from the landing. When the hawsers drew tight, a pyramid of ironstone mugs chuckled once. The mill manager imagined the carnivorous swamp he was traveling toward, this new place he had seen only in photographs in *Lumber World Magazine*. He wondered how his brother, the smart brother with the best books in his head, the finest notions, was handling the mill saloon. He heard again the thump of the shotgun barrels on the skulls of the roustabouts, and he looked up to where the clerestories gathered first light spangling in their textured glass, sooty greens and golds flaring dim like fire seen through mica. The arch of windows at the front of the salon grayed off like lead, and there was light enough for him to go down on the foredeck and stand among the freight boxes and sacks and wait for his trunks. The first person he saw was the rouster who had been cut in the face. He was sitting back against a pile of rice sacks, making a sound like a running-down record. The mill manager raised a deck lamp off its hook and walked back among the crates. He was thinking that it would be a shame for the man to be ruined. He was not old and had years of work left in him.

He raised the light. "Is someone going to get a doctor for you?"

A pair of eyes opened, boiled eggs floating in a tabasco of pain. "Ain't one'll come."

Speck, the waiter, suddenly loomed at the mill manager's back. "You want me to carry these up to the depot on the dolly, sah?"

Randolph stooped down. "Do you have any alcohol and bandages on board?"

Speck sniffed. "Seem like some niggers done had enough alcohol."

"He needs some for the outside. And bring me a roll of gauze and a strip of salt meat from the galley." He looked up at Speck and could hardly see him but could smell his sour black uniform. "There'll be more than a dime under a plate."

"Sah," he said, turning for the staircase.

Typescript page, with revisions by Alfred A. Knopf editor Gary Fisketjon, for Gautreaux's 2003 novel,
The Clearing, *about a shell-shocked World War I veteran who becomes a lawman in Louisiana*
(courtesy of the author)

body parts programmed by DNA and neural chains, but also for the spiritual mysteries of grace and redemption. A *New Orleans Magazine* interviewer suggested to Gautreaux in 1998, without incurring objection, that his "recurring motif of machinery" could be viewed as "a parallel to Catholicism—the possibility of fixing things."

Things soon need fixing beyond Paul's expert skills when Colette abandons him to move to California. He follows her to Los Angeles with the hopes of winning her back, but despite a one-night reconciliation that leaves her pregnant, she proceeds with divorcing him. The increasing sadness of events is counterpointed by the humorous glimpses of California culture as viewed through a homesick Cajun's eyes. The latter device allows Gautreaux to contrast Paul's values of love, family, commitment, religion, tradition, honesty, and work for work's sake against the postmodern "values" of materialism and consumerism, a clash that is also symbolized by the opposition of Paul's used Ford sedan with Colette's new Mercedes.

When the oil industry collapses in Louisiana, destroying the economy of Paul and Colette's hometown, it becomes clear that there can be no going home again for the main characters, at least not to the way things used to be. But they do go home, separately, to a ruined landscape where even their old dance hall has been burned for the insurance money. In relating the catastrophic effects of the recession upon multiple generations of families and upon every element of the town's identity, from the bottle-denuded front window of the liquor store to the rafts of tugboats tied up idle along the river, Gautreaux demonstrates a broad-canvas narrative range toward which his short stories only hinted. "The novel's triumph," wrote *Booklist* reviewer Frank Caso (1 January 1998), "is its sense of community." Other reviews, equally positive, emphasized the "star-crossed lovers" theme and Gautreaux's rich evocation of Cajun culture. The novel won the 1999 Southeastern Booksellers Association "Novel of the Year" Award.

One year after the publication of his first novel, Gautreaux came forth with a second collection of short stories, *Welding with Children*. Archetypes recognizable from his first collection and from the novel populate these narratives as well: men who are good with machines, repairmen who cannot help meddling in their clients' lives, elderly grandfathers trying to parent the abandoned children of the "me generation," canny blue-collar Cajuns matching wits with academic poseurs, sociopaths preying upon the elderly, and kindly old priests wielding the power of forgiveness from sin. Absent, however, is the "hardhearted

woman" who stood as a foil to Gautreaux's sentimental men in the earlier works. The hardhearted women in these stories—like the ten-year-old daughter of neglectful parents who has a science-fair project due, or the woman who pretends to be a lesbian and African American to enhance her appeal to a university tenure committee—are putting on an act to mask their emotional vulnerability.

As in *The Next Step in the Dance,* the overarching theme of these stories is the return of the lonely or outcast individual to the shelter of community. At the end of the story "Good for the Soul," a parish priest looks out from his Sunday pulpit to spot the low-stakes sinner and nonchurchgoer Clyde Arcenaux, an elderly Cajun man now dying of emphysema, slumped in a pew: "He was asleep, pale, two steps from death, his head resting against the wall, but at least he had finally come inside."

For the first time, a few reviewers took issue with the craftsman-like plotting that had been praised in Gautreaux's first collection and in his novel. When plotting becomes too machine-like, too far from the randomness of life, it can appear contrived, and Gautreaux skates a thin line between intricacy and artifice. Whereas earlier reviews had been unanimous in praising Gautreaux's moral vision, a few now sensed undertones of moralizing or judgmentalism. Overall, however, the critical reception for *Welding with Children* was good. Gautreaux is "rapidly becoming a major American writer," declared *Kirkus Reviews* (1 August 1999), voicing the majority opinion. The collection was named a *New York Times* Notable Book of 1999.

The Clearing, Gautreaux's second novel, was published by Knopf in 2003. It marks a departure from his earlier fiction: it is set in the past, and the two main characters are Northerners. Once again, however, Gautreaux tackles the theme of an individual estranged from the community and the efforts of others to restore the broken bonds of human connection. In this case, the lost sheep is Byron Aldridge, the son of a Pittsburgh timber baron. Shell-shocked and despondent from the horrors of World War I, Byron has fled his future as the heir to his father's business and has gone into hiding from his family. But the father pays an investigator to track Byron down to a remote cypress swamp in Nimbus, Louisiana, where he is working as the constable for a rough-and-tumble logging operation. The senior Aldridge then sends his younger son, Randolph, to Louisiana to coax Byron back to the fold.

The task is not an easy one. Randolph must leave his bride, Lillian, and his comfortable Northern lifestyle behind and settle in for a long stay in the hot, humid, disease-ridden, alligator- and snake-infested mill town. Although Byron has married and is carrying out his law-enforcement duties, he seems interested only in listening to sentimental songs on a Victrola for hours on end, ostensibly to drive the refrains of patriotic songs from his memory. Eventually the birth of a child to Randolph's light-skinned black housekeeper, who has slept with both Aldridge brothers, and the murderous excesses of the Sicilian gang who run the only tavern in Nimbus combine to force Byron out of his alienated death-in-life state–but at great cost to Randolph.

Gautreaux's human-like machines take on sinister personality traits in this work. Developments in technology–the machine gun, poison gas, aerial bombing–have caused the mass slaughter of millions in World War I, and now a stand of cypress trees as old and magnificent as the California redwoods is falling prey to the forces of industrialism. When the so-called Last Tree is felled and sawn into boards, the mill-hands strip off their gloves and walk outside "like mourners leaving a funeral." Even the music Byron plays on his Victrola is not a symbol of spiritual longing but a substitute for human communication.

One review in *The New Yorker* (30 June 2003) likened Gautreaux to "some Bayou Conrad." Certainly the remote swamp setting, the search of one man for another who has lost his senses, and the moral ambiguities of the plot are meant to evoke Joseph Conrad's *Heart of Darkness* (1899). Unlike Conrad, however, Gautreaux believes in the redemptive power of love, and the moral choices for his characters are clearly delineated. "The alertness to good and evil is constant and you feel–almost–that language itself is a moral tool," observed a reviewer for *The Spectator* (4 October 2003).

A critic for *Publishers Weekly* (26 May 2003) stated that "Gautreaux is perhaps the most talented writer to come out of the South in recent years." With the publication of *The Clearing,* Tim Gautreaux has made a bid to be considered not only as a Southern and American writer but also as a world writer in the regionalist tradition of William Faulkner and Gabriel García Márquez.

Interviews:

Katie Bolick and David Watta, "A Conversation with Tim Gautreaux," *Atlantic Unbound* (14 March 1997) <http://www.theatlantic.com/unbound/factfict/gautreau/tgautr.htm>;

Elizabeth Arnold, "Best American Short Stories 1997: An Interview with Tim Gautreaux," National Public Radio, 15 December 1997, transcript 121504np.212;

Christina Masciere, "Novel Approach: Tim Gautreaux Takes *The Next Step,*" *New Orleans Magazine,* 32, no. 6 (March 1998): 31+;

Christopher Joyal, "An Interview with Tim Gautreaux," *New Delta Review,* 16, no. 1 (Fall/Winter 1998): 87–97;

Jennifer Levasseur and Kevin Rabelais, "Tim Gautreaux," *Mississippi Review,* 27, no. 3 (1999): 19–40;

Greg Langley, "Gautreaux Doesn't Need a Label Other Than 'Writer,'" *Baton Rouge Advocate* (10 October 1999): 11;

Julie Kane, "A Postmodernist Southern Moralist and Storyteller: Tim Gautreaux," in *Voices of the Americas,* edited by Laura Alonso Gallo (Cádiz, Spain: Aduana Vieja, forthcoming 2004).

Kaye Gibbons

(5 May 1960 –   )

Suzanne Disheroon-Green
Northwestern State University

BOOKS: *Ellen Foster* (Chapel Hill, N.C.: Algonquin Books, 1987; London: Cape, 1988);

How I Became a Writer: My Mother, Literature, and a Life Split Neatly into Two Halves: A Nonfiction Piece (Chapel Hill, N.C.: Algonquin Books, 1988);

A Virtuous Woman (Chapel Hill, N.C.: Algonquin Books, 1989; London: Cape, 1989);

Birth of a Baby, So Lovely (Chapel Hill, N.C.: Mud Puppy Press, 1990);

Family Life (Rocky Mount, N.C.: Wesleyan College Press, 1990);

A Cure for Dreams (Chapel Hill, N.C.: Algonquin Books, 1991);

Charms for the Easy Life (New York: Putnam, 1993; London: Abacus, 1994);

Sights Unseen (New York: Putnam, 1995; London: Virago, 1996);

Frost and Flower: My Life with Manic Depression So Far (Decatur, Ga.: Wisteria Press, 1995);

Pete and Shirley: The Great Tarheel Novel, by Gibbons, David Perkins, and others (Asheboro, N.C.: Down Home Press, 1995);

On the Occasion of My Last Afternoon (New York: Putnam, 1998; London: Virago, 1999);

Divining Women (New York: Putnam, forthcoming 2004).

RECORDINGS: *Charms for the Easy Life,* read by Gibbons, New York, Simon & Schuster Audioworks, 1994;

Sights Unseen, read by Gibbons, New York, Simon & Schuster Audioworks, 1995;

Ellen Foster, abridged, read by Gibbons, New York, Simon & Schuster Audioworks, 1996.

OTHER: "My Mother, Literature, and a Life Split Neatly into Two Halves," in *The Writer on Her Work, Volume II: New Essays in New Territory,* edited by Janet Sternburg (New York: Norton, 1991) pp. 52–60;

Kaye Gibbons (photograph © McIntyre Photography Inc.; from the dust jacket for On the Occasion of My Last Afternoon, *1998; Richland County Public Library)*

"It Had Wings," in *The Rough Road Home: Stories by North Carolina Writers,* edited by Robert Gingher (Chapel Hill: University of North Carolina Press, 1992);

"Ellen Foster's Christmas," in *Twelve Christmas Stories by North Carolina Writers: and Twelve Poems Too,* edited by Ruth Moose (Asheboro, N.C.: Down Home Press, 1997);

"The First Grade, Jesus, and the Hollyberry Family," in *Southern Selves: From Mark Twain and Eudora Welty to Maya Angelou and Kaye Gibbons: A Collection of Autobiographical Writing,* edited by James H. Watkins (New York: Vintage, 1998) pp. 70–82.

North Carolina writer Kaye Gibbons has overcome a great deal of adversity in her life: losing her mother to suicide; moving from one family member to another after her abusive father's death from alcoholism; suffering the effects of manic depression; and finding salvation from her ambivalent birth family, finally, in the care of a foster mother. Despite the challenges of her young life—or more likely because of them—Gibbons has developed into a writer with a distinctive voice. In her work, Gibbons delves into what she described to Liz Seymour in a 1999 *Book* magazine interview as "the extraordinary subterranean world that lies behind the action" of a story. Drawing heavily from her Southern background, as well as from her personal experiences, Gibbons is a writer who has, as Julian Mason has pointed out, successfully "taken the perseverance of the human spirit . . . for her continuing literary domain." Her firmly grounded sense of place, combined with believable and often heartrending characterizations, has won for Gibbons a significant readership.

Gibbons was born Bertha Kaye Batts on 5 May 1960 in the small rural community of Bend of the River, in Nash County, North Carolina. Her father, Charles Batts, was a tobacco farmer, and her mother, Alice, was a housewife. Kaye Batts and her siblings—a brother thirteen years her senior, and a sister nine years older—are descendants of the first permanent white settler in North Carolina, Nathaniel Batts. As the child of a farmer, Kaye Batts grew up in a poor family, residing in a frame farmhouse. She looked up to her mother; according to Mason, Alice Batts provided "order and stability through perseverance and hard work," serving as a role model to her young daughter. Kaye's childhood came to an abrupt end, however, when she was not quite ten years old: her mother committed suicide in March 1970. After staying with her abusive, alcoholic father for a brief period, Kaye went to live with her mother's sister but quickly found this arrangement unworkable, later describing the "various bizarre, kleptomaniac, hypochondriac, pathological-liar, sociopath relatives" among whom she was passed around until she "found a safe haven with a foster mother." These experiences, to some degree, inform the narrative that evolved into Gibbons's first novel, *Ellen Foster* (1987).

Kaye Batts graduated from Rocky Mount Senior High School in 1978, enrolled in classes at North Carolina State University on a partial scholarship, and later transferred to the University of North Carolina. But she left the university without taking a degree because of perpetual illnesses that plagued her eldest daughter. Batts had married Michael Gibbons while pursuing her degree, had three daughters, and also experienced a bout of severe depression that led to her first hospitalization.

During her matriculation at North Carolina State, Gibbons became familiar with the work of Louis Rubin, a renowned teacher and noted scholar of Southern literature. She became determined to study with Rubin, and upon enrolling in his class at the University of North Carolina in 1985, she found him to be a supportive mentor who encouraged her early creative-writing efforts. In fact, Gibbons wrote her first novel, *Ellen Foster,* as a result of Rubin's encouragement. She told Seymour that she trusted Rubin—"He doesn't lie"—so she decided to show him a poem that she had written from the point of view of an African American girl, who later became Ellen's friend Starletta. Rubin told Gibbons to go home and finish the work, and she presented him with a manuscript two months later. *Ellen Foster* was published by Algonquin Books, the publishing house that Rubin founded, in 1987.

Ellen Foster tells the story of a young girl with a background that shares many attributes with Gibbons's own. The novel opens with the ten-year-old Ellen sharing one of her earliest memories with the reader: "When I was little I would think of ways to kill my daddy . . . But I did not kill my daddy. He drank his own self to death the year after the County moved me out . . . All I did was wish him dead every now and then. And I can say for a fact that I am better off now than when he was alive." The story rapidly unfolds, demonstrating the truth of Ellen's matter-of-fact statements. Her mother, recently returned from a stay in the hospital as a result of her heart condition, is immediately set upon by her father, who demands that the gravely ill woman prepare an evening meal and hints with little subtlety that she should also tend to the weeds that have grown up in the yard. The mother—who is never given a name in the narrative beyond that of "my mama"—is soon overcome by her husband's drunkenness, his abuse, and his constant complaints and demands, so she swallows a nearly full bottle of her heart medicine. Ellen prepares to go to the local store to call a doctor, but since her father threatens to kill her mother and her if either of them leaves the house, Ellen is left with no alternative but to lie down next to her mother, offering what little comfort she can as her mother's heart slowly stops beating.

After her mother's death, Ellen remains with her father until she is removed from his custody and often escapes the threats posed by him and his

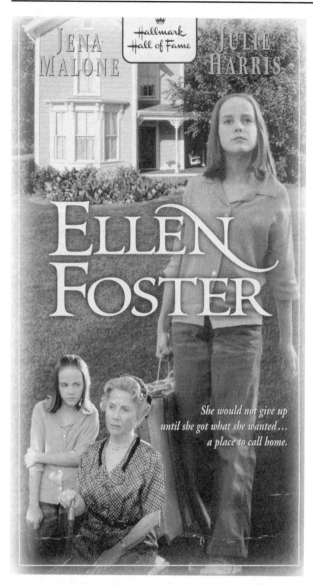

Cover for the home-video version of the 1997 television movie of Gibbons's first novel (1987), a semi-autobiographical story of a girl who builds a new life for herself after her abusive, alcoholic father drives her sickly mother to suicide (Richland County Public Library)

whiskey-drinking friends by going down the road to stay with her friend Starletta. The relationship between Ellen and Starletta is a complicated one, for although she is in many ways the only friend Ellen has until the end of the novel, Ellen looks down on Starletta and her family because they are black; she refuses, at first, to eat or use the bathroom at their house. As Ellen grows, she realizes that Starletta and her family are decent, caring people, while her father is nothing more than the "trash" that his sister-in-law calls him. Ellen lives for a time with her mother's sister, where she encounters a jealous female cousin who still wets herself on occasion.

Tiring of being treated like a poor relative and a burden, she contrives to remove herself from her aunt's home. Ellen becomes enamored of a woman who takes in children with nowhere else to go; she believes the woman's name to be Foster, not realizing that the "Foster" she keeps hearing associated with the woman has to do with her occupation rather than her surname. Unable to forge an identity of her own that satisfies her because of the separation and isolation she experiences, the best life that Ellen can envision for herself—and that she in fact actively covets—is that of a foster child.

By the end of the novel, Ellen has essentially placed herself in the foster home, and for the first time, she begins to feel that she is appreciated, wanted, and cared for. Much of the sense of security that the reader sees developing in Ellen is the result of the nurturing of Ellen's "new mama," and the fact that she not only allows Ellen to continue her friendship with Starletta but also opens her home to the girl, treating her like a welcomed guest when she comes to spend the night with Ellen. Despite the horrific events that Ellen endures in the course of her young life, she finally finds a place where she believes she may belong.

Ellen Foster demonstrates many of the themes that Gibbons has employed over the course of her career, including an individual's alienation from society and the ways in which class status serves to limit the choices available to individuals. The issue of alienation is one that Gibbons was well acquainted with as a girl, since she was the child of a poor, rural family and was further stigmatized by her mother's suicide. She has described the experience of trying to exist on the margins of her small, Southern community, telling Seymour, "Because of my childhood and being country-come-to-town I never fit in with any social group . . . But the thing about the South is that if you don't fit into one group, you can fit in anywhere. I think it's the peculiar situation of writers in the South that we can be part of the community and not part of the community at the same time." Inherent in this sense of alienation and separation based on class and background are issues of abuse that often accompany difficult financial situations and family relationships. In addition to her depictions of psychological abuse and its effects, especially on the young, Gibbons also examines the effects of mental illness on the family members who must coexist with a loved one suffering from such an affliction. She demonstrates the ways in which the mother-daughter relationship, specifically, may become fractured by circumstances that cannot be controlled by either woman, and the monumental effort that it requires to overcome the mistrust and fear that may color such relationships. Gibbons extends her examination of mother-daughter relationships into many of her works, demonstrating such relationships from a variety of perspectives.

In large part because of Gibbons's adept handling of such sensitive themes, critics were lavish in their praise of *Ellen Foster*. Eudora Welty called Gibbons a "stunning new writer . . . the honesty of thought and eye and feeling and word mark the work of this talented writer." Walker Percy praised the novel as the "real thing. Which is to say, a lovely, sometimes heart-wrenching novel" that is "as much a part of the back-woods South as a Faulkner character–and a good deal more endearing." Alice Hoffman, writing for *The New York Times Book Review* (31 May 1987), described the book as "filled with lively humor, compassion and integrity," suggesting that Ellen Foster is possibly "the most trustworthy character in recent fiction." Pearl K. Bell, in a review for the *New Republic* (29 February 1988), agreed with Hoffman's assessment:

> Ellen has a rare capacity for seeing through phonies and figuring things out, but Gibbons never allows us to feel the slightest doubt that she is only 11. . . . The voice of this resourceful child is mesmerizing because we are right inside her head. The words are always flawlessly right. . . . Ellen is an original who remains sweet and loving through the worst of times. Thus does Gibbons persuade us, as few writers can, that even a terrible childhood can be a state of grace.

The almost universally positive reception of *Ellen Foster* was not limited to published reviews; the novel was chosen in 1997 as a selection of the Oprah Winfrey book club, which led to the sale of nearly 800,000 additional paperback copies several years after its initial publication. In 1987 Gibbons was also awarded the Sue Kaufman Prize for first fiction from the American Academy and Institute of Arts and Letters and a citation from the Ernest Hemingway Foundation.

Gibbons's next fiction effort, *A Virtuous Woman*, appeared in 1989. Continuing Gibbons's emerging interest in issues raised by class and family, *A Virtuous Woman* focuses on the ways in which a young woman's choice of a husband–in this case, a low-class, money-seeking drifter impetuously chosen by the pampered daughter of a wealthy landowner–will devalue the woman's existence by lowering her to the level of the man with whom she associates herself. Ruby Pitt suffers just such a fate when she chooses to marry John Woodrow despite the fact that she knows her parents would strongly disapprove of the match. Woodrow rapidly shows himself to be greedy and resentful, verbally abusing Ruby for being spoiled, accusing her family of having raised her to believe she was "Little Miss Vanderbilt." Despite her husband's mistreatment, however, Ruby is too proud to return to her parents, carry-ing the burden of life as the wife of an abusive migrant worker with relative grace. After Ruby catches him engaged in an affair with a trashy woman with whom he has sired a child, Woodrow leaves Ruby; but three days after his departure, he sustains fatal injuries in a knife fight.

Much of the story of Ruby's disastrous first marriage is narrated after her death by her second husband, in an act of despair and grief as he attempts to recover from losing her. Shortly after Woodrow's death, Ruby agrees to marry Jack Stokes, another migrant farmworker who, in contrast to Woodrow, is hardworking, kind, and honest. In fact, when Ruby inherits a portion of her parents' estate upon their deaths, Jack refuses to move to the land because it does not belong to him.

Jack tries to give Ruby a good life and in many ways is a good husband to her. She quickly realizes that Jack is utterly dependent on her for his day-to-day needs. When she knows that her death from lung cancer–the result of a lifelong smoking habit–is imminent, she cooks and freezes enough meals to see Jack through the first months following her death, because she knows that otherwise, he will not eat. Jack views Ruby's actions as signs of love, and he sees her value as a person deriving from the ways in which she nurtures him. The tragedy of Ruby's life, however, is that neither of her husbands understands her or ever really knows her needs and desires. Ruby remains an unfulfilled woman, despite the kindness of her second husband, her affection for him, and her gratitude for his willingness to take care of her after the demise of Woodrow. Ruby's virtue comes not from having survived the trauma of her first marriage but from keeping her promises, accepting the consequences of her actions with dignity, and refusing to ask for help from others in the process.

In *The New York Times Book Review* (30 April 1989) Padgett Powell said of *A Virtuous Woman*: "This compact, complex novel is a somewhat stripped-down descendant of Faulkner's *As I Lay Dying*. . . . the architecture of this novel is remarkable." Roz Kavaney, reviewing the novel for *TLS: The Times Literary Supplement*, observed that it "has the simplicity of a good Country-and-Western song . . . *A Virtuous Woman* dares to do the ordinary thing, to transfigure the common-place into a plain language that speaks with as much complexity as the rococo might, but with more appropriateness." Marilyn Chandler, in *The Women's Review of Books* (July 1989) noted the disparity in the type and intensity of affection shared by Jack and Ruby:

> Gibbons' short novel about a dying woman and her husband's unhappy survival provides an unsentimental tribute to and reminder of the old virtues of loyalty, tol-

Dust jacket for Gibbons's 1995 novel, in which a girl narrates her mother's struggle with manic depression (Richland County Public Library)

for storytelling lasts to the moment of her death, leading her own daughter to describe her as "chattering like a string-pull doll. I had spent my life listening to her, sometimes all day, which often was my pleasure during snow and long rains. I would need only say to her, Tell me about your mother and you. . . . Tell me about the years that made you." Despite the fact that Lottie begins her married life greatly enamored with her husband, she soon comes to realize that he is not the gallant savior of whom she dreamed in her youth. Instead, he moves her away from her family to North Carolina, where he expects sixteen-year-old Lottie to work alongside him on the farm: "work and toil may have been my father's bloodtraits but he counted overmuch in the idea that my mother should care as much about making something from nothing as he did." The solid work ethic of Lottie's husband allows the family to experience a modest degree of financial success, even during the years of the Great Depression, but leaves the youthful Lottie feeling lonely. She soon "silently withdrew her affections" from her husband—a phrase that Gibbons is especially fond of using—and devotes her entire attention to the care and raising of her young daughter and to developing a cohesive community of women who share similar backgrounds and experiences. By the end of the novel, the reader has a sense that the ways in which the stories are told by Gibbons's narrators are as important as the narratives themselves.

If critics were less enthusiastic about *A Cure for Dreams* than they were about Gibbons's first two novels, it is perhaps because they had come to expect a fast-paced story from Gibbons. When confronted with a folksy narrative presented in a style that seemed a throwback to a nineteenth-century literary style, they were understandably jarred. However, as Tonita Branan argued in her essay "Women and 'the gift for gab': Revisionary Strategies in *A Cure for Dreams*," Gibbons creates a community in which women's stories and voices are privileged over men and their narratives. Rather than drawing on traditional Southern approaches to writing about small-town life, Gibbons uses women's voices to relate the events of this small, Depression-era town, demonstrating the transformations that may occur when women talk freely among themselves. Overall, the reviews that the novel received were positive. Josephine Humphreys remarked, in a review for *The Los Angeles Times* (19 May 1991), that the novel is "Full of unforgettable scenes and observations, characters drawn surely and sharply, and writing that is both lyrical and lightning-keen, this is a novel of vision and grace. It *shines*." Anne Tyler praised the novel in a review for the *Chicago Tribune* (24 March 1991), saying that: "When it comes to hearing and replicating the way

erance, compassion and forgiveness that are the real stuff of workable, if limited, partnerships. . . . The power of Gibbons' art lies largely in the remarkable tension she sustains between the simple language and categories available to these characters and the depth and magnitude of the feelings and questions they manage to evoke.

Like its predecessor, *A Virtuous Woman* was an Oprah Winfrey book-club selection in 1997.

A Cure for Dreams (1991) departs from the theme of abuse, delving instead into the intricacies of familial relationships and focusing specifically on the ways in which mothers and daughters relate to each other. Drawing from the long-standing Southern tradition of storytelling, Gibbons makes clear early in the novel that its central concern is the community of women that develops under the encouragement of the matriarch, Lottie O'Cadhain Davies. Lottie's stories are related by her daughter, Betty Davies Randolph, whose penchant

people speak, Kaye Gibbons has perfect pitch." Similarly, a reviewer for *Publishers Weekly* (25 January 1991) also remarked on Gibbons's well-deserved "reputation as a chronicler of small-town life in the South," pointing out that although the novel is a "series of loosely connected vignettes," they are "enlivened by Betty's tart comments and the pithy aphorisms of plain country folk." Doris Lynch, in a review for *Library Journal* (1 February 1991), credited Gibbons with having "captured magnificently the dailiness and sense of community of rural life . . . Gibbons's voice reveals life's truths."

Gibbons's first marriage ended, and in 1993 she married Frank Ward, an attorney. (This marriage ended in divorce by 2002). In her next novel, *Charms for the Easy Life,* published that same year, Gibbons continues her examination of women's communities and familial relationships, drawing upon women's traditions and the power of natural healing as strong subtexts to her primary narrative. The novel focuses on three generations of women: Charlie Kate, a healer and midwife; her daughter, Sophia; and her granddaughter, Margaret. The three women spend much of their lives under the same roof, sharing the trials and tribulations of daily living and building a life that is, for the most part, companionable, but marked by its absence of men. In her youth, Charlie Kate marries a ferry operator, who soon deserts her and her young daughter. Charlie Kate supports herself and the child through her unconventional medical practices and her willingness to deliver babies, even if her patients cannot pay. The Native American women indigenous to this rural area of North Carolina admire Charlie Kate's work as well: "grandmother continued to nurse people who lived across the river, and soon Indian women in the vicinity came to prefer her root cures to their own." By the time Sophia is old enough to begin to understand what Charlie Kate does for a living, many people in their community trust Charlie Kate's judgments of how to treat a particular illness over those of the formally educated and state-licensed physician.

Sophia and Charlie Kate share a relationship that could be described as tempestuous, in large part because Sophia feels that she must have a man in her life, even if it is the wrong man. Some critics, such as a writer for *Variety* (15 August 2002), suggested that the "primary drive of the story remains getting them matched up with men, who always seem to be of the proper class." While *Charms for the Easy Life* demonstrates one of Gibbons's recurrent themes–the unhappy consequences befalling women who choose, or settle for, the wrong man–to say that the book is only about women attempting to catch a man is misleading. Charlie Kate learns early in her life that an identity that is built around a man, around being his wife, is no kind of identity for a woman, as there is no surety or stability in it. Sophia, however, longs for a relationship with a man, and as a result of her haste suffers in her first marriage. Mother and daughter are frequently at odds over Sophia's choices, a situation that is not improved by Sophia's resentment of what she perceives as Charlie Kate's interference in her life. Margaret, in many ways, more closely resembles her grandmother than her mother. Whereas Sophia is disinterested in Charlie Kate's healing methods, Margaret is fascinated by them. While Sophia's interests lie in securing a husband, Margaret demonstrates more of an interest in self-improvement and in developing an identity of her own. The relationships among these three women lead to a substantial amount of conflict, but the conflicts result from loving, albeit stormy, relationships.

Critics received *Charms for the Easy Life* more warmly than its predecessor. Called a "touching picture of female bonding and solidarity" by a *Publishers Weekly* reviewer (11 January 1993), *Charms for the Easy Life* concerns a central theme in all of Gibbons's work: "Southern women who shoulder the burdens of their ordinary lives with extraordinary courage," as Bob Summer pointed out in a second *Publishers Weekly* review (8 February 1993). In the *Memphis Commercial Appeal* (28 March 1993) Frederic Koeppel remarked that "Gibbons has crafted this delicate balance of fear and confidence, reason and passion with exquisite deftness. Eccentricities and all, Charlie Kate, Sophia and Margaret are as believable and irresistible as any heroines in contemporary literature." Similarly, in *The New York Times* (11 April 1993), Stephen McCauley called the novel "haunting and beautiful," finding it "an evocative and gracious novel."

Gibbons's next book, *Sights Unseen* (1995), brings to the reader's mind some of the circumstances of Gibbons's own early life, as she relates the experiences of the young daughter of a mentally ill mother. Called by *Publishers Weekly* "Gibbons's best novel since *Ellen Foster,*" *Sights Unseen* demonstrates the destruction that a mental illness can wreak on an entire family. Young Hattie possesses a matter-of-fact voice similar to that of Ellen Foster; she reports similarly horrific events from the perspective of a preteen, albeit with less evidence of the toughness and presence of mind that sees Ellen through her hardships. The book opens with Hattie's stark thoughts on the treatment of the illness of her mother, Maggie, and despite Hattie's even tone, the fear and insecurity underlying her words are apparent:

Had I known my mother was being given electroconvulsive therapy while I was dressing for school on eight consecutive Monday mornings, I do not think I could

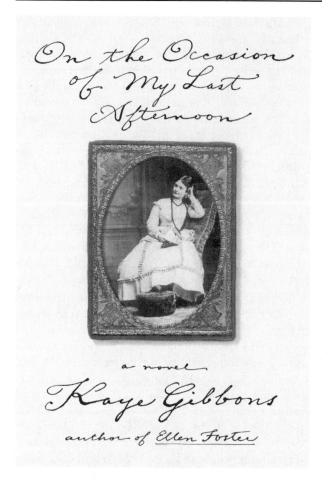

Dust jacket for Gibbons's 1998 novel, about a Virginia belle who marries a Yankee surgeon during the Civil War (Richland County Public Library)

have buttoned my blouses or tied my shoes or located my homework. . . . I was twelve, deemed too young to be told what was happening to her and in fact too innocent to surmise it.

The story progresses through Maggie's struggles to regain her sanity and her frequent slides back into mania. Maggie's difficulties are exacerbated by the fact that she lives in a small, Southern town in which everyone is aware of the actions of the neighbors; because of her often unseemly behavior, she becomes known as "the Barnes woman with all the problems." The never-ending pressure to conform, to behave appropriately to her position in the town, and to become well enough to care for her daughter, push Maggie into a complete breakdown on more than one occasion. Hattie's father is alternately resigned to and angered by Maggie's situation, and even when she has been successfully treated as an inpatient, allowing her to gain control of her illness, he is at first wary of believing that

the change is permanent. On one occasion he tells Hattie that, despite the fact that he is grateful for the respite Maggie's reestablished sanity allowed him,

> When she was home from the hospital . . . I would still have the same dream. I had the dream for months, the very one I had before she was hospitalized. . . . I go outside to see what's happening, and there she lies at the foot of the steps. They've pulled her out of the irrigation pond and brought her to me and just dropped her body there the way a cat deposits a mouse.

The trauma that Hattie's father suffers is indicative of that suffered by the family as a whole. But ultimately Maggie is able to stay sane: "There was never any more havoc, never any more terror in our house. Every day she tried to be well, the earnest way a child will try to be good on the days before Christmas. Only Mother was uniformly successful." Unlike Gibbons's mother, whose story ended far more bitterly, Maggie is able to overcome her illness, to remain stable, and to reestablish a relationship with her daughter, without recriminations or anger, and with catharsis serving as the reward for telling the difficult story.

Gibbons's efforts to make Maggie believable yet sympathetic are bolstered by her own experiences, but critic Gale Harris pointed out in a review for *Belles Lettres* (January 1996) that if Gibbons had provided "more narrative concerning the eventual reconciliation between Hattie and Maggie, readers might be able to develop greater affection and sympathy for the mother." Harris added that "the almost exclusive focus on Maggie's behavior in her manic states creates an alienating effect that is not alleviated by brief portraits displaying the other side of Maggie's character."

Called by the *Knight-Ridder News Service* (20 September 1995) an "unflinching portrait of a family's struggle with mental illness, of life with a mother so savaged by inner demons that she cannot be a parent," the book caught the literary world off guard. One critic for *The New York Times* (24 September 1994) praised Gibbons's "natural gift for telling stories," and a *Washington Post* reviewer argued that "there is something enduring, genuine, and original in Kaye Gibbons's work." A writer for *Kirkus Reviews* (1 June 1995) summed up the reaction to the book aptly, stating that Gibbons tells a "tale of exasperation and juvenile confusion mixed with unquestioning love. . . . Gibbons finds the perfect voice: manic behavior captured in beautifully modulated, tranquil prose." According to *Publishers Weekly* (5 June 1995), *Sights Unseen* is a "haunting story that begs to be read in one sitting," in large part because of the pathos that is implicit in the narrative itself.

Since the appearance of this novel, Gibbons has been quite open about her own battle with manic depression, and her efforts to share her condition with others has led to another autobiographical work, titled *Frost and Flower: My Life with Manic Depression So Far* (1995). In the interview with Seymour, she also discussed how her manic stages became part of the writing of her next novel, *On the Occasion of My Last Afternoon* (1998). In January 1998 she completely deleted a nine-hundred-page novel draft that had become too bogged down to salvage; but since Putnam was advertising her next novel as a summer release, she was determined to produce a book by March. As Seymour reports:

> The whole household reshaped itself around Gibbons' literary marathon. Mary, 14, Leslie, 12, and Louise, 10, would often come downstairs on a school morning to find their mother standing in the backyard with a coffee cup in her hand after an all-night writing session. "I had 300 pages of legal notes taped on the kitchen walls and cabinets and on the floor," says Gibbons. "To get to the coffeemaker in the morning my husband Frank had one little path." Dressed in a serviceable uniform of sweatshirt and sweatpants ("It was more time-effective to write than to bathe," she says) Gibbons sat up night after night on the kitchen stool with a laptop on her knees, tapping out [protagonist] Emma Garnet's story in bursts of chapters that she e-mailed off to New York as soon as they were done. Some days she would get no more than three or four hours of sleep; in one feat of endurance she stayed up for 65 hours straight.

Gibbons further explains: "I write best when I'm just a little bit manic—not full blown let's-go-out-and-buy-500-pairs-of-red-shoes manic, but enough so that I see connections, and images come to me." But she acknowledges that it is "a very dangerous game," and finishing this novel took its toll: "I feel like writing that book blew some pistons and rods. . . . I will never do that to my body again."

On the Occasion of My Last Afternoon is set during the Civil War era on a plantation in Tidewater Virginia. The novel tells the story of Emma Garnet Tate Lowell, the daughter of a wealthy intellectual with the morals of a Dorian Gray. Samuel Tate, Emma Garnet's father, is the product of a poor household but educates himself extensively and discovers a personal penchant for art and literature; he then sets his sights upon ascending the ranks of the Southern aristocracy. After making his fortune under dubious circumstances, he marries the daughter of a well-known and equally well-respected family in order that he might capitalize socially on his association with the family. Given the Southern hierarchy of the time, only one reason exists that would allow a man like Tate, who lacks family name, honor, and integrity, to marry into an old aristocratic family. The family is land rich but extremely cash poor, and in a transaction not uncommon during the antebellum era,

they sell their daughter in marriage to the man who can save their financial necks.

Emma Garnet's refined and gentle mother suffers mightily under the tyranny of her husband, watching him abuse his slaves and treat everyone around him with disdain. However, she devotes herself to her children, Emma Garnet, her elder son, Watley, and two younger daughters. When Emma Garnet decides to marry Quincy Lowell, a Yankee surgeon with whom she falls deeply in love, her mother supports her, despite her father's threats to disown her. Emma Garnet leaves with her husband, setting up housekeeping with him in North Carolina with the able assistance of a family servant who loves Emma Garnet like her own child. Her marriage takes her away from her horrid father but also forces her to leave her mother. Mrs. Tate dies not long after Emma Garnet's marriage, ostensibly because of poor medical care and an ignorant doctor, but Gibbons strongly suggests that the basis of Mrs. Tate's illness is a pervasive loneliness, since both of her children have left home.

When the Civil War breaks out, the Lowells spend their time tending to wounded, with Quincy acting as surgeon and Emma Garnet working as his nurse. During the war years, Emma Garnet gives birth to three daughters, with whom Quincy cannot spend much time because of the demands of his wounded patients. As the war ends, Emma Garnet and Quincy have an opportunity to establish a cohesive family, but this hope is cut short when Quincy dies unexpectedly, having literally worked himself to death during the war. Emma Garnet is devastated by this turn of events, but she is sustained by the support of her sister, with whom she has come to an understanding over the years, and Clarice, the free woman of color who, out of love, stays with the Lowells until her death.

The narrative is bracketed as the remembrance of an elderly woman just before her death; Emma Garnet recounts her early life and marriage as if she were watching her life pass before her for inspection. Gibbons draws on her now-familiar themes of family, the strength that can be derived from women's communities, and the ways in which people survive trauma, both individually and collectively. *On the Occasion of My Last Afternoon* is also in many ways a book about memory—the ways in which memories are constructed, the reliability of those memories, and the influence that memories have on the ways that an individual develops as a person. As with *Charms for the Easy Life,* Gibbons draws on nineteenth-century literary traditions, as well as Southern cultural traditions, to lend veracity to her story.

Critics offered mixed opinions of *On the Occasion of My Last Afternoon.* While Gibbons's mastery of the historical-novel form won praise, Jane Fisher, in a review for *America* (2 January 1999), remarked that the novel suffers from a "lack of narrative suspense, due mainly to the depiction of a life already completed, which dispenses with the openness and sense of future possibilities so often found in her works." Nonetheless, Fisher called *On the Occasion of My Last Afternoon* a "lively and readable novel" that "becomes more interesting when read in conjunction with Gibbons's other novels or against the background of the ongoing American obsession with race, status, and truth." Joanna M. Burkhardt, in a review for *Library Journal* (15 September 1999), stated that Gibbons "relates a touching, evocative story with crystal clarity and brilliant realism." Donna Seaman of *Booklist* (15 May 1998) pointed out that Gibbons "has evolved a distinctive narrative style based on the poignant eloquence and acuity of young female narrators struggling to transcend the moral and spiritual failings of their troubled families." A reviewer for *Booklist* (20 April 1998) noted the political significance of the novel as well: "A plea for racial tolerance is the subtext of Gibbons's estimable new novel, her first foray into historical fiction." *On the Occasion of My Last Afternoon* garnered award nominations from the Northern California Independent Booksellers Association and the SEBA Books Awards. The novel was also named a Notable Book of the Year in 1998 by *The New York Times*.

Kaye Gibbons is an author who has come of age at the opening of a new century, and her work is indicative of themes that will continue to intrigue writers in the twenty-first century. Gibbons looks at difficult issues squarely and depicts them with her brand of reality. Whether showing the ways in which women's communities can serve to bolster women's sense of self-identity and self-worth, or offering a different perspective on abuse, mental illness, or historical events, Gibbons has already proven herself to be an influential novelist of the new century.

Interviews:

Bob Summer, "Kaye Gibbons: Her Fourth Novel Brought Unexpected Challenges to This Southern Writer," *Publishers Weekly* (8 February 1993): 60–62;

Shirley Marie Jordan, "Kaye Gibbons," in *Broken Silences: Interviews with Black and White Women Writers* (New Brunswick, N.J.: Rutgers University Press, 1993), pp. 65–82;

Dannye Romine Powell, "Kaye Gibbons," in *Parting the Curtains: Interviews with Southern Writers* (Winston-Salem, N.C.: J. F. Blair, 1994), pp. 115–132;

Liz Seymour, "Kaye Gibbons—Making It Up As She Goes Along," *Book* (May/June 1999) <http://www.book magazine.com/archive/issue4/gibbons.shtml>;

Jan Nordby Gretlund, "'In My Own Style': An Interview with Kaye Gibbons," *South Atlantic Review*, 65, no. 4 (2000): 132–154;

Seymour, "Oh, Kaye!" *Book* (November/December 2002).

References:

Tonita Branan, "Women and 'the gift for gab': Revisionary Strategies in *A Cure for Dreams*," *Southern Literary Journal*, 26 (1994): 91–101;

Julian Mason, "Kaye Gibbons," in *Contemporary Fiction Writers of the South: A Bio-Bibliographic Sourcebook*, edited by Joseph M. Flora and Robert Bain (Westport, Conn.: Greenwood Press, 1998), pp. 156–168;

Sharon Monteith, "Between Girls: Kaye Gibbons' *Ellen Foster* and Friendship as a Monological Formulation," *Journal of American Studies*, 33, no. 1 (1999): 45–64.

Elizabeth Gilbert

(1969 –)

D. Mesher
San José State University

BOOKS: *Pilgrims* (Boston: Houghton Mifflin, 1997; London: Picador, 1998);
Stern Men (Boston: Houghton Mifflin, 2000; London: Picador, 2000);
The Last American Man (New York: Viking, 2002).

SELECTED PERIODICAL PUBLICATIONS–
UNCOLLECTED: "Buckle Bunnies," *Spin,* 10 (September 1994): 78–82, 154;
"The Muse of the Coyote Ugly Saloon," *GQ,* 67 (March 1997): 252–257;
"Eustace Conway Is Not Like Any Man You Know," *GQ,* 68 (February 1998): 176–183;
"Chicks with Decks," *GQ,* 70 (August 2000): 164–169, 189–191;
"The Ghost," *GQ,* 70 (December 2000): 304–311, 346–349;
"My Favorite Martian," *GQ,* 71 (March 2001): 330–335.

Elizabeth Gilbert (photograph © Jerry Bauer; from the dust jacket for Stern Men, *2000; Richland County Public Library)*

When Elizabeth Gilbert's first story, "Pilgrims," was published in 1993, the editors at *Esquire* subtitled it "The Debut of an American Writer." A decade into her professional writing career, her diverse résumé included short fiction, a novel, creative nonfiction, drama, and journalism–and the awards she has garnered include several prizes for best new fiction writer, a National Magazine Award, and a nomination for a National Book Award. Whatever the genre, however, there is a consistency of theme and subject matter in almost all of Gilbert's writing: hers is a distinctive voice in contemporary American letters, mixing antisocialist working-class heroes with antiliberal frontier values, in service of a feminism that is anything but antimale.

Gilbert was born in Waterbury, Connecticut, in 1969, and raised outside of nearby Litchfield. Many of the specific details of her biography are kept private. She is the daughter of John Gilbert, a chemical engineer, and Carole Gilbert, a nurse; the family also farms Christmas trees at their isolated country home, and as a child Gilbert lived without conveniences such as televi-

sion. Not surprisingly, that upbringing influenced her early writings, not only in her occasionally remote settings but also in her patent distrust of the creature comforts of American life and those who enjoy them.

Gilbert majored in international relations at New York University. After graduating, she financed trips of exploration across the United States and abroad by working in a Philadelphia diner. "Everything I did in my twenties was with an eye toward creating experiences to write about, gathering landscapes and voices," Gilbert told Frank Bures for a 2002 profile in *Poets & Writers;* "I went West for the same reason I worked at a diner and in bars, the same reason I talked to every single person: just to learn." Gilbert's apprenticeship in human experiences began to pay off when, in 1993, *Esquire* published "Pilgrims," set in Wyoming. Gilbert managed to parlay that story into a three-year stint as a staff writer for *Spin* magazine, where her first piece was about rodeo groupies known as "Buckle Bunnies." The success of her journalism at *Spin* helped land Gilbert a position as writer-at-large for *Gentlemen's Quarterly (GQ)* beginning in 1997. Her first article for *GQ*, "The Muse of the Coyote Ugly Saloon," was based on her own turn as a waitress at that New York establishment shortly after she came back from Wyoming; it became the inspiration for the 2000 motion picture *Coyote Ugly*.

Gilbert's best journalism often focuses on barrier-breaking situations, such as challenging the male bastion of high-stakes professional poker in "Chicks with Decks" (2000), or on individuals with a sense of originality that has placed them beyond the bounds of middle-class America, such as cult science-fiction figure Forrest Ackerman in "My Favorite Martian" (2001) or country-music bad boy Hank Williams III in "The Ghost" (2000). The last piece won a National Magazine Award and was anthologized in *Best American Writing 2001*.

Shortly after she began writing for *GQ*, Gilbert published her first book, a volume of stories collected under the title *Pilgrims*. Reviewing the collection for *The Boston Globe* (12 October 1997), Robert Taylor found elements of Gilbert's prose style rooted in her journalism: "Many of her nonfiction strengths carry over: She draws her characters beautifully, and her sentences are sharp and bright." In addition to the *Ploughshares* prize, *Pilgrims* won "first fiction" awards from *The Paris Review* and *The Southern Review* and was a finalist for the PEN-Hemingway Award. Several of the stories in *Pilgrims* were also brought to the stage in 2001, under the same title, by the Water Theatre Company, adapted and directed by Shira Piven, for two runs at the Tribeca Playhouse in New York, the second with the backing of Mike Nichols.

In her short fiction Gilbert eschews the surprise or ironic ending championed by O. Henry—a technique that has become increasingly predictable and artificial in the postmodern period. Without the contrived cleverness of that technique, however, Gilbert's short fiction seems more often to fade out than to climax, working best when the absence of any final closure operates to enhance the central elements of the story. In "Elk Talk," for example, the first story in *Pilgrims* after the title tale, Jean and her young nephew, Benny, are spending the weekend alone at their remote Wyoming cabin while Jean's husband, Ed, who works for the Fish and Game Department, travels to Jackson to give a talk on poaching. The sense of isolation Jean prizes is disrupted by a family of refugees from urban life, who

have moved into a camper a half-mile down the road. The dangerousness of that family—L.D., Audrey, and their daughter, Sophia—is suggested when they first appear in the story, driving recklessly enough on the dirt road to force Jean to swerve off into the underbrush. Later, at Jean's cabin, the uninvited L.D. and Audrey expect to be greeted with hospitality, as if Jean, who has chosen to live miles from the next house, ought to be excited about having new neighbors.

The self-centeredness apparent in the expectations of L.D.'s family and in his driving is confirmed by the central incident of the story, in which L.D. uses a mating call to attract three moose, including a bull, out of the woods, catching all five characters in exposed positions, too far from the safety of Jean's cabin. L.D. and Audrey, naive urban-dwelling lovers of an unrealistic, romanticized nature, have no idea of the danger in which they have put themselves, Jean, and the two children. After the moose finally wander off without doing any harm, Audrey turns to Jean and says, "Have you ever . . . in your entire life felt so privileged?" What Jean feels, in fact, is anger and a sense of having been manipulated. The story ends with Jean wishing, "briefly, that her husband was with her, a thought she immediately dismissed on the grounds that there were already far too many people around."

That last line fails to create the same level of finality provided by the ironic reversals with which so many earlier American stories conclude. Yet, the lack of closure accurately portrays Jean's situation. Her life has been disturbed by the type of unthinking, liberal, formally educated but worldly ignorant, middle-class boors that Gilbert loves to pillory in her fiction, and any suggestion of an easy solution for Jean's anger would only undercut it. Instead, Gilbert ends "Elk Talk" on an almost digressive note, leaving the central issues of the story unresolved. Conclusions without closure are common in Gilbert's work; other stories with endings that flatline instead of spike include "Bird Shot" and "At the Bronx Terminal Vegetable Market." But the ending of "Elk Talk" does manage to suggest not only Jean's continuing frustration but also a sense of the traditional frontierswoman's self-reliance.

More controversial than the endings of Gilbert's fiction is her fondness for politically incorrect humor. Typically, such humor appears in the conversations of those rural, working-class characters that Gilbert prefers over the usually urban, middle-class antagonists of her stories. The confrontation between working-class heroes and middle-class interlopers is not presented as class warfare in any direct sense, since the two groups usually have little or no economic relationship. Instead, the occasionally self-congratulatory, often contradictory, and always oversimplified values of liberal, middle-class America–moral, social, sexual, political, and environmental–are the targets of Gilbert's stylized redneck humor and satiric attacks.

A third feature of Gilbert's fiction is her use of misdirection as both theme and narrative technique. Thus, "The Many Things That Denny Brown Did Not Know," one of the more experimental narratives in the collection, actually turns out, in the last paragraph, to concern things that Denny's friend Russell Kalesky did not know about Denny Brown. And "Come and Fetch These Stupid Kids," which seems to be about the dangerous decision of an aimless group of college friends to go for a swim during a summer-ending storm, ends not with the death by drowning of Peg and Margie, caught out beyond the breakers, but with Peg's realization that her boyfriend, J.J., will hate her. He might swim out to save them or he might telephone the coast guard, but "it didn't matter what he decided, because he would hate Margie and Peg either way. Whatever he decided, he would certainly hate them for it. . . . Peg hated J. J. for standing on the beach while she herself got dragged out deeper to sea. She hated him for being a strong swimmer. She hated him for wondering what to decide and for catching his breath, and she hated him (most of all) for hating her." Stopping the story short of Peg's impending death removes the possibility of closure and allows Gilbert to suggest that Peg has been drowning, in figurative ways, all along.

Gilbert's first novel, *Stern Men* (2000), continued Gilbert's fascination with self-reliant workingmen and with women who challenge traditional gender roles, in a story about the isolated, dangerous, and impoverished lives in the Maine lobster fishery. *Stern Men* takes place on two small Maine islands, Fort Niles and Courne Haven–the fictional geography of which "closely resembles that of Vinalhaven and North Haven," according to John Robinson of the *Portland Press Herald* (18 June 2000). The lobster fishermen on the islands are engaged in a long-standing battle over fishing rights in the surrounding waters. The novel shares many of the qualities of her short fiction: Ruth Thomas, the protagonist, is a more complex and more realized version of Gilbert's earlier headstrong but insightful female characters; the politically incorrect humor is supplied by the lobstermen, especially the rude Angus Addams; and the ending, which avoids addressing some of the issues the novel has raised, offers a curious reconciliation of sorts between Ruth and Lanford Ellis, a rich, elderly man who has manipulated her with the same paternalism that generally marks his relations with the other island residents.

While an American novel about any fishery might, eventually, be compared to *Moby-Dick* (1851), the use of the lobster industry in *Stern Men* seems to be much more reminiscent of later works such as Graham Swift's novel of the English Fens, *Waterland* (1983), and E. Annie Proulx's Pulitzer Prize–winning novel set in Newfoundland, *The Shipping News* (1993). Despite chapter epigraphs from such suitably antiquated sources as William B. Lord's *Crab, Shrimp, and Lobster Lore* (1867) and Francis Hobart Herrick's *The American Lobster: A Study of Its Habits and Developments* (1895), Gilbert fails to convert historical and professional information about the fishery into striking symbols and metaphors, as do Herman Melville and Swift.

Although the title suggests both the hired hands who work in the stern of a lobster boat as well as the attitude of the males with whom Ruth must deal on the islands of Fort Niles and Courne Haven, *Stern Men* is really about Ruth Thomas's personal and family problems–problems that are, at best, tangentially related to lobsters and the men who trap them. In the novel, a lobster "sternman" tends to be a teenage helper, often immature or incompetent, usually despised and mistreated by the boat owner, and thus not a stern man at all. Nor are the other men notably stern. Chief among them is Ruth's father, Stan Thomas, who says to her repeatedly, "I don't care who you spend your time with." Stan's purported indifference to his daughter's behavior is, in many ways, central to the novel, since it serves to connect one of Ruth's main problems–her relationship with her parents–to the larger history of the two islands. Stan is bitter because Ruth's mother, Mary, has left him and returned to work for Vera Ellis. Vera and her brother, Lanford, who continues to summer on Fort Niles, are the last generation of a mainland family who once exploited the islands for their granite deposits, leaving the deep scars of abandoned quarries behind. Ruth's grandmother had been adopted into a kind of servitude to Vera, making her at once a stepsister and an unpaid employee; Ruth's mother was raised to fulfill that same function, from which she escaped to marry Stan, and to which she returned after the birth of Ruth's severely deformed brother, Ricky.

In an interview with Daphne Uviller of *Newsday*, Gilbert traces Ruth's character to two rather different antecedents: the Book of Ruth and Henry James's *Portrait of a Lady* (1881). Like her biblical namesake, Ruth cleaves to a surrogate mother, neighbor Mrs. Pommeroy; unlike James's Isabel Archer, Ruth avoids a tragic ending. According to Gilbert, "Ruth is sort of a redeemed Isabel Archer. . . . Isabel is ruined, but I couldn't do that to Ruth. I had to leave her triumphant." In the novel, to reject the Ellis claim on her, Ruth feels she must assert her Fort Niles connection: "It was important to Ruth in principle that she feel happy on Fort Niles, although, for the most part, she was pretty bored there." But she cannot alienate the Ellises com-

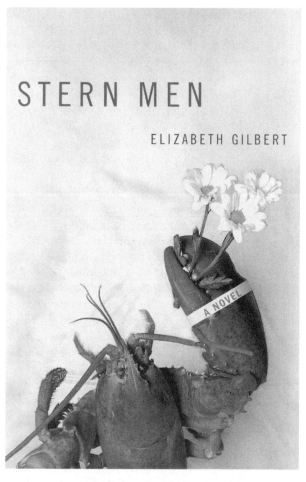

Dust jacket for Gilbert's 2000 novel, about a woman who ends a long-standing feud between lobstermen on two small neighboring islands off the Maine coast (Richland County Public Library)

receives–the Ellises' holdings on Fort Niles as, she tells Lanford, "restitution to my family for the lives of my mother and my grandmother. And for my life, too." Such indemnification would be meaningless, however, without Ruth's personal sense of liberation.

This outcome might seem a happy ending, were it not disturbed by a revelation Ruth receives prior to that exchange, when Lanford tells Ruth that her decision to "stay here and organize these islands" was precisely his intention in controlling the way she was raised and educated. Ruth clearly understands the implications:

> *Big deal,* she thought. So he'd been manipulating her whole life. He'd manipulated the life of everyone he had sway over. It was no surprise, really; in fact, it was edifying. And in the end–*what of it?* Ruth came to this conclusion rapidly and with no fuss. She liked knowing at last what had been going on all these years. There are moments in a person's life when the big understanding arrives in a snap, and this was such a moment for Ruth Thomas-Wishnell.

The idea that Ruth should put her victimization behind her and get on with her life is probably part of the political incorrectness of so much of Gilbert's fiction. Nor does it hurt that Ruth's "restitution" demand not only will allow her to share in the Ellises' wealth but also will free her from any further influence, since they will be banished from Fort Niles. Nevertheless, Lanford's manipulations and Ruth's quick reconciliation–she kisses "the old dragon right on the forehead" in the last line of the novel–mean that the novel ends with a sense that, at least in this case, such paternalism is not only acceptable but in some way endearing.

The complexity of that ending notwithstanding, Ruth Thomas is a wonderfully realized character, and certainly the best expression of Gilbert's unconventional and innovative insights into contemporary women's roles. Describing one of the honors the novel has received, Florence Shinkle wrote in the *St. Louis Post-Dispatch* (18 April 2001) that "Elizabeth Gilbert has won what you hope will be the first annual Kate Chopin Literary Award, given to the author of a female character who 'best exemplifies the spirit of Chopin's heroine Edna in going beyond the boundaries of cultural expectations to claim a life on her own terms.'" Gilbert herself, in St. Louis to accept the award from the Kate Chopin Society, compared her protagonist to Edna Pontellier from Chopin's *The Awakening* (1899): "Edna drowns herself in the sea. A century later, Ruth kind of comes out of the sea, forms her life out of it. You could say she lives as a redemption to that previous woman. It took a century, but she found a way to make it all work."

pletely, because her mother works for them and because they not only provide care for Ricky but also paid for Ruth's education at an exclusive boarding school.

By the end of the novel, Ruth has almost single-handedly rewritten the history of the islands by fostering trust and community in the place of suspicion and enmity. She does so first by marrying into the Wishnells, the dominant family on rival Courne Haven. Her romantic attachment to Owney Wishnell, who is quiet to the point of passivity but a prodigious lobsterman, prompted Ron Charles, reviewing *Stern Men* for the *Christian Science Monitor* (20 July 2000), to describe the novel as "'Romeo and Juliet' with a Maine drawl and a much happier ending."

Ruth also brings peace in a more public way, by creating a successful cooperative that ends a century of always wasteful and sometimes deadly feuds between individual lobstermen as well as the whole islands. Unlike the childless Ellises, who represent barren exploitation, Ruth gives birth to a son and then demands–and

Gilbert's cast of quirky characters earned praise from John Stickney, who in a review for the Cleveland *Plain Dealer* (2 July 2000) described *Stern Men* as a "skilled portrait" of "an eccentric community." Not as successful as her best short fiction, the novel nevertheless suggests its author's considerable range and inventiveness. "Sophisticated yet ribald, comic yet serious," according to *Kirkus Reviews* (1 March 2000), *Stern Men* is "an exceptional debut from a writer to watch." A critic for *The San Francisco Chronicle* (9 July 2000) termed the work a "sometimes howlingly funny first novel."

Gilbert followed *Stern Men* with *The Last American Man* (2002), a nonfiction study that attempts to shed new light on the history of the American pioneering spirit by examining the life of a contemporary frontiersman, Eustace Conway, whom Gilbert first profiled in a 1998 magazine article. The product of a contemporary middle-class suburban upbringing, Conway rejected those values and adopted the lifestyle of an isolated, self-reliant frontiersman, living off the land in the Carolina mountains. He began running a camp to teach backwoods skills and values and proselytizing among the nature-starved urban dwellers of America. In *The Last American Man* Gilbert examines not only the troubled origins of Conway's personal quest but also the equally troubled origins of American frontier history and the men who made it. As Gilbert explained in an interview with Alex Chadwick for National Public Radio, "we have this kind of idea of American masculinity and manhood that's built up on these 19th century ideals about the frontier and about being a pioneer and a cowboy and standing tall in the saddle and mending fences and striking a claim. We still use that vocabulary in American culture. But with Eustace Conway, when you use that vocabulary, it's literal."

The Last American Man continues the exploration of ideas familiar from Gilbert's earlier journalism and fic-tion, but does so in a more accomplished and consistent manner, as its nomination for the National Book Award for nonfiction suggests. As Heather Hewitt described it for *The Christian Science Monitor* (9 May 2002), "Gilbert examines America's ongoing infatuation with the frontier and leaves no stone unturned in her exploration of the cultural landscape of masculinity." The similarities between author and subject also were not lost on reviewers. Janet Maslin, for example, writing in *The New York Times* (3 June 2002), made the point that "Gilbert is clearly, almost boastfully, one of Mr. Conway's tough kindred spirits," and that, in her writing, the author "treads as thin a line between honesty and self-conscious myth making as Mr. Conway does."

In *The Last American Man* Gilbert contends that "the history of Eustace Conway is the history of man's progress on the North American continent"—a notion that suggests Gilbert also sees fictional protagonists such as Ruth Thomas and her father in *Stern Men* and Jean in "Elk Talk" as embodying core American values that have become lost in the empty affluence of modern America. Fervent in those convictions, Elizabeth Gilbert may soon earn a place among the important American novelists of the early twenty-first century.

Interviews:

Daphne Uviller, "Talking with Elizabeth Gilbert: A Fishy Tale," *Newsday* (2 July 2000): B11;

Alex Chadwick, "Elizabeth Gilbert Discusses Her New Book, *The Last American Man,*" *Morning Edition,* National Public Radio, 13 May 2002.

Reference:

Frank Bures, "In Search of the Last American Man: A Profile of Elizabeth Gilbert," *Poets & Writers* (May/June 2002): 32–39.

David Guterson

(4 May 1956 –)

Jeffrey F. L. Partridge
Central Connecticut State University

BOOKS: *The Country Ahead of Us, The Country Behind* (New York: Harper & Row, 1989; London: Bloomsbury, 1996);

Family Matters: Why Homeschooling Makes Sense (New York: Harcourt Brace Jovanovich, 1992);

Snow Falling on Cedars (New York: Harcourt Brace, 1994; London: Bloomsbury, 1995);

East of the Mountains (New York: Harcourt Brace, 1999; London: Bloomsbury, 1999);

Our Lady of the Forest (New York: Knopf, 2003).

SELECTED PERIODICAL PUBLICATIONS–
UNCOLLECTED: "Northwest Passage: The San Juans," *New York Times,* 15 May 1994, VI, Part 2: 34;

"Apples," *Granta,* 54 (Summer 1996): 125–142.

David Guterson gained a reputation through his first two novels for poignant, elegiac prose, morally rooted subject matter, carefully researched details, and, perhaps most of all, a sense of place. Guterson considers himself a "traditional" novelist, and he often eschews the description of postmodern fiction writer in interviews. His first novel, *Snow Falling on Cedars* (1994), "runs counter to the post-modern spirit," as he told Ellen Kanner of *BookPage* (January 1996). Guterson suggests that "Post-modernism is dead because it didn't address human needs. The conventional story endures because it does." Guterson's embrace of the "traditional" story can be traced back to his university years, when he found himself particularly drawn to Russian writers such as Leo Tolstoy, Anton Chekhov, and Ivan Turgenev. He explained to Bill Donahue in a 2000 interview for *Book* magazine that "stories will always matter–stories that present human beings in crisis, deciding how to confront their struggles, how to be fully human. Stories deliver us the heroes of the common people. Without them, we wouldn't have culture. We wouldn't know who we are." Guterson's fiction is rooted in a storytelling tradition, in a definable moral universe, and in a physical space.

David Guterson (photograph by Jill Sabella; from the dust jacket for Snow Falling on Cedars, *1994; Richland County Public Library)*

David Guterson was born in Seattle, Washington, on 4 May 1956. His father, Murray Guterson, is a criminal-defense lawyer whose expertise and moral character later provided the model for the fictional Nels Gudmundsson, the aged defense attorney in *Snow Falling on Cedars.* Murray Guterson and his wife, Shirley (Zak) Guterson, had five children, of whom David was the third. Guterson's affinity for nature, so apparent in his novels, began in his childhood years as his family spent time outdoors enjoying the woods and mountains of Washington. A favorite vacation spot was a resort at Soap Lake, located east of Seattle in Grant County. This region, together with the Columbia River basin, where Guterson spent time in his twenties hunting and exploring, later provided the setting for the fictional hunting trip of Ben Givens, the protagonist of Guterson's 1999 novel, *East of the Mountains.*

Guterson described himself to John Blades of *Publishers Weekly* as a mediocre student who showed little interest in his studies until he entered the University of Washington in 1974. The university sparked his interest in a variety of subjects, an enthusiasm that has carried over into his mature fiction as he describes topics such as human anatomy, botany, Asian American history, and veterinary science. While authors from Chekhov to William Shakespeare engaged his attention as an English major, Guterson did not lose touch with life beyond books. He spent summers clearing brush and fighting fires for the United States Forest Service.

After graduating in 1978 from the University of Washington with a B.A. in English, Guterson married Robin Ann Radwick, whom he had known since high school, on 1 January 1979. Guterson had begun writing short stories at the age of twenty-one, while still an undergraduate, and his desire to pursue his writing more seriously led him to enroll in the creative-writing master's program at Brown University soon after his wedding. Finding Brown "too experimental" for his liking, Guterson withdrew and later enrolled in the creative-writing program at the University of Washington, where he studied under prominent writers, including Charles Johnson. "Some students take classes to see if they're writers," Johnson told Donahue, but "David was different. He just knew; he was serious. He understood that good writing is about specificity." Guterson's aspirations to be a writer had as much to do with moral conviction as they did with sensing his own talent; he wanted to contribute to society in the way his father had as a criminal-defense attorney.

Guterson completed his M.A. at the University of Washington in 1982. With their newborn son, Taylor, the Gutersons toured Europe in a Volkswagen van and returned to Seattle bankrupt four months later. In 1984, the year their second child, Travis, was born, the Gutersons moved to Bainbridge Island, located thirty-five minutes west of Seattle by ferry. Bainbridge High School hired him as an English teacher, a position he held until 1994, and Guterson settled down to family life on the island. A third son, Henry, was born in 1986, and a daughter, Angelica, in 1993.

Guterson achieved his first major publishing breakthrough in 1989 after several of his early stories had appeared in magazines such as *The Seattle Review,*

The Iowa Review, and *Prairie Schooner.* Guterson compiled his best stories and sent them to book publishers. The collection was accepted by Harper and Row and was published in 1989 under the title of *The Country Ahead of Us, The Country Behind* to scant but positive reviews.

The Country Ahead of Us, The Country Behind, later republished by Vintage after the success of *Snow Falling on Cedars,* is a collection of ten stories focusing on the lives of young men and boys at defining moments in their lives. The stories reminisce about the days of youth in a bittersweet tone of nostalgia and regret. "Wood Grouse on a High Promontory Overlooking Canada," for instance, tells the story of a boy on a camping trip with his older brother, who has just returned from the Vietnam War. The boy is shocked by his brother's uncontrolled fit of tears when he is asked if he killed anyone in Vietnam. The story suggests the terror and anguish of a young man upon his return from war without overstating and sentimentalizing those feelings.

In a 1999 interview with *Publishers Weekly* Guterson indicates his feeling that the stories in this collection are too heavily influenced by other writers in comparison to his later fiction, and that perhaps the stories should be seen as the work of a writer seeking his own vision and voice. Lois E. Nesbitt suggested in a *New York Times* review (3 September 1989) that the stories are "often submerged under the influence of Hemingway and Faulkner," while others noted the influence of Raymond Carver. Guterson remarks, "That period of intense derivation is a necessary and inevitable step for a writer. Eventually you just plain outgrow it. You mature, your sensibilities become refined, you find your own voice." Guterson may speak dismissively of these stories, but the collection is more than a trial run by an author in the making. The stories are sharply written, and most are noteworthy in their own right. In "American Elm," for instance, Guterson captures in words and syntax the gasping last thoughts of an elderly man who drowns himself: "in a swirl that contained him bottomlessly he pondered what might be the right last thoughts to have and they were all of them, all of them, trivial." In such passages Guterson displays empathy for the lives of his characters and showcases the crafted prose that readers have come to expect from him.

After the publication of *The Country Ahead of Us, The Country Behind,* Guterson began researching and writing his first novel, but he was also finding success with nonfiction during this period. His articles on topics such as environmental issues and travel appeared in *Esquire, Sports Illustrated,* and *The New York Times,* and he served as a contributing editor for *Harper's.* A book editor took notice of an article Guterson wrote on homeschooling for *Harper's,* and as a result, *Family Matters: Why Homeschooling Makes Sense* was published by Harcourt Brace Jovanovich in 1992. But the publication of *Snow Falling on Cedars* in 1994 was what brought Guterson's writing widespread recognition.

Guterson's first novel has the same empathy for and insight into human character as *The Country Ahead of Us, The Country Behind.* The novel, however, sheds the minimalist style of Carver and Ernest Hemingway, though losing some of its suggestiveness in the process, and reveals an artist developing a distinctive voice. Described in a review for *Time* (26 September 1994) as "a tender examination of fairness and forgiveness," *Snow Falling on Cedars* tells the story of small-town prejudice on an island in Puget Sound. The novel is set in the 1950s, with several flashbacks to events in the World War II period: prominent among these flashbacks are the teenage love affair between the white protagonist, Ishmael Chambers, and his Japanese schoolmate, Hatsue Imada; a battle against Japanese troops in the Pacific in which Ishmael loses his arm; and the internment of Hatsue's family and other Americans of Japanese ancestry under Executive Order 9066.

The narrative follows the trial of Hatsue's husband, Kabuo Miyamoto, a first-generation Japanese American accused of murdering Carl Heine, a first-generation German American and fellow salmon gillnetter. A wound found on Carl's head after the sheriff pulls the man's drowned body from the nets of his drifting fishing boat provides the evidence: the gash in Carl's head reminds the coroner, Horace Whaley, of wounds inflicted by Japanese soldiers that he observed as a medic in the Pacific theater during World War II. Almost in passing, Horace remarks to the sheriff that the wound looks like "one of those *kendo* strikes the Japs used," adding that "Japs are trained in it from when they're kids. How to kill with sticks." The comment raises the sheriff's suspicions of foul play. An old family feud supplies the motive: many years before, Carl's father had agreed to sell a plot of land to Kabuo's father. The agreement skirted discriminatory laws of the time that did not allow immigrant Japanese to own property in the state of Washington by putting the property in Kabuo's name once he turned eighteen. Carl's father died, however, while the Miyamotos were interned at Manzanar during World War II, and Carl's mother promptly sold the farm to Ole Jurgensen. Ishmael Chambers, a reporter and the sole proprietor of the island newspaper, covers the murder trial. Ishmael discovers evidence that would likely exonerate Kabuo, but partly because he resents Hatsue for jilting him to marry Kabuo years before, Ishmael sits on the information until it is almost too late.

Drawing on his experience living on Bainbridge Island, Guterson brings to life in *Snow Falling on Cedars* a composite island of cedars and wild strawberries, farmers and gillnetters, and European and Japanese immigrants in the northern reaches of Puget Sound. Guterson's San Piedro Island is so palpable that it functions almost as a protagonist. Despite the centrality of Kabuo's trial to the story, the reader cannot help but sense the preeminence of the natural world of the island over all the aspirations and folly of its people. The woodlands of the Pacific Northwest, in Guterson's view, are a pervading element in the lives of its inhabitants. In a conversation with Linda Mathews of *The New York Times* (29 February 1996) Guterson said, "The cycle of decay is so overwhelmingly present here. Everything human disappears in this landscape." This "cycle of decay," and the concomitant understanding that all human drama is absorbed by the fog and dense forests of San Piedro Island, permeates the novel. Hatsue's walk in the woods demonstrates both her familiarity with the island and her helplessness before the rot and decay of nature:

> Everything was familiar and known to her here—the dead and dying cedars full of punky heartwood, the fallen, defeated trees as high as a house, the upturned root wads hung with vine maple, the toadstools, the ivy, the salal, the vanilla leaf, the low wet places full of devil's club.

Such atmospheric description lends an exotic quality to the novel. Location, however, is more than atmosphere for Guterson. A sense of place that derives from location is intimately connected to Guterson's ethos, as he reveals in his interview with *Book* magazine: "I think that people don't have enough of a sense of place these days. That's why we have so much environmental devastation: People don't live in the landscape; they just live temporarily on it. They don't care about it." The sense of connection between the story and the natural world of the region becomes as important as the events of the story.

Further, Hatsue's relationship with the woods defines her youthful love for Ishmael Chambers as natural, despite the prevailing prejudice against interracial affairs in the 1940s island community. Her feelings for the woods extend the connection between the Japanese immigrant community and the island in ways that the European immigrants and their descendants fail to recognize. Throughout the novel, the white islanders demonstrate distrust of the Japanese that surpasses even their distrust of the reporters from Seattle and other nonislanders. They view the Japanese as outsiders, even though Japanese have lived on the island for as long as European immigrant families.

The whites constitute the majority of the island community and clearly form the center of island life. The commercial center of the island, located on Amity Harbor, is dominated by European immigrant proprietors, as indicated by shop names such as "Petersen's Grocery," "Fisk's Hardware Center," and "Larsen's Pharmacy." The Japanese-owned stores are located in what is known on the island as "Jap Town." The map provided in the front of the novel reveals that Amity Harbor is located at what is called "Island Center," and Jap Town is located on the extreme northern tip of the island on a small, triangular point. All the farms that occupy the center of the island are owned by whites, while the Imada and Miyamoto homes are on the south and north ends of the island, respectively—segregated from the white community by both geography and emotion.

San Piedro's racial division is not only represented geographically but also enacted socially, as seen, for instance, in the arrangement of the courtroom during Kabuo's trial. The Japanese audience members sit at the back of the courtroom "because San Piedro required it of them without calling it a law." This segregation of whites and Japanese is played out time and again in the social relationships on the island. When Kabuo goes to visit Carl Heine, he does not expect to be invited into the living room, offering instead to wait on the porch. He is surprised when Susan-Marie Heine invites him in to wait for her husband. Among the fraternity of gillnetters who dock in Amity Harbor, Kabuo is treated as an outsider. Most poignantly, the ill-fated love of Ishmael and Hatsue serves to dramatize this segregation. The only way they can be together is to hide from the rest of society inside a hollow cedar trunk, which becomes an emblem in the novel of their rotting Edenic world—a world of youthful innocence and shamelessness eroded by the bigotry and suspicion of adults.

Similar to the trial scene in *To Kill a Mockingbird,* the 1960 novel by Harper Lee that Guterson assigned for years to his English class at Bainbridge High School and that he has cited as a profound influence on *Snow Falling on Cedars,* the trial of Kabuo is an examination of racial prejudice and of the ways in which notions of race influence people's judgment. Kabuo's "silent" and "imperial" demeanor in the courtroom leads the white onlookers in the gallery, as well as eleven of the jurors, to believe he is capable of cold-blooded murder. The prosecutor's closing argument ends with this appeal to the jury: "Take a good look, ladies and gentlemen, at the defendant sitting over there. Look into his eyes, consider his face." Defense attorney Nels Gudmunds-

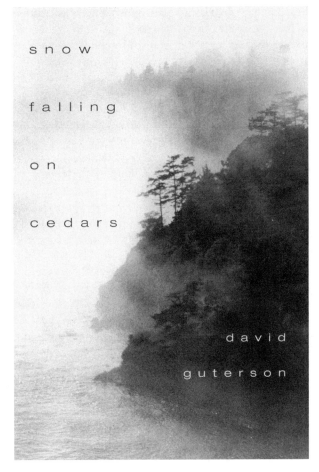

Dust jacket for Guterson's first novel, in which a Japanese fisherman stands trial for the murder of his German neighbor on a Puget Sound island during the 1950s (Richland County Public Library)

son objects that the prosecutor wants to connect Kabuo in the jurors' minds with the enemy the United States faced in the war in the Pacific. He reminds the jury that Kabuo is connected with the war—not as an enemy, but as an American soldier. Despite this appeal, the jury's conversation in the deliberation room comes back to the face of Kabuo. While the islanders may regard the silence, pride, and mysteriousness of Carl or Ishmael as products of war or of the gillnetters' profession, Kabuo, who is both veteran and gillnetter, is defined as an enemy and an outsider simply because of his ethnicity.

The white islanders see Kabuo as indistinguishable from those Japanese who bombed Pearl Harbor and waged war in the Pacific theater. When Kabuo returns from the European theater to try to reconstruct his life on San Piedro, he goes to Etta Heine to inquire about the property that she unfairly sold to Ole Jurgensen upon her husband's death. She tells him, "Carl junior's fighting the Japs." When Kabuo replies that he heard about Mr. Heine's passing while he was fighting in Italy, the irony of who the enemy was in the European theater is either missed or ignored by the Bavarian-born woman. Kabuo speaks more bluntly with Carl, however. When Carl tells him the property transaction occurred while he was "fighting you goddamn Jap sons a–," Kabuo retorts that he was fighting Germans in Europe, "so don't you talk to me about Japs, you big Nazi son of a bitch." In a review for *TLS: The Times Literary Supplement* (26 May 1995), Stephen Henighan claimed that "Guterson's handling of the theme of racial bigotry is effectively low-key."

Guterson spent more than five years researching and writing *Snow Falling on Cedars,* pursuing accuracy in his details about the Japanese internment, forensics, gill-netting, America's war in the Pacific, and botany. Bainbridge Island provided more than physical background for the fictional San Piedro Island. For instance, Arthur Chambers, Ishmael's father and founder of the local paper, is modeled after Walt Woodward, who ran the *Bainbridge Review* during World War II and openly questioned the constitutionality of the Japanese internment. Guterson also learned about salmon fishing in Puget Sound firsthand, and he traveled to the San Juan Islands in order to experience life on islands more remote and sparsely populated than Bainbridge. He wrote a travel piece based on one of these journeys for *The New York Times* just months before *Snow Falling on Cedars* appeared. Many reviewers expressed admiration for Guterson's attention to the details of location and history, but Susan Kenny of *The New York Times* (16 October 1994) claimed that the novel "hovers on the verge of digressiveness," and Henighan complained that Guterson failed "to distinguish between telling detail and information." Nonetheless, Guterson's scrupulous concern for detail and technical information is a hallmark of his first novel.

Snow Falling on Cedars quickly became number one on *The New York Times* best-seller list, and the paperback edition spent seventy-eight weeks on *Publishers Weekly* charts–thirty-seven weeks at number one. The book garnered rave reviews from critics, winning such prizes as the PEN/Faulkner Award (1995), the American Booksellers Book of the Year Award (1995), and the Pacific Northwest Booksellers Award (1995). By the end of the decade, Vintage, which owned the paperback rights to the book, had sold more than three million copies of the novel, making it the most successful novel in the history of the imprint. By the same year, translations had appeared in thirty languages. Universal Pictures produced a movie version (with screenplay by Ronald Bass and Scott Hicks) that premiered in 1999, the same year that Harcourt Brace published Guterson's second novel, *East of the Mountains.*

The verisimilitude of *East of the Mountains* depends upon the same attention to detail that Guterson exhibited in *Snow Falling on Cedars.* Guterson traveled to the sage deserts of eastern Washington to conduct research; he immersed himself in the study of apple farming and veterinary science, interviewed migrant fruit pickers from Mexico, and traveled to the Dolomites in Italy to prepare for a flashback sequence. Once again, place is significant in the novel, leading Pico Iyer in his review for *Time* (26 April 1999) to comment that "its protagonist, in fact, is really the land itself." Guterson told Alden Mudge of *BookPage,*

> I've only recently come to realize that I start just as powerfully with a sense of place and, ultimately, with a love of place, which seeks expression, which wants to use me to express itself. I felt that way about western Washington when I wrote *Snow Falling on Cedars,* and I felt that way about eastern Washington when I wrote *East of the Mountains.* It's almost as if I'm compelled to sing these places. I can't seem to stop them from becoming central. Even though I may not intend it when I set out to write the book, these places just emerge as major players in what I'm doing, almost as if they are insisting on it.

As with *Snow Falling on Cedars,* the setting of *East of the Mountains* functions as a protagonist, but the location of the second novel is vastly different.

Reviewers were generally surprised that Guterson's second novel abandoned the foggy, densely wooded islands of Puget Sound that brought him so much success in his first novel. They were even more surprised that he chose to write about the journey of a seventy-three-year-old man dying of cancer, a radical thematic departure from the furtive love affair and dramatic murder trial of *Snow Falling on Cedars.* Many recognized this departure as a bold and necessary step for a serious artist wishing to explore his craft rather than repeat a formula for popular success. Iyer remarked in his review for *Time,* "as a response to best-sellerdom, the book–and its author–has the bravery to strike off in a new direction." As this comment suggested, expectations were high for this follow-up novel. *Publishers Weekly* reported that Harcourt Brace ran a first printing of five hundred thousand hardbound copies, with a promotional budget of $500,000, and Guterson's agent sold rights to the United Kingdom, Germany, France, Italy, Japan, Holland, Norway, Finland, Sweden, and Denmark before publication.

The critical response to *East of the Mountains,* however, was mixed. Robert Sullivan, in a review for *The New York Times* (9 May 1999), praised Guterson's "smooth and pleasing and often sensual prose," and Bill Broun of *TLS* (11 June 1999) conceded in an otherwise negative review that "there are enough instances of fine writing here to assure us that Guterson's talents have not disappeared." Michiko Kakutani wrote in *The New York Times* (9 April 1999), however, in one of the most negative of all the reviews, that the plot is unconvincing and the characters "feel like cardboardy mouthpieces." The negative reviews seemed to confirm Iyer's prediction in an otherwise positive review that "some readers may find the novel a little too sweetspirited and lacking in a strong enough sense of evil to make the triumphs of goodness seem earned." Positive reviewers praised Guterson's prose and eye for detail. A reviewer for *Publishers Weekly* (11 January 1999) wrote that Guterson's "unsparingly direct, beautifully observed and meticulously detailed prose creates an almost palpable atmospheric background." A critic from *Library Journal* (15 February 1999) praised Guterson's "compelling characters" and "passionate prose," recommending the book highly.

East of the Mountains is about the journey of a retired and cancer-ridden heart surgeon, Ben Givens, who sets out one morning on a hunting trip that he intends to be his last. Lonely for his recently deceased wife, Rachel, and hopeless about his own future, Ben plans to take his own life in the sage-lands east of the mountains, making it look like a hunting accident. Guterson skillfully explores Ben's motivation; Ben's experience as a surgeon has taught him that "nothing could stop his death, no matter how hopeful he allowed himself to feel, no matter how deluded." Rather than embracing an egotistical confidence in the power of science over nature, Ben holds an almost nihilistic appreciation of nature's course and the inevitability of death.

With nearly three hundred pages to go, the reader knows that the end will not come as soon for the aged doctor as he plans. The novel is not, in fact, about his suicide, but about how the "accidents" on his journey convince him of the value of his life. Ben begins to have misgivings about his decision even before the real events of the novel exert any influence on him. Just being out in the open country hunting birds induces doubts, and he feels "he could not understand the end he'd chosen except as an act of stoic machismo, and that was not enough." A run-in with a pack of hounds leaves his dog, Rex, in need of a doctor, and the owner of the hounds makes off with Ben's shotgun after Ben shoots the hound that nearly takes Rex's life. Concern for his dog and lack of an adequate weapon provide at least two preliminary reasons for Ben's change in plans. Ben also meets a young couple who helps him after his vehicle is wrecked on a mountain pass just hours into his trip; a drifter who gives him three marijuana joints; an illegal-alien fruit picker; and a Mexican woman whose life he saves by delivering her baby. Each char-

acter provides a lesson, perhaps too predictably for some readers, until Ben returns to his Seattle home with a new vision of the world and his place in it.

Perhaps the most poignant moments of the novel are the flashbacks and memories that force themselves upon Ben during his journey. Some are extended, and three are even drug-induced, but often the sudden, free association opens the heart of the protagonist to the reader. While walking among the sage early in his journey, Ben touches his shotgun, which sparks memories of Italy, where he was stationed during World War II, and to a train trip he took with Rachel into the Italian countryside:

> The land outside seemed to travel with them, as did the sun and the violet sky, against which a church spire rose high, slim, pale as the moon. Only the birds, swooping south from tree to tree, seemed free of the force that propelled the fabric of the world northward.

The description of this memory clearly carries more weight in the narrative than simply to fill in the details of Ben's history. As with the description of Hatsue in the forest in *Snow Falling on Cedars,* Guterson melds descriptions of nature with deeper themes within the narrative: the free-flying birds bring to mind the yearnings of the human spirit in the face of the relentless progress of time.

East of the Mountains, like its predecessor, reveals the sensibilities of a serious writer with a clear moral vision. For some critics, however, Guterson's first two novels verged on the moralistic. His third novel, *Our Lady of the Forest* (2003), dispels any such criticism. In a positive review for *The New York Times* (2 November 2003), Claire Dederer claimed that through *Our Lady of the Forest,* Guterson "overcomes his virtue problem, writing with more humor than ever before. For the first time he seems interested in the mess and mud of real life." While his first two novels present characters who are, in Dederer's words, "tinged with nobility living in places carved out of beauty," Guterson's third novel explores sordid people in a morbid place.

The depressed logging town of North Fork, Washington, and its surrounding rain-soaked forest is the setting. Rank mildew invades the homes, minimarts, laundromats, hotels, bars, and churches of North Fork like an encroaching evil. Each character is likewise tainted: Father Donald Collins, the local priest, suffers from guilt at his carnality and lust; Ann Holmes, the sixteen-year-old runaway whose visions of the Virgin Mary ignites the plot of the novel, endures the trauma of rape and emotional abandonment as well as failing health; Carolyn Greer, Ann's impromptu spokeswoman, struggles with greed; and Tom Cross, a

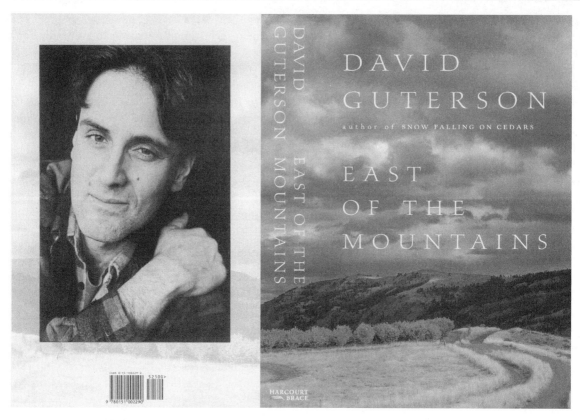

Dust jacket for Guterson's 1999 novel, in which an elderly widowed doctor with terminal cancer sets out on a hunting
trip during which he intends to commit suicide but has experiences that give him a reason to go on living
(Richland County Public Library)

former logger down on his luck, carries shame and guilt over a tragic accident that left his son paralyzed. All struggle with issues of faith and redemption.

The novel begins with Ann's vision of the Virgin Mary while picking mushrooms deep in the Washington rainforest. Ann confides in fellow mushroom-picker Carolyn, who cynically advises the girl to seek psychological treatment. Ann takes her story to Father Collins, who lacks the faith to believe in the veracity of Ann's vision and the restraint to ignore his sexual attraction to the teenaged visionary. News of the apparition spreads rapidly by word of mouth and by a cyber-network of fanatical Catholics hungry for visions of Mary and miraculous healings. Before long, a throng of zealots invades North Fork, transforming the hapless town into a momentary Mecca.

While Ben Ratliff complained in a negative review for *The New York Times* (18 November 2003) that "the novel lacks a single likable character," other reviewers praised Guterson's boldness and craft. Iyer wrote in *Time* (10 November 2003) that the novel is "a group of portraits of beat-up, lived-in lives that amounts to a group portrait of America today" and that Guter-

son effectively brings Nathaniel Hawthorne's symbolic forests and historical witch trials into the twenty-first century. Andrea Hoag, writing for the Minneapolis *Star Tribune* (5 October 2003), found "brilliance" in Guterson's ability to elicit the reader's empathy for Tom Cross, the violent and acerbic Catholic who claims to hate his son.

Our Lady of the Forest asks deep questions about the human desire for the spiritual and the miraculous. For most of the novel, the reader teeters on the edge of faith: is it all delusion, or does God invade this time and space? Ann's insistence on the reality of her visions, her thrall-like state and near-levitation posture witnessed by acolytes and cynics alike, and the rumors of miraculous healings lend credence not only to Ann's visions but also to the claims of Christianity. As Tom Cross puts it in his frenzied interrogation of Ann just before her death, "if Mary's real then all of it's real. God, Jesus, all of it."

Unfortunately, at least according to critics such as Sarah Churchwell of *TLS* (21 November 2003), Guterson throws a wet blanket over the nascent flames of religious faith in the last three pages of the novel. In an ending that Randy Michael Signor of the *Chicago Sun-Times* (21 September 2003) described as "too pat," Carolyn returns to North Fork after a long absence, on the day of dedication of Our Lady of the Forest Church, to inform Father Collins that Ann had been taking heavy doses of an allergy medicine that is known to induce hallucinations. "Mary was just a big Phenathol overdose," says Carolyn. "Phenathol's behind this massive spectacle. This multimillion-dollar film-set church. That's what you are presiding over, Father. A Phenathol trip."

Perhaps the biggest surprise to the reader is that Father Collins is not surprised by Carolyn's revelation. He has known since Ann's autopsy that there was a medical explanation for her visions, but somehow he found a reason to continue with the church-building project. Somehow he found the possibility of faith. "Her brain was cooked by her fever," says Father Collins. "An adverse reaction to Phenathol, perhaps. But maybe, too, the hand of God." Churchwell maintained that *Our Lady of the Forest* is an unsatisfying "literary version of Pascal's wager, believing in faith only as far as it seems wise." She added, "by restricting his miracle, David Guterson has constricted his art." Some readers may share her disappointment. However, Guterson's exploration of downtrodden people besieged by doubt might redeem the novelist in the eyes of those who saw his fictional world as unrealistically hopeful. With his versatile exploration of the human condition, elegant prose style, insight into human character, and a traditional sense of the value of a good story, David Guterson is a novelist to watch in the twenty-first century.

Interviews:

Ellen Kanner, "A Wonderful Irony: The Quietest of Books Makes the Splashiest Debut," *BookPage* (January 1996) <http://www.bookpage.com/9601bp/fiction/snowfallingoncedars.html>;

Linda Mathews, "At Home with David Guterson: Amid the Cedars, Serenity and Success," *New York Times,* 29 February 1996, p. C1;

Mary Ann Gwinn, "After 'Snow Falling on Cedars,' David Guterson Won't Be Sneaking Up on Success," *Seattle Times,* 28 March 1999, p. 16;

John Blades, "David Guterson: Stoic of the Pacific Northwest," *Publishers Weekly* (5 April 1999): 215–217;

Alden Mudge, "Guterson Offers a Moving Story of One Man's Final Pilgrimage," *BookPage* (April 1999) <http://www.bookpage.com/9904bp/david_guterson.html>;

Bill Donahue, "David Guterson," *Book* (March/April 2000) <http://www.bookmagazine.com/mar2000/guterson.shtml>.

Reference:

Paul Heike, "Old, New and 'Neo' Immigrant Fictions in American Literature: The Immigrant Presence in David Guterson's *Snow Falling on Cedars* and T. C. Boyle's *The Tortilla Curtain,*" *Amerikastudien* (Amsterdam), 46, no. 2 (2001): 249–265.

Kent Haruf

(24 February 1943 –)

Michael R. Molino
Southern Illinois University

BOOKS: *The Tie That Binds* (New York: Holt, Rinehart
& Winston, 1984);
Where You Once Belonged (New York: Summit, 1990);
Plainsong (New York: Knopf, 1999);
Eventide (New York: Knopf, forthcoming 2004).

PRODUCED SCRIPT: *Private Debts,* motion picture,
Chanticleer Films, 1989.

SELECTED PERIODICAL PUBLICATIONS–
UNCOLLECTED:

FICTION

"Now (And Then)," *Puerto del Sol,* 17 (Summer 1982):
39–42;
"The Autopsy of Sam Adams," *Grand Street,* 5 (Spring
1986): 7–18;
"Private Debts/Public Holdings," *Grand Street,* 6
(Autumn 1986): 18–32;
"Dancing," *Prairie Schooner,* 66 (Summer 1992): 53–65;
"Inside T.O. Judy's Mouth," *Gettysburg Review,* 7 (Sum-
mer 1994): 483–495.

NONFICTION

"To See Your Story Clearly, Start Pulling the Wool
over Your Own Eyes," *New York Times,* 20
November 2000, p. E1;
"What We Did for Love," *More* (October 2001): 66–
68.

*Kent Haruf (photograph by Cathy Haruf; from the dust
jacket for* Plainsong, *1999; Richland
County Public Library)*

Kent Haruf's novels relay the struggles of high-
plains farmers and teachers, children and parents, husbands and wives, whose lives proceed along differing
trajectories. Like William Faulkner's Yoknapatawpha
County or Sherwood Anderson's Winesburg, Ohio,
Haruf's fictional Holt, Colorado, is a place where
momentary kindnesses and abiding despair intersect in
the lives of small-town people. Collectively, the stories
of these people create a history that all the inhabitants
of Holt share as they seek emotional connections to sustain them through long winters and years of hard work
in this isolated region of northeast Colorado. In a profile published in the *Omaha World Herald* (19 December

1999), Haruf revealed that he has created a map of
Holt in his mind and carefully located the homes, businesses, and even the water towers that mark the landscape of his fictional town. Holt is based in part on the
real Colorado towns of Yuma, Wray, and Holyoke,
where Haruf lived as a child; he says that Holt

seems like home to me. There seems to be plenty to
write about there. . . . You know their family stories.
You know the connections between people. You know

148

how society works. You know whose pickup is parked in somebody's driveway where it doesn't belong, and you know whose dog is loose and whose bicycle is parked in front of the bakery. All those things are important to a writer.

The sudden and unexpected acclaim afforded Haruf's 1999 novel, *Plainsong*, belies the gradual and assiduous efforts of its author to tell the seemingly simple story of Holt.

Haruf was born Alan Kent Hoerauf in Pueblo, Colorado, on 24 February 1943. (The family name was changed in the 1940s by Haruf's father; Haruf's grandfather had immigrated to America from Germany in the 1880s and found that no one could pronounce Hoerauf.) Haruf is the son of Eleanor V. (Shaver) Haruf, a teacher, and Louis A. Haruf, a Methodist minister who moved his family to various small Colorado towns where the populations rarely exceeded two thousand people. Haruf spent his childhood riding his bicycle and exploring the countryside with his brother, sitting in church while his father preached, and reading avidly. Haruf's parents were book lovers and nurtured their son's desire to read. Storytelling was also part of family life; after dinner Haruf's father would recall tales of his childhood on a remote North Dakota homestead. In such family sessions, Haruf first heard stories of a place like Holt.

Haruf enrolled in Nebraska Wesleyan University, where he majored first in biology before discovering writers such as Ernest Hemingway and Faulkner. From the former, Haruf learned the power of a clear and direct prose style, while from the latter he discovered the value of stories set in a small town populated by hardworking people. After graduating in 1965 with a degree in English, Haruf spent two years in the Peace Corps teaching English to children in Turkey. He returned to the United States intent upon pursuing graduate studies in English. He entered the University of Kansas but left quickly, displeased with the way literature was taught. A conscientious objector to the Vietnam War, Haruf spent the next two years working in a hospital as an orderly and in an orphanage as a house parent in lieu of military service.

After one failed attempt to gain entrance into the prestigious Writers Workshop at the University of Iowa, Haruf was admitted in 1971. He was twenty-eight years old. Haruf's classmates at Iowa were such now notable authors as Tracy Kidder, Stuart Dybeck, T. Coraghessan Boyle, and Ron Hansen. In the *Omaha World Herald* profile, Hansen identified a difference between Haruf and his classmates: "He was a quiet, reserved, but friendly guy, and when he had something to say, it had resonance. He was older and seemed more assured about what he wanted to do as a writer." After graduating with an M.F.A. from Iowa in 1973, Haruf needed to support his growing family—he had married Virginia K. Koon in 1967 and had three daughters—so in 1974 he began teaching in an alternative high school in Madison, Wisconsin. In 1978 the Harufs moved back to Colorado. After several lean years working construction, Haruf earned a teaching certificate and began teaching English to farm kids in several rural schools, spending his summers writing what became his first novel, *The Tie That Binds* (1984).

In 1982, at the age of thirty-nine, Haruf published his first piece of fiction: a four-page, stylistically self-conscious story titled "Now (And Then)," in which the narrator recounts his mother's drive home from Wisconsin through Iowa. Shortly thereafter, John Irving, one of Haruf's teachers at Iowa, encouraged Haruf to contact his agent, John Matson, with the new novel, warning Haruf that Matson had rejected the past fifty authors Irving had sent to him. Matson, however, liked Haruf's novel and quickly found a publisher in Holt, Rinehart, and Winston. *The Tie That Binds* appeared in 1984.

In *The Tie That Binds* Haruf employs a circular narrative structure in which the narrator, Sanders Roscoe, tells the story of a woman, Edith Goodnough, who has been charged with murder and lies in the Holt hospital awaiting trial. Edith's situation is complex, though, and Roscoe feels compelled to tell her whole story because he knows that a reporter from the *Denver Post* has been collecting information for a story about Edith. Roscoe thinks the city reporter, foolishly wearing yellow pants to interview people living on a ranch, has no clear sense of either Edith or the town where she has lived for more than seventy years. Thus, after snubbing the reporter, Roscoe begins his story in the present but in the course of relaying events quickly retreats into the past. For Roscoe, in order to understand Edith Goodnough and the events that led to her current state, one has to begin back in 1895, when her parents, Roy and Ada Goodnough, got married and moved from Iowa to Holt. The past is not a distant abstraction for Roscoe but a series of events that both link him with the Goodnough family and cast light on Edith's recent transgressions. Events that impact the country as a whole are not ignored, but the real history Roscoe presents involves people whose lives are inseparably interconnected. Roscoe seems to have learned the importance of the small stories within a larger one from his father, whom he recalls saying, "Well, this is a piece of history that won't appear in no history books."

The story revolves around siblings Edith and Lyman Goodnough, their overbearing father, and the meager land they farm. Edith and Lyman's story is one

*Dust jacket for Haruf's 1984 novel, in which the narrator
explains why an elderly woman tried to burn down her
family home with her brother and herself inside
(Richland County Public Library)*

of joyless forbearance as they suffer the rage and intolerance of their loveless father. Edith represents a recurring type of female character in Haruf's fiction—hardworking, enduring, and faithful, surviving on brief moments of affection and emotional connection. When Lyman, who is particularly persecuted by his father, has the chance to escape the farm, he does so with apparent detachment, leaving the sister who loves him and not returning home until twenty years later, well after his father's death. In the interim, Edith patiently braves the life given her, remembering the brief love affair she had with Roscoe's father and watching Roscoe grow into a man. Though not her biological child, Roscoe becomes a figurative son for her. The interaction between the aging woman and growing boy and then the old woman and adult narrator poignantly reveals Edith as a woman who has spent her life caring

for an emotionally and physically crippled father while quietly observing the life and son she might have had.

Roscoe is in many ways a typical Haruf narrator: simple, direct, and scrupulous in his own sense of accuracy. To some extent, Roscoe resembles F. Scott Fitzgerald's Nick Carraway in *The Great Gatsby* (1925): both men articulate a clear sense of right and wrong that springs from their middle-American roots; both participate from the periphery in the stories they tell; and both bring their own sense of morality to bear upon the events of the story. The similarities between Nick and Roscoe end there, for Roscoe is different from Nick in terms of reliability. In Haruf's novel Roscoe eagerly, if not longwindedly, distinguishes between what he knows with certainty because he witnessed it; what he believes happened based on long experience; and what he assumes happened based on speculation. For example, early in the novel when Roscoe explains why the sheriff, Bud Sealy, arrested Edith and then discussed her story with a reporter, Roscoe presents his version of events and adds: "But I can't say for sure that's how Bud was thinking. What I've suggested is based only on what I know about him after these fifty years of seeing and talking to him about once every week." That fifty years of experience qualifies Roscoe to explain why last month Edith burned down the Goodnough house with herself and Lyman still in it. Roscoe is willing to share what he knows with anyone willing to sit, wait, and listen to the entire story—just as long as he or she is not a reporter from the *Denver Post* wearing yellow pants.

The Tie That Binds received qualified but favorable reviews and quite a bit of critical acclaim. One critic for *The Los Angeles Times Book Review* (27 January 1985) referred to the novel as "an impressive, expertly crafted work of sensitivity and detail, absent the hokum that usually accompanies sad tales of simple women and their domineering fathers." A critic for *The New York Times Book Review* (6 January 1985) acknowledged Haruf's work as a "fine novel that dramatically and accurately explores the lives of people who work the land in the stark American Middle West." For Haruf, though, the greatest praise for his fiction came one evening at a party while he was visiting friends in Colorado. A farmer Haruf knew approached him and read aloud two paragraphs from the novel, about milking a cow whose tail is covered with a grotesque mixture of feces and afterbirth. Completing the passage, the farmer boldly proclaimed it exactly right. *The Tie That Binds* went into three paperback reprints and won the $25,000 Whiting Writers' Award. The novel was a runner-up for the prestigious PEN/Hemingway Award for first fiction. On the strength of his first effort, Haruf secured a teaching position at Nebraska Wesleyan in 1986; he then began work on his second novel.

Where You Once Belonged (1990) began as two short stories published in *Grand Street* magazine in 1986. One of those stories, "Private Debts/Public Holdings," which eventually became chapter 8 of the novel, was reprinted in *Best American Short Stories 1987* and made into a prizewinning motion picture (*Private Debts*, Chanticleer Films, 1989). *Where You Once Belonged* received good reviews but sold poorly. In the *Omaha World Herald* profile Haruf admits ambivalence over his second novel: "I was really in despair when I finished that book. I had three daughters by then, all in school, all hungry. I was teaching a lot, and I was under pressure to get it done. There are good things in it, but I wanted it to be better than it turned out to be." Despite Haruf's feelings about the novel, a reviewer for *The Los Angeles Times* (11 February 1990) regarded the final product positively: "Haruf's writing has a disciplined economy that sets off its power. Each phrase is spare and straightforward, yet out of all of them together . . . an extraordinary poetry emerges."

Where You Once Belonged employs the same narrative technique as *The Tie That Binds*. Beginning in the present with the return of a local hero turned thief, Jack Burdette, the novel then retraces Burdette's steps, from his childhood in Holt to his flight from town and his eventual return to terrorize the town once again. Burdette takes advantage of the goodness and vulnerability of others and thus brings out the worst in them. The novel explores the frustration of people whose faith in a hero is shattered and who then have no just outlet for their anger over that loss of faith. For many in Holt, their anger at Burdette festers or finds inappropriate outlet until Burdette returns to town and the story of *Where You Once Belonged* begins.

Everything comes too easily for Jack Burdette. A high-school sports hero, Burdette finds that he can rely on the tolerance and praise of the townspeople and the loyalty and love of a local beauty. All changes when Burdette and the narrator, Pat Arbuckle, go off to the University of Colorado in Boulder. Arbuckle studies journalism to pursue a career in the family business—the local newspaper, the *Holt Mercury*. Burdette, on full athletic scholarship, treats the university much in the way he treated everything in Holt, with callow indifference. Burdette neither shines athletically nor succeeds academically: he is not the largest or fastest athlete on the team, and without his girlfriend, Wanda Jo Evans, to complete his homework, Burdette cannot pass his courses. Eventually, on the verge of failing out of school, Burdette is expelled for stealing, an event that leaves him nonplussed and foreshadows behavior that will alter Holt's perception of the local hero forever.

Like Roscoe, Pat Arbuckle presents the facts of Burdette's easy success and eventual disgrace in a manner that weaves together the stories of many Holt citizens. While Roscoe was preoccupied with telling the story correctly because of his love for Edith Goodnough, Arbuckle is a journalist whose father taught him the value of listening to every version of an event without assuming any one of them is flawlessly accurate. Thus, Arbuckle carefully tells the story of Burdette's betrayal and its impact on the citizens of Holt. Like the story told by Roscoe in *The Tie That Binds*, Arbuckle's large story includes many smaller stories. Like Roscoe, Arbuckle is involved in the story, because Arbuckle loves the woman abused and rejected by Burdette, whose fate he is powerless to alter.

Haruf creates characters in *Where You Once Belonged* who echo characters from *The Tie That Binds* and foreshadow characters in *Plainsong*. Nora, Arbuckle's quiet and distant wife, is a character who psychologically recoils in the isolated and unrefined world of Holt. Like Lyman Goodnough in *The Tie That Binds* and Ella Guthrie in *Plainsong*, Nora finds no life and no story of her own amid the stories of Holt. She, like Lyman and Ella, must leave Holt in order to survive and have any hope of happiness. Their stories lie elsewhere. Conversely, Haruf populates his novels with strong women who persevere even in the most hostile situations, adapting to their circumstances and accommodating others in their lives. For instance, Jessie Burdette suffers her husband's abuse and faces the misdirected hostility of Holt's citizens when Burdette skips town after embezzling money from the grain elevator. Maggie Jones in *Plainsong* cares for her ailing and senile father, takes in the pregnant Victoria Roubideaux, and waits for Tom Guthrie to recognize her for the good woman she is. In turn, Victoria Roubideaux is a younger version of these women, making mistakes early in her life from which she suffers the consequences, emerging stronger, wiser, and experienced enough to perceive the good in those around her.

The principal male characters in all three novels resemble one another: Roscoe, Arbuckle, and Guthrie struggle to maintain a sense of equilibrium and honesty in the face of dishonesty and ruthlessness in others. Each has a wife or mother from whom he feels estranged; each, in turn, finds companionship and love, if only fleetingly enjoyed, in the arms of another woman. Each knows he does not deserve the good woman he finds; as Guthrie admonishes his own image in the mirror, "'You don't deserve it [Maggie Jones's love],' he said aloud. 'Don't ever even begin to think that you do.'"

In 1991, shortly after publishing his second novel, Haruf accepted a faculty position at Southern Illinois

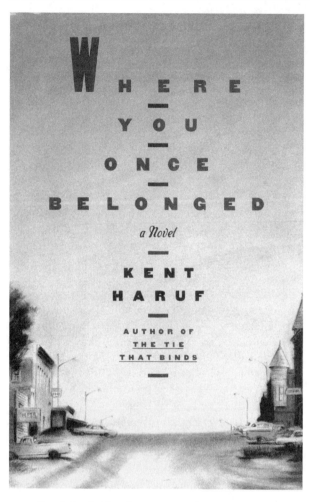

Dust jacket for Haruf's 1990 novel, about the decline of a former local hero in the fictional town of Holt, Colorado (Richland County Public Library)

University at Carbondale, where he could teach fiction workshops and work with students in a growing M.F.A. program. After his first marriage ended in divorce, Haruf married Catherine S. Dempsey in 1995. The lightened teaching load at Southern Illinois gave Haruf the opportunity to work on the novel that moved him from a solid "mid-list" author to a best-selling one. In 1999 Haruf published *Plainsong*, which won early praise from independent booksellers. Word-of-mouth recommendations spread until Haruf found himself on *The New York Times* best-seller list and short-listed for the National Book Award. *Plainsong* went on to win the Regional Book Award in fiction from the Mountain and Plains Booksellers Association; a Salon.com Book Award; the American Booksellers Book Award; and awards from *The New Yorker* and *The Los Angeles Times*.

Readers and reviewers responded approvingly to Haruf's direct, plainspoken narrative and his story of people surviving adversity. Haruf eschews quotation marks throughout the novel, which underscores the connection between what the characters think and what they say. While many of the traits reviewers championed in *Plainsong* were present in his earlier novels, *Plainsong* represents a clear departure for Haruf.

In his first two novels, Haruf's first-person narrator begins with an event in the present and explores relevant past events leading back to the present. In contrast, the third-person narrative of *Plainsong* follows a linear development. An impending sense of anticipation and trepidation recurs throughout the early chapters as the central characters begin their daily routines. The novel then charts the lives of its characters over a nine-month period from early fall until late spring. The past is less relevant in *Plainsong* than in Haruf's earlier novels. The reader learns little about the past lives of Tom Guthrie, Victoria Roubideaux, and the McPheron brothers. The reader never learns why Guthrie's wife, Ella, has retreated into an isolated and lonely world, why she moves out of the house, or why she moves to Denver to live with her sister. Rather than explain in detail why a single event occurred, as he does in *The Tie That Binds* and *Where You Once Belonged,* Haruf reveals little more than what happens to each character in *Plainsong*.

The structure of *Plainsong* complements its narrative. The central characters' stories are told in recurring self-titled chapters, intersecting occasionally as characters interact with one another. The novel revolves around the lives of Tom Guthrie; elderly farmers Raymond and Harold McPheron; Victoria Roubideaux; and Guthrie's sons, nine-year-old Bobby and ten-year-old Ike. Guthrie's story is told in eight chapters scattered through the novel, the McPheron brothers' in nine chapters, Victoria's in twelve, and Ike and Bobby's likewise in twelve. These stories constitute forty-one of the forty-four chapters. Of the remaining three chapters, one presents Ella Guthrie's life of lonely detachment from her husband and children. Later in the novel, the chapter titled "Maggie Jones" reveals a strong and determined woman for whom things just may be looking up. The psychologically downward trajectory of Ella's life in contrast to the potentially upward direction of Maggie's life denotes not turning points in a plot but coincidental contrasts in two women's lives. These two women represent recurring types of female characters in Haruf's fiction—one who suffers from a life on the plains and one who perseveres.

In the final chapter, titled simply "Holt," the key characters meet at the McPheron ranch on a peaceful

May evening. In contrast to its beginning, the novel ends with a sense of contentment as the characters watch the setting sun and await dinner. Although the birth of Victoria's baby suggests the joyful prospects of a new life, the novel does not proffer a resolution to all conflicts: Guthrie still faces problems with his student Russell Beckman; Guthrie and Maggie's budding romance is far from guaranteed; and Victoria faces the challenge of being a teenage single mother without a high-school diploma.

Throughout his fiction, but particularly in *Plainsong,* Haruf explores the way communities are formed outside traditional societal institutions. Despite his father's calling as a minister, Haruf does not present the church as the focal point in his characters' lives nor as the place where lasting bonds are formed. Rather, community bonds are formed in Haruf's fiction naturally by people willing to connect with others and give of themselves. At times, this bond is a natural one, such as a father's love for his sons, a mother's love for her unborn child, or the alliance between siblings. Most others, though, occur in unexpected ways among unlikely people. For example, the McPheron brothers are willing to help Victoria, a girl they do not know, and take her in again after she indifferently casts off their friendship. Ike and Bobby find themselves unwittingly attached to Iva Stearns, an elderly woman who becomes something of a surrogate grandmother to them; but her sudden death stuns the boys. Unable to verbalize the inexplicable sense of loss they feel over Stearns's death, the two silently ride their horse to the ranch of their older counterparts, Raymond and Harold McPheron, seeking solace.

The critical praise for Haruf's third novel centered on the author's style of storytelling. A critic for *The New York Times Book Review* (3 October 1999) articulated what most reviewers believed:

> It is the triumph of *Plainsong* that here [the final chapter], where the novel turns and the reader might have felt the author's hands clutching his lapels, you feel instead the McPherons' self-knowledge—their plain intent to change without knowing why—passes effortlessly into your own self-knowledge. You are convinced that if there really were a Holt, Colo., this is how things would be in that town, truant and forgiving at the same time. The tide of judgment has washed away here, leaving a world that is only what it is, with lives to be made or squandered as they will.

Despite such praise for the empathic connection between reader and character, Haruf's fiction never presents an idealized vision of the world or a mythic connection between the individual and the land.

Dust jacket for Haruf's award-winning 1999 novel, about the dismal lives of several Holt families (Richland County Public Library)

Haruf's fiction often involves the sense of community that links people both to each other and to the land; these communal bonds hold despite the many disappointments and accommodations exacted on the individual. Haruf's stories are not the stories of people inspired by a myth of progress and exploration, of the heroic dream of taming a wild frontier. These stories are the offspring and grandchildren of people who dreamed those large dreams. Both an attraction to and a repulsion from the land recur in Haruf's characters. People are transformed by the land they work and the space they occupy rather than the other way around. Any promise of material wealth, social advancement, or spiritual rejuvenation that may have motivated the ancestors of Haruf's characters lingers only as a dimly remembered dream annulled. Many of Haruf's characters oscillate merely between work and rage or work and drink. Even the houses in which Haruf's characters live do not offer a sense of solace or refuge from the world but rather instill a sense of psychological entrapment. At its best, the house is a place where objects of practical use stand ready for service while objects that recall past happiness haunt closed rooms or closets. At times, the house seemingly constricts the lives of its occupants. In contrast to the vast plains and infinite sky, the house, particularly for females, draws its occupants into a sense of isolation from the world outside. In the case of Edith Goodnough, the house eventually becomes the tomb that inters Lyman and nearly inters her.

Plainsong was made into a television movie by Hallmark Hall of Fame Productions, with screenplay by Oliver Goldstick; it is scheduled to air on CBS in May 2004 and stars Aidan Quinn and Rachel Griffiths. Haruf's next novel, *Eventide,* is also scheduled for publication by Knopf in 2004. Like *Plainsong,* the novel is set in Holt and shifts among three sets of characters in a third-person narrative that spans nine months. Characters such as Victoria Roubideaux and the McPheron brothers recur in the novel, though the story is darker than that of *Plainsong.*

Like the fiction of Douglas Unger, James Welch, Patricia Henley, Craig Lesley, William Kittredge, Louise Erdrich, and David Quammen, the novels of Kent Haruf do not tell the story of heroic idealism on the American plains but rather reveal the isolated acts of kindness, love, loyalty, betrayal, and desperation defin-ing the lives of those whose ambivalent affection for the land is won at great cost and with even greater labor. This hard-won sense of place that comes to characters in Haruf's fiction is summed up by Sanders Roscoe: "Course it's not fair. There ain't none of it that's fair. Life ain't. And all our thinking it should be don't seem to make one simple damn." Nonetheless, Roscoe stays true to Edith and conceives his life bound up in hers and with the lives of others who live in Holt, Colorado.

Interviews:

Hillel Italie, "Author's Rural Story Causing a Buzz in Book Circles: Murphysboro Writer Harks Back to Colorado Childhood and Strikes a Chord," *Peoria Journal Star,* 31 October 1999, p. B7;

John Mark Eberhart, "Simple and *Plainsong:* Kent Haruf Wanted His Celebrated Book to Capture Quiet but Real Lives without the Quote Marks," *Kansas City Star,* 19 August 2000, p. E1;

Michael McGregor, "An Interview with Kent Haruf," *Writer's Chronicle,* 33 (March/April 2001): 38–45.

References:

Nelson Limerick, Clyde A. Miller II, and Charles E. Rankin, *Trails: Toward a New Western History* (Lawrence: University of Kansas Press, 1991);

Diane Dufva Quantic, *The Nature of the Place: A Study of Great Plains Fiction* (Lincoln: University of Nebraska Press, 1994).

Carl Hiaasen

(12 March 1953 –)

J. Rocky Colavito
Northwestern State University

BOOKS: *Powder Burn,* by Hiaasen and William D. Montalbano (New York: Atheneum, 1981);

Trap Line, by Hiaasen and Montalbano (New York: Atheneum, 1982);

A Death in China, by Hiaasen and Montalbano (New York: Atheneum, 1984);

Tourist Season (New York: Putnam, 1986);

Double Whammy (New York: Putnam, 1987);

Skin Tight (New York: Putnam, 1989);

Native Tongue (New York: Knopf, 1991);

Strip Tease (New York: Knopf, 1993);

Stormy Weather (New York: Knopf, 1995);

Naked Came the Manatee, by Hiaasen and others (New York: Putnam, 1996);

Lucky You (New York: Knopf, 1997);

Team Rodent: How Disney Devours the World (New York: Ballantine, 1998);

Kick Ass: Selected Columns of Carl Hiaasen, edited by Diane Stevenson (Gainesville: University Press of Florida, 1999);

Sick Puppy (New York: Knopf, 2000);

Paradise Screwed: Selected Columns of Carl Hiaasen, edited by Stevenson (New York: Putnam, 2001);

Basket Case (New York: Knopf, 2002);

Hoot (New York: Knopf, 2002);

Skinny Dip (New York: Knopf, forthcoming 2004).

Carl Hiaasen, October 2003 (courtesy of the author)

Based in South Florida, where he is a columnist for the *Miami Herald,* Carl Hiaasen has always exhibited an unbridled interest in the landscape of that state. This interest in and love of the land fuels his darkly tinted novels, which pull no punches and are populated by bizarre characters who find themselves in situations that border on the surreal. However, the characters and situations are just plausible enough to keep his works planted in the realm of realistic fiction. Given his warts-and-all approach to characterization, setting, and plot, Hiaasen's work is probably better characterized in a naturalistic vein similar to the earlier works of Frank Norris, Upton Sinclair, and other writers who were not reluctant to paint man, his works, and his foibles and failings in an ultrarealistic fashion.

Carl Andrew Hiaasen (pronounced "hiya-sun") was born on 12 March 1953 in Plantation, Florida, a suburb of Fort Lauderdale in the then-rural outer fringes of Broward County. His parents were lawyer K. Odel Hiaasen and Patricia Moran Hiaasen. He has two sisters, Judith and Barbara, and a brother, Rob. Hiaasen forged his ecological consciousness as a child with mischief that included stealing survey markers for new developments in his community. In her introduction to *Kick Ass: Selected Columns of Carl Hiaasen* (1999) Diane Stevenson writes that Hiaasen learned to read at age four, using *Miami Herald* sports stories and Florida maps as primers. After receiving his first typewriter in 1960, he taught himself to type and ultimately produced a neighborhood sports page. He began to form his satirical voice while attending Plantation High School, publishing an underground newsletter called *More Trash* that examined the current teen culture and depicted teachers and administration in a comical light.

Hiaasen started college in 1970 at Emory University, where, according to Stevenson, "he ghostwrote a doctor's memoirs . . . married his high school sweetheart [registered nurse and attorney Constance Lyford], and became a father" in the space of two years. (He and Lyford, who divorced in 1996, have a son, Scott.) He then attended the University of Florida, graduated with a degree in journalism in 1974, and began writing for *Cocoa Today* (now *Florida Today*). Moving to the *Miami Herald* in 1976, he found fame as an investigative reporter and became a finalist for the Pulitzer Prize in 1980 and 1981 for series on doctors who committed malpractice and on the drug-smuggling industry, respectively. Since 1985 Hiaasen has been a regular columnist for the paper, appearing twice weekly in the local section. His columns have occasionally raised the ire of regional developers and bureaucrats, who blame him for discouraging tourism. Hiaasen welcomes these charges and openly discusses his activism and his dedication to preserving Florida's ecology. Articles and reviews have noted time and again the saturating presence of crimes against nature in Hiaasen's work, while also calling attention to his penchant for developing bizarre villains, even more bizarre situations involving those villains that usually turn out badly, and almost poetically just resolutions to sometimes complex plots.

Hiaasen's early novels, written collaboratively with William D. Montalbano (former editor of the *Miami Herald*), rely more heavily on the formulas of detective and adventure fiction and less on what became his characteristic motifs. *Powder Burn* (1981) uses the tried-and-true formula of a crime witness in jeopardy because of his potential to draw out criminals who are of greater interest to the police. *Trap Line* (1982) draws upon Hiaasen's experience reporting on smuggling in South Florida; its protagonist, a fishing-boat captain, tries to avoid becoming caught up in smuggling activities, which earns him the wrath of a local drug organization. The organization begins undermining the protagonist's life, threatening his son in the process. In true pulp fashion, the protagonist turns violent in an effort to save his son.

These two early works show some affinity with Hiaasen's favored settings in Florida and their associated crime-related issues. *A Death in China* (1984) moves its action from South Florida to the Far East, where the familiar displaced character must surmount the wall of secrets that is commonly erected when murders are committed on foreign soil. Inklings of Hiaasen's now characteristic perversity are apparent—for example, a character dies a painful death after being bitten by a cobra—but the novel, along with *Powder Burn* and *Trap Line*, seems to show more of the writer's early formation and is not fully representative of the characteristics that have come to make Hiaasen's current body of work noteworthy.

In 1986 Hiaasen published *Tourist Season*, his first solo novel. This novel chronicles the efforts of an inept group of activists who terrorize Florida tourists and developers in an effort to rid the state of all that ails it. Tourists are kidnapped, thrown into a pool containing an alligator, and awarded their freedom if they are able to successfully swim across the pool; the alligator, of course, always wins. A local politician is found neatly folded up in a suitcase with a toy alligator stuffed down his throat. The novel culminates with a successful kidnapping of the Orange Bowl Queen by one of the terrorists, who happens to be a former football player for the Miami Dolphins. The leader of this band is Skip Wiley, a former columnist for the *Miami Sun*, and he serves as the mouthpiece for many of what appear to be Hiaasen's own attitudes toward Florida's overdevelopment. The protagonist, Brian Keyes, a reporter turned private investigator, eventually unravels the mystery and confronts both the demons that forced him out of reporting and his former mentor, Wiley, on an island slated for development. In a last bit of ecoconsciousness, Wiley, incapacitated by a leg wound, climbs a tree in an effort to frighten an eagle away from its nest because the island is set for rezoning via dynamite. Tony Hillerman, in *The New York Times Book Review* (16 March 1986), noted that the novel "is full of . . . quick, efficient, understated little sketches . . . of the sort of subtle truth that leaves you grinning."

Hiaasen followed *Tourist Season* with *Double Whammy* (1987), a mystery combining intrigue in bass-fishing tournaments and the overdevelopment of the Florida landscape. Once again, the protagonist, R. J. Decker, is something of a reluctant private eye. Similar to the protagonist of *Tourist Season*, Decker has a former life in journalism, this time as a news photographer, and he confronts a variety of adversaries, the strangest of whom is a violent kidnapper who carries out his mission with the disembodied head of a pit bulldog dangling from his arm. Readers are also introduced to a recurring character in Hiaasen's work: Clinton "Skink" Tyree, a Florida governor who suddenly vacates the office after the corruption around him becomes too much to bear. Tyree ultimately flees into the swamps and becomes something of an ecoterrorist or prankster,

Dust jacket for Hiaasen's 1997 novel, in which the heroine pursues a pair of white supremacists
who stole her winning lottery ticket (Richland County Public Library)

a role often taken up by characters in later works, sometimes after direct contact with Skink, who appears to mature into a teacher figure.

The plot of *Double Whammy* involves the machinations of a corrupt televangelist and his efforts to sell interests in a Florida waterfront development. His comeuppance includes the exposure on national television of his inability to heal, along with his subsequent arrest for fraud. Hiaasen's familiarity with the subject and setting was singled out for praise by critics. In a *Sports Illustrated* review (11 April 1988) Bob Brown notes that Hiaasen "displays a comprehensive knowledge of the elaborate cheating schemes that have plagued many bass fishing tournaments, and of the political corruption that has deprived Florida of much of its wetlands." Walter Walker, of *The New York Times Book Review* (16 March 1988), also praised some of the more technical aspects of the novel: "the writing style is macabre-funny and it delivers the plot's myriad twists and turns with breathtaking speed." Thus, in these two works Hiaasen's favored subjects, his soon-to-be characteristic plot structures, and his radically different characters begin to coalesce.

Skin Tight (1989) continues in its reliance upon a reluctant protagonist (Mick Stranahan, a former investi-

gator for the state) and makes his opponents two of the more stereotypically salacious business types to be found in a sunny climate populated by aging tourists/transplants and criminals: a plastic surgeon, whose ineptitude is exacerbated by less-than-steady hands, and a personal-injury lawyer. Along for the ride are a Hispanic television host specializing in shock-news reporting and the soon-to-be characteristic Hiaasen villain who improvises in the face of injury: in this case, the villain fashions a prosthetic limb out of a weed-whacker to replace an arm chewed off by a barracuda. The dark humor that characterizes Hiaasen's work is also readily apparent; an intruder is impaled on a stuffed trophy fish, and the television host, who is seeking to expose the plastic surgeon, meets his demise via uncontrolled liposuction on live television. Hiaasen's propensity for creating beyond-the-pale villains caught the attention of Katherine Dunn, who noted in *The New York Times Book Review* (15 October 1989), "no one has ever designed funnier, more terrifying bad guys, or concocted odder ways of doing away with them."

The oddness continues in Hiaasen's next work, which relies on familiar South Florida institutions as the source of its plot. In *Native Tongue* (1991) Hiaasen takes on the multiple issues of theme parks, endangered spe-

Dust jacket for Hiaasen's 2000 novel, about an ecoterrorist waging war against developers building on an island toad sanctuary (Richland County Public Library)

cies, and overdevelopment in his home state. The protagonist, Joe Winder, is thrust into a distasteful new environment: he is a former investigative reporter reduced to writing public-relations material for the theme park. He is shaken from his mundane life by the theft of two endangered mango voles that are part of a popular exhibit at the park. The intrigue culminates in the park burning down and the landscape being left alone for the time being. The deformed villain in this novel is a steroid-addled chief of security, who becomes so reliant on the drugs that he drags an IV along with him. He meets a perverse fate: he falls into the dolphin tank and drowns while being sodomized by the park's performing dolphin. The other villain, a ruthless developer with past organized crime connections, wants to destroy the Florida landscape further by building a golf complex next to the already intrusive theme park. He meets his demise at the hands of a hired hit man who also happens to be the prizewinning five-millionth visitor to the park. Skink also reappears as a helper in Winder's quest to unravel the labyrinthine twists of the plot. *Publishers Weekly* (12 July 1991) favorably compares Hiaasen's writing with that of Edward Abbey and termed the novel "sometimes scattershot, but always inventive." Other reviewers focused on the satirical ele-

ments and the level of conviction in conveying its environmental message.

Strip Tease (1993) was the first of Hiaasen's novels to make the best-seller list. The novel was later adapted for the screen in 1996 with Demi Moore, Burt Reynolds, Armand Assante, and Ving Rhames starring in the poorly executed and badly received film. Significant because it marks the first appearance of a woman as a protagonist in Hiaasen's work, the novel intertwines political intrigue and impropriety, Cuban interests in the sugar industry, custody battles, and some feminist thinking about women forced by circumstance into stripping to earn a living. Among the blackly humorous elements in this novel are death by golf club and sugar-refining equipment, a widely known congressman slathered from head to foot in Vaseline, and the mad search for a snake to replace the suspiciously deceased prop of one of the strippers. With regard to his first female protagonist, Erin Grant, Hiaasen remarked to Charlie Huisking in an interview in the *Sarasota Herald Tribune* (2 November 1997): "I operate on the theory that women are more interesting than men and generally sharper . . . they often face burdens greater than their male counterparts, yet they end up outliving us. I find them inspiring and mysterious, and I like that air of mystery." Walter Shapiro's review in *Time* magazine (20 September 1993) was mixed, describing the plot as "bare-bones" and suggesting that one must identify with specific characters in order to get full enjoyment from the work. In contrast, *Kirkus Reviews* (1993) was more forgiving, calling the novel a "marvelous madcap yarn" and adding that "Hiaasen's satire is more barbed than ever here . . . prime Hiaasen, and with a new edge: sexier, more violent, more political, but just as funny."

Hiaasen followed *Strip Tease* with *Stormy Weather* (1995), which intertwines the stories of different opportunists who seek to capitalize on the aftermath of a destructive hurricane. Multiple subplots about insurance swindles, inept housing inspection, grief peddling to television networks, and environmental protection, courtesy of the reappearing Skink, combine to give an all-too-accurate picture of the grotesque opportunism that arises after natural disasters. In typical Hiaasen fashion, the most villainous characters meet ghastly comeuppances: the builder guilty of shoddy construction practices is killed by flying debris at one of his sites, and the home inspector who approved many of the faultily constructed homes dies from a bite by a rabid rabbit intended to be part of a Santeria ritual. However, many of the less savory characters manage to escape fairly unscathed; for example, the opportunistic advertising executive who speeds to the disaster site with a video camera makes good at his agency, and a gold-digging woman desperately seeking a Kennedy scion for a mate finds happiness with the advertising executive. In an interesting twist, the novel concludes by letting the reader know that a group of nonindigenous wild animals, which had been released from an illegal zoo by the hurricane, has taken up residence in and around Dade County, thus representing a lasting impression of the power of nature to initiate change.

Hiaasen's approach found favor with reviewers. Bill Ott commented in *Booklist* (July 1995) on Hiaasen's ability to unite "slapstick nightmare, black comedy, and moral outrage in just the right proportions" and suggested that "Hiaasen's surrealistic vision of Florida on the brink of Armageddon bears comparison to Nathanael West's Hollywood and Malcolm Lowry's Mexico." Peeter Klopvillem, in a review in *Maclean's* (16 October 1995), praised Hiaasen's novel as a "wild, manic romp through the wasteland that remains after [Hurricane] Andrew's destructive passage" and notes that "with a keen sense of dialogue and detail," Hiaasen brings to life "a world of substandard homes reduced to kindling [and] uprooted trees . . . where the daytime sound of chainsaws gives way to the crackle of gunfire at night."

Though not torn straight from the news like *Stormy Weather,* Hiaasen's next novel, *Lucky You* (1997), relies upon occasional news items that provoke strange behaviors. The plot of *Lucky You* tackles the issue of lottery winnings and the greed that so often infects multiple winners who must split the jackpot. Hiaasen once again has a female protagonist, JoLayne Lucks, who is joined by another displaced investigative reporter who is reduced to writing happy human-interest stories for a regional daily. JoLayne echoes Hiaasen's fondness for all things natural: her intention is to use the lottery winnings to preserve a forest that is slated for cutting so a new strip mall can be built. The antagonists, two white-supremacist yokels looking to use the funds to bankroll a militia, represent what money can do to blind its holders. The yokels steal the heroine's ticket, dragoon a convenience-store clerk into joining them, kidnap a Hooters waitress, and finally are confronted by the heroes on an island with a high population of vultures, which inevitably figure into the demise of one of the villains while the other is done in by the stinger of a manta ray, which pierces his femoral artery. The waitress and the store clerk end up with one of the winning tickets; the protagonist secures her own; and all is right with the world.

Though some critics made observations about the unevenness of the plot, *Lucky You* was praised by reviewers on several counts. Tom DeHaven of *Entertainment Weekly* (28 November 1997) cited the intensity of the humor: "everything from survivalist folly to religious fanaticism is lampooned with gusto . . . the sledgehammer wackiness never flags." Charles Salzberg of *The New York Times Book Review* (16 November 1997) lauded the "witty dialogue that crackles" and noted that "his characters are eccentrically colorful." *Kirkus Reviews* (1997) was similarly complimentary: "the whole sideshow seethes and boils with all the grinning vitality of a 'Have a Nice Day' poster imagined by Hieronymous Bosch." Finally, *Publishers Weekly* (15 September 1997) praised the "crackling pace," "fall-down funny dialogue," and the "sweet and offbeat spirit" of the novel. *Lucky You* seems to mark the most successful fusion of the elements that characterize Hiaasen's work up to this time.

Prior to *Lucky You,* Hiaasen had deviated somewhat from his normal output with *Naked Came the Manatee* (1996), a mystery jointly written by Hiaasen and twelve other authors from South Florida, including Dave Barry and John Dufresne. Originally published in serial form in the *Tropic* magazine section of the *Miami Herald,* the novel brings together noted characters associated with each author, rushing them through a fast-paced and playful mystery with an emphasis on showcasing each author's propensity for having fun and developing quirky characters within the parameters of serial fiction. The manatee of the title, Booger, even has an individual chapter in which he shares his soul-

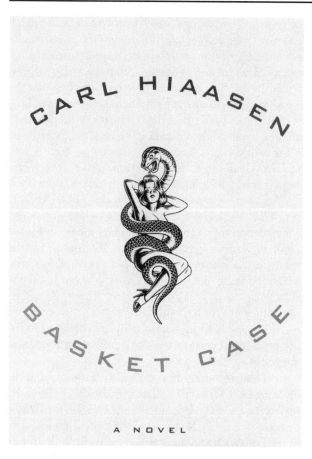

*Dust jacket for Hiaasen's 2002 novel about a reporter
investigating the death of a former rock star
(Richland County Public Library)*

searching with the audience. Hiaasen supplies the concluding chapter. *Publishers Weekly* (13 January 1997) terms the work "a successful experiment in the art of absurdity . . . [which] should be read for the pure fun of it."

Hiaasen continued in his experimental phase with a brief turn from fiction in 1998 when he published *Team Rodent: How Disney Devours the World*. Part of Ballantine's Library of Contemporary Thought series, *Team Rodent* is an unabashed and unforgiving attack on Disney World and its influence in Florida. In keeping with the series aim "to say things that need saying," Hiaasen examines—albeit with the bias of someone whose stated goal in life is to be "banned forever from Disney World"—the intrusions of Disney into Times Square, the improprieties that permeate the operation of Disney World (including the highly publicized incident involving the hidden camera in the locker room where female characters changed into their outfits), and the negative impact of the theme park on the Florida landscape. Described by Andrew Paxman in *Variety* (13 January 1998) as "a provocative overview of how Walt

[Disney] and his successor have turned a swath of central Florida into a candy-coated Orwellian state," the work is also praised by Paxman for comic treatment of Disney's all-consuming desire for secrecy and its fantastic visions of ecoterrorism that are right out of one of Hiaasen's fictional works.

Readers were given more of Hiaasen's nonfiction in *Kick Ass*. Editor Stevenson collects some of Hiaasen's *Miami Herald* columns on a variety of subjects, which are all united by Hiaasen's characteristic vitriol. Subjects include South Florida life ("Carl Hiaasen's South Florida Stress Test"), crime and punishment, and Hiaasen's favorite topic, urban development. Included in the collection is a comprehensive introduction with an overview of Hiaasen's life and career, giving readers a peek at the forces that have shaped Hiaasen's thinking and concerns and providing insight into the shape of his writing. Stevenson cites Dave Satterfield, a former *Miami Herald* city editor, who offers the characterization of Hiaasen's writing as "a baseball bat to the forehead" and observes that "Hiaasen looks at issues in terms of right and rather than according to some narrower agenda, he appeals to a wide audience." Doug Clifton, former executive editor of the *Miami Herald*, is also interviewed by Stevenson. He suggests that "people read Hiaasen to be outraged, to experience the same emotion he directs toward those who have violated the public trust." *Kick Ass* was well received. *Publishers Weekly* (25 October 1999) lauded Hiaasen's ability to overcome the limitations of his setting and specificity, noting that "Hiaasen's columns demonstrate a talent for expressing frustration with the status quo that will resonate well beyond the Miami city limits" and praising the writing as exhibiting "an old-time columnist's sense of righteous rage and an utterly current and biting wit." David Zucchino, reviewing the collection for *Southern Cultures* (Fall 2000), called Hiaasen one of the best newspaper columnists, praising him for performing "the columnist's sacred duty: to hold politicians and the powerful accountable, to expose society's flaws and foibles, to ridicule the artificial and the pompous, to lampoon the preposterous, to speak on behalf of the powerless and dispossessed."

In Hiaasen's next work of fiction, *Sick Puppy* (2000), he creates a protagonist, Twilly Spree, who most consistently mirrors the potential for ecoterrorism that permeates his work. Returning to territory explored in *Native Tongue*, *Sick Puppy* focuses on efforts by developers to build on Toad Island—so named for the thousands of oak toads that populate it—and Twilly's counterefforts to stymie the political and literal machines that seek to facilitate this development. Skink returns and becomes something of a father figure for Twilly; the novel concludes with the two of them in hot pursuit of a speeding Pontiac Firebird whose passengers are tossing beer bottles and other garbage out the windows. In keeping with past works, nature has a hand in the demise of several antagonists: one victim is found in the cab of a submerged bulldozer with several tadpoles alive and well in his throat; the developer is gored to death by a rhinoceros whose horn he covets to please his twin mistresses who like to dress up like perverted versions of Barbie dolls; and the rhino deals the corrupt politician backing the development deal a similar fate by trampling him to death. Ellen Moses, of *The Sarasota Herald Tribune* (30 January 2000), cited the "genuinely outrageous players" and "colorful backdrop" as factors in overcoming what may be seen as a "predictable plot." *Publishers Weekly* (8 November 1999) stated that "Hiaasen has refined his knack for using this gloomy but persistent state of affairs as a prime mover for scams of all sorts" and added that he "shows himself to be a comic writer at the peak of his powers." This peaking suggests Hiaasen's firm entrenchment within the mainstream framework of contemporary American fiction.

The favorable reception of *Kick Ass* led to additional dissemination of Hiaasen's columns: *Paradise Screwed,* another collection, appeared in 2001. Compiled once again by Stevenson, *Paradise Screwed* offers more coverage of the world of South Florida through the eyes of one of its most acerbic critics, including more contemporary issues such as the Elian Gonzales situation and the 2000 election fiasco. David Pitt of *Booklist* (15 September 2001) praised the collection, calling it "reminiscent of the snarky, opinionated newspaper articles of the great Mark Twain" and adding that "Hiaasen's columns are finely crafted little gems." Pitt declared *Paradise Screwed* and *Kick Ass* "the best collections of occasional journalism published in recent years" and praised Hiaasen for his ability to give issues most familiar to south Floridians "universality with his style and point of view." *Publishers Weekly* (2001) echoed Pitt's enthusiasm, calling the work "a head-shaking romp through a south Florida that they won't find in any tourist brochure." This review compared Hiaasen to Jimmy Breslin and Pete Hamill, describing him as "an old-school columnist who can't stomach greed or hypocrisy, pulls no punches, and keeps his sense of humor and outrage firmly intact."

With the publication of *Basket Case* (2002), Hiaasen presents his first novel that does not rely solely on ecological issues for its theme or structure. Set instead against the backdrop of the music industry, the novel chronicles the efforts of another former investigative reporter, Jack Tagger, to unravel the suspicious death of the lead singer of a once-popular rock band. The novel is also a departure in its use of first-person point of view (third-person omniscient is the norm in Hiaasen's other works). Tagger pursues the master copy of the victim's soon-to-be released comeback song while dealing not only with a parasitic hanger-on who seeks to capitalize on the victim's demise by releasing the song as her own but also with a burgeoning relationship between himself and his editor. In keeping with the characteristic Hiaasen reliance upon perverse injury and death, the victim is killed by a bait truck that backs over him, and Tagger fends off an attacker with the frozen carcass of a large lizard. The book was generally well received, despite its apparent movement away from Hiaasen's past topics. *The Economist* (30 March 2002) noted its "affectionate swipe at the pop-music crowd, and a more sincere jab at avaricious media tycoons . . . his rambunctious plot is largely a vehicle for snappy dialogue, snide parody, and wicked one-liners." The review also praised the book for its "offhand and compulsive social satire" and "marvelous sense of the absurd." Dan DeLuca of *The Philadelphia Tribune* (13 February 2002) provided some insight into the creation of the protagonist by interviewing Hiaasen and linking Tagger's personal obsessions to Hiaasen's reflections on his own mortality and the early demise of his father. Several interviews also focus on the uncharacteristic use of first-person narrative, which Hiaasen describes as "comfortable" but also "fun and scary." In a *Publishers Weekly* interview (12 November 2001) Hiaasen offers insight into the construction of the novel: "with each novel I like to do something a little different . . . I thought it would be interesting . . . to spend a whole novel inside one character's head . . . I actually wrote the first five chapters two different ways [first and third person] . . . I mulled both over and decided I liked the first-person better."

Hiaasen's next work, *Hoot* (2002), his first attempt at a book for children, marks a return to his favored subjects. This book is a coming-to-consciousness story involving a transplanted protagonist, a kid named Roy Eberhardt, who falls in with a young ecoprankster named Mullet Fingers. The plot involves their efforts to save a clutch of burrowing owls on a site earmarked for a chain restaurant while avoiding capture attempts by local officials, all of whom are inept and hypocritical. The work reflects Hiaasen's sentiments about educating the youth about nature and its fragility: he believes that such education is a vital necessity because it may lead to a heightened environmental consciousness in later generations, which he sees as one sure way of there being change for the better.

The reviews of *Hoot* were generally favorable; in *Publishers Weekly* (24 June 2002) Ott cited the "characteristically quirky characters and comic twists" that overcome the "intermittently protracted focus on several

/

CHAPTER ONE

At the stroke of eleven on a cool April night, a woman named Joey Perrone went overboard from a luxury deck of the cruise liner M.V. *Sun Duchess*. Plunging toward the dark Atlantic, Joey was too dumbfounded to panic.

I married an asshole, she thought, knifing headfirst into the waves.

The impact tore off her silk skirt, blouse, panties, wristwatch and sandals, but Joey remained conscious and alert. Of course she did. She had been co-captain of her college swim team, a biographical nugget that her husband obviously had forgotten.

Bobbing in its fizzy wake, Joey watched the gaily lit *Sun Duchess* continue steaming away at twenty nautical miles per hour. Evidently only one of the other 2,049 passengers was aware of what had happened, and he wasn't telling anybody.

Bastard, Joey thought.

She noticed that her bra was down around her waist, and wriggled free of it. To the west, under a canopy of soft amber light, was the coast of Florida. Joey began to swim.

The water of the Gulf Stream was actually warmer than the air, but a brisk northeasterly wind had kicked up a messy and uncomfortable chop. Joey paced herself. To keep her mind off sharks, she replayed the noteworthy events of the week-long cruise, which had begun almost as unpromisingly as it had ended.

The *Sun Duchess* had departed Port Everglades three hours late because a raccoon had turned up berserk in the pastry kitchen. One of the chefs had wrestled the frothing critter into a sixty-gallon tin of

Typescript page for Hiaasen's novel Skinny Dip, *forthcoming from Knopf in 2004 (courtesy of the author)*

adults." Ott noted that "several suspenseful scenes build to the denouement involving the sitcom-like unraveling of a muckity-muck at the pancake house; these, along with dollops of humor, help make the novel quite a hoot indeed." *Kirkus Reviews* (15 July 2002) lauded Roy, the protagonist, calling him "surprisingly engaging . . . it's his kind of determined innocence that sees through the corruption and compromises of the adult world to understand what must be done to make things right." *Hoot* was named a Newbery Honor Book in 2003.

Occasional interviews and profiles of Hiaasen dot the Internet. Hiaasen's official website, <http://www.carlhiaasen.com>, includes multiple interviews with the author, as well as links to individual works and tour information. Lengthy interviews with Hiaasen also appear in *The Armchair Detective* (1996) and in the on-line magazine *Salon* (2000). Most discussions of Hiaasen's work are found in reviews culled from the popular press, but he is slowly finding a place within critical discussions. One critical study of note is Julie Sloan Brannon's 1997 article on Hiaasen, the grotesque, and regional noir fiction. Dana Phillips's 1994 article "Is Nature Necessary?" contrasts Hiaasen's work with that of Ernest Hemingway in an effort to fix the writing within the realm of "postmodernist views of nature." In a 1990 essay Peter Jordan addresses Hiaasen's combining of ecological concerns within the milieu of crime fiction. Ott offers a brief discussion of Hiaasen's techniques of characterization, particularly of his "bad guys," in "Hiaasen's People" (2001). The most lengthy and thoroughgoing treatment of his early years is Joanne Kenen's "Carl of the Wild" (1993). Though slightly out of date with respect to the more mature novels, the piece offers both biographical data and examples of Hiaasen's passion about the subjects he holds dear.

Carl Hiaasen still lives in Florida with his wife, Fenia, whom he married in 1999, and their son, Quinn. With the positive reception of his work and his ongoing output in the *Miami Herald,* Hiaasen's place in the canon of contemporary American authors seems assured. Marked by their ability to transcend both time and place, his words tweak the sensitivities of those disinclined to take his ecological messages seriously. Hiaasen's characters, bizarre as they may be, are accessible to a wide audience. Hiaasen's experience as a journalist has exposed him to the "news of the weird" on a constant basis, and this knowledge has a palpable influence on his plots and characters. His works show the reader in no uncertain terms that strange things do happen, and strange people usually have a hand in such occurrences. Hiaasen also reveals that nature is a harsh critic of human folly and takes no prisoners in dealing out punishments to those who would trespass against her.

Interviews:

Charles Silet, "Sun, Sand, and Tirades: An Interview with Carl Hiaasen," *Armchair Detective,* 29 (Winter 1996): 8–18;

"The Interview: Carl Hiaasen," *Bon Appetit* (August 1997): 122;

Charlie Huisking, "Following in His Footsteps," *Sarasota Herald Tribune,* 2 November 1997, p. 1E;

Jay Lee MacDonald, "Carl Hiaasen Takes a Bite Out of Crimes Against the Environment," *BookPage,* January 2000 <http://www.bookpage.com/0001bp/carl_hiaasen.html>;

David Bowman, "Carl Hiaasen," *Salon,* 31 January 2000 <http://www.salon.com/people/lunch/2000/01/31/hiaasen/print.html>;

Adam Dunn, "PW Talks with Carl Hiaasen," *Publishers Weekly* (12 November 2001).

References:

Julie Sloan Brannon, "The Rules Are Different Here: South Florida Noir and the Grotesque," in *Crime Fiction and Film in the Sunshine State,* edited by Steve Glassman and Maurice O'Sullivan (Bowling Green, Ohio: Popular Press, 1997), pp. 47–64;

Christina Cheakalos, "Hurricane Hiaasen," *People Weekly* (15 May 2000): 139;

Peter Jordan, "Carl Hiaasen's Environmental Thrillers: Crime Fiction in Search of Green Peace," *Studies in Popular Culture,* 13, no. 1 (1990): 61–71;

Joanne Kenen, "Carl of the Wild," *American Journalism Review,* 15 (October 1993);

Bill Ott, "Hiaasen's People," *Booklist,* 97 (1 May 2001): 1600;

Dana Phillips, "Is Nature Necessary?" *Raritan,* 13 (Winter 1994): 78–100;

Susan Schindehette and Meg Grant, "Tree Hugger From Hell," *People Weekly* (21 October 1991): 95.

Alice Hoffman

(16 March 1952 –)

Kate Cochran
Northern Kentucky University

BOOKS: *Property Of* (New York: Farrar, Straus & Giroux, 1977; London: Hutchinson, 1978);

The Drowning Season (New York: Dutton, 1979; London: Hutchinson, 1979);

Angel Landing (New York: Putnam, 1980; London: Severn House, 1982);

White Horses (New York: Putnam, 1982; London: Collins, 1983);

Fortune's Daughter (New York: Putnam, 1985; London: Collins Harvill, 1985);

Illumination Night (New York: Putnam, 1987; London: Macmillan, 1987);

At Risk (New York: Putnam, 1988; London: Macmillan, 1988);

Seventh Heaven (New York: Putnam, 1990; London: Virago, 1991);

Turtle Moon (Franklin Center, Pa.: Franklin Library, 1992; New York: Putnam, 1992; London: Macmillan, 1992);

Second Nature (New York: Putnam, 1994; London: Macmillan, 1994);

Practical Magic (New York: Putnam, 1995; London: Macmillan, 1996);

Here on Earth (New York: Putnam, 1997; London: Chatto & Windus, 1997);

Fireflies: A Winter's Tale (New York: Hyperion, 1997);

Local Girls (New York: Putnam, 1999; London: Chatto & Windus, 1999);

The River King (New York: Putnam, 2000; London: Chatto & Windus, 2000);

Horsefly (New York: Hyperion, 2000);

Aquamarine (New York: Scholastic, 2001; London: Egmont, 2003);

Blue Diary (New York: Putnam, 2001; London: Chatto & Windus, 2001);

Indigo (New York: Scholastic, 2002);

Green Angel (New York: Scholastic, 2003);

The Probable Future (New York: Doubleday, 2003; London: Chatto & Windus, 2003);

Moondog, by Hoffman and Wolfe Martin (New York: Scholastic, forthcoming 2004).

PRODUCED SCRIPT: *Independence Day,* motion picture, Warner Bros., 1983.

OTHER: Excerpt from *Second Nature,* in *Women on Hunting,* edited by Pam Houston (Hopewell, N.J.: Ecco, 1995);

"Advice from My Grandmother," in *Connecting: Twenty Prominent Authors Write About Relationships That Shape Our Lives,* edited by Lee Gutkind (New York: Putnam, 1996);

John Miller and Tim Smith, eds., *Cape Cod Stories: Tales from Cape Cod, Nantucket, and Martha's Vineyard,* introduction by Hoffman (San Francisco: Chronicle, 1996);

Scribner's Best of the Fiction Workshops 1997, edited by Hoffman (New York: Scribners, 1997);

Entry by Hoffman, in *Thirty-Three Things Every Girl Should Know,* edited by Tonya Bolden (New York: Crown, 1998);

Maclin Bocock, *A Citizen of the World,* introduction by Hoffman (Cambridge, Mass.: Zoland, 1999);

Harvey Oxenhorn, *Turning the Rig: A Journey to the Arctic,* introduction by Hoffman (Cambridge, Mass.: Zoland, 2000);

Washington Irving, *The Legend of Sleepy Hollow and Other Stories,* introduction by Hoffman (New York: Modern Library, 2001);

Emily Brontë, *Wuthering Heights,* introduction by Hoffman (New York: Scholastic Classics, 2001);

Ploughshares, 29 (Fall 2003), edited by Hoffman.

SELECTED PERIODICAL PUBLICATIONS–UNCOLLECTED:

FICTION

"Kindness," *Fiction,* 4, no. 2 (1976): 28–30;

"Sleep Tight," *Ploughshares,* 15 (1989): 102–112;

"The Secret Soup," *New York Times Book Review: A Gorey Christmas,* 2 December 1990, pp. 16–18;

"Rose Red," *Ladies' Home Journal* (July 1996): 92–96;

"Local Girls," *Cosmopolitan* (October 1996): 250–254;

"Dream Girl," *Redbook* (February 1997): 128–131;

Alice Hoffman (photograph © Debi Milligan; from the dust jacket for
Blue Diary, *2001; Richland County Public Library)*

"Bake at 350," *Agni,* 45 (1997): 94–100;

"The Man Who Could Eat Fire," *Story Quarterly,* 33 (1997): 25–34;

"Still Among the Living," *Boulevard,* 12, no. 1–2 (1997): 112–121;

"The Rest of Your Life," *Boulevard,* 12, no. 3 (1997): 88–94;

"True Confession," *Southwest Review,* 82 (1997): 531–543;

"How to Talk to the Dead," *Kenyon Review,* 20 (1998): 93–100;

"Examining the Evidence" and "Devotion," *Five Points,* 3, no. 3 (1999): 93–102;

"Gretel," *Literary Cavalcade,* 52 (2000): 6–10.

NONFICTION

"The Book That Wouldn't Die: A Writer's Last and Longest Voyage," *New York Times,* 22 July 1990, p. 14;

"Provider," *New York Times Magazine,* 1 November 1992, pp. 22–24;

"It's a Wonderful House," *Architectural Digest* (December 1993): 30–32;

"Reviving the Spirit of a Cape Cod Farmhouse," *Architectural Digest* (February 1997): 36–41;

"What Grandma Knows," *Ladies' Home Journal* (September 1997): 184;

"Hot Potato Wisdom," *Utne Reader,* 90 (1998): 37–39;

"Summertime on Cape Cod," *Gourmet* (August 1999): 58–60;

"A Cure for Self-Loathing," *Self* (October 1999): 144;

"Sustained By Fiction While Facing Life's Facts," *New York Times,* 14 August 2000, p. E1;

"Aquamarine" (April 2001) <http://www.alicehoffman. com/aquamarine.html>;

"What I Wish I'd Told My Mother," *Redbook* (August 2003): 106–109;

"People in Glass Houses Shouldn't Throw Stones," *Good Housekeeping* (September 2003): 152.

Alice Hoffman developed a taste for the magical at an early age from reading Grimm's fairy tales and stories by Ray Bradbury; an affinity for magic permeates all of her fiction. Her novels, short stories, and children's books revolve around archetypal symbols, fairy-

*Dust jacket for Hoffman's first novel (1977), written while she
was a student at Stanford University, about a teenage girl
who becomes involved with a street gang (Richland
County Public Library)*

interview in *The New York Times* she said of her childhood, "Unhappiness was trapped in the house like a bubble. My mother was a teacher and a social worker, and my father wasn't there. My brother was the smart one, the scientist." She received a B.A. in English and anthropology from Adelphi University in 1973, writing short stories and subsequently earning an Edith Mirrielees Fellowship to the Stanford University Creative Writing Center, from which she received an M.A. in creative writing in 1975. After beginning a doctoral program at SUNY Stony Brook and briefly living in Manhattan, Hoffman married Tom Martin; the couple and their two sons live outside Boston. Despite her literary acclaim, Hoffman prefers to live a quiet life. As Ruth Reichl observed in "At Home with Alice Hoffman: A Writer Set Free by Magic" (*The New York Times,* 10 February 1994), Hoffman is one of the most private authors in the United States. She told Reichl, "I think the book should just be the book, not the author."

Hoffman has spoken often about the influence Grace Paley's work had on her. In the 1994 *New York Times* interview Hoffman stated, "Before I read her, I thought I didn't have anything to write about. I was a young woman; I had never been to war. Reading Grace Paley changed a lot of things. I began to write." While Hoffman was still at Stanford, she wrote and published her first novel, *Property Of* (1977). The story is told by a teenage girl infatuated with gang life and with McKay, the leader of the "Orphan" gang, a band of pseudochivalric knights obsessed with honor. The narrator and McKay explore sex and drugs and ultimately confront addiction, murder, abortion, rape, and incarceration. In his *New York Times* review (10 July 1977) Michael Mewshaw observed of the narrator, "Addicted to love, she becomes addicted to heroin, because she cannot stand to be outside, alone. In the end when she kicks both habits, the reader is moved, but cannot understand why she took so long." The narrator does realize that her magical thinking, code of silence, steadfast loyalty, and dragon's tooth charm fail to keep her connected to McKay, and she thereby succeeds in her own quest for identity, eschewing becoming the "property of" anyone but herself—the first to do so in the succession of Hoffman's female protagonists.

The reader never learns the name of the narrator of *Property Of* nor the surname of the family of characters in Hoffman's next novel, *The Drowning Season* (1979), indicating that external signifiers such as names define neither identity nor family connection for Hoffman. In *The Drowning Season* the family matriarch, Esther the White, traveled from Russia to Marseilles and London, finally settling in New York, where she Anglicized her last name and constructed a family "Compound" on the coastline. The security and pres-

tale structures, and the interweaving of the fantastic with the quotidian. Her novels have been named notable books of the year by *The New York Times, The Los Angeles Times,* and *Library Journal.* Although her use of fairy-tale structures allies her with authors such as Angela Carter, Robert Coover, and Gregory Maguire, most reviewers classify her writing as magic realism, descended from Nathaniel Hawthorne and related to Gabriel García Márquez, Salman Rushdie, and Isabel Allende. Her characters navigate Romantic landscapes haunted by ghosts, animals, or other wild creatures and often must resolve the almost Gothic grip the past holds on their lives and souls. The melding of the Romantic, the Gothic, fairy tales, and magic realism within a quest to understand identity and human relationships characterizes Hoffman's fiction.

Born in New York City on 16 March 1952, Hoffman grew up in Valley Stream, Long Island. When she was eight years old, her parents divorced; in a 1994

tige of the Compound is threatened, however, by the legend of the Drowned Man, the frequent suicide attempts of her son, Phillip, and her tenuous control over her family. Jerome Charyn noted in his *New York Times* review (15 July 1979) that "*The Drowning Season* is a touching and startling novel by a young writer who has a feeling for myth, genuine wickedness and the nagging perversity of love." Esther the White learns that only by connecting with her rebellious eighteen-year-old granddaughter, Esther the Black, can she attain the sense of family that the Compound and her manipulations of Phillip as well as of her daughter-in-law, Rose, and her husband, Mischa, are intended to provide. Although Carol L. Cardozo's *Library Journal* review (15 June 1979) stated that the "constellation of bizarre people and strange events . . . doesn't gel into a coherent whole," James N. Baker's review in *The Nation* (15 September 1979), noted that *The Drowning Season* "betrays a talented writer's eagerness to try something different. But her book is finally a study of redemption, as moving as John Cheever's *Falconer*." Redemption ultimately takes the form of surrendering control, as Esther the White and Esther the Black learn to rely on each other.

With *Angel Landing* (1980) Hoffman experiments with interweaving first- and third-person narration. Most of the novel is recounted by an omniscient narrator, but in the course of counseling sessions and conversations, Natalie Lansky, a social worker, listens to Michael Finn's history firsthand. Finn is guilty of blowing up the nuclear power plant Angel Landing III, and Natalie is responsible for both healing and saving him. Larry McMurtry stated in his *New York Times* review (30 June 1981), "Alice Hoffman . . . is very good at describing emotional pain. Since Michael Finn has lived with emotional pain all his life she has, in this novel, plenty to describe." But Hoffman's use of marginal characters—Natalie's Aunt Minnie, her former boyfriend Carter, and her colleague Lark—reveals the thematic thrust of this novel: one must choose a reason to live that is somehow bigger than oneself in order to survive spiritually. Frances Esmonde de Usabel of *Library Journal* (1 October 1980) observed that "Hoffman is talking about the courage to be, to feel, to act": the characters choose separate paths, mainly inspired by social activism or romantic love, but all have in common the fierce desire to establish control over their own lives. Unlike most of Hoffman's other novels, *Angel Landing* does not employ many supernatural elements. Instead, the author seems more interested in the power of psychology and the ways in which family, the past, loss, and love coalesce into a coherent identity for the individual.

In *White Horses* (1982) Hoffman returns to describing the ineluctable hold of family that she examines in *The Drowning Season*. For the Connors of Santa Rosa,

family identity is rooted in history, isolation, storytelling, and incest. In her *New York Times* review (28 March 1982) Anne Tyler observed that this novel marks a significant change in Hoffman's writing because of its balance of magic and the everyday: "The overall impression is one of abundant life, masterfully orchestrated by the author." *White Horses* is the first novel in which Hoffman reveals her interest in the manifestations of desire, a motif that reoccurs frequently in her fiction. For Teresa and her brother Silver, desire is embodied in the legend of the Arias, a group of daring night riders who traverse the desert on white horses. Their mother, Dina, tells them this story so compellingly and so often that it seems clear to them that Silver is an Aria and thus cannot be denied, even when he seduces his sister. Most reviewers focused on the depiction of longing and enchantment in the novel rather than on its representation of molestation; *White Horses* portrays incest as the interplay of desire, dysfunction, and psychic dis-ease. Jackie Cassada commented in her 15 March 1982 *Library Journal* review, "Teresa's inevitable love affair with her brother affords further protections from the choices she must make as an adult." Teresa develops a sleeping sickness in response to her family dynamic; in later works Hoffman's female protagonists often experience somatic manifestations of their psychic discontent. This novel also represents the first time that Hoffman uses a detective as a main character, balancing the magical pull of desire with clinical investigations of that desire.

Hoffman's fifth novel, *Fortune's Daughter* (1985), manipulates the magnetism of both the past and the future in the relationship of Rae Perry and Lila Grey. The story is set in Hollywood during earthquake season, and Hoffman uses the natural environment to provide some of the magical power that exudes influence over her characters. Rather than legends of chivalric knights, the Drowned Man, or night rider Arias, the characters' own lives provide the mythic background for this novel. Hoffman concentrates her depiction of desire in this novel on the desire of the mother. Lila relives the experience of giving up her own daughter for adoption as she develops a friendship with the pregnant and abandoned Rae. Lila is a fortune-teller; she reads tea leaves, conjures up the ghost of her baby, and bakes wishes and lessons into a cake for Rae. In "The Grip of Family in the Novels of Alice Hoffman and David Small" (1997), Sanford Pinsker describes Rae as suffering "from all the usual Hoffmanesque conditions (pregnant by a cruel and dangerous man, cut off from her parents, seeking the aid and comfort of an older, fortune-telling woman)" and notes that the novel exhibits "the way that magical transcendences fuse with

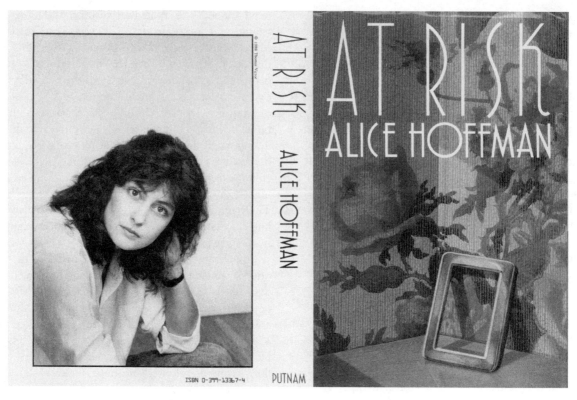

*Dust jacket for Hoffman's 1988 novel, about an eleven-year-old girl who contracts
AIDS through a blood transfusion (Richland County Public Library)*

aspects of the ordinary to provide something akin to closure."

Illumination Night (1987), the first book that Hoffman wrote after becoming a mother herself, also focuses on motherhood, but in it she broadens her examination to include parenting by fathers and grandparents. In presenting different portrayals of parenting, Hoffman highlights the terror of being a child but also emphasizes another consistent theme: the struggle between fate and free will. Andre and Vonny are worried about their four-year-old son Simon's lack of growth and the tenuous state of their own marriage. Vonny's resulting agoraphobia reveals how an individual must confront his or her own limitations; after she is finally able to leave her house, Vonny realizes: "By the time you have made your third run down the driveway you have stopped asking yourself why you have to start all over again. You are simply a woman practicing the art of real life." Practicing the art of real life, for Hoffman, means dealing with what is, like Vonny's agoraphobia, and with what was, like Andre's brief affair with sixteen-year-old Jody, in order to synthesize an understanding of self in the present. The characters' struggle between the past and the present, fate and free will, and dreams and reality is reflected in the magic

realism of Hoffman's writing. Pinsker asserts of *Illumination Night,* "Life and dreams might well intertwine . . . but there is surely enough surface grit, enough sense that her characters are connected by human threads, for her eccentrics to seem normal, and for the 'normal' to seem eccentric." Hoffman manipulates the tension between eccentricity and normalcy by juxtaposing the supernatural and the quotidian.

Hoffman received increased critical attention for *At Risk* (1988), in which she recounts the events that ensue after an eleven-year-old, Amanda, is diagnosed with AIDS. Some reviewers, such as Ann H. Fisher of the *Library Journal* (1 July 1988), applauded Hoffman's focus on issues of AIDS as both topical and cathartic. However, since Amanda is doubly innocent, as a child and by contracting AIDS from a blood transfusion, activists and critics faulted Hoffman's examination of AIDS as too neat. In his *New York Times* review (4 July 1988), Christopher Lehmann-Haupt called the novel "touching but too schematic," adding, "The problem is that even though *At Risk* seems spontaneous and original, a reader never escapes the sense of a blueprint behind it." This impression may be caused in part by the patterns of scientific inquiry appearing in the novel, both in facts surrounding Amanda's medical condition

Dust jacket for Hoffman's 1995 novel, about a pair of sisters who use the family gift for witchcraft to cope with the complications of love (Richland County Public Library)

and her father's profession as an astronomer, and in dreams, as when her younger brother, Charlie, has a nightmare about being one of the last dinosaurs. Science acts as a kind of detective work in Hoffman's fiction, since both pursuits base hypotheses in empirical evidence and use facts to deduce theories about reality. However, Hoffman shows that rational explanations are often insufficient: there exists a truth that rationality cannot approach. Laurel Smith, a psychic who communes with the dead, provides a counterpoint to rationality in this novel, but Hoffman also shows that dreams, magic, and the paranormal can prove just as inconclusive. The grief her characters endure is much more powerful than the rationality of science or the magic of the paranormal because it is rooted in their love for Amanda.

Hoffman's eighth novel, *Seventh Heaven* (1990), takes place in a sanitized 1950s Long Island subdivision undergoing a magical transformation. By the time the protagonist, Nora Silk, rids Hemlock Street of its bothersome crows and takes a seventeen-year-old as a lover, marriages have dissolved; housewives have gotten jobs; and the ghost of a dead girl walks down the street in red

high heels. According to J. H. Korelitz of *TLS* (15 February 1991), *Seventh Heaven* is a coming-of-age tale in which every character matures; for Barbara Ann Schapiro, Nora Silk is "the agent of desire." Hoffman uses the staid environment of a 1950s suburb to show what happens—to individuals, to relationships, and to whole communities—when desire goes unfulfilled. In a 2000 interview for *Bookreporter.com* Hoffman said: "Every time I write a novel it begins in a different way. Sometimes with a character, as in *Seventh Heaven,* which began with Nora Silk, a woman who arrives in a neighborhood and shakes up the residents' lives. Sometimes with a place, as in *Turtle Moon,* where the invented town of Verity came to be all at once, as if a map had been delivered to me in the middle of the night." In *Turtle Moon* (1992) the main characters live in an apartment building populated by thirteen divorced women in Verity, Florida. Hoffman again uses landscape and season to imbue the novel with magic, as the first line of the novel indicates: "Every May, when the sea turtles begin their migration across West Main Street, mistaking the glow of streetlights for the moon, people go a little bit crazy." Despite a murder, two missing children, and an angel

*Dust jacket for Hoffman's 2001 novel in which a woman discovers
that her loving husband is not the person he appears to be
(Richland County Public Library)*

haunting a gumbo-limbo tree, the main characters come to a clearer understanding of self by exploring their pasts and giving in to their desires, learning how to forgive themselves for both their past wrongs and their human frailties.

With *Second Nature* (1994), Hoffman again examines self-forgiveness, but she also focuses on the ways in which people underestimate the power of nature. Robin Moore rescues the Wolf Man, a man raised by wolves and caught by trappers. She teaches him to read, to drive, and to live in a community of people. But the opening quotation from Jean-Jacques Rousseau– "Nature never deceives us; it is always we who deceive ourselves"–foreshadows the Wolf Man's integrity of self and his eventual return to the woods. In "'To Build is to Dwell': The Beautiful, Strange Architectures of Alice Hoffman's Novels" (1996), Terri Brown-Davidson notes: "*Second Nature* is a more fantastic yet ultimately less imaginative and satisfying exploration of a world ripe for

peeling back to expose its spiritual/supernatural core." Stephen, the Wolf Man, is untouched by society; his time with Robin in the Nassau County suburbs reveals the sickness inherent in human society which mandates (self) deceit, a repeated message in Hoffman's works.

Practical Magic (1995) is Hoffman's best-known novel because of its adaptation as a motion picture starring Sandra Bullock and Nicole Kidman in 1998. In a review of *Practical Magic* in the *Antioch Review* (Winter 1996), Suzann Bick wrote: "Hoffman's likable novel mimics the plot of many 19th-century narratives using paired protagonists: the 'bad' sister emerges as more interesting than the good one." The "good" sister, Sally, becomes a slave to domesticity while Gillian, the "bad" sister, flees human connection and responsibility. Raised by their witchy maiden aunts in Massachusetts, the two girls took separate but parallel directions in life, only to meet again after Gillian's diabolical lover dies. The two aunts, Gillian and Sally, and Sally's two daughters represent generational pairs whose life choices, largely based in defense mechanisms, work against their growing sense of family, acknowledgment of true love, and individual destinies. Barbara Hoffert of the *Library Journal* (15 May 1995) observed that the theme of *Practical Magic* "that we must follow our destinies is not entirely original, but Hoffman gives it a nice twist in this charming, readable tale."

Here on Earth (1997) is inspired by Emily Brontë's *Wuthering Heights* (1847), with the Earnshaws and the Lintons represented by the Murrays of Fox Hill and the Coopers of Guardian Farm, respectively. In her review of *Here on Earth* in the *Women's Review of Books* (March 1998), Rebecca Steinitz stated: "Despite its temporal and physical transmutations, this novel ultimately . . . seeks to fill in the gaps, here to answer the question of what might have happened if Catherine and Heathcliff had reunited." March Murray returns to her Massachusetts childhood home for a funeral and is reunited with the Heathcliffesque Hollis, ultimately moving in with him and enduring his abusive temperament. Gwen, March's daughter, and Hank, Hollis's ward, become the more promising couple, according to Steinitz, since "Gwen and Hank have their own redemptive stories that depart significantly from those of their fictional forebears, Cathy and Hareton, and offer a powerful counterpart to their own older generation." Nancy Pate of the *Orlando Sentinel* noted in her review (18 March 1998), "Although darker than some of Hoffman's other works, *Here on Earth* has a similar fablelike air." As in *White Horses,* the seductive male character smells of fire; as in *Fortune's Daughter,* home is represented by a lemon tree; and, as in all of Hoffman's novels, fear is finally understood to be the driving force behind the characters' belief in fate.

Hoffman's *Local Girls* (1999) is usually characterized as a collection of short stories rather than as a novel, although each story follows the Samuelson family in the suburb of Franconia. The collection reveals the influence not only of fairy tales, such as Rose Red and Hansel and Gretel, but also of stories from Scripture, such as Jacob wrestling with the angel of God. Valerie Miner's review in the *Women's Review of Books* (November 1999) found in *Local Girls* the ontology of female friendship: "Hoffman's snappy, conversational style in the early chapters belies the depths of philosophical inquiry, intelligent humor and profound grief conveyed by her book as a whole." Hoffman received much attention for donating the proceeds from this novel to breast cancer research and care; the character of Frances Samuelson is diagnosed with breast cancer, as was Hoffman in 1998. In the "Frequently Asked Questions" section of her official website, <http://www.alicehoffman.com>, Hoffman explained:

> The first profits have gone to a local hospital to start a Breast Center, so that women who are diagnosed will be guided by experts, such as oncology nurses, as they make their decisions for their treatment. In the past, I donated my advance from my novel *At Risk* to AIDS research and funding for People with AIDS. I have always believed there is a connection between literature and social action, and so this is my way of trying to make a difference.

She is following the models of her literary heroes, Paley and Tillie Olsen, whom she esteems not only for their artistic achievements but also for their activism.

With *The River King* (2000), Hoffman revisits her themes of powerfully deliberate natural landscapes, damaging human cruelty, intimacy as the sharing of secret pain and an involuntary pull to mutual vulnerability, and hauntingly profound desire. As in previous novels, Hoffman shows that the founder of a place in part determines its magic-filled landscape, community personality, and the grip of the past on the characters. In this case, Dr. Howe is the first headmaster of the Haddan School, and his mistreatment of his wife, Annie, sets up both the combative relationship between the school and the town as well as a legacy of meanness for the students. This meanness gives rise to hazing, exclusion, and ultimately the mysterious drowning of a student. In part, the characters in this novel try to shed Dr. Howe's legacy through Hoffman's characteristic path to human connection via desire. Amanda Fortini's *New York Times* review (16 July 2000) lauded Hoffman's realistic mix of the Gothic and the Romantic: "good old-fashioned storytelling . . . is Hoffman's strength."

The figure of a cruel and powerful man, a constant in Hoffman's fictions, again takes center stage in

Blue Diary (2001), in which she retells the story of Bluebeard. Jorie Ford discovers that her loving husband of thirteen years, a pillar of the community, has all that time been hiding the truth of a rape and murder he committed in his youth. Hoffman adds the subplots of a breast cancer survivor finding true love and a twelve-year-old boy struggling with the truth about his father. She maintains a consistent magical atmosphere not only with the skeleton of Bluebeard's plot but also with her depiction of the pervasiveness of nature: the universe interacts with the characters. Although some critics faulted Hoffman's overuse of environment, Hoffman consistently establishes a contrast between nature and humanity. Individuals' actions can be futile or ineffective, backfiring because they act out of desire and need. Nature is self-contained but always influential, god-like in its mysterious power over the individuals who must navigate it.

Hoffman has also written several children's books—*Fireflies: A Winter's Tale* (1997), *Horsefly* (2000), *Aquamarine* (2001), *Indigo* (2002), and *Green Angel* (2003)—that explore her appreciation for magic, fairy tales, and the mystery of human relationships. Moreover, these books portray children who achieve compassion through caring for disempowered and enchanted creatures: fireflies, a mermaid, a flying horse, a magical puppy-cum-werewolf. Hoffman notes in the brief on-line essay "Aquamarine" (2001) that she enjoys writing children's books, since "Introducing someone to the world of literature and to a writer whose books have been meaningful to you is a treasured gift. I hope that *Aquamarine* will be a way for mothers and younger daughters to share my work and to share the joy of reading." *Green Angel* was included on the *Publishers Weekly* list of top books for teens in 2003, and the author's advance for this book was donated to the New York Women's Foundation to benefit young women and girls in lower Manhattan.

Hoffman's next novel, *The Probable Future* (2003), recounts the story of three generations of women in the Sparrow family. Rebecca Sparrow was persecuted as a witch in eighteenth-century Unity, Massachusetts, and her descendants discover paranormal powers on their thirteenth birthdays: grandmother Elinor can detect others' lies; mother Jenny can see others' dreams; and Stella can foresee others' deaths. When Stella tries to change "the probable future" by warning a woman of her imminent death, Stella's father is accused of the woman's murder, and the three generations of Sparrow women must relive their ancestral past. Starr E. Smith of the *Library Journal* (15 March 2003) called *The Probable Future* "another over-the-top yet thoroughly appealing fictional confection," while Molly Haskell's *New Leader* review (May/June 2003) deemed the novel "a feminist folk tale" in which Hoffman "counters the many featherbrained and girly-chick images of teenage girls with her fierce and intelligent young women, whose gifts got them into trouble, whose wills clashed with men, but who refuse to be silenced anymore." In *The Probable Future,* as in most of Hoffman's other novels, female characters feel that they are under a spell, and that spell feels like fate. However, in the end, each understands that she makes her own fate by choosing either to remain spellbound or to transcend the legacy of her past.

In "Sustained By Fiction While Facing Life's Facts" (2000) Hoffman explains how writing nourished her during her battle with cancer:

> I wrote to find beauty and purpose, to know that love is possible and lasting and real, to see day lilies and swimming pools, loyalty and devotion, even though my eyes were closed and all that surrounded me was a darkened room. I wrote because that was who I was at the core, and if I was too damaged to walk around the block, I was lucky all the same. Once I got to my desk, once I started writing, I still believed anything was possible.

The reader finds in Alice Hoffman's novels the same sustenance that writing brought to her. Through exploring intersections of the supernatural and everyday, Hoffman's fiction depicts characters in the process of learning about change, chance, loss, and desire, all of which one must embrace as a part of the tapestry of magical human connection.

Interviews:

"'At Risk' Author Discusses Fears About AIDS," *New York Times,* 18 July 1988, p. C15;

Ruth Reichl, "At Home with Alice Hoffman: A Writer Set Free by Magic," *New York Times,* 10 February 1994, p. C1;

Rose Martelli, "What Makes a Family Strong?" *Redbook* (July 1999): G1–G3;

Ellen Kanner, "Making Believe: Alice Hoffman Takes Her Practical Magic to the River," *BookPage* (August 2000) <http://www.bookpage.com/0008bp/alice_hoffman.html>;

Jana Siciliano and Dana Schwartz, "Interview" (10 August 2001) and "Past Interview" (4 August 2000), *Bookreporter.com* <http://www.bookreporter.com/authors/au-hoffman-alice.asp>;

Zoe Frechette, "Talking with Alice Hoffman," *Story Quarterly,* 38 (2002): 228–236;

Judith Gaines, "Alice Hoffman," *Yankee,* 67, no. 10 (2003): 18;

Melissa Mia Hall and Jeff Zaleski, "The Quest for Blue Rose and Other Unexpected Gifts," *Publishers Weekly* (5 May 2003): 196.

References:

Terri Brown-Davidson, "'To Build Is to Dwell': The Beautiful, Strange Architectures of Alice Hoffman's Novels," *Hollins Critic,* 33 (1996): 1–15;

Joseph Dewey, "Music for a Closing: Responses to AIDS in Three American Novels," in *AIDS: The Literary Response,* edited by Emmanuel S. Nelson (New York: Twayne, 1992);

Katie Hogan, "Speculations on Women and AIDS," *Minnesota Review,* 40 (1993): 84–93;

Maryanne O'Hara, "About Alice Hoffman," *Ploughshares,* 29, no. 2–3 (2003): 194–198;

Judith Lawrence Pastore, "Suburban AIDS: Alice Hoffman's *At Risk,*" in *AIDS: The Literary Response,* edited by Nelson (New York: Twayne, 1992);

Sanford Pinsker, "The Grip of Family in the Novels of Alice Hoffman and David Small," *Critique: Studies in Contemporary Fiction,* 38 (1997): 251–261;

Barbara Ann Schapiro, "Desire and Uses of Illusion: Alice Hoffman's *Seventh Heaven,*" in her *Literature and the Relational Self* (New York: New York University Press, 1994).

Josephine Humphreys

(2 February 1945 –   )

Joan Wylie Hall
University of Mississippi

BOOKS: *Dreams of Sleep* (New York: Viking, 1984; London: Collins, 1985);

Rich in Love (New York: Viking, 1987; London: Collins Harvill, 1988);

The Fireman's Fair (New York: Viking, 1991; London: Harvill, 1991);

Nowhere Else on Earth (New York: Viking, 2000; London: Heinemann, 2001).

RECORDINGS: *Josephine Humphreys Reads* Dreams of Sleep *and* Rich in Love, excerpts read by Humphreys, Columbia, Mo., American Audio Prose Library 8061, 1988;

Josephine Humphreys Interview and Reading, read by Humphreys, New Letters 101488, 1988;

Josephine Humphreys Reading and Interview, read by Humphreys, Columbia, Mo., American Audio Prose Library 8063, 1988;

Rich in Love, read by Humphreys, St. Paul, Minn., Penguin HighBridge Audio, 1992.

OTHER: "My Real Invisible Self," in *A World Unsuspected: Portraits of Southern Childhood,* edited by Alex Harris (Chapel Hill: University of North Carolina Press for the Center for Documentary Photography, Duke University, 1987), pp. 1–13;

"A Disappearing Subject Called the South," in *The Prevailing South: Life & Politics in a Changing Culture,* edited by Dudley Clendinen (Atlanta: Longstreet, 1988), pp. 212–220;

"The Epistle of Paul to Titus: Liars and Beasts," in *Incarnation: Contemporary Writers on the New Testament,* edited by Alfred Corn (New York: Viking, 1990), pp. 247–256;

"Bells," in *The Wedding Cake in the Middle of the Road,* edited by Susan Stamberg and George Garrett (New York: Norton, 1992), pp. 48–57;

Ruthie Bolton, *Gal: A True Life,* preface by Humphreys (New York: Harcourt Brace, 1994);

Rosa Shand, Scott Gould, Deno Trakas, and George Singleton, *New Southern Harmonies: Four Emerging*

Josephine Humphreys (photograph © Joyce Ravid; from the dust jacket for The Fireman's Fair, *1991; Richland County Public Library)*

Fiction Writers, introductions by Humphreys, Shelby Hearon, Fred Chappell, and Bret Lott (Spartanburg, S.C.: Hub City Writers Project, 1998);

Susan Sully, *Charleston Style: Past and Present,* foreword by Humphreys, photography by John Blais (New York: Rizzoli, 1999).

Josephine Humphreys anchors her best-selling novels firmly in the South, and scholars identify her interest in place, family, race, and history as Southern concerns; but hers is not the "Christ-haunted" South of Flannery O'Connor, and her characters are more likely to be urban than rural. Mystery and ritual are nevertheless familiar presences in her fiction. In her essay "The Epistle of Paul to Titus: Liars and Evil Beasts" (1990) Humphreys says that the unorthodox quality of her belief keeps her "awake and on the lookout." She associates this anticipatory spirit with an almost pantheistic love of nature and also with her love of the written word, affections shared by many of her characters. Humphreys believes that true fiction is rooted in "the mystery and power" of place, and in the essay "A Disappearing Subject Called the South" (1988), she urges writers to defend this "lifeblood" against the threat of so-called development. Environmental awareness allies her with such Southern contemporaries as Wendell Berry and Barbara Kingsolver, although her work has received less attention than theirs in the ecocriticism of scholars who study literary depictions of nature.

Humphreys is notable among her contemporaries for creating plots with multigenerational, multiracial communities, culminating in the large family tree (with Indian, black, and white members) that fills the endpapers of *Nowhere Else on Earth* (2000). In contrast to the Native American heroine of this book, protagonists of the three earlier novels are urban and suburban Caucasians, but Humphreys's communities always extend beyond the domestic circle to include at least one significant interracial friendship. Like William Faulkner's Yoknapatawpha County, which she mentions in her essay on the changing South, Humphreys's fictional Carolinas are visibly multiethnic, and she has demonstrated a sensitivity toward the heterogeneous culture of the region since the beginning of her career. The recipient of many regional and national awards, Humphreys is one of the South's most respected novelists at the start of the twenty-first century.

Josephine Trenholm Humphreys was born in Charleston, South Carolina, on 2 February 1945, the oldest of three daughters of William Wirt Humphreys, director of the Charleston Development Board, and Martha Lynch Humphreys. In her foreword to the coffee-table book *Charleston Style: Past and Present* (1999), she recalls that she was entranced by the view of trees and harbor from a garret window in her grandmother's big house at the corner of Church and Water Streets: "I felt the town was all mine—its secrets, its constantly surprising beauty, faults both tragic and comic, depths of vanity and stamina, ruthless pride and startling good-heartedness." Among Humphreys's ancestors were such prominent leaders as her great-great-grandfather George Trenholm, secretary of the treasury for the Confederacy; and her maternal grandfather, head of the Medical University of South Carolina and vice president of the American Medical Association. Humphreys has always been intrigued by physicians, a fascination that could account for the several doctors in her stories of psychological wounds and healing.

After her grandfather abandoned his wife, however, Humphreys's middle-class parents became so suspicious

of rich doctors that they avoided physicians whenever possible. If Josephine or her sisters needed medical care, they were taken to "the scuzziest-looking doctors in the worst part of town" on the assumption that patients were the chief concern of such practitioners, Humphreys told interviewer Dannye Romine Powell in 1994. Humphreys's fiction displays a similar distrust of ostentation and a related fear of betrayal. In *The Fireman's Fair* (1991), for example, protagonist Rob Wyatt seems noble rather than foolish when he moves out of his Charleston condominium and into a shabby beach bungalow, then resigns his position as a divorce specialist for a top law firm. Rewarding the reader's faith in him, Rob eventually opens a low-paid legal business in a shed, with a clientele that includes the Vietnamese owner of a tiny restaurant/bait shop, as well as the jailed father of Rob's best friend and fellow volunteer fireman, an African American named Albert Swan. "Rob believed in salvage," Humphreys remarks in the opening paragraph of *The Fireman's Fair* as her central character surveys the wreckage left by Hurricane Hugo and the internal wreckage of his life.

Humphreys expresses the same theme of ruin and rescue in the essay on Paul's epistle when she articulates her personal credo: "I believe in the salvageability of humanity, and that's what I try to write about." The earliest supporters of her writing, before she even went to grade school, were her mother and her divorced grandmother, Neta, women whose strong artistic sensibility found limited outlet in their domestic lives. Her grandmother is the focus of Humphreys's "My Real Invisible Self" (1987), an essay about Neta's inventive staging of the annual family Christmas picture. The photography session became tense the year Josephine turned thirteen because she was sullenly convinced that she was beginning to "resemble a pony," with her long face, teeth in need of braces, and a gumline that showed when she smiled. Not only did her childhood good looks fail her, but she actually feared she might lose Neta's interest and love since she had also proven a failure at piano, ballet, and painting.

To her great relief, Neta commanded her to write stories, forcefully reminding Josephine that she did have a special talent and lifting her from a "self-doubt so deep it is indistinguishable from vanity." In a 1994 interview with Alphonse Vinh, Humphreys said she grew up in a happy nuclear family, but the collapse of her grandparents' marriage made her uncomfortably aware that "even a family that looks okay, that looks secure, can really fall apart overnight." This realization is shared by the dazed Lucille Odom in *Rich in Love* (1987) when her mother leaves a purse and a grocery bag with melting ice cream in her parked car and walks out on a marriage that has become unbearably dull to her. Lucille, a high-school senior, sees Helen Odom's quest for a new life as a betrayal of the family. When Vinh told Humphreys that all her novels seem to focus on households at the point of disintegration, and that loneliness is "a recurring companion" to her characters, she responded that loneliness was always her "closest companion," starting with her extremely shy childhood and continuing to the present, since writing is such an isolated profession.

Like Lucille Odom's father in *Rich in Love,* Humphreys's father always preferred nonfiction to fiction, but both of her parents came from families of readers, and both were steady patrons of the public library. As a girl, Humphreys was aware that the state had a literary tradition, even though she never read any South Carolina writers and did not learn about the Pulitzer Prize–winning novelist Julia Peterkin until she was in her twenties. Her grade-school teachers praised her writing, and at her single-sex high school, Ashley Hall, she worked on the literary magazine and participated in weekly exchanges with other young writers. "We had a teacher who made writing seem like the most important thing that you could do," Humphreys recalls in the interview with Vinh, "and it never was presented as a sort of girl's hobby." Humphreys attended Duke University in Durham, North Carolina, as an Angier B. Duke Memorial scholar. William Blackburn and Reynolds Price were outstanding professors and mentors who influenced her not with particular directives but, as she told Powell, "because I loved them so much I ended up writing for them." Humphreys describes Blackburn as a "gruff" man whose Renaissance literature exams were notoriously hard; yet, students "adored him," and Humphreys dedicated her first novel to him as a belated present.

She uses the word "magical" to suggest the impact of Price, to whom she dedicated *The Fireman's Fair.* In an interview with Rosemary M. Magee in 1991, Humphreys said she read Price's first novel at seventeen and "never recovered." When she received her bachelor's degree Phi Beta Kappa from Duke in 1967, however, Humphreys declined a Mary Duke Biddle fellowship that would have allowed her to work on a novel for a year. Instead she went to the English department at Yale University on graduate fellowships from the Woodrow Wilson and Danforth Foundations. Perhaps reflecting the author's sense of a regional divide, Rob Wyatt of *The Fireman's Fair* feels that his own Yale degree makes him a misfit among Charleston attorneys. Humphreys completed the master's degree program at Yale in 1968 and moved to the University of Texas at Austin for a doctorate, but she never finished her dissertation on the eccentric British religious poet William Cowper.

After she married Thomas A. Hutcheson, a Duke graduate and Chicago attorney, on 30 November 1968, the couple moved to Charleston at her husband's suggestion. Humphreys was reluctant to raise children in the city

Dust jacket for Humphreys's first book (1984), a novel about a dysfunctional family in Charleston, South Carolina, that won the Ernest Hemingway Foundation Award (Richland County Public Library)

she remembered as narrowly conformist, but she found that both she and Charleston had changed. Her son Allen was born there in 1973, followed by William in 1974; both attended Harvard University after growing up in their mother's hometown. In a 1990 interview with Mickey Pearlman, Humphreys said that she had never held a baby until she had one of her own, so her love of children, which expanded to include all children, came as "one of the nicest surprises" in her life. From 1970 to 1977, Humphreys taught English at Baptist College in Charleston and served as a volunteer in the psychiatric ward at the county hospital, where she was intrigued by the patients' visions. She has compared her own mental state while writing to meditation or a sort of deliberate hallucination that is analogous to such disorders as schizophrenia. Despite her early attraction to authorship and the encouragement she received in college, Humphreys did not publish her first novel until she was almost forty. It took an epiphany with mythic overtones and then a major restructuring of her life for her to commit herself to a writing career.

Humphreys credits a trip to Crete with her art-loving mother as the impetus for her decision. Before the dramatic visit to the ruins at Knossos, Humphreys's exhausting round of college teaching, family activities, entertaining, and community service led to nightmares and severe chest pains that a doctor labeled "anxiety reaction." At home, she had viewed writing as a risky enterprise for a conservative Southern woman from an Episcopalian background; but standing in the small sunlit spaces of the Queen's Megaron, surrounded by paintings of winged dolphins and flying men, Humphreys reflected that an artist's lies can get at the truth. In "The Epistle of Paul to Titus: Liars and Beasts" she explains that not only did writing seem less "dangerous" but "It seemed like the only thing to do. When I got home, I started." Humphreys's life-changing journey may have influenced some of her allusions to myth and ritual in *Dreams of Sleep* (1984), her first book, but all of her novels delineate characters in terms of legends, ceremonies, and heroes. Like the Southern writers Eudora Welty, Ellen Douglas, Elizabeth Spencer, and Anne Tyler, she draws on a wide range of fairy tales and other old narratives to add resonance to her stories of modern life.

In *Dreams of Sleep,* allusions include Sleeping Beauty and Aladdin as well as Adam and Eve, Odysseus, bears and hunters in constellations, and the legendary freed slave Dave-Nero Jones. Elizabeth A. Ford suggests, in *Southern Writers at Century's End* (1997), that Humphreys's use of Dave-Nero's story introduces "historic issues of silence and recovery" relevant to the portrayal of African American characters in the book—a portrayal that some commentators consider to be weak and underdeveloped. Humphreys's allusions raise other social issues as well. When the protagonist, Alice Reese, accidentally breaks her daughters' Donald Duck soap and forbids them to eat Count Chocula cereal, the implication is that these figures of modern American popular culture are more flimsy and even more sinister than earlier heroes. Like many characters in Southern literature, Alice struggles with present-day changes by idealizing the past. She remembers that the dolls of her girlhood were "babies or storybook characters like Cinderella and Snow White who though past childhood were somehow not yet into the world, girls who kept themselves apart from the world without knowing what for." At four and six, Marcy and Beth are dumbstruck when their failure to pick up their curvaceous fashion dolls prompts Alice to dump the toys into the trash while chiding the girls in a "witchy voice" that makes her a villain for trying to preserve the children's innocence.

Alice and Will Reese's substantial Charleston house, with its two-foot-thick walls and iron gates, seems to be an enchanted castle, its queen (with her dreams about "sleep's ease") transformed into a monstrous mother because its king has turned knave through his affair with Claire Thibault, the nurse who manages his medical office. Will's old friend and fellow gynecologist Danny Cardozo taunts him: "Not a chink in the old armor, is there?" Images of fertility—the obstetrics practice, the Reeses' children—are offset by images of destruction, including Alice's three miscarriages and Claire's abortion, all four fetuses engendered by Will. "How effortlessly and smoothly things go from ripe to rotten," Alice reflects as she empties limp carrots and a collapsing cucumber from the refrigerator crisper. Briefly revived by the abundant offerings at the America Street supermarket, she cries when she sights an obscenity carved neatly as cuneiform into the back of the plump chicken she has chosen, a "bad omen" in a "wasteland" of a store whose food, she now realizes, "will never make her family healthy and hearty." With the mocking laughter of the butcher and his assistant in her ears, Alice is already dazed when she glimpses Claire kissing the divorced Danny Cardozo over a bag of groceries. Accidentally signaling her shock, Alice sets off the orange-colored Shrieker that she keeps in her purse as a defense against danger. The vividness of the scene in the grocery store typifies a style that is "dense with observation and detail," as Joan Philpott says in her April 1984 review of the book for *Ms.* magazine.

The good fairy who restores a tenuous order to the Reeses' beleaguered kingdom is Iris Moon, a seventeen-year-old whose name Alice considers a "perfect emblem" and good portent. Alice recognizes the girl's unusual gift of sympathy when she goes to Iris's boardinghouse room to interview her for a babysitting job. Gathered for supper under Iris's supervision are three disabled men, the first of several oddly assorted little communities that appear in Humphreys's novels. The rapt Alice identifies the household as Snow White's: "Dwarfs, ugly and alone in the woods, despairing of ever winning love, resigned to their own company; and along comes a girl fit for a prince, taking over their lives." So, too, does Iris take over the Reeses' lives, bringing with her an energy that the depressed and depleted Alice has lost over the course of Will's affair. Kathryn B. McKee observes in *Mississippi Quarterly* (1993) that Iris is "interconnected" with people—including her African American friend Emory—in ways that Alice and Will are not because "Iris understands more about love than any other character in the novel." McKee also sees both Reeses, the Phi Beta Kappa mathematician Alice and the physician Will, as heirs to "the legacy of Southern male introspection" exemplified in the novels of one of Humphreys's favorite authors, Walker Percy. In *Mississippi Quarterly* (1994), Susan H. Irons argues that *Dreams of Sleep* is a subversive rewriting of several Percy texts, particularly *The Last Gentleman* (1966), whose Allison and Will Barrett are parodied by Humphreys, even to the names Alice and Will Reese. In a review for *The New York Times* (13 May 1984) that praised *Dreams of Sleep* as "the best first novel I've read in years," Ellen Douglas detected echoes of Percy's "nostalgic, bewildered, ironic men and women," though Douglas added that such people are not rare in modern society.

Humphreys told Vinh that *The Last Gentleman* impressed her tremendously as the first "real" treatment she had read of the urban South, and she admitted that Percy's Will Barrett might have influenced the development of her Will Reese; but she also pointed out that both her father and her son are called Will. In the same interview Humphreys recalled that sadness was "the huge emotion" in her life when she began writing *Dreams of Sleep* because she felt that, at thirty-three (also Alice's age), she had wasted time and utterly failed to achieve her early dream of becoming a writer. Alice in particular bears the weight of Humphreys's sorrow, a melancholy that lessens in her subsequent work; and the enthusiastic response to *Dreams of Sleep*—which won the PEN American Center's Ernest Hemingway Foundation Award for the best first novel of 1984—was an affirmation of her identity as an author.

Nevertheless, Humphreys believes "there is a great deal of sadness in women's lives that really has no outlet and it is both an unknown factor and an unknown quality." In her second novel, *Rich in Love,* the runaway Helen Odom embodies the built-up sorrow that Humphreys perceives in many mothers and housewives; and Helen's newly married and pregnant daughter Rae is so unhappy about the coming birth that she withdraws into depression. Parallel to Iris Moon of *Dreams of Sleep,* Helen's younger daughter Lucille (also seventeen and "rich in love") is the steadying force in the disintegrating family. Several reviewers and scholars have noted Humphreys's sympathetic exploration of the social and domestic pressures on mothers and daughters in the American South, the region that is still most often associated with traditional gender roles.

Written with a grant from the John Simon Guggenheim Foundation, *Rich in Love* is Lucille's first-person narrative, in contrast to the third-person viewpoint (shifting among Alice, Will, and Iris) that Humphreys employs in the earlier book. Girls like Iris, Lucille, and Billie Poe of *The Fireman's Fair* "strike me as insistent presences who will show up whether I plan them or not, as bearers of hope in an adult world of despair," says Humphreys in the Magee interview. Lucille's youthfulness also underscores Humphreys's recurring and related themes of vulnerability and identity. Elinor Ann Walker suggests in *Mississippi Quarterly* (1994) that the "adolescent voice" of *Rich in Love* is an apt vehicle for "a redefinition of Southern narrative—a narrative that validates, not the public self

Dust jacket for Humphreys's 1987 novel, in which a teenage girl tries to help her family through domestic upheavals (Richland County Public Library)

that is buffeted by the past and reclaimed through memory and the untangling of history, but the private self that is created very much in the present." Immersed in the here and now, Lucille nevertheless displays a fascination with the past and a concern about the future that opens out the present action in both directions.

The final scene of the novel smoothly conveys this triple consciousness. Savoring the contact with her setting, Lucille rides her bike, as she does in the first chapter; but now she lives in a different home with her divorced mother, and now she pedals with her niece, Phoebe, in a baby carrier on the back. Lucille leans into the curves, wondering what the coming years will bring for her and her small passenger. She thinks back to "ancient times, long before Latin," when "'family' meant people in a house together. But that was in a language so far back that all its words are gone, a language we can only imagine." With the next generation literally kicking behind her, Lucille rides into adulthood, accepting the painful changes of the past year and alert to "the strength and fragility of things, the love and the luck hidden together in the world." Although she loved the twenty-five-year collection of family artifacts in the Odoms' Mount Pleasant home across the water from Charleston, she also loves the unfinished concrete block "exoskeleton of a house" near the Wando River where Helen finds sanctuary from her insulated domestic life.

Dramatic transformations in the Odom family are set against the changes that Lucille and her historian brother-in-law, Billy McQueen, observe in the bigger world. Humphreys refers to Charleston's Old Slave Mart, the Confederate flag, and statues of the Native American chief Osceola and the secession supporter John C. Calhoun not simply to create a Southern ambience but to hint at the South's tumultuous history. The impingement of the New South is comically evident in Lucille's reaction to the blank expressions of Charleston tourists: "I could tell what the trouble was: they had been to Epcot. After Epcot, Charleston is hardly worth seeing; no dinosaurs are going to lunge at you on the Battery, no music comes out of the azaleas." Music does come out of another unexpected place, however: a century-old African Methodist Episcopalian church that has been made over into Fishbone's, a black club where Rae—whose best friend Rhody is African American—used to sing with the band.

At Fishbone's, bandleader Tick Willis and the Yankee outsider Billy engage in a sarcastic verbal joust with motifs of race, region, sex, and violence; but the tension vanishes when Rae suddenly steps onto the stage and becomes a "sorceress" who dazzles each man and woman, black and white, with her voice. Lucille is startled by her epiphany that every woman, including herself, probably has a "singing self," and that Rae's singing is not just singing but "a way to let out something." Rae has a disturbing epiphany, too, the awful perception that "she'd miss her single self as she'd known it." Billy cannot convince her that she can go on singing; and, driving home through the dark and the fog, Lucille realizes that the young couple's faces are "wide-eyed with despair." Rae's despair does not lift until three weeks after Phoebe's premature and traumatic delivery, but a tentative sense of healing extends to the rest of the family and to a whole network of minor characters, from Lucille's former boyfriend, Wayne Frobiness, to her father's former secretary, Sharon. Alfred Uhry, the well-known author of *Driving Miss Daisy* (1987), wrote the screenplay for the 1992 movie adaptation of *Rich in Love,* featuring Albert Finney, Jill Clayburgh, and Alfre Woodard. Popular in both book and movie versions, *Rich in Love* broadened Humphreys's audience while also drawing praise, as *Dreams of Sleep* did, from fellow writers, reviewers, and literary critics. Fred Chappell, in *The New York Times* (13 September 1987), compared the novel to Candace Flynt's *Mother Love* (1987) and Marianne Gin-

gher's *Bobby Rex's Greatest Hit* (1986) because of "a willingness on the part of the authors to allow their characters to master their lives and to accept the inevitable responsibilities." Like many other commentators on Humphreys's first two books, Chappell also praised her skillful style.

In 1987, the year *Rich in Love* was published, the Lyndhurst Foundation awarded Humphreys a three-year stipend in recognition of her contribution to the arts. Based in Chattanooga, Tennessee, the private foundation has a special interest in the "social, natural, and built environment" of the surrounding Southeastern area. Humphreys's similar concern is evident in her 1988 essay on the "disappearing" South, where she remarks that "the first gradual and now swift metamorphosis of our geography has changed our literature." To Humphreys, "development" is an ironic term for the destruction of Southern towns and rural areas. Will Reese in *Dreams of Sleep* deplores plans for a pirate theme park on the Charleston riverfront, and he calls a resort at Sea Island a "fake place," agreeing to spend the family vacation there only because the hotel at least is old and historic sites are close at hand. Rob Wyatt of Humphreys's third novel, *The Fireman's Fair,* is from a generations-old Charleston family and wonders why he has never felt at ease in the city. Even as a boy, he spent days in the woods of Francis Marion National Forest, watching for unusual birds. Rob identifies not with his fellow lawyers but with Odysseus, Ishmael, and Huck Finn—adventurers who take to the water. "Mad voyage has its appeal," he reflects, remembering the Sewee Indians' "last-ditch effort to escape the misery of life in white Carolina" by heading for England in canoes to trade deerskins directly to the British.

Humphreys told *Contemporary Authors* interviewer Jean W. Ross in 1989 that she tries to "write something different every time," at least in respect to tone and point of view. *Rich in Love* is less gloomy than *Dreams of Sleep,* for example, and she shifts from a first-person account in *Rich in Love* to a third-person narrative in *The Fireman's Fair.* Although imagery of disaster and destruction is a constant in all three novels, Humphreys has wryly commented that in *The Fireman's Fair* she finally had an excuse for such ominous figures. Humphreys is accustomed to writing several drafts for each book, but she had already completed the first draft of *The Fireman's Fair* before Hurricane Hugo struck the Carolinas in 1989, and the devastating storm provided her with the "initiating spark" for Rob's radical transformation from upscale lawyer to unemployed thinker. Humphreys told Powell that survivors commonly experienced a "process of clarification" after the hurricane: "It became clear to us that you can lose all your material possessions, and that wouldn't matter very much." Not only does Rob move into his beach bungalow with Speedo, a big dog he found starving in the National Forest nine years earlier, but he also sells his Alfa Romeo and drives an old Toyota pickup truck.

Even though *TLS: The Times Literary Supplement* (29 November 1991) reviewer Abigail Levene was at first annoyed by the "folksy, story-telling tone" and finally unimpressed by the "obligatory happy ending" to the "Boy Meets Girl" formula, she nevertheless fell under Humphreys's "powerful spell." Levene concluded that "The charm of the novel underlines the truth of its central premise: beauty may be found everywhere, even amidst ruin." Such unexpected gifts come in several forms, from Rob's nineteen-year-old love interest Billie Poe (a girl on the run) to Rob's amazed recognition that his elderly parents too are bound by a tie of love–despite Jack Wyatt's earlier affairs and despite Maude Wyatt's seeming indifference to her husband's anxieties about aging and abandonment. Maude's extensive genealogy project hints at the importance of family in *The Fireman's Fair,* but Rob realizes that families can take unusual shapes. Walking down the street with his black friend Albert (whose parents are institutionalized) and with the exuberant Billie (whose parents abandoned her), Rob decides they are a "trio of misfits" that compose a new type of family, "joined not by blood or sex but by pure shared loneliness, which makes strong bonds." Even though many bonds in the novel become almost hopelessly tangled, a climactic scene at the annual fireman's fair conveys a carnivalesque mood of release, followed by further entanglements before the contrite Rob arrives at a subdued but happy conclusion.

Like *Dreams of Sleep* and *Rich in Love, The Fireman's Fair* was named a *New York Times* Notable Book of the Year. Novelist Frank Conroy called this third novel "good craft" and "deftly constructed," aside from an occasional implausible scene; however, his review for *The New York Times* (19 May 1991) ends with a hope that the talented author will "aim higher" than a "beach book" next time. Considerably more enthusiastic were novelist Oscar Hijuelos's dust-jacket comment that *The Fireman's Fair* is "a joyful, strong and elegant book" and Patrick H. Samway's remark, in a review for *America* (31 August 1991), that "Humphreys is fast becoming an important American novelist as she explores the love relationships that have the power to revitalize the lives of her characters."

Early in 1994 Humphreys was inducted into the South Carolina Academy of Authors. That same year she wrote the foreword to *Gal: A True Life* by the pseudonymous Ruthie Bolton, an African American woman from the Charleston area whose "strong voice" Humphreys admired so much that she helped Bolton to get her story into print after a mutual acquaintance put them in contact with each other. Their unusual collaboration produced an account of childhood and spousal abuse alien to the families in Humphreys's fiction, and the kindness of Bolton's second husband transformed her life in ways more dra-

matic than any transformations experienced by Humphreys's characters. Humphreys recognized the power of Bolton's story as soon as she read the fifty-eight-page, handwritten manuscript, but she helped to bring the events to life by subsequently meeting with the young woman twice a week for several weeks. After recording Bolton's spoken account, transcribing the tapes, and typing the chapters, Humphreys modestly described herself as "only a witness and a secretary," but her suggestion that the novice writer "try another way of telling, the way southern stories are best told: out loud, teller-to-listener" was the catalyst for *Gal* to become a *New York Times* bestseller, reviewed from Atlanta to Los Angeles.

In an interview for *BookPage* in 2000, Humphreys told Michael Sims that her fourth book is "almost a total change for me, in terms of subject, method–everything's different." She contrasted the "process of discovery" in the earlier fiction, written with no pre-established plots, to the narration of the real Rhoda Strong's life, a familiar story in eastern North Carolina. Humphreys originally heard about Rhoda and her outlaw husband Henry Berry Lowrie in 1962, when a Lumbee girl sitting next to her on a train through North Carolina told her about them. The thoroughness of her research on the Lumbees is obvious in the details, from Humphreys's depiction of a turpentine camp and her knowledge of foodways to her use of words such as "withy" and "foggying" and her precise descriptions of the plant life in Robeson County. In 1985 she made the first of many visits to the Indian community in Pembroke, North Carolina, and met the Native American historian Adolph Dial. Because the verifiable facts about Rhoda would fill only a few pages, Humphreys emphasizes that, although her characters are historical, *Nowhere Else on Earth* is an imaginative reconstruction of their lives.

Humphreys credits the Scuffletown heroine with changing her ideas on "Southernness," race, community identity, and the plight of Native Americans. *Nowhere Else on Earth* made its author conscious of the large difference between "private dreams" (such as fifteen-year-old Rhoda's yearning for romantic love) and "community dreams" (specifically, the Indian cause to which the newly-wed teenager irrevocably commits herself). The importance of working for a world beyond the family and the neighborhood is implicit in Humphreys's earlier novels, but she describes a "wonderful crossover between me and Rhoda, a connection that I haven't had in any of my earlier books with characters." The crossover extends to Rhoda's perception of herself as a writer, expressing her story on paper over the course of many years and many lonely hours.

Humphreys's ambitious scope, her skill in developing Rhoda's nineteenth-century Lumbee voice, and her serious themes evoked high praise for *Nowhere Else on Earth,* including Gibbons's opinion, quoted on the dust

Dust jacket for Humphreys's 1991 novel, about a lawyer who quits his job and moves into a beach bungalow to sort out his life (Richland County Public Library)

jacket, that the novel is a "masterpiece." In the *Chicago Tribune* (17 September 2000) Kathryn Rhett said Humphreys's "dazzling creation" is a "thoroughly satisfying" novel in which the attention to women's vulnerability, "the nature of cruelty," attachment to home, and other thoughtful motifs "resonate beyond its historical setting." In contrast, Michael Upchurch in *The New York Times* (17 September 2000) judged most of the characters to be caricatures of heroes and villains, and he was irritated by the "retroactive political correctness." While complimenting Humphreys's poetic evocations of nature, her unusual choice of subject matter, and her memorable scenes of civilian suffering in *Nowhere Else on Earth*, Upchurch nevertheless has a decided preference for "the sassy sophistications" of *Rich in Love* and *The Fireman's Fair*, books that, in his opinion, showcase the author's "natural strengths." Upchurch's negative review is in the minority, however, and Humphreys is in no hurry to return to the contemporary Charleston of her previous work.

Humphreys is a popular reader on her extensive book tours, and she has been a featured speaker in many academic settings, including Furman University in Greenville, South Carolina, which awarded her a doctor of humanities degree in 1996. In October of 2000 Humphreys spoke to creative-writing classes and dined with Angier B. Duke scholarship winners at her alma mater, Duke University, where she has deposited much of her correspondence and literary material. She was inducted into the Fellowship of Southern Writers in Chattanooga, Tennessee, in 2001; the fellowship, founded in 1987 by twenty-seven distinguished Southern authors, awarded Humphreys its Hillsdale Prize for fiction in 1993.

As a book reviewer for the *Atlanta Journal-Constitution*, the *Nation*, the *Chicago Tribune*, and *The New York Times*, Humphreys has discussed the works of many important authors since the mid 1980s, including Price, Amy Tan, Jane Smiley, Dennis McFarland, May Sarton, Allan Gurganus, and Alice Munro. In her first three novels, Humphreys portrays the fragility of families, couples, and landscapes, chronicling Charleston's transformation by hurricane winds, Yankee investors, and the Southern upper class. Reviewers of these mildly satiric comedies of manners occasionally complained that her white males were voyeuristic, her African American characters stereotypical, and her endings unreal. More typically, however, Humphreys was admired for her relaxed but graceful style, her articulate young protagonists, and her balanced representation of the South. The Charleston plots reveal "both criticism of and nostalgia for the southern past without damning it completely or revering it without question," Walker concludes in *Studies in the Literary Imagination* (1994). The balance becomes much more tenuous in *Nowhere Else on Earth*. The Lumbees' losses are of a magnitude unprecedented in Humphreys's earlier novels, and although she once again rescues her central character from final despair, the redemptive vision of human suffering that distinguishes her fiction is at its dimmest in the swamps of Scuffletown. This volume has both fortified and complicated Humphreys's reputation as one of the best writers of the contemporary South.

Interviews:

Mickey Pearlman, "Josephine Humphreys," in *Inter/View: Talks with America's Writing Women,* by Pearlman and Katherine Usher Henderson (Lexington: University Press of Kentucky, 1990), pp. 157–162;

Rosemary M. Magee, "Continuity and Separation: An Interview with Josephine Humphreys," *Southern Review,* 27 (1991): 792–802;

Shirley M. Jordan, "Josephine Humphreys," in *Broken Silences: Interviews with Black and White Women Writers,* edited by Jordan (New Brunswick, N.J.: Rutgers University Press, 1993), pp. 111–128;

Dannye Romine Powell, "Josephine Humphreys," in *Parting the Curtains: Interviews with Southern Writers,* interviews by Powell and photographs by Jill Krementz (Winston-Salem, N.C.: John F. Blair, 1994), pp. 182–195;

Alphonse Vinh, "Talking with Josephine Humphreys," *Southern Quarterly,* 32 (1994): 131–140;

Michael Sims, "Historical Fiction Presents New Challenges for Josephine Humphreys," *BookPage* (September 2000) <http://www.bookpage.com/0009bp/josephine_humphreys.html>.

Bibliography:

John S. Spencer and Mary O'Neill, "Josephine Humphreys," *Bulletin of Bibliography,* 50 (1993): 325–329.

References:

Barbara Bennett, "Making Peace with the (M)other," in *The World Is Our Home: Society and Culture in Contemporary Southern Writing,* edited by Jeffrey J. Folks and Nancy Summers Folks (Lexington: University Press of Kentucky, 2000), pp. 186–200;

William G. Chernecky, "Josephine Humphreys and the Problem of the New South," *POMPA: Publications of the Mississippi Philological Association* (1998): 68–73;

Dawn Ann Drzal, "Casualties of the Feminine Mystique," *Antioch Review,* 46 (1988): 450–461;

Elizabeth A. Ford, "Josephine Humphreys: 'Hope's Last Stand,'" in *Southern Writers at Century's End,* edited by Jeffrey J. Folks and James A. Perkins (Lexington: University Press of Kentucky, 1997), pp. 201–211;

Jan Nordby Gretlund, "Citified Carolina: Josephine Humphreys' Fiction," in *Southern Landscapes,* edited by Tony Badger, Walter Edgar, and Gretlund (Tübingen, Germany: Stauffenburg, 1996), pp. 254–265;

Michael A. Griffith, "'A Deal for the Real World': Josephine Humphreys's *Dreams of Sleep* and the New Domestic Novel," *Southern Literary Journal,* 26 (1993): 94–108;

Ann Henley, "'Space for Herself': Nadine Gordimer's *A Sport of Nature* and Josephine Humphreys' *Rich in Love,*" *Frontiers,* 13, no. 1 (1992): 81–89;

Susan H. Irons, "Josephine Humphreys's *Dreams of Sleep:* Rewriting Walker Percy's Male Gaze," *Mississippi Quarterly,* 47 (1994): 287–300;

Shelley M. Jackson, "Josephine Humphreys and the Politics of Postmodern Desire," *Mississippi Quarterly,* 47 (1994): 275–285;

Lewis A. Lawson, "Introduction to Essays on Josephine Humphreys," *Mississippi Quarterly,* 47 (1994): 273–274;

Kathryn B. McKee, "Rewriting Southern Male Introspection in Josephine Humphreys' *Dreams of Sleep,*" *Mississippi Quarterly,* 46 (1993): 241–254;

Elinor Ann Walker, "'Go with What Is Most Terrifying': Reinventing Domestic Space in Josephine Humphreys' *Dreams of Sleep,*" *Studies in the Literary Imagination,* 27 (Fall 1994): 87–104;

Walker, "Josephine Humphreys' *Rich in Love:* Redefining Southern Fiction," *Mississippi Quarterly,* 47 (1994): 301–315.

Papers:

Duke University in Durham, North Carolina, holds a large collection of Josephine Humphreys's manuscripts and correspondence. The papers include business contracts for publication and movie rights, handwritten and typed book manuscripts and proofs, book reviews of others' work by Humphreys, clippings of interviews and reviews of her work, audiotapes, photographs and negatives, books inscribed to Humphreys, and seven scrapbooks with additional letters and reviews. The bulk of the collection dates between 1983 and 1987. Humphreys is a major correspondent in the Reynolds Price papers, also held by Duke University.

Tama Janowitz

(12 April 1957 –   )

J. Rocky Colavito
Northwestern State University

and

Ashley Minton

BOOKS: *American Dad* (New York: Putnam, 1981;
London: Picador, 1988);

Slaves of New York (New York: Crown, 1986; London:
Picador, 1987);

A Cannibal in Manhattan (New York: Crown, 1987; London: Pan, 1988);

The Male Cross-Dresser Support Group (New York: Crown,
1992; London: Picador, 1992);

By the Shores of Gitchee Gumee (New York: Crown, 1996;
London: Picador, 1998);

A Certain Age (New York: Doubleday, 1999; London:
Bloomsbury, 1999);

Hear That? (New York: SeaStar, 2001);

Area Code 212: New York Days, New York Nights (London:
Bloomsbury, 2002);

Peyton Amberg: A Novel (New York: St. Martin's Press,
2003; London: Bloomsbury, 2003).

PRODUCED SCRIPT: *Slaves of New York,* motion picture, Merchant-Ivory, 1989.

Tama Janowitz's collection of short stories, *Slaves
of New York* (1986), thrust her into the celebrity spotlight. Prior to its publication she had written one book,
American Dad (1981), which received little critical attention. The appearance of her second book, however,
was coupled with author tours, interviews, and radio
spots. The attention continued through the next year,
as R. Z. Sheppard chronicled in *Time* magazine (19
October 1987):

> She attracted attention in 1986 when she crashed the
> Four Seasons restaurant with handouts promoting her
> short story collection *Slaves of New York.* . . . Janowitz
> has appeared in magazine articles for Amaretto and
> Rose's Lime Juice. Her face pops up with increasing
> frequency in newspapers and magazines, and she has
> given the MTV generation its first performance-writer

*Tama Janowitz (photograph by Marion Ettlinger; from the
dust jacket for* A Certain Age, *1999; Richland
County Public Library)*

by making videotapes to plug *Slaves.* . . . Janowitz has a
catchy style and achieves her satiric effects with a sly
Valley-girl delivery.

Julia Reed's "Publishing's New Starlets" (*U. S. News &
World Report,* 1 December 1986) was one of the first
mainstream articles to afford Janowitz wide attention,
and in this article Janowitz offers an apt description of
the nature of her work: "I'm trying to record social
mores of the time, and I don't feel qualified to offer
solutions. This is just something that I saw over and
over in the small world I live in, and I wrote it down."

Janowitz was born on 12 April 1957 in San Francisco, California, to highly successful parents. Her father, Julian Frederick Janowitz, was a psychiatrist; her mother, Phyllis Winer Janowitz, was a poet and professor. Janowitz attended Barnard College, where she received her B.A. in 1977. While at Barnard, she was awarded the Breadloaf Writer's Conference Prize in 1975 as well the Elizabeth Janeway Fiction Prize in 1976 and 1977. In 1977 she was also awarded the Amy Loveman Prize for poetry. She earned an M.A. in 1979 from Hollins College, where she was awarded an institutional fellowship. Upon completing her studies at Hollins, she attended the Yale University School of Drama from 1980 to 1981. She moved on to Columbia University and was awarded two National Endowment for the Arts Grants (1982, 1986), the CCLM/General Electric Foundation Award (1984), and the Ludwig Vogelstein Foundation Award (1985). In 1985 she received her M.F.A. from Columbia University, and she spent the 1986–1987 academic year at Princeton University as an Alfred Hodder Fellow in the Humanities.

In 1992 Janowitz married Tim Hunt, who now serves as curator of the Andy Warhol Foundation. The two met when Hunt came to the United States to handle Warhol's estate and a mutual friend set them up on a blind date. Warhol and Janowitz had been friends and often fixed one another up on blind dates; Janowitz told Laura L. Buchwald in 1999 about meeting Hunt, "I consider this Andy's final gift to me." Janowitz, Hunt, and their adopted daughter, Willow, reside in an apartment in Brooklyn.

Janowitz's first book, *American Dad,* was written when she was just twenty-three, and her own upbringing figured heavily in the novel: the protagonist's parents are a psychiatrist and a poet. *American Dad* might best be described a coming-of-age novel; yet, Janowitz's style makes it more than a bland variation on this genre. She livens up a seemingly bleak novel–centered on family, philandering, divorce, and murder–with an edgy humor.

American Dad centers on the life of Earl Przepasniak, born to a couple with more pressing concerns than parenting. Robert Abraham Przepasniak, psychiatrist, is an overwhelming presence in his family's life. Earl and his brother, Bobo, live in a state of combined awe and dread of their father. Their mother, Mavis, a dreamy woman who writes poetry, lives in a world of denial regarding her marriage and family. When she can no longer tolerate her husband's philandering, the couple separates, and the subsequent divorce affects the brothers in drastically different ways. Earl becomes extremely emotional, looking for something outside of himself to fill the empty place left in the wake of his father's absence and his mother's weakness. Bobo, on the other hand, withdraws into himself to such an extent that he is of no help to Earl either.

Earl is intimidated by his father's extreme prowess with women. He feels weakened in relation to Robert's virility. Robert's need to possess and control women leads to his accidental murder of Mavis as the two argue over alimony payments. Janowitz indicates that it is not just alimony that enrages Robert; apparently, Mavis's emerging independence is more than the doctor can bear. Earl's father is subsequently convicted of murder.

Because of his tumultuous and troubled childhood, Earl is overwhelmed by feelings of living in his father's shadow, which has become increasingly sinister. Earl sets off on a quest for self-knowledge, which takes him to London, where he has two ill-fated affairs but does indeed appear to come into his own. With his father safely removed from the dating pool and in another country, Earl discovers his own character. Predictably, following his misadventures abroad, Earl is on his way to self-actualization.

Not much critical attention was given to *American Dad.* Garrett Epps, reviewing the novel for *The New Republic* (6 June 1981), did offer high praise for the work, terming Janowitz "an extremely gifted writer" and the novel "a memorable and original portrait of an authentic American type, the monster shrink." He added that it was "one of the most impressive first novels I've read in a long time."

In dealing with coming-of-age issues alongside familial dysfunction, Janowitz tapped into American disillusionment. Her next work, *Slaves of New York,* made her the spokeswoman for young New York, while the 1989 Merchant-Ivory movie adaptation, for which Janowitz wrote the screenplay, made her a star. As the book became a best-seller, she found herself compared to her male contemporaries such as Jay McInerney and Bret Easton Ellis; critics liked to refer to them as "the literary brat pack." While McInerney and Ellis were also writing about young Manhattanites and their Ronald-Reagan-economy lifestyles, their novels were written from a masculine perspective, and the overall tone of their respective works was generally less optimistic than Janowitz's more bohemian collection of short stories. Her characters, at least in *Slaves of New York,* are more artistic than Ellis's or McInerney's young urban professionals.

Slaves of New York is a series of loosely connected short stories following members of the struggling, young, bohemian community in Manhattan. Sheppard suggested in *Time* (19 October 1987) that "*Slaves* cartoons the downtown-Manhattan art scene, where Janowitz . . . understands that people will look at anything rather than nothing: art-like artifacts if there is no art,

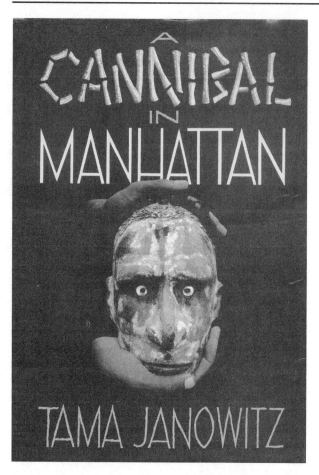

Dust jacket for Janowitz's 1987 novel, about a South Seas native adjusting to life in New York as the husband of a bored socialite (Richland County Public Library)

and book-like objects if there is no literature." The characters are mainly artists and musicians. Janowitz has described Eleanor, the recurring protagonist, as being a composite of herself and her female friends of the time. Eleanor is looking to find her place in the world. She stays with Stash, her emotionally unavailable boyfriend, as much out of fear of being homeless in the city as out of love. For all of the trappings of the 1980s, Janowitz touches on some timeless aspects of urban living and dating in *Slaves of New York*. As Elizabeth Young notes in her essay on Janowitz, Mary Gaitskill, and Catherine Texier in *Shopping in Space: Essays on America's Blank Generation Fiction* (1992), *Slaves of New York* "mirrors the moral and intellectual flexibility required for survival in a multi-textured, frequently nonsensical and paradoxical environment." Michael Dibdin, in the *London Review of Books* (5 February 1987), noted that "Janowitz avoids the risk of anecdotalism" and succeeds in "making her subject matter thematic: her characters create a bewildering range of 'art objects,' but first and foremost they create themselves."

A Cannibal in Manhattan (1987), her follow-up novel to *Slaves of New York,* was not so well received. The story centers on a cannibal who finds himself on the island of Manhattan and unwittingly becomes the pawn of a derelict heiress who wants his recipe for a powerful hallucinogenic drug made by his tribe. Through a series of mishaps and misadventures he finds himself not only fitting in with the New York jet set but also actually becoming one of the most desirable bachelors in the city. The story is a rigorous tale of independence and of total submersion in a new culture, told in satirical fashion.

In many ways, *A Cannibal in Manhattan* is a twisted retelling of Daniel Defoe's *Robinson Crusoe* (1719). Mgungu, the cannibal, happens onto an island that is heavily populated, yet is as lonely as Crusoe's deserted one. Thinking he has been brought to Manhattan to marry the heiress, who is in many ways his captor, he tries to acclimate himself to her world. He finds that he has lost more than his culture and the familiarity of his homeland; he has been stripped of his identity. In Manhattan he is a novelty, or worse, a freak.

Janowitz is quick to clarify that Mgungu is essentially no different from his new acquaintances and neighbors. The novel ends with a gruesome dinner party at which Mgungu's new bride and captor is served up as the main course in response to a bizarre plot twist involving the underworld. *A Cannibal in Manhattan* begs the question of what darkness lurks in the heart of humans, whether ostensibly civilized or not. Furthermore, what constitutes civility? Janowitz asks of her readers, "who are the true cannibals?" Peter Reading, of *TLS: The Times Literary Supplement* (4–10 March 1988), lauded the novel for its setting: he said the novel "is at its best when dealing with the seedy. The cartography of garbage-and-stray-dog waste land is impeccable."

Like *A Cannibal in Manhattan,* Janowitz's next novel, *The Male Cross-Dresser Support Group* (1992), asks some sensitive questions of contemporary society by exploring concepts of community and culture in ways that reflect badly on both. Neither men nor women are spared the social microscope through which Janowitz views her characters. The novel revolves around Pamela Trowel, a woman employed to sell advertising space in a hunting magazine. Her day-to-day existence is bleak until nine-year-old Abdhul follows her home. She is at first annoyed and frightened by this new and unwanted responsibility. Her maternal instinct quickly kicks in, however, and she develops a deep and powerful love for the boy. A series of unfortunate incidents, including unemployment, force Pamela and Abdhul to flee the city.

Through biting satire, Janowitz asks her readers to think about the ways in which women, particularly single women with children, are forced into oppression in a male-dominated society. Pamela ultimately must pose as a man to protect herself as well as her charge. But Janowitz also explores the ways in which women contribute to their own oppression. In *The Male Cross-Dresser Support Group* readers are given a strong lesson in gender equality along with an examination of the concept of family and human relations. Janowitz's style is noteworthy; Tom Shone of the *Spectator* (14 November 1992) stated, "the reader is happy to tag along . . . largely due to Janowitz's narrative tone." He added that "Pamela's schtick is engagingly dippy," and "Janowitz's humour has that pleasingly raddled logic of a drunkenly told shaggy dog story."

Janowitz's fourth novel, *By the Shores of Gitchee Gumee* (1996), is her first one not set in Manhattan or its surrounding areas. This novel, like *American Dad* or *The Male Cross-Dresser Support Group,* centers around family. Evangeline Slivenowicz is the single mother of five children, each of whom has a different father. Maud, Evangeline's eldest daughter, narrates the family's squalid and outrageous story. The Slivenowiczes are an eccentric group of independent beings, each with his or her own talent and ambition, living together in a trailer at the edge of Lake Gitchee Gumee in upstate New York. Evangeline trains her children in the ways of the world as best she can, which is not nearly well enough. As with the Przepasniaks of *American Dad,* a dysfunctional undercurrent exists within the Slivenowicz household. The lines between parent and children are blurred, leaving the reader wondering who exactly is in charge. Janowitz is clever in her insidious critique of the American family and how society determines what is appropriate or "normal" in terms of parenting. The novel combines screwball comedy with surreal parody. Maud, the teenage cynic, leads the reader through contemporary culture as well as the life of her dysfunctional family.

By the Shores of Gitchee Gumee is a clever novel if somewhat exhausting. Some reviewers found the Slivenowicz family and all of their idiosyncrasies and talents to be occasionally overwhelming, although Todd Tamsin of *The Washington Post Book World* (20 October 1996) noted the presence of "moments of incisive satirical observation" in the novel. Donna Seaman in *Booklist* (1 June 1996) complimented Janowitz's "nimble, satisfyingly nasty, and wholly unexpected humor" and characterized "life in a Janowitz book" as "chaotic and smart-ass but precocious, indefatigable, funny, and somehow optimistic."

Janowitz revised her vision of the human condition somewhat with her next novel, *A Certain Age* (1999), perhaps the most complex of her works. Influenced by Edith Wharton's *The House of Mirth* (1905),

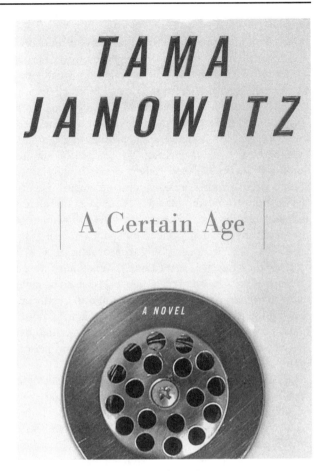

Dust jacket for Janowitz's 1999 novel, influenced by Edith Wharton's The House of Mirth *(1905), about an auction-house employee in desperate search of a husband (Richland County Public Library)*

this work focuses on the life of Florence Collins, a thirty-two-year-old woman making the wrong choices. She is slowly losing control of her life and apparently does not want to suffer alone. She is an auction-house assistant director who cannot handle her money, her men, or even her daily existence. She is motivated more by greed than love, and her search for a husband is dependent upon her spiritual depravity. A. J. Jacobs of *Entertainment Weekly* (30 July 1999) termed Florence "one of the least likeable characters in modern fiction history. More self-obsessed than Portnoy, more marriage-crazed than Bridget Jones." Most of the characters in the novel are similarly devoid of real emotion. They are not without their charm, though; if nothing else, Florence and her cohorts serve as a cautionary tale to postmodern society. Florence, and women like her, represent a large and somewhat underground segment of urban society that enables gender wars to continue unfettered. Both sexes participate in a sort of matrimonial bargaining that goes on until one party folds or bottoms out. *Publishers Weekly* (31 May 1999) called the novel an "unflaggingly downbeat comedy of manners" and suggested that "what poignancy the novel offers is continuously undercut by the author's arch contempt for virtually every character."

Janowitz's next work, the children's book *Hear That?* (2001), represents a sharp deviation from her previous output. In a dimly lit apartment on a rainy evening, a mother and her son are startled by sounds coming from the hallway. Relying on the interplay of sounds with a child's imagination, the story builds to the revelation that the intruder is, in fact, the child's father. Along the way the reader sees the by-products of the child's imagination, done in two-page renderings by Tracy Dockray that, according to Maryann H. Owen of the *School Library Journal* (2001), "maintain interest and show the disorder of a house in which a child lives." *Publishers Weekly* (2001) also noted the contributions of the illustrations, saying that "the fantasy noise-makers amuse rather than frighten" and suggesting that the suspense of the tale "depends on read-aloud performance, ideally on a rainy evening."

Area Code 212: New York Days, New York Nights (2002) is a nonfiction collection chronicling Janowitz's experiences in the city. She returned to fiction with *Peyton Amberg* (2003), a modern retelling of Gustave Flaubert's *Madame Bovary* (1857). Peyton is a beautiful, restless travel agent who drifts from affair to affair. Meredith Parets, in *Booklist* (2003), noted that "Janowitz's eye for the sordid detail is as merciless as ever" but that ultimately "Peyton is so ineffectual and passive, and the supporting characters so uniformly unappealing, that there is little to care about in the story of her downfall." A reviewer for *Publishers Weekly* (2003) wrote, "Peyton's overactive id and sense of dissatisfaction seem a bit contrived at times, and her comeuppance rather old-fashioned, but Janowitz's trademark mix of humor and gross-out realism give the novel a queasy charge."

Janowitz's rapid ascension in the 1980s cemented her place among the contemporary authors who rose to fame with works that were one with their times. Her use of the rich tapestry of urban New York City as a setting links her to regional writers who mined this territory as a literary environment. Her characters come to represent the types and stereotypes associated with the period. Her work, the influence of which is still developing, is a significant marker of times, places, and people in the late twentieth century and serves as a helpful guidebook to those seeking insight into the psyches and lives of characters of that era.

Interviews:

John Bellante and Carl Bellante, "A Chic, Cheeky Chat with Tama Janowitz," *Bloomsbury Review* (May/June 1993): 13–14, 20;

E. Paul Driscoll, "Going to the Opera with Tama Janowitz," *Opera News,* 61 (November 1996): 26–30;

Laura L. Buchwald, "My Lunch with Tama," *Bold Type* (August 1999) <http://www.randomhouse.com/boldtype/0899/janowitz/interview.html>;

"Tama Janowitz," *Momstown* (February 2000) <http://newyork.urbanbaby.com/community/momstown_main.html>.

References:

Julia Reed, "Publishing's New Starlets," *U.S. News & World Report* (1 December 1986): 61;

R. Z. Sheppard, "Yuppie Lit: Publish or Perish," *Time* (19 October 1987): 77ff;

Patricia Stubblefield, "New York's 'Brat Pack' and the Postmodern Novel of Manners," dissertation, University of South Carolina, 2001;

Elizabeth Young, "Library of the Ultravixens," in *Shopping in Space: Essays on America's Blank Generation Fiction,* edited by Young and Graham Caveney (New York: Atlantic Monthly Press, 1992), pp. 142–194.

Ha Jin

(21 February 1956 –   )

Robert D. Sturr
Kent State University, Stark Campus

See also the Jin entry in *DLB 244: American Short-Story Writers Since World War II, Fourth Series.*

BOOKS: *Between Silences: A Voice from China* (Chicago: University of Chicago Press, 1990);

Facing Shadows (Brooklyn, N.Y.: Hanging Loose Press, 1996);

Ocean of Words: Army Stories (Cambridge, Mass.: Zoland, 1996);

Under the Red Flag (Athens: University of Georgia Press, 1997);

In the Pond (Cambridge, Mass.: Zoland, 1998; London: Vintage, 2001);

Waiting (New York: Pantheon, 1999; London: Heinemann, 2000);

The Bridegroom (New York: Pantheon, 2000; London: Heinemann, 2001);

Wreckage (Brooklyn, N.Y.: Hanging Loose Press, 2001);

The Crazed (New York: Pantheon, 2002; London: Heinemann, 2002).

Ha Jin has published volumes of poetry, collections of short stories, and novels. His short fiction in *Ocean of Words: Army Stories* (1996) and *Under the Red Flag* (1997) won praise from critics and two prestigious literary prizes, the PEN/Hemingway and Flannery O'Connor Awards, while an even wider popular acclaim followed the publication of his best-selling novel *Waiting* (1999), which won the National Book Award. Jin's spare prose style in narrating the lives of ordinary individuals trapped in political and moral ambiguities has led to comparisons with Nikolai Gogol and Anton Chekhov. Indeed, he explores a world as unfamiliar to most of his readers as Tsarist Russia: the Maoist Chinese culture of his youth.

Much of Jin's work is set in Manchuria, the forbidding yet strategically important northeastern region of China, and his stories generally take place in the turbulent period from the mid 1960s to the mid 1980s. His writing focuses on the human cost of ideological conflicts or social upheavals, such as the Sino-Soviet rift,

Ha Jin (photograph by Nancy Scherm; from the dust jacket for In the Pond, *1998; Richland County Public Library)*

Mao Tse-tung's Cultural Revolution, and Deng Xiaoping's reforms. His characters struggle to know how to behave and even how to think in order to meet the constantly changing demands of communist orthodoxy. Open resistance could lead to immediate danger, and yet adopting obedient silence in the face of a stifling and dehumanizing ideology only leads to a slow obliteration of self. In his review of *Ocean of Words* in *World Literature*

Today (Autumn 1997), Timothy Wong noted that Jin "challenge[s] Marxist (or Maoist) political ideology not by declaring allegiance to some other ideology but by demonstrating again and again the complexity of human emotion which defies simplistic dogma." In returning to the scenes of his youth, Jin seeks to recover and memorialize the many voices and lives that were sacrificed in the name of class struggle.

Ha Jin is the pen name of Xuefei (pronounced shu-FAY) Jin, born on 21 February 1956 in the city of Jinzhou in Liaoning province to Danlin Jin, an officer in the People's Liberation Army (PLA), and Yuanfen (Zhao) Jin. The arrival of the Cultural Revolution in 1966 ended Jin's formal education when schools were closed. Jin witnessed the rise of the cult of Mao and even joined a youth auxiliary to the Red Guards, but he also experienced the cruelty and hysteria of attacks on those accused of counterrevolutionary thinking when his family was publicly criticized and harassed because his maternal grandfather had once been a landholder. Jin felt pressure to prove his devotion to Mao and to China. "Like everyone else," he revealed in a *New York Times Magazine* profile (6 February 2000), "I wanted to be a hero, a martyr." Thus, in late 1969, just a few months before turning fourteen, he enlisted in the army.

Initially assigned to an artillery company on the Sino-Soviet border, Jin later trained as a telegraph operator. After five and a half years of service, he left the army and worked as a telegrapher for the Harbin Railroad Company from 1974 to 1977. He began a process of intense self-education, particularly in the classics of Chinese literature, and slowly improved his reading and writing skills. He also began to study English by listening to an educational radio program. When the universities were reopened at the end of the Cultural Revolution, he enrolled in Heilongjiang University to study English. He graduated in 1981 and moved south with his family to begin graduate study in American literature at Shangdong University. While earning a master's degree, he met Lisha Bian, a mathematician. They were married in 1982, and their son, Wen, was born in 1983.

Jin arrived in the United States in 1985 to pursue a Ph.D. in English at Brandeis University in Boston, with the expectation that he would return to China as a teacher or translator. Although the Chinese government initially kept his family behind, his wife was allowed to join him in 1987, and, surprisingly, his young son was granted an exit visa just a few weeks after the 1989 massacre of students and protesters at Tiananmen Square. The repression of China's prodemocracy movement was a turning point for Jin because it convinced him, as he explained in a 1999

profile in the *St. Louis Post-Dispatch,* that "it would be impossible to write honestly in China." Accordingly, he began to think of himself as a permanent exile, and this new identity profoundly changed the direction of his career.

While finishing his doctoral research on modernist poetry, Jin worked as a busboy, housecleaner, and night watchman to help support his family. He also enrolled in creative-writing courses at Boston University and made the decision to write and speak exclusively in English. "The process was excruciating," he noted in the *Post-Dispatch* profile, "like changing my blood. I was full of anxiety as if I were running a fever all the time." When *The Paris Review* accepted his first poem, he chose the pseudonym Ha because Xuefei was so difficult for English-speaking readers to pronounce. The name Ha was taken from the first Chinese character for Harbin, where he had first studied English.

In his first book of poems, *Between Silences: A Voice from China* (1990), Jin offers a preview of the different themes, characters, and situations that fill his later work. In the preface he writes that his interest is not merely to describe the tragic events of modern Chinese history but also to "speak for those unfortunate people who suffered, endured or perished at the bottom of life and who created the history and at the same time were fooled or ruined by it." He begins the volume with "The Dead Soldier's Talk," which is based on the famous true story of a young soldier who drowned in the Tuman River in 1969 while trying to save a plaster statue of Mao. The soldier was celebrated as a great hero during the Cultural Revolution, but in Jin's poem, which takes place six years after his death, the young martyr is restless in his grave and feels embittered that no one brings him news of "our Great Leader." He is unaware that the Cultural Revolution will soon end and that Mao is near death. A similar dramatization of frustration and disillusionment appears in the poem "Marching Towards Martyrdom," in which the narrator says sarcastically that "It was so easy to become a martyr, and there were so many ways." Writing in *World Literature Today* (Winter 1992), K. C. Leung praised Jin as "a master of understatement" who expresses a "quiet cynicism about the military that recalls the World War I poets." Far from noble, the sacrifice of young lives for the sake of Maoist orthodoxy seems like a terrible waste, according to Jin.

Between Silences also focuses on the consequences of the Cultural Revolution on everyday life in villages and towns, especially from the perspective of children. Jin presents horrifying moments of children publicly denouncing those who care for them, as in the poem "A Thirteen-Year-Old Accuses His Teacher." Young people growing up in the society portrayed in *Between*

Silences are either silenced through intimidation or death, or they learn how to use words and half-truths as weapons in the struggle to survive. Later poems in *Between Silences* focus on artistic expression and the restrictive intellectual and literary environment Jin experienced in China. Gail Mazur observed in *Ploughshares* (Spring 1991) that Jin's poems seem to have been "forged under the most intense pressure to remain silent, in the certainty that to speak freely is to court calamity."

Following the success of *Between Silences* and the completion of his doctorate in 1993, Jin was hired as an assistant professor of creative writing at Emory University and moved to Atlanta. *Facing Shadows* (1996), his second collection of poems, includes responses to the Tiananmen Square massacre as well as depictions of the uncertainty of a new life in the United States. In "A Child's Nature" Jin describes the arrival of his son in San Francisco, including his dismay that the Chinese media, along with his own family, had taught the boy that the students in Tiananmen Square were hooligans who deserved to be killed. However, despite such flashes of anger at the Chinese government, most of the poems in *Facing Shadows* focus on personal feelings of regret and guilt stemming from the sacrifices made by Jin's wife, memories of youthful enthusiasm for Maoist ideology, and embarrassment that, unlike dissidents in China, he had not taken a more definitive stand against the government. Other poems focus on new challenges, such as Jin's struggle to secure a teaching job and support his family. In "War," for example, Jin writes that when he was young and in the army, "The targets were clear: / Russian Tartars, American wolves, / Japanese devils, / Taiwanese bandits." But now that he is "Here" rather than "Back there," Jin sees that "No enemy is visible" and that "Small supple hands / toting tiny bundles of cash / stroke my throat and pat my hair, / ready to pin me to the ground / and turn me into a happy worm." Similar expressions of disorientation, entrapment, and suffocation fill the second half of *Facing Shadows*.

Published in the same year as *Facing Shadows,* the twelve stories in *Ocean of Words* all occur during the period of simmering tension in the late 1960s and early 1970s along the border between China and the Soviet Union. The forbidding setting of Jin's tales serves as a symbol of the even icier grip of political indoctrination. As Andy Solomon observed in *The New York Times,* Jin's diverse characters "form a group portrait that suggests how an entire people struggles to keep its basic humanity within the stiff, unnatural confines of Maoist ideology." In some stories, Jin focuses on the precarious position of low-level officers and party officials who must indoctrinate and lead young recruits. "A Report,"

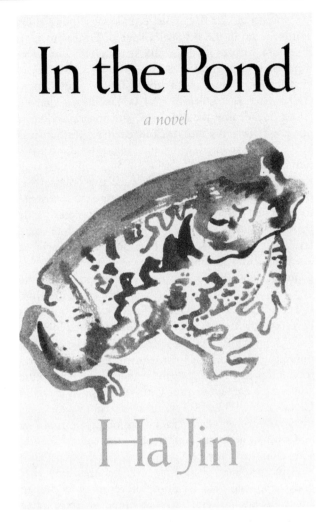

Dust jacket for Jin's first novel, about a dissatisfied fertilizer-plant worker who becomes a political cartoonist (Richland County Public Library)

for example, is written from the perspective of Chen Jun, the political instructor of a reconnaissance company, who must explain why, during a parade through a local city, new recruits began to cry while singing a song about saying goodbye to their mothers. The emotion is, in Chen Jun's mind, not merely an embarrassment but also an instance of counterrevolutionary thinking that must be explained lest he be punished. The PLA does not allow for any other images of its men than those of brave and self-sacrificing soldiers, and so, in a chilling line, Chen Jun suggests that the authorities "ban this poisonous song and investigate the family and political backgrounds of its author and its composer." As is often the case in the world that Jin creates in his writing, characters must anxiously deny the reality of their experience in order to construct an appropriate and safe narrative of events that will confirm the false but dominant ideology of their society.

Under the Red Flag, Jin's second collection of short stories, is set in the fictional village of Dismount Fort. The book focuses on the traditional harshness of life in a poor, rural town as well as on the disruptive social changes that came with the Cultural Revolution. Katherine Riegel noted in *Crab Orchard Review* that Jin "does not idealize the old ways, and the Red Guards are not always the most vicious enemy." Rather, it is the "cultural splintering" brought about by the frustration of the inhabitants of Dismount Fort combined with the implementation of cold and destructive political theories about modernization and progress that contribute to what she describes as "a sense of hollowness inside these characters as if each one were lost in a lost country." Jin's genius, according to Fatima Wu in a *World Literature Today* (Spring 1998) review, is rooted in his genuine sympathy for the ordinary people whom he chooses as protagonists. Wu favorably compared him to Lu Xun and wrote that "Ha Jin is a satirist, but at his best he is a writer of compassion, warmth, and love."

A few stories in *Under the Red Flag* go beyond the immediate and personal consequences of the Cultural Revolution and investigate the maneuvering behind the scenes by local Communist Party officials. "Winds and Clouds over a Funeral" reveals the extent to which survival and even political victory can obliterate morality and truth. The dying mother of a local cadre begs her son, Ding, to bury her in the ground, in accordance with the tradition of filial piety, rather than have her body cremated. He is aware of recent government edicts demanding cremation in order to save arable land, and realizes that his political adversaries will seek to trap him—either Ding will violate party policy or he will be a disloyal son. Despite his promise and what he knows to be the truth, Ding eventually declares that his mother actually wanted to be cremated. In an exchange of articles in local and regional newspapers, he outflanks his opponents who had printed articles highlighting Ding's disrespect toward his mother. Using his contacts at more respected papers, Ding publicly reiterates the notion that his mother welcomed cremation, thus turning his convenient lie into the authorized truth. His son, Sheng, a recently discharged soldier, is angry about the deception but remains silent because "His experience in the army had taught him that disaster always comes from the tongue." To simply speak or record the truth as an individual is futile because Ding, who is a clear reminder of the Orwellian resonances in Jin's writing, controls the way information is shaped and preserved.

The manipulation of information, particularly through the media, is the focus of Jin's first novel, *In the Pond* (1998). Its setting is also Dismount Fort, but the action takes place after the close of the Cultural Revolu-tion. In a *World Literature Today* (Spring 1999) review, Jeffrey Kinkley praised Jin's "mischievous prose" that so accurately captures the tone and rhetoric of the period. He noted that "The book satirizes a world of Maoist human relationships and views that was about to vanish just as Ha Jin left China." Compared to Jin's earlier work, the tone of the novel is somewhat lighter as Jin depicts the attempt by the leadership of a rural commune to silence a pompous yet likable gadfly.

The protagonist, Shao Bin, works at a fertilizer plant and is a self-taught artist and aspiring scholar. At the urging of his wife, he tries to ingratiate himself to the factory director, Ma Gong, and party secretary, Liu Shu, but they eventually deny him a spot in a new housing complex. Outraged at the unfairness, he uses his artistic talent to strike back. Bin imagines that his struggle is connected to the ancient traditions of scholarly learning as he recalls that "the materialist thinker Wang Chong of the Han Dynasty had said something about punishing the evil with the writing brush." This fuzzy recollection of a passage from a paperback anthology of philosophical writing is typical of the way Bin thinks. He is rarely accurate or even articulate, but he is filled with fantasies about the power that might flow from his art. Blending earnestness and idealism with a touch of vanity and buffoonery, Bin remains a likable and sympathetic character. The novel is not just a satire on the petty squabbles within communes but also a work that challenges the well-meaning pretensions of writers, artists, and intellectuals who dabble in politics.

When his first drawing appears in the local newspaper, Bin becomes frightened after Ma and Liu publicly denounce him, but he refuses to write the self-criticism that they demand and continues to insinuate that the commune leadership is corrupt. The struggle escalates as Ma and Liu accuse Bin of mental instability and block his attempts to transfer to another job. Jin gives these low-level officials enough depth so that despite their cruelty, readers see their vulnerability in dealing with a disobedient worker. They become desperate as they try to avoid the charge of corruption that, in the reform-minded era of the novel, would earn them serious punishment. As novelist Phyllis Alesia Perry noted in her *Atlanta Journal-Constitution* (10 January 1999) review of *In the Pond,* Bin and his enemies are "locked in a miserable cycle of attack and counterattack," which allows Jin to expose the commune as the "stagnant little puddle" that it is. Although readers can "grasp Bin's need to cling to fading images of pure socialist ideals," his fight is still revealed as a petty and futile struggle.

In the closing chapters Bin reaches beyond Dismount Fort to express his anger in the pages of a reformist academic journal in Beijing. The ripples from his initial defiance in the small pond of Dismount Fort seem serious enough that his agitation might actually do harm to the careers, and even lives, of his supporters. In this way the comedy of *In the Pond* is always mixed with a sense that something could go terribly wrong. In an ending that deflates Bin's position as a crusading hero, Ma and Liu buy his silence when they give him a new job in the propaganda office of the factory. He is flattered to receive recognition as an artist and quickly forgets about his wife's dreams of a new apartment and the reforms trumpeted by his supporters in Beijing. He believes that he has won but has yet to see that he will never escape Dismount Fort and that his scathing wit will always be at the service of Ma and Liu. Writing in *The Baltimore Sun* (29 November 1998), critic Joan Mellen summed up the ending by noting that "Jin eschews all sentimentality" and that his conclusion is filled with "sheer irony, devastating in its unrelenting finality." In the closing scene Bin sees a flock of geese fly overhead on the first morning of his new job and he lifts up his arm "as if he too had wings." Bin's comic travails give way to an aching sense that even in the post-Maoist era, social forces in the "new" China will rarely allow for true autonomy or fulfillment. He is aware of the folly and chaos at the center of his world, but he does not possess enough power or even self-awareness to overcome it.

As a bittersweet love story, Jin's novel *Waiting* has a different tone than *In the Pond,* but Jin continues to explore themes of entrapment, powerlessness, and self-delusion. *Waiting* covers more than two decades, from the early 1960s to the mid 1980s, and includes scenes in both a tradition-bound rural village and a modern city. In a prologue set in the early 1980s, Lin Kong, an army doctor, is caught between those two worlds. He is assigned to a hospital in Muji City and only returns to his home village once a year. During recent visits he has tried but failed to secure a divorce from his wife. The first chapter moves back to the beginning of the story to reveal that Lin and Shuyu were married many years before as part of an arrangement to please his parents. Following his parents' deaths and the birth of a daughter, Lin stopped thinking of Shuyu as his wife. Her bound feet symbolize a way of life that he rejects, and because of both her illiteracy and servility, he is embarrassed to bring her to the city. As the novel progresses, Lin becomes attached to Manna Wu, a nurse in the hospital, but he cannot obtain a divorce without Shuyu's consent, which is always withheld at the instigation of her brother. Lin cannot bring himself to push Shuyu to agree, even though he probably has the power to do so. Instead, he allows eighteen years to go by until, according to the law, he can be granted a divorce without her agreement. In the meantime, army

regulations strictly forbid an affair with Manna, and because the Muji City hospital is a confining place lacking in privacy, they can be nothing more than guarded friends and good Maoist comrades.

As with Jin's earlier fiction, this situation can be read as a political parable that dramatizes the stifling consequences of both the traditional Chinese value of filial piety and more modern notions of Maoist purity. Lin is a good son, but his willingness to marry the bride his parents chose has led to a lifetime of unhappiness. He is a good PLA officer and says the right things in political meetings. Consequently, he creates a safe zone in the hospital where he can live quietly and enjoy reading books from his secret library, so long as they are kept hidden. He enjoys Manna's company and, surprisingly, comes to accept their inability to pursue a relationship far more readily than she does. His response to the denial of their love is to withdraw into a comfortable yet passionless lifestyle. Lin's situation is, as Kinkley noted in his review for *World Literature Today* (Summer 2000), "an absurd impasse of the sort the author excels at creating, quintessentially Maoist but also universally human." Lin ultimately finds, however, that a habitual self-denial of love and pleasure makes him unable to fully understand or express his feelings for Manna Wu, even though they wait for one another for nearly two decades.

Lin's emotional paralysis is revealed slowly over the course of the novel and elicits a certain degree of sympathy. However, Lin's passivity—his willingness to leave Manna in an undecided, socially powerless position for nearly two decades—leads to much harsher consequences for her. Most notably, she is brutally raped by Geng Yang, a patient in the hospital who had befriended Lin. She is unable to report the crime because of her shame and the uncertainty of an investigation that might probe her relationship with Lin as much as the rape.

In the surprising conclusion of the novel, Lin is finally granted a divorce, but he is unable to open himself emotionally to Manna. Even though political and social restrictions are removed, he remains uncomfortable and undemonstrative in their marriage. In response, Manna instigates frantic and exhausting lovemaking, but rather than bring them closer, this sexual intensity drives Lin further away. In fact, it deepens their lingering frustration and loneliness. Lin can sense Manna's anger and desperation, and yet he cannot change. The sadness of this situation highlights the universality of the story. In praising the novel in *The New York Times* (24 October 1999), Francine Prose echoed a familiar comparison: "What happens to Lin and Manna has as much to do with who they are as with the times they live in, and *Waiting* is as much and as lit-

*Dust jacket for Jin's 1999 novel, about a man who must wait
eighteen years to divorce his wife and marry the woman
he loves (Richland County Public Library)*

tle about 20th-century Communist China as Chekhov's story 'The Lady with the Pet Dog' is about 19th-century Yalta." While Chekhov's story ends with the frustration of two lovers who cannot be together, the final chapters of *Waiting* present two lovers who are together but cannot find happiness.

The birth of twin boys—an event viewed enviously and as a sign of great fortune by other characters—also reveals a serious heart condition in Manna that leaves her with perhaps only months to live. Surprisingly, Shuyu becomes important to Lin once again. In order to help his daughter, Hua, Lin settles her and Shuyu in the city, even though he had resisted that step for so many years. While in Muji City, Shuyu becomes more modern and begins to appear as a younger, more vibrant woman. Uncertain and filled with regret about Manna, Lin appears in the end to turn back to Shuyu. With an open-ended conclusion that does not reveal

either how long Manna will live or if Lin truly wishes to reconstitute his first family, Jin leaves only the bittersweet mood of regret. Critic Linda Simon, writing in *World & I* (May 2000), highlighted the circular nature of the story: "Manna is waiting, only now, she awaits death; Shuyu is waiting, hopefully, as ever, for her husband to return; and Lin is waiting: for love, liberation, or perhaps an inner revolution that, Ha Jin implies, is the only real basis for cultural enlightenment." Lin, who has spent a lifetime carefully regulating his thoughts and behavior, does not know how to undertake such a transformation. He only knows how to wait.

In the year following the success of *Waiting,* Jin was awarded a Guggenheim Fellowship, and the novel received the PEN-Faulkner Award. He also published *The Bridegroom* (2000), a collection of short stories set in Muji City that focuses on China in the early 1980s. It won the Asian American Literary Award in 2001 and the Townsend Prize in fiction in 2002. The collection probes the transition from Maoist orthodoxy to an entrepreneurial socialism and presents characters who expect that their lives will change—that opportunity will be expanded and justice upheld. However, they are invariably disappointed by official corruption and the abuse of power. As Jodi Daynard noted in a *Boston Globe* review (22 October 2000), Jin's characters are "spiritually distorted and disfigured." Because they are "unable to triumph over adversity, they become experts at revenge instead." For instance, in "Saboteur," a college professor, Mr. Chiu, is harassed by the police while on his honeymoon and arrested on the false charge of sabotage. He expects that his status as a scholar and party member will save him from such an obvious and petty abuse of power. Because he senses a flare-up of his hepatitis, Mr. Chiu agrees to confess to a lesser crime. However, as a way to exact revenge, he visits four restaurants on his way out of town and uses shared cups and bowls in order to spread his disease. More than eight hundred fall ill and six die as Mr. Chiu is so warped by his anger at the police that he does, in fact, become a saboteur.

The depiction of cruel and arbitrary authority is made specific in several stories that depict the repression of sexuality. The management of marital relationships and the punishment of adultery figure prominently in *Under the Red Flag* and *Waiting,* and in *The Bridegroom* Jin more explicitly demonstrates that deviance from sexual norms in Chinese culture—or in many other places—is often seen as more than just the violation of a moral code; it is also considered a dangerous assertion of individual will that threatens political order. Sex creates a secret, interior life that leads individuals to withdraw and conspire with one another.

Even after the Cultural Revolution, the government and party officials described in *The Bridegroom* find this kind of freedom intolerable.

In the closing stories of *The Bridegroom,* Jin moves closer to the time of his departure from China as he describes economic and cultural changes of the mid 1980s. "After Cowboy Chicken Came to Town" depicts the arrival of a Western fast-food restaurant in Muji City. Told from the workers' perspective, the story details the ways that ordinary Chinese had to adapt to new economic rules. Despite the strange business practices of their bosses at Cowboy Chicken, the employees feel a sense of loyalty—just as though they were part of a communist-era commune. However, when they fight against salary inequity, they are shocked to find themselves fired and their strike suppressed by local officials who are more interested in placating American investors than in supporting workers.

Although the liberalizing of China is hinted at in *The Bridegroom,* its focus is on the frustration and repression of ordinary citizens. Because of this criticism—as well as the stark view of China presented in Jin's other books—the Chinese government has not allowed his work to be translated or published, and he is generally unknown in his native country. Even though Jin has become an American citizen, he has not returned to China since he left. He stated in the many interviews following his National Book Award that he might soon turn his attention to writing about the experience of exiles and immigrants in the United States. Jin's third collection of poetry, *Wreckage,* appeared in 2001. Frank Allen wrote in *Library Journal* that the subjects of many of the poems are "both stunning and horrific" and that the volume "bears witness to a sad, troubled bond with his [Jin's] homeland."

In 2002 Jin published his next novel, *The Crazed.* It is set against the background of the Tiananmen Square massacre and tells the story of Jian Wan, a Chinese graduate student who becomes a caregiver to his literature professor and future father-in-law, who has suffered a stroke. The stricken professor's ravings about his political past, as well as the massacre, lead to life-changing decisions for Jian Wan. A reviewer for *Publishers Weekly* noted that the novel "is permeated by a grief that won't be eased or transmuted by heroic images of resistance" and that Jin "continues to refine his understanding of politics as an unmitigated curse." In *Booklist* Donna Seaman observed that Jin writes "with a searing restraint born of long-brewing grief over the Chinese government's surreal savageness" but added, "Jin's dramatic indictment does not preclude love, or the ancient power of story to memorialize, awaken compassion, and shore up hope."

Ha Jin has continued to focus on all three literary modes—poems, short stories, and novels—in which he has had previous success. In 2001 he left his teaching position at Emory and after a short sabbatical began teaching at Boston University in 2002, thus continuing his career at the place where he first took courses in creative writing. It is where he made the decision to write solely in English, to resist the silence imposed in China, and to become an important new voice in American literature.

References:

Martha Baker, "Award-Winning Author Articulates Misfortunes of Chinese in English," *St. Louis Post-Dispatch,* 6 December 1999, p. D3;

Dan Cryer, "A Writer's Dedication," *Newsday* (6 December 2000);

Dwight Garner, "Ha Jin's Cultural Revolution," *New York Times Magazine,* 6 February 2000;

Chen Jianguo, "Against Silences: The Cultural Revolution and Literary Memory," in *The Conscience of Humankind: Literature and Traumatic Experiences,* edited by Elrud Ibsch (Amsterdam: Rodopi, 2000);

Jerome V. Kramer, "Ha Jin of America," *Book* (January 2000);

Judy Stoffman, "Author Finds Chinese Essence in English," *Toronto Star,* 13 November 2000;

John D. Thomas, "Across an Ocean of Words," *Emory Magazine* (Spring 1998).

Randall Kenan

(12 March 1963 –   )

Keith E. Byerman
Indiana State University

BOOKS: *A Visitation of Spirits* (New York: Grove, 1989;
    London: Abacus, 1996);
Let the Dead Bury Their Dead and Other Stories (New York
    & San Diego: Harcourt Brace Jovanovich, 1992;
    London: Abacus, 1994);
James Baldwin (New York: Chelsea House, 1994);
*Walking on Water: Black American Lives at the Turn of the
    Twenty-First Century* (New York: Knopf, 1999;
    London: Little, Brown, 1999).

Randall Kenan is emerging as one of the foremost
young African American writers. Using a mixture of
realistic detail and often surrealistic narrative, he creates
the world of Tims Creek, North Carolina, a space occupied by demons, ghosts, and ordinary residents. He
incorporates into this portrayal the difficult and sometimes tragic experiences of homosexuals. At the same
time, his stories do not fit the conventional modes of
either racial or gay fiction. As a reviewer for the *Virginia
Quarterly Review* has suggested, "The old tropes and conventions (and clichés) are only tools now." Nonetheless,
Kenan has embraced these aspects of his identity, especially his racial identity, through nonfiction books on
James Baldwin and on African American experiences
across the United States. A consistent theme in Kenan's
body of work is the breaking of boundaries, whether in
literary expression or personal identity.

This violation of rules can be seen from his birth as
an illegitimate child in Brooklyn on 12 March 1963. At the
age of six weeks, Randall Garrett Kenan was taken by his
paternal grandfather to Wallace, North Carolina, and
then, a short time later, to Chinquapin in rural Duplin
County to be raised by his father's relatives, his great-aunt
functioning as his primary caregiver. The name Kenan
has long been associated with the county, from a white
immigrant slaveowner by that name appearing in the
county census of 1790. Some of the Kenan slaves appear
to have been the ancestors of the author. The county seat
is called Kenansville after the family name. The white
Kenans married into Standard Oil money, thus extending
their influence in the local community. Similarly, the

Randall Kenan (from the dust jacket for A Visitation of
Spirits, *1989; Richland County Public Library)*

world of the black Kenans was one of prosperous farmers
with a staunchly conservative religious faith. Randall
Kenan asserted in a 1993 interview with Dorothy Allison
that he knew from early childhood that he was gay; hence,
he always felt like an outsider in this social and spiritual
environment, even as it nurtured him in other ways—care
by extended family, storytelling, and education.

Although he was raised primarily by women, one
of the strong influences of Kenan's childhood was his
cousin's husband, John W. Brown, who made frequent
visits from New York and eventually moved to Chinquapin. Brown was a former boxer who also had a
broad education and was a storyteller. Through both

example and instruction, he taught young Randall the importance of persistence, self-awareness, and social responsibility. These attributes became significant themes in Kenan's fiction.

More formal schooling came first in a segregated kindergarten class, then in integrated public schools. His interaction with whites provided a split in his life, since his family had few interracial contacts, while he had many. This dual existence was highlighted by the fact that he was known as Randall at school and Garrett at home. This division becomes an issue in his novel, *A Visitation of Spirits* (1989), as the family of the protagonist, Horace, is enraged by his friendships with white schoolmates. Kenan's childhood reading also reflected this larger perspective. While part of his interest in writing came from the oral tradition within the black community, his personal preferences for reading were science fiction and fantasy. As he told Don Belton in an interview in *Speak My Name: Black Men on Masculinity and the American Dream* (1995): "I had been a dreamy kid, aloft in fantasy and make-believe. Comic books, fairy stories, tales of the amazing and especially of the fantastic were my real world. Paying little attention to the outside world, I lived for Star Trek and Spiderman and the vampires, werewolves, and bigfoots of horror novels." He also played trumpet and was a Smithsonian scholar, graduating from East Duplin High School in Beulahville in 1980.

Kenan's interest in science led him to major in physics when he enrolled at the University of North Carolina at Chapel Hill at the age of seventeen. In addition to science courses, he took classes in African American studies, and as a diversion during his sophomore year, he signed up for a creative-writing class with H. Maxwell Steele. His dream was that he would write science fiction on the side during his career as a physicist. He also began reading Toni Morrison's novels, and this combination steered him away from physics and toward a major in English. The summer following his junior year, he went to Oxford University to study British literature. According to Doris Betts, by the time he arrived in her senior honors writing course, "he had already developed the style and tone he needed." He graduated from the University of North Carolina with a B.A. in English and a minor in physics in December 1985.

The following February, with a letter of introduction from Betts to Morrison, who was then an editor at Random House, Kenan landed a job as a receptionist. Within a year, he had been promoted first to the position of assistant to the vice president and then to assistant editor at Knopf. During this time, he began working on a novel, *A Visitation of Spirits,* which was published by Grove Press in 1989.

A Visitation of Spirits is set in Tims Creek, a rural North Carolina community much like Chinquapin. Its central family is the Crosses, who—similar to the Kenans—

are prominent in the town, have white and black branches, and have a town named after them. In creating this community, which he continued to develop in his later fiction, Kenan was influenced by William Faulkner's Yoknapatawpha County; he invented a history, a culture, and a set of recurring characters to populate his creation. Kenan has also acknowledged the importance of Katharine Anne Porter, Gabriel García Márquez, Yukio Mishima, and Baldwin on his writing.

A Visitation of Spirits alternates between two days, 29 April 1984 and 8 December 1985, and between the perspectives of two characters, Horace Cross and his cousin, James Malachai Greene. The earlier date is the day on which sixteen-year-old Horace commits suicide after realizing that he can neither deny his homosexuality nor escape the homophobic world of his family and community. On the later day, James, a minister and school principal, takes his elderly great-uncle Zeke and Zeke's sister-in-law, Ruth, to visit a hospitalized cousin. The journey, the memories, and the conversations that occur during the trip help to establish the family context for the Horace narrative.

Having reached an impasse in his life, Horace has decided to use the knowledge he has acquired through books of fantasy and magic to transform himself into a bird and thus escape his situation. He waits until his grandfather, Zeke, falls asleep and then goes into the woods to perform his ritual. Instead of changing himself, however, he calls forth demons, which then take him on a Dickensian journey to the sites and moments that are the sources of his inner conflict. He repeatedly wonders if he has gone insane but feels compelled to follow the voices in his head and the ghosts that seem to populate the night. Each of the sections of the book is given a title appropriate to this phantasmagorical feature: "White Sorcery," "Black Necromancy," "Holy Science," "Old Demonology," and "Old Gods, New Demons." This uncertainty about reality and fantasy, madness and reason, memory and hallucination gives this part of the novel its surreal or magical realist quality.

The demons take Horace through his youth. He visits the church that his family helped to establish. He sees both the living and the dead he has known there. He also hears again one of Reverend Barden's sermons attacking homosexuality. Like Baldwin's John Grimes in *Go Tell It on the Mountain* (1953), Horace reexperiences his deep ambivalence about religious belief. He goes to the elementary school, where he feels again his love of books and, by implication, his love of modernity. He recalls his first encounter with gay identity, which is embodied in Gideon Stone, a "pretty boy" who has accepted his homosexuality and has learned to defend himself with words against the taunts of other students. Unlike Horace's friends, Gideon sees through the protagonist's reluctant participation in "queer-baiting," recognizing their shared orientation.

As the novel continues, Horace visits his high school, which was the site of struggles over both his sexual and racial identities. Gideon again plays a crucial role in his development as Horace now finds himself infatuated, so much so that the young men begin a sexual relationship. At the same time, his grandfather asks him about girlfriends and tells stories in Horace's presence that help to define "normal" manhood. To comply with his grandfather's perception of normalcy, the younger man begins dating and even having sex with girls, and he eventually breaks off his association with Gideon, violently. These actions, however, intensify rather than ameliorate his conflict. He becomes an athlete but is aware of his desire for the other males on the teams. His increased friendliness with white students in this context provokes a negative response from his family. Later in the novel, James recalls that at the Thanksgiving before Horace's death, the young man was criticized at dinner, ostensibly for getting an earring but more deeply for having white companions. To establish such relationships, in some sense, is to violate the wisdom of the black Crosses, who have made their way in the world by distrusting and ignoring whites. To willingly identify with members of that group is tantamount to betrayal of the family and the race.

The last major Horace section describes his experiences in a world in which his sexual orientation is accepted. A theater group comes to town to perform an historical pageant written by one of the white Crosses. Several of the actors are gay or bisexual, and they draw Horace into their sexual activities. In an effort to bring together race and orientation, Horace confesses his love for the principal black actor but is brutally rejected. He finds more agreeable companions among the others, but instead of providing a sense of the possibilities for his life, this period of fulfillment only aggravates his sense of isolation from his own community. After the troupe leaves and his family forces him to give up his white friends, he begins to ignore his schoolwork and to search for a way to escape.

In the last scene, he is discovered by James, who tries to talk him out of suicide. Horace explains to James that he cannot live in the world as defined by family, church, and community—in essence, all of those who make him hate himself for the life he has been given. The section ends, first by questioning whether the demons guiding Horace are real, and then by pointing out that it does not really matter since Horace kills himself, an action that is described in clinical terms.

This stark ending brings readers back into harsh reality and suggests the need for the James Greene narratives. The Horace sections are so inward that an externalized perspective is needed to make some sense of that

narration. By depicting an ordinary day in the Cross family, a day during which Horace is barely mentioned, the author provides a context of memory and conflict that demonstrates the obsessions with death and control that would have made it difficult for the young man to live the kind of life he needed. Zeke and Ruth are constantly at odds, and nothing James says or does can reconcile them. Readers gradually learn that Zeke holds Ruth responsible for the miserable life and early death of her husband, who was his brother. By the end of the day, they seem to have gained some peace, though it is unarticulated and thus becomes part of what is repressed. By implication, the text ends by asking: if this world could destroy a "normal"—in this instance black-identified and heterosexual—man because of his perceived weaknesses, what would it do to a Horace? Only James Greene has any glimmerings of the question, to say nothing of the answer.

A Visitation of Spirits received few reviews when it was published, though it has received some critical attention. An anonymous reviewer in the *Virginia Quarterly Review* called it "Tightly structured but highly original." In *The Richmond Review,* an on-line publication, Adam Baron stated that the novel "is a very honest, moving book, which takes big risks in both its subject matter, and in its fantastical form which could have appeared contrived and sensational in less capable hands." In a critical essay, Robert McRuer points out that setting the novel in rural North Carolina breaks with the conventional view of black gay life as limited to urban areas. By doing so, McRuer argues, Kenan challenges assumptions about the nature of that identity.

The publication of the novel opened new career possibilities for Kenan. He left the publishing world in 1989 to begin teaching at Sarah Lawrence and Columbia University. In 1994 he became the first William Blackburn Visiting Professor of Creative Writing at Duke University, and the next year he was the Edouard Morot-Sir Visiting Professor at the University of North Carolina. A position as the John and Reneé Grisham Writer-in-Residence at the University of Mississippi preceded his job as professor of creative writing at the University of Memphis.

During this time Kenan pulled together some of the stories he had begun in Betts's writing class along with material originally intended as part of *A Visitation of Spirits.* The collection was published in 1992 as *Let the Dead Bury Their Dead and Other Stories.* The volume was nominated for the *Los Angeles Times* Award, was a finalist for the National Book Critics Circle Award, and was named a Notable Book for 1992 by *The New York Times.*

Let the Dead Bury Their Dead is composed of a series of short stories about Tims Creek and a long oral history, ostensibly collected by James Malachai Greene of the earlier book. As in the novel, the central themes are death and desire, in the context of the supernatural. "Clarence and the Dead," for example, involves a talking pig and a boy who brings messages from the dead to the living. Much of the story, in fact, is about the ways a community "naturalizes" that which it considers unnatural. Wilma's claims that her hog, Francis, talks to her are explained by the difficulties of her life; in addition, the people do not seriously consider having her committed to an institution because she owns the property on which their homes sit. They have more difficulty with Clarence, since he offers advice and information beyond the knowledge level of most children. They use devices of avoidance and counterconjuration to prevent any harmful effects from his words, but they are also fascinated by his abilities. Trudier Harris has pointed out that the narrator uses a humorous narrative technique as one means of evading the more troubling implications of Clarence's powers.

A more serious engagement with death is evident in "Things of This World," in which an Asian man suddenly appears one day on the farm of John Stokes, an elderly black man. After attending to the injuries of the stranger, Stokes continues to care for him, though he has little information about him other than his name, Chi. The black man mostly continues with what has obviously been a quiet life, until the day the racist sons of Terrell, the richest landowner in town, kill his old dog. Stokes takes his gun to Terrell's house and kills one of the white man's prized coon dogs. He is arrested and then released on bail. When he returns home, he sits on his porch and tells Chi that he wishes he could die so as to rob Terrell of the satisfaction of a trial. The next morning, his neighbors find him dead in the same chair, "his eyes stretched wide with astonishment." Chi is never seen again. His name, in both African and Chinese contexts, suggests that he is a spirit, perhaps sent to grant Stokes his last wish. Such supernaturalism, however, operates within the context of a realistic presentation of racial discrimination. This juxtaposition of the normal and the paranormal has led reviewers to categorize Kenan's work as magical realism.

The stories that focus on desire are much more conventionally realistic, though their subject matter has generally been considered taboo, especially among African American writers. "The Foundations of the Earth," for example, tells of Maggie MacGowan Williams's developing friendship with the white gay lover of her grandson, Edward. Gabriel comes to Edward's funeral and reveals the truth about their relationship, a truth Maggie angrily rejects. She then experiences emotional depression followed by a dream about the experiences of Job. Later, she invites Gabriel to visit her again, and they begin talking about Edward, about homosexuality, and about the struggles of living an honest life.

As a counterpoint to this conversation, the local preacher and Maggie's neighbors get into an argument

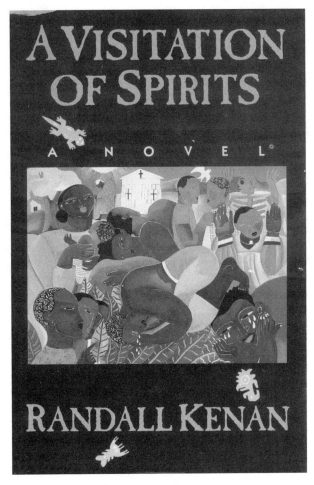

Dust jacket for Kenan's first novel, set in the fictional North Carolina community of Tims Creek, about a homosexual teenager who commits suicide after taking a fantastic demon-guided journey through his past (Richland County Public Library)

about the Sunday work being done by the white man to whom Maggie has leased her land. Their debate, which eventually leads to a confrontation in the fields, demonstrates the narrowness of the world of Tims Creek and thus how difficult it would have been for Edward to have revealed the truth of his orientation. By the end of the story, Maggie has come to see the silliness of those restrictions; she sympathizes with the farmer and Gabriel and begins to mourn Edward properly.

The final story, or more properly novella, is also the most radical in terms of structure. "Let the Dead Bury Their Dead" is set up as a book put together by James Malachai Greene, later found and edited by Reginald Gregory Kain, who has the same initials as Kenan. Composed of oral history, diary entries, letters, and various passages of academic discourse on a variety of subjects, it also makes use of footnotes with references to actual and fictional sources. The story is told primarily by Zeke from *A Visitation of Spirits,* who provides the history of Tims Creek.

The narrative is filled with magic, racial violence, and a community created by escaped slaves, which eventually develops into the town. The narrative relates the story of Pharoah, a wizard who escapes from the Cross Plantation, as well as the story of Phineas Cross, the owner's gay son who becomes a botanist prominent in scientific societies. The narrative also incorporates the diary of Rebecca Cross, Phineas's mother, which provides the slaveholder's perspective on events. Ruth, who also appears in the novel, repeatedly challenges the legends told by Zeke. "Let the Dead Bury Their Dead" was originally intended to be part of *A Visitation of Spirits,* but Kenan deleted it during the development of that earlier work.

Let the Dead Bury Their Dead received more critical attention than the earlier work, and the reviews were consistently positive. Frank Mosher, in *The New York Times Book Review,* called it "nothing short of a wonder-book," while the critic from *Library Journal* saw him as "a daring writer who fully explores his genre." The strongest comment came from Valerie Miner in *Nation:* "Kenan explores the territories between the living and the dead, between the fantastic and the mundane in an energetic, inventive prose that never descends to contrivance of sentimentality. These sensual, humorous, eventful stories mark Randall Kenan as a writer of startling, imaginative compassion." *Let the Dead Bury Their Dead* was nominated for the 1993 National Book Critics Circle Award and won a Lambda Award for best gay men's fiction.

Kenan's writing efforts since *Let the Dead Bury Their Dead* have focused on nonfiction. In 1994 he published a short biography of Baldwin as part of the Lives of Notable Gay Men and Lesbians series, designed for young adult readers. In this work Kenan focuses on the importance of understanding individual differences, using Baldwin's life as an example. While the emphasis is on the theme of homosexuality, both in Baldwin's life and in his writing, Kenan makes it clear that his subject did not define himself in terms of a single category, nor did he deny any aspect of his identity.

Walking on Water: Black American Lives at the Turn of the Twenty-First Century (1999) addresses the question of what it means to be black in America, through interviews with dozens of people from locations as diverse as Martha's Vineyard, Massachusetts, and Anchorage, Alaska, and from all walks of life. In an interview about the project, Kenan noted that assertions about the meaning of black identity tended to be associated with a particular region, such as the Deep South or the urban North. While he included these areas in his fieldwork, he also explored racial experience in areas not normally associated with African Americans, such as Coeur d'Alene, Idaho, and North Battleford, Saskatchewan. As with all of his work,

Kenan focuses on the diversity within black life as much as the difference it makes in the nation. As he makes clear in the introduction to the volume, he does not believe that race is a fixed biological category, but rather that it is a product of history and culture. Thus, readers would expect what Kenan finds—that like other human beings, African Americans are shaped largely by what exists in their environment. In a review appearing in the 14 March 1999 issue of *The New York Times Book Review,* Alan Wolfe points out that Kenan's approach to his material "violates every rule of the sociologist" but then asserts that this tactic "may be just the reason his book succeeds so well as a work of insight and compassion."

In long and short fiction, Randall Kenan has successfully combined the realistic with the fantastic, traditional storytelling with experimentation, and the spiritual with the mundane. He has also been recognized for his achievements in biography as well as oral history. He is coming into his own as a teller of remarkable tales.

Interviews:

Dorothy Allison, "Spies Like Us: Talking Between the Lines," *Voice Literary Supplement,* 188 (September 1993): 26;

V. Hunt, "A Conversation with Randall Kenan," *African American Review,* 29, no. 3 (1995): 411–420;

Don Belton, in *Speak My Name: Black Men on Masculinity and the American Dream,* edited by Belton (Boston: Beacon, 1995);

Charles Rowell, "An Interview with Randall Kenan," *Callaloo,* 21, no. 1 (1998): 133–148.

References:

Doris Betts, "Randall Garrett Kenan: Myth and Reality in Tims Creek," in *Southern Writers at Century's End,* edited by Jeffrey J. Folks and James A. Perkins (Lexington: University Press of Kentucky, 1997);

Trudier Harris, *The Power of the Porch: The Storyteller's Craft in Zora Neale Hurston, Gloria Naylor, and Randall Kenan* (Athens: University of Georgia Press, 1996);

Sharon Patricia Holland, "(Pro)Creating Imaginative Spaces and Other Queer Acts: Randall Kenan's *A Visitation of Spirits* and Its Revival of James Baldwin's Absent Black Gay Man in *Giovanni's Room,*" in *James Baldwin Now,* edited by Dwight A. McBride (New York: New York University Press, 1999), pp. 265–288;

Robert McRuer, "A Visitation of Difference: Randall Kenan and Black Queer Theory," *Journal of Homosexuality,* 26, nos. 2–3 (1993): 221–232.

Dean Koontz
(David Axton, Brian Coffey, Deanna Dwyer, K. R. Dwyer, John Hill, Leigh Nichols, Anthony North, Richard Paige, Owen West, Aaron Wolfe)
(9 July 1945 –   )

Jennifer Vance

BOOKS: *Star Quest,* [bound with *Doom of the Green Planet,* by Emil Petaja] (New York: Ace Double, 1968);

The Fall of the Dream Machine [bound with *The Star Venturers,* by Kenneth Bulmer] (New York: Ace Double, 1969);

Fear That Man [bound with *Toyman,* by E. C. Tubb] (New York: Ace Double, 1969);

Anti-Man (New York: Paperback Library, 1970);

Beastchild (New York: Lancer, 1970); revised and republished (New York: Charnel House, 1992);

Soft Come the Dragons [bound with *The Dark of the Woods,* by Koontz] (New York: Ace Double, 1970);

The Dark Symphony (New York: Lancer, 1970);

Hell's Gate (New York: Lancer, 1970);

The Pig Society, by Koontz and Gerda Koontz (Los Angeles: Aware Press, 1970);

The Underground Lifestyles Handbook, by Koontz and Gerda Koontz (Los Angeles: Aware Press, 1970);

Bounce Girl, by Koontz and Gerda Koontz (North Hollywood: Cameo [Aware Press], 1970); republished as *Aphrodisiac Girl* (New York: Oval Press, 1973);

Hung, as Leonard Chris (New York: Cameo, 1970); reprinted (New York: American Art Enterprises, 1989);

The Crimson Witch (New York: Curtis, 1971);

Demon Child, as Deanna Dwyer (New York: Lancer, 1971);

Legacy of Terror, as Deanna Dwyer (New York: Lancer, 1971);

Chase, as K. R. Dwyer (New York: Random House, 1972);

Children of the Storm, as Deanna Dwyer (New York: Lancer, 1972);

The Dark of Summer, as Deanna Dwyer (New York: Lancer, 1972);

Dean Koontz (photograph by Jim McHugh; courtesy of the author)

Dance with the Devil, as Deanna Dwyer (New York: Lancer, 1972);

A Darkness in My Soul, as Deanna Dwyer (New York: DAW, 1972);

The Flesh in the Furnace (New York: Bantam, 1972);

Starblood (New York: Lancer, 1972);

Time Thieves, as Leigh Nichols [bound with *Against Arcturus,* by Susan K. Putney] (New York: Ace Double, 1972); published separately, as Koontz (London: Dobson, 1977);

Warlock (New York: Lancer, 1972);

Writing Popular Fiction (Cincinnati: Writer's Digest Books, 1972);

Blood Risk, as Brian Coffey (Indianapolis: Bobbs-Merrill, 1973; London: Barker, 1974);

Demon Seed (New York: Bantam, 1973; London: Corgi, 1977; revised edition, New York: Berkley, 1997; London: Headline Feature, 1997);

Hanging On (New York: M. Evans, 1973);

The Haunted Earth (New York: Lancer, 1973);

Shattered, as K. R. Dwyer (New York: Random House, 1973; London: Barker, 1974); republished, as Koontz (London: W. H. Allen, 1983; New York: Berkley, 1985);

A Werewolf Among Us (New York: Ballantine, 1973);

After the Last Race (New York: Atheneum, 1974);

Strike Deep, as Anthony North (New York: Dial, 1974);

Surrounded, as Coffey (Indianapolis: Bobbs-Merrill, 1974; London: Barker, 1975);

Dragonfly, as K. R. Dwyer (New York: Random House, 1975; London: Davies, 1977);

Invasion, as Aaron Wolfe (New York: Laser, 1975); revised and republished as *Winter Moon,* as Koontz (New York: Ballantine, 1994; London: Headline Feature, 1994);

The Long Sleep, as John Hill (New York: Popular Library, 1975);

Nightmare Journey (New York: Berkley, 1975);

The Wall of Masks, as Coffey (New York: Bobbs-Merrill, 1975);

Night Chills (New York: Atheneum, 1976);

Prison of Ice, as David Axton (Philadelphia: Lippincott, 1976; London: W. H. Allen, 1976); revised and republished as *Icebound,* as Koontz (New York: Ballantine, 1995; London: Headline Feature, 1995);

The Face of Fear, as Coffey (Indianapolis: Bobbs-Merrill, 1977); republished, as K. R. Dwyer (London: Peter Davies, 1978);

The Vision (New York: Putnam, 1977);

The Key to Midnight, as Nichols (New York: Pocket Books, 1979; London: Magnum, 1980); republished, as Koontz (Arlington Heights, Ill.: Dark Harvest, 1989; revised and republished edition, New York: Berkley, 1995);

The Funhouse, as Owen West (New York: Jove, 1980; London: Sphere, 1981); republished, as Koontz (London: Headline, 1992; New York: Berkley, 1994);

The Voice of the Night, as Coffey (Garden City, N.Y.: Doubleday, 1980); republished, as Koontz (New York: Berkley, 1991);

Whispers (New York: Putnam, 1980);

The Eyes of Darkness, as Nichols (New York: Pocket Books, 1981; London: Piatkus, 1981); revised and republished, as Koontz (Arlington Heights, Ill.: Dark Harvest, 1989; revised and republished edition, New York: Berkley, 1996);

The Mask, as West (New York: Jove, 1981); republished, as Koontz (New York: Berkley, 1988; London: Headline, 1989);

How to Write Best-Selling Fiction (Cincinnati: Writer's Digest Books, 1981);

The House of Thunder, as Nichols (New York: Pocket Books, 1982; London: Piatkus, 1983); republished, as Koontz (Arlington Heights, Ill.: Dark Harvest, 1988);

Phantoms (New York: Putnam, 1983);

Darkfall (New York: Berkley, 1984); republished as *Darkness Comes* (London: W. H. Allen, 1984);

Twilight, as Nichols (New York: Pocket Books, 1984); republished as *The Servants of Twilight* (London: Piatkus, 1985); republished, as Koontz (Arlington Heights, Ill.: Dark Harvest, 1988);

The Door to December, as Richard Paige (New York: Signet/New American Library, 1985); republished, as Nichols (London: Fontana, 1987; London: Inner Circle, 1988); revised and republished, as Koontz (New York: Signet/New American Library, 1994);

Twilight Eyes (Plymouth, Mich.: Land of Enchantment, 1985; London: W. H. Allen, 1987; revised and republished edition, New York, Berkley, 1987);

Strangers (New York: Putnam, 1986; London: W. H. Allen, 1986);

Shadowfires, as Nichols (New York: Avon, 1987; London: Collins, 1987); republished, as Koontz (Arlington Heights, Ill.: Dark Harvest, 1990);

Watchers (New York: Putnam, 1987; London: Headline, 1987);

Lightning (New York: Putnam, 1988; London: Headline, 1988);

Oddkins: A Fable for All Ages (New York: Warner, 1988; London: Headline, 1988);

Midnight (New York: Putnam, 1989; London: Headline, 1989);

The Bad Place (New York: Putnam, 1990; London: Headline, 1990);

Cold Fire (New York: Putnam, 1991);

Hideaway (New York: Putnam, 1992; London: Headline, 1992);

Dragon Tears (New York: Putnam, 1993; London: Headline, 1993);

Mr. Murder (New York: Putnam, 1993; London: Headline, 1993);

Dark Rivers of the Heart (New York: Knopf, 1994; London: Headline, 1994);

Strange Highways (New York: Warner, 1995; London: Headline, 1995);

Intensity (Franklin Center, Pa.: Franklin Library, 1995; London: Headline, 1995; New York: Knopf, 1996);

Santa's Twin (New York: HarperPrism, 1996; London: HarperCollins, 1996);

Ticktock (London: Headline Feature, 1996; New York: Ballantine, 1997);

Sole Survivor (London: Headline Feature, 1997; New York: Knopf, 1997);

Fear Nothing (London: Headline Feature, 1997; New York: Bantam, 1998);

Seize the Night (London: Headline Feature, 1998; New York: Bantam, 1999);

False Memory (London: Headline Feature, 1999; New York: Bantam, 1999);

From the Corner of His Eye (New York: Bantam, 2000; London: Headline Feature, 2000);

The Book of Counted Sorrows (New York: Barnes & Noble Digital, 2001);

The Paper Doorway: Funny Verse and Nothing Worse (New York: HarperCollins, 2001);

One Door Away From Heaven (New York: Bantam, 2001; London: Headline, 2001);

By the Light of the Moon (New York: Bantam, 2002; London: Headline, 2002);

Every Day's a Holiday: Amusing Rhymes for Happy Times (New York: HarperCollins, 2003);

The Face (New York: Bantam, 2003; London: HarperCollins, 2003);

Odd Thomas (New York: Bantam, 2003);

Robot Santa: The Further Adventures of Santa's Twin (New York: HarperCollins, 2004);

The Taking (New York: Bantam, forthcoming 2004).

OTHER: "Koontzramble," "My First Short Story," and "Kittens," in *The Dean Koontz Companion,* edited by Martin H. Greenberg, Ed Gorman, and Bill Munster (New York: Berkley, 1994), pp. 149–154, 187–198;

David Robinson, *Beautiful Death: Art of the Cemetery,* foreword by Koontz (New York: Penguin Studio, 1996);

Patricia Dibsie, *Love Heels: Tales from Canine Companions for Independence,* foreword by Koontz (New York: Yorkville Press, 2003).

SELECTED PERIODICAL PUBLICATIONS–
UNCOLLECTED: "A Genre in Crisis," *Proteus: A Journal of Ideas,* 6 (Spring 1989): 1;

"Why We Love Horror," *TV Guide,* 41 (23 October 1993): 22–24+;

"Koontz on Koontz," *Mystery Scene,* 59 (1997): 30–33.

Dean Koontz is one of the best-known names in popular fiction. He is a prolific writer with more than seventy novels to his name in addition to nonfiction books, articles, and short stories. While he considers himself mainly a suspense author, his novels are usually cross-genre, blending elements of suspense, horror, supernatural, and romance literature. Though finding a publisher for this type of fiction was difficult when Koontz began his career, he now often hears editors ask other authors to include elements of more than one genre in their novels. Throughout his career Koontz has built a large and supportive fan base while still garnering surprisingly little critical attention except for the many book reviews published as each of his novels hits bookstore shelves.

Dean Ray Koontz was born on 9 July 1945 in Everett, Pennsylvania, to Florence and Ray Koontz. Though poor, his parents were overjoyed at the long-anticipated birth of their only child. Soon they moved to a three-bedroom apartment in nearby Bedford, Pennsylvania, where they lived until Dean was five. At his father's insistence, he became the mascot for the Blue Devils, Bedford's football team, when he was three. Florence Koontz, usually called Molly, was a sickly woman, and Ray Koontz was often abusive; so it is not surprising that Dean relished the escape he found through books. When Dean was four, his mother was hospitalized for ten weeks, during which time he went to live with Bird and Louise Kinzey, his mother's friends. According to Katherine Ramsland's *Dean Koontz: A Writer's Biography* (1997), Koontz credits his stay with the Kinzeys for instilling in him a love of books and remembers the time spent with them as one of the happiest periods of his young life.

In 1950, when Dean was five years old, his parents could no longer afford to pay the rent on their Bedford apartment and moved into a house built by Dean's maternal grandfather, John Logue, as a summer home. The house was smaller than the apartment; it had only two bedrooms and an outhouse for a bathroom, was not particularly well built, and was in the less desirable part of town. Both the house and the fairgrounds it overlooked find their places in Koontz's fiction. Biographer Ramsland explains how Koontz uses this house in the title story of *Strange Highways* (1995): "It is the childhood home of Joey Shannon, who reluctantly returns to it only after his parents have died. . . . The only fictional addition to this house is the bedroom in the basement for PJ, Joey's brother, who grew up to be a psychopathic killer." While the Koontz home is most vividly portrayed in this story, it

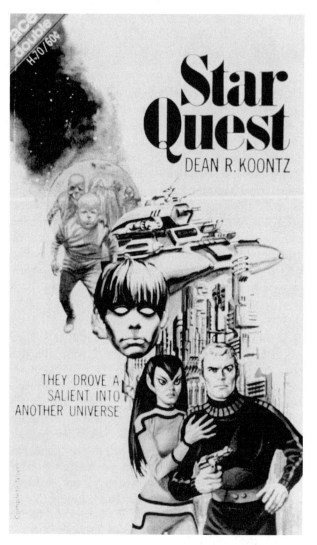

*Paperback cover for Koontz's first novel, published in 1968, about
an attempt to end a thousand-year interplanetary war
(Collection of Bryan Moose)*

is neither the first nor the last time the house finds its way
into Koontz's fiction.

At best, Koontz's relationship with his father can be
described as troubled. In a 1994 interview with Ed Gorman, Koontz says, "My father never met a vice he didn't
like, and sometimes it almost seemed that he took pride in
the fact that he succumbed to every temptation." During
Koontz's young life he was plagued by his father's pen-
chants for violent drunken rages and womanizing, a pattern of behavior that only worsened with age and was
finally diagnosed as borderline schizophrenia, now more
commonly called schizotypal personality disorder. According to Ramsland, Koontz's villains often mirror Ray
Koontz, exhibiting patterns commonly associated with
schizotypal personality disorder.

With Koontz's troubled home life, he sought an
escape in books, comic books, and movies. At the age of

eight he began selling homemade books, which he wrote,
illustrated, and fashioned himself. According to Ramsland,
"Bored with the simplistic books that taught him to 'look
and see,' he filled tablets of paper with exotic tales influenced by watching television and reading comics. He
remembers that they had robots and monsters in them like
the stories that young Joey writes in *The Funhouse* [1980]."
However, in "My First Short Story" (1994), Koontz deval-
ues these first attempts at writing "because the nickels
were gifts given out of affection or pity, not because anyone actually saw value in what I had written." At twelve,
Koontz entered a contest sponsored by a local newspaper
in which he won $25.00 and a watch for his essay and
thus began his writing career.

Although he loved reading, grades were unimportant to Koontz, as indicated by his mediocre performance
throughout high school. Bored with the traditional classroom setting, Koontz fervently absorbed everything that
interested him through the public library. Socially, Koontz
and his best friend, Larry Johnson, were accepted as the
class clowns, but Koontz floundered in his romantic pursuits because of low self-esteem. During his senior year,
however, he met Gerda Ann Cerra, then a junior. When
Koontz graduated from high school in 1963 and left Bedford to attend Shippensburg State College (later Shippensburg University) about an hour away, Cerra feared their
newfound romance might falter, but Koontz proposed
during his freshman year of college. They were married
on 15 October 1966, shortly before Koontz graduated
from Shippensburg with a major in English and a minor in
communications.

Koontz's junior and senior years in college were
eventful not only because of his marriage but also
because, unbeknownst to him, one of his English professors, Mabel Lidner, submitted his short story "The Kittens" (later just "Kittens") to a national writing
competition sponsored by *The Atlantic Monthly*. When
Koontz won one of the five prizes for fiction, his professors were impressed; no one from his college had ever
received any recognition from the contest. "The Kittens"
was accepted for publication in the May 1966 issue of
Readers and Writers, and Koontz received $50.00 for his
submission–his first professional monetary gains as a
writer. In "My First Short Story," which was published
along with "Kittens" in *The Dean Koontz Companion* in
1994, Koontz remarks, "In defense of the story, I can say
it exhibits the macabre sensibility and love of unexpected
but well-seeded narrative turns that are among the qualities that mark my fiction all these years later."

After college, Koontz took a teaching position with
the Appalachian Poverty Program with the intention of
aiding economically less fortunate but intelligent children
to realize their educational goals. However, he quickly
became disenchanted with the program as he learned that

its actual practice fell drastically short of its stated goals and that his predecessor had been hospitalized after being beaten by his students. The children Koontz was attempting to educate were not the purported smartest in their disadvantaged school systems but rather those with the worst discipline problems. Koontz stayed with the program for the remainder of the academic year, but when the new school year began in 1967, he took a position teaching English at another high school in Mechanicsburg, Pennsylvania. Throughout Koontz's teaching career, he spent almost all of his spare time writing.

Koontz's efforts were rewarded with several short-story publications in 1967, and his first novel, *Star Quest,* was published by Ace in 1968. *Star Quest* was part of an Ace Double (two paperbacks published together in the same binding) and paid only $1,000 despite Ace's promise to pay $1,250 for the completed novel. Like most of Koontz's early works, this novel escaped critical attention upon publication; but in explaining its significance, Ramsland writes, "*Star Quest* takes up a theme that would reverberate throughout many of Dean's later novels. Living in a culture of hypocritical political duplicity, wherein covert and morally hypocritical actions of the government were being exposed and denounced, Dean used the story to indicate how one end of the political spectrum had mirrored the other" in their manipulation of the masses. Members of the high-school administration perceived the novel as controversial, as Ramsland reports: "the principal said that the part where a childlike character sucks on the breast of a woman—not in a sexual sense, but for comfort—was obscene." Their protests about it and about other things, such as their belief that Koontz did not spend enough time on the classics, made Koontz's job as a high-school English teacher all but unbearable.

Though Koontz continued to teach and diligently wrote on nights and weekends, he knew he could not be truly successful as an author until he devoted himself to writing on a full-time basis. In January of 1969, Gerda Koontz offered to support her husband for five years while he tried to make something of his writing career. Koontz published two novels that year, *The Fall of the Dream Machine* and *Fear That Man;* both presented a dark picture of God, a result of the anger Koontz felt as a result of his mother's death that February. *The Fall of the Dream Machine,* another half of an Ace Double, plays upon the fears of the electronic age. According to Ramsland, "It is about a village society in which people are so subliminally connected that they lose their individuality and meld together into a single consciousness. The implication is that they return to their origins, God." The novel is the logical extreme of Marshall McLuhan's notion of a "global village" and reflects Koontz's fear of this concept and the social sterility inherently possible in it. Koontz's third novel, *Fear That Man,* combined two earlier short stories,

"In the Shield" and "Where the Beast Runs." Ramsland argues that this novel shows not only anger against God but also "a desire to replace the chaotic, destructive deity with a moral rational humankind." Several more short stories were published that year, but by the end of the year, rejection slips were more abundant than acceptances. Koontz knew he could no longer market his own novels, so in early 1970 he hired the Scott Meredith Agency to represent him.

Koontz's fourth novel was published by Paperback Library in 1970 and was originally titled "The Mystery of His Flesh" after an earlier short story on which the novel is based. However, as Koontz told Gorman, the editor thought that title made the novel sound homosexual and so renamed it *Anti-Man.* Though Koontz did not approve of the new title, he had no title control and so submitted to the editor's wishes. Ramsland argues that *Anti-Man* continues the theme found in *Fear That Man* "that God might be psychotic and therefore dangerous."

Though Koontz published several novels during 1970, his most important contribution that year was *Beastchild.* The novel was a finalist for the prestigious Hugo Award for best novella of the year. According to Ramsland, it was "a social commentary on the evils of capitalism, such as greed and the soulless pursuit of one's own advantage." *Beastchild* is one of Koontz's best works from his early career and was revised as a limited-edition hardcover in 1992. *The Dark of the Woods, Soft Come the Dragons, Hell's Gate, Bounce Girl,* and *Hung* were also published in 1970. The first three are similar in style to his previous works, while *Bounce Girl* (later titled *Aphrodisiac Girl*) and *Hung* are both erotic novels and are out of print at the author's request.

After Koontz's brief stint as an erotic novelist, he returned to his science-fiction roots with *The Crimson Witch* in 1971. Like much of Koontz's early fiction, this novel, too, is out of print. The work itself is an interplanetary drama and a study in Freudian psychology. While Koontz often uses psychological approaches in his novels, *The Crimson Witch* is the only space opera he has written. Ramsland evaluates the novel thus: "The action speeds along with only superficial character development. The plot is a straight quest fantasy based on a power struggle and resulting in the triumph of the hero and his lover."

After the publication of *The Crimson Witch,* Koontz was faced with a difficult decision. He was not making enough money from his writing to pay the bills. When his new agent, Henry Morrison, suggested he write Gothic romance novels because they were quick, fairly easy to write, and were in high demand at the time, Koontz originally refused because he did not want to write formulaic novels and was unsure about writing from a feminine perspective. However, as the year progressed, he felt he could make one of two choices: either write Gothic romances

*Poster for the 1977 movie version of Koontz's 1973 novel in which a supercomputer wants
to impregnate a scientist's wife (Collection of Paul Talbot)*

and treat them as practice, or get a part-time job so he and his wife would be able to support themselves. In researching Gothic novels, Koontz found that most were written by men using female pseudonyms. His first Gothic romance, *Demon Child,* was published using the pseudonym Deanna Dwyer in 1971. During 1971 and 1972, Koontz wrote *Legacy of Terror, Children of the Storm, The Dark of Summer, Dance with the Devil,* and *A Darkness in My Soul,* all Gothic romances using the same pseudonym.

While writing these novels, Koontz also wrote and published *Chase* (1972) under the name K. R. Dwyer. In the *Dean Koontz Companion* interview, Gorman comments that *Chase* "is perhaps the most pessimistic" of Koontz's early novels: "Despite a reasonably happy ending, the reader is left with the sense that Benjamin Chase will probably never banish his personal demons." Koontz replies that Benjamin Chase reflects how he was feeling during that time period.

Koontz began using pseudonyms more frequently in 1971 because his reading and writing interests varied so greatly. By the time *A Darkness in My Soul* (Koontz's last Deanna Dwyer novel) appeared, Koontz had already published ten science-fiction novels under his own name. Editors and publishers of the time expected the same kind of writing from him, and since his interests varied outside these expectations, he was forced to use different names for different genres. Dean Koontz wrote science fiction; Deanna Dwyer wrote Gothic romances; K. R. Dwyer was a realist; John Hill used more philosophy in his fiction; Leigh Nichols wrote large suspense novels with intermingled love stories; Brian Coffey wrote short suspense novels; Anthony North wrote one novel, a military thriller titled *Strike Deep* (1974); Richard Paige wrote in a similar style to Leigh Nichols but under a different publisher; Owen West wrote horror novels; and Aaron Wolfe wrote one novel, *Invasion* (1975; republished as *Winter Moon,* 1994) about an extraterrestrial attack in Maine.

Throughout the early 1970s, Koontz continued his rigid writing schedule, and by late 1974–the end of the five-year period his wife had given him to explore his writing–Koontz was successful enough that he and Gerda Koontz were able to move into a more luxurious apartment, and she was able to quit her outside job. From that moment on, Gerda Koontz submitted Koontz's manuscripts to overseas markets, handled most of his correspondence, proofread, and did research for his upcoming projects.

Though Koontz continued to use pseudonyms throughout the 1970s and into the late 1980s, by the mid 1970s he also began using his own name for what he deemed "cross-genre" pieces. The first of these was *Night Chills,* published in 1976 by Atheneum. According to Koontz's interview with Gorman, this new type of fiction was not well received by editors and publishers because it

confused readers, and there was no single place for such volumes in bookstores. Publishing houses were convinced that non-genre-specific fiction could not last.

After *Night Chills,* Koontz decided to adopt new representation because he felt Morrison's ambitions for his career did not match his own. He chose Claire Smith of the Harold Ober Agency after investigating several other agents. On a more personal level, Koontz and his wife also decided to leave Pennsylvania in search of a sunnier location in 1975. The couple decided on Las Vegas, Nevada, but had horrible luck finding a suitable living space. The first house they tried to rent reeked of animal waste because of the previous owners' pets. The inhabitants of the second pretended to own the house when they placed it on the market, but they were delinquent renters who were to be evicted the same day Koontz was to take possession of the house. The third seemed habitable except that it was haunted. The Koontzes lived in the third house for about a year before they decided to buy their own, but before they could move into their new purchase, Koontz witnessed a crime and feared for his and his wife's safety because of it. So they continued their pilgrimage west to southern California, where they now live.

During that same year, 1976, Koontz published *Prison of Ice* under the name David Axton. The original novel was only about 50,000 words and was revised and republished under Koontz's own name as *Icebound* in 1995. The story line is essentially the same for both novels, but *Icebound* is much more developed at 135,000 words. According to *The Dean Koontz Companion, Prison of Ice* "seems something of a tribute to the early adventure novels of Alistair MacLean." Early critics heralded it as one of the most suspenseful novels of the time.

The Face of Fear was published in 1977 as by Coffey. Graham Harris, a psychic who is helping the police find a serial rapist and murderer, is trapped by the killer at the top of an empty office building, along with his girlfriend. According to the editors of *The Dean Koontz Companion,* "It is a tight, fast-paced suspense novel, significant because it is an early indication of the unique imaginative story lines that were to be a feature of the author's later work and because it was a precursor of the many serial-killer novels that were to become increasingly popular through the eighties and nineties." Like most of Koontz's suspense novels, *The Face of Fear* was touted in original book reviews as one of the best suspense novels of the year.

The Vision, published by Putnam in 1977, was originally promised to Random House. However, Random House did not like the new novel as written and wanted Koontz to rewrite it. Because he thought the novel could sell as it was, Koontz opted to pay back the advance he had received from Random House and gave the work to Putnam instead. The novel began as a horror novel but ended up as Koontz's second cross-genre novel, combin-

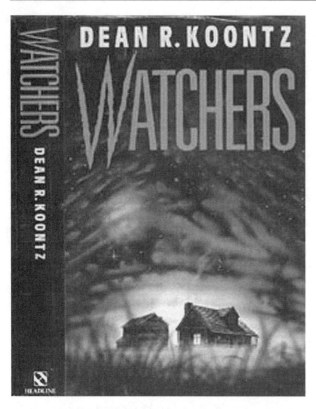

*Dust jacket for the first British edition of Koontz's 1987 novel about
a genetically manipulated dog with human intelligence and
an evil creature created by the same laboratory
(SA Book Connection, Johannesburg)*

ing the classic suspense novel with the plain language normally associated with detective fiction.

In 1977 the movie version of Koontz's 1973 novel *Demon Seed* (screenplay by Robert Jaffe and Roger O. Hirson), starring Julie Christie, opened in movie theaters across the United States. It was the first of Koontz's novels to be turned into a motion picture. However, despite Koontz's apparent success with a motion-picture release and two novels, 1977 was not a good year for him personally. Ray Koontz could no longer take care of himself, so Koontz and his wife sent him money and an airplane ticket and found an apartment for him close to them in Irvine, California. Though Gerda Koontz became her father-in-law's primary caregiver so Koontz could continue writing, Ray Koontz's intrusive phone calls during the middle of the night affected both of them. By 1979, Ray Koontz was diagnosed as having borderline schizophrenia with violent tendencies. At that time, Koontz was also told that his father could possibly be a sociopath in addition to his other psychological problems. Though it was difficult for Koontz to hear this diagnosis, he was not surprised and was somewhat relieved to be able to put a name to what he had always understood as his father's abnormal behavior.

In 1979 Koontz adopted another pseudonym, Leigh (originally Lee so as to be genderless) Nichols, for a new paperback, *The Key to Midnight*. In June of 1979 the novel became a paperback best-seller, a first for Koontz under any name. The novel, primarily set in Kyoto, Japan, is an action-filled suspense story involving international intrigue and some romance. The pace that eventually became a trademark in Koontz's fiction began to take form in *The Key to Midnight,* as did his detailed characters and twisted plots.

Koontz published *The Funhouse* under the name Owen West in 1980. It was his second paperback best-seller. The novel relied heavily on Koontz's childhood memories of the fairgrounds in Bedford, Pennsylvania, and his subsequent fascination with carnivals and carnies. When Ellen Straker gives birth to a hideous child, whom she destroys, her husband, Conrad, leaves her and vows to destroy any of her future children. Conrad spawns another deformed child, Gunther, while Ellen has two children, Joey and Amy, and undergoes a religious conversion. Despite Ellen's best attempts at separating her children and Conrad, the three converge at a carnival as adults, and Conrad plots to kill Amy and Joey by releasing his own son upon them. *The Funhouse* was originally a screenplay written by Lawrence Block on which Koontz was supposed to base the novel. Book and movie were to be released at the same time, but when the novel was released three months earlier, it became an almost immediate best-seller. However, the movie received such poor reviews that Koontz's sales dropped dramatically upon the release of the movie.

Whispers, published in 1980, is the dividing line between Koontz's early and later careers. Like *The Key to Midnight, Whispers* relies heavily upon psychology in creating well-defined characters. Screenwriter Hilary Thomas killed a man who had attacked her because he believed she was a reincarnation of his mother. When the attacker inexplicably returns, police officer Tony Clemenza helps Hilary uncover what really happened. Because it was the first novel published under Koontz's own name to reach best-seller status and was a prime example of Koontz's cross-genre style, it somewhat eased the criticism Koontz so often received from editors about writing this type of fiction. In Gorman's interview Koontz describes the central point of the novel as an exploration of "all of the ways that our lives are influenced by events of which we are often unaware or which we only dimly perceive." Though Ramsland praises the novel overall, she still finds some fault: "One flaw in this novel is the degree of explanation indulged in by characters who otherwise give no clue that they can be as sophisticated about complex psychological conditions as Hilary and Tony seem to be." Neither of these characters seems to gain any in-depth psychological understanding from their pasts, but together they analyze the antagonist's motives in order to solve the mystery that the entire novel revolves around.

Despite the commercial success of *The Key to Midnight,* the next novel published as Nichols, *The Eyes of Darkness* (1981), was not as successful because of printing delays at Pocket Books. Subsequently, the remaining Nichols books—*The House of Thunder* (1982), *Twilight* (1984), and *Shadowfires* (1987)—were also not as successful. Ramsland describes *The Eyes of Darkness* as "a dramatic tale of the unprotected child, violated not by parents but by the government as a parental symbol." When Koontz rereleased *The House of Thunder* under his own name in 1988, it reached number one on the best-seller lists. Like *The Eyes of Darkness,* it is a novel overrun with government conspiracies. *Twilight* brought Koontz his first $100,000 advance. *Shadowfires* did not do well commercially until it was republished under Koontz's own name in 1990. At that time, it was rated number one on the best-seller list after only one week and remained on the list for eight weeks. Though critics found the book compelling, they also took issue with the amount of violence in the novel.

The Mask, published by Jove in 1981, was Koontz's last novel written as Owen West. Though the novel was on the best-seller list for eight continuous weeks, it was not as commercially successful as Koontz expected, given the initial success of *The Funhouse,* West's previous novel. *The Mask* is primarily a horror novel: protagonist Laura dies in a fire in 1865 after being trapped in a cellar. Laura blames her mother for her death because her mother gave her the chore of cleaning the cellar. Laura is subsequently reincarnated several times, with the goal of killing her mother's reincarnation before Laura's sixteenth birthday. After publishing this novel, Koontz became disenchanted with Freudian psychology. He began rereading Charles Dickens's novels and subsequently started to reconsider his characters' motivations. Whereas Freudian psychology dictates that a character's motivation can be explained by experiences in the character's past, thus removing any accountability for one's own actions, Dickens's characters do not act because of something their parents did or did not do or because of some childhood drama. They are simply what they are.

Phantoms is the only novel Koontz published in 1983. While critics deemed the novel a classic horror story, the perceived supernatural elements of the novel were closer to classic science fiction, according to Ramsland. Phyllis Grann, longtime publisher at Putnam, felt the novel did not live up to Koontz's trademark cross-genre style and so published only about five thousand copies during the first printing. *Phantoms* was originally intended to be a monster tale; the monster turned into a thing with a logical explanation for its existence, one that could eventually be destroyed by human technology, which made the novel more like classic science fiction.

The publication of *Phantoms* as a genre piece inspired Koontz to stop using the pseudonym Owen West and publish novels with horror elements under his own name instead. *Darkfall* (1984), originally titled "The Pit," was the first novel initially intended for Owen West but published under Koontz's own name. The novel is written as a police procedural with strong horror elements and a love story that forms between Jack Dawson and Rebecca Chandler as they attempt to solve several murders in Manhattan. *Darkfall* posits a dichotomy of evil in which the more malignant type can only be overcome by people caring for one another. Doubleday Book Club featured the novel as an alternate selection, and it reached number ten on the paperback best-seller list.

In 1985 Koontz launched a new pseudonym, Richard Paige, for the publication of *The Door to December.* The editors of *The Dean Koontz Companion* place the novel high in their evaluation of Koontz's body of fiction: "Its exploration of the corrupting influence of power and the totalitarian urge is as dark as anything the author has written, but this is nicely offset by the character of Dan Haldane, whose dialogue is frequently as witty as it is acerbic." When Dylan McCaffrey kidnaps his young daughter, Melanie, to perform psychological experiments on her and then is murdered, Laura, Melanie's mother, and Dan Haldane, a police officer, are dragged into the middle of a murder investigation and become targets of a stalker themselves. The novel was republished twice: in 1988, Inner Circle of London published it under the Nichols name for British audiences, and in 1994 it was revised and republished by New American Library under Koontz's real name.

Twilight Eyes, Koontz's second novel published in 1985, continued to explore Koontz's fascination with carnivals and carnies. Koontz wrote *Twilight Eyes* to give himself an outlet for the vast amount of knowledge he amassed on the subject. For him, *Twilight Eyes* was an undertaking of pure amusement, and he decided to publish it as a limited edition through a small press called Land of Enchantment.

Koontz's next mass-market undertaking was *Strangers* (1986). The novel was a departure from Koontz's normal fiction and therefore surprised many of the critics who thought they could predict his work. Putnam paid Koontz $275,000 for *Strangers,* and the novel was chosen as a main selection for both the Literary Guild and Doubleday Book Club. Less than a month after its first printing, the novel was on *The New York Times* and *Publishers Weekly* best-seller lists. It was Koontz's first hardcover to be on any best-seller list. The novel features an enormous cast of characters and covers several diverse issues, but its major theme is friendship. One reviewer for the *Wichita Falls Times* (4 April 1986) praised the novel: "Dean Koontz is a master storyteller. He has absolutely amazing knowledge of his

Dust jacket for Koontz's 1993 novel about a writer pursued by his doppelgänger (Richland County Public Library)

as a patient, Koontz put his father in the psychiatric unit of the county hospital while he searched for a more suitable place. Within a week, Ray Koontz convinced a county agent that he was able to care for himself and should be released. An uncertain court battle ensued in which Ray Koontz was eventually remanded back into the psychiatric hospital. Koontz placed him in Buena Vista Care Home on 7 October 1988.

During this ordeal with his father, Koontz continued to work as he had for the past eleven years. After the success of *Strangers,* a new group called the Horror Writers of America was forming and convinced Koontz to become their first president. Though Koontz definitely did not want to be marked as a horror writer, he took the position thinking he would not be pigeonholed as a horror writer for the rest of his career. To his consternation, he was mistaken, and he continues to struggle with the label. Koontz later regarded this move as one of the biggest mistakes of his career. The organization did not represent the solidarity of like-minded individuals as Koontz had originally hoped but was instead fraught with derision and politics.

Watchers (1987) is one of Koontz's favorite novels of those he has written. It is the story of Einstein, a genetically engineered dog who possesses human-equivalent intelligence and has escaped from a research laboratory. But another creature, one far more malevolent, has also escaped from the lab, and Einstein's human protectors Travis and Nora must help him defeat it and elude the human agents who seek to recapture him. According to *The Dean Koontz Companion,* the novel is an integral one in Koontz's career because

> it embodies all of the major themes with which he is obsessed: the healing power of love and friendship; the struggle to overcome the past and change what we are; the moral superiority of the individual over the workings of the state and large institutions; the wonder of both the natural world and the potential of the human mind; the relationship of mankind to God; transcendence; and how we sustain hope in the face of our awareness that all things die.

Since the publication of *Watchers,* critics and avid Koontz fans have been asking for a sequel. While Koontz has toyed with the idea, he has no definite plans for a sequel because he has yet to find an idea for it that would be equal to its predecessor.

In 1988 Koontz republished *The Mask* and wrote a children's book, *Oddkins: A Fable for All Ages,* but published only one new novel, *Lightning.* Koontz felt the novel was a stretch of his creative ability, but Grann disliked the book because it did not have the usual frantic pace that marks so much of Koontz's fiction. However, when the book was released, bookstores could barely keep their shelves stocked, and it quickly reached the best-seller lists. *Light-*

subject matter, whether it be religion, military weapons, medicine, or an understanding of human nature. *Strangers* is absolutely enthralling." *Strangers* received similar reviews throughout the country, and, more important to Koontz, it proved to those who doubted he could ever be successful as a hardcover novelist that he could indeed.

In 1987 Koontz's father was diagnosed with degenerative alcohol syndrome and hospitalized for ten days after he tried to stab Koontz with a fishing knife. Koontz and his wife decided his father should no longer live by himself and so placed him in the Casa Orange Retirement Home. The staff had difficulty controlling Ray Koontz's violent behavior and called Koontz after his father punched another resident on 22 September 1988. When Koontz arrived, his father tried to stab him a second time with a knife bought during an outing and sharpened for the purpose. The police arrived soon after Koontz wrestled the knife from his father. They mistook Koontz for the culprit and almost shot him before he convinced them that his father was the dangerous one. Since Casa Orange would no longer accept Ray Koontz

ning has a strong, credible female protagonist, a convoluted plot, and a twist to which readers and reviewers responded well.

In 1989 the stress in Koontz's life caught up to him, and he was taken ill as he prepared to promote his newest book, *Midnight,* in England. His doctor, Steven Ducker, ordered him to see his father for only fifteen minutes every six weeks instead of the two ninety-minute visits per week Koontz was used to making. Under Ducker's care, Koontz made a full recovery, and Ducker became his personal physician. *Midnight,* like Koontz's other novels, met with success as a mainstream cross-genre novel. It was his first number-one best-seller on *The New York Times* best-seller list. Also in 1989, Shippensburg University awarded Koontz an honorary doctorate of letters.

Koontz followed this accomplishment with the publication of *The Bad Place* in 1990. The novel features Thomas, a boy with Down's syndrome; Thomas's sister, Julie, and her husband, Bob, are detectives hired by a man who keeps waking up with amnesia and possessing strange items he cannot explain. *The Bad Place* was received well critically and quickly soared to the top of *The New York Times* best-seller list. *The Los Angeles Book Review* called the novel "as close to physical terror as the printed word can deliver."

Cold Fire, based on Jungian synchronicity, was published in 1991. Social commentary is essential to the novel; reporter Holly Thorne tries to find meaning in her life as she investigates Jim Ironheart, a man inexplicably drawn to rescue people in danger. Like *The Bad Place* and *Midnight, Cold Fire* was number one on *The New York Times* best-seller list. It was also a main selection of the Literary Guild and Doubleday Book Club and remained a best-seller for three months. Early reviews called the book a classic because of the extreme range of emotions and characters. Susan Pierce of the *Arkansas Democrat* wrote, "It's in the descriptions of emotional states–from love to despair–that Koontz consistently hits bull's-eyes, evoking reactions of, 'Yes! I know exactly how that feels!'"

Koontz continued to develop his principal themes and vivid characterization with *Hideaway* in 1992 and *Dragon Tears* in 1993. Critics continued to praise him for the emotional clarity in his books and his use of intricately placed plot twists. However, Koontz's personal life was changing. Ray Koontz died of degenerative alcohol syndrome on 16 September 1991. Koontz had his father cremated the night he died and sealed the ashes in a mausoleum in Fullerton, California. Ray Koontz had few friends in life and none in California, so when Koontz prepared a memorial service, he and his wife were the only ones there. According to Ramsland, Koontz used *Hideaway* and *Dragon Tears* to explore the feelings he had about the strained relationship he and his father had always shared. By the time Koontz wrote *Dragon Tears,*

his fifth number-one best-seller in a row, he dropped the "R.," for Ray, from his name as a way to put his father behind him.

After *Hideaway* and *Dragon Tears,* Koontz changed agents and publishers because he felt Putnam was no longer following through on their promotional promises. When Koontz's longtime agent insisted on attempting to pacify him instead of taking action with the publisher, he left for Robert Gottlieb of the William Morris Agency. When Putnam said they did not have the money needed to comply with the new contract terms, Gottlieb procured a better contract with the Knopf Publishing Group.

Mr. Murder (1993) was the last book Koontz published with Putnam. It is the story of a novelist, Marty Stillwater, battling a relentless doppelgänger in an effort to save his family and his sanity; his foe, in turn, is being pursued by the agency that created him. The novel is filled with autobiographical references and displays elements of dark humor while still maintaining a highly suspenseful pace. In "The 10 Questions Readers Most Often Ask Dean Koontz," published in *The Dean Koontz Companion,* Koontz cites *Mr. Murder* as one of his favorite books out of those he has written. In the same book, the editors write, "At times this is one of the most humorous novels he has ever done–especially in the scenes with the two young girls, Charlotte and Emily [Marty's daughters], and with the two bureaucratic villains, Oslett and Clocker–but *Mr. Murder* is nevertheless fast-paced and almost unbearably suspenseful."

Ramsland describes Koontz's next book, *Dark Rivers of the Heart* (1994), as a "cathartic experience" for Koontz as, for the first time, he began directly to "dig into the psychological ramifications of being the son of a sociopath." In a 27 February 1997 interview, Koontz recalls how long it took him to write the novel: "11 months and 3 weeks. I remember the exact period of time because I slept one night out of two during the final week as I was so deeply involved." The main character, Spencer Grant, forces himself to cope with an even more traumatic childhood than Koontz's own, while he and a woman he has just met flee from killers working for a sinister security agency. Spencer fears the genetic legacy of his father, who murdered forty-two women. As Koontz acknowledges in Ramsland's biography, *Dark Rivers of the Heart* is full of water and blood images–which, to Koontz, are connected to destiny:

> First, destiny is our blood, our family. Second, destiny is in the stars, our own course set within us when we were born, because life has a spiritual purpose. Third, destiny is a result of how we choose to exercise our free will, for we can reject the power of blood (genetics) if we are strong enough to be what we want to be. All three of those are reflected in the book.

Dust jacket for Koontz's 1994 novel, about a sociopathic killer's son who is fleeing from assassins sent by a sinister security agency (Richland County Public Library)

The novel remained on best-seller lists for three months, and reviewers compared it to Stephen King's fiction and George Orwell's *Nineteen Eighty-Four* (1949) while declaring the mix of optimism and pessimism in the novel more substantial than Koontz's previous work.

Koontz's second novel for Knopf, *Intensity,* appeared first in a limited edition in 1995. Chyna Shepherd, the heroine, is a twenty-six-year-old graduate student in psychology who still carries scars from an abusive childhood. She is staying with her best friend's family when a psychopathic killer, Edgler Foreman Vess, murders everyone else in the house. Through the events of the novel, Chyna learns that she must take risks if she is to survive. She cannot continue to hide beneath the bed, both literally and figuratively, if she hopes to overcome Vess, who considers himself above the laws of good and evil and therefore bears no accountability for his actions to any higher authority. Chyna prevails in her struggle to understand the human condition and her attempt to save Ariel, Vess's next intended victim. The novel relies heavily on psychology but dismisses Koontz's earlier Freudian vision, illustrated so clearly in *Whispers.* Though some reviewers

noted the excessive, even gratuitous, violence, *Intensity* became an immediate best-seller and was celebrated by most critics.

Ticktock (1996) and *Sole Survivor* (1997) were both published in England before they debuted in the United States. As Koontz explained in a December 1998 interview with Joe Hartlaub, when his novels are set for release during the early part of the year in the United States, they are often published in England first because the Christmas season has a much larger effect on hardcover book sales in England. *Ticktock* is lighter than most of Koontz's fiction and shows some of the same spirit as *Mr. Murder.* The central character is a Vietnamese American named Tommy Phan who is a journalist and crime novelist. He desires to be an American like the ones about whom he writes, but he is pursued by a demonic doll that is sent by Tommy's mother to bring him back into the family. An adventurous chase ensues, during which Tommy meets a waitress named Deliverance Payne who proposes to him at the end of the tale. Upon publishing *Ticktock,* Koontz received many fan letters asking him to write a sequel or turn the novel into a series.

Sole Survivor was Koontz's third novel for Knopf, thus fulfilling his contract with them. When no further offer was made to extend the contract, Koontz listened to the offers Gottlieb presented him while drafting a proposal detailing a trilogy wherein each book could be read in the series or stand on its own, but the main character would repeat throughout. While debating his publishing-house future, Koontz shaved off his trademark mustache and got hair implants; the personal change inspired him to make a bigger change in his career. Though not dissatisfied with Knopf or Ballantine, Koontz sold his three-book series to Bantam Books of the Bantam Doubleday Dell Publishing Group.

Sole Survivor debuted in the United States on 6 February 1997 and quickly rose to the tops of the best-seller lists. Unlike earlier novels, Sole Survivor posits the existence of a benign deity. Ramsland explains, "For Dean, while God may have a dark side, the most profound morality nevertheless is rooted in the spiritual, so each person must come to grips with the reality of suffering without losing hope." In the novel, Joe Carpenter struggles to recover from grief at the loss of his wife and daughters in a devastating airplane crash in which most victims were so badly mangled that their bodies could not be identified. When he meets a mysterious woman who claims to have survived the crash, Joe finds his life's meaning in trying to differentiate between the official story of the crash and what really happened and in rescuing a girl he does not know but feels strangely drawn toward. Koontz expected that the novel would receive unfavorable reviews because of its ingrained spirituality, but he was pleasantly surprised when critics seemed impressed with the very thing he thought would cause a negative reaction. Although some wanted a return of the pace of Intensity and thought Koontz's descriptions were sometimes overdone, most reviewers called Sole Survivor one of Koontz's best novels.

Fear Nothing (1997) and Seize the Night (1998) are the first two installments of the trilogy Koontz sold to Bantam in 1996. The third novel, tentatively titled "Ride the Storm," has yet to be published. The protagonist of all three novels is Christopher Snow, a twenty-eight-year-old writer and surfer who suffers from xeroderma pigmentosum, a rare skin condition that means he must avoid any exposure to sunlight. Despite his condition, Christopher does not pity himself and lives a full life with his girlfriend, Sasha Goodall, who is a disc jockey at the Moonlight Bay radio station; his dog, Orson; and his best friend, Bobby Halloway. Both Fear Nothing and Seize the Night were best-sellers when they were published and well received by critics and fans alike. Jeff Zaleski of Publishers Weekly wrote, "Fear Nothing matches in depth of character and sophistication of technique anything Koontz has written, and its suspense is high-wire." Patricia Pearson of The National Post (27 March 1999) was less

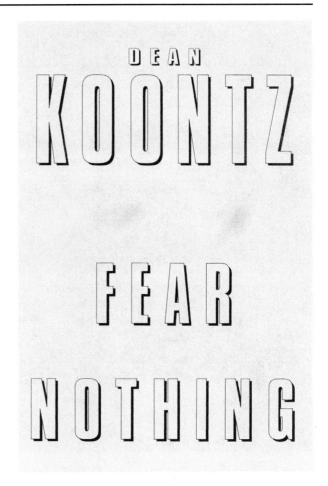

Dust jacket for the 1998 American edition of Koontz's novel (first published in Britain in 1997), the first volume of a trilogy about a writer who cannot tolerate sunlight (Richland County Public Library)

enthusiastic: "Uncharacteristically, Koontz fails to seize the pace for the first third or so of the novel, lingering way too long on descriptions of plumbing, wiring, engineering, and his narrator's childhood."

False Memory (1999) is a classic example of Koontz's cross-genre writing, complete with vivid characters and suspense. In this novel Martie Rhodes develops a rare but real psychological condition called autophobia, which literally means fear of one's self. During the course of the novel, Martie and her husband, Dusty, try to find the meaning behind her sudden fear. Although several reviewers noted that the story could have been told more economically, a critic for Library Journal praised "the vilest villain Koontz ever created" and the "compelling" story, while a writer for Kirkus Reviews observed, "Koontz deftly sidesteps clichés of expression while nonetheless applying an air pump to the suspense."

From the Corner of His Eye (2000) was an instant number-one best-seller on The New York Times best-sellers list. The

*Dust jacket for Koontz's 2003 novel in which a security guard tries to protect a movie star's
son from a kidnapper (Collection of Paul Talbot)*

novel features three separate story lines that eventually converge. Bartholomew Lampion, blinded by age three, has beautiful eyes. While he cannot see, he has been given the gift of second sight. Junior Cain, the villain, is convinced that someone named Bartholomew will destroy him. And Angel White, a child born of rape, is linked to them both. Chris Nelson of *The Calgary Sun* (4 February 2001) called the novel "a marked improvement from recent novels" but disliked the conclusion: "it ends far too quickly and the book falls away into a type of mysticism." Jeff Ayers noted in *Library Journal:* "Though over 600 pages, the book never seems long. The characters are vivid and emotionally exciting, creating a fast and compelling read."

Koontz frequently uses epigraphs to set the tone for his novels, and in doing so with early novels, he sometimes had difficulty finding exactly the right passage to express himself. When that happened, he created something to fit and attributed the passage to a fictitious work titled *The Book of Counted Sorrows*. Koontz received many letters from fans who had started searching for this book and wanted to know where they could get a copy. Since so many people were interested in *The Book of Counted Sorrows,*

Koontz promised he would publish it. After many false starts, the work was finally published as an electronic book by Barnes and Noble Digital in 2001. According to Michael Fragnito at Barnes and Noble Digital, *The Book of Counted Sorrows* was the first eBook to get promoted in retail stores.

In his next novel, *One Door Away From Heaven* (2001), Michelina "Micky" Bellsong moves in with her Aunt Geneva in a dusty California trailer park. When nine-year-old Leilani Klonk and her family move into the trailer next door, Michelina and Leilani forge a friendship that will lead them on an incredible, life-changing quest. A reviewer for *Publishers Weekly* noted that "Koontz's once form-fitting style has gotten baggy of late" but that nevertheless, "the novel is surprisingly focused on its inspirational message—'we are the instruments of one another's salvation and only by the hope that we give to others do we lift ourselves out of the darkness into light'—and conveys it with such conviction that only the most critical will demur."

An endangered child is also the focus of *The Face* (2003). Ten-year-old Aelfric "Fric" Manheim, the son of a movie star renowned for his looks, is the target of a kid-

4

1

My name is Odd Thomas, though in this age when fame is the altar at which most people worship, I am not sure why you should care who I am or that I exist.

I am not a celebrity. I am not the child of a celebrity. I have never been married to, never been abused by, and never provided a kidney for transplantation into any celebrity. Furthermore, I have no desire to be a celebrity.

In fact I am such a nonentity by the standards of our culture that *People* magazine not only will never feature a piece about me but might also reject my attempts to subscribe to their publication on the grounds that the black-hole gravity of my noncelebrity is powerful enough to suck their entire enterprise into oblivion.

I am twenty years old. To a world-wise adult, I am little more than a child. To any child, however, I'm old enough to be distrusted, to be excluded forever from the magical community of the short and beardless.

Consequently, a demographics expert might conclude that my sole audience is other young men and women currently adrift between their twentieth and twenty-first birthdays.

In truth, I have nothing to say to that narrow audience. In my experience, I don't care about most of the things that other twenty-year-old Americans care about. Except survival, of course.

I lead an unusual life.

Typescript page for Koontz's 2003 novel Odd Thomas, *about a young man who communicates with the dead. Koontz does all revising on the computer and does not save early drafts (courtesy of the author).*

napping plot by anarchist Corky Laputa. Fric is protected by security chief Ethan Truman as well as a mysterious guardian angel who sends the boy warnings. A reviewer for *Publishers Weekly,* while once again observing that Koontz can sometimes be guilty of overwriting, had praise for his use of language and offered "great kudos to Koontz for creating, within the strictures of popular fiction, another notable novel of ideas and of moral imperatives."

Publishers Weekly also had high praise for Koontz's next novel, *Odd Thomas* (2003). The title character is a twenty-year-old fry cook with whom the dead can communicate. When they begin sending him warnings about a stranger in town–one who idolizes serial killers–Odd Thomas must find a way to avert the impending disaster. The reviewer for *Publishers Weekly* noted not only the "electrifying tension and suspense" but also the fact that "the author has recently added humor to his arsenal of effects, and this thriller also stands out for its brilliant tightrope walk between the amusing and the macabre."

With a career that has spanned more than thirty years, Dean Koontz has firmly established his place among noteworthy American novelists at the end of the twentieth century. The *Publishers Weekly* reviewer of Koontz's 2002 novel, *By the Light of the Moon,* observed, "Perhaps more than any other author, Koontz writes fiction perfectly suited to the mood of America post-September 11: novels that acknowledge the reality and tenacity of evil but also the power of good; that celebrate the common man and woman; that at their best entertain vastly as they uplift." In the 27 February 1997 interview Koontz noted, "Most of my life has been spent writing. And I can't think of anything more interesting to do with my time."

Interviews:

Lisa See, "PW Interviews: D. Koontz," *Publishers Weekly,* 232 (18 December 1987): 44–45;

Ed Gorman, "Interview with Dean Koontz," in *The Dean Koontz Companion,* edited by Martin H. Greenberg, Gorman, and Bill Munster (New York: Berkley, 1994), pp. 1–56;

"The 10 Questions Readers Most Often Ask Dean Koontz," in *The Dean Koontz Companion,* edited by Greenberg, Gorman, and Munster (New York: Berkley, 1994), pp. 275–282;

Marlene Taylor and Sean Doorly, "Author Profile: Dean Koontz," *Bookreporter.com* (27 February 1997) <http://www.bookreporter.com/authors/au-koontz-dean.asp>;

Joe Hartlaub, "Author Profile: Dean Koontz," *Bookreporter.com* (December 1998) <http://www.bookreporter.com/authors/au-koontz-dean.asp>;

Hartlaub, "Author Profile: Dean Koontz," *Bookreporter.com* (14 January 2000) <http://www.bookreporter.com/authors/au-koontz-dean.asp>.

Biography:

Katherine Ramsland, *Dean Koontz: A Writer's Biography* (New York: HarperPrism, 1997).

References:

Paul Alexander, "Dean Koontz," *Rolling Stone,* 789 (25 June 1998): 46–47+;

Andrea Chambers, "Best-selling Novelist Dean Koontz May Be a Titan of Terror But He's a Timid Type at Heart," *People Weekly,* 27 (13 April 1987): 77–78;

Michael Collings, "Dean Koontz," *Mystery Scene,* 45 (January–February 1994): 46–50;

Matthew J. Costello, "Films, Television, and Dean Koontz," in *The Dean Koontz Companion,* edited by Martin H. Greenberg, Ed Gorman, and Bill Munster (New York: Berkley, 1994), pp. 101–107;

"Dean Koontz Traveling Many Roads to the Top of the Charts," *Publishers Weekly,* 245 (14 December 1998): S1–S18;

Nick Gillespie and Lisa Snell, "Contemplating Evil: D. Koontz," *Reason,* 28 (November 1996): 44–49;

Elizabeth Gleick, "Family Secrets: D. Koontz," *People Weekly,* 42 (28 November 1994): 141–142;

Joan G. Kotker, *Dean Koontz: A Critical Companion* (Westport, Conn.: Greenwood Press, 1996);

Bill Munster, *Sudden Fear: The Horror and Dark Suspense Fiction of Dean R. Koontz,* Starmont Studies in Literary Criticism, no. 24 (Mercer Island, Wash.: Starmont House, 1988);

David B. Silva, "Keeping Pace with the Master," in *The Dean Koontz Companion,* edited by Greenberg, Gorman, and Munster (New York: Berkley, 1994), pp. 57–73;

Karen Springen, "The Cheery Titan of Terror: D. Koontz," *Newsweek,* 117 (11 February 1991): 62.

Lorna Landvik

(12 December 1954 –)

Suzanne Leonard
University of Wisconsin–Milwaukee

BOOKS: *Patty Jane's House of Curl* (Bridgehampton, N.Y.: Bridge Works, 1995; London: Virago, 1997);

Your Oasis on Flame Lake (New York: Fawcett Columbine, 1997);

The Tall Pine Polka (New York: Ballantine, 1999; London: HarperCollins, 2001);

Welcome to the Great Mysterious (New York: Ballantine, 2000);

Angry Housewives Eating Bon Bons (New York: Ballantine, 2003).

RECORDINGS: *Patty Jane's House of Curl,* abridged, read by Landvik, St. Paul, Minn., HighBridge, 1996;

Your Oasis on Flame Lake, abridged, read by Landvik, St. Paul, Minn., HighBridge, 1997.

Lorna Landvik's blend of homespun humor and eccentric characterization has led critics to compare her prose with that of Midwestern notable Garrison Keillor. Like Keillor, Landvik has an affinity for describing the vagaries of life in Middle America, and she displays an obvious affection for the offbeat characters that populate her fictionalized Minnesota towns. She uses her fiction to underscore the importance of strong community bonds, and her characteristic blend of comedy and tragedy illustrates, above all, that the darker moments of life are best navigated in the presence of good friends and supportive family members. Although her characters face their share of mishaps, Landvik is frequently optimistic and relies on humor to grant her characters reprieves from their troubles. This penchant for comedy notwithstanding, Landvik has a keen sense of the heartaches, both big and small, that can afflict American lives.

Landvik was born in Grand Forks, North Dakota, on 12 December 1954 and moved to Minnesota with her family when she was three years old. Raised outside of Minneapolis, Landvik often entertained classmates with her comic abilities and was par-

Lorna Landvik (photograph by Jennifer Bong; from the dust jacket for Patty Jane's House of Curl, *1995; Richland County Public Library)*

ticularly adept at mimicking foreign accents. A fourth-generation Norwegian, she often used her heritage to poke fun at herself and later made this blend of parody and self-effacement a mainstay of her fiction. After high school, Landvik traveled through Europe with a friend, and the two worked as chambermaids and English tutors in Bavaria. When she returned from Europe, Landvik spent a year studying at the University of Minnesota, then left the state to pursue a career as an actress and comedian in California.

While living in San Francisco, Landvik performed her comedy routines in several different venues, including one club in the basement of a church. This underground locale provided the inspiration for the basement performance space in her second novel, *Your Oasis on Flame Lake* (1997). Landvik later moved to Los Angeles, where she performed comic sketches and stand-up routines at the Comedy Store and Comedy Improv. Her skits were populated with quirky oddballs such as Mrs. Olsen, the coffee lover driven insane by caffeine, and Frau Kuchenschnitter, a manic German cook, and were based on people Landvik met during her travels in Europe. Landvik won praise for her ability to transform herself into these characters while onstage, and her impersonation skills were credited to her astute powers of observation. Though these stage characterizations were sometimes too long-winded to satisfy punchline-hungry audiences, they have translated easily into fictional representations. Landvik's writing style, in fact, is often praised for its careful attention to the details of character.

In 1984 Landvik married musician and artist Chuck Gabrielson, and their first daughter was born in 1986. Shortly after the birth, the family participated for nine months in the Great Peace March for Global Disarmament, walking from California to Washington, D.C., to protest federal spending on nuclear weapons. Less than a year later, Landvik and her husband decided to move back to Minnesota. Three days before leaving California, Landvik began writing what became her first book, *Patty Jane's House of Curl* (1995). This literary effort represented the fulfillment of a lifelong ambition. As Landvik told an interviewer for Nashville Public Radio in 1999, she had planned to be a writer since she was in the sixth grade.

Patty Jane's House of Curl initiated Landvik's signature style, featuring dialogue-heavy prose that pairs humor with bittersweet revelations about the nature of love, community, friendship, and family. The novel chronicles thirty years in the lives of two sisters, Patty Jane and Harriet Dobbin, and the tale begins when Patty Jane is deserted by her Norwegian husband, Thor. Fearful at the prospect of becoming a new father, Thor goes out for a walk one night and never returns. Patty Jane's abandonment is not the first heartache the sisters have experienced: their alcoholic parents both died when the girls were teenagers, and the sisters virtually raised themselves. After Thor's departure, Patty Jane suffers an emotional breakdown and becomes a social recluse, although she does still manage to take care of her newborn daughter, Nora. Shortly after Nora's birth, Harriet's millionaire fiancé, Axel, dies in a plane crash. To combat their collective grief, Harriet, Patty Jane, and Patty Jane's mother-in-law, Ione, move

in together, and the women survive tragedy by relying on the calming effects of domestic harmony. In their household, good coffee and generous helpings of sentiment soothe many tearful moments and put the women on the path to emotional recovery.

One of the major themes of the novel is the healing power of familial bonds, which Landvik traces through her description of each character's idiosyncratic contribution to the maintenance of a collective household. Heavy on domestic detail, the novel chronicles the nuances of daily living: Harriet's daily harp recitals, Patty Jane's sharp witticisms, and Ione's frequent articulation of the all-purpose Norwegian epithet "Uff-da" are used to show how the rhythms of the everyday become a collective source of strength for the women. Patty Jane's decision to open a beauty shop, called Patty Jane's House of Curl, signifies an attempt to transplant this living arrangement into the public sphere. Providing a good haircut as easily as she offers a piece of down-home advice, Patty Jane becomes a model of female empowerment. She treats her customers like family, providing scented kerchiefs for each of them, serving homemade banana bread, and even offering regulars their own monogrammed smocks. The rest of Patty Jane's family also participates in the business— Harriet plays her harp in the shop, Ione bakes homemade cookies and gives crochet lessons, and Patty Jane's daughter, Nora, answers the phone when she is not at school. Clyde Chuka, the Indian manicurist, adds an element of cultural diversity and a masculine perspective to what is an otherwise homogenous group. His addition is structurally important, for it suggests that the beauty shop is a comfortable, welcoming space for all.

After the House of Curl becomes a commercial success, Patty Jane decides to initiate a lecture series in the shop. Featuring topics that range from "Legends of Hollywood" to "Decorating with Fabrics," the series is intended to lend a more intellectual atmosphere to her small town and also help patrons find what Patty Jane calls "a sense of self. A sense that we're not just mothers or children or wives or girlfriends." Patty Jane's design for the series is clearly well-meaning, although its execution is rendered in Landvik's characteristically humorous terms. The viewing of the first presentation, a short movie made by a local avant-garde artist, results in more than half the attendees rising up in a swarm of protest when they notice that the movie features nudity. While Landvik sketches these characters lovingly, she also pokes fun at their insularity and at Patty Jane's attempts to fashion them into more cultured individuals.

More heartbreak is on the horizon for the family, however, when Harriet follows in the footsteps of her parents, becomes an alcoholic, and deserts the family in a haze of drunken desperation. After bouts with prostitution and homelessness, Harriet meets a recovered alcoholic named Reese, discovers the virtues of Alcoholics Anonymous, and returns to her family in a tearful reunion. Meanwhile, Thor also comes home after it is revealed that he suffered extensive brain damage from an accident he had on the night he deserted Patty Jane. Although Thor is welcomed back with open arms, the family is not all under one roof for long. In the final sequence of the novel, Harriet, who has been a chain-smoker all her life, gets diagnosed with lung cancer and dies.

This stockpiling of tragedies has led some reviewers to liken *Patty Jane's House of Curl* to a soap opera and to point out that its melodramatic aspects detract from its ability to portray tragedy in a realistic way. This critique of Landvik's fiction is fairly common, which may help to explain why none of Landvik's work has drawn scholarly regard or academic attention to date. Her novels do consistently garner interest from the popular press, however, and *Patty Jane's House of Curl* has been recognized for its poignant depiction of the restorative and regenerative power of female communities. A critic for *Kirkus Reviews* (1 July 1995) wrote that although "the elaborately crafted wackiness and cloying coziness of the beauty parlor scene will annoy some, readers hungry for an easy-to-swallow tale of female, not feminist, solidarity may find this a satisfying sugary treat." The novel is similar in some respects to Robert Harling's drama *Steel Magnolias* (1987), which also featured a beauty parlor as the central meeting and healing place for an intergenerational group of women. Like the Southern belles depicted in *Steel Magnolias,* Landvik's characters are feisty and forthright, and the *Denver Rocky Mountain News* (20 April 1997) praised Landvik for creating "colorful, believable, often eccentric characters." Although the heavily plot-driven ending of the novel has come under scrutiny, Landvik's depiction of the deep and lasting bonds forged between women has been viewed favorably by critics and readers alike.

Landvik's second novel, *Your Oasis on Flame Lake,* earned a nomination for the Minnesota Book Award in 1997. In this novel Landvik uses multiple narrators, focusing on a year in the lives of two adult best friends, Devera and Bidi, and their respective families. Landvik originally wrote the tale as a short story, but an editor at *The Atlantic* told her that although the writing was good, he could not follow the story line. She reworked and expanded the text into a novel, using a narrative style that rotates among five central characters: Bidi; Devera; Bidi's husband, Sergio; Devera's husband, Dick; and Devera's twelve-year-old daughter, Darcy. Because of this revolving cast, the novel has been characterized as "an intimate conversation with several smart and inter-

esting men and women. They all seem familiar. Each possesses a keen sense of humor and some knowledge of his or her flaws," according to Carol Connolly in the 13 July 1997 *Minneapolis Star Tribune.*

The book opens as Bidi and Devera attend their twentieth high-school reunion and are both voted the "least changed." While Bidi, who is obsessed with maintaining her size-five figure, wears this distinction proudly, it precipitates a crisis of identity for Devera, who muses, "Being a wife and mother, I still believe, is the main entrée on life's plate, but I'm starting to think I missed out on some of the more exotic side dishes. Where's the hot pepper relish? The garlic pilaf? Can I get a helping of that mango aspic, please?" Devera decides that having an affair with the man who teaches her nighttime history class might spice things up, so she begins sneaking around with him instead of spending time with her husband, Dick. Meanwhile, Dick opens a weekend nightclub in the basement of the couple's suburban home, which is the realization of his lifelong dream. In the club, called Your Oasis on Flame Lake, Dick croons out parodies of show tunes and provides the neighborhood with a popular weekend watering hole.

While rendering the disjunction between Dick's outwardly directed need for public performance and Devera's secret inner life, Landvik meditates on the difficulties of sustaining a long-term marriage, especially when the participants' inclinations are at cross-purposes. Both Devera and Dick seek a change in their routine, although they look for variation in different places. The passage of time becomes a central preoccupation of the novel, for while characters like Bidi are fighting to preserve the past, or at least the figure she had in the past, Devera becomes despondent when she realizes that everything that she thought would happen in her life has already happened. As Devera states, "Dick and I knew we were getting married from the eleventh grade on." When she wants to alter her life, Devera is at a loss. She wonders: Should she become a vegetarian? Take a night class? Leave her family? Although Devera chooses to have an affair to fill this void, the experience wreaks havoc on her emotional life. She alternates between feeling exhilarated by her daring and guilty for her betrayal. Landvik deftly uses this story line to explore middle-age malaise and suggest that serious issues frequently percolate below the surface of a seemingly happy family.

Besides exploring Devera's betrayal, *Your Oasis on Flame Lake* addresses other ambitious and provocative topics surrounding the issue of personal identity. Bidi is so concerned about her weight that she becomes addicted to diet pills, and her narcissism compels her to contemplate an abortion when she becomes pregnant unexpectedly. Similarly, her image consciousness com-

Dust jacket for Landvik's first novel, about two sisters who help each other survive a series of tragedies during a period of thirty years (Richland County Public Library)

pels a complete lack of sensitivity toward the feelings of her stocky, hockey-playing daughter, Franny. In one of the more troubling story lines, Franny makes the winning goal for the men's hockey championship and then gets beaten up by the rival team's players, while her boyfriend, one of her own teammates, looks on. Franny refuses to name her attackers, but Landvik renders this reluctance not as a weakness but rather as a sign of personal integrity and suggests that Franny is one of the more self-realized characters.

Like Landvik's first novel, *Your Oasis on Flame Lake* illustrates that even when people age and grow, female friendships like the one between Bidi and Devera remain constant. However, *Your Oasis on Flame Lake* pays more attention to exploring issues of gender, the nuclear family, and the many permutations of that term than does *Patty Jane's House of Curl,* which focused more singularly on female solidarity. Unlike its predecessor, *Your Oasis on Flame Lake* sketches male characters who have a capacity for introspection and emotionality comparable to that of the women: Dick, as well as Bidi's husband, Sergio, both narrate their own sections.

In one section, Sergio describes his affection for Franny, whom he has decided to adopt. On the heels of this decision, Franny's biological father, who has been absent for most of her life, comes back into town in order to contest the adoption. Sergio's pain is skillfully depicted, as is his role in defending his family from outside intrusion. Sergio and his blended family are further tested when Bidi's baby is born prematurely and the doctors tell them that the baby may not survive. After a tense period, the family learns that the baby will live.

Common to the various story lines in *Your Oasis on Flame Lake* is the awareness of the ambiguities and ambivalences that family commitments engender. Devera ultimately decides to terminate her affair, which implies that her impulse to drastically alter her life is checked by her loyalty to the people with whom she has chosen to spend that life; yet, the decision is not made without struggle. When Dick finds out about her betrayal, the couple pledges to work together to repair their broken marriage. Throughout this narrative, Landvik suggests that fragile relationships are either shattered or maintained depending on one's ability to negotiate the commonplace disappointments and frustrations characteristic of family life.

Besides its poignant handling of family-related issues, a major appeal of *Your Oasis on Flame Lake* is its conversational tone. Although the book has been criticized for ending too neatly, Landvik is credited with having created warm and engaging characters and finding complexity in the simplest details of everyday lives. Sybil Steinberg of *Publishers Weekly* (5 May 1997) commented on Landvik's "quirky and passionate characters, and her ardent determination to give them dignity." Landvik's attempts at characterization have often been the focus of critical attention, although there is some debate over how well-developed these characters are. Nancy Pearl of the *Library Journal* (15 May 1997) wrote that the weaknesses of the book are its "rather unbelievable plot; the pedestrian writing; and the less than three-dimensional characters." Conversely, Carol Connelly of the *Minneapolis Star Tribune* (13 July 1997) commented, "a host of finely wrought characters roams here," suggesting that Landvik courts comparison with "Maeve Binchy, Jon Hassler and all the great storytellers who bring you to the heart of their home places." Despite these differing opinions, critics seem to agree that Landvik has a knack for rendering local settings and characters that are both familiar and likable.

Landvik's third novel was also well received, and it, too, was nominated for a Minnesota Book Award. Inspired by the time that Landvik spent in California, *The Tall Pine Polka* (1999) tells the story of Tall Pine, a small Minnesota tourist town that gets invaded by Hollywood movie moguls. Landvik's longest book to date, the novel centers on the customers who frequent the town coffee shop, the Cup O'Delight Café. Like the beauty shop in *Patty Jane's House of Curl,* the café serves as a welcome gathering space in which the wayward residents of Tall Pine share their troubles and joys. Owned by Lee O'Leary, a forty-year-old redhead who buys the restaurant after fleeing from her abusive husband, the café plays regular host to Lee's best friend Fenny Ness, a twenty-two-year-old whose parents died the previous year in a bizarre cycling accident. Regulars also include Pete, who expresses his unrequited love for Fenny by making her shoes; Slim, the Vietnam veteran who barks like a dog; Mary Gore, famous for her erotic poetry and 1960s hairdo; and Frau Katte and Miss Penk, the town's one lesbian couple. The characters are so integral to life at the café that they "sat at the counter on the same regular basis that students sit at their desks. When one didn't show up, telephone calls were made to the truants to assure that no one was having chest pains or lying prostrate from a stroke." As in *Patty Jane's House of Curl,* Landvik develops each of these eccentric characters through dialogue rather than description; in *The Tall Pine Polka* she relies more on characters' words than on the kind of first-person interior monologues found in *Your Oasis on Flame Lake.* This conversation-laden narrative approach produces a slightly unwieldy text, however, as Landvik tries to combine a large cast of characters with a more central story line focusing on Fenny.

Fenny's adventure begins when a talent scout looking to cast the movie *Ike and Inga,* a tale about a feisty Norwegian mail-order bride, spots her in Tall Pine. Although still devastated from the unexpected loss of her parents, Fenny reluctantly agrees to travel to Hollywood for a screen test, and there her habit of innocently saying whatever is on her mind surprises several self-important moviemakers. Fenny's lack of pretension lands her the leading role in the movie, and her forthright manner contrasts the many hypocrisies she witnesses in Hollywood. Landvik said in a 1999 interview for Nashville Public Radio, "I know what a heapin' helping of surrealism Hollywood serves up . . . I wanted to write about the many paradoxes of Hollywood that I'd seen." Despite Landvik's firsthand knowledge of the entertainment industry, her portrayal of Hollywood veterans as ruthlessly self-involved has been regarded by some critics as excessive. Karen Hanna of the *Cleveland Plain Dealer* (13 September 1999) wrote of the novel, "as it labors to mock Hollywood, it most mimics it." Such comments suggest that Landvik's attempts at parody are not always successful.

Fenny returns to Tall Pine for the filming of the movie, which also brings to town Big Bill, a half-Polynesian, half-Chippewa musician and athlete. His arrival precipitates a crisis between Fenny and Lee when they both fall in love with him, and the struggle to win his affection produces a rift in their friendship. In addition to the many mishaps suffered by the cast and crew of the movie, the book climaxes with a shoot-out. Lee's former husband comes back to attack her, and Pete is killed when he takes a bullet meant for Lee. Fenny ends up with Bill, but thanks to one night he spends with Lee, she becomes pregnant with his child. Through it all, Fenny retains her good-natured, down-home values, and by the end of the book, she pledges that she will not leave Minnesota again.

Landvik's skill in creating a sense of place in *The Tall Pine Polka* has led to comparisons with Fanny Flagg's *Fried Green Tomatoes at the Whistle Stop Café* (1987) as does her celebration of the virtues of friendship. Landvik again earned approval for writing a novel wherein "comedy and tragedy blend seamlessly," according to Susan Kelly of *USA Today* (4 October 1999). Other reviewers pointed out, however, that the book focuses on plot over all else, which results in the production of a cast of one-dimensional characters. Hanna wrote in the *Cleveland Plain Dealer,* "Landvik comes undone recounting the stories of seemingly dozens of characters and seems never to know who her story is about." Similarly, Susan C. Thompson of the *St. Louis Post-Dispatch* (14 November 1999) said, "Her people, Fenny included, have no inner lives and are knowable only by what they do and say." Other reviewers had more patience for the attempt to handle a multitude of peoples and story lines; the *Kirkus Reviews* critic described it as "an appealingly wacky frolic."

Those who praised the book complimented its boundless ambition, and Steinberg contended in *Publishers Weekly* (19 July 1999) that although it does not "add up to much in terms of character development," the lengthy novel is nevertheless "good-natured and zooms along, fueled by zany Minnesota energy." Similarly, Joyce Slater of the *Minneapolis Star Tribune* (5 September 1999) found it to be "a big boisterous novel that rarely stops to catch its breath," adding, "even those who find the plot sprawling and the ending impossibly happy must recognize the author's exuberance." As with her other novels, Landvik earned accolades for understanding the importance of community gathering places—Patty Jane's beauty shop, Dick's basement performance space, and Lee's café all serve as sites for the formation of lasting friendships and remind characters and readers alike that there is often strength in numbers.

Landvik's next novel, *Welcome to the Great Mysterious* (2000), is narrated by its main character, Broadway actress and self-proclaimed diva Geneva Jordan.

Dust jacket for Landvik's 1999 novel, in which a small-town Minnesota girl is selected for a Hollywood movie role (Richland County Public Library)

and contemplating a rapidly approaching menopause, Geneva decides that it might be an opportune time to take a break from New York. Once in Minnesota, Geneva begins caring for Rich, and in the process of living with him, she learns several lessons about the value of doing things for people other than herself. She also comes to realize that she has paid a price for leaving her Midwestern family for the lure of the big city.

Geneva's journey of self-revelation is assisted by the discovery of a scrapbook that she and her sister constructed long ago, suggestively titled "Welcome to the Great Mysterious." Filled with her family's answers to philosophical questions like "What is true love?" and "What is the meaning of life?," the scrapbook helps Geneva to reconnect with her younger self and also to realize she has lost sight of the person she once was. She reminisces about long-gone parents, aunts, uncles, and grandparents via the scrapbook, and their answers remind her that a cherished family is not something that fame or fortune will ever provide. At the same time that she reassesses her life priorities, she befriends mailman James, who is also a concert pianist with a fear of performing. Despite a short-lived move back to New York City and an unexpected proposal from her former boyfriend, Geneva ultimately returns to Minnesota to be with her family and marry James.

Although Geneva admits to her own self-absorption, Landvik's portrayal nevertheless makes her a surprisingly likable character. Steinberg in *Publishers Weekly* (31 July 2000) found that the "voice of the self absorbed Broadway diva . . . holds ingratiating charm." This charm can be credited in part to Geneva's treatment of Rich, for the two share a special bond. Rich is rendered lovingly; Pamela Miller of the *Minneapolis Star Tribune* (10 September 2000) wrote, "to Landvik's credit, Rich is a rounded character, alternately annoying and endearing." Miller added, "Landvik celebrates kindness in a way that may seem trite on the surface, but there is a lot to it. In her books, community is more than a buzzword."

Despite the poignancy of these portrayals, Landvik's choice to have Rich help teach Geneva "life lessons" is perhaps a bit overdone, considering how commonplace it has become to feature a disabled person who helps a more functional character learn something about himself or herself. Furthermore, Landvik's comparison of the down-home values of the Midwest and the callous selfishness of the East tends to be rather predictable: she lauds pure, good Minnesotan values and vilifies New York for promoting superficiality and selfishness. Nancy Pearl of *Library Journal* (13 August 2000) added that the novel does not share "the vigor, delightful characters, and goofy plot" of *The Tall Pine Polka*, but admirers such as Linda Duval of the *Col-*

Geneva has a winsome, if self-centered, tone and is charming despite her pretentiousness:

> All right, so I'm a diva. There are worse things—a mass murderer, a bigot, a telephone solicitor.
>
> I'm surprised my sister even uses the word as an insult. Why should I be offended by the truth? My dictionary defines *diva* as a "distinguished female singer." I certainly am that. The word, however, is cross-referenced with *prima donna,* defined as "a temperamental person; a person who takes adulation and privileged treatment as a right and reacts with petulance to criticism or inconvenience."
>
> Well, I might ask, who likes criticism or inconvenience? And why shouldn't one take privileged treatment as a right? A little self-esteem is *not* a bad thing.

Glamorous Geneva gets asked to do a surprising favor, however, when her sister requests that Geneva visit Minnesota for a month to care for her thirteen-year-old nephew, Rich, who suffers from Down's syndrome. Reeling from the breakup with a longtime boyfriend

orado Springs Gazette-Telegraph (12 November 2000) disagreed: "This is not the first time Landvik has written the Hollywood-meets-the-Heartland theme, which she did so hilariously in *The Tall Pine Polka*. But she keeps it fresh with vivid characters and new scenarios."

Landvik's next novel, *Angry Housewives Eating Bon Bons* (2003), tackles the familiar theme of female friendship she made popular in *Patty Jane's House of Curl* and *The Tall Pine Polka*. Using a narrative format that focuses separately on each of its five main characters, the novel employs the organizing device of a book club to both structure and comment on the experiences of the women over three decades. (Although the group initially calls itself the Freesia Court Book Club, the more derogatory moniker "Angry Housewives Eating Bon Bons" is bestowed upon them by a surly husband.)

The book-club aspect does more than provide the novel with its title, however, for each chapter is structured around a particular novel and the woman who chose it. Book selections from the women serve to showcase both their individual experiences and the current social climate—for example, Slip, who is an avid political activist, selects Eldridge Cleaver's controversial *Soul on Ice* (1968), and during the torrid 1970s the group reads Erica Jong's salacious *Fear of Flying* (1973). As reviewer Robin Vidimos wrote in the *Denver Post* (9 March 2003), "The picks are as diverse, and as telling, as the membership," and Jeff Zaleski of *Publishers Weekly* (10 March 2003) added, "their personal dramas are regularly punctuated by reflections on political milestones."

The group's friendship begins in 1968 when Faith, a lonely housewife and newcomer to Freesia Court, finds her backyard host to an impromptu snowball fight between her neighbors. This spontaneous event introduces her to the rest of the cast, including Audrey, a voluptuous woman with a voracious sexual appetite; Merit, the doctor's wife who quietly suffers from her husband's physical abuse; Kari, a thoughtful and lonely widow; and Slip, the antiwar activist. Together the women support each other through heartaches and triumphs, including Audrey's and Merit's respective divorces, the adoption of Kari's niece's illegitimate baby, cancer, and the women's various attempts to secure employment outside their homes.

The scope of the book is ambitious, although Landvik's treatment of the topic of female friendship at times too closely echoes the portrayals that appear in other popular novels about aging female friends, specifically Whitney Otto's *How to Make an American Quilt* (1992) and Rebecca Wells's *The Divine Secrets of the Ya-Ya Sisterhood* (1996). *Angry Housewives Eating Bon Bons* is perhaps a bit too reliant on its predecessors to set the parameters for a novel about female friendship—the similarity to Wells's best-seller led Carol Haggas to write in *Booklist* (1 February 2003), "so dysfunctional and dramatic are their lives, so witty and wise are these women, Landvik could just as easily have titled the book *Divine Secrets of the Uffda Sisterhood*." Nevertheless, those who praised the book and others like it noted that although "none of these books explores the human condition in ways that literary judges deem important," they nevertheless have a gift for portraying women "who are, for the most part, as unremarkable and normal as the people living down the street" (*Denver Post*, 9 March 2003).

Ultimately, Lorna Landvik's literary reputation hinges on her ability to successfully blend likable characters with comic circumstances. She formulates characters who are interesting and at times insightful, and she allows them to laugh at their own foibles and those of their neighbors and friends. Although her stories frequently treat wild eccentricities as commonplace qualities, which sometimes detracts from the force of her wit, Landvik is consistently admired for her imagination and creative energy. Although she usually entertains rather than enlightens, her stories nevertheless emphasize the virtues of friendship and family and pay particular attention to the bonds among women. Taken as a whole, Landvik's novels celebrate the existence of community and familial ties and underscore the warmth, compassion, love, and support provided by these relationships.

Interview:

"A Conversation with Lorna Landvik," Nashville Public Radio (1999) <http://www.josephbeth.com/html/landvikarchive.html>.

Mark Leyner

(4 January 1956 –)

Roy C. Flannagan
South Carolina Governor's School for Science and Mathematics

and

Eileen A. Joy
Southern Illinois University–Edwardsville

BOOKS: *I Smell Esther Williams and Other Stories* (New York: Fiction Collective, 1983);

My Cousin, My Gastroenterologist (New York: Harmony Books, 1990; London: HarperCollins, 1991);

Et Tu, Babe (New York: Harmony Books, 1992; London: Flamingo, 1993);

Tooth Imprints on a Corn Dog (New York: Harmony Books, 1995); republished as *A Dream Date with Di* (London: Picador, 1996);

The Tetherballs of Bougainville (New York: Harmony Books, 1997; London: Random House, 1997).

RECORDINGS: *My Cousin, My Gastroenterologist,* read by Leyner, Studio City, Cal., Dove Books on Tape, 1990;

I Smell Esther Williams, read by Leyner, Beverly Hills, Dove Audio, 1991.

OTHER: *American Made: New Fiction from the Fiction Collective,* edited by Leyner, Curtis White, and Thomas Glynn (New York: Fiction Collective, 1986).

Mark Leyner (photograph © by Robin Thomas; from the dust jacket for Et Tu, Babe, *1992; Bruccoli Clark Layman Archives)*

By turns imaginative, verbose, and iconoclastic, Mark Leyner is a humorist and experimentalist who tackles the often ridiculous products of postmodern culture and squeezes new hybrids out of them, ranging from military academies of beauty to weight-loss camps for terrorists to custom-built designer electric chairs. Leyner has also crafted a postmodern world citizenry made up of methedrine-suppository-ingesting haiku poets, transsexual teamsters, samurai tetherball players, and every gene-spliced person in between. One cannot help but laugh at such outrageous creations, but not without also pausing to consider the incisive critique of the excesses of contemporary American life that lies beneath what David Foster Wallace, in an interview with Larry McCaffery, once termed Leyner's "hip cynicism." Leyner's fiction speaks the lingua franca of the MTV generation, and it utilizes stylistic techniques derived from such forms of mass communication as television, advertising, software programs, technical manuals, informational brochures, and exercise videos. While some critics have accused Leyner of pandering to the short attention span and mindless tastes of his youthful readers, his work actually suggests new and liberating ways for negotiating the information overload of a technologically saturated consumer society.

For much of his career, Leyner has spent so much time poking fun at himself as an author and cult celebrity, both in interviews and in his fiction, that it has been difficult for reviewers and critics to pin down his work and to properly assess its literary and socially edifying merits. One of Leyner's chief artistic aims is the elimination of the distinction between high and low art—between, for instance, novelists and tabloid journalists, Greek tragedy and television game shows, or French symbolist poetry and pop music. No subject is too sacred for Leyner's satire, including himself and the literary arts—in *Tooth Imprints on a Corn Dog* (1995), for example, his fictional alter ego, "Mark Leyner," has been commissioned by *Der Gummiknüppel* ("the German equivalent of *Martha Stewart Living* but with more nudity and grisly crime") to write "1,000 lines of free verse in the *poète maudit* tradition of Arthur Rimbaud, but infused with the ebullience and joie de vivre that made ABBA so popular in the 1970s." The result of this violent and humorous yoking together of such disparate cultural figures is that some critics doubt Leyner's sincerity as commentator on the human condition or as an important literary innovator; they see, instead, mere sophomoric high jinks. Most famously, fellow experimental writer Wallace dubbed Leyner an "antichrist" figure, apparently because, for Wallace, Leyner's irony is of a "poisonous" variety that is not able to critique commercial culture because it has been so wholly absorbed by that culture. Conversely, Curtis White, one of the directors of the avant-garde press Fiction Collective 2 and editor with Leyner of *American Made: New Fiction from the Fiction Collective* (1986), has written that "Leyner's comic coup is to ironize postmodern irony. By virtue of that double negative, he is impossibly sincere." Despite White's positive assessment, Leyner has not yet received as much scholarly reflection as other contemporary experimental writers such as Wallace, Kathy Acker, and Paul Auster.

Mark Leyner was born in Jersey City, New Jersey, at the Margaret Hague Maternity Hospital on 4 January 1956 to Joel Leyner, a successful lawyer, and Muriel (née Chasan) Leyner, a real estate agent and designer. A sister, Debbie, was born six years later. Two of Leyner's earliest formative memories are seeing the ticker-tape parade for astronaut John Glenn in New York City in 1962, which inspired Leyner to want to be similarly celebrated and famous, and watching the Beatles on *The Ed Sullivan Show* in 1963, which led him to want to become an "unduplicatable" artist. As a result of his father's financial successes, the family traveled to Europe on occasion; they lived in West Orange and, when Leyner was in the eighth grade, in Maplewood, both in New Jersey. Leyner's artistic influences in middle and high school included the Rolling Stones (Keith Richards's violent guitar playing, in particular), Percy Bysshe Shelley and John Keats, Rimbaud and Charles Baudelaire, baseball players, Marcel Duchamp, Paul Bowles, William Seward Burroughs, and James Dean. At Columbia High School, Leyner wrote a column titled "This Side of Paradise" for the school newspaper, in which he chronicled the adolescent social scene and—according to an old friend from those days, John Carlin—attempted to "squeeze some *fin-de-siecle* decadence" out of mundane parties and gossip about who was interested in whom. During his junior year he ran for vice president of the student body in a campaign he described to William Grimes as "no issues . . . exclusively spin."

Leyner went on to study literature and creative writing at Brandeis University, where he worked with novelist Alan Lelchuk and had his first publishing success with a poem dedicated to Tina Turner in *Rolling Stone* in 1974. After finishing his B.A. in 1977, he accepted a fellowship to study creative writing at the University of Colorado at Boulder, where he gained the attention of Ronald Sukenick, an experimental novelist and one of the directors of the Fiction Collective, an independent writer-owned press dedicated to promoting avant-garde literature. Leyner received his M.F.A. in 1979 and then moved to Washington, D.C., where he began writing *I Smell Esther Williams and Other Stories,* published by the Fiction Collective in 1983. Leyner later moved back to New Jersey and worked as an editor for *The Hoboken Reporter,* but he soon found that medical-advertising copywriting suited his talents better. In a 1995 interview with Jonathan Bing of *Publishers Weekly,* Leyner noted that writing ad copy allowed him to "spend a lot of time musing about language and doing research in arcane medical books . . . while seeing, in sharp relief, the rich absurdities of the ad industry." In 1984 Leyner married Arleen Portada, a psychotherapist. Portada shows up often as a character in Leyner's first three books, and he even mentions their divorce in *Et Tu, Babe* (1992).

In more than one interview, Leyner has characterized his first book, *I Smell Esther Williams and Other Stories,* as juvenile. He told Grimes that he "almost can't bear to look at it" and indicated that the book was overly pretentious and "nakedly derivative." An extremely difficult work to describe, it is neither a collection of short stories nor a novel, and the chapter headings, such as "The Tao of Being White" and "Blue Dodge," often give the reader no indication of what is coming. Shortly after writing *I Smell Esther Williams and Other Stories,* Leyner said in an interview for *Contemporary Authors* that he did not have the "patience for those lax transitional devices of plot, setting, character, and so on that characterize the awful *longuers* of traditional fiction," and consequently the book is focused more upon the immediacy of a scene, and upon tone and language, than on narrative sense. Divided into twenty-six brief chapters–some no more than one paragraph–the pieces include prose poems, letters, diary entries, movie treatments, songs, short plays, and longer pieces of prose that blend several genres together, all written in a free-associative, disjunctive style, sometimes without punctuation. The entire book, in which Esther Williams never actually appears, consistently subverts narrative convention and adheres to Leyner's often-expressed desire to write fiction of unrelenting intensity. Furthermore, he indicated that he would not settle for anything less than "maximum, flatout drug overkill." Indeed, the book takes this principle to its extreme limits.

Although Leyner views his first book as immature, its iconoclastic humor, dream logic, and abrupt shifts in tone hold in embryo many of the themes and formal innovations that he develops more fully in his later work. For example, in the title piece, Leyner combines haiku, a dialogue titled *Teenage Christ Killers,* two movie treatments–one about talking shampoo bottles and another about George Washington Carver being gang-raped and then attacked by Blacula–and Peter Jennings explaining the "Principle of the Graduated Hostility of Things," among many other chaotic assemblages of language and persons both real and invented. The longest piece in the book, "I Smell Esther Williams" encapsulates all of the forms and stylistic innovations found elsewhere in the collection, and there is no obvious connection between the seemingly random "bits" collected there. Themes that recur throughout the book and his later works include biology and strange science; "Mark Leyner" as protagonist and *Überman;* the absurdity of advertising and marketing language; the blurring of the lines between historical, literary, and pop-culture figures; parodic pornography; altered states of mind; and muscular bodies.

Since *I Smell Esther Williams and Other Stories* had a small pressrun, it received limited critical attention. Writing for *American Poetry Review* (March/April 1984), Charlotte M. Meyer praised the book as "the funniest, most innovative fiction around." Acknowledging the "insanely disjointed . . . surface, on the level of logic,"

she nevertheless found "an internal consistency . . . [that] originates more out of tone and mood than content." Ultimately, she noted that "the stories are finally about language," and therefore, Leyner's work is part of a high literary tradition that includes the formally innovative work of John Donne and T. S. Eliot. Meyer asserts that Leyner's book provides more than a mere link to his predecessors; it "confidently points toward the future of fiction." In a 1996 article appraising the history of the Fiction Collective, Michael Berube, a well-known cultural critic, viewed *I Smell Esther Williams and Other Stories* as having offered the public what Frederic Jameson (in another context) called "surrealism without the unconscious." Ultimately, Berube saw the Fiction Collective, which gave Leyner his start and continues to keep his first book in print, as performing the "critical task of sustaining this nation's weirder literary heritages against the logic of Time-Warner and the Sears Financial Network." Even though Leyner thoroughly dislikes his earliest work, it is considered by some critics to be a significant moment in the history of experimental American fiction.

Leyner's big break came in 1988 when McCaffery chose one of Leyner's stories, "I Was an Infinitely Hot and Dense Dot," for a special cyberpunk issue of *The Mississippi Review. Harper's* magazine reprinted the story, and Leyner soon signed a book contract with Crown publishers. The success of the publication of *My Cousin, My Gastroenterologist* (1990), especially with college students who regarded him as a cult figure, allowed Leyner the freedom to write for a living, and since then he has supported himself with his books and also by writing occasional humor pieces for major magazines such as *Esquire* and *The New Yorker.* His second wife, Mercedes Pinto-Leyner, and their daughter, Gabrielle, often appear in these pieces.

Published by Harmony, a division of Crown, and aggressively marketed as a cult novel to MTV-loving college students, *My Cousin, My Gastroenterologist* was, in the words of Wallace, a kind of *Dharma Bums* (1958) of its day, combining insider references to pop culture with a rebellious hipness in a slightly more coherent point of view, although the collection shares with its predecessor a complete impatience with traditional narrative staples such as plot, continuity, and characterization. Similar to Hunter S. Thompson's writing, the supposedly drug-influenced quality of the prose made it all the more irreverent and appealing to younger readers and led the *Village Voice* reviewer to say that the novel "Kicks with the amphetamine-addled impact of a Hong Kong gangster flick, leaving your head buzzing for days." Written while Leyner was working as a medical-advertising copywriter in semiobscurity, *My Cousin, My Gastroenterologist* is the

Dust jacket for Leyner's 1992 novel, in which he parodies his own celebrity
(Bruccoli Clark Layman Archives)

most television-influenced of his works, and reading it gives one the dizzy sensation of channelsurfing at top speed, demonstrating how much of the American consciousness is full of popular-culture trivia that has encroached upon older frames of reference, such as painterly landscapes and traditional social distinctions. Leyner shows how adopting the style of the rapid-fire, jump-cut editing associated with music videos can reshape fictive syntax and keep the reader consistently off balance in the midst of a blur of images. In the McCaffery interview, Leyner claimed that he wanted the collection to "be like a colonoscopic examination of my insides—and of the insides of this body of information I've been swimming in." The title stems from the banal reality that Leyner does, in fact, have a cousin who is a gastroenterologist, but he uses the mechanics of an intestinal examination as a metaphor for the imaginative process of writing fiction. Ultimately, *My Cousin, My Gastroenterologist* reads like the uncontrolled data flow of an undiscriminating imagination steeped in the electronic media, and it remains in many ways Leyner's most influential work.

Described by Welch D. Everman in the *American Book Review* (November–December 1990) as "a kind of postmodern *Arabian Nights*," *My Cousin, My Gastroenterologist* looks and feels more like a short-story collection than *I Smell Esther Williams and Other Stories*, although some chapters, such as "colonoscope nite" and "ode to autumn," can only be described as free-associative prose poems. While several of the pieces stand out as strongly plotted narratives, there is almost never a page that goes by without several story lines impinging upon each other at once. For example, "fugitive from a centrifuge" follows the narrator from childhood to his graduation from the Wilford Military Academy of Beauty to his execution in a Miës van der Rohe Barcelona-style electric chair. Along the way, he works at McDonald's selling McHaggis sandwiches; travels to an asteroid with his girlfriend, Olivia; inherits the DeFrancesco diamond; thwarts a kamikaze pilot's plan to crash a commercial jet into a luxury cruise ship; and is then wrongly charged with conspiracy to commit murder. Although the story follows the arc of one man's ridiculous adventures, and could even be called a Surrealist picaresque, several times within the chapter the narrative briefly veers off on other courses. In addition to the narrator's life story, readers encounter the ninety-four-year-old godfather of the Louisiana Mafia, who is crowned Miss Universe in Taiwan; the great peripatetic teacher, Uchitel, who teaches rich children in the open-air squalor of sludge barrels on the outskirts of a nameless city; and seven-year-old Trevor, who "could barely concentrate long enough to comprehend a three-word sentence" but who "was accepted into a postdoctoral high-energy physics program at Stanford." Even though many random sketches throughout the story seem unrelated to the main plot, Leyner neatly stitches together the discontinuous elements of his narrative.

Leyner told Grimes that when he turned in his first story to his writing teacher at Brandeis, Lelchuk called it a "real tour de force" but did not think Leyner could keep up that pace "beyond one story." Nevertheless, much of the writing in *My Cousin, My Gastroenterologist* shows that Leyner was able to sustain the intensity of his writing and language play at a high level. For example, in a brief interlude titled "Idyll," Leyner begins with a semi-autobiographical reverie concerning a pastoral scene that warps into a consideration of both the environmental destruction of the Earth and Leyner's concomitant future literary reputation:

> I was reading an article that contained the words "vineyards, orchards, and fields bountiful with fruits and vegetables; sheeps and goats graze on hillsides of lush greenery" and I realized that in five months none of these things would exist and I realized that as the last sheep on earth is skinned, boned, filleted, and flash-frozen, Arleen and I would probably be making love for the last time, mingling–for the last time–the sweet smell of her flesh which is like hyacinths and narcissus with the virile tang of my own which is like pond scum and headcheese and then I realized that the only thing that would distinguish me in the eyes of posterity from–for instance–those three sullen Chinese yuppies slumped over in their bentwood chairs at the most elegant McDonald's in the world is that I wrote the ads that go: "Suddenly There's Vancouver!"

In one sentence, Leyner not only gives free rein to his signature stylistic excesses but also provides, in a compressed form, both a self-involved apocalyptic sexual fantasy and a socio-environmental critique in which he satirizes his own narcissism as well as the careless commodification of capitalist culture.

The critical reception of *My Cousin, My Gastroenterologist* was, for the most part, extremely positive. William Kowinski, in *The Bloomsbury Review* (January–February 1991), called Leyner "a voice to watch in the nineties. He may even be a new type of writer." Writing for *Publishers Weekly* (16 March 1990), Penny Kaganoff raved about the "exuberant, adventurous and audacious collection." *The Los Angeles Times* writer Irene Lacher pointed out how Leyner had become "the spiritual stepson of William Burroughs and Lenny Bruce, only with a high-tech sheen." Everman praised *My Cousin, My Gastroenterologist* for its "new hyperreality"and was also impressed by the way Leyner's work shows how "the media work to flatten and homogenize culture," with the "difference between metaphor and the literal" disappearing in the surface sheen of his prose. In his 1993 essay for *The Review of Contemporary Fiction*, "E Unibus Pluram: Television and U.S. Fiction," Wallace placed *My Cousin, My Gastroenterologist* at "the far, dark frontier of the fiction of image–literature's absorption of not just the icons, techniques, and phenomena of television, but of television's whole *objective*." Although Wallace found Leyner's "vignettes" to be "dazzlingly creative" and the book as a whole to be "the best image-fiction yet," he also feared that Leyner's work was equally "forgettable" and "oddly hollow." Meanwhile, the marketing campaign for the book was so successful that its sales exceeded Harmony's expectations for a relatively new author.

Et Tu, Babe was Leyner's first full-blown novel. It depicts the megalomaniacal fantasy of one celebrity author's world domination, personal dissipation, and eventual disappearance. While enjoying the cult status of *My Cousin, My Gastroenterologist*, Leyner took his delusions of grandeur and converted them into a book that wholly consists of jacket copy for itself, with "Mark Leyner" starring as the protagonist who claims, "Today I *am* the most intense, and in a certain sense, the most significant young prose writer in America." In this manner, *Et Tu, Babe* blurs the line between art and marketing, making it difficult to draw distinctions between Leyner the serious author, deftly parodying a popular commercial genre, and Leyner the cult celebrity, giving in to the superlatives heaped on him by reviewers and turning that hype into a marketing campaign disguised as fiction. In the interview with Bing, Leyner said that he wrote the novel at a time "when I was intoxicated with my own portrayal of myself" but also "very proud of having accommodated my very unhinged style to a narrative." Furthermore, in a 1993 interview with John Bellante and Carl Bellante in *The Bloomsbury Review*, Leyner remarked that the tight plotting of *Et Tu, Babe* reminded him of Jane Austen and that it was "the most novelistic" of anything he had ever written. Leyner explained to Grimes that he wrote the book in order to demonstrate how the "simulacrum [of celebrity images] is becoming indistinguishable from the reality." The constant pronouncements of its own brilliance throughout *Et Tu, Babe* struck some reviewers as tiresome, but others viewed it as a hilarious and insightful send-up of the apparatus of celebrity-making.

The story line reads like a tabloid exposé on the rise and fall of an increasingly paranoid superstar author, "Mark Leyner," albeit told from the superstar's point of view. Emphasizing the fact that readers often want to know more about the personal life of the writer than about his or her works, Leyner embellishes and mythologizes his private life for mass consumption, blending together real biographical facts, such as his passion for bodybuilding, with more preposterous scenarios. Raised in orphanages, reform schools, and prisons, and treated for many psychological illnesses, Mark lives in a compound surrounded by "punji sticks and claymore mines" to protect him from his many enemies. Disdainful of the "self-marginalization" of other "whining" writers, Mark assembles a Team Leyner of marketers, spies, and elderly but physically enhanced bodyguards to help promote his image. A "bar/pistol range" helps Team Leyner staffers relax after a hard day's work. Mark conducts workshops with young writers, so he can isolate those who might conceivably become competitors, and then kidnaps and brainwashes them into never writing again, and when the government confiscates his laptop, riots break out throughout the world. Mark is the most logocentric and commercially savvy of writers, using computer software to emend his books for different demographics of readers, publishing a coffee-table book of high-resolution nude pictures of himself taken from a spy satellite, and mailing out Team Leyner belt buckles and other fan-club-like memorabilia to his consumers. Given to every form of celebrity excess, Mark snorts a vial of "Lincoln's Morning Breath" as a hallucinogenic aid to marathon bouts of sex with his then-wife Arleen, plots damage-control strategies with his staff, and performs minor surgery on himself in his free time. Perhaps the most significant trope in the book, in fact, is the always-present image of the author's muscle-bound and self-transmogrifying body as a commodity fit for public consumption. The author's body, as fantasized upon in the novel, could well stand in for the idea of the celebrity as being "all surface," as well as for Leyner's idea of himself as a writer so intense he literally becomes gigantic.

Toward the end of the narrative, Mark disappears from his own memoir, and the book resorts to a mock oral history of other celebrities who recount the author's tailspin decline, during which his entourage, one by one, gradually desert him. Without admirers or sycophants, his fortunes wane, and the book comically illustrates both the in vitro creation of a celebrity as well as the yawning absence that lies beneath his carefully orchestrated image. At the same time, by virtue of having the protagonist disappear without a trace, thereby setting into motion the kind of dis-

course that always surrounds the secretive, reclusive celebrity—such as J. D. Salinger or Greta Garbo—Leyner both parodies and sets into motion a mythology that keeps Mark, no matter how dubious his accomplishments, alive. The book became, in Leyner's own words, a "self-fulfilling prophecy," leading him to appear on *Late Night with David Letterman* and also in a cover story for *The New York Times Magazine*.

As a result of the ambiguities and self-indulgences in the novel, reviews were mixed, and for the first time, some critics began to express annoyance at Leyner's endlessly ironic prose. While the reviewer for *Publishers Weekly* (24 August 1992) found Leyner's "relentless assault on the ways in which celebrity now drives the literary world . . . ingenious and on target," critic John Skow in *Time* (12 October 1992) saw the book as a "comic train wreck" ultimately aimed at a reading public that "a generation of hotshot young editors earnestly believes, won't and can't pay attention to more than 200 consecutive words." Writing for *The New York Times Book Review* (27 September 1992), Lewis Frumkes found the book, if unrelentingly narcissistic, at least "genuinely creative and amusing." In *The New York Times* (13 October 1992) Michiko Kakutani praised Leyner's "vitality as a writer—his inventiveness, irreverence and shrewd ability to satirize the wretched excesses of a society obsessed with fame," but stated that Leyner leaves readers "reeling from anecdote overload and more than a little sick of the author's willful hipness." In Grimes's cover article on Leyner for *The New York Times Magazine*, written shortly after publication of *Et Tu, Babe*, Wallace admitted being a fan of Leyner's novel, but he also stated that after reading Leyner, he thought of the culture "as a cancer patient with a terminal diagnosis." Furthermore, Wallace worried that "If the purpose of art is to show people how to live, then it's not clear how he does this." Leyner has never responded directly to Wallace's criticism of his writing, but he did tell Grimes that the only way to get young people not to abandon literature is to speak their language and to engage them on their level.

In his next collection of essays, stories, and occasional magazine pieces, *Tooth Imprints on a Corn Dog*, Leyner displays a slightly mellower style that reflects more mature concerns, such as his new fatherhood. He wonders, for instance, how a father can maintain the "aura of danger and delinquency . . . an indispensable constituent of a man's sex appeal" while carrying his daughter in a Snugli. Adding some literary gravitas to his writing, he includes a short play based on Nathaniel Hawthorne's 1835 story "Young Goodman Brown," only now the satanic forests of the Puritan era have been transposed to the lower floors of the

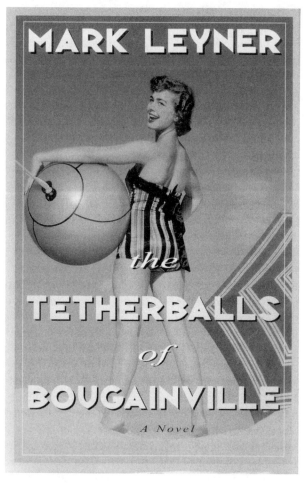

Dust jacket for Leyner's 1997 novel, in which thirteen-year-old "Mark Leyner" reviews a movie written and directed by another "Mark Leyner" in which yet another "Mark Leyner" is the main character (Richland County Public Library)

"hulk couture," in which he argues that he is "All Beast . . . with style." Other, shorter pieces in the collection concern secret tattoos worn by United States senators, a sperm-donor clinic in the Empire State Building, a pitch to include contemporary product inserts in classic works of literature, and fantasies about snuggling with Princess Diana. Although *Tooth Imprints on a Corn Dog* could be described as a collection of random humor pieces, it is not without its social critique; in "oh, brother," a satire of the sensational and much-publicized murder trials of Lyle and Erik Menendez for the 1989 murders of their parents, Leyner lampoons a society overly indulgent of its adolescent whims. In addition, the book reflects Leyner's interest in blurring the line between fact and fiction, thereby calling into question how fixed literary genre distinctions really are.

For the most part, critics liked *Tooth Imprints on a Corn Dog* but were again leery of the superficiality and scattershot organization of the collection. Writing for *Newsweek* (27 March 1995), Rick Marin praised the book for its accessibility, "pumped-up prose and steroidal satire," but he also found that Leyner's "semiautobiographical style is his strength and weakness." In *The New York Times* (7 March 1995), Kakutani, usually impressed by Leyner's writing skills, found that each piece in the book "is really just an excuse for Mr. Leyner to joke around and free-associate about his favorite preoccupations: namely, arcane skin diseases, bizarre technological innovations and the consequences of contemporary celebrity." Furthermore, while Kakutani found many of the pieces "laugh-out-loud funny," the critic felt that they had "the emotional afterlife of a mayfly" and were "willfully superficial." Arguing for the important literary merits of *Tooth Imprints on a Corn Dog* in the *Review of Contemporary Fiction* (Fall 1995), Steven Moore lauded Leyner for capturing the "disorienting melange of media overkill, global awareness, hyperconsumerism, and sensory overload that makes up postmodern life." Moore discussed Leyner's collection within the context of McCaffery's term for a new genre of writing—Avant-Pop, an "art that mixes pop or low culture with serious, high culture concerns" and can be traced back to James Joyce's *Ulysses* (1922). Ultimately, Moore judged Leyner's writing to be better crafted than most so-called serious contemporary fiction.

The Tetherballs of Bougainville (1997) is the most unified of Leyner's books in terms of its formal structure and theme. In an interview with Laura Miller of the on-line magazine *Salon*, Leyner commented, "It's the first book I've written with a continuous story, and with somewhat stable characters. To me that's a huge leap." The book satirizes the conventional bil-

Bergdorf Goodman department store in New York. *Tooth Imprints on a Corn Dog* also continues Leyner's project of skewering the myth of the famous author as seen in *Et Tu, Babe;* the title story details the hyper-writing process of "Leyner," who holes up in the Chateau Marmont in Hollywood, California, to crank out a commissioned thousand-line poem on his laptop, clearing, as he puts it, the "Augean stables of contemporary literature" and "slashing the rank vegetation of American popular culture with the warped machete of my mind." Just as Gustave Flaubert suffered while writing *Madame Bovary* (1857), "Leyner" goes through manic highs and lows, writer's block, and bouts of despair until an inspiring breeze blows into the room and helps him complete the poem.

Leyner's preoccupation with bodybuilding shows up throughout the book, most noticeably in

dungsroman, complete with adolescent antihero (the thirteen-year-old "Mark Leyner"), the death-exile of the father (who, in Leyner's twisted version, refuses to die), and the rites of sexual initiation with an older woman. Leyner told Miller that he was irritated by the reviews of *Tooth Imprints on a Corn Dog* that characterized his writing as more emotionally mature, and he decided to "do a book that was inimical to that. I couldn't think of a creature more diametrically opposed to the good father than a 13-year-old boy." Although *The Tetherballs of Bougainville* is tightly focused upon what might be called "a day in the life" of one character filtered only through that character's emotionally unhinged and pharmaceutically altered consciousness, the book also incorporates a wide array of genres, including handheld video-game scenarios, a "Q & A" brochure, a music video, television newsmagazine dialogue, a movie review, advertising copy, and a screenplay. Ultimately, the book creates a narrative claustrophobia in which the reader could easily feel trapped within the cognitive spasms of a grossly immature mind; at the same time, using a thirteen-year-old as his mouthpiece, Leyner once again accomplishes the feat of showcasing everything that is wrong with America's self-obsessed culture.

The Tetherballs of Bougainville is divided into two sections—the first is an "autobiographical" account of Mark's witnessing his PCP-addict father's failed execution for "killing a security guard who'd apprehended him shoplifting a Cuisinart variable-speed hand blender and Teflon-coated ice-cream scooper from a vendor's kiosk in an outlet in Secaucus." He then witnesses his father's resentencing to New Jersey State Discretionary Execution (NJSDE): "Joel Leyner" is allowed to leave the prison, but the State reserves the right to "execute said inmate immediately upon his . . . release into the community or at any time thereafter." The second section comprises a screenplay written by Mark titled "The Vivisection of Mighty Mouse Jr.," which details the druggy sexual orgy that occurs once Mark is left alone with the female warden and also includes the longest review ever written for a movie never made—*The Tetherballs of Bougainville*. In the fifty-three-page review itself, which is read aloud to the warden, Leyner indulges his penchant for high-speed, outlandish writing. Readers follow the adventures of another fictionalized Mark Leyner, writer and director of *The Tetherballs of Bougainville*, starring yet another Mark Leyner, this one "played with pitch-perfect menace by Chandrapal Ram, a 16-year-old contortionist dwarf from the Great Raj Kamal Circus in Upleta, India." In the movie, that version of Mark, whose father has also been sentenced to NJSDE, wants to make a movie that "will do for

tetherball what *The Poseidon Adventure* did for synchronized swimming," and he travels to the Solomon Islands, where tetherball is a national sport. Once there, he establishes a public-relations agency for Bougainville's dictator with Polo, a genetically altered Bonobo chimp. The book itself comes to a complete halt when Joel manages to get himself executed by B-52 bombs in such close proximity to the penitentiary that his son is killed at the same instant.

Critical reaction to *The Tetherballs of Bougainville* was mostly positive, but with some reservations. *Publishers Weekly* reviewers (24 July 1997) raved that "Leyner is one of our most talented comic writers . . . at his horny, hip, encyclopedic best." Writing for the *Review of Contemporary Fiction* (Spring 1998), Trevor Dodge praised *The Tetherballs of Bougainville* as "both postmodern product and parody, a full-blown riot in the coffers of the New York publishing industry and a testament to Leyner's whipsmart comedic genius." Jonathan Yardley of *The Washington Post* dubbed Leyner a "provocative social critic," and in *Salon* (6 October 1997) Ben Marcus observed that "certain smart writers . . . will be crippled with envy by Leyner's surpassing ability to coax vibrant new worlds out of the scraps and refuse that litter our own." In contrast, Matthew DeBord, writing for *The Boston Phoenix* (20 October 1997), tempered his praise with the observation that "Leyner now reads like a writer in a rut," but he did give credit to Leyner for showcasing "a sophisticated late-century understanding of the means by which ego is constructed . . . through marketing." Although critics continued to wrestle with ways to reconcile Leyner's humor with the more serious ideas that might lie beneath, in the interview with Miller, shortly after publication of *The Tetherballs of Bougainville,* Leyner stated that he did not feel that the entertainment value of a work and its integrity as a piece of art should be mutually exclusive.

Serious scholarly attention to Leyner's work has been minimal, but some critics have examined the ways in which his fiction highlights a consumer culture that increasingly impinges upon and redefines the possibilities for art and self-actualization. In *Blank Fictions: Consumerism, Culture and the Contemporary American Novel* (1998), James Annesley categorizes Leyner as a writer of "blank fiction," a new type of prose that is intensely aware of its position within the larger cultural matrix of movies, television, and popular music and that demonstrates "the ways in which it is still possible to engage with mass culture without being integrated and incorporated by these supposedly rigid and commercial experiences." In "Figuring Out Mark Leyner: A Waste of Time" (1996) William G. Little focuses primarily on *Et Tu, Babe,* and he holds up Leyner's work as a savvy defense of artistic heterogeneity in a capitalist culture that "rushes to repress aesthetic difference." Likewise, Little views Leyner's fiction as creating "ecstatic experiences" in which high literary aims are maintained in the midst of a culture addicted to speed and mindless waste. Ultimately, in Little's view, reading Leyner is a "socially responsible waste of time." Leyner himself has often been reticent about his literary status, but he is, finally, among the preeminent postmodern humorists working in contemporary American letters, and in a world that is becoming increasingly hypertextual, his fiction offers a means to navigate the complicated relationship between the marketplace and private life.

Interviews:

John Bellante and Carl Bellante, "A Leaner and Meaner Mark Leyner," *Bloomsbury Review,* 13 (July–August 1993): 5–7;

Jonathan Bing, "Mark Leyner: 'Completely Committed to Being Funny,'" *Publishers Weekly* (6 March 1995): 44–45;

Larry McCaffery, "Maximum, Flat-Out Drug Overkill," in *Some Other Fluency: Interviews with Innovative American Authors,* edited by McCaffery (Philadelphia: University of Pennsylvania Press, 1996), pp. 219–240;

Laura Miller, "Untethered Ego," *Salon* (8 December 1997) <http://www.salon.com/books/int/1997/12/cov_si_08leyner.html>.

References:

James Annesley, *Blank Fictions: Consumerism, Culture and the Contemporary American Novel* (New York: St. Martin's Press, 1998);

Michael Berube, "Straight Outta Normal," *Critique: Studies in Contemporary Fiction,* 37 (Spring 1996): 188–205;

William Grimes, "The Ridiculous Vision of Mark Leyner," *New York Times Magazine,* 13 September 1992, pp. 34–35, 51, 64, 66;

William G. Little, "Figuring Out Mark Leyner: A Waste of Time," *Arizona Quarterly: A Journal of American Literature, Culture, and Theory,* 52 (Winter 1996): 136–163;

Christian Moraru, "Intertextual Bodies: Three Steps on the Ladder of Posthumanity," *Intertexts,* 5 (Spring 2001): 46–60;

David Foster Wallace, "E Unibus Pluram: Television and U.S. Fiction," *Review of Contemporary Fiction,* 13 (Summer 1993): 151–194.

Alice McDermott

(27 June 1953 -)

Susan Farrell
College of Charleston

BOOKS: *A Bigamist's Daughter* (New York: Random House, 1982);
That Night (New York: Farrar, Straus & Giroux, 1987; London: Hamilton, 1988);
At Weddings and Wakes (New York: Farrar, Straus & Giroux, 1992; London: Hamilton, 1992);
Charming Billy (New York: Farrar, Straus & Giroux, 1998; London: Bloomsbury, 1999);
Child of My Heart (New York: Farrar, Straus & Giroux, 2002; London: Bloomsbury, 2003).

RECORDING: *At Weddings and Wakes,* read by McDermott, Beverly Hills, Dove Audio, 1992.

OTHER: "Books and Babies," in *Women, Creativity, and the Arts: Critical and Autobiographical Perspectives,* edited by Diane Apostolos-Cappadona (New York: Continuum, 1997), pp. 196–198;
"Bend Sinister: A Handbook for Writers," in *Sewanee Writers on Writing,* edited by Wyatt Prunty (Baton Rouge: Louisiana State University Press, 2000), pp. 125–137.

SELECTED PERIODICAL PUBLICATIONS– UNCOLLECTED:
FICTION
"Simple Truth," *Ms.,* 7 (July 1978): 73–75;
"Romantic Reruns," *Seventeen,* 38 (June 1979): 150–151;
"Small Losses," *Ms.,* 8 (August 1979): 60–62;
"Deliveries," *Redbook,* 155 (July 1980): 29+;
"Summer Folk," *Ms.,* 9 (April 1981): 69+;
"She Knew What She Wanted," *Redbook,* 166 (February 1986): 44+;
"Robert of the Desert," *Savvy Woman,* 10 (July 1989): 62+;
"Enough," *New Yorker,* 76 (10 April 2000): 82+.
NONFICTION
"Not a Love Story," *Mademoiselle,* 88 (February 1982): 90+;

Alice McDermott (photograph by Mimi Levine; from the dust jacket for At Weddings and Wakes, *1992; Richland County Public Library)*

"*That Night* and the Link to the Storyteller's Life," *New York Times,* 9 May 1987, p. 13;
"Teen-age Films: Love, Death, and the Prom," *New York Times,* 16 August 1987, p. H1;
"Dark Domestic Visions? So What Else Is New?" *New York Times,* 13 October 1991, p. H32;
"In Praise of Great Teachers; Three Students Recall Lessons of a Lifetime," by McDermott, Byron Janis, and Carl Sagan, *Washington Post,* 6 November 1994, p. ER1;
"The Annual Sermon, Retold," *New York Times,* 25 December 1997, p. A15;

231

"What (and Why) Mothers Always Know," *Washington Post,* 10 May 1998, p. C01;

"Night Without End, Amen: What Was One Shuddering Fan Sucking the Heat Out of the House, When All of Manhattan Was Pumping It Back in Again?" *Washington Post,* 12 July 1998, p. W11;

"Confessions of a Reluctant Catholic," *Commonweal,* 11 February 2000, p. 40.

Alice McDermott has developed a reputation as the premier chronicler of the ordinary lives of Irish Catholic New Yorkers in the twentieth century. Though reluctant to be categorized as either an Irish American writer or a Catholic writer, McDermott explained in a 2002 interview with Teresa K. Weaver that she writes about what she knows: "In fiction you have to be fairly specific," she points out, "And I know how Irish-Americans in the New York area talk, what kind of couches they buy, and what kind of plastic slipcovers they put on the couches. . . . But you know, I'm more interested in what's going on in their heads than what's going on their couches. I don't want to be a social scientist." She adds, "The spirituality that is tied to Catholicism is much more important to me." McDermott probes this spirituality in each of her thoughtful and compelling novels. Sometimes described as a "quiet" writer whose main purpose is to examine the emotional depth in ordinary lives and commonplace events, McDermott often takes a wistful, elegiac tone in her work. Her novels generally explore the lives of a large community of family members and neighbors, and her books are noteworthy for evoking the feel and texture of suburban life on Catholic Long Island in the 1950s and 1960s. McDermott's style tends to be nonlinear; she often shifts between generations, weaving back and forth between the past and the present as she explores the ties of love and sorrow that bind people together and keep them apart.

Like many of her characters, McDermott grew up in a middle-class Irish Catholic family on suburban Long Island. She was born on 27 June 1953, the third child and only daughter of Mildred Lynch McDermott, a secretary and homemaker, and William J. McDermott, who worked for Con Edison. Because both parents were first-generation Irish Americans who were orphaned in their youth, McDermott grew up never knowing any of her biological grandparents. She was, however, part of a large Catholic community, which led her parents to send her to elementary school at St. Boniface in Elmont, Long Island, where classes were taught by nuns. She later attended high school at Sacred Heart Academy in nearby Hempstead. McDermott claims to have been an indifferent student: "I liked to read books," she told Dan Cryer of *Newsday,* "but I

wasn't really a good student. I was not engaged, let's say, with what was going on in the classroom in high school. I was just interested in having a good time." McDermott also remembers filling up notebooks with stories as a nine- or ten-year-old. Writing was a way of expressing herself privately when dinner-table conversation was dominated by her two older brothers, who both became lawyers. "Writing was a way for me to make my own world and work out my thoughts," she recalls.

After graduating from Sacred Heart in 1971, McDermott entered the State University of New York at Oswego. During her undergraduate years, her interest in writing crystallized. Although books and reading were important in her family, McDermott remembered in an interview with Wendy Smith of *Publishers Weekly* that her parents did not encourage her to be a writer:

> I think my family, with completely good intentions, discouraged me because it seemed so removed to them; they saw me starving in a garret and tried to steer me away from it the same way they tried to steer me away from cocaine; I know it sounds very appealing right now, but believe me, you'll regret it! Their big thing was that I should go to Katie Gibbs and learn shorthand; If you really love books, you can get a good job in publishing if you have your secretarial skills. Then maybe you can be an editor and if you really want to write, you can write at night. But you'll have health insurance!

At Oswego, McDermott took her first writing class with Paul Briand, who became her mentor. Briand and the other instructors in Oswego's well-regarded writing program offered encouragement, helping her to think of herself as a writer and teaching her to analyze her own writing carefully and closely on the sentence level. "I took a tutorial with him one year, and we would take an hour in his office and go over a draft," McDermott told Greg Rienzi in an interview appearing in the Johns Hopkins University newspaper, "And he would say, 'Red dress. Why not yellow? What are you thinking? Why not a comma there? Now read the sentence through.'" From this experience, McDermott commented, "I realized that writing was sentence by sentence work."

Despite the support she received, McDermott still contemplated other career options after graduating from Oswego with a B.A. in 1975. For a time, she considered following in the path of her older brothers and attending law school. She settled, instead, on moving to New York for a brief stint as a clerk-typist at Vantage Press, a vanity publishing house that supplied much of the inspiration for the fictional Vista Books of her first novel, *A Bigamist's Daughter* (1982). Soon, though,

McDermott enrolled in the master's program in fiction writing at the University of New Hampshire (UNH), where she met a second mentor, Mark Smith, whom she describes as "a good, good novelist." Smith was key in persuading McDermott to start sending out manuscripts for publication. "In my second year," she told Smith, "he asked me what I had sent out. When I admitted I hadn't submitted anything, he said, 'Look, you've got the talent but you've got to take yourself seriously. Is this a career, or just something that you're doing?' He treated me as a colleague," McDermott remembered, "which was a wonderful confidence-builder; he helped me see myself as something other than apologetic about what I did." Acting on Smith's advice, McDermott began sending stories to potential publishers. Her first short story, "Simple Truth," was published in *Ms.* magazine in July 1978. In the next few years, she published two more stories in *Ms.* and placed others in *Seventeen, Redbook,* and *Mademoiselle.* Meanwhile, UNH had hired McDermott as a lecturer after she completed her M.A. degree in 1978. She taught English at UNH during the 1978–1979 academic year. Also during this period, McDermott met her future husband, David Armstrong, at a bar while she was celebrating the publication of her first short story. The couple married on 16 June 1979, and they have three children—sons Will and Patrick, and a daughter, Eames.

Inspired by her first taste of literary success, McDermott decided to write a novel. She and her new husband moved to New York, where Armstrong finished medical school and McDermott met Harriet Wasserman, an established literary agent who agreed to represent her. Smith had written a letter of introduction to Wasserman in which he lauded his former student, even beginning the letter with the line: "You're going to kiss my feet in Macy's window," according to Cryer in the *Newsday* interview. With Wasserman's help and the editing of Jonathan Galassi, whom McDermott later followed to Farrar, Straus, and Giroux and who edited each of her subsequent books, *A Bigamist's Daughter* was published in 1982 by Random House.

The novel examines ways in which the past shapes people: the stories they create about their pasts, the ways they romanticize their lives, and the deceptions necessary to maintain these stories. *A Bigamist's Daughter* tells the story of Elizabeth Connelly, a young editor in chief at Vista Books. While her friends and family are impressed by her new, lofty title and seeming success in her mid twenties, Elizabeth, along with her Vista coworkers, lives a carefully spun lie. Her job does not involve much actual editing–in fact, she never finishes reading the books she publishes. Rather, she is hired to puff up the dreams and soothe the fragile egos

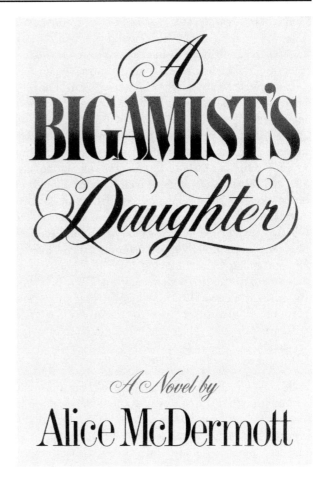

Dust jacket for McDermott's first book, a 1982 novel about an editor whose affair with one of her authors inspires her to seek the truth about her father's past
(Richland County Public Library)

of the foolish and somewhat pathetic aspiring writers Vista attracts: among them, Margaret Alice Greer, author of *Gouged of Womanhood: Poems of Two Mastectomies,* who wants T-shirts printed with the title of her book to help attract beach readers; Jonathan Whitney Peale Palmer, author of *Apocalyptic Calculations Based in the Third Dimension,* who seems to have been working on his book for the entire sixty years since he graduated from Harvard; and several people purporting to be prophets or the Holy Spirit himself. Elizabeth is the deal closer–she charms potential authors into signing the large checks that make up Vista's profit.

When Elizabeth becomes romantically involved with one of Vista's authors, Tupper Daniels, a Southerner who has written a novel about a bigamist, she begins for the first time to confront larger deceptions in her own life and her family's past. Tupper's fictional story begins to merge with Elizabeth's life as she explores her own father's long absences and her suspicions about his secret life. Was he, too, a bigamist, with a second or third family he visited and loved? And if so, was he like Beale in Tupper's book, a man of "great integrity," "infinitely moral," who marries again and again because his capacity for love is so great? Tupper's interest in the past, combined with his interest in finding an ending for his as-yet-unfinished novel, encourages Elizabeth to revisit her relationships with both her mother, who has recently died, and with a previous live-in boyfriend to whom Elizabeth is still emotionally attached. Elizabeth's romance with Tupper, though, is no panacea for her loneliness and isolation. In the end, Elizabeth truly becomes the bigamist's daughter of the title in a way deeper than a simple filial bond implies. She chooses to leave Tupper behind to travel for her job, imagining herself moving from one anonymous hotel room to another, perhaps meeting a new lover she will invite to share a bottle of wine with her, a lover she may lie to about her past to retain mystery and romance—her life, finally, "a hall of mirrors and secrets."

A Bigamist's Daughter was critically well received; reviewers often mentioned that the book was unusually accomplished for a first novel. Anne Tyler, writing in *The New York Times Book Review* (21 February 1982), argued that McDermott "sounds like anything but a first-time novelist." Rather, she asserted that McDermott "writes with assurance and skill" and creates a "fascinatingly prismatic story." Stephen Harvey of *The Village Voice* (23 February 1982) complimented McDermott for writing a tale "which sounds, for a change, like truth" though it grows from "commonplaces mined in so much undistinguished fiction." He admires the author's "spare, acidic prose" as well as her refusal to succumb to romantic illusions on the one hand or to maudlin depression on the other. Le Anne Schreiber in *The New York Times* (1 February 1982) described the book as a "shrewd, sad first novel" written by "a very tough-minded and talented young writer." The reviewers, however, did not see the book as flawless. Several commented that Tupper and Elizabeth are not always believable, with Tyler going so far as to say that the book "is almost done in, at times, by the fatuousness of its two central characters." She was particularly bothered by Tupper's proclivity to recite large chunks of his novel from memory at the slightest excuse. Nevertheless, McDermott counts herself lucky in the reviews she received for her first novel. Much of her success, she modestly told Rienzi, is "just good fortune. . . . it's the right person at the right time. They gave my first novel to Anne Tyler, and she was kind in her review." McDermott also credits her agent and editor for their key roles in her early success.

Following the release of *A Bigamist's Daughter*, McDermott and her husband moved to La Jolla, California, where Armstrong, by then a neuroscientist, conducted research while McDermott taught at the University of California, Davis. During this time, she worked on her second novel, *That Night* (1987). The book was published by Farrar, Straus, and Giroux to glowing reviews. A finalist for the National Book Award, the Pulitzer Prize, the PEN/Faulkner Award, and the *Los Angeles Times* Book Award, the novel is set in a sleepy Long Island suburb in the early 1960s. It begins with the incidents of one particular summer night that have permanently marked the mind of the narrator, a ten-year-old girl. Rick, the leader of a group of young, black-jacketed hoods, arrives with his friends on the narrator's street to claim his fifteen-year-old girlfriend, Sheryl, from her family, not realizing that Sheryl became pregnant and has been sent to relatives in the Midwest. Echoing Stanley Kowalski in Tennessee Williams's *A Streetcar Named Desire* (1947), Rick stands before Sheryl's house, bellowing her name "with such passion that even the friends who surrounded him, who had come to support him, to drag her from the house, to murder her family if they had to, let the chains they carried go limp in their hands." The neighborhood fathers, clad in Bermuda shorts, gray suit pants, and chinos, and wielding baseball bats and snow shovels, gather to confront the boys and to protect Sheryl. The romantic, impressionable narrator whose "ten-year-old heart was stopped by the beauty of it all" describes the awkward fight that ensues. The rest of the novel circles around this central incident, describing events leading up to it and resulting from it.

That Night is a novel about loss, about growing up, about the impossibility of holding onto love and romantic illusions. The skinny, tough-talking, heavily made-up Sheryl, traumatized by the recent and unexpected death of her father, believes that she can defeat death by loving someone enough: "I mean how logical is it for you to love somebody and then they just die?" she asks the much younger narrator in a fit of girlish confidence. "That's why it wouldn't matter if Rick got killed or something," she continues, "I guess it would be lonely, but it wouldn't be like I'd never see him again or anything. It would be just like with me and my father. I miss him, but I know I'm going to see him again because I think about him all the time. And you don't keep loving someone who doesn't exist anymore." Sheryl hypnotizes her boyfriend, Rick, with similar talk, telling him that, without her love, he would be forgotten when he dies: "If he had died then, before he met her, who would have loved him enough to make his disappearance from the earth illogical?"

Despite all her cool adolescent assurance, Sheryl is defeated by the stringent morals of her time and her community. When she finds herself pregnant, she is sent to live with relatives in Ohio, where she will have her baby but will not be allowed to keep it. A "good Catholic family" adopts the child immediately after the birth. Sheryl's dreams are crushed: "It was not logical for love to come to nothing," McDermott writes, but Sheryl "must have admitted then, for the first time, that it was certainly possible that it could, like grief, grow forgetful and weary and slowly wear away. She would get older. She would love someone else." As McDermott pointed out in an interview with Mervyn Rothstein on 9 May 1987, the tragedy of the novel "isn't in death, the tragedy is in living." Youthful romance must give way to adult practicality.

That Night laments the loss not only of a certain adolescent purity and passion, but it also evokes the passing of a particular time and place as well. One way that the novel succeeds is in its ability to re-create the feel of early 1960s suburbia: the intense friendships between the suburban mothers that flower and fade as they talk in kitchens with cigarettes in hand and children underfoot; the fathers who seem somewhat out of place as they return from work in the evening, "huge and foolish, like fullbacks on tricycles"; the sounds of lawn mowers on long summer nights. Several reviewers praised McDermott's ability to refresh a commonplace story and locale. Richard Eder of the *Los Angeles Times* (26 April 1987), for instance, pointed out that "these things should be as familiar as a television serial. But McDermott makes them seem new. We have never seen them before; and as with any new life, our own lives have to shift a little to make room for them." David Leavitt of *The New York Times* (19 April 1987) agreed, arguing that the novel "is an original, a work that, in spite of its much-exploited subject, revels in a rich, discursive prose style that belongs entirely to Alice McDermott, and that stands completely out of sync with contemporary literary trends." McDermott, in an interview with Kim Heron, explained that she was fully aware of the potential banality of her plot but that the very ordinariness of the story appealed to her:

I had the idea that this was the kind of story a serious writer would probably feel was unworthy. A fairly simple, even cliched story of a teen-age pregnancy and the false drama it might have elicited. But, I'm trying to retrieve situations and characters that I feel have been poorly handled in soap operas and TV movies and lousy fiction. In *That Night,* I was sort of stubbornly trying to take very simple emotions and redeem them, to show that they are still serious, or can be.

Most reviewers agreed that McDermott succeeds in this attempt.

In her next novel, *At Weddings and Wakes* (1992), McDermott similarly explores the deep emotional resonance of ordinary lives and commonplace events. Published by Farrar, Straus, and Giroux after McDermott had moved back east with her husband and family, the book unfolds the lives of three generations of an Irish Catholic family in Brooklyn, New York. The novel is told from the perspective of the youngest members of the family, the three children of the former Lucy Towne, who live in suburban Queens in the early 1960s but who are hauled into the city twice weekly, over two buses and two subways, to visit their maternal relatives. Living in the Towne apartment in Brooklyn are Momma, the family matriarch, and Lucy's three unmarried sisters, who are in their forties. As the novel carefully interweaves the past and present, readers discover that Momma is not the biological mother of the four Towne sisters. Their mother, Annie, died giving birth to her youngest daughter, and the girls have been raised by Annie's younger sister, Mary, who had arrived from Ireland to help out a few weeks before her sister's death. Mary and Jack Towne, the girls' father, eventually marry, making the story partly theirs.

These long afternoons in the Brooklyn apartment unfold with dull regularity for the children. Lucy begins her litany of complaints about her husband while her sister Mary listens patiently. Momma cooks a heavy dinner in the steaming apartment, and the children listlessly thumb through old copies of *National Geographic* and *Life* magazines. When the oldest sister, Agnes, returns from her job as an executive secretary, and the youngest sister, Veronica, emerges from her room and the alcoholic stupor of the previous evening, it is time for the cocktail hour and the fighting and recrimination among the sisters that routinely accompany it. McDermott writes, "it seemed to the children that the only way they could clearly account for the sudden anger that struck the four sisters at this time of day was that it was somehow prescribed, part of the daily and necessary schedule, merely the routine." Each of the sisters, as well as their stepmother, harbors regrets and disappointments that must be aired. Momma, whose married life consisted of bitter arguments with her husband, is nonetheless heartbroken when he dies "right outside this apartment door." Agnes's robust energy has been directed into learning about and acquiring the best material objects available. Veronica compensates for the pain and embarrassment of her disfigured face with alcohol, and Lucy petulantly complains that her husband is not the man she married.

*Dust jacket for McDermott's 1987 novel, about the impact of
a teenage girl's pregnancy on the ten-year-old narrator and
on their sleepy suburban neighborhood in the 1960s
(Richland County Public Library)*

Particularly well drawn is the character of May, the most appealing of the Towne sisters, a former nun who is conducting a shy, middle-aged courtship with Fred, her mailman. The wedding and wake of the title are both May's. She dies unexpectedly from an aneurysm four days after marrying Fred, losing the sort of life she had always longed for as soon as she attains it. May's story suggests the larger stories of families everywhere. The novel probes the bitterness of family relationships and the ways that family can constrict its members, obligating them and narrowing their lives. As Paul Baumann pointed out in his *Commonweal* review (22 May 1992), "the novel is eager to show how people are as much tied to one another by shared loss as by any transitory triumph or joy." Michiko Kakutani, reviewing the novel for *The New York Times* (24 March 1992), recognized the intermingling of joy and sadness in the novel: "the story of these three children and their family assumes a kind of mythic reso-

nance: it becomes a parable about all families and all families' encounters with love, mortality and sorrow." Kakutani praised McDermott's "rich, supple prose" and "quiet, emotional wisdom." Baumann called the novel "stunning." Jill Smolowe of *Time* (20 April 1992) declared McDermott a "mesmerizing and innovative storyteller." Like McDermott's previous novel, *At Weddings and Wakes* was named a finalist for the Pulitzer Prize in fiction.

During the 1990s, McDermott held a variety of academic positions while raising her children and continuing to write. She taught briefly at American University in 1992, was writer-in-residence at the Virginia Center for the Creative Arts in 1995 and 1997, and settled into a long-term position as creative-writing professor at Johns Hopkins University in 1996, where she was hired to replace the retiring John Barth. Although each of her first three novels was quite successful and helped secure McDermott a solid reputation among a small circle of literary critics, writers, and academics, her fourth novel, *Charming Billy,* published by Farrar, Straus, and Giroux in 1998, was the one that won her popular acclaim and a much wider readership. After *Charming Billy* unexpectedly won the 1998 National Book Award (Tom Wolfe's *A Man in Full* was considered the strong favorite that year), McDermott found herself in demand as a speaker, reader, and interview subject. The book spent several weeks on *The New York Times* best-seller list, became the number-two seller at Amazon.com, and ranked in the top ten at Barnes and Noble.

Set in Irish Catholic Long Island, like McDermott's previous novels, *Charming Billy* opens by describing the funeral lunch for Billy Lynch, a charming, yet maddening, alcoholic with a tragic past, much beloved and much indulged by his family and friends. As the book reveals the story of Billy's life and of the close-knit community in which he moved, McDermott revisits some of the occupations evident in her previous fiction: the human longing for romance; the deceptions people work on themselves and others; the inescapable loss and sorrow of ordinary lives; and the evocation of a particular community and place.

Told largely in flashbacks and digressions, Billy's story begins in 1945, when he and his cousin, Dennis, return from World War II and spend the summer repairing the beach cottage of Dennis's new stepfather, Mr. Holtzman. Billy falls in love that summer with Eva, an Irish girl working as a nursemaid for a large, wealthy family vacationing in East Hampton. When summer ends and Eva must return to Ireland and family responsibilities, Billy takes two jobs to save enough money to bring her—and her entire family if necessary—back to New York. "'I'll send for them all,'

Billy tells Eva, 'your parents and your sisters and the next-door neighbors if you want me to. Does your town have a pastor—I'll send for him. A milkman? Him too.' She was laughing now. 'Is there a baker you're particularly fond of? Any nuns? Cousins? We'll bring them over. We'll bring them all over.' It was what his life had held for him all along."

Billy's life does not work out as he dreams it will, however. Before long, Eva stops answering Billy's letters. When Eva's sister, Mary, tearfully confesses to Dennis that Eva has married an old boyfriend back in Ireland and spent the five hundred dollars Billy had sent her on a gas station and cafe, Dennis cannot bear to tell Billy the truth. He lies, telling Billy that Eva has died of pneumonia. The lie Dennis tells shapes the rest of Billy's life, perhaps pushing him into the alcoholism that eventually kills him.

The myth of Billy's tragic past also affects the other characters, who invest Billy with the romance their own lives are lacking. His suffering is noble and tragic, while theirs often seems mundane. Rand Richards Cooper, reviewing the novel for *Commonweal* (27 March 1998), pointed out that Billy becomes an almost Christ-like figure in the book: there is a "redemptive, sacrificial quality to Billy's passion," he argued. Billy's "goodness of heart gets soaked up by friends and relatives whose hurting he does for them: he loves and loses, he keeps the faith." Of course, Billy's great tragedy is based on the lie Dennis tells because he cannot bear for his friend to be reduced to the ordinary, the pitiable, the jilted lover. The novel, then, is as much about Dennis as it is about Billy. As Lois Wadsworth of *Biblio* (March 1999) pointed out, *Charming Billy* "expresses how complicated loyalty and friendship can be." She continued, "the reader gradually comes to realize" that the story "is not Billy's at all. Dennis is the star, the prime mover. The stories are about him and his family—his mother, Sheila; his dad, Daniel; his stepfather, Mr. Holtzman; his wife, Claire, and their children."

The book, in fact, is narrated by Dennis's daughter, an elusive character who has married and moved to Seattle and largely left the world she describes behind her. As in her previous two novels, McDermott chooses a narrator who is part of the community, yet also somewhat removed from it, thus achieving a certain amount of narrative distance and objectivity while retaining an intimate knowledge of the characters and a real sense of affection for them. As Penny Perrick put it in her *Sunday Times* (19 September 1999) review, *Charming Billy* "is an extraordinary novel about ordinary people, who, although unimportant as far as the world is concerned, feel themselves to exist in God's eye." The novel explores human frailties such as the tendency to lie to oneself and others. In pointing out such weaknesses, however, McDermott transforms them, proposing that it may be this very frailty that leads people to great acts of kindness and love and redeems them in the end.

While grateful for the attention generated by winning the National Book Award, McDermott keeps her success in perspective. When asked by Elizabeth Farnsworth of *The NewsHour with Jim Lehrer* what winning the award meant to her, McDermott replied, "It means a couple of very busy days and lots of phone calls and a lot of excitement, and I hope a return to work fairly soon." In several interviews, McDermott points out that the responsibilities of being a suburban wife and mother keep her grounded. "If you really want to be brought back to Earth," she told Rienzi, "have a 5-year-old throw up on you at 8 o'clock in the morning. Then you can say, National Book Award, my eye." McDermott and her family live in Bethesda, Maryland, outside Washington, D.C. McDermott continues to squeeze writing in when her children are in school and between volunteer work, teaching, and speaking engagements.

McDermott's fifth novel, *Child of My Heart*, was published by Farrar, Straus, and Giroux in December 2002. While the extended family and community networks of her earlier novels fade partially into the background in *Child of My Heart*, McDermott still evokes the wistful nostalgia of her earlier works. She also returns to familiar themes: intense love mingles with inevitable sorrow, and characters weave deceptions to make the pain of loss easier to bear, at least temporarily. Narrated by fifteen-year-old Theresa, the novel re-creates a magical summer in the early 1960s on the far end of Long Island. Theresa's life has elements of the fairy tale about it. She is the almost impossibly beautiful and kind only daughter of middle-aged parents; her good looks, her mother believes, are the gift of a generous saint. Her parents make great sacrifices for their beloved daughter, moving to the outskirts of the ritzy East Hamptons from their own working-class neighborhood: "They moved way out on Long Island because they knew rich people lived way out on Long Island, even if only for the summer months, and putting me in a place where I might be spotted by some of them was their equivalent of offering me every opportunity." The move, though, requires Theresa's parents to rise at 5:00 in the morning for their long commutes to work in the city; they do not return home until after 7:00 in the evening. Since she is left alone much of the time, Theresa's imagination runs wild; she creates an enchanted world of lollipop trees, magical shoes, and dreams of the future that she shares with the animals and children she takes care of during the long summer days.

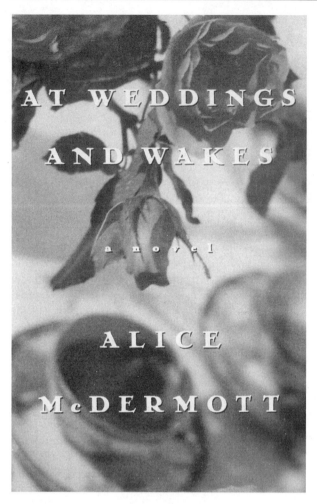

*Dust jacket for McDermott's third novel, about the dismal
lives of four sisters and their stepmother as witnessed
by one sister's three children (Richland
County Public Library)*

The fairy tale has its dark side, though. Adults
in the novel are habitually negligent or absent. The
Morans, a hard-drinking and hard-fighting couple
who pay little attention to their five grubby and needy
children, live next door to Theresa. Petey Moran,
whom Theresa describes as perhaps "the loneliest kid
on earth," is particularly attached to her, following her
around, promising presents, and constantly asking if
she likes him and his family. Theresa babysits daily
for Flora, the two-year-old daughter of a famous and
aging artist whose fourth wife has just left him.
Largely ignored by her father, who is conducting an
affair with the French housekeeper, and abandoned by
her natural mother, Flora relies on Theresa for the
affection she does not receive from her own family.
But the story revolves mostly around the summer visit
of Theresa's eight-year-old cousin Daisy, one of eight
siblings from Queens, often overlooked by her own
harried mother and policeman father. A somewhat

forlorn child who tires easily and hides bruises that
never seem to heal, Daisy worships Theresa as both
the dashing and magical older sister and the beautiful
and loving mother she lacks in real life. The novel
carefully builds the loving relationship between the
two cousins, all the while showing its fragility. Despite
Theresa's struggles to invent a happy, enchanted, and
safe place for her cousin, it is finally a world that cannot last. Theresa's own burgeoning sexuality leads her
firmly into the world of adults, while the cause of
Daisy's symptoms becomes apparent. The book
chronicles both Theresa's coming-of-age and the intrusion of reality into a world of fantasy and imagination.

McDermott's novel received mixed, though
mostly favorable reviews, with several critics noting
the new direction she had taken. Joan Acocella of *The
New Yorker* (11 November 2002) observed that *Child of
My Heart* leaves behind the precise realism and rigidly
controlled point of view of McDermott's earlier
works. In fact, Acocella argued, this book "is not just
not realism; it's almost not a novel. It's more like a
poem or a dream. Theresa obsessively tells us what
she did this day and the next, but the narration is just
a sort of bass line. The melody is something else.
Events are set off not so much by prior events as by
images." Other reviewers noted that the novel is told
in a more chronologically straightforward way than
McDermott's earlier works, and that the first-person
narrative voice is also more straightforward because
this narrator is the main character in the story rather
than an outside observer. The most often cited criticism of the work, however, had to do with the narrative voice. Several reviewers argued that Theresa is
not a believable character. Malcolm Jones of *Newsweek*
(18 November 2002), for instance, wrote that Theresa
"is simply too good to be true." Michiko Kakutani of
The New York Times (18 November 2002) called the
narrative "flatfooted and unconvincing" and the narrator herself "opaque and annoying." Gail Caldwell of
the *Boston Globe* (1 December 2002) and Carolyn See,
writing in the *Washington Post* (8 December 2002), both
admired the novel greatly but also pointed out that
Theresa is not at all a realistic adolescent girl, which,
according to See, is "a bit of a problem." Nevertheless,
most of the reviewers agreed that the book resembles
McDermott's other works in its artistry–the careful
crafting of sentences, the use of small details that tell
readers so much about the lives of her characters, and
the beauty and haunting sadness of its theme.

Perhaps McDermott's greatest contribution to
fiction of the twenty-first century is her ability to
evoke a particular time and mood. McDermott's work
brings to life Irish Catholic Long Island and New
York of the 1950s and 1960s in the same lovingly

detailed way that Jane Austen's work depicts the subtle manners and morality of British country life in the early nineteenth century. McDermott's novels often seem small, wistful, or quiet initially, but they open out and deepen to explore the largest questions of human existence. As Acocella writes about McDermott's accomplishments, "the smallest gesture, the briefest remark, speak volumes. Manners equal morals, and morals equal spiritual truth."

Interviews:

Kim Heron, "Redeeming Simple Emotions," *New York Times,* 19 April 1987, sec. 7, p. 1;

Mervyn Rothstein, "The Storyteller Is Part of the Tale," *New York Times,* 9 May 1987, I: 13;

Sally Levitt Steinberg, "L.I. Streets Inspire a Novelist," *New York Times,* 29 October 1989, sec. 12LI, p. 23;

Wendy Smith, "Alice McDermott," *Publishers Weekly,* 30 March 1992, p. 85+;

Dan Cryer, "Will Success Spoil Alice McDermott?" *Newsday* (New York), 25 March 1998, p. B06;

Elizabeth Farnsworth, "Online Focus: *Charming Billy,*" television, *NewsHour with Jim Lehrer,* 20 November 1998;

Greg Rienzi, "Charming Alice McDermott: Writing Sems Professor Brings Home National Book Award for Fiction," *Gazette Online: The Newspaper of the Johns Hopkins University* (7 December 1998) <http://www.jhu.edu/~gazette/octdec98/dec0798/07alice.html>;

Mary Ann Gwinn, "A Top Book Award Brings Changes to the 'Ordinary' Life of Alice McDermott," *Seattle Times,* 31 January 1999, p. M1;

Mary Jo Dangel, "Charming Alice McDermott: Award-winning Novelist," *St. Anthony Messenger* (May 2001) <http://www.americancatholic.org/Messenger/May2001/feature1.asp>;

Teresa K. Weaver, "Books: Multilayered Stories Are Writer's Forte," *Atlanta Journal-Constitution,* 21 April 2002, p. F4.

Jay McInerney

(13 January 1955 –   )

Robin Miller

BOOKS: *Bright Lights, Big City* (New York: Vintage, 1984; London: Cape, 1985);

Ransom (New York: Vintage, 1985; London: Flamingo, 1987);

Story of My Life (New York: Atlantic Monthly Press, 1988; London: Bloomsbury, 1988);

Brightness Falls (New York: Knopf, 1992; London: Bloomsbury, 1992);

The Last of the Savages (New York: Knopf, 1996; London: Bloomsbury, 1996);

Model Behavior: A Novel and 7 Stories (New York: Knopf, 1998; London: Bloomsbury, 1998);

Bacchus & Me: Adventures in the Wine Cellar (New York: Lyons Press, 2000);

How It Ended (London: Bloomsbury, 2000).

OTHER: John Dos Passos, *Manhattan Transfer,* introduction by McInerney (London: Penguin, 1987);

Cowboys, Indians and Commuters: The Penguin Book of New American Voices, edited by McInerney (London: Viking, 1994);

Dressed to Kill: James Bond: The Suited Hero, edited by McInerney (Paris: Flammarion, 1996).

Jay McInerney (photograph by Dan Borris; from the dust jacket for Model Behavior: A Novel and 7 Stories, *1998; Richland County Public Library)*

Jay McInerney's works document the urban world of New York and provide a peek into the glitzy, sometimes overly consumerist existence about which average Americans know little. Although he is often categorized with other chroniclers of the New York scene such as Bret Easton Ellis and Tama Janowitz, younger writers known as the literary "brat pack," McInerney resists the label. As he explained to Ron Hogan in a 1996 interview, "I was the first writer in that bunch. . . . I never particularly felt I was part of a group." He added, "Really, I just see my career as a succession of books, each one of which has been an attempt to do something different, maybe a bit more ambitious than the book before it."

John Barrett McInerney Jr. was born on 13 January 1955 in Hartford, Connecticut, to John Barrett McInerney, an international sales executive for Scott

Paper, and Marilyn Jean (Murphy) McInerney. After completing his B.A. in 1976 at Williams College in Williamstown, Massachusetts, McInerney spent two years teaching English in Japan and returned to the United States in 1979. He did some postgraduate work at Syracuse University in 1983. His graduate-school years are summarized in his essay "Raymond Carver, A Still, Small Voice," which first appeared in *The New York Times* (6 August 1989):

I was knocking around between graduate schools and the New York publishing world in the late 1970's and early 80's. . . . Having fallen under Carver's spell on reading his first collection, *Will You Please Be Quiet, Please?*, a book I would have bought on the basis of the title alone, I was lucky enough to meet him a few years later and eventually to become his student at Syracuse University in the early '80s.

McInerney took only six weeks to write his first and best-known novel, *Bright Lights, Big City,* in 1983. The book was published in 1984, when McInerney was twenty-nine years old. The novel has since sold more than one million copies. A movie adaptation was released in 1988, starring Michael J. Fox as the main character, who is never named in the book. The story is told in second person and spans three days in the protagonist's life. He combs the bar scene and snorts cocaine by night with friend Tad and daydreams through his working hours as a fact checker for a major magazine. He mourns his divorce from his supermodel wife and avoids his family. He is eventually fired from his job and realizes that his best friend and former wife are shallow, uncaring people. The story seems hopeless, but McInerney injects a note of hope at the end. Wandering the New York streets in the early morning hours, the protagonist sees a man unloading bags of warm bread from the back of a truck. He trades his expensive sunglasses for one of the bags, which becomes symbolic of his realization that he has to rebuild his life: "You get down on your knees and tear open the bag. The smell of warm dough envelopes you. The first bite sticks in your throat and you almost gag. You will have to go slowly. You will have to learn everything all over again."

William Kotzwinkle's review of *Bright Lights, Big City* in *The New York Times* (25 November 1984), "You're Fired, So You Buy a Ferret," praised the novel:

> Mr. McInerney's strong suit is humor, and there is lots of it in *Bright Lights, Big City*—a fast-paced book that also introduces us to such figures as the Ghost, a recluse in the magazine's office who has been working on a single article for the past seven years, and an inventor responsible for the automatic toilet-bowl cleaning revolution, who has now received a patent for a rotary nose-hair clipper. To all this zaniness, Mr. McInerney brings a strong sense for big-city sights. Here a ride in another limo: "you are moving only by the passage of lights across the tinted windows. Some of the lights have dim halos and others spill crystalline shards into the night." One can't improve on that.

The book made McInerney a celebrity, giving him, as he told an interviewer for *Publishers Weekly* (14 September 1998), "the French Kiss of popular acceptance . . . You never know what you'll do until you're in that embrace,"

he told the magazine. The article continued: "What McInerney did was party." Gossip columnists made him as much a celebrity for his well-known drug use and romantic entanglements as for his writing. He had been married briefly before the novel appeared; his second marriage, to Merry Reymond (now novelist Merry McInerney-Whiteford) in 1984, also ended in divorce.

McInerney's next novel, *Ransom,* was released by Vintage Books in 1985. It is the story of Chris Ransom, a young American in Kyoto who hates his first name and has spent two years in a karate dojo trying to purge himself of his past and reclaim the spiritual bearings he has lost. Ransom had imagined Japan as "a place of austere discipline which would cleanse and change him." He takes up karate as a form of penance and purification. He feels guilty about the flabby privilege of his upper-middle-class background, and guilty by association with his father, a playwright who sold out years before, getting rich writing scripts for television sitcoms. But mostly he embraces the pain and asceticism of karate as a "partial redemption" after a tragedy involving his two closest friends.

In his *New York Times* (29 September 1985) review of the novel, Ron Loewinsohn noted the influence of Ernest Hemingway:

> It [*Ransom*] is concerned with a group of young, rootless American expatriates in an exotic foreign land where one of them attempts to reconstruct his ravaged self in a corrupt and corrupting environment, and it reads like a transistorized version of *The Sun Also Rises*—that is, miniaturized, reduced. Hemingway set his action in Paris and Spain; Mr. McInerney places his characters in Japan. Where bullfighting provided Hemingway with a central metaphor, karate does the same for Mr. McInerney.

Like Hemingway, McInerney employs the pastime to show, as Loewinsohn stated, "the purity and intensity of commitment to this violent art as a gauge of his various characters' human worth. Both books focus on male companionship and competitiveness, and in both books the protagonist acts as a pimp—selling or giving the woman he is involved with to another man."

McInerney had said that he began writing *Ransom* first, and before completing it was inspired to write *Bright Lights, Big City.* Loewinsohn said the book reads like a first novel; it explains too much, "summarizing when it needs to render, and [is] deaf to its own lame phrases. It has none of the linguistic brio or Raymond Chandler-style humor of *Bright Lights, Big City*."

Story of My Life, McInerney's third novel, was published in 1988 and features a female narrator, twenty-year-old Alison Poole, who describes two months of high living on the Upper East Side of New York City.

Cover for the paperback original for McInerney's first book, a novel about the self-destructive behavior of a young fact checker at a prestigious New York City magazine. The 1984 work made McInerney a celebrity at twenty-nine (Thomas Cooper Library, University of South Carolina).

She is overprivileged, undereducated, and unhappy. Michiko Kakutani's review of *Story of My Life* in *The New York Times* (20 August 1988) was less than complimentary. The review, titled "Gold Cards, Parties and Late Rent," stated:

> Mr. McInerney's earlier novels (*Bright Lights, Big City* and *Ransom*) attested to his playful sense of humor, his observant, well-trained eye; and *Story of My Life* once again demonstrates his gift for capturing the clever banter that passes for conversation among the knowing young. There are some quick, funny portraits of club denizens in this volume, and some satiric renditions of the stoned dialogue that can accompany the ingestion of chemical substances. In the end, though, none of this makes us care about Mr. McInerney's characters. It simply leaves us depressed at the shallowness of these people's lives, and at the author's failure to find a worthy showcase for his talents.

McInerney was unhappy with the bad reviews received by these books, telling the *Publishers Weekly* interviewer, "I got a bad rap." He attributes some of his bad press to resentment: "I think a lot of the people who write about me think that if they had to write fewer interviews then they would transcribe their life-story and it would be a big success. Or should be." The interviewer asked if the bad reviews and profiles were products of jealousy. McInerney answered, "No, it's something else, too. I collaborated in the creation of my own image as a generational spokesman. It was very easy to read me as the protagonist of my own book, as the symbol of the very thing I claimed to be criticizing."

McInerney received somewhat better reviews for his 1992 satire of the publishing world, *Brightness Falls*. As Patricia Ross noted in *Library Journal,* in this novel "McInerney wryly examines the dilemma of people in their 30s who came of age with sex, drugs, and rock and roll and must now come to grips with adult responsibilities." Russell Calloway is an editor for a major publishing house, and his wife, Corrine, is a stockbroker. At first they appear to be a blissful New York couple; but Russell has an affair with his investment banker, Trina, after organizing a hostile-takeover bid for his publishing company. The consequences include Corrine's leaving him and his best friend's suicide. Cathline Schine hailed the novel in *The New York Times* (31 May 1992):

> An ambitious satire addressing almost as many talk-show topics as Oprah herself (bulimia, heroin, celebrity drug rehabilitation, AIDS, adultery, a miscarriage and more), *Brightness Falls* hits all its targets with great accuracy. . . . The glancing delicacy of this writing is in sharp contrast to the obvious blows of the more rhetorical sections of the book, but even at his worst Mr. McInerney is disarmingly openhanded.

Schine concluded that "Jay McInerney's delight in telling a story, even one heard before, is contagious." A critic for *Kirkus Reviews* was less kind: "With all its soap-opera turns, it's hard to take this thirtysomethingish novel seriously." *Publishers Weekly* noted: "While the strengths of McInerney's writing are in evidence, the characterizations in this well-plotted generational portrait of late-'80s Manhattan yuppies fail to convince." Ross, however, found the novel "Replete with ironic insight, wit, and style."

McInerney's personal life was changing during this period. In 1991 he had married jewelry designer Helen Bransford, who was seven years his senior, and the couple bought a ranch outside of Nashville, Tennessee, Bransford's home state. His next novel, *The Last of the Savages* (1996), is set in the South. The story takes place over three decades, beginning in the 1960s, and focuses on the friendship between Patrick Keane, an Irish Catholic boy from a dull New England mill town, and Will Savage, charismatic son of an old-money, Old South family. Will tries to put behind him his forebears' associations with slavery by forming a blues record company and marrying a black woman. The novel ends with Patrick as a corporate lawyer and Will as a promoter of soul music.

The Last of the Savages received mixed reviews. In *Library Journal* Wilda Williams called it "easily a candidate for the worst novel of 1996," adding that McInerney's "saving grace as a writer–his satirical wit–is missing in this tale." In contrast, a reviewer for *Publishers Weekly* called the novel a "warm, wondrously empathetic work." A writer for *Booklist* commented, "Although never heavy-handed or pretentious, McInerney touches on too many ideas and covers too much ground to be entirely successful at the task," while another critic for *The Boston*

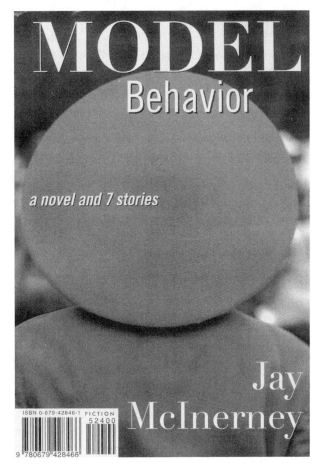

Dust jacket for McInerney's 1998 collection, in which the title piece is a novel about a celebrity-magazine writer dealing with a supermodel girlfriend who leaves him, a best friend who is a brilliant author on the edge of insanity, and an anorexic sister (Richland County Public Library)

Review claimed, "A novel applying McInerney's glibness to a subject as hazardous as the decline of sixties-era idealism has the potential to be achingly awful, but *The Last of the Savages* is a triumph."

McInerney's marriage to Bransford lasted nine years, and the couple had twins, Maisie and John Barrett McInerney III, through a surrogate mother. McInerney moved back to New York, and Bransford settled in Tennessee with the children. His next book, *Model Behavior: A Novel and 7 Stories,* published in 1998, was set again in New York. In the title novel, Connor McKnight is a writer for the fashion magazine *CiaoBella!* He struggles to cope with his girlfriend, model Philomena, who leaves him for an actor; his best friend, Jeremy, a writer who walks the line between genius and madness; and his sister, Brooke, who is so sensitive to the suffering of others that she is starving herself. The seven stories in the volume were collected with three new ones as *How It Ended* in 2000.

Some critics called the book shallow: Gary Krist, in a review for *Salon* magazine (22 September 1998), wrote that "the title novel is a sporadically entertaining comedy that ends up trying for an emotional heft its thin plot line can't support." He concluded, "the book exudes an aura of disingenuousness that dulls its satiric bite." Several other critics were more enthusiastic; a reviewer for *Publishers Weekly* stated, "McInerney impresses here with his trenchant humor and keen eye for detail, as he vengefully skewers the New York literary scene and other, equally unforgiving cliques"; this critic added, "Say what you will, McInerney has few peers in chronicling a certain segment of contemporary society that he loves and hates at the same time." Donna Seaman of *Booklist* said that with this "brisk, thoroughly entertaining novel" and the "impeccable short stories," McInerney "returns to his forte: tightly constructed and viciously funny satires of the high life of New York and Hollywood."

McInerney, meanwhile, started writing columns about wine for *House & Garden* magazine, and in 2000 he published the book *Bacchus & Me: Adventures in the Wine Cellar*. The book is a compilation of forty-nine columns of detailed information on the different aspects of wine. The author explains the book in his introduction:

> This wine critic gig began as a form of moonlighting. On my passport it says I'm a novelist, and my previous books have all been works of fiction. . . . It all started about five years ago with a phone call from Dominique Browning, an old friend who'd recently been given the mandate of resurrecting *House & Garden,* the venerable *Conde Nast* shelter magazine.

Browning decided to make the magazine more modern by hiring a wine enthusiast who was not necessarily an expert. McInerney's conclusion to his introduction is simple: "After almost five years of writing about wine, I feel less confident of my grasp of the subject than I did when I began. But I think that, on the day I feel confident in my expertise, I'll stop writing about it."

McInerney continues to write book reviews and articles for *The New York Times* and other publications. Because of his attention to detail and commitment to the subgenre of the urban novel, McInerney's novels have contributed to broadening the span of twenty-first-century American literature.

Interviews:

Dwight Garner, "Bright Lights, Bad Reviews," *Salon* (27 May 1996) <http://www.salon.com/weekly/mcinerney1960527.html>;

Ron Hogan, "Jay McInerney," *Beatrice.com* (1996) <http://www.beatrice.com/interviews/mcinerney/>;

Lorin Stein, "Jay McInerney: N.Y. Confidential," *Publishers Weekly,* 245 (14 September 1998): 39–40;

Lynn Barber, "The Beautiful and the Damned," *Guardian UK* (10 September 2000) <http://jaymcinerney.com/aboutjguardian.html>.

Papers:

A collection of Jay McInerney's papers from 1971 to 1989, including manuscripts, personal and professional correspondence, and photographs, is housed at the Division of Rare and Manuscript Collections at Cornell University Library.

Terry McMillan

(18 October 1951 –   )

Laurie Champion
San Diego State University, Imperial Valley

BOOKS: *Mama* (Boston: Houghton Mifflin, 1987; London: Cape, 1987);

Disappearing Acts (New York: Viking, 1989; London: Cape, 1990);

Waiting to Exhale (New York: Viking, 1992; London: Doubleday, 1992);

How Stella Got Her Groove Back (New York: Viking, 1996; London: Viking, 1996);

A Day Late and a Dollar Short (New York: Viking, 2001; London: Viking, 2001).

PRODUCED SCRIPTS: *Waiting to Exhale,* by McMillan and Ronald Bass, motion picture, 20th Century-Fox, 1995;

How Stella Got Her Groove Back, by McMillan and Bass, motion picture, 20th Century-Fox, 1998.

RECORDINGS: *Waiting to Exhale,* abridged, read by McMillan, St. Paul, Minn., Penguin HighBridge Audio, 1992;

Disappearing Acts, abridged, read by McMillan and Avery Brooks, St. Paul, Minn., Penguin High-Bridge Audio, 1993.

OTHER: *Breaking Ice: An Anthology of Contemporary African-American Fiction,* edited by McMillan (New York: Viking, 1990; London: Vintage, 1992).

Terry McMillan (photograph © 1996 Jonathan Exley; from the dust jacket for How Stella Got Her Groove Back, *1996; Richland County Public Library)*

Terry McMillan's novels explore issues relevant to African Americans in contemporary American society. McMillan is interested especially in African American women, and her female characters struggle with and celebrate motherhood, cope with troubled romantic relationships, look for successful careers, and search for both personal and cultural identity. The commercial success of McMillan's novels began with *Waiting to Exhale* (1992), which stayed on *The New York Times* bestseller list for several months, sold nearly four million copies, and earned McMillan $2.64 million for paperback rights, the second-largest amount in publishing history. McMillan continues to entertain her readers with realistic portrayals of contemporary African American society, depictions of resilient women, and humor.

Terry L. McMillan was born on 18 October 1951, the first of five children born to Edward Lewis McMillan and Madeline Washington Tillman. She grew up in Port Huron, Michigan, a suburb roughly sixty miles outside of Detroit. Her parents divorced when she was thirteen, and McMillan's mother, who worked in an auto factory as well as performing domestic jobs, assumed almost full responsibility for raising the children. (Edward McMillan died three years later.) When McMillan was sixteen years old, she began a job at the city library in Port Huron, where she discovered books by African American authors; reading these works gave her a sense of black pride and helped her become aware of issues relevant to African American culture.

In 1968 McMillan left her hometown and moved to Los Angeles. She enrolled in Los Angeles City College, where she studied classic texts by black authors. In 1973 she transferred to the University of California at Berkeley, where she studied journalism and writing and met Ishmael Reed, a well-known author and poet. After receiving her bachelor's degree in journalism, McMillan moved to New York City, where she studied film at Columbia University. In 1979 she earned her M.F.A. from Columbia and participated in the Harlem Writers Guild workshop, which was crucial to her development as a writer. She completed a draft of her first novel, *Mama* (1987), at the MacDowell Colony, where she stayed for two weeks in 1983.

Dedicated to McMillan's mother, *Mama* is the story of Mildred Peacock, the mother of five children. The story is set in Point Haven, Michigan, about ninety miles from Detroit. The novel begins during the civil rights era, when Black Power encouraged blacks to affirm and celebrate their cultural identity and heritage, and during the second wave of feminism in the United States. The novel spans twenty years and deals with social changes affecting both African Americans' rights and women's rights. The powerful opening of the novel establishes Mildred's condition: her husband, Crook, has beaten her severely the night before, and she contemplates revenge. The narrator says that if it were not for her five children, she would have left Crook a long time ago. The opening further establishes that Mildred is poverty-stricken and has few options available to her. Mildred had her first child, Freda, when she was seventeen, and she has been married to Crook for ten years. Now, at twenty-seven, she vows to leave him for good. She throws Crook out of the house and tells his longtime mistress, Ernestine, that he is now free to marry her. In order to provide for herself after divorcing Crook, Mildred performs various jobs such as working at the Diamond Crystal Salt Factory, cleaning private homes, waiting tables, and even engaging in prostitution. Lacking economic opportunities, she eventually seeks welfare assistance. Despite her hardships, Mildred never regrets having left Crook.

McMillan's portrayal of Mildred's relationship with Crook shows how difficult it is for abused women to leave their husbands. Unable for many years to support herself and her five children, Mildred feels she must stay in the abusive marriage; however, her personal strength and courage eventually manifest themselves. Mildred suffers from oppression not only because she is a woman but also because she is black

and poor. If economic opportunities were difficult during this time period for white women, they were almost impossible for African American women.

Although Crook severely mistreats Mildred, she refuses to give up hope, self-respect, and her desire for male companionship. Although the title of the novel is *Mama,* and Mildred is a mother in every sense of the word, she is also a woman, with sexual desires and individuality. When she starts dating a man named Sonny, she feels rejuvenated as a woman. When he has to go to Okinawa for military service, she thanks him for the time she has spent with him rather than clinging to him or regretting their time together. She is obviously not dependent on a man. As Rita B. Dandridge points out in her essay "Debunking the Motherhood Myth in Terry McMillan's *Mama*" (1998), "Mildred's circumstances differ significantly from the traditional assumptions that motherhood occurs within a traditional family, that males and females have rigid sex roles, and that mothers are financially dependent on their husbands." Later, when Freda protests because Mildred is dating Spooky, a married man, Mildred defends herself and remains ruled by her own heart and conscience, not her children or society. When Spooky leaves Mildred to return to his wife, she feels defeated and vows never to love again. She then marries Rufus simply so he will help support her. Feeling unfulfilled emotionally, she divorces Rufus because she realizes she wants more than an economic helpmate. He threatens Mildred with a knife when she announces her plans to divorce him, and Freda comes to Mildred's aid.

Although Mildred marries Rufus for economic security, her renewed sense of strength will not allow her to remain in the relationship. Her decision to leave Rufus after only a brief marriage demonstrates her personal growth. She has learned that she can survive alone, and she is not willing to tolerate living with a man whom she does not love. Later, Mildred marries a much younger man, Billy, who eventually leaves her because he claims the family is too much responsibility.

Freda gets a job at a library, where she becomes familiar with books written by African Americans. Later, she moves to Los Angeles, attends a community college, and becomes enlightened about issues relevant to blacks and women. Wanting to act upon this knowledge and share it with others, Freda begins to demonstrate black pride and tells her mother about books that she has read, such as *The Autobiography of Malcolm X* (1965). On her thirtieth birthday, Freda decides to change her life and calls Alcoholics Anonymous to seek treatment for her drinking problem. She returns to her hometown, where Mildred is now living, and announces that she has received a writing fellowship; Mildred announces her plans to move so that she can attend college. The novel ends with Freda and Mildred celebrating their life-changing decisions together.

Mama chronicles the development of the complex relationship between Freda and Mildred. At different points, their roles seem to reverse: Freda sometimes acts as mother and nurturer to Mildred. For example, after witnessing Mildred's psychological breakdown, Freda not only rescues her by bathing her and calling Mildred's father, but she also tends to the house and the other children while Mildred recuperates. Most of the time, however, Mildred cares for Freda and teaches her truths by bluntly stating lessons she should learn. For example, when Freda sees the big house in which Mildred works, Freda vows to be rich when she grows up and promises to provide for Mildred so she will not have to clean white people's houses. Rather than encouraging Freda to strive for economic success, Mildred says, "And baby, let me tell you something so you can get this straight. That big fancy house ain't the only thang in life worth striving for. Decency. A good husband. Some healthy babies. Peace of mind. Them is the thangs you try to get out of life. Everything else'll fall in place. It always do. You hear me?"

McMillan helped promote *Mama* herself. Instead of relying on publishers to organize readings and market the novel, she called bookstores and African American organizations and offered to present readings of the book. *Mama* received quite a bit of critical attention, especially for an author's first novel. Although some reviewers pointed out flaws, it was received favorably for the most part. Many reviewers praised *Mama* for its realistic portrayal of the struggles of an African American family in the 1960s and 1970s. After the publication of *Mama,* McMillan was offered a position as an instructor at the University of Wyoming at Laramie, where she taught from 1987 to 1990. McMillan also taught writing at Stanford University and the University of Arizona. She received the American Book Award of the Before Columbus Foundation (1987) and a National Endowment for the Arts Grant (1988).

McMillan's next novel, *Disappearing Acts,* was published in 1989 and became a national best-seller, with more than one hundred thousand paperback copies sold. *Disappearing Acts* chronicles the tumultuous relationship between Zora Banks and Franklin Swift. Told from Zora's and Franklin's alternating first-person points of view, the novel reveals both characters as they explain their perspectives on their relationship, their goals, and their philosophies of life. The opening chapters introduce the characters and give brief histories of their lives, emphasizing particularly their past romantic involvements. These summaries provide readers with sketches of the characters prior to their meeting. They also offer reference points for the psychological states of mind of

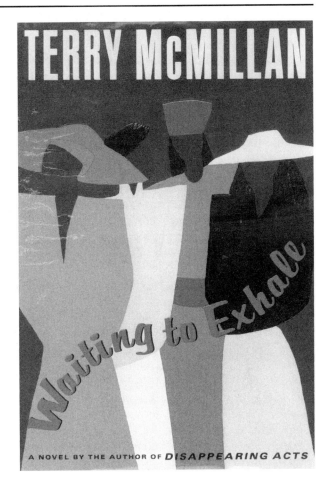

Dust jacket for McMillan's 1992 novel, which chronicles the friendships and romantic involvements of four African American women (Richland County Public Library)

each of the characters. Franklin says of himself: "My life is pretty simple. I like to get drunk on Friday nights, but only if I worked a full week. No pay, no play." After describing his relationship with his estranged wife, Pam, he explains why he does not have a woman in his life: "And that's exactly why women ain't in the picture right now. They complicate shit. Fuck up my whole program. All they do is throw me off track. It takes me too damn long to swing back." In her introduction Zora describes the type of man she wants:

I like a clean, tall, smart, honest, sensuous, energetic, aggressive man with white teeth who smells good and reads a good book every now and then, who votes and wants to make a contribution to the world instead of holding his hands out. A man who stands for something. Who feels passion for more than just women.

The end of Zora's narrative focuses on her desire to become a singer. She says she is not looking for a relationship, but if she meets a man who wants to join her while she pursues her singing career, she might welcome him.

Zora, a teacher and aspiring musician, meets Franklin while looking at rental houses. The fact that Franklin is unable to maintain a steady job frustrates him. Frequently, he brings his frustration into his relationship with Zora, who soon begins to feel discouraged because she is unable to understand Franklin's predicament. However, one Thanksgiving she visits Franklin's family and comes to understand the myriad of problems Franklin has experienced. As her compassion for him grows, he becomes aware of her physical impairment–epilepsy. Later, during Christmas, Franklin meets Zora's family. He sees that Zora's family seems peaceful and notices the differences between her family and his own.

The major obstacle in Franklin's relationship with Zora is that he is married to another woman. Although he does not interact with his wife, he remains married because he cannot afford a divorce. However, he is ashamed to admit to Zora that he is unable to pay for a divorce. Zora becomes pregnant, has an abortion, and does not tell Franklin. Although they have reasonable explanations for not sharing these important aspects of their lives with each other, the secrets cause them to grow farther apart instead of bringing them closer together. Their relationship seems doomed because the very solutions they create for their problems only make their problems worse. When Zora becomes pregnant the second time, she tells Franklin, and he persuades her to have the baby.

When Franklin experiences a major identity crisis, Zora's personal identity fades into her efforts to help him. After Zora finally asks him to leave, both she and Franklin begin to achieve goals more successfully apart than they did together. Franklin enrolls in college and gets a steady job, while Zora decides to become a songwriter. Three months later, Franklin visits Zora, and she promises that she will reunite with him as soon as he is economically and psychologically stable. The ending is ambiguous: they could be starting a pattern of breaking up and reuniting, or they could reunite and create a harmonious, successful relationship. In any case, Zora acknowledges a major element of their relationship when she tells Franklin, "Our lives need to keep going, Franklin. That's been a big part of our problem. I think we both just kind of disappeared somewhere along the way and just stopped moving altogether." This type of dialogue, in which Zora and Franklin analyze their relationship, occurs throughout the novel and reflects contemporary habits and perspectives. The hip attitude expressed by the characters is one element that places *Disappearing Acts* in "a whole new literary category–the post-feminist black urban romance novel," as David

Nicholson noted in a 27 August 1989 review for *The Washington Post*. Zora's and Franklin's philosophies about love are similar to the types of insights one might hear on a contemporary talk show.

The name Zora Banks makes clear that *Disappearing Acts* also pays homage to Zora Neale Hurston, one of the most well-known women writers of the Harlem Renaissance. Banks is the last name of the characters in "The Gilded Six-Bits" (1933), one of Hurston's most significant short stories. The couple in "The Gilded Six-Bits" shares a remarkably romantic marriage until the wife has an affair; however, by the end of the story the couple has reunited, and the story is about forgiveness as well as endurance. Both "The Gilded Six-Bits" and *Disappearing Acts* reveal the intense emotions often felt by those struggling to make relationships last. Incidentally, *Disappearing Acts* ends with Zora and Franklin preparing to play a game of Scrabble, an ending similar to the coin-tossing game that the couple plays at both the beginning and the end of "The Gilded Six-Bits." Both endings suggest positive growth and imply that playfulness is essential for maintaining romantic relationships.

The publication of *Disappearing Acts* sparked a lawsuit: Leonard Welch, McMillan's former boyfriend and father of her son, Solomon (born in 1984), sued her and her publisher, Viking, for defamation of character. He claimed she modeled Franklin–and the character's disagreeable behavior–on him and thus acted maliciously when she wrote the novel. The suit drew national attention, and writers feared that a victory for Welch would set a dangerous precedent that would deny creative license to writers across America. The New York Supreme Court ruled in McMillan's favor, however; among other reasons, the judge noted differences between Franklin and Welch.

McMillan's third novel, *Waiting to Exhale*, appeared in 1992. As Edward M. Jackson notes in his 1993 analysis, part of the commercial success of the novel can be attributed to McMillan's portrayal of "many themes universal to the contemporary America experience. She wrote about the subjects of divorce, single parenting, weight problems among women, health problems of elderly parents, the insensitivity of males, and the tensions of female friendships." The subjects Jackson describes run throughout McMillan's novels. However, among her novels, *Waiting to Exhale* most vividly explores female bonding and advocates the need for women to support each other.

Waiting to Exhale, like *Disappearing Acts*, shifts first-person points of view to reveal various accounts of events that unfold. *Waiting to Exhale*, however, also uses the third-person point of view to describe some of the events more objectively. *Waiting to Exhale* tells the story of four African American women who live in Phoenix.

The narrative flashes back and forth to show how each of the women's particular predicaments has brought her to Phoenix. Although the four women argue and disagree and form subgroups among themselves, their friendships endure.

Waiting to Exhale opens with Savannah Jackson's first-person account of her life. She explains that she is tired of living in Denver and plans to move to Phoenix. She has taken a significant cut in pay to move but is willing to do so in her self-proclaimed search for peace of mind. She is thirty-six years old, has never been married, and is preparing to go to a New Year's party when her narrative begins. The event is symbolic of the reassessment she makes of her life. Like Zora in *Disappearing Acts,* Savannah describes what type of man she seeks. Reviewing the men her prayers to God have sent her, she says she left out the details of what she is looking for—a little compassion, some pride as opposed to cockiness, some confidence as opposed to arrogance:

> Now I'm more specific: Could you make sure he talks about what he feels and not just about what he thinks: could he have a genuine sense of his purpose in life, a sense of humor, and could he already *be* what he aspired to? Could he be honest, responsible, mature, drug-free, and a little bit spontaneous? Could he be full of zest, good-enough-looking for me, and please let him be a slow, tender, passionate lover?

She vows that the next man with whom she lives she will also marry.

The next chapter of *Waiting to Exhale* introduces Bernadine Harris, Savannah's former college roommate, from the third-person point of view. Her husband has just left her for a white woman. After describing the upper-middle-class private schools her children have attended, Bernadine accuses her husband of aspiring to live like the upwardly-mobile-driven whites he has seen on television. Throughout their eleven-year marriage, her husband has always managed the money and invested it. Bernadine has come to realize that she has given up her own identity to help him achieve his own self-interested goals. Although she acknowledges that she and her husband do not share the same worldviews or goals, she is terrified at the thought of being a thirty-six-year-old divorcée.

The third chapter returns to the first-person point of view, with thirty-five-year-old Robin Stokes's narrative. She reveals that she has broken up with her live-in boyfriend, Russell, and recently has met Michael. The action proper begins with her statement: "So here I am, waiting." Robin mentions Bernadine and Gloria Matthews as close friends who have helped her since her breakup with Russell. Gloria, who owns a hair salon, is introduced in the fourth chapter, through a third-person

Dust jacket for McMillan's 1996 novel, in which an overworked divorcée vacations in Jamaica and finds love with a man twenty-one years her junior (Richland County Public Library)

narrative that demonstrates her relationship with her son, Tarik. Gloria hears the news that Bernadine's husband has left her and reveals that her own former husband wants nothing to do with her because he is gay.

The situations of the four friends begin to develop plots and subplots in which the action parallels that of soap operas. The novel not only explores the women's relationships with men and their struggles to succeed at romance but also reveals conflicts they have with each other. Chronicling these women's lives, the narrative also includes details about each of their families. For example, Savannah's mother is on social security and receives food stamps. Her sister feels trapped in an unhealthy marriage because she cannot afford to leave her husband. Also, Robin's mother is overwhelmed from caring for Robin's father, who has Alzheimer's disease. The family struggles emotionally when they feel they have no choice but to send him to a nursing home for medical care.

The four women all experience significant life-changing events throughout the course of the novel. While showing their individual tribulations and successes, the novel also weaves their stories together to become a story about friendship between women. Susan Dodd's assessment in *Bookworld* (24 May 1992) captures the essence of the story: "*Waiting to Exhale* is less a book about life's hardships than lifetime friendships. The men may come and go—and they do. But through it all, these four vibrant and durable women are there for one another. It is a vision to cheer and console a reader yearning, as most of us are, for innuendoes of redemption in an era when hope suffers too many pratfalls." The women in *Waiting to Exhale* encourage each other, listen to each other, support each other, and even argue with each other. Relationships with men are still important to the women in *Waiting to Exhale,* but the women do not depend on men for self-fulfillment. As Janet Ellerby points out in a 1997 article, "McMillan draws vivid portraits of women who are successful at liberating themselves from the desire for the patriarchal family, replacing that delusional construct with African America patterns of communal interdependence."

McMillan's fifty-nine-year-old mother died of an asthma attack in 1994, and the following year McMillan's best friend died of cancer. She was unable to write after the trauma of these two events. Faced with writer's block, she visited Jamaica to try to overcome her grief; there she met Jonathan Plummer, a twenty-two-year-old resort worker. Although McMillan is twenty years older than Plummer, the two became lovers and eventually married in 1998.

McMillan's fourth novel, *How Stella Got Her Groove Back* (1996), is loosely based on her experience in Jamaica and the beginnings of her relationship with Plummer. Like the women in *Waiting to Exhale,* Stella has experienced difficulties with romantic relationships. When *How Stella Got Her Groove Back* opens, Stella has been divorced for almost three years and has given up hope for a meaningful marriage, but she wants to do something interesting during the two weeks her son will be visiting his father in Colorado. She contemplates how she can "put the fizz back into" her life. Stella admits with a tinge of guilt that she is relieved that her son is gone and that she has time for herself. She understands that she is tired from days spent carpooling and coping with the stress of her high-powered job. While contemplating how much stress she has experienced recently, she sees a television ad about visiting Jamaica. She asks herself why she should not go to Jamaica, and instead of looking for reasons and affirmations why she should do something, she decides she is unable to articulate a reason not to go.

The central plot of *How Stella Got Her Groove Back* concerns Stella's romance with Winston Shakespeare, whom she meets on her trip. The central conflict of Stella's newly found romance is the age difference: she is forty-two, and Winston is twenty-one. One of the reasons this fact becomes such an issue for Stella is because her age concerns her even before she meets Winston. At the beginning of the novel, she refers to her age repeatedly when she reassesses her life:

> I can't believe I'm really forty-fucking-two years old because people tell me all the time I don't look forty-two and to be honest I don't have any immediate plans of really acquiring the *look* if there is a way to look when you're forty-two and I certainly don't feel forty-two even though I don't know how I'm supposed to feel being forty-two and what I do know is that I'm not angry about being forty-two but it feels like I'm slowly but surely catching up to my mama because she was only forty-two when she died and I'm thinking how is this possible that I could ever be the same age as mama? I wonder if I could secretly be having a midlife crisis?

Eventually, she overcomes her doubts and can enjoy her relationship with Winston. When people question her about her younger boyfriend, she finally concludes, "Men have been dating younger women for fucking centuries and does anybody say anything to them?" The novel ends with Stella's decision to marry Winston.

Paralleling the theme of romantic relationships, *How Stella Got Her Groove Back,* like many of McMillan's works, explores the relationship between a mother and a child. Stella's son, Quincy, is eleven years old, and he sometimes assumes the parental role in his relationship with Stella. However, unlike the parent-child role reversal portrayed in *Mama,* the role reversal in *How Stella Got Her Groove Back* is comical. For example, Quincy leaves Stella and Winston alone so they can have privacy; he cautions Stella about safe sex; and he refuses her offer to cook eggs for breakfast because they are not healthy. *How Stella Got Her Groove Back* received mixed reviews. Some critics faulted the novel for its style, which presents stream-of-consciousness narration without regard to punctuation, and for its shallow themes. However, many reviewers praised the novel, primarily for its humor and for its portrayal of women from a feminist perspective that encourages empowerment of women.

McMillan's next novel, *A Day Late and a Dollar Short* (2001), features themes, subjects, and narrative techniques found in her earlier books. The novel portrays a variety of characters in a soap-opera manner: some of their predicaments are melodramatic, and frequently characters from one subplot relate to those in other subplots. Like *Waiting to Exhale* and *Disappearing Acts, A Day Late and a Dollar Short* is told from various first-person points of view.

Viola Price is the family matriarch in *A Day Late and a Dollar Short*. The novel opens with her summary of her life, including her role as a mother:

> Can't nobody tell me nothing I don't already know. At least when it comes to my kids. They all grown, but in a whole lotta ways they still act like children. I *know* I get on their nerves—but they get on mine too—and they always accusing me of meddling in their business, but hell, I'm their mother. It's my job to meddle. What I really do is worry. About all four of 'em. Out loud. If I didn't love 'em, I wouldn't care two cents about what they did or be the least bit concerned about what happens to 'em. But I do. Most of the time they can't see what they doing, so I just tell 'em what *I* see. They don't listen to me half the time no way, but as their mother, I've always felt if *I* don't point out the things they doing that seem to be causing 'em problems and pain, who will?

Viola is especially close to her oldest daughter, Paris. In one scene, shortly after Viola has been hospitalized for a severe asthma attack, Paris is lying in bed with her mother. Viola asks Paris to take responsibility for the family if something should happen to her, challenging her daughter to consider what she wants out of her own life.

The characters in *A Day Late and a Dollar Short* represent various lifestyles and different strata of society. As reviewer Greg Tate noted in the *Village Voice* (30 January 2001), "McMillan fires off rounds of mordant moral and social observation here that are damn near Whartonian in their dissection of African American manners and appearances." The characters range from those who succeed in opening their own businesses to child molesters and drug addicts. In the opening chapter, Viola humorously describes differences between her four children: "I had 'em so fast they felt more like a litter except each one turned out to be a different animal. Paris is a female lion who don't growl loud enough. Lewis is a horse who don't pull his own weight. Charlotte is definitely a bull, and Janelle would have to be a sheep—a lamb is closer to it—because she's always being led out to some pasture and don't know how she got there." Each of the children and some of the grandchildren are introduced in the first chapter; at the end, the novel comes full circle with letters Viola has written to them.

A Day Late and a Dollar Short is also about the aging process. The several generations represented in the novel provide insights about differences in ways people act and think at various life stages.

The characters in *A Day Late and a Dollar Short* support each other, but also experience conflicts with each other. However, McMillan suggests that the fact that they are related by blood helps them overcome all sorts of differences. As Viola says, "Friends come and go, but family is forever. . . . You don't have to like your kinfolk, but accept them—faults and all—because they're your flesh and blood." Even though at the end of the novel Viola is no longer alive to maintain the family unity, the family comes together at Thanksgiving to celebrate family ties.

Terry McMillan continues to intrigue readers with her characters, her plots, and her sense of humor. She writes daily, enjoys skiing, and spends time at her home near Lake Tahoe. Her novels have happy endings, and her characters, especially her women characters, triumph over sometimes incredible odds. As McMillan herself said in a 29 April 1996 *Newsweek* interview, "I don't write about victims. They just bore me to death. I prefer to write about somebody who can pick themselves back up and get on with their lives. Because all of us are victims to some extent." Her novels continue to inspire readers to set and achieve goals and to encourage women to defy roles prescribed for them by patriarchal societies.

Interviews:

Ray Sawhill, Allison Samuels, and Sherry Keene-Osborne, "How Terry Got Her Groove," *Newsweek* (29 April 1996): 76–79;

Maya Jaggi, "The Song of the Uncaged Birds," *Guardian UK*, 26 May 2001.

References:

Rita B. Dandridge, "Debunking the Beauty Myth in Terry McMillan's *Waiting to Exhale*," in *Language, Rhythm, and Sound: Black Popular Cultures into the Twenty-First Century*, edited by Joseph K. Adjaye and Adrianne R. Andrews (Pittsburgh: University of Pittsburgh Press, 1997), pp. 121–133;

Dandridge, "Debunking the Motherhood Myth in Terry McMillan's *Mama*," *CLA Journal*, 41, no. 4 (1998): 405–416;

Janet Ellerby, "Deposing the Man of the House: Terry McMillan Rewrites the Family," *MELUS*, 22 (1997): 105–117;

Tina M. Harris, "Interrogating the Representation of African American Female Identity in the Films *Waiting to Exhale* and *Set It Off*," *Popular Culture Review*, 10, no. 2 (1999): 43–53;

Harris and Patricia S. Hill, "*Waiting to Exhale* or 'Breath(ing) Again': A Search for Identity, Empowerment, and Love in the 1990's," *Women and Language*, 21, no. 2 (1998): 9–20;

Edward M. Jackson, "Images of Black Males in Terry McMillan's *Waiting to Exhale*," *MAWA Review*, 8, no. 1 (1993): 20–26;

Charles Whitaker, "Exhaling! Terry McMillan Hits Jackpot in Romance and Finance," *Ebony* (April 2001): 154–157.

Robert Morgan

(3 October 1944 –)

Cecelia Conway
Appalachian State University

See also the Morgan entry in *DLB 120: American Poets Since World War II.*

BOOKS: *Zirconia Poems* (Northwood Narrows, N.H.: Lillabulero, 1969);

The Voice in the Crosshairs (Ithaca, N.Y.: Angelfish Press, 1971);

Red Owl: Poems (New York: Norton, 1972);

Land Diving: New Poems (Baton Rouge: Louisiana State University Press, 1976);

Trunk & Thicket (Fort Collins, Colo.: L'Epervier Press, 1978);

Groundwork (Frankfort, Ky.: Gnomon Press, 1979);

Bronze Age (Emory, Va.: Iron Mountain Press, 1981);

At the Edge of the Orchard Country (Middletown, Conn.: Wesleyan University Press, 1987);

The Blue Valleys: A Collection of Stories (Atlanta: Peachtree, 1989);

Sigodlin: Poems (Middletown, Conn.: Wesleyan University Press, 1990);

Green River: New and Selected Poems (Middletown, Conn.: Wesleyan University Press, 1991);

The Mountains Won't Remember Us, and Other Stories (Atlanta: Peachtree, 1992);

Good Measure: Essays, Interviews, and Notes on Poetry (Baton Rouge: Louisiana State University Press, 1993);

The Hinterlands: A Mountain Tale in Three Parts (Chapel Hill, N.C.: Algonquin Books, 1994);

The Truest Pleasure (Chapel Hill, N.C.: Algonquin Books, 1995);

Wild Peavines: New Poems (Frankfort, Ky.: Gnomon Press, 1996);

Gap Creek: The Story of a Marriage (Chapel Hill, N.C.: Algonquin Books, 1999; London: Fourth Estate, 2000);

The Balm of Gilead Tree: New and Selected Stories (Frankfort, Ky.: Gnomon Press, 1999);

Topsoil Road: Poems (Baton Rouge: Louisiana State University Press, 2000);

This Rock: A Novel (Chapel Hill, N.C.: Algonquin Books, 2001);

Robert Morgan (photograph by David G. Spielman; from the dust jacket for Gap Creek: The Story of a Marriage, *1999; Richland County Public Library)*

Brave Enemies: A Novel of the American Revolution (Chapel Hill, N.C.: Algonquin Books, 2003);

The Strange Attractor: New and Selected Poems (Baton Rouge: Louisiana State University Press, 2004).

OTHER: "Landscape of the Blue Ridge," in *A Place Not Forgotten: Landscapes of the South from the Morris Museum of Art* (Lexington: University of Kentucky Art Museum, 1999);

"Nature Is a Stranger Yet," in *The Jordon Lectures, 1998–1999,* edited by Robert Denham (Salem, Va.:

Roanoke College, Department of English, 1999), pp. 27–42;

"Cormac McCarthy: The Novel Raised from the Dead," in *Sacred Violence*, volume 1: *Cormac McCarthy's Appalachian Works*, edited by Wade Hall and Rick Wallach (El Paso: Texas Western Press, 2002), pp. 9–22;

Leatha Kendrick and George Ella Lyon, eds., *Crossing Troublesome: Twenty-Five Years of the Appalachian Writers Workshop*, preface by Morgan (Nicholasville, Ky.: Wind Publications, 2002).

SELECTED PERIODICAL PUBLICATIONS– UNCOLLECTED:

FICTION

"Bishop's Tours," *Pembroke Magazine* (2000): 87–97;

"Church of the Ascension," *Pembroke Magazine* (Spring 2003).

NONFICTION

"Never Confuse a Fact with the Truth," *Mississippi Quarterly* (Winter 1992–1993): 115–120;

"Remembering William Stafford," *Christian Science Monitor*, 26 October 1993, p. 16;

"Work and Poetry, the Father Tongue," *Southern Review*, 31 (Winter 1995): 161–179;

"The Greatest Novel Ever Written," *Raleigh News & Observer*, 5 May 1996, pp. G1, G5;

"The Tribe of Tiger," *NCLR* (Summer 1996): 113–116;

"Note on Shovel," *Poetry East* (Fall 1996): 25–26;

"Clearing Newground: A Tribute to Jim Wayne Miller," *Appalachian Heritage* (Fall 1996): 5–7; expanded, *Appalachian Heritage* (Fall 1997): 24–30;

"Thomas Hart Benton and the Thresholds of Expression," *Southern Cultures*, 3, no. 2 (Spring 1997): 38–42;

"The Medicine Rock," *Algonkian* (Summer 1998): 36–37;

"Visions, Haints and Fever Wit," *Algonkian* (Summer 1999): 8–9;

"You Can't Get There From Here: Essay on Carl Sandburg," *Appalachian Journal*, 28 (Winter 2001): 222–226;

"A Noble and Dangerous Tradition," *Algonkian* (Fall 2001): 4–5;

"Writing the Living Voice: The Achievement of Lee Smith," *Pembroke Magazine*, 33 (2001): 182;

"Notes from Underground: Homer Hickam's Sky of Stone," *New York Times*, 21 October 2001, VII, p. 22;

"The Bill of Rights Belongs to North Carolina," *New York Times*, 22 August 2003, p. A23.

Raised in the mountains of North Carolina, Robert Morgan is an award-winning poet, critic, short-story writer, teacher, and novelist. Although he has spent more than thirty years at Cornell University, where he became Kappa Alpha Professor of Writing and American Literature, the wellspring of Morgan's art has remained his Green River homeplace. In *Kirkus Reviews* (1 September 1999) a critic identified him as "the poet laureate of Appalachia." In the 1999 lecture "Nature Is a Stranger Yet" Morgan describes writing as enabling him "to see the wilderness better" and to explore and dream wildernesses that he "would never otherwise know." He explores the values and fears of diverse people who choose to return or remain rooted to their mountain homeplace, create community and art, offer hospitality to strangers, and continue to survive despite harsh challenges. Morgan's writings offer overlooked, but viable, human approaches for dealing with modernist responsibilities amid fragmented cyberspaces and mallscapes in disconcerting millennial and multinational times.

Morgan considers his ability to listen his best talent as a writer; his dramatic storytelling, he explains at readings, is "voice-driven" fiction. His mountain characters become so vivid that he says he hears them speak the novels.

The Morgan family arrived from Wales in the eighteenth century, and Robert Ray Morgan grew up on a mountain homeplace where his ancestors cleared the forest in 1840 for new ground to farm. Born on 3 October 1944 to farmer Clyde R. and Fannie Levi Morgan, the writer was raised near Hendersonville, North Carolina. The family's knowledge of folklore, storytelling, and sacred traditions of the region offered him vital cultural resources. His mother worked in cotton mills and beauty shops but loved gardening and was familiar with flowers and herbs, medicinal roots and barks. His father recounted sometimes gruesome historical stories from the American Revolution and the Civil War, and he loved to read aloud and debate theology. His grandfather terrified Morgan and his sister, Evangeline, with bedtime tales of ghosts, snakes overtaking the hearth, and panthers chasing, capturing, and clawing early and recent settlers.

The arrival of the bookmobile when he was in the sixth grade allowed Morgan to start reading Jack London's novels and other frontier adventure stories of the far north. He soon turned to Charles Dickens, Leo Tolstoy, Fyodor Dostoevsky, William Faulkner, and Ernest Hemingway, as well as local mountain writers Thomas Wolfe and Carl Sandburg. Later that year, his class went to the Biltmore House, the improbable French chateau on the Vanderbilt estate in Asheville. Morgan did not have the $3 admission and remained

Dust jacket for Morgan's 1992 collection. In the title novella an elderly widow makes peace with the memory of her first love, who was killed in a plane crash during World War II (Richland County Public Library).

behind. His resourceful teacher did not want Morgan to waste the day and told him to write a story about a man lost in the wilderness. After an hour of thought, Morgan began to write the details of sharpening a stick for a spear.

Morgan left hard work on the one-horse family farm in the Blue Ridge Mountains to seek the intellectual life of the university. He originally planned to become an aeronautical engineer, but he transferred from North Carolina State University to the University of North Carolina at Chapel Hill, from which he graduated with a B.A. in English in 1965. He earned a master of fine arts degree at the University of North Carolina at Greensboro in 1968. In 1965 he married Nancy Bullock, with whom he has three children: Benjamin, Laurel, and Katie. Joining the faculty of Cornell University in 1971, Morgan became a modernist scholar of Ameri-

can literature as well as an accomplished poet and teacher of writing. Cornell initially hired Morgan to replace established poet A. R. Ammons for one year. That position evolved into a tenured Kappa Alpha Professorship and a distinguished career at Cornell. During his first twenty years as a poet, Morgan began to reflect upon the art of words in essays, interviews, and notes on poetry collected later in *Good Measure* (1993); this record of his thought provides an invaluable intellectual context for all of his writings.

The bedrock of Morgan's writing rests upon his insider mountain and outsider scholarly perspectives. Leaving home sharpened his view, but Morgan observes in "Nature Is a Stranger Yet" that he "continued to live" in his Carolina mountains in "the imagination, in the geography and landscape of language." He also maintains a farmer's work schedule by writing from 6:00 to 8:00 A.M. every day. His poetry explores everyday life in the Blue Ridge, and he says that his poems of the mountains often begin with a specific object or process described clearly and closely. In the early collections *Zirconia Poems* (1969), *The Voice in the Crosshairs* (1971), and *Red Owl* (1972), Morgan explores objects and entities from gems to owls. As he observes in *Good Measure,* these poems "seemed to be spoken against the silence of all eternity." Morgan recalls that he began to reconnect with childhood memories of how his "great aunts had spoken, and the smells of old houses heated by cooking stoves and fireplaces." He explains in an interview that, surrounded by writers at Cornell, he began to understand poetry as "voice" and conversation and to remember family and regional stories. By his fourth collection, *Land Diving* (1976), Morgan turns from crystalline imagist poems to a dramatic mode. The poems, as he says in *Good Measure,* "began to sound like someone talking on a given afternoon." Morgan begins to counterpoint his early examination of inspirations from nature with the hard work and endurance of mountain people conversationally presented.

Professor and poet William Harmon criticized the Robert Bly–like poems in *Zirconia Poems* but, like most others, he also praised the short early poems. In *The Virginia Quarterly Review* (1970) Sherer James said that Morgan's poems "place him in the vanguard of the fruitful revolution going on in American poetry today." By the time of *Red Owl,* first-person voice has disappeared from the poems, and most critics found Morgan's vision, methods, and eloquence well set by *Land Diving.* In the mid 1970s Morgan's interest in narrative poetry turned toward "Rhymed forms and balladic horror and compression." In *Groundwork* (1979), for example, "When the Ambulance Came" tells how that "day in Easter snow" the "driver cursed the torn / roads over the mountain / when he slammed the spattered door" on Grandma's "seventy years of staying home." By 1980, Morgan said, "My first principle of versification was, make something happen in every line." *Bronze Age* (1981) and *At the Edge of the Orchard Country* (1987) won praise from critics. Morgan's honors for poetry include National Endowment for the Arts Grants (1968, 1974, 1982, 1987); the Southern Poetry Review Prize (1975); the Eunice Tietjens Prize (1979); a New York Foundation for the Arts Fellowship (1986); the Hawthornden Castle Fellow in Poetry at the International Writers Retreat, Scotland (1986); and the Amon Liner Poetry Prize (1989).

As a recipient of Guggenheim and Bellagio Fellowships (1988–1989), Morgan applied his gifts as a poet and insights as a modernist intellectual to his fiction. In the collection *The Blue Valleys* (1989), ranging in setting from Civil War prison camps to trailer parks, Morgan's first stories maintain the narrative thrust, suspense, and compression of ballads. Based on family remembrance, "A Brightness, New and Welcoming" is characteristic of the collection. The story weaves themes of planting, harvest, and sustenance with suspense. The time shifts of a Civil War prisoner's feverish mind, from his gruesome, wounded present to memories of home, set the realistic, counterpoint pattern typical of Morgan's storytelling. Morgan introduces a mountain spring as a symbol of the homeplace that offers imaginative promise to the wounded soldier: "Spring water was touched by all the mineral wealth it had passed through, the gold and rubies, silver and emeralds in the deep veins. The water was a cold rainbow on the tongue." Remembrance transports the prisoner from his agonizing pain to soothing meditations upon the spring, intimacy in the laurels, and blooming sunflowers.

A critic in *Publishers Weekly* (31 March 1989) declared the collection "formidable," and a reviewer for *The New York Times* (10 December 1989) observed that "This beautifully crafted collection" is "rich with native detail and character, told in language as plain and deep as the hills . . . weighted with an awareness of death that looms over the struggle for a meaningful life." The story "A Brightness, New and Welcoming" won the *Jacaranda Review* Fiction Prize (1988), and the American Academy of Arts and Letters nominated *The Blue Valleys* for its First Fiction Award; the collection also received the North Carolina Award in literature in 1991.

With Morgan's next collections of poetry, *Sigodlin* (1990) and *Green River* (1991), Roger Jones observed in *Contemporary Authors* (1992) that beneath his "plainspoken colloquial diction" Morgan's poetry moves increasingly toward "musical, lyrical precision" and "vibrancy." In the *Southern Review* (Autumn 1992) Dara Wier noted of *Green River* that "individual poems maintain a steady,

staunch, evenhanded repose." Morgan received the James G. Hanes Poetry Prize from the Fellowship of Southern Writers in 1991.

In his second collection of stories, *The Mountains Won't Remember Us* (1992), Morgan addresses imagination's inspiration from nature and its grounding in the ritual of work, and he explores complex relationships between people. The stories clarify identity, offer cautions, and sometimes heal the teller. "Poinsett's Bridge" began Morgan's publishing relationship with Algonquin when it was selected for publication in their *New Stories from the South* in 1991. This initial story retains the suspense, narrative complexity, and explorations of the wilderness of earlier work but expands the storytelling and occupational folklore. The protagonist, an accomplished and self-reflective stonemason, speaks directly to his son to create a conversational style and an intimate tone. On the way home from constructing a new, handsome bridge, the mason is beset by two robbers. To calm himself, the craftsman's mind flashes between the present threat and memories of his accomplished work. The stonemason entrances himself with the ritual of hard work and how man crafts natural resources. Ultimately, the value of the construction is not the money earned but the craftsmanship gained and the story told. The mason's sacraments of stonework carefully crafted with his hammer are, rock by rock, not unlike the wordsmithing of the poet and storyteller.

Morgan's radical expansion and dramatic turn of voice appears in the title story that concludes the collection. "The Mountains Won't Remember Us" is Morgan's first novella told from a woman's point of view. Early on, Morgan had written a poem about his influential Uncle Robert, who died in a plane crash during World War II. After vast library research and oral histories with Air Corps crew members, Morgan felt "hung up on runways and flight plans" and decided to tell the story of Uncle Robert's fiancée. The ruminating female, Sharon, reflecting upon her early lost love, allows Morgan to move beyond his own voice into an intense counterpoint between her present fears and past delights and horrors. After a depressing first and a satisfying second marriage, the now elderly widow is dealing with a foot amputation and revisiting her romantic and tragic past. She confronts the specter of the lost Robert, now dead more than four decades. Sharon faces self-doubts and realistic fears and lets go of her loneliness.

At various readings, the author has spoken of writers as "actors" and the delight of leaving one's ego to explore another character's voice. Morgan has commented on the artistic discipline required to maintain a character's voice and the need to "erase oneself" to genuinely hear the voice of any character. This shift

*Dust jacket for Morgan's 1994 volume, a series of stories about
life on the North Carolina frontier between 1772 and 1845
(Richland County Public Library)*

becomes especially intense when crossing the gender
barrier. Morgan has said that the shift for this story was
so alarming and thrilling that he probably worked twice
as hard on it. He has observed also that women make
exceptional storytellers because they notice details—
from the design on the wallpaper to the gossip of a holiday party—and especially because, unlike many of his
male characters, women are willing to talk about their
relationships and feelings. These attributes allow Morgan to explore extensively the intimate communication
between a woman and a man.

Many considered this novella his best fiction at
the time. In the *Atlanta Journal-Constitution* one critic
commented that Morgan "writes with beauty and precision" and offers "much to ponder." Another reviewer
for *The Asheville Citizen-Times* said the stories of the collection "sweetly sing of the universal range of human
emotion, from love to hate, doubts to perseverance,"
and observed that Morgan "has chiseled and sweated
out hard-won stories that won't be readily forgotten." A
reviewer for *Publishers Weekly* (27 April 1992) said "Mor-

gan brings authority to . . . varied periods" and gives
characters "spontaneity and depth."

The Hinterlands: A Mountain Tale in Three Parts
(1994) serves as a transition between Morgan's collections of short stories and his novels. Set from 1772 to
1845 and told by three generations of speakers who settle near Green River, North Carolina, the tales of this
cycle dramatize frontier adventure. Their local history
illustrates the sweep of national settlement. The tales
have traditional roots in nature lore, family and
regional legends, ballads, tall tales, and ghost stories. In
Booklist (1 September 1995) Theresa Duncan described
The Hinterlands as "a richly textured family saga" that
"forebodes . . . the ecological changes that civilization
has brought to our wilderness."

Petal's 1772 tale, "The Trace," introduces themes
of the romance of the frontier wilderness and of love, as
Petal tells her grandchildren about her life with her husband. In the second tale, Solomon recounts the hilarious, true story of blazing "The Road" in 1816. To
mark the best passable road, he uses the folk wisdom of
grabbing the tail of a hungry pig headed for home. In
the third tale, "The Turnpike," after helping build the
road in 1845, Richards tells of being chased home by
Old Trifoot the Panther and flinging off his clothes to
distract the mountain lion.

Without the humorous distance maintained by
the two male narrators in their tall tales, Petal earnestly
discusses the personal challenges of romance, introduced by earlier female narrators. She faces the realities
of women's work, including the consequences of
romance—childbirth. Petal explains that she tells this
tale of her marriage so that her grandchildren will
remember it after she is gone: "Your Grandpa's gone
and he can't tell you. He always had trouble speaking
his affections anyway, though he could charm anybody
in a friendly way." Faltering communication provides
the main obstacle to intimacy. Grandpa has red-faced
sensitivity but little voice; he is often inaudible. Many
of Morgan's complex men are competent and skillful
on the frontier but typically shy and personally inarticulate as they struggle to find voice.

Grandpa tricks Petal about where they have settled, and he keeps the secret for years because he is
afraid she will leave him. To make amends, he offers
her a witch-hazel branch, the last bloom of winter; with
this gift, Grandpa is able to move beyond silence and
express his affections and desire for forgiveness, without words. Petal eventually seeks reconnection with
Grandpa after his betrayal of silence: "Now a touch
speaks far beyond any words, children. A touch is a little thing, but at the right time it's like a current pours
through. People ain't whole unless they're connected,
and a touch is the first and true sign of that connec-

tion." The connection of touch prefigures the theme of sensuality in later novels as crucial communication between people. Couples often survive the extensive external crises they encounter and internal crises they create when they connect physically and emotionally through work and sexuality.

Critics generally praised this cycle of tales. In *The New York Times* (24 July 1994) Thomas H. Cook observed the "intensely stoical philosophy," and the "fortitude and self-reliance" of the characters. Novelist Lee Smith called the book "Required reading for anyone who would know what it was to be a pioneer. Robert Morgan's lyric mountain language is equal to the epic sweep of history, to the grandeur of the land itself."

While he was writing these regional tales with increasing confidence and skill, Morgan was also working on the novel *The Truest Pleasure* (1995), in which he again writes convincingly and eloquently from a woman's point of view. Inspired by the lives of his paternal grandparents, the novel extends the family saga introduced in earlier short stories and tales. Morgan explores intimate communication, refines his storytelling, and incorporates laconic dialogue with traditional ballads, tales, and sacred songs intended to be heard aloud. Before the final revisions in 1992 and 1993, Morgan wrote third-person drafts filled with extensive dialect, but he eventually discarded them. Following Eudora Welty's lead, he settles upon distinctive phrases and syntax to create hallmarks of regional speech.

In this novel, for the first time in his fiction, Morgan tackles the subject of the religious enthusiasms that surrounded his upbringing. Morgan remembers being afraid of his Pentecostal father and "others speaking in tongues, shouting, and . . . being especially terrified of the phrase 'baptism of fire.'" The protagonist, Virginia "Ginny" Peace Powell, speaks in tongues, but her religious ecstasy does not always provide solace—especially in her marriage.

Morgan has said at readings that he relished being able to return, from his acquired King's English, to the academically forbidden mountain speech of his boyhood. He adds that once he began to hear Ginny's voice, the novel came alive and began to take shape. The voice of devout, well-read Ginny echoes the lush and pristine poetry of the speech of the King James Version of the New Testament, which Morgan read daily as a child, and of Ralph Waldo Emerson, whose every sentence the novelist considers "a work of art in itself." In contrast to his clean, precise, personal style, Morgan creates the voice of Ginny with eloquent and expansive flourishes.

Morgan approaches his subject not with ironic distance or disdain but as an insider, and the sacred tra-

ditions of his childhood provide rich resources. The novel begins with the motherless Ginny attending a Pentecostal or Holiness brush-arbor meeting with her father; Morgan provides one of the few sympathetic and realistic descriptions of Holiness religion in American fiction. Filled with folksinging and the "white hot" language of preaching and prayer, the service begins with the hymn "Revive Us Again." Enchanted with words, Ginny feels the outpouring of spirit for the first time and cherishes the expressiveness of the meeting. The preacher says, "Through you has flowed the sweet honey from the rock and in your mouth is the light of stars." Glossolalia, or speaking in tongues, is believed language incarnate; it also becomes a symbol for poetry—for understandable imagination and spirit incarnate.

Walking to the spring after church and sitting by the river on Sunset Rock during "the minute . . . when the sky shone side to side," and then watching the fireworks of falling meteors, Ginny falls in love with Tom Powell, who is the son of the prisoner in "A Brightness, New and Welcoming." The connections between family members and generations weave Morgan's poems, stories, and novels into an intricate tapestry. He creates an epic saga of the community on Green River and of their extended families back to the wilderness and the Cherokees.

Tom and Ginny have a practical marriage. Ginny understands even as they court that "Tom didn't have any land. It made sense that he would fall in love with the land as much as with" her. Tom works hard to put her father's homestead back in shape, and he brings in extra cash with molasses, firewood, and produce from folks who work in the new mill. Tom and Ginny work well together, have children, and often enjoy a satisfying love life.

Morgan directly faces the readers' potential resistance to the Pentecostal subject matter by making religion the central conflict of Ginny's marriage. Tom is Baptist and Ginny is Pentecostal, and both are stubborn. Ginny finds the expressiveness of brush-arbor Holiness religion a blessing, but Tom, raised too poor to attend school long enough to read well, considers the camp meetings a frenzied embarrassment. Ginny's brother Locke describes the generational parallels: "I guess what Mama feared most" about their father's religion and "what Tom fears most is loss of control and reason. If somebody that close to them can lose their willpower and dignity then they might also." Tom believes people "have no business working themselves up crazy" at services.

Work and lovemaking are the main ways that the couple reach around the extended withdrawals and silences that arise from their conflicts. Ginny says,

"That's when I feel the best when I don't even think about myself but about what needs to be done." As with the stonemason, the ritual of work stabilizes her identity and Tom's. Work also helps Ginny heal after the loss of their third baby and helps her reconnect with Tom: "If you have a cold or feel like you're taking sick sometimes a good sweat will heal you. As I worked in the dirt by Tom I felt I was being cleansed from inside." Morgan is sensitive to women who do not distance or sever the world of spirituality from sensuality. Ginny also thinks, "as we loved, I felt I was right, and in the right place, even as I did at the revival services. And I thought how the thrill of loving was almost the same as communion with the Spirit and the thrill of solitude by the river, but I didn't understand how it could be. It was a mystery." With these thoughts, Ginny connects major sources of reassurance in Morgan's fiction–nature, intimacy with another, and spirit.

More fully than the members of her family, readers become the trusted listeners to Ginny's intimate story. Near the end of this novel of incomplete conversations, when Tom faces a life-threatening illness, Ginny says, "Suddenly I saw all the things I had hated about Tom I could just as well have loved. Maybe that was me seeing through other eyes." In a cigar box, Ginny finds Tom's treasures, which include more than his yearned-for and hard-earned gold pieces. Just as Tom had never told her of "the faded bone button from his Papa's Civil War uniform" or showed her the faded newspaper clipping announcing their marriage on Green River, so Ginny now regrets her own silences: "saddest of all was that I could never . . . thank him, or tell him that I loved him. I wanted to say we accepted his gifts." From potential loss, she learns understanding of another.

The first runner-up for the Southern Book Critics Circle Award and a *New York Times* Notable Book, *The Truest Pleasure* is a favorite of Morgan's mother, and many critics consider it the author's best novel to date. Richard Bausch, in *The New York Times Book Review* (29 October 1995), called it "Marvelously vivid . . . a quietly audacious book." Jeff Mason, in *The Boston Book Review* (October 1995), said that Morgan writes "with an authority usually associated with the great novelists of the last century" and added, "this book is astonishing." Karen Angel for *The Washington Post Book World* (4 February 1996) commented, "Morgan's simple eloquent language grounds the story in a tough farm life, yet his language pulses with poetry." In the *News and Record* (26 September 1999) Merritt Moseley found the Pentecostal Ginny "credible, interesting, and sympathetic" and thus perhaps Morgan's "greatest achievement." He added that Morgan's "skill with language is at the heart" of the novel.

Like Ginny Powell and many Appalachian women, Julie Harmon, the protagonist of Morgan's 1999 novel, *Gap Creek: The Story of a Marriage,* is hardworking and competent. She feeds the stock, carries water from the spring, gathers and splits the wood. Where Ginny turns to religion, Julie turns more to the ritual of work. Julie's mother defines mountain community by explaining why the girl must do difficult chores: "Because you're the strongest one in the family. . . . And because everybody has to do what they can." Julie realistically frets, "Mama always did know how to make me ashamed when I tried to get out of a job," but the girl understands survival. She serves the family, and she steadies and expresses herself through work.

Though not well-read, poetic, or confident like Ginny, Julie narrates the novel. Morgan explains at readings that like an actor who has played the same role for a long time, he found it hard at first to make room for any voice but Ginny's. Once he realized that Julie's reluctance to speak was part of the character and heard her stripped-down mountain voice, however, the novel wrote itself quickly.

Julie begins the story with a testament to experience: "I know about Masenier because I was there. I seen him die. . . . It was too awful to describe to other people. But I was there, even though I didn't want to be." In a feverish, prophetic dream, her stricken little brother, Masenier, hollers out, "There is snakes dancing!" Carrying him from the doctor's house four miles back up the wooded moonlit mountain, Julie "thought he was throwing up milk or some white gravy. But what come out of his mouth was gobs of squirming things. They was worms, wads and wads of white worms." Science and the doctor's sweet syrup have not saved the boy but drawn the worms into his throat, so that he choked to death.

Masenier's death is the first of an awful chain of disasters that has led North Carolina poet laureate Fred Chappell to say to Morgan the novel should be called "Job Had It Easy." About the crises and graphic details, critic Dwight Garner wrote in *The New York Times Book Review* (10 October 1999) that "the sense of doom can be overwhelming" and that, as with the work of Cormac McCarthy or Harry Crews, the reader can "begin to feel . . . that the author has been typing with blood on his hands and some of it has rubbed off onto your shirtsleeves."

Like Ginny, Julie sometimes finds reassurance in nature and sexual intimacy, but her marriage separates her from her family. Julie falls in love with the handsome, good-humored, bold banjo player Hank Richards. As he says, he likes to sing, "Better than I like to eat peaches." Hank takes Julie down the mountain to Gap Creek, South Carolina, and into the strangeness of marriage. He thinks that Gap Creek is pretty and that his work building the new mill will also help him to escape his mother. Julie thinks he is "wise and on his way to riches," but she soon faces hog killing, humoring their crotchety landlord, a deadly fire, con artists, a flood, and the alarming arrival of Hank's Ma Richards. Hank loses his job, and the couple loses their first baby not long after Julie gives birth alone. Author and critic Donald Seacrest observes that perhaps the greatest strength of the book is Julie's "growth from maidenhood to womanhood, from hardworking child to wise wife."

After a horrendous year in Gap Creek, the couple returns home to the North Carolina mountains. They have endured silences and fractured intimacy, but both characters have grown. Julie has learned to understand Hank and how her strengths complement his. Her expression and connection to others by service and rituals of work now also includes inspiration from the land and intimacy with her love. Though often stymied, Hank has learned to calm a contentious alcoholic neighbor and sometimes has spoken his feelings, cared for their endangered baby, and now playfully teases Julie. Pregnant with the promise of spring and a new baby, the couple journeys up the mountain.

In 2000 *Gap Creek* received the Southern Book Critics Circle Award; it was selected a Book of the Year by the Association of Appalachian Writers and a Notable Book by *The New York Times;* it was featured in Oprah Winfrey's book club; and it became a *New York Times* best-seller. Stewart O'Nan described the novel as "intimate and eternal," and in the *Charlotte Sun Herald,* Polly Paddock Gossett called it "Pure as a mountain stream, haunting as a mountain melody." Garner observed that Morgan's "plain people stubbornly refuse to become archetypes" and that Morgan is "among the relatively few American writers who write about work knowledgeably, and as if it really matters." Seacrest observed that Morgan's dominant theme is "the glow of the human spirit against the indifferent grandeur of nature and the indecipherable tribulations of religion." He noted that Morgan uses economical and precise images that move from sensory perception to emotion to create his complex, changing characters.

While a few critics do not appreciate Morgan's fascination with details, most remark on the contribution of details to character and theme. Garner said that "in Morgan's hands . . . details become the stuff of stern, gripping drama." Others compare his work to that of Crews, McCarthy, Larry McMurtry, or Charles Frazier. A critic from the *Baltimore Sun* compared Morgan's writing to "the same . . . clear, clean prose and often disturbing imagery" of James Dickey.

Dust jacket for Morgan's 1995 novel, about the religious conflicts of an otherwise happily married mountain couple (Richland County Public Library)

When Winfrey invited Morgan to appear on her television show, the author, who does not watch television, thought *Gap Creek* might sell another twenty thousand copies. Within the week Algonquin shipped five hundred thousand books. More than two million have been sold, and the novel has been translated into foreign languages. The success of Morgan's novel, along with the National Book Award–winning *Cold Mountain* (1997) and the Grammy Awards for the soundtrack of *O Brother, Where Art Thou?* (2000), has made popular critics notice what some have analyzed for almost three decades—that the diversity of Appalachia is a lightning rod and wellspring of American culture.

Morgan continued to develop his short fiction with *The Balm of Gilead Tree: New and Selected Stories* (1999) and his poetry with *Topsoil Road* (2000). Arranged chronologically, the stories in *The Balm of Gilead Tree* explore the self and the unfamiliar other, mostly in first-person narratives. They begin with the sixteenth-century Cherokee Purple Grass in "The Tracks of Chief de Sota" and range into the 1960s with "A Taxpayer & A Citizen." In *Publishers Weekly* (13 September 1999) Sybil Steinberg observed that "Morgan displays an impressive command of American history and of language." The title story won a 1997 O. Henry Award. The first section of *Topsoil Road* follows history from the Cherokees living on the land to the settlement of the poet's Welsh forebears; the second part depicts eloquently the intricacies and processes of nature and man's hand upon them. One critic in *The Virginia Quarterly Review* (Autumn 2001) wondered if some poems have "an excess of craft," but he observed that the best, like "Grain of Sound," "begin with the timbre of hickory and poplar, and end opening out into a vaster territory of vein, and singing blood, and bone." Filled with lyrical vibrancy, the poems of *Topsoil Road,* as the critics and sales figures attest, are among Morgan's most melodic and luminous.

Until his 2001 novel, *This Rock,* Morgan avoided the stereotyped subject of moonshining. In "A Noble and Dangerous Tradition" for the *Algonkian* (2001), the author discusses liquor making and his extended family connections with the trade: "There were no poets in my ancestry but many artists of the still." Long "relishing the metaphor of making," Morgan emphasizes his companionship with distilling: "As I began in the art of words, I enjoyed the striving for the luminous phrase, the living sentence." With this novel, a sequel to *The Truest Pleasure,* Morgan brings together several narrators and previous themes.

The book is divided into "Readings" (1921, 1922, and 1923). In a prologue, the compelling, steadying voice of widowed Ginny Powell identifies the talents and weaknesses of her two sons, as different as Cain and Abel. Muir was "the buildingest boy you ever saw," but from the first "log cabin, like Daniel Boone made," Muir's "worst enemy . . . was his own lack of patience. The backyard was littered with things he had started and abandoned." His jealous and irreverent brother, Moody, seems the worst enemy when he sets fire to Muir's carefully constructed cabin. As they grow older, Muir continues to struggle with Moody, whose angry manner covers a soulful voice heard in two letters. As these fatherless young men try to move beyond silence, a matured Hank Richards returns from Gap Creek to mentor Muir.

For the first time, Morgan turns most of the novel over to a male protagonist. Muir pursues two goals: to preach and to someday marry fourteen-year-old Annie Richards. Muir's obsession with his destiny dominates the novel. Preaching will require this shy boy, born "so tongue-tied he couldn't even cry," to search for a voice publicly as well as privately. Muir gets permission to preach a sermon on "mountainism"—"to say any mountain could be a holy mountain." With childhood longing, he understands "the desire to build something

sacred" and has "studied about building almost as much as about trapping and preaching." Muir is skilled at building and trapping, and the planned sermon is good; but Muir freezes and makes a mess of the preaching. Then he makes a mess of trapping by spraining his ankle. Hank, Annie's father, carries the hurt boy home and tries to ease Muir's embarrassment over the preaching disaster.

Muir thinks intimacy might help: "Only walking with Annie would help me redeem myself." On the way home from church, Muir finally gives Annie a first "spicey" kiss. Immediately Moody, who earlier punctuated Muir's unwieldy preaching with a fart, again thwarts his brother. Moody sweeps Annie off for a ride in the Model T and soon entangles the family in more serious troubles. While Muir stumbles through the wilderness of the Lord and the backwoods, sixteen-year-old Moody has been running liquor. He works out of Peg Early's tavern full of girls and gamblers in Dark Corner. When he turns up missing, Ginny and her nephew, the storekeeper, find Moody and a young tavern girl lying near a spring. For "cutting the liquor" with water, each has been busted and beaten by Peg herself. Ginny takes Moody home and offers to take his girl, but the girl returns to Peg's. When Moody refuses to let Ginny wash him and clean the bloody knife wound in his groin, she is reminded of a mother's limits: she can raise a boy to be a person but not to be a man.

The novel focuses increasingly on Muir and on themes of parenting, brotherly conflict, and Muir's search for destiny—his desire to build something sacred to benefit the community. Like his mother, Muir is well read. While recovering from the sprained ankle, he finds his grandfather's copy of Henry Adams's *Mont-Saint-Michel and Chartres* (1904) and grows mesmerized by talk about "cathedrals 'flinging stones against the sky.'" In the 1922 "Reading," after a scrape with the law over Moody's moonshining, Muir sets out to seek his fortune. Filled with doubts, he journeys north until he meets gangsters and then goes trapping down east in North Carolina on the Tar River until he nearly drowns. Finally home and envisioning himself excruciatingly trapped on Green River, Muir gets drunk on Moody's liquor for the first time. Instead of falling into disaster or a brawl, he revises the moonshining stereotype by having a sacred vision. Ever improbable, he starts to build a church by hauling huge rocks from the river up to the mountaintop.

Eventually, Muir must preach his first real sermon, at a funeral in the unfinished mountain church. He offers comfort and says that the departed "is gone beyond the wall of time. He is gone beyond the sky. But in our sadness we are more alive than ever before."

Echoing Ginny's beliefs and words from the end of the first "Reading," Muir says, "The loved dead are with us at our moments of greatest happiness, and they are with us in our days of greatest sorrow. They will not desert us as we step forward in our lives." With the next line, "The dead loved ones give dignity and weight to our confused lives," Muir finds his own voice. This passage on loss and "the loved dead," who remain with those bereaved, became a comfort to widespread audiences during national book-tour readings after the 11 September 2001 terrorist attacks.

Finally Morgan returns to the theme of all of his writing—the vibrant art of words. As Muir preaches, he realizes, "I had spent my whole life preparing for this moment. . . . As I talked I seen I was building an altar of words in the air. I was building a church of words a sentence at a time. It was slow humble work, like digging a grave or a foundation."

In *The New York Times* (14 October 2001) Katherine Whittemore, who still "hasn't shaken" the opening death scene of "the harrowing" *Gap Creek,* declared the prologue of *This Rock* "hellbent and excellent," and says that "no one writes with more rough, intuitive grace about tending crops and tending animals (Cain's and Abel's callings)." She concluded that the novel is "resonant" and "moving" and that readers will be "amply rewarded" by Morgan's "intensely anthropological prose," from which they learn such details as the word "sigodlin," which means "out of place" or "confused," and the fact that "molasses scum 'looks both green and purple and shines like it was boiling metal.'"

Morgan's next novel, *Brave Enemies* (2003), begins on 17 January 1781, during the turning point of the American Revolution, in a wooded pasture on the northern border of South Carolina at the horrendous Battle of Cowpens. In *The New York Times Book Review* (9 November 2003) critic Will Blythe noted Morgan's "command of the details of daily life in the past" and said he "writes terrifically well of battle, portraying the tactics, equipment and close-range terror of eighteenth-century fighting." As the novel opens, the patriot narrator is seriously wounded and talking wildly. The novel is structured with a memory loop, and when readers return, near the end of the novel, to the climactic battle, the remembering or rereading of the prologue reveals subtle foreshadowing and intentional ambiguity.

After the prologue, the novel immediately personalizes history by introducing vibrant, sixteen-year-old Josie Summers, who lives in a cabin on the frontier north of Charlotte. Josie's stepfather, a Tory sympathizer, stomps on terrapins and says, "Let that be a lesson, Josie. . . . Can't nothing hide in this world." During any disagreements, Josie's mother also "pulled herself

Dust jacket for Morgan's critically praised and commercially successful novel about a mountain girl who matures through a series of disasters (Richland County Public Library)

into a shell just like a terrapin. She hunkered down in a corner and wouldn't say a thing." Like Morgan's best mountain women, Josie is hardworking and competent—even when she has to "scoop up the bloody pieces" of the stepfather's terrapin mess. She is also curious, bold, and a quick learner, but she cannot hide from this man or the war. Outside in the mud near the hog pen, the stepfather rapes her. She finally escapes to her mother for protection, but this woman, whose mind is fading, accuses Josie of being a "hussy." Unlike Morgan's former heroines, Josie cuts her hair and runs away from the domestic sphere; she dresses like a boy and calls herself Joseph to avoid the dangers of traveling alone as she adventures into the world of men—at war.

Brave Enemies is narrated primarily by Josie with a clear, straightforward voice, but later a compelling young man adds counterpoint. After crossing the

Catawba River, hungry and lost in the snow, Josie takes refuge in a small church, where the well-educated John Trethman of Virginia is an itinerant preacher. In the wilderness, where patrols and sometimes neighbors are taking revenge on opposing sympathizers by burning homes and hanging families, he preaches forgiveness. Trethman is an avowed nonpartisan, but both the Crown and patriots suspect him of being a spy. Glad for company, he takes Joseph back to his cabin to be an assistant. Amid the brutality of colonial and English terrorists, John and Joseph offer moments of peace and relief to various wilderness congregations.

John's narrative begins, "I always loved to watch clouds." He is a good singer, and his flute, "soft as the voice of a little stream," seems "to answer the splash of the branch and the chirp of crickets." Joseph is also a good singer and makes hoecakes, and John asks Joseph to read eloquent passages of Scripture aloud each day. They develop a soulful friendship. When John sees the Northern Lights one night and tries to wake Joseph to see them, John feels her breast and discovers that Joseph is Josie. In shock, the man spends a night wandering in the woods, worried and furious that his congregations will think he has intentionally misled them. But he cherishes his companion. Not trusting himself to speak to Josie, he writes a letter that expresses his guilt-ridden fears but also acknowledges that he loves Josie. He finally marries her, serving as both reverend and groom, and together they achieve sustained emotional and sexual intimacy, but they maintain her disguise to avoid explanations.

Soon the British, "who think neutrality is an act of treason," seize John to minister to the wounded and bury the dead in Colonel Banastre Tarleton's cavalry. Morgan portrays the brutal Tarleton as an avid chess player who is smart, cruel, and dangerous but also personable and sometimes considerate or respectful to John. Searching for her husband and still disguised as Joseph, although she is now pregnant, Josie joins the local rebel militia to avoid being hanged as a traitor. For the last third of the novel, both pacifists reconverge unawares, on opposing sides, at the Battle of Cowpens. Josie says, "I wanted to do my part, but I didn't want to kill anybody." But she is on the patriot front line, scrutinized and bullied by a sergeant who has learned her secret and attempts to force his sexual advances upon her.

Soon readers realize they have arrived at the events that introduced the novel and that the feverish patriot who calls out "Where's Mama?" and "Is my baby all right?" is Josie. Carried in a wagon, the seriously injured Josie hears the voice of John as he preaches a funeral. The battered couple have survived being placed as brave enemies and learned more of their capacity for human failing and dignity. In the fierce struggle to build a new homeland of freedom, Josie and John connect intimately and carry songs and words of forgiveness to the fearful settlers and to each other.

This novel is the author's most intricate weave of history, folklore, and love story. In a letter to Algonquin, author Reynolds Price wrote that "One of the rarest of Robert Morgan's many gifts is his ability to embody the minds and voices of strong women," and that Josie "is Morgan's richest yet, and her story is steadily compelling." In the *Christian Science Monitor* (2 December 2003) book editor Ron Charles said readers "are unlikely to take their eyes off the page–or even take a breath" during this "relentlessly exciting story." In the *Washington Post* (16 November 2003) reviewer Noel Perrin wrote that Morgan is "a very good writer" and often creates "outrageous," sometimes shuddering "tall tales" and still has "the reader coming back for more." In a starred review, the critic for *Publishers Weekly* (2003) said Morgan "delivers a rousing and affecting tale of the American Revolution" and a "gripping story of love and desperation."

In his novels, Robert Morgan shows readers the inspiration of a mountain spring, the ritual of stonework, the resonances of storytelling, the connection of intimacy to glossolalia and to homemaking, and the communion of prayers and preaching in alarming times. Morgan's fictional landscape is a Blue Ridge Mountain epic and cultural history.

Interviews:

David L. Elliot, "An Interview with Robert Morgan," *Chattahoochee Review,* 13 (Winter 1993): 78–97;

Tal Stanley, "Robert Morgan," *Appalachian Journal* (Spring 1996): 276–292;

Robert West, "The Art of Far and Near: An Interview with Robert Morgan," *Carolina Quarterly,* 49 (Summer 1997): 46–68;

Cecelia Conway, "Readings and Conversations on Video," Cane Creek & ASU (Fall 2000);

John Doherty, "Homes and Haunts: Robert Morgan: Speaking on His Life and Work to ASU Librarians," Belk Library (Fall 2000);

Peter Josphy, "Getting the Voices Right: A Conversation with Robert Morgan about the Gardener's Son," *Southern Quarterly,* 40 (Fall 2001): 121–131;

"Jimmy Carter and Robert Morgan Revisit the Revolution," *Book* (November/December 2003): 49–52.

Bibliographies:

Stuart Wright, "Robert Morgan: A Bibliographical Chronicle, 1963–1981," *Bulletin of Bibliography,* 39 (September 1982): 121–131;

"Cornell Writers: Robert Morgan," <http://www. writers.cornell.edu/morgan.html#Bibliographies>.

References:

David Baker, "*Topsoil Road,*" *Poetry,* 181 (February 2003): 285–298;

Suzanne Booker-Canfield, "Robert Morgan and the American Romantic Tradition," dissertation, University of North Carolina at Greensboro, 1998;

Fred Chappell, "Double Language: Three Appalachian Poets," *Appalachian Journal,* 8 (1980): 55–59;

Cecelia Conway, "Robert Morgan's Mountain Voice and Lucid Prose," *Appalachian Journal,* 29 (Fall 2001/Winter 2002): 180–198;

Conway, "Robert Morgan's *The Truest Pleasure,*" *Appalachian Journal,* 27 (Spring 2000): 214–217;

Thomas Dilworth, "Morgan's 'Mountain Graveyard,'" *Explicator,* 4 (Summer 1999): 248–249;

William Harmon, "Robert Morgan's Pelagian Georgics: Twelve Essays," *Parnassus,* 9 (Fall/Winter 1981): 5–30;

Gina Herring, "Climbing Paradox Mountain: The Stories of Robert Morgan," *Appalachian Journal,* 27 (Spring 2000): 260–271;

Iron Mountain Review, special Morgan issue, 6 (Spring 1990);

John Lang, "'He Hoes Forever': Robert Morgan and the Pleasures of Work," *Pembroke Magazine,* 31 (1999): 221–227;

William Matthews, "Land Diving," *Meridian,* 1 (1980): 8–10;

Jim Wayne Miller, "Groundwork," *McGill Literary Annual* (1981): 388–390;

Rita Sims Quillen, "Robert Morgan," in *Looking for Native Ground: Contemporary Appalachian Poetry* (Boone, N.C.: Appalachian Consortium Press, 1989), pp. 50–62;

Robert Morgan: Official Author Web Site, <http://www.people.cornell.edu/pages/rrm4/index.htm>;

Robert Schultz, "Recovering Pieces of the Morgenland," *Virginia Quarterly Review,* 64 (Winter 1988): 176–188;

Donald Seacrest, "The Gap in the Circuit," *World & I,* 15 (July 2000): 232–240.

Papers:

Collections of Robert Morgan's papers are housed at Emory University in Atlanta, Georgia, and the University of North Carolina at Chapel Hill.

Mary McGarry Morris

(10 February 1943 –   )

Roxanne Harde
Queen's University

BOOKS: *Vanished* (New York: Viking, 1988; Harmondsworth, U.K.: Penguin, 1990);

A Dangerous Woman (New York: Viking, 1991; London: Macmillan, 1991);

Songs in Ordinary Time (New York: Viking, 1995; London: Fourth Estate, 1995);

Fiona Range (New York: Viking, 2000; London: Fourth Estate, 2000);

A Hole in the Universe (New York: Viking, 2004).

SELECTED PERIODICAL PUBLICATIONS–
UNCOLLECTED: "Some Small Requiem," *Northeast* (September 1989);

"Bingo," *Story* (Winter 1990);

"No Other Death," *Santa Monica Review* (Spring 1991);

"The Perfect Tenant," *Glimmer Train,* 1 (1991): 7–25;

"A Man of Substance," *Ploughshares,* 19 (Fall 1993): 105–117;

"My Father's Boat," *Glimmer Train,* 9 (1993): 43–60.

Mary McGarry Morris (photograph by Melissa Morris Danisch; from the dust jacket for Fiona Range, *2000; Richland County Public Library)*

Since the 1988 publication of her first novel, Mary McGarry Morris has earned critical praise for the quality of her writing, along with mixed criticism of its content. Her novels have gained increasing popular attention, with respectable sales for each hardcover edition and subsequent paperback. When Oprah Winfrey selected *Songs in Ordinary Time* (1995) for her book club, the resulting paperback sales exceeded one million copies. A former caseworker, Morris writes fiction notable for its examination of the essences of human behavior, the needs and desires that motivate men and women, and the ways in which people respond to their circumstances and to the consequences of their own actions. Her prose is remarkable for the subtlety with which she draws her characters. Even as critics note her lapses into melodrama and contrivance, they appreciate the ways in which her sometimes extraordinary plots startle the reader into awareness of the characters' circumstances.

Mary Joan McGarry was born in Meriden, Connecticut, on 10 February 1943, to John C. McGarry and Margaret Coursey McGarry, who separated when Mary was young. The oldest of four children and the only girl, Mary grew up in Rutland, Vermont. Her mother held factory and clerical jobs as she raised her family, then ran a restaurant with her second husband, Vincent Chiriaco, until they retired. Morris attended the University of Vermont (1960–1962) and the University of Massachusetts (1962–1963). Married to lawyer Michael W. Morris since 1961, she has five adult children: Mary Margaret, Sarah, Melissa, Michael Jr., and Amy. The Morrises live in Andover, Massachusetts, in a rambling old house that was once a girls' dormitory for Abbot Academy and is somewhat similar to the Birds' home depicted in her first novel, *Vanished* (1988). From 1980 to 1986, Morris worked for the Massachusetts Department of Public Welfare, and while she had always written creatively, employment as a caseworker provided her with narratives that she felt compelled to tell. Her work for the Department of Public Welfare led directly to *Vanished* and then to her career as a writer of fiction.

Morris combines subtly drawn characterization with surprising and grittily realistic plots. While she usually narrates her stories with an omniscient voice, Morris aligns her audience's perspective with that of one particular character. The reader learns about key characters both through careful layers of descriptions and through dialogue as they react to and interact with other characters. Morris's characters are complicated and disquieting. *A Dangerous Woman* (1991) begins and ends with title character Martha Horgan, a woman who "made people nervous because they made her nervous, and on the rare occasion when she met someone she liked, her attention was so rapt as to be frightening." Morris draws Martha in such a way that she definitively engages the reader's sympathies, even as her odd behavior engenders a high level of discomfort. Her "tics and rituals," the stuff of other people's uneasiness, are shown to be "parts of other things, engine-revving incantations against fear and failure," things to which most readers can relate. Morris depicts Martha's aunt, the beautiful and wealthy Frances, in a similarly paradoxical fashion: her personality and behavior are understandable and attractive, even as her motives are clearly cold and selfish.

Furthermore, Morris writes these complex characterizations in a forthright manner with diction that is often highly poetic. In his review of *Vanished* for *The New York Times Book Review* (3 July 1988) Harry Crews described her language as "precise, concrete and sensual. Her eye for telling detail is good, and her ear for the way people talk is tone-perfect." For example, rather than a bland direct narrative to relate how the confidence man Omar Duvall ingratiates himself with the Fermoyle family in *Songs in Ordinary Time,* Morris shifts from the present to the future tense as the broke and battered Duvall picks himself up and begins again:

As he made his way to the lilac shrub, and broke off the thickest blooms, he knew, not with his brain, but from deep in his belly, what he would do next, and where he would go, and what he would say to her. . . . The lilacs would stand in a milk bottle . . . he saw how easy the next request would be.

However, even as Duvall's insidiousness permeates the scene, Morris makes the reader aware of and sympathetic to the "abject and limitless hunger" stirred inside him by his view of the Fermoyle family.

This type of profound loneliness demonstrated by Duvall forms the matrix of Morris's thematic concerns. Compared by several reviewers to Carson McCullers, Morris depicts spiritual isolation and the attempt to overcome this isolation through love. The characters in her novels are rarely alone physically, but the inability to connect with others becomes a trait in her protagonists. Despite the bleakness with which the first two novels end, Morris's next two allow for the possibility of human connection, an end to loneliness, and happiness.

Morris sets her stories primarily in southwestern Vermont and northeastern Massachusetts. Landscape and setting are not focal points of the novels, but characters, events, and actions are connected to and shaped by place. In a personal interview Morris explained that she has to "feel the place" for other aspects of the novel to work and that her "characters are who they are because of place." For example, the forest adjacent to Morris's fictional town of Atkinson, Vermont, where her first novel begins and the next two are set, plays a recurring role. Morris's settings add a depth of accuracy and reality to her work. The Vermont mountains provide the backdrop as *Vanished* gets under way, and the towns of northern Massachusetts figure in its ending. While *Fiona Range* (2000) is set mainly in a small city near Boston, the fictional Dearborn, the countryside and its quarries are crucial to the climax of the novel.

Morris's reluctance to set her work in areas that she does not know well has been clear since her first novel, *Vanished*. The novel begins with a prologue in which Aubrey Wallace, a man of severely limited intelligence, is working on a highway crew outside of Atkinson when he encounters Dotty, a crazed teenager who has just murdered her abusive father. Dotty steals Aubrey's father-in-law's truck—and Aubrey himself, when he jumps in to stop her—and they begin a journey that ends in tragedy in Massachusetts. Seen as "a pastiche of those mid-1970's movies about disaffected couples on the lam" by reviewer Michiko Kakutani (*The New York Times,* 4 June 1988), the novel skips forward five years between the prologue and the first chapter, which opens at the beginning of their journey back north to the Massachusetts town from which they stole a baby as they left New England. All the places they visited in those five years, mainly in the southern United States, are left out of the novel and are mentioned only through the ways in which those places shaped the characters' lives.

Morris introduces her protagonists and builds knowledge of them slowly: the narrative voice reveals

Dust jacket for Morris's 1995 novel, about a divorcée who is victimized by a confidence man but rescued
by her two teenage sons (Richland County Public Library)

past events in infrequent snippets and flashes that build the story until the reader can make sense of the character's actions and motivations. Although Crews cautioned that Morris "has to learn that until we know the motives out of which people are acting we don't have people at all, only ciphers, characters with names," in the course of daily interaction, people always begin as ciphers to each other, until further communication allows understanding. On the first page of *Vanished* Dotty is introduced through the description of her father's murder, "his pants half-burned and the mound of spent matches the deputies found on his crotch." She is described by the men in Aubrey's road crew as a "crazy little bitch" who should be shot on sight. Given the loaded description, it comes as no surprise when, near the end of the novel, Dotty tells the story of a young girl she knew who had been brutally raped by her father from the age of ten until she killed him, and "so everyone'd know, so he'd know, she lit a match and tried to set him on fire—there." Her appearance to Aubrey and her continued crazed activity depict her as a young woman frozen into a childish worldview that dictates her actions as motivated by survival, self-interest, and without consideration of any type of consequence or repercussion.

While Dotty's behavior is erratic throughout the novel, her actions become horrific at the end as she is abused by former convict Jiggy Huller, with whom she forms a plan to return Canny—the stolen child, now almost six years old—to her family for the reward money. Dotty murders again, and these killings become bookends in the novel. The latter answers the former in a sort of rough justice for the girl who was permanently damaged by her father. Just as she accepts the knowledge that she will be punished for killing her father, knows that "they'd call her names, and they'd never believe her," at the beginning, she is perfectly happy to accept the role of victim and heroine assigned to her by the legal and journalistic misreading of the outcome of events.

In *Vanished,* as in all her novels, Morris sets forth harsh details and gritty realities with veracity. Morris began writing before she became a caseworker, and her affinity for both professions is clear in the way that she depicts the dark truths of some people's lives with sympathy and without judgment. As she told interviewer Caryn James, "I would recognize my characters sometimes across the desk." Morris makes Dotty's experiences with abuse believable and immediate to her readers.

The richness of Aubrey's character is one of the triumphs of *Vanished*. Gary Davenport described Aubrey as having "the mind of a child" (*Sewanee Review*, March 1989). Similarly, Kakutani described Aubrey as a sort of Faulknerian character, "an innocent, a kind of holy fool, whose disordered mind, filled with fairy tales and dreamlike memories, only dimly processes the grim realities around him." The fairy stories told by his wife to his sons haunt him and the book, and Aubrey remembers his inability to correct the bad endings she creates to frighten them. He sees Canny as a fairy child, and he wishes to give her a happy ending. Even with his severely limited mental abilities, Aubrey realizes that "all he ever had to worry about was the present," that first his wife, Hyacinth, and then Dotty "kept track of the past and presided over the future." In light of that conclusion, Aubrey maintains a steady, if passive, activity through the novel. He is the primary caregiver for Canny and Dotty, then for Huller's wife and daughters. Morris makes *Vanished* both horrifying and touching by writing from Aubrey's perspective. In *TLS: The Times Literary Supplement* (5 February 1990) Tamara Jane Smith noted that "in spite of all the unpleasantness, *Vanished* is in some ways an uplifting work." The narrative convinces through Aubrey's transparently good intentions and his great-heartedness. His death is particularly telling as he is swept along by circumstance until he dies in a hail of gunfire, but "not a bullet had hit his heart. Not a one." *Vanished* was nominated for the National Book Award and the PEN/Faulkner Award.

The characters in Morris's second novel, *A Dangerous Woman,* are similarly overtaken by circumstance: options are swept away by events, hope is exhausted, and violence is both inevitable and pervasive. In *The New York Times* (4 January 1991) Kakutani noted the similarities between Aubrey Wallace and Martha Horgan, calling them dangerous innocents and outsiders. Similarly, in *The New York Times Book Review* (13 January 1991), Alice McDermott suggested that both novels hold their characters in "traps of circumstance and personality" against which they struggle, "not nobly but with an animal desperation." *A Dangerous Woman* is told in long, chronologically organized chapters that are framed between crimes: the opening scene is the sexual assault of the teenage Martha by a group of young men, and the novel climaxes as the thirty-one-year-old Martha murders her most recent tormentor, a loutish petty criminal named Getso, then spirals into madness. In between, the novel moves with Morris's usual rapid pace as she stages the actions and develops her characters through a series of detailed scenes. Kakutani calls the action "at once thrilling and deeply affecting" and says that although it has "the sort of violent, melodra-

matic climax that makes newspaper headlines," there is "not a shred of sensationalism."

Martha, bespectacled, awkward, and brutally honest, lives a kind of shadowy existence after the assault, until her father dies. Caretaker for the wealthy Horace Beecham, her father had brought his younger sister, Frances, down from the Flatts into Atkinson to care for Martha when her mother died. Frances marries Beecham, inherits his fortune, and becomes Martha's guardian. At the same time, having pulled herself from the poverty of the Flatts into the upper class, Frances has a sharp-edged practicality and awareness of her social position that precludes her from actually caring for the lonely younger woman. Frances sees the assault as an embarrassment and is largely unsympathetic to the difficult and quick-tempered Martha. She finds her niece problematic: "every incident was high drama, every confrontation a disaster, every slight a blow. Such an exhausting life, without subtleties, propelled by fear and anxiety." When Mack, an itinerant would-be writer, comes into their lives, he feels sympathy for Martha, and like her friend, Birdy, he shows patience with her. However, Mack also seduces her when he is drunk and treats her with cruelty as often as with kindness. When he becomes Frances's lover and begins to enjoy the opportunities the affair provides him, Martha's fate seems sealed.

Morris depicts Martha as a lonely ogre whom cruel children love to taunt and adults need to shun. The most notable achievement of the novel is Morris's ability to make Martha both repugnant and pitiable, to make readers understand that they too would be uncomfortable in her presence, even as they sympathize with her desperate loneliness. Morris summarizes Martha's motivations and frustrations near the end, when Martha prepares to confess that Mack is the father of her baby. She

> watches his face twist with the same frustration she had seen in her father, in teachers who had all thought she should have some control over the fiasco that was her life. Of course she should. She wanted to, but did not, never had, and probably never would. And because there seemed to be no reasons for this, no mark they could see, no disfigurement or missing limb, one by one they would abandon her. That was the reason she always reacted so suddenly, loving so fiercely those who would be kind, so that in order to part they would have to tear themselves away from the ancient battlefield that was her heart.

Morris resists sentimentality and makes clear that Martha's complete isolation is inevitable, that the tastes she has had of happiness will only fuel the anger and

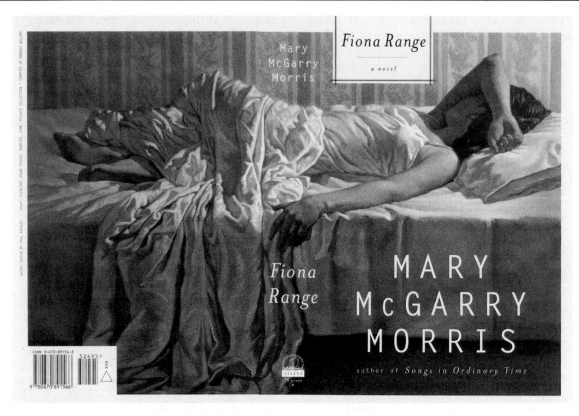

Dust jacket for Morris's 2000 novel, about a troubled young woman who tries to change her life by establishing a relationship with the man she thinks is her father (Richland County Public Library)

despair that drives her to violence and then into complete withdrawal.

In 1993 *A Dangerous Woman* was adapted for the screen by Naomi Foner, who also produced the motion picture. Directed by Stephen Gyllenhaal, the movie starred David Strathairn, Gabriel Byrne, Barbara Hershey, and Debra Winger.

Morris's third novel was her first best-seller. Propelled into the spotlight by Winfrey, *Songs in Ordinary Time* marks a stylistic departure for Morris. Rather than long, internally divided chapters, this novel is told in a series of short vignettes, and its episodic nature is further complicated as the reader is given the story from the perspective of many characters, although Morris focuses on the Fermoyle family, particularly twelve-year-old Benjy. While the novel found popular acclaim, reviewers panned it for its attempt to tell many stories in somewhat melodramatic plotlines. In *The New York Times* (4 August 1995) Kakutani charged Morris with losing her "magical sympathy for her characters" and with peopling her town with "characters whose lives are a tangled and unbelievable mess of felonies, suicide attempts, sexual indiscretions and betrayals."

However, Morris has always attempted to tell many stories, giving more background than is needed for secondary and peripheral characters.

Songs in Ordinary Time is also set in Atkinson, but in 1960, before the time of Morris's first two novels. However, where the earlier novels feature characters from the Flatts and the upper class, Morris focuses largely on the Catholic working and middle class in her third. She includes characters mentioned previously: the pig man from *Vanished* is given a name and a love story, and the sheriff from *A Dangerous Woman* returns in one of the most poignant stories of the novel. At the heart of *Songs in Ordinary Time*—which also begins with a crime, a murder in this case—is the Fermoyle family. Marie is the bitter, lonely head of the household, a woman who bears the weight of her divorce and her poverty with anger. Morris makes clear how deeply Marie cares for her children and how the burdens she bears cause her to lash out at them, and this verbal abuse is realistic and disquieting. At the same time, she works overtime so that Alice, just finishing high school, can go to college. She does her best to quell her own anger so that her teenage son, Norm, will learn to curb the anger that is his legacy from his alcoholic father, and she forces Benjy to take swimming lessons in an effort to toughen him up and to teach him to face his fears. Marie's pride and strength ensure that most of her relationships will be fraught with difficulty. Morris draws Marie as a complex and realistic character, the type of woman readers can admire and find sympathetic even as they are made uncomfortable by some of her actions and choices.

As Marie falls under the spell of the con man Duvall and goes into debt to buy into his scheme, her children make poor choices of their own. Alice, waiting to leave for college and questioning her sexual orientation, has an affair with an emotionally unstable priest, who suffers a nervous breakdown when the monsignor catches them in bed. Norm, with his own anger and drinking problems, is initially resistant to Duvall but is lured into the scheme by Duvall's promise of easy money and the hope of happiness for his mother and family. Similarly, Benjy, hoping for his mother's happiness, hides what he knows about Duvall, just as he hides the abuse and harassment he receives from Sam, his drunken father. Like Aubrey and Martha, Benjy is a difficult character. On the one hand, his lies and silence seem subversive to his family's interests, and his comfort level with Duvall, whom he knows to be a violent liar, seems unbelievable. On the other hand, Benjy is "fixed, immured in the vastness that time becomes when you are twelve. . . . untouched, and for days on end, ignored, he was not a child and not a man." Morris makes clear that Benjy sees Duvall's coming as "inevitable as the summer's fiery sun, and as unstoppable." Throughout the novel, Benjy holds Duvall at arm's length, doing his bidding and hoping for his mother's continued happiness. He sees Duvall as a catalyst and welcomes any changes this villain may bring about—changes to his mother's cold bitterness, his brother's anger, and his own inertia.

Duvall does change their lives. As Norm realizes that the con artist has tied them up "with their own fears, hopes, and sins," he and Benjy make the definitive move to free their family from Duvall. The results are more positive than Morris's earlier novels. Marie remains unable to trust her reformed former husband, but she is able to forgive him and able to accept help from others. She remains single, but no longer alone, even as her children get on with their lives. Morris resolves the rest of the stories in a variety of imaginative ways, remaining true to the unsentimental and tough-minded vision of her earlier work.

In her next novel, *Fiona Range,* Morris continues to explore her thematic concerns of spiritual isolation and the ways in which people overcome it with love, and of the moral consequences of things done for love.

Morris maintains her fast-paced narrative but draws her eponymous protagonist with broader brush strokes than she has used in her prior work. By the end of the first chapter, Fiona has had a one-night stand with a married man, dated her cousin's former lover, had an altercation with the man she thinks is her father, and revealed herself to be a deeply troubled and lonely young woman. Abandoned by her mother shortly after her birth, Fiona was raised by her aunt and uncle alongside their own three children. Because the identity of her father has been kept secret and because she has never felt herself to be a wanted member of the Hollis family, Fiona has been a hell-raiser most of her life. Morris presents her hero as bright, beautiful, and kind, but deeply flawed by her perpetual isolation. At one point Fiona muses that "the past was with her everyday and everywhere"; she thinks that "she might be able to change what she became, but nothing could change what she came from. And to tell the truth, most days she didn't give a damn." The plot gets under way as Fiona, sickened by her own irresponsible behavior and ready to change, embarks on a quest to bond with Patrick Grady, the scarred, angry veteran she thinks is her father.

Like Duvall, Grady is both threatening and understandable. Grady is deeply disturbed and isolated, and he knows all the secrets that are revealed in the harrowing climax of the novel. *Fiona Range* begins and ends more like romance fiction than Morris's other novels. As reviewer Maggie Paley pointed out in *The New York Times* (4 June 2000), the novel is Morris's "lightest and in many ways not her best. Sometimes its plot contrivances make it hard to take seriously." While the plot, centered in the secrets held by Grady and by Fiona's uncle, is gripping yet less compelling than her earlier novels, Morris demonstrates finesse in depicting Grady and his attraction for Fiona. Like Martha, he is frightening in the enormity of his loneliness and his need. Unlike Martha or Aubrey, however, someone tries to save Grady with love. Convinced that all he needs is a daughter's love to repair his damaged psyche, Fiona battles his pain and rage with patience and affection. Further, with Grady, Morris adds the element of suspense to her fiction. His immense anger is attributed by Fiona and most of the other characters to his stint in Vietnam and to Fiona's mother's running away, leaving him and her baby behind. However, Grady is haunted by the secrets he shares with Charles Hollis: that Hollis is Fiona's father and that Grady murdered her mother when he found out the baby was not his. As Fiona rushes headlong into a relationship with Grady, she becomes the catalyst that brings about changes in many relationships, the violent climax, and the series of happy endings in the low-key denouement.

In an interview with Roger Cohen, Morris said of *Fiona Range,* "I am very aware that it is an extremely lonely work, and of how fragile a normal life can be, how loosely held together certain things are that we take for granted." In Morris's fictional worlds, humanity's worst fears are realized: children are stolen, abandoned, neglected, or abused; the emotionally disturbed and mentally deficient remain lost and hopeless; sex is often a smokescreen masquerading as love; and good intentions are misunderstood and bad ones attractive. Morris's work offers a candid view of these realities. Morris's next novel, *A Hole In the Universe,* forthcoming in 2004, is set in a once-prosperous Massachusetts mill town, and like *Fiona Range,* it features a decades-old murder and its continuing effect on the living.

While her work has always combined solid characterization and attention to detail in a fast-paced plot, as she matures as an artist, Morris shows increasing ability to build suspense and to draw her readers into the story as much as into concern for her characters. The growth of her continued popular and critical acceptance is evidenced by the translation of her novels into many languages and by their increasing use in the academic classroom. Even as critics draw attention to problematic aspects of some of Morris's approaches to plot, organization, and other aspects of her work, they consistently look forward to more of her writing.

Interviews:

Caryn James, "A Writer Is Author At Last," *New York Times,* 20 June 1988, p. C17;

Roger Cohen, "Author's Worlds: Benign Reality and Violent Fantasy: Mary McGarry Morris's Life Contrasts with Her Fiction," *New York Times,* 28 January 1991, pp. C19–C22;

Linda Davies, *Glimmer Train,* 10 (1993): 124–131.

Jayne Anne Phillips

(19 July 1952 –)

Suzanne Disheroon-Green
Northwestern State University

BOOKS: *Sweethearts* (Carrboro, N.C.: Truck Books, 1976);

Counting (New York: Vehicle Editions, 1978);

Black Tickets (New York: Delacorte/Seymour Lawrence, 1979; London: Allen Lane, 1980);

How Mickey Made It (St. Paul, Minn.: Bookslinger Editions, 1981);

The Secret Country (Berkeley, Cal.: Palaemon Press, 1982);

Fast Lanes (New York: Vehicle Editions/Brooke Alexander, 1983; expanded edition, New York: Dutton/Seymour Lawrence, 1987; London: Faber & Faber, 1987);

Machine Dreams (New York: Dutton/Seymour Lawrence, 1984; London: Faber & Faber, 1984);

The Last Day of Summer, text by Phillips, photographs by Jock Sturges (New York: Aperture Foundation, 1991);

Shelter (Boston: Houghton Mifflin/Seymour Lawrence, 1994; London: Faber & Faber, 1995);

MotherKind (New York: Knopf, 2000; London: Cape, 2000).

RECORDING: *Jayne Anne Phillips Reads Souvenir and Machine Dreams* [excerpts], Columbia, Mo., American Audio Prose Library, 1991.

OTHER: "Something That Happened," in *The Best American Short Stories 1979,* edited by Joyce Carol Oates and Shannon Ravenel (Boston: Houghton Mifflin, 1979);

Ploughshares (Winter 1980–1981), edited by Phillips and Lorrie Goldensohn;

Stephen Crane, *Maggie: A Girl of the Streets and Other Short Fiction,* introduction by Phillips (New York: Bantam, 1986);

"Premature Burial," in *Bloodroot: Reflections on Place by Appalachian Women Writers,* edited by Joyce Dyer (Lexington: University Press of Kentucky, 1998), pp. 209–217;

Jayne Anne Phillips (photograph © Jerry Bauer; from the dust jacket for Shelter, *1994; Richland County Public Library)*

"Why She Writes," in *Why I Write: Thoughts on the Practice of Fiction,* edited by Will Blythe (Boston: Little, Brown, 1998), pp. 188–195;

"On Not Having a Daughter," in *Mothers Who Think: Tales of Real-Life Parenthood,* edited by Camille Peri and Kate Moses (New York: Villard, 1999), pp. 36–44;

"The Widow Speaks," in *The Eleventh Draft: Craft and the Writing Life from the Iowa Writer's Workshop,* edited by Frank Conroy (New York: Norton, 1999), pp. 41–49.

SELECTED PERIODICAL PUBLICATIONS–
UNCOLLECTED:

FICTION

"Obsession: A Simple Story," *Critical Quarterly,* 37 (Winter 1995): 49–51;

"Mothercare," *Granta,* 55 (Autumn 1996): 49–72;

"Home After Dark: Letter from Paducah," *Harper's* (November 1997).

NONFICTION

"A Project for Artforum: Half-Life," *Artforum International,* 31 (March 1993): 66–70;

"Outlaw Heart," *Critical Quarterly,* 37 (Winter 1995): 43–48.

Praised by such literary notables as Raymond Carver, Tillie Olsen, and Nadine Gordimer, novelist and short-story writer Jayne Anne Phillips has garnered attention from both the literary establishment and popular readers. Phillips's body of work, which includes three novels and four collections of short fiction, draws upon themes that have come to be associated with the twentieth-century American literary tradition, including the effects of psychological damage, communication failures within families and between lovers, danger to children, women's lack of fulfillment in marriage, and the ways in which sex is used and abused in modern society. As critic Meredith Sue Willis has argued, however, Phillips's approach does not "depend so much on her subjects as on a fictional strategy of recreating moments of being. These moments, sometimes almost painful in their intensity, are passages of heightened sense observation that create breakthroughs to the reality underlying the everyday." Phillips has been acclaimed for her ability to speak for the downtrodden and has been called a "poet of deprivation and desire" by Nicci Gerrard of *The Observer* (29 January 1995). Book critic Michiko Kakutani of *The New York Times* (12 June 1984) described Phillips as having stepped "out of the ranks of her generation as one of its most gifted writers," making her a writer to watch as the twenty-first century unfolds.

Phillips was born on 19 July 1952 in Buckhannon, West Virginia, to Martha Jane Thornhill Phillips, a schoolteacher, and Russell R. Phillips. She was raised with two brothers, one elder and one younger; their parents divorced in 1972, when Phillips was twenty. She reports having literary aspirations at the age of nine, when she wrote what she has described to Dorothy Combs Hill as a "kind of serial novel, starring myself and my friends, about a girl who moves to New York City and falls in love with a kid gang leader. I did that to entertain people." She grew up in a small West Virginia town characterized by many Southern attributes, not the least of which was the propensity of

its citizens to share stories. In the Hill article, Phillips described her experience as a child in a town where her family had lived for almost three hundred years:

everyone knew everyone's stories, but the stories were secret. As the writer in my family, I felt that I was the person who was charged with making sure all these stories and ideas survive, but at the same time you're not allowed to tell anyone. Writing is the telling of secrets. Secrets have to be told. It's terrible if they're not, but if you tell the secrets, they can transform and unite one moment with another, and bridge the gulf between time, distance, difference.

Willis has described Phillips as having a "preternatural ability to create such moments from decades before she was born," and forming this bridge between then and now is one of the more notable elements of Phillips's craft.

Upon graduation from high school, where she found encouragement for her creative efforts from English teacher and poet Irene McKinney, Phillips enrolled at West Virginia University. She earned her bachelor's degree in 1974. During this period, she successfully published some of her poems in little magazines. Upon completion of her degree, Phillips spent some time traveling and living in Oakland, California, and later in Colorado, where she became friends with Annabel Levitt, the founder of Vehicle Editions. Together, the women founded a writer's workshop that nurtured Phillips's interest in fiction, for despite the fact that she was writing what Hill has described as "long narrative poems," many of these eventually evolved into pieces of short fiction. Vehicle Editions later published two of Phillips's early works: *Counting* (1978), a collection of short pieces that garnered the St. Lawrence Award for fiction, and the first edition of *Fast Lanes* (1984), a critically acclaimed volume of short stories. Phillips found herself drawn toward home, however, returning to West Virginia for part of a year while she applied to graduate school in the prestigious University of Iowa Writers' Workshop.

During the summer of 1976, while Phillips was preparing to leave for Iowa, Truck Books in Carrboro, North Carolina, published *Sweethearts* (1976). Hill describes the collection as an "edition of twenty-four one-page prose pieces," and despite the relative obscurity of the press, the collection garnered a Fels Award in fiction from the Coordinating Council of Literary Magazines, and selections from *Sweethearts* were anthologized in *Pushcart Prize II: The Best of the Small Presses* (1977).

Phillips enrolled in the writing program at the University of Iowa, earning a master of fine arts degree in 1978. She studied with Frank Conroy while at Iowa, and she credits his workshop with providing the environment in which she wrote some of the stories that later appeared in *Black Tickets* (1979). After graduation she accepted a teaching position at Humboldt State University in California, and as she was preparing to depart West Virginia to assume her duties, she received word that *Black Tickets* had been accepted for publication. Hill describes Phillips's "now much-celebrated and much-repeated exchange" with Seymour Lawrence of Delacorte, a conversation that led to the publication of *Black Tickets*. Phillips reportedly asked Lawrence if he published short stories, and received the curt response, "Not if I can help it." Nonetheless, Lawrence departed with a copy of *Sweethearts,* and Phillips soon received word from him that she was a "real writer." *Black Tickets* brought Phillips a Yaddo Corporation fellowship as well as the first of two prestigious National Endowment for the Arts fellowships.

Black Tickets offers an eclectic group of stories, ranging from impressionistic flash fiction that describes a fleeting moment to fuller treatments of emotionally wrenching situations. The stories vary from the opening vignette, a child's impressions of her youthful mother in "Wedding Picture," to overtly erotic dialogue found in "Slave" and "Accidents." Others present the more deeply troubling side of humanity, exemplified by the musings of a mass murderer and the decision of a girl to abandon foster care in favor of life with two drug addicts. There are stories that elucidate the interminable period preceding the death of a sick old man and depict the awkward relationship between a daughter and her divorced father. Carver called *Black Tickets* "a crooked beauty," finding the collection "unlike any in our literature." The variety of the collection led Gordimer to credit Phillips's "exquisite and terrible insight" and to call her the "best short-story writer since Eudora Welty," praise that was used in dust-jacket blurbs.

Critics applauded the collection, although it received greater attention in later years than on its first appearance. Gail Caldwell of the *Boston Globe* (21 May 2000) noted the "trance-like ferocity" of the narratives. Gerrard of *The Observer* (29 January 1995) noted that "Jayne Anne Phillips came from nowhere, and surprised the American literary scene like an exotic hybrid in a well-bred shrubbery," adding that *Black Tickets* "spoke for disenfranchised America." David Remnick of the *Washington Post* (26 April 1987) pointed out that "her keenest asset is her ear, her ability to make art of the desperate, nervous voices in the nether corners of America." Remnick went on to praise the size of Phillips's collection "in this era of

Dust jacket for the U.S. edition of Phillips's 1984 first novel, about the breakup of a marriage as seen from the perspectives of the husband, wife, son, and daughter (Richland County Public Library)

the anemically thin," remarking on her "talent for voices, a talent rarer than might be imagined." The almost unanimously positive critical response to Phillips's first effort culminated when she was awarded the first-ever Sue Kaufman Prize for First Fiction from the American Academy and Institute of Arts and Letters in 1980.

While polishing the final portions of *Black Tickets,* Phillips fulfilled her commitment to Humboldt but quickly realized that she did not want to devote her energy to full-time teaching. The Provincetown Fine Arts Center previously had offered her a fellowship, which she had declined because she had already accepted the position at Humboldt, but within the year, she asked to be considered again for the fellowship. By 1979 she had returned to the East Coast, settling in Cape Cod. She followed the year at Provincetown with a year at Radcliffe College on a Bunting Institute fellowship, and during this period she published two additional books with small presses:

Dust jacket for Phillips's novel about lust, insanity, and violence at a girls' summer camp (Richland County Public Library)

How Mickey Made It (1981), a short story that also appeared in the 1987 collection *Fast Lanes,* and *The Secret Country* (1982). Phillips also began working on what became her first novel, *Machine Dreams* (1984), which took her four years to complete.

Relationships challenged by changing times and social values form the core of the narrative of *Machine Dreams.* Structured as a sequence of interrelated remembrances, some of which take the form of letters or telegrams, the story is related from the perspectives of four members of the Hampson family: the father, Mitch; the mother, Jean; the daughter, Danner; and the son, Billy. The novel begins with Jean's reminiscences of the World War II years and the necessary adjustments when the men returned home. Jean married Mitch largely out of fear: she had recently lost the love of her life to a sudden heart attack when he was only seventeen, and her mother was dying of cancer. The much older Mitch, who himself was orphaned at a young age and was raised by an older but loving

cousin, seemed steady and caring, never voicing any resentment of Jean's responsibilities and treating her mother with kindness. As life wears on, however, Jean becomes increasingly frustrated by having her efforts to maintain the family thwarted. At first, she fills a traditional woman's role, caring for her family physically, spiritually, and emotionally and acquiescing to her husband's wishes. She gradually becomes the family's primary source of financial support when Mitch's once-prosperous business fails—a loss from which he never fully recovers, either financially or personally. When her children are grown, Jean divorces Mitch, leaving him to return to his cousin's home, where he lives in the basement, alienated from the family of which he is no longer the head.

Danner and Billy relate their experiences growing up with these parents, attempting to please and establish a relationship with each of them, yet finding communication difficult. The children perpetually feel that they have disappointed their mother, and they cannot penetrate the distance that their father wraps around himself. As the novel draws to a close, the Vietnam era has dawned, causing Billy to be drafted and Danner to become involved in a legal scrape in a mistaken attempt to escape from the realities that she cannot control. Phillips's characters seek a sense of belonging and a sense of purpose, yet none of the primary characters in *Machine Dreams* achieves either—they only dream of reaching a place where they will belong, will have control over their own destinies, and will not find themselves subjected to the whims of wars and social expectations.

Critics were pleased with *Machine Dreams,* although several have speculated about the extent to which the book is autobiographical, given the similarities between Bellington, the setting of the *Machine Dreams,* and the small West Virginia town of Phillips's youth. The characters share similarities with members of Phillips's family—her father was a business owner turned road-crew foreman, and her mother earned a degree later in life and worked up to the position of school administrator. Phillips followed a similar academic course to that of Danner, who also attends West Virginia University to study English. Despite these similarities, however, Phillips is adamant that the book is not entirely autobiographical, remarking that "More often than not, the reaction I get from my family is, 'Well, that's not what happened.'" Phillips's narrative strategy moves the novel further away from the autobiographical. Each of the four narrators speaks from a slightly different point of view. Danner's sections, for example, are most often related in the third person, while Jean's stories are told in first person, and Mitch's reflect a distance that is in keeping with his characterization. The varying narrative voices serve to emphasize the strengths of each character and the difficulties that they have in building trusting relationships with each other. Barbara Liss in the *Houston Chronicle* (2 July 2000) characterized the novel as one in which "parents and children lose their illusions and their innocence. At risk is their very sense of where they belong in the world." R. D. Pohl of the *Buffalo News* (21 October 2001) remarked that the novel became an "instant classic" that "continues to be regarded as one of the best American novels of the 1980s." *Machine Dreams* was nominated for a National Book Critics Circle Award.

Phillips also published a collection of short stories, *Fast Lanes,* in 1983, expanding it in 1987. Once again Phillips makes use of a wide variety of voices, relating stories of the untimely death of a child, the rise and demise of a love affair, and the reasons that a young girl, Alma, becomes her mother's confidante. A combination of new and previously uncollected material, the 1987 *Fast Lanes* found favor with critics. The review in *Publishers Weekly* (27 February 1987) extolled the collection for demonstrating "the evolution of the author's gifted style and subject matter. . . . The dazzling play of language and reckless protagonists of such tales as 'How Mickey Made It' and 'Bluegill' show a young writer in love with words and perhaps a little too enamored of life in the fast lane." Similarly, Paul E. Hutchison said in *Library Journal* (1 March 1987) that as a "West Virginian, Phillips is often strongest when treating the isolation of that state's rural communities, as in 'Bess,' a woman's reminiscence of life in turn-of-the-century Coalton. But the author's voice now broadens . . . Phillips's perspective on contemporary life is refreshingly honest, her style engaging." In *The New York Times* (11 April 1987) Kakutani called Phillips's ear "almost unerring . . . as ever, she writes beautifully, capturing elusive moods with startling images and scenes."

In 1985 Phillips married Mark Stockman. She has one son and two stepsons.

Hill has argued that the major focus of Phillips's fiction is the "deracination of her generation and the tragedy the traditional male-female roles wreak on people when those roles no longer exist in society." The author herself remarked in a 1998 interview that she is "interested in what home now consists of. Because we move around so much, families are forced to be immediate; they must stand on their relationships, rather than on stereotypes or assumptions of a common history." This interest in what constitutes family can be seen in her next novel, *Shelter.* Published in 1994, *Shelter* offers a stark and often startling look at the ongoing struggle between good and

evil. Parson is a simple, uncommunicative, and possibly schizophrenic religious fanatic who hears voices and believes that he has encountered the devil incarnate in former fellow prison inmate Carmody. Parson feels it is his responsibility to rid the world of Carmody's evil. A deeply troubled alcoholic, who is by turns abusive and emotionally and physically needy, Carmody spends what turn out to be the final days of his life moving ever closer to sexually abusing his only son, the illiterate, alienated Buddy. The boy's mother, the cook at Camp Shelter, attends to the salvation of her son's soul but is unable to improve his worldly lot, in large part because of their poverty. Buddy spends the summer running wild in the woods surrounding Camp Shelter. Shelter is a residential camp for girls, offering them the opportunity to hike, swim, canoe, and commune with nature, all while being thoroughly indoctrinated in the evils of communism by the camp director.

In a narrative style similar to that of *Machine Dreams,* the events that take place at Camp Shelter are told from multiple viewpoints. Parts of the narrative are related by Alma and her older sister, Lenny, and their respective friends, Delia and Cap. Phillips draws the reader into the girls' experiences as they encounter Carmody and Parson. The subplot of the novel involves the older girls' exploration of their sexual urges, which at one point leads Lenny and Cap into a brief and unexpected sexual encounter with a young man, Frank, who lives in the woods surrounding the camp. The girls yearn for more freedom than is allowed them; their boredom and their interest in the strange emotions that Frank arouses in them lead them unwittingly into Carmody's path. When Carmody encounters the four girls, he is on his way to force his abused son, Buddy, to perform a robbery so that he can leave Shelter and his family responsibilities behind. However, his lust overtakes him when he catches sight of the innocent and nubile girls, and he attempts to rape Lenny. The other girls, with the help of Parson, kill Carmody and hide his body in a cave, where it will likely never be found. By the end of the novel, Buddy is enjoying the freedom from his father, whom he had feared yet had been unable to escape. The girls leave town and enroll in boarding school, yet the alienation and inability to communicate that ensues from their experiences at the camp continue to haunt these young women.

Evocative of the American and the Southern literary traditions, *Shelter* addresses issues of what constitutes sin and how forgiveness may be attained. Even more important, it focuses on the ways in which sexuality may become overwhelming, leading individuals into unsatisfying situations in their searches for

Dust jacket for Phillips's 2000 novel, about a poet who tries to balance her new marriage, which includes two stepsons and a baby of her own, with her responsibilities as caregiver for her cancer-stricken mother (Richland County Public Library)

writing about swollen adolescent urges, and never does she allow us to step back into the detachment of adulthood." Phillips's "coming of age" presents her readers with characters who are complex and who achieve some level of connectedness that has been denied her previous characters.

MotherKind (2000), Phillips's third novel, tells the story of Kate, who learns that she is pregnant by her soon-to-be-divorced fiancé, Matt. When they are able to marry, she attempts to blend his family, consisting of two sons from his first marriage, with theirs. Her efforts are temporarily stymied by the antagonism of Matt's former wife, who insists on blaming the breakup of their family on Kate, despite the fact that Matt's former wife engaged in an extramarital affair that destroyed the marriage. Kate's attempts to fuse her new family into a cohesive unit are further complicated by her mother's terminal cancer and Kate's role as her primary caretaker. Kate and her mother, Katherine, share a warm relationship, yet it is not without its stressful moments. Kate also strives diligently to establish a positive relationship with her stepsons, all while dealing with the loss of her creative outlet. Kate is a poet, but with all of the demands on her time, she finds herself perpetually unable to write, and at times she desperately misses her writing and her former life. As Katherine weakens and declines, Kate is pulled in too many directions, and the result is that on the heels of the birth of their son and the death of Kate's mother, Matt expresses doubts that he and Kate will find their way back to each other as a couple after all of the interferences in their relationship. The book ends on a hopeful note, with Kate expressing confidence in her marriage and her new family, which includes her stepsons, but the reader is left wondering just how deep the ambivalence of Kate's husband runs, and if their relationship will continue to deteriorate because he has felt neglected for an extended period of time.

Although Pohl of the *Buffalo News* (21 October 2001) described *MotherKind* as having a "completely transparent" plot, he added that this transparency is not a weakness in the novel, because the "emotional trajectory of the characters provides the narrative with its sense of drama." Pohl suggested that, in some fashion, "*MotherKind* is a literary self-help book written for men and women who are living those stories right now." Gerrard pointed out in *The Observer* (24 September 2000) that "Kate is the woman who loses a mother as she becomes one," and this condition is one Phillips sets out to examine. In the same article Phillips remarked that in *MotherKind,* she "was asking: what is death? What is being alive? I wanted to write about that milky, sensual space in an infant's life, and in the mother's,

love, and the ways in which sexuality may be manipulated into an evil force. Critics acknowledged the visceral nature of *Shelter,* appreciating Phillips's use of suspense. Marie Arana-Ward described the book in *The Washington Post* (16 October 1994) as "an eerie tale about the origins of evil and the very human hunger for redemption," concluding that "the task Phillips has set for herself is nothing short of mapping the geography of the soul." In Willis's 1996 article, Phillips said of *Shelter* that "I wanted to think about evil . . . about whether evil really exists or if it is just a function of damage, the fact that when people are damaged, they damage others." Evil certainly plays a significant part in Phillips's narrative, leading Gerrard to remark in *The Observer* (29 January 1995) that although the "camp seems at first like Eden . . . shocking violence begins to transform the camp into a kind of Hades." Gerrard pointed out that "in all of Phillips's fictions, sex and danger are embraced . . . she's where identities are melted." Phillips told Melissa Falcon, the reviewer for the *Austin American-Statesman* (12 September 1999), that "*MotherKind* is very much about place, or lack of it. The novel deals with what 'home' is when so many of us move frequently, or live our lives far from where we started. . . . Family themes have always been central to my work."

Jayne Anne Phillips describes herself as a "slow" writer, yet the body of work that she has produced at this relatively early point in her career is impressive. Critics agree that her mastery of voice, of narrative techniques that demonstrate a variety of points of view, and of the painful places in the human psyche that bear examination place her among the foremost writers of her generation. Phillips continues to write and serves as writer-in-residence at Brandeis University in Waltham, Massachusetts.

Interview:

Bonnie Lyons, "The Mystery of Language," in *Passion and Craft: Conversations with Notable Writers,* edited by Lyons and Bill Oliver (Urbana: University of Illinois Press, 1998), pp. 159–170.

References:

James Grove, "'Because God's Eye Never Closes': The Problem of Evil in Jayne Anne Phillips's *Shelter,*" in *The World Is Our Home: Society and Culture in Contemporary Southern Writing,* edited by Jeffrey J. Folks and Nancy Summers Folks (Lexington: University Press of Kentucky, 2000), pp. 73–92;

Dorothy Combs Hill, "Jayne Anne Phillips," in *Contemporary Fiction Writers of the South: A Bio-Bibliographical Sourcebook,* edited by Joseph M. Flora and Robert Barnes (Westport, Conn.: Greenwood Press, 1993), pp. 348–359;

Catherine Houser, "Missing in Action: Alienation in the Fiction of Award-Winning Women Writers," *Mid-America Review,* 14, no. 2 (1994): 33–39;

Meredith Sue Willis, "Witness the Nightmare Country: Jayne Anne Phillips," *Appalachian Studies Journal: A Regional Studies Review,* 24, no. 1 (1996): 44–51.

Jodi Picoult

(19 May 1966 –   )

J. Elizabeth Clark
LaGuardia Community College

BOOKS: *Songs of the Humpback Whale* (Boston: Faber & Faber, 1992);

Harvesting the Heart (New York: Viking, 1993);

Picture Perfect (New York: Putnam, 1995);

Mercy (New York: Putnam, 1996);

The Pact (New York: Morrow, 1998; St. Leonards, N.S.W.: Allen & Unwin, 1999);

Keeping Faith (New York: Morrow, 1999);

Plain Truth (New York: Pocket Books, 2000);

Salem Falls (New York: Pocket Books, 2001);

Perfect Match (New York: Atria Books, 2002);

Second Glance (New York: Atria Books, 2003);

My Sister's Keeper (New York: Atria, forthcoming 2004).

SELECTED PERIODICAL PUBLICATIONS– UNCOLLECTED: "Keeping Count," *Seventeen,* 46 (February 1987): 126;

"Road Stop," *Seventeen,* 46 (August 1987): 330.

With ten novels published by the time she was thirty-seven, Jodi Picoult ranks among the more prolific and ambitious young American writers. She has been characterized by critics as a women's fiction author; she contests this label, however, citing her popularity with both male and female fans. Her novels cross many genres, including literary fiction, legal thrillers, psychological portraits, romances, and ghost stories. In reviews, her body of work, themes, and writing style have been compared to authors as diverse as Alice Hoffman, John Grisham, and Daphne du Maurier. As this varied group of comparisons suggests, Picoult creates a new reading experience for her audience with each book.

Jodi Lynn Picoult was born on 19 May 1966 and grew up in Nesconset, Long Island, with her parents, Myron Michel Picoult, a securities analyst on Wall Street, and Jane Ellen Friend Picoult, a nursery-school teacher. She has one younger brother, Jonathan Paul Picoult. On her official website, <http://www.jodi-picoult.com>, Picoult says jokingly of her childhood, "I had such an uneventful childhood that much later,

Jodi Picoult (photograph by Joseph Mehling; from the dust jacket for Salem Falls, *2001; Richland County Public Library)*

when I was taking writing classes at college, I called home and yelled at my mother, wishing for a little incest or abuse on the side." She continues, "Good writers, I thought at the time, had to have something to write about. It took me a while to realize that I already did have something to write about—that solid core of family, and of relationships, which seem to form a connective thread through my books." Picoult's happy childhood included writing stories, which her grandmother still keeps as examples of her "early" work, and a job as a library page. These youthful interactions with professional writing compelled Picoult to move toward a career as a novelist.

278

She earned a B.A. in English in 1987 from Princeton University, where she studied creative writing with writers Robert Stone and Mary Morris. Under their guidance, Picoult had her first publishing success. She submitted a short story, "Keeping Count" (February 1987), to *Seventeen,* which published it and a subsequent story, "Road Stop" (August 1987).

Despite these early writing successes, Picoult went to work on Wall Street in New York City after her graduation. She then worked at a publishing company and later at an advertising agency. Finally, Picoult returned to the classroom to pursue a master's degree in education at Harvard University, earning an M.Ed. in 1990. Concomitant with her graduate education, Picoult taught creative writing at the Walnut Hill School for the Arts in Natick, Massachusetts from 1989 to 1991.

On 18 November 1989, Picoult married Timothy Warren van Leer, whom she met when both were members of the heavyweight men's crew team at Princeton. Picoult jokes, "I was a manager/coxswain, and I was the first person with two X chromosomes to set foot in a men's crew shell at the university!" Picoult's first novel was published following her marriage. Written while Picoult was six months pregnant with the first of her three children, *Songs of the Humpback Whale* (1992) establishes Picoult's primary theme for each of her subsequent novels: the love between family and friends. Her novels probe the key idea of what it means to love someone.

Songs of the Humpback Whale tells the same story from the perspectives of five related narrators: Jane Jones, the primary narrator; her daughter, Rebecca; her husband, Oliver; her brother, Joley; and her lover, Sam. The novel begins by following Jane, who decides to leave Oliver, a marine biologist who researches the songs of humpback whales. Jane and Rebecca set out on a cross-country trip to Stow, Massachusetts, where they will visit Joley, who works in an apple orchard. Jane narrates the trip from San Diego to Stow.

Rebecca's narrative follows her mother's, telling the story in reverse after the mother-daughter pair arrives in Stow. The perspectives of the three men play a less central role in the narrative, interwoven into Jane's and Rebecca's narratives and serving to move the plot along by speculating or commenting about Jane's and Rebecca's whereabouts. Picoult explores the relationship of family traditions and stories and the ways in which history is formed from the perspectives of different narrators.

Songs of the Humpback Whale sets the trajectory for Picoult's subsequent novels, which focus on protagonists facing a crucial moment of self-determination in their lives. As these protagonists explore the greater questions of their own subject positions and identities, they engage their immediate communities—groups of relatives or strangers who become parts of a greater narrative—in their considerations of life, love, and future decisions.

Publishers Weekly (10 February 1992) called *Songs of the Humpback Whale* a "powerful and affecting novel that demonstrates there are as many truths to a story as there are people to tell it" and cites Picoult's talent for creating strong, individual characters. The critical reception for this novel, however, was uneven. Susan Spano of *The New York Times Book Review* (6 September 1992) commented, "Picoult has created some characters whose voices ring true, but she doesn't seem to trust them enough to tell a more simply structured and more compelling tale." Critical receptions of some of Picoult's later novels followed a similar pattern: the books largely found favor with industry publications but encountered a more mediocre reception from literary reviewers.

Harvesting the Heart (1993) proves an exception to this trend, however. Karen Ray of *The New York Times Book Review* (16 January 1994) lavished praise on Picoult's second book. *Harvesting the Heart* demonstrates Picoult's character-driven angst most poignantly through the coming-of-age story of Paige O'Toole Prescott. Much of Paige's personal struggle stems from the crucial historical detail that Paige's mother deserted her when she was a child; Paige is determined to establish her own life, separate from the father who raised her and from the painful legacy of an absent mother. Told in flashbacks, the novel explores Paige's journey, which begins when she is eighteen, moving from her father's home in Chicago to Cambridge, Massachusetts, where she works while saving money to attend the Rhode Island School of Design.

Unable to afford art school, Paige works at the Mercy Diner, where she sketches the customers as part of the "Chicken Doodle Soup Special." Once Paige marries medical student Nicholas Prescott, she still works as a waitress in order to pay Nicholas's school bills. One of the central themes in the book revolves around Paige's struggle to understand and accept her own role as a mother. The *Publishers Weekly* reviewer (13 September 1993) commented, "this is a realistic story of childhood and adolescence, the demands of motherhood, the hard paths of personal growth and the generosity of spirit required by love. Picoult's imagery is startling and brilliant; her characters move credibly through this affecting drama." Paige's marriage to Nicholas leads to her second pregnancy, the first (by a former boyfriend) having ended in an abortion while Paige was still living in Chicago.

*Dust jacket for Picoult's first book, a 1992 novel in which five
narrators tell the story of a woman who leaves her
marine-biologist husband, taking their daughter
with her on a cross-continental journey
(Richland County Public Library)*

Overcome with her new responsibilities as a mother to baby Max and as a wife to Nicholas, Paige eventually abandons her child and husband to search for her long-estranged mother. Paige is torn by feelings of inadequacy resulting from her fractured experiences with motherhood on both sides of the relationship. Ultimately, her story becomes a search for self-discovery as she seeks out her own mother for answers about their lives, their separation, and the emotional connections that continue to exist in spite of physical absence. Paige eventually reunites with Nicholas and Max, determined that the best way to interrupt her mother's legacy is to embrace her role as a mother.

Harvesting the Heart was partially inspired by Picoult's own transition to new motherhood. Part of Picoult's craft depends on her ability to fully research her characters and to understand their lives. In order to better comprehend all of her characters and not just rely on the affinity of experience she imagined with

Paige, Picoult delved into medical-school research, even observing cardiac surgery to more realistically portray Nicholas's course of study.

The publication of Picoult's third book, *Picture Perfect* (1995), brought the beginning of critical attention to her work. This novel received recognition as a featured alternate selection of the Literary Guild and a Doubleday Book Club selection. In *Picture Perfect* Picoult demonstrates a clear commitment to exploring social issues that are prominent in cultural discussions, such as divorce, child custody, AIDS, rape, abuse, media culture, and in the case of *Picture Perfect,* domestic violence.

Protagonist Cassie Barrett, an anthropologist on location in Kenya as a scientific consultant to a movie, enters a world of glamour and high society when she marries movie star Alex Rivers. As with previous novels, Picoult uses flashbacks as a stylistic tool to unravel her story, so *Picture Perfect* begins with Cassie wandering through the streets of Los Angeles with amnesia. After her husband arrives at the police station to identify her, Cassie tries to reconcile her privileged lifestyle with the feelings of apprehension she has about her home and husband. The plot moves from California to a Native American reservation in South Dakota as Cassie flees memories of an abusive relationship. With a compassion common to Picoult's women characters, Cassie eventually returns to Los Angeles from the perceived safety of the reservation and her relationships there, to try to reconcile with Alex. His inability to face his violence and rage, however, lead Cassie to publicly expose his secret life as an abusive spouse. In a 1 January 1995 review, Dawn L. Anderson of the *Library Journal* praised the novel highly as "an important book from a talented writer we hope to hear from again and again."

Picoult's fourth book, *Mercy* (1996), is another story testing the bounds of love and compassion, and it illustrates her growth as a writer. *Mercy* places two cousins, Cameron and Jamie McDonald, at opposite ends of the spectrum of love and sacrifice. Set in Wheelock, Massachusetts, a town where the largely Scottish inhabitants adhere to clan law and their clan leader, police chief Cameron, the novel begins as Jamie arrives at the police station in his truck with his dead wife, Maggie, beside him. He confesses that he has killed his wife, as she wished, rather than letting her suffer with terminal cancer. This opening scene sets the tone for a novel in which the main characters confront the conflict between law and morality as they struggle with ethics, social taboos, and desire.

Cameron struggles with his conflict of interest in investigating a murder case in which the accused is his cousin. As Jamie stands trial for killing his wife out of love and dedication, however, Cameron practices selective ethics as he begins an affair with his wife's new assistant, Mia. Ultimately, Picoult argues that love is never an equally shared venture; in *Mercy*, Jamie and his cousin-in-law—Cameron's wife, Allie—serve to represent those who love more in their respective relationships, because their love forgives and endures despite the extraordinary pain of death and betrayal.

Booklist critic Donna Seaman (July 1996) wrote: "A graceful stylist, Picoult entertains her readers not only with feel-good story-telling and irresistible characters but with consideration of such serious moral dilemmas as euthanasia and forgiveness." Seaman praised Picoult's ability to interrogate human weakness and desire in *Mercy*, observing that one of Picoult's strengths as a writer lies in her ability to confront difficult social issues through powerful characters.

The transformative power of relationships between people—both the renewing possibilities of love and support and the dangers of deception and hurt—remains a constant thematic focus for Picoult. *The Pact* (1998), her fifth novel, exposes the power in a relationship between two teenagers who enter a suicide pact. As with *Harvesting the Heart*, Picoult relied heavily on research to better understand her characters. While Picoult spent a day in jail researching *The Pact*, her brief incarceration is not the most interesting element of her preparation to write this novel. Her interview with a policeman proved to be a crucial part of the development of the novel, leading to a radical reconceptualization of the entire plot. Picoult explains on her website:

> I was going to write a character-driven book about the female survivor of an unfinished suicide pact, and I went to the local police chief to do some preliminary research. "Huh," he said, "it's the girl who survives? Because if it was the boy, who was physically larger, he'd automatically be suspected of murder until cleared by the evidence."

With this revelation, Picoult focuses on Chris Harte, who survives an alleged suicide pact that leaves his girlfriend, Emily Gold, dead.

Picoult alternates the timeline of the narrative between Chris and Emily's love story and the aftermath of Emily's death. The novel follows their childhood friendship, which leads to young love, intimacy, pregnancy, the suicide pact, the eventual breakdown in the friendship between the Harte and the Gold families, the police investigation, and the suspicion of murder eventually facing Chris. Considered Picoult's "breakout novel" by *People Weekly* (8 June 1998) because of its sales (it has sold more than three hundred thousand copies), *The Pact* led to further acco-

Dust jacket for Picoult's 1996 novel, about euthanasia and adultery in a Massachusetts town (Richland County Public Library)

lades, including critical attention as a featured alternate selection of the Literary Guild, a selection of the Doubleday Book Club, and an Australian edition of the book, published by Allen and Unwin in 1999, which reached the best-seller list in that country. Since *The Pact*, her novels have been translated into a variety of languages. *The Pact* was made into a Lifetime television movie that aired in November 2002, with screenplay by Will Scheffer; it starred Megan Mullally and Juliet Stevenson.

The critically pleased reception of *The Pact* extended to *Keeping Faith* (1999), Picoult's sixth novel, which was also selected as a featured alternate selection of the Book of the Month Club. In a 15 May 1999 review, Margaret Flanagan of *Booklist* wrote: "Picoult blends elements of psychology and spirituality into a mesmerizing morality play, where conventional notions of faith and honesty are put to the test." *Keeping Faith* develops the relationships between protagonist Mariah White, her mother, her lover, her estranged husband, and their child, Faith. The crux of this novel

Dust jacket for Picoult's 1999 novel, about a custody battle over a girl who has mysteriously acquired supernatural healing powers (Richland County Public Library)

lies in Faith, who talks with her "guard," a being invisible to those around Faith but who allows the child to help and heal other people. Raised in a nonreligious household, young Faith begins to quote from the Bible, to exhibit stigmata on her hands, and to demonstrate the ability to heal people—of AIDS-related complications, of heart attacks, and of any other ailment they suffer—despite her lack of religious training and her lack of a substantive belief system.

Keeping Faith again demonstrates Picoult's keen ability to focus on human relationships and their sustaining power. The novel begins with the devastating affair of Colin, Mariah's husband, which results in the disintegration of their marriage. As the public becomes aware of Faith's new power to heal, the Whites' front lawn becomes a postmodern carnival of news media, the ill, and the curious. In a fierce custody battle for Faith, Colin uses the media spectacle to accuse Mariah of Munchausen syndrome by proxy, a condition in which parents hurt their children for attention. During this difficult period, Mariah finds that her relationships

with her mother, child, and new lover sustain her and lead her to self-confidence and independence.

Picoult's fifth and sixth novels attest to her regional appeal; her work is often cited as New England fiction because of its geographic specificity. In *The Concord Monitor* (24 December 2000), Rebecca Mahoney observed that "Both *The Pact* and *Keeping Faith* take place in fictional New Hampshire towns, her characters often drive on Route 4 and Interstate 93, and legal scenes are played out in state courts, including a custody battle in Carroll County in *Keeping Faith*." While the New England landscape has been an important part of Picoult's fictional landscape, she has also demonstrated experimentalism in her approach to each new novel. She tries different genres, different contemporary social issues, and with the publication of her seventh book, a new geography.

Continuing Picoult's exploration into issues of faith, *Plain Truth* (2000) takes readers to Pennsylvania Amish country. Picoult became interested in the Amish and posted a message on an Internet message board. A woman who read Picoult's query arranged for her to visit and stay with an Amish family as part of the research for her seventh novel, which included milking cows, attending Bible study, and participating in the life of the Amish household.

In this novel Picoult delves into the story of Katie Fisher, a young Amish woman who is accused of killing her newborn child. Ellie Nathaway, a Philadelphia defense attorney vacationing in Paradise, Pennsylvania, defends Katie. The novel becomes both the gripping tale of the collision of Katie's past and future and also of Ellie's growth as she enters a new culture and has to find ways of integration and assimilation. A review in the *Christian Science Monitor* (22 June 2000) demonstrates the critical praise for *Plain Truth:* "The solidly drawn cast of characters and supporting story lines boost the mounting cultural tension initiated by the criminal trial. There's the rigid father, an outcast son, and a hidden love. And through Katie's Amish community, Picoult creates a poignant portrait of the nature of deeply held beliefs." Patty Engelmann, in *Booklist* (15 April 2000), agreed that "Picoult does a wonderful job describing the Amish world and the desires these two different women share while presenting a gripping legal murder mystery." A 20 March 2000 *Publishers Weekly* reviewer offered the only mixed review, commenting that "Perhaps the story's quietude is appropriate, given its magnificently painted backdrop and distinctive characters, but one can't help wishing that the spark igniting the book's opening pages had built into a full fledged blaze." *Plain Truth,* like *The Pact,* has attracted considerable cross-over attention and is also under development as a television movie for Lifetime.

Picoult's next novel, *Salem Falls* (2001), also explores relationships in small-town America. *Salem Falls,* a contemporary revision of Arthur Miller's historical drama *The Crucible* (1953), pits the individual against the community. Picoult introduces Jack St. Bride, a teacher and soccer coach fleeing his tarnished reputation after a rape accusation. A group of young women in the town of Salem Falls, notably Gillian Duncan, whose father is a powerful local mogul, target St. Bride as the object of their pubescent curiosity. At a Wiccan ceremony in the woods late one evening, Gillian is assaulted. The ensuing story finds St. Bride at the center of accusations reminiscent of the ones that brought him to Salem Falls seeking anonymity and a chance to start his life over. In a *Denver Post* review (22 April 2001), Robin Vidimos observed:

> Not the least of Picoult's story-telling gifts is her ability to convey the natural tension in a small town between knowing enough to care and knowing so much as to be fearful. Much of her plot turns on the townspeople's blind distrust of Jack once they realize that he's been convicted and jailed as a sexual predator. It's a label he is unable to avoid, given the requirements of Megan's law. In this case, the label is unjust, but he's facing a conflict built on sly whispers and supposition. He is left with no way to respond.

Vidimos's commentary demonstrates that Picoult's power comes from her ability to understand small towns and how they operate.

St. Bride is both enigma and obvious victim. Jeff Zaleski, in a 19 February 2001 *Publishers Weekly* review, questioned Picoult's attempt to elucidate St. Bride's situation and offered mixed praise for the novel: "Genuinely suspenseful and at times remarkably original, this romance-mystery-morality play will gain Picoult new readers although her treatment of the aftermath of rape may also make her a few enemies." Picoult uses St. Bride's situation to reveal the relationships around him as well as the true nature of the town and its citizens.

Picoult's ninth novel, *Perfect Match* (2002), also examines the relationship between the individual and the community, focusing upon a timely character—a child-molesting priest. Picoult narrates from the perspective of attorney Nina Frost of York County, Maine. Nina and Caleb Frost are happy parents to their young son, Nathaniel. Early in the novel, the child is molested, and the trauma of the incident prevents the five-year-old child from speaking. He indicates that "father" committed the crime, so initially his father, Caleb, is arrested. After Nathaniel regains his power of speech, however, he reveals that his abuser is "Father Gwen"—

Dust jacket for Picoult's 2001 novel, about a modern-day "witch hunt" in which a teacher with a prior conviction as a sex offender is falsely accused of raping a rich man's daughter (Richland County Public Library)

and Father Glen Szyszynski heads the local Catholic church. DNA evidence corroborates Nathaniel's story.

As Nina struggles with this crime, she realizes that the only way to convict Father Szyszynski is to put Nathaniel on the stand, compelling him to relive the horrific incidents that drove him into prolonged speechlessness. Nina acts on her sense of rage against the injustice of a legal system that would revictimize her son, and she shoots Father Szyszynski in public before his arraignment. After she kills Father Szyszynski, she stands trial, and during the trial, further DNA tests (thus the title, *Perfect Match*) show that Father Szyszynski is not the molester. Suspicion then falls on Father Szyszynski's half-brother, Father Gwynn. Nina is found guilty of manslaughter, is given probation, and loses her license to practice law.

Denver Post reviewer Vidimos commented that Picoult's novel was begun long before the 2002 public scandal about Catholic clergy and pedophilia. Vidimos wrote in her 21 April 2002 review that "The danger of focusing on the sensationalized part of the novel is that its deeper, more difficult, questions will be ignored. Nina is sure she is doing the best for those she cares about when she kills the alleged perpetrator. She is certain she has the right man and that the testimony needed to convict him would destroy her son." As with other Picoult novels, *Perfect Match* is an exploration of social mores and personal responsibility in the context of intense personal relationships. Nancy Pearl of the *Library Journal* (1 May 2002) disagreed, however, arguing, "the usually reliable Picoult fails to deliver. . . . Nina is a truly dislikable heroine (her justifications for the murder are both laughable and frightening), and the truly meaningless subplots distract from, rather than add to, the main story." At the heart of *Perfect Match,* as with most of her novels, Picoult questions the ways in which people come to know one another in a community and within their relationships. She presents the main character in conflict with society in order to explore the depths of her character's convictions.

Picoult's tenth novel, *Second Glance* (2003), a featured selection of the Literary Guild, is set in Comtosook, Vermont, and follows the story of ghost hunter Ross Wakeman. Mourning the loss of his fiancée, Aimee, in a car accident, Ross tries unsuccessfully to commit suicide. His desperation is replaced by his fascination with the paranormal as a way to contact Aimee. As with other novels, Picoult weaves in real-life controversies, such as eugenics projects carried out in Vermont in the 1930s, as a way of exploring deeper issues of truth. Following the publication of this novel, Picoult was awarded the 2003 New England Bookseller Association Award in fiction.

My Sister's Keeper (2004) also explores real-life controversies as well as the bonds between siblings. Thirteen-year-old Anna was conceived by her parents specifically as a bone-marrow donor for her sister, Kate, who has leukemia. Anna's life is dictated by her sister's ill health. The novel focuses on Anna's search for identity in a life that was predetermined by her genetic ability to help her sister. In an author's note on her website, Picoult writes that "Today's political and scientific battles over cloning and DNA and gene replacement therapy led me to think about some of what the future might hold, on a personal level, for people." She asks, "If you use one of your children to save the life of another, are you being a good mother . . . or a very bad one?" Picoult is currently at work on her twelfth novel, "Vanishing Acts," due in 2005.

Picoult's novels rely on her ability to engage the reader with "what if" situations. In each of her novels, ordinary characters face the kinds of events that readers and characters think will never happen to them. The ability of readers to connect with Picoult's wide range of characters is evident in Picoult's wide popular appeal. She is a featured author in many public libraries; the virtual community of the Internet has embraced her work with chat rooms and messages posted about her latest books; and her fans stave off their impatience for new books by sending her e-mail, which she answers faithfully.

Given Picoult's prolific career, her contribution to the American literary canon as a twenty-first-century novelist promises to be significant. Picoult offers her readers a look inside relationships, inside communities, and inside the hearts and minds of characters with whom they share common ground. Picoult focuses on the collision between the everyday and the unexpected; she renders her characters capable survivors in the midst of tragedy, imperfect creations in an imperfect world.

Interviews:

Rebecca Mahoney, *Concord Monitor,* 24 December 2000;

"An Interview with Jodi" and "Frequently Asked Questions" <http://www.jodipicoult.com>.

Anna Quindlen

(8 July 1952 –)

Lisa Abney
Northwestern State University

BOOKS: *Living Out Loud* (New York: Random House, 1988);

Object Lessons (New York: Random House, 1991; London: Arrow, 1996);

The Tree That Came to Stay (New York: Crown, 1992);

Thinking Out Loud: On the Personal, the Political, the Public, and the Private (New York: Random House, 1993);

One True Thing (New York: Random House, 1994; London: Chatto & Windus, 1995);

Naked Babies, text by Quindlen, photographs by Nick Kelsh (New York: Penguin Studio, 1996);

Happily Ever After (New York: Viking, 1997);

Siblings, text by Quindlen, photographs by Kelsh (New York: Penguin Studio, 1998);

Black and Blue (New York: Random House, 1998; London: Chatto & Windus, 1998);

How Reading Changed My Life (New York: Ballantine, 1998);

A Short Guide to a Happy Life (New York: Random House, 2000; London: Century, 2002);

Blessings (New York: Random House, 2002; London: Hutchinson, 2002);

Loud and Clear (New York: Random House, 2004).

RECORDING: *Thinking Out Loud,* read by Quindlen, New York, Simon & Schuster Audio, 1994.

During the last decades of the twentieth century, Anna Quindlen emerged as an important novelist. Her works address a variety of topics, ranging from the maturation of a girl in a large Irish Italian family to sobering depictions of fatal diseases and domestic violence. While Quindlen has sometimes been viewed as a novelist addressing women's issues, her work possesses universal appeal.

Anna Quindlen was born on 8 July 1952 in Philadelphia, Pennsylvania, the oldest of five siblings. Her father, Robert V. Quindlen, was a management consultant of Irish extraction, and her mother, Prudence Quindlen, came from an Italian family and worked in

Anna Quindlen (photograph by Maria Krovatin; from the dust jacket for Blessings, *2002; Richland County Public Library)*

the home. Even as a youth, Quindlen found herself drawn to writing. Raised in the upper-middle-class neighborhood of Drexel Hill, Quindlen attended private parochial schools and earned her B.A. in English literature from Barnard College in 1974. Quindlen's

285

Dust jacket for Quindlen's 1991 first novel, which chronicles the
lives of three generations of an Irish-Italian American
family through the eyes of an adolescent girl
(Richland County Public Library)

Quindlen gave birth to her first son, Quin, in 1983 and another son, Christopher, in 1985. By that time Quindlen felt drawn to stay home with her children, and she decided to resign from the newspaper. Her editor, however, offered her a chance to write a weekly column, which later turned into "Life in the 30s." Quindlen's columns became enormously popular and soon gained syndication across the United States. Her topics ranged from reminiscences about her childhood to difficulties in raising children and working outside the home to pro-choice issues. While some readers hailed her work as brilliant and interesting, others found it tedious and self-absorbed. Her columns were largely drawn from personal experience and addressed subjects that she found important—primarily issues affecting women and children. Her dedication to women's issues stemmed largely from her experiences with sexism; in an interview with Karen Winegar of the Star Tribune (17 September 1995), Quindlen remarked:

> Younger women get clonked on the head later than I did. If you are my age and you weren't a total moron, by the time you were 18 or 19 years old sexism hit you upside the head a number of times, ranging from the fact that there were certain colleges you couldn't go to. And there were certain ways you were going to be treated like garbage, and you were either gonna put up with it and therefore be lauded as one of the boys or you wouldn't put up with it and therefore be classified as a bitch.

> For younger women, the moment of truth doesn't come now until they are in their 30s, because they can go to any of these colleges or graduate schools, get good jobs and move through and don't have to put up with some of the sexual harassment and name calling that we did.

Comments such as these sparked violent reactions from the conservative Right, and Quindlen often received scathing letters of disagreement regarding her views about politics and women's issues. For the most part, however, her writing appealed to many who became loyal readers. In 1988 Quindlen retired her column, and in the same year, she published her first work, *Living Out Loud,* which was a collection of her "Life in the 30s" pieces. Her daughter, Maria, was born that same year, and Quindlen felt that it was time to move toward fiction writing rather than journalism, though she still wrote freelance pieces. In 1992 Quindlen was honored with the Pulitzer Prize in commentary.

While writing her "Life in the 30s" column, she had begun work on a novel, *Object Lessons,* which was published in April 1991. *Object Lessons* chronicles the

upbringing was steeped in the strong traditions of Catholicism, as manifested in her parents.

When she was just eighteen, Quindlen was hired by the *New York Post* as a part-time reporter, and by the time she completed her degree at Barnard, she had earned a spot as a full-time reporter. While Quindlen was at Barnard, her mother was diagnosed with cancer and died when Quindlen was nineteen. In 1977 Quindlen left the *New York Post* for a job with the prestigious *New York Times.* She began work there as a general-assignment reporter and was soon assigned to City Hall, which she covered until 1981. In 1978 Quindlen married Gerald Krovatin, a criminal-defense attorney. By 1983, Quindlen had been promoted to deputy metropolitan editor and was contributing two editorial columns a week in addition to her other writing duties at *The New York Times.*

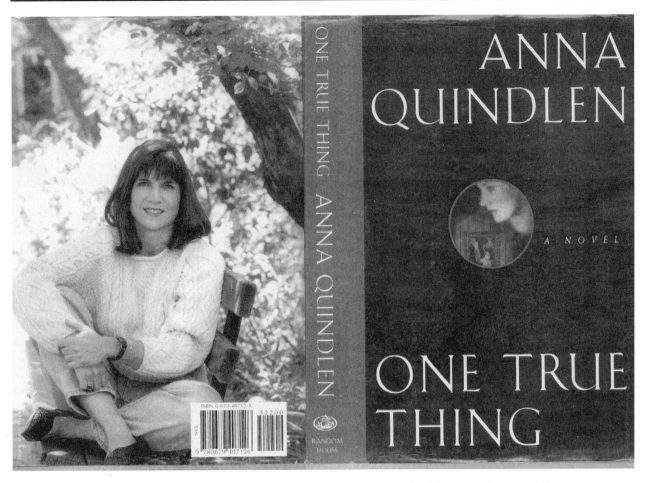

Dust jacket for Quindlen's 1994 novel, about a woman who gives up a prestigious job to care for her cancer-stricken mother and is accused of the latter's mercy killing (Richland County Public Library)

lives of three generations of the Scanlans, an Irish Italian American family. The novel is related through the perspective of Maggie Scanlan, a thirteen-year-old observing the activities of adults who perplex her as she watches them. John Scanlan, the patriarch of the family, becomes the central figure around whom all the others revolve: "That was what impressed Maggie most about her grandfather Scanlan: not that he dispensed down payments, tuition money, doctor's fees. . . . It was that he could, almost magically, make his children bob and move and sway like marionettes." This pivotal summer of Maggie's life includes her grandfather's death, the revelation of family secrets, and her own coming of age. *Object Lessons* presents characters who are interesting and vivid, and who endure a variety of tragedies and disappointments. Quindlen's journalist eye for detail is mirrored in her fiction, and Maggie's narrative is realistic and readable.

Object Lessons received favorable acclaim from readers; yet, critics often panned the book for its inadequacies. Louise Kennedy of the *Boston Globe* (22

April 1991) commented: "Unfortunately, the novel is not nearly as good as it could have been. . . . What trips Quindlen up is the gap between nonfiction and fiction. It may all be 'writing,' but Quindlen has not yet mastered the skills that are particular to fiction." Further, Kennedy argued that Quindlen's too-frequent use of the flashback technique is distracting to readers. Alex Madrigal, in a review for the *San Francisco Chronicle* (26 May 1991), wrote: "Anna Quindlen is best known for her *New York Times* syndicated columns, especially the 'Life in the 30s' pieces of a few years back. Warm and wry, they offer accessible, thoughtful, down-home wisdom, also a characteristic of her first novel, *Object Lessons*. It must also be said that for all its charm, *Object Lessons* never goes much deeper than the columns." On the whole, Quindlen's first work of fiction failed to bring strong critical reviews, but stalwart fans and new readers enjoyed the novel.

Quindlen's next project was a children's book, *The Tree That Came to Stay,* published in 1992. It was followed by *Thinking Out Loud: On the Personal, the Polit-*

*Dust jacket for Quindlen's 1998 novel, about a woman's
attempt to escape her abusive husband
(Richland County Public Library)*

der, but she did not deliver the morphine to her mother. She suspects that her father gave her mother the overdose in her last meal of rice pudding. After Ellen escapes indictment, she returns to New York, and after a period of confusion and a series of temporary jobs, she enters medical school and becomes an adolescent psychiatrist. Only by chance does she meet her father on the street in New York and discover that he did not give her mother the morphine—that, in fact, her mother committed suicide in order to spare Ellen and her father the pain of further caring for her.

Critics hailed the book as astounding and triumphant, and that same year, a movie version with screenplay by Karen Croner and starring Renée Zellweger and Meryl Streep premiered. Donna Seaman wrote in *Booklist* (December 1994):

> It isn't easy reading of Ellen's once radiant and ever-nurturing mother, but it is eminently satisfying to witness Ellen's transformation from an often glib, emotionally suppressed overachiever into a woman who begins to fathom the meaning of love. Quindlen also gets in some good jabs at the media for its feverish appetite for easy scandal and its irrelevance to the truth manifest in genuine tragedies."

Another reviewer with the *Wellington Evening Post* (12 February 1999) asserted that *One True Thing* "may not be Great Literature but it is a satisfying and multi-layered exploration of a mother-daughter relationship. . . . What impresses is Quindlen's even-handed portrayal of the two, very different women." Sylvia Sachs wrote in the *Pittsburgh Post-Gazette* (9 October 1994):

> As she proved in her years as a columnist for the *New York Times,* Anna Quindlen has an innate understanding of and feeling for contemporary life and the people who live it. The family in *One True Thing* is very like those the reader may know as neighbors or acquaintances. And in her current role as novelist, Quindlen is free to delve into secrets not usually revealed about the real folks next door.

Quindlen's exploration of controversial issues and secrets reappears in her third novel, *Black and Blue* (1998), which followed another children's book (*Happily Ever After,* 1997) and two coffee-table books with photographer Nick Kelsh (*Naked Babies,* 1996, and *Siblings,* 1998). *Black and Blue* recounts the story of Fran and Bobby Benedetto's painful and turbulent marriage. After almost twenty years of domestic violence, nurse Fran finally endures enough beatings, and she contacts a battered women's organization. Fran and her son, Robert, escape to Florida under the

ical, the Public, and the Private* (1993), an essay collection in which Quindlen examined a range of social issues. Quindlen's second work of fiction, *One True Thing,* is a loosely autobiographical depiction of the lives of an upper-middle-class family dealing with the mother's diagnosis of cancer. Ellen Gulden gives up a prestigious job to care for her dying mother, for whom she has possessed little respect over the years. While caring for her mother, Ellen learns about herself and the family that she has long taken for granted. Quindlen illustrates the demands placed upon women in familial relationships and explores the controversial topic of euthanasia.

The novel, recounted through Ellen's perspective, demonstrates the growth that the self-absorbed and ambitious character undergoes as she learns about the value of her mother's life. When her mother dies from an overdose of morphine in the later stages of her illness, Ellen is charged with mur-

assumed names of Elizabeth and Robert Crenshaw, and Fran begins to create a new identity. She forms a close relationship with the mother of one of her son's schoolmates, Cindy Roerbacker, and their friendship, along with Fran's job as a home health attendant, make Fran's new life bearable. Fran and Robert cannot leave their old lives behind, however; on Thanksgiving night, she calls her sister to reminisce, and Robert, after a traumatic fight at school, calls his father. Bobby, by tracking the phone number, comes to Florida to reclaim his son, and for one last time, he brutalizes his wife. Fran is beaten severely, and when she awakens, her son has been kidnapped, and she is left to start her life over once more.

Literary critics were more pleased with *Black and Blue* than the previous two novels, although some reviewers were less welcoming of the social critiques. Betsy Taylor, writing for the *Buffalo News* (26 April 1998), argued: "In this novel, Quindlen skillfully shows the strange combination of passion, fear and familiarity that binds a dysfunctional family together, even as it rips it apart." Laura Green, writing for the on-line *Salon.com* (10 February 1998), asserted: "Like other contemporary domestic novelists, such as Anne Tyler and Anne Lamont, Quindlen balances her readers' longing to experience the protagonist's triumph with the knowledge that to end by simply rewarding virtue would betray the very realism we enjoy." Barbara Liss, writing for the *Houston Chronicle* (1 March 1998), found the novel unoriginal: "the characters do not resolve conflict; they struggle with an issue. . . . If Quindlen wants to use fiction to explore social issues, she must say something new and unexpected. It is distressing she has not yet done so." The majority of the reviews, however, have been positive, and readers embraced the work, leading to its presence on many best-seller lists. It became a television movie in 1999, with screenplay by April Smith and starring Mary Stuart Masterson and Anthony LaPaglia.

In 2000 Quindlen published *A Short Guide to a Happy Life,* which was an expanded version of a commencement speech. With that work, Quindlen became the first writer ever to have books appear on the fiction, nonfiction, and self-help *New York Times* best-seller lists. Following this book, Quindlen wrote another novel, *Blessings,* which was published in 2002.

Blessings presents Lydia Blessing, a rigid and slightly haughty elderly woman, and her handyman, former convict Skip Cuddy. One morning while doing his chores, Skip discovers an abandoned baby. Trying to put his past transgressions behind him, he values his second chance. Once he finds the box with the baby in it, he attempts to care for her on his own;

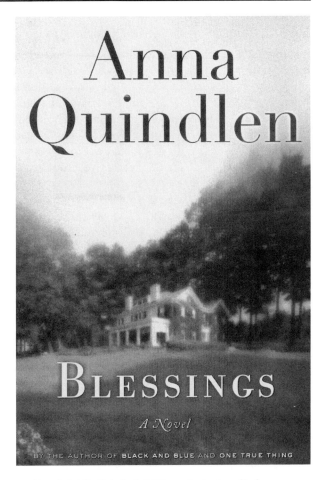

Dust jacket for Quindlen's 2002 novel, about an elderly woman and her handyman, who undertake to raise an abandoned baby (Richland County Public Library)

however, because of his work, he cannot hide the child. Together, he and Lydia bond with the abandoned baby girl, whom they name Faith and raise for a short time, forming a nontraditional family unit. After several twists in the story, the child is reunited with her biological mother, and Skip and Lydia are left to continue their lives. The 2003 CBS television-movie version, with screenplay by Joyce Eliason, starred Mary Tyler Moore and Liam Waite.

Critics have, as with Quindlen's other novels, been split over their perceptions of *Blessings.* Amanda Heller, writing for the *Boston Globe* (13 October 2002), regarded the novel as implausible: "The central characters—the solitary hired hand, the frigid dowager—seem products of guesswork, not creative intuition. And the descriptive passages bulge with gassy, misplaced lyricism." Carole Goldberg differed in her assessment of the novel for the *Star Tribune* (13 October 2002): "An old-fashioned romanticism, a fairy-tale sweetness permeates Anna Quindlen's *Blessings,* a novel of love, sacrifice and redemption." Claire Dederer wrote for *Amazon.com:* "Quindlen wrings a remarkable amount of pathos from this somewhat simple setup. . . . Best of all is her flair for observation. The book wouldn't work at all if she couldn't make us feel Skip and Lydia's amazement at the small joys of a baby ('The deep pleat in the fat at her elbow made her arms look muscled'). Here is a book that lives up to its title." With this mixed critical acclaim, *Blessings* has yet to attain the success of Quindlen's previous novels.

Anna Quindlen's fiction maintains a strong social agenda, and throughout all her novels, she emphasizes the importance of realistic and believable characters. Her novels have drawn legions of loyal readers; and critics, while sometimes not entirely impressed with Quindlen's plots, almost always praise her ability to create interesting stories and strong characters.

Interviews:

Brian Lamb, *"Thinking Out Loud: On the Personal, the Political, the Public and the Private,"* C-Span (16 May 1993) <http://www.booknotes.org/Transcript/?ProgramID=1149>;

Karen Winegar, "Ex-Columnist Anna Quindlen Continues Fight for Feminist Causes from Speaker's Podium," *Star Tribune,* 17 September 1995, p. E1;

"Life in the 40s: Writer Anna Quindlen is Enjoying the Relative Anonymity of Her Celebrity Life," *St. Louis Post-Dispatch,* 11 March 1998, p. E1;

"Breakfast with Anna Quindlen," *Pittsburgh Post-Gazette,* 29 October 2001, p. D2;

"Conversations with Anna," Random House website <http://www.randomhouse.com/features/aquindlen/conversations.html>.

Anne Rice
(A. N. Roquelaure, Anne Rampling)
(4 October 1941 –)

Betsy Bryan Miguez

University of Louisiana at Lafayette

BOOKS: *Interview with the Vampire: A Novel* (New York: Knopf, 1976; London: Raven, 1976);

The Feast of All Saints (New York: Simon & Schuster, 1979; London: Penguin, 1982);

Cry to Heaven (New York: Knopf, 1982; London: Chatto & Windus, 1990);

The Claiming of Sleeping Beauty: An Erotic Novel of Tenderness and Cruelty for the Enjoyment of Men and Women, as A. N. Roquelaure (New York: Dutton, 1983; London: Macdonald, 1987);

Beauty's Punishment, as Roquelaure (New York: Dutton, 1984; London: Macdonald, 1987);

Exit to Eden, as Anne Rampling (New York: Arbor House, 1985; London: Futura, 1986);

Beauty's Release, as Roquelaure (New York: Dutton, 1985; London: Macdonald, 1988);

The Vampire Lestat: The Second Book in the Vampire Chronicles (New York: Knopf, 1985; London: Futura, 1986);

Belinda, as Rampling (New York: Arbor House, 1986; London: Macdonald, 1987);

The Queen of the Damned: The Third Book in the Vampire Chronicles (New York: Knopf, 1988; London: Macdonald, 1989);

The Mummy, or Ramses the Damned (New York: Ballantine, 1989; London: Chatto & Windus, 1989);

The Witching Hour (New York: Knopf, 1990; London: Chatto & Windus, 1991);

The Tale of the Body Thief (New York: Knopf, 1992; London: Chatto & Windus, 1992);

Lasher (New York: Knopf, 1993; London: Chatto & Windus, 1993);

Taltos: Lives of the Mayfair Witches (New York: Knopf, 1994; London: Chatto & Windus, 1994);

Memnoch the Devil (New York: Knopf, 1995; London: Chatto & Windus, 1995);

Servant of the Bones (New York: Knopf, 1996; London: Chatto & Windus, 1996);

Anne Rice (photograph by Mary Ellen Mark; from the dust jacket for Taltos: Lives of the Mayfair Witches, *1994; Richland County Public Library)*

Violin (New York: Knopf, 1997; London: Chatto & Windus, 1997);

The Anne Rice Reader, edited by Katherine Ramsland (New York: Ballantine, 1997);

Pandora: New Tales of the Vampires (New York: Knopf, 1998; London: Chatto & Windus, 1998);

The Vampire Armand: The Vampire Chronicles (New York: Knopf, 1998; London: Chatto & Windus, 1998);

Vittorio, the Vampire: New Tales of the Vampires (New York: Knopf, 1999; London: Chatto & Windus, 1999);

Merrick: A Novel (New York: Knopf, 2000; London: Chatto & Windus, 2000);

Blood and Gold, or, The Story of Marius: The Vampire Chronicles (New York: Knopf, 2001; London: Chatto & Windus, 2001);

Blackwood Farm (New York: Knopf, 2002; London: Chatto & Windus, 2002);

Blood Canticle (New York: Knopf, 2003).

PRODUCED SCRIPT: *Interview with the Vampire: The Vampire Chronicles,* motion picture, Warner Bros., 1994.

OTHER: "Elliott: The Garden and the Bar" and "Elliott: Below Stairs," in *Flesh and the Word: An Anthology of Erotic Writing,* edited by John Preston (New York: Plume, 1992), pp. 189–212;

Alice Borchardt, *Devoted,* introduction by Rice (New York: Dutton, 1995);

Franz Kafka, *The Metamorphosis, In the Penal Colony, and Other Stories,* foreword by Rice (New York: Schocken, 1995);

Kelly Klein, *Underworld,* introduction by Rice (New York: Knopf, 1995);

Borchardt, *Beguiled,* introduction by Rice (New York: Dutton, 1997).

SELECTED PERIODICAL PUBLICATIONS–UNCOLLECTED: "David Bowie and the End of Gender," *Vogue,* 173 (November 1983): 432–434, 498;

"The Master of Rampling Gate," *Redbook,* 162 (February 1984): 50–58.

Anne Rice is a best-selling author of Gothic novels, historical fiction, and erotica under her own name and two pseudonyms. Interest in Rice's life has earned her celebrity status among her fans. Not only does Rice intertwine the past and present, but her vampires, witches, ghosts, and human "outsiders" travel around the world as she tells tales that never shy away from taboo subjects. A thread of philosophy runs through her writing, as themes concerning immortality and morality are repeated using different genres, subjects, and writing styles. Rice puts herself into her novels, allowing characters to live her experiences and voice her thoughts. The history of her writing is thus the history of her own journey of self-discovery. In fact, Rice has described her writing as a therapeutic process that has helped bring together a personality fragmented by several losses in her early years. Rice's books have attracted a huge following of diverse readers and have gained attention from the academic community as well.

Anne Rice was named Howard Allen Frances O'Brien when she was born in New Orleans on 4 October 1941. Howard (who gave herself the name Anne when she entered school) was the second of four girls who were raised in an environment influenced by the teachings of the Catholic Church. While her father,

Howard J. O'Brien, encouraged her creativity and contributed to her literary education, her mother, Katherine Allen O'Brien, consciously set out to raise geniuses. Volumes of Charles Dickens and Edgar Allan Poe filled the house, and storytelling was common among the Irish relatives who came to visit. Also inspired by the rich home environment, Anne's older sister became a successful author of historical romances and fantasy novels, writing as Alice Borchardt.

At the Catholic school Anne O'Brien attended, she never felt that she fit in. Her family was poorer than most of the other families, and her large vocabulary, her knowledge of literature, and her individuality made her stand out. The rigidity of school rules was a direct contrast to the relative freedom of her home. Although her mother believed girls could do anything, O'Brien observed different expectations for boys and girls at school.

O'Brien's mother was often "sick" as she succumbed to alcoholism, and O'Brien's father was absent from the chaotic household much of the time working two jobs. O'Brien filled her time with walks, taking in the beauty and mystery of New Orleans with all her senses. Death was a natural part of life in the city where cemeteries house aboveground tombs and where funerals are family events. O'Brien developed intricate fantasy worlds to feed her imagination. She and her cousins explored the supernatural in library books. From Dickens, she developed her interest in the human conflict between good and evil. O'Brien was the family playwright and journalist. She sent novels to publishers at an early age, hoping to save the family from its problems.

Attending mass daily, O'Brien was surrounded with the beauty and the restrictions of the Catholic Church. O'Brien developed a fascination with the female saints who had suffered self-inflicted wounds and stigmata. She spent many hours of her youth praying in a makeshift oratory, a retreat her father built for her. O'Brien's devotion to the Catholic Church was complicated by her sensuous response to the mass and its symbolism. The conflict between pleasure and fear of punishment led to masochistic fantasies she later developed in her erotic novels. Her fascination with androgyny, which later pervaded her writing, also started at church, where she was surrounded with priests and nuns in robes to their ankles and asexual statues of saints.

When O'Brien was fourteen years old, her mother died of alcoholism. This devastating loss contributed to a fear of death that influenced her adult life and writing. Characters in her novels often experience their own sense of loss as they deal with alcoholic mothers, death, and growing up without a mentor or teacher.

O'Brien's father remarried a year after her mother died, and the family moved to Richardson, Texas, a suburb of Dallas. O'Brien felt like a transplant in her new environment. She soon met fellow writer Stan Rice, who was drawn to O'Brien's vitality, but they drifted apart when she entered Texas Women's University in 1959. O'Brien worked hard to finance her education, believing that education was the key to the greatness her mother had inspired in her. While in college, O'Brien's curiosity led her to explore ideas that were contrary to the teachings of the Catholic Church. Seeking a freer environment, O'Brien moved to the Haight-Ashbury area of San Francisco in 1960.

O'Brien and Stan Rice renewed their relationship and were married in October 1961. They worked and attended college, both graduating from San Francisco State College (later University) in 1964. By graduation, Stan Rice was respected as a poet. He earned a master's degree and began teaching at San Francisco State College.

Anne Rice's college major was political science. After graduation, Rice continued her studies at San Francisco State College, where she completed an M.A. in creative writing in 1972. She submitted an erotic novella titled "Katherine and Jean" for her thesis. She published two short pieces in *Transfer,* the school literary magazine. "October 4, 1948," an autobiographical story describing a day in New Orleans through the eyes of a young girl, appeared in the May 1965 issue. The first chapter of a romantic novella titled "Nicholas and Jean" was published in June 1966. Both of these were later collected in *The Anne Rice Reader* (1997).

On 21 September 1966 the Rices' first baby, Michele, was born. The family moved to Berkeley, where Rice worked on several literary pieces. In the summer of 1970, her full attention turned to Michele, who was diagnosed with acute granulocytic leukemia. Despite intense research over the next two years, Rice found no way to save her child. Michele died in 1972. After losing her mother and her daughter, Rice no longer believed in God. She turned toward humanism, seeking goodness separate from religion, and she began to place more value in human experience than in abstract ideas.

Rice sank into a deep depression and drank alcohol daily. Out of her pain and loss came her first successful novel. She picked up a vampire story she had started before Michele's illness. Working relentlessly for five weeks, she completed the 338-page manuscript of *Interview with the Vampire* (1976) in early 1974. In *Prism of the Night: A Biography of Anne Rice* (1991), Katherine Ramsland says that writing the novel was therapeutic and that many of Rice's struggles and thoughts are

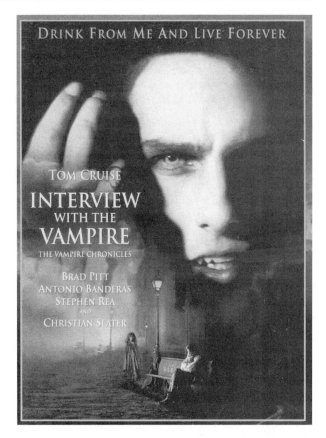

Poster for the 1994 movie version of Rice's best-selling 1976 first novel, in which the vampire Louis de Pointe du Lac tells the story of his life (Collection of Paul Talbot)

expressed through Louis de Pointe du Lac, the vampire who relates the story of his life. Louis wrestles with the existence of God, the concepts of good and evil, and the nature of his own immortality. At that time, Rice refused to acknowledge that the character of Claudia, a small blonde girl who is given immortality through life as a vampire, was in any way connected with her daughter, Michele. The vampire Lestat de Lioncourt, who later became Rice's most popular character, mentors Louis in this novel.

Despite many rejections by publishers, Rice believed *Interview with the Vampire* was worthy of publication. Rice, who has described herself as a gay male trapped in the body of a female, breathes sensuality into the interactions of same-sex vampires. Her voluptuous style heightens erotic scenes. The New Orleans setting described through many sensory experiences underscores the theme of immortality and the questions of morality posed by the vampire Louis. In this book Rice began her creation of the vampire myth that she expanded as the Vampire Chronicles continued. Telling the story from the vampire's point of view, which Rice continued to do in later novels, provided an avenue for exploration of philosophical ideas.

In late 1975, Alfred A. Knopf bought publication rights to *Interview with the Vampire* for $12,000. Paramount bought the movie rights for $150,000. The paperback rights sold for $700,000, the greatest sum ever paid for a paperback at that time. *Interview with the Vampire* was released in May 1976.

Interview with the Vampire attracted the attention of seventy-five reviewers, most of whom viewed it favorably. "While not for the squeamish, it *is* spellbinding, eerie, original in conception, and deserving of the popular attention it appears destined to receive," wrote Irma Pascal Heldman in *The Village Voice* (10 May 1976). In the *Wall Street Journal* (17 June 1976) Edmund Fuller praised Rice's originality, her Gothic style, the philosophical content of the book, and the "incredibly controlled craftsmanship for a first novel." One objection voiced in several reviews was the fact that the bloodsucking Louis was so concerned with the concept of morality. "What makes *Interview* so bad is not that the erotic content is so explicit, but that the morbid context is so respectable," complained Edith Milton in *New Republic* (8 May 1976). Despite her objections, Milton predicted that the book was "headed for almost certain success." The book sold slowly at first; its popularity grew as fans spread its reputation by word of mouth.

Money from the rights for *Interview with the Vampire* gave the Rices freedom to travel and buy their own home. For the next few years, Rice and her husband lived in several houses in Berkeley and Oakland, California. Rice preferred the area to San Francisco because of the milder climate and greener landscape. The Rices' second child, Christopher, was born on 11 March 1978. Rice was no longer drinking, and she had become a full-time writer. Utilizing research about New Orleans she had been collecting for years, Rice wrote *The Feast of All Saints* (1979).

The Feast of All Saints brings to life the *gens de couleur libre* (free people of color) who lived in New Orleans in the 1840s. Like the vampires of her first novel, the free people of color were outsiders; they were suspended without power between the white and black worlds. Rice strove to make her characters interesting, entertain her readers, and comment on the human experience. She believed that this story, which centers on a boy's sexual and intellectual development, would be a success. Simon and Schuster agreed and offered her a $150,000 advance. The novel was published at the end of 1979.

The Feast of All Saints attracted only half the number of reviews *Interview with the Vampire* had, and critics were mixed in their opinions. Fewer than twenty thousand copies of the hardcover book were sold, and paperback rights garnered only $35,000. The book eventually went through several printings as Rice's reputation grew.

In 1980 the Rices moved to the Castro district of San Francisco. Rice's next major undertaking was the historical novel *Cry to Heaven* (1982). Rice consciously laid out the historical background at the beginning of the novel in an attempt to appeal to her American audience. The main characters of the novel are Italian castrati, boys castrated to preserve their perfect soprano voices. Rice depicts the main character's search for personal and sexual identity. Alfred A. Knopf offered Rice a $75,000 advance by the time the novel was two-thirds complete.

Cry to Heaven received mixed reviews when it was published in October 1982. *The New York Times* reviewer Michiko Kakutani praised Rice's use of research about eighteenth-century Venice but attacked her "lush, portentous style" and described the novel as "a dark, humid melodrama filled with assassinations, attempted suicides and incestuous couplings, and animated by such operatic passions as ambition and revenge" (9 September 1982). When the *San Francisco Chronicle* ran Rice's picture with a negative review, she felt alienated from the local literary community. Depression followed, and Rice vowed never to write another historical novel. She spent time taking care of her four-year-old son. Readers, however, offered support through book purchases, letters, and phone calls.

While visiting a pornography shop with her husband, Rice was inspired to write pornography for women that they could identify with and enjoy. She decided to share her own fantasies, describing sadomasochistic relationships from the tactile rather than visual point of view. She placed her characters in situations where they could surrender themselves without fear of harm. Rice supported the idea that sexually explicit literature should be available in mainstream bookstores.

To give herself complete freedom for this project, Rice used the name A. N. Roquelaure. (A roquelaure is a type of cloak that was created in eighteenth-century France.) For the first time, Rice's main character was female. *The Claiming of Sleeping Beauty: An Erotic Novel of Tenderness and Cruelty for the Enjoyment of Men and Women* (1983) begins where the traditional story of Sleeping Beauty ends. Instead of living happily every after, the prince tells Beauty that she must be his slave. The story concerns surrender, but it is also about Beauty's discovery of the power she has to arouse desire in the prince. Through a variety of sexual tortures, Rice depicts the close relationship between fear and arousal. There is religious symbolism in the fact that total surrender brings the slave closer to the ruler. The book ends with Beauty in a cart bound for greater punishments.

Simon and Schuster turned down *The Claiming of Sleeping Beauty,* but E. P. Dutton enthusiastically accepted it. Negotiations led to a three-book contract. *The Claiming of Sleeping Beauty* was published in 1983. Rice quickly finished the sequel, *Beauty's Punishment,* which was published in 1984. In the second book, Beauty and a prince named Tristan are aroused and punished so often that they can no longer tell punishment from pleasure. There are homosexual overtones, as Tristan and his master Nicolas enter a deep sadomasochistic relationship involving love. This relationship draws a parallel with man's relationship to God. As this book ends, Beauty and Tristan are on a ship traveling to a sultan's palace, where they will be treated as animals. The first two books about Beauty sold well.

Rice began work on another erotic novel, *Exit to Eden* (1985), under the pseudonym Anne Rampling. She took the last name from actress Charlotte Rampling, who starred as a masochistic concentration-camp survivor in the 1974 movie *The Night Porter.* The Anne Rampling style, which Rice describes as her California voice, uses more vernacular, making the novel sound as if it were spoken. For the first time, Rice uses a first-person female point of view as Lisa, the main character, speaks to the reader in a breezy, nonchalant style.

Exit to Eden takes place in a Caribbean island club, a safe environment where the wealthy may rent slaves to satisfy their sexual desires. The themes that emerge are ones with which Rice often deals: freedom to define oneself versus the responsibility that comes with making choices, and the theme of dominance versus submission. Through Lisa and other characters, Rice explores her belief that outsiders, people who live outside the norm, can enjoy life and that they often experience the greatest rejection from their families. The club is described in religious terms and with religious imagery.

Exit to Eden was rejected by Dutton, but Arbor House offered $35,000 for the hardcover rights. The book was published in June 1985. Rights for the paperback went to Dell for $150,000. Most mainstream critics ignored *Exit to Eden.* A few reviewers acknowledged that the book was well-written erotica. While the *San Francisco Chronicle* gave it a positive review, *Publishers Weekly* dismissed it as pornography. Publicity for *Exit to Eden* targeted housewives, and it did not sell well. A 1994 movie adaptation by Deborah Amelon and Bob Brunner, starring Dana Delany and Paul Mercurio, was a major box-office flop.

Rice planned more Rampling novels and had a contract with Dutton for the final Roquelaure book. She also pursued an interest in writing for magazines. *Redbook* published a vampire story titled "The Master of Rampling Gate" in February 1984. Rice wrote a nonfic-

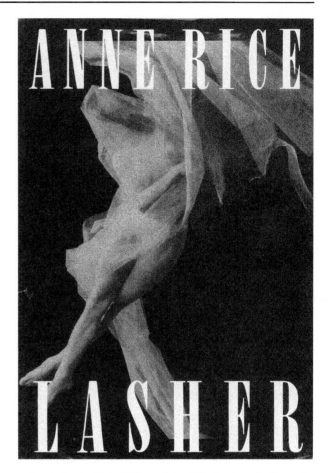

Dust jacket for Rice's 1993 novel, in which she relates the history of the bisexual spirit who has accompanied thirteen generations of a family of witches (Richland County Public Library)

tion article for the November 1983 issue of *Vogue* on David Bowie, her ideal androgynous male, in which she discussed her ideas on gender. John Preston, a gay activist and writer, included chapters cut from *Exit to Eden* in a gay men's pornography collection titled *Flesh and the Word: An Anthology of Erotic Writing* (1992).

Rice completed the Roquelaure trilogy with *Beauty's Release* (1985). In this book the slaves are treated as animals and must endure greater punishments than ever before. Beauty ends her story with Laurent, a prince who commands her to be his wife and secret slave. As king and queen, they live happily ever after. The suffering in this book is, once again, compared to Christians who suffer in order to gain the acceptance of God. Some readers were not pleased with the happily-ever-after ending of the Beauty series.

In *Prism of the Night* Ramsland points out that "the *Beauty* books helped Anne to work out some of her sexual alienation. She was not yet aware of it, but she had brought the Roquelaure voice to a cathartic completion." Rice's works are unified by her own development. Through her erotic writing, she brought together

her male/female and dominant/submissive sides. Growing awareness of the AIDS epidemic in the 1980s discouraged Rice from continuing the Beauty series. The trilogy continued to be published as sales slowly climbed and a cult following emerged among readers.

Rice then turned her attention to a book about Lestat, who begins telling his own story in *The Vampire Lestat: The Second Book in the Vampire Chronicles* (1985). She had to rework some details of *Interview with the Vampire* in order to present Lestat as she envisioned him. The Lestat who awakens in 1985 is a flashy showman who embraces contemporary culture, rides a Harley, listens to Johann Sebastian Bach on his Walkman, and watches the 1979 movie *Apocalypse Now*. He calls on humans to look for goodness outside their old gods. Rice once again describes meetings of same-sex vampires in sensuous terms. Lestat uses his autobiography and his status as a rock star to reveal his own story and secrets of vampire lore to humans. This causes hoards of vampires to descend on him in the concert that concludes the book. Lestat escapes, and the book ends with the promise of a sequel.

Most reviewers had mixed feelings about *The Vampire Lestat,* but the book was a hit with readers. Two weeks after the book was published, it made *The New York Times* best-seller list, and it stayed on the list for seven weeks. A book tour put Rice in touch with her readers, who came from many segments of society.

By 1986 eight-year-old Christopher Rice was beginning to write his own stories. Stan Rice was chairperson of the creative-writing department at San Francisco State University. Fans clamored for a sequel to *The Vampire Lestat,* but Rice began working on a second Rampling book, *Belinda* (1986). This story is about Jeremy Walker, a children's book illustrator who falls in love with and paints a young female model. He is torn between the safe career he has established and painting the erotic visions he feels called upon to produce. Rice took a step toward writing about reality when she used her own house and a real hotel for the setting of *Belinda.*

Jeremy's feelings about meeting the public and about the content of his artwork express Rice's feelings about her own work. Jeremy and Belinda romp through New Orleans, getting closer and closer to the Irish Channel, the area where Rice grew up. Religious images mix with the characters' sexual experiences. Although the book is erotic, the tone is more romantic than *Exit to Eden,* the previous Rampling novel.

Arbor House gave Rice a $60,000 advance for *Belinda,* a low figure considering her reputation and the fact that her own name would be on the cover, exposing the Rampling pseudonym. The few reviews of *Belinda* were mostly favorable, but the book did not sell well in hardcover or paperback.

In 1987 the Rices moved to Sonoma County in California. The forest and creeks surrounding her house inspired Rice as she worked on *The Queen of the Damned: The Third Book in the Vampire Chronicles* (1988). In this book a complicated plot traces vampire history back to its beginning with Akasha, the mother of all vampires, also known as the Queen of the Damned. Many characters tell stories within stories as Rice weaves mythology into vampire history. Lestat is caught up in a plot to rid the world of violence by wiping most men off of the face of the earth. While the violent psychological makeup of men is explored, Rice's belief that humanity is developing in a positive way emerges. Although *The Queen of the Damned* seems to complete the history of Lestat, on the last page of the book, Rice promises her readers that the Vampire Chronicles will continue.

When it was published in 1988, *The Queen of the Damned* went straight to number one on *The New York Times* best-seller list, and it remained there seventeen weeks. The book was number seven in fiction sales that year. Several reviewers commented that the story dragged in places, and they criticized the graphic descriptions of violence committed in order to bring peace to the world. Writing for *The New York Times Book Review* (27 November 1988), Eric Kraft captured many of Rice's positive attributes: "She has a masterly way with language, works on a broad canvas, has a vast range of knowledge, brings exotic settings vividly to life and is wonderfully clever, but," he wrote, "these gifts are wasted on vampires."

"The third in the vampire series, *The Queen of the Damned,* is the novel that truly catapulted Rice to superstardom," explains Ramsland in *The Anne Rice Reader.* A national fan club based in New Orleans was growing quickly. Rice's books were being assigned in college classes. Psychologists and scholars were corresponding with the author. Rice was realizing her dream of reaching a popular audience while being taken seriously.

Rice's next novel started as the script for a television miniseries. When conflicts with the producers halted the endeavor, Rice turned the plot of *The Mummy, or Ramses the Damned* (1989) into a novel. Rice concentrated on making the characters real and evoking the atmosphere of a grade-B horror movie. In this action-packed adventure, the mummies of the Egyptian king Ramses and his former lover Cleopatra rise from the dead. Ramses' exploits center around his secret elixir of life and involve an archaeologist's daughter, her former fiancé, and his aging, bisexual father. The book treats themes of bisexuality, androgyny, and human morality. Ballantine released *The Mummy, or Ramses the Damned* in paperback in May 1989, and it stayed on *The New York Times* paperback best-seller list for eighteen weeks. Despite some negative comments, most reviews were positive.

In July 1988 the Rices sold their Sonoma County house and bought a house in New Orleans. For years, Rice had longed to return to the warmth of the climate and to the people with whom she shared a common background. She was working on *The Witching Hour* (1990) and wanted to be in New Orleans, where the story takes place.

The Witching Hour takes place in the Rices' house. This book presents the history of the Mayfair family, thirteen generations of witches. Michael Curry, the character Rice uses to describe her own feelings about New Orleans and San Francisco, learns the history of the Mayfair family from files provided by the Talamasca, a group that has explored paranormal events for centuries. Michael is already involved with the powerful witch Rowan when she falls under the spell of Lasher, the bisexual spirit that has accompanied the most powerful Mayfair witches for generations. Rowan's desire to destroy Lasher and her attraction to him, followed by his successful attempt to enter the body of her unborn child, reflect the same tension between dominance and submission that is found in earlier books by Rice. At the end, Michael is left alone to philosophize about the possibility of good in Rowan's future and about his belief in the goodness of humanity.

Bisexuality, homosexuality, and incest play strong roles in the history of the Mayfair family. In *Prism of the Night* Ramsland reports that Rice became consciously aware of the link between fear and eroticism while writing this book. The fact that Rice speaks through a strong, masculine male is evidence that she was piecing together the life she had once described as fragmented. In this book and its sequels, she explores her feminine side through the female members of the Mayfair family. Rice's interest in family members connected through hundreds of years reflects the peace Rice found surrounded by her extended family in New Orleans. One new philosophical element that enters Rice's writing in *The Witching Hour* is a willingness to acknowledge the possibility of God's existence.

When it was published in 1990, *The Witching Hour* stayed on *The New York Times* best-seller list for five months. Warner Bros. paid $1,000,000 for rights to a movie, which was never completed. The review in *The New York Times* (4 November 1990) described *The Witching Hour* as "pleasantly creepy entertainment," and articles about Rice appeared in *The New York Times Magazine* and *Newsweek*. Besides the usual publicity tour, Rice was featured on several television shows. For fiction that year, *The Witching Hour* ranked ninth in sales.

Dust jacket for Rice's 1997 novel, about a woman who is tormented by a violin-playing ghost while she is grieving over the deaths of her mother, her daughter, and her husband (Richland County Public Library)

Visiting Miami on a book tour inspired Rice to begin her next vampire novel there. *The Tale of the Body Thief* (1992) opens with Lestat in Miami, where he agrees to change bodies temporarily with a mortal vampire hunter. When the vampire hunter absconds with Lestat's vampire body, Lestat calls on David Talbot, an aging member of the Talamasca, for assistance. Through several twists and turns, Lestat retrieves his body, and David inhabits the twenty-five-year-old body Lestat had occupied as a human. Despite David's objections, Lestat turns him into a vampire. Lestat reiterates the thought he had at the end of *The Queen of the Damned:* that he actually likes the evil that comes with being a vampire.

Reviews of *The Tale of the Body Thief* were mostly positive. Patricia Corrigan in the *St. Louis Post-Dispatch* (27 September 1992) wrote, "Rice tells an exciting, fast-paced story in 'The Tale of the Body Thief,' at the same time providing further explorations of her favorite themes: good vs. evil, immortality vs. the human condition, conventional values vs. exciting lives." *The Tale of the Body Thief* was number one on *The New York Times* best-seller list for four weeks in 1992 and remained on the list for fifteen weeks.

While writing *The Tale of the Body Thief,* Rice suffered from unexplained fatigue and depression. When her father was hospitalized on the evening of her fiftieth birthday celebration, Rice and other relatives took turns staying with him twenty-four hours a day until his death two months later. During her night shift, Rice found that her thoughts about her father were similar to the ones she had created for Lestat concerning his aging friend David Talbot in the book she had just finished writing, *The Tale of the Body Thief.*

Rice finished writing the screenplay for *Interview with the Vampire* in 1992. When the movie went into production, Rice strongly voiced her objections to Tom Cruise playing the androgynous Lestat, but she changed her mind and wrote retractions after she saw the movie, for which she had high praise. Released in 1994, the movie *Interview with the Vampire* brought in more than $100 million in the United States, and it was an international success.

Responding to fans who clamored for a sequel to *The Witching Hour,* Rice continued the story of the Mayfair witches in a book titled *Lasher* (1993). Lasher's history and his race, the Taltos, are explained through stories of the past and through genetic research. Lasher, in the flesh, becomes Rowan's grown child, her lover, and her captor. As he struggles to procreate, the Talamasca and the Mayfair family join forces to annihilate him. They depend on Michael, whom they see as the good man described in the prophecy of Lasher's demise. Many of the scenes take place in Rice's own home on St. Charles Street in New Orleans.

Taltos: Lives of the Mayfair Witches (1994) followed *Lasher.* Lasher's background is further developed as Rice weaves Taltos mythology with the history of the British Isles and early Christianity there. Rice's belief that teenage girls should be allowed to express their sexuality is conveyed through the lives of the young Mayfair witches.

Critics generally agreed with Donna Seaman's evaluation in the *Chicago Sun-Times* (9 October 1994) that *Lasher* was excessive in its "bloody eroticism," and they found it lacking in character development and in the sensuous tone of earlier books. Reviews of *Taltos* were mixed, with complaints that the history of the Taltos was too drawn out. Seaman's prediction that Rice's followers would "devour" *Taltos,* however, was true. Both *Lasher* and *Taltos* stayed on best-seller lists for months. Maureen O'Brien, writing in *Publishers Weekly*

(19 September 1994), described Rice's readers as an "enormous global network of rabid fans."

Rice returns to her character Lestat in *Memnoch the Devil* (1995). As Lestat joins the devil (Memnoch) on a trip to heaven and hell, Rice presents her visions of the Creation, evolution, and the crucifixion of Christ. She ponders the meaning of human life on earth. Rice wrote the 354-page book in one month. When she finished, she announced that she did not expect to write about Lestat again.

Reviewers pointed out that *Memnoch the Devil* lacked the usual eroticism and double-sided characters typical of the Vampire Chronicles. They were surprised to find the brazen Lestat cowering and observing much of the activity. Reviewers continued to praise Rice's storytelling ability and to criticize the lack of editing in her books. *Memnoch the Devil* sold well, earning the top spot on *The New York Times* best-seller list three of its fourteen weeks on the list.

In a 1995 interview in *Rolling Stone* (13–27 July), Rice said she was immersed in research concerning God, the Bible, and Catholicism. Her interest in near-death experiences, angels, ghosts, and other spiritual forces reflected a trend in society at that time. She explained that her writing was therapeutic: "When I write," she said, "I explore my worst fears and then take my protagonist right into awful situations that I myself am terrified by."

Rice's fascination with spirits also influenced her next book, *Servant of the Bones* (1996), in which a 2,600-year-old ghost named Azriel tells his story to a modern Jewish scholar. The book went straight to the top spot on the *Publishers Weekly* fiction chart. Meredith Renwick, writing for *The Toronto Sun* (6 October 1996), described the novel as "part ghost story and part murder mystery, and an extensive meditation on the nature of good and evil." Renwick pointed out that Rice embraced movies, television, and rock music as twentieth-century art forms, and that her writing had the "energy and dazzle" of these forms. She attributed Rice's personal appeal to her ability to be herself and to share her eccentricities with her fans. Renwick compared Rice's fame to that of rock stars and movie queens of bygone days.

Rice completed a forty-city publicity tour for *Servant of the Bones* in forty-five days. In *Publishers Weekly* (19 August 1996) Daisy Maryles described Rice's customized bus as having "all the amenities befitting a superstar." In *The Tampa Tribune* (15 September 1996), reviewer Elizabeth Hand added that Rice's work had impacted pop culture in music, comic books, and movies.

In 1996 Linda Badley published *Writing Horror and the Body: The Fiction of Stephen King, Clive Barker, and Anne Rice.* Badley explains that Rice introduced her vampire tales in the 1970s and 1980s, when the Goth movement was entering pop culture. Badley feels that, although Rice's historical fiction and pornography were out of step with the times, her life and other books reflect the age and the culture in which she lived. For a variety of readers, "Rice functions as a sort of New Age priestess, psychoanalyst, and storyteller," says Badley.

In 1996, writers taking a scholarly perspective offered explanations for the many negative reviews Rice attracts despite her large following among readers. In her *Toronto Sun* review Renwick wrote, "The books really defy any conventional labelling, and I suspect that—and her success—may be a major reason Rice's work gets trashed." In the introduction to *The Gothic World of Anne Rice* (1996) Gary Hoppenstand and Ray B. Browne agree that Rice's books often receive negative reviews because they do not fit most reviewers' definition of horror fiction. Hoppenstand and Browne explain, "When Rice's story meets the critics' formulaic expectations, they enjoy what they see, but when she moves her plot away from conventional expectations into a different, more abstract philosophical area, they find fault with her efforts."

When movie rights to *Servant of the Bones* were not sold before its publication in 1996, Rice set up her own company, Kith & Kin, LLC, to develop merchandise supporting her books. This business soon included Garden District and New Orleans area tours, a merchandise catalogue on the Internet, and wines decorated with paintings created by Stan Rice. To expand her options, Rice purchased the merchandising rights to the Vampire Chronicles and the Lives of the Mayfair Witches from Warner Bros. Hiring relatives for Kith & Kin helped fulfill Rice's desire to be surrounded by family. Rice funneled her time and money into preservation efforts in New Orleans. Over the years, she purchased and restored the Redemptorist Chapel, St. Elizabeth's Orphanage, and houses on St. Charles Avenue and First Street. She amassed a large collection of pre–Vatican II parish art.

For her next ghost story, *Violin* (1997), Rice returned to the lyric style of *Interview with the Vampire* to relate the tale of the guilt-ridden Triana grieving over the deaths of her alcoholic mother; her daughter, who died of cancer; and her husband, who has recently died of AIDS. Rice wrote the book to rid herself of memories that had haunted her since her return to New Orleans. She incorporated her love of the violin, which she had studied in her youth: Triana is tormented by a violin-playing specter. While critics attacked the book for wordiness, repetition of themes from previous novels, and a meandering plot, fans bought it eagerly.

In December 1998 Rice acted on her growing desire to return to the Catholic Church. She was drawn

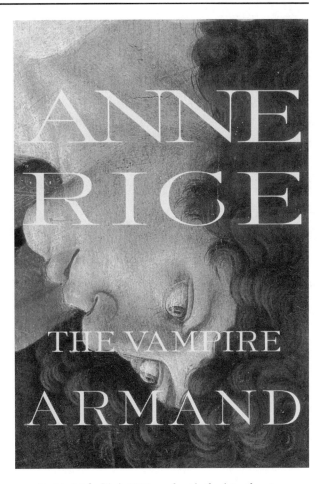

Dust jacket for Rice's 1998 novel, set in the sixteenth century, about a Russian boy who is kidnapped, taken to Italy, and turned into a vampire to save him from being murdered (Richland County Public Library)

back by a yearning to experience Communion and by the Mystery of the Incarnation, the concept of God taking on human form in Jesus Christ. Rice went to confession, received Communion, and had her marriage to Stan Rice blessed in the Catholic Church. Two days after her Catholic wedding, Rice slipped into a diabetic coma and almost died. Sitting at his mother's bedside, her son, Christopher, conceived the idea for a semi-autobiographical novel. Christopher Rice's *Density of Souls* hit *The New York Times* best-seller list when it was published in 2000.

When she recovered, Rice realized that she could continue the Vampire Chronicles by expanding the stories of individual vampires. *Pandora: New Tales of the Vampires* (1998) was the first of these. The two-thousand-year-old vampire Pandora, first mentioned in *The Queen of the Damned*, tells her story to David Talbot, the former Talamasca member who was transformed into a vampire by Lestat in *The Tale of the Body Thief*. Pandora, a reclusive vampire living alone in Paris, shares the history of her mortal life as the daughter of a Roman senator. When most of her family is murdered, she joins the followers of the Egyptian goddess Isis. Pandora's childhood sweetheart, who has become the vampire Marius, initiates her into the vampire world. The story centers on Pandora's life, adding pieces of vampire lore to the myth Rice started constructing in *Interview with the Vampire*. This book addresses two of Rice's familiar themes: the search for meaning in the lives of immortals and a preference for knowledge that comes from experience rather than from abstract ideas.

In late 1998 *The Vampire Armand: The Vampire Chronicles* appeared. This novel is the story of the young, angelic-looking Armand, who was first introduced in *Interview with the Vampire*. Once again, David Talbot records his story. Kidnapped from his Russian homeland, Armand joins a company of boys under the care of Marius in sixteenth-century Italy. When Armand is almost murdered, Marius turns him into a vampire to save him from death. Rice traces the loss and recovery of Armand's religious beliefs and his path from pupil to mentor, two themes derived from struggles in her own life.

In *Vittorio, the Vampire: New Tales of the Vampires* (1999), the main character is similar to many Rice creations. Vittorio, a beautiful, rich, young man, is turned into a vampire against his will. Sumptuous details of Florence, Italy, in its golden age serve as a background. After his family is destroyed by renegade vampires, the vampire Ursula saves Vittorio from death in the renegades' black mass. Vittorio's story explores the nature of good and evil as it depicts his desire for revenge and his passion for Ursula. Rice's fascination with spiritual forces emerges as Vittorio receives the ability to see and talk with angels.

Merrick (2000) weaves together the worlds of the Vampire Chronicles and *Taltos*. Merrick is a descendant of the free people of color first described in *The Feast of All Saints,* and she is related to the Mayfair witches. David Talbot narrates Merrick's tale, reviewing her life for the vampire Louis de Pointe du Lac. Louis wants Merrick to call his vampire-daughter Claudia from the dead. *Merrick* is filled with voodoo and magic, concentrating on the powers Merrick has inherited from her Creole background. As reviewers pointed out, Merrick's characterization is well developed, and action at the end of the book creates an exciting ending.

Marius, who was introduced in earlier books through his involvements with Lestat, Pandora, and Armand, is the central character of *Blood and Gold, or, The Story of Marius: The Vampire Chronicles* (2001). Marius reveals his personal history, sharing the memories he has accumulated in a life that stretches from ancient Egypt to modern times. Marius's journey reflects Rice's research and interest in many historical periods and

places. She has often expressed a preference for reading historical nonfiction; she says that stories spring from her mind as she reads. Even though some critics attacked the slow start and wordiness of *Blood and Gold,* they offered praise for what Rebeca Rodriguez, in the *Fort Worth Star-Telegram* (4 November 2001), called "Rice's rich presentation of history and her ability to conjure lush scenes."

All of the books written to expand the Vampire Chronicles, from *Pandora* in 1998 through *Blood and Gold* in 2001, stayed on the best-seller lists for six weeks or more. Reviewers continued to praise Rice's lavish descriptions, sensuous tone, and dynamic storytelling. They found that some of the characters remained flat despite revelations of their life stories, but the main complaint concerned the pace of the books. Reviewers continued to comment that the books suffered from lack of editing.

In *Conversations with Anne Rice* (1996) Michael Riley records Rice's thoughts about editing. "It's really take it or leave it. It's been that way since *The Queen of the Damned,*" says Rice. She feels that authors are vulnerable, not knowing whether their manuscripts will be accepted or rejected, during the editorial process. She also feels strongly that she should have the right to make the final decision on the content of her books. Rice has worked with Knopf editor Victoria Wilson for many years. The only editing Rice allows is correction of mistakes.

Vampires, Mayfair witches, and spirits meet in *Blackwood Farm* (2002). Rice uses a familiar structure, having the main character describe his life to a willing listener. This time the listener is none other than the famous Lestat. Fledgling vampire Quinn Blackwood enlists Lestat in his attempt to rid himself of a doppelgänger named Goblin, a spirit Quinn fears will overtake him and destroy his loved ones. As Quinn reveals family secrets, familiar Rice motifs—incest, murder, and bisexuality—become a part of the story. Despite these similarities to other books, *Blackwood Farm* is a departure from Rice's vampire and witch series. Quinn is a contemporary character whose story takes place in rural Louisiana. Reviewers praised Rice for creating new characters with a fresh story line. "But it's intrigue, eroticism and obsession that fans want, and they'll find plenty of all three," wrote Jeff Zaleski in *Publishers Weekly* (2 September 2002).

When Knopf released Rice's twenty-fifth novel, *Blood Canticle,* on 31 October 2003, Rice announced that this volume completed the story of her witches and vampires. The book brings together characters from the Vampire Chronicles, the Mayfair Witch saga, and *Blackwood Farm.* Reviewers agreed that it was time for these tales to come to an end, although they predicted

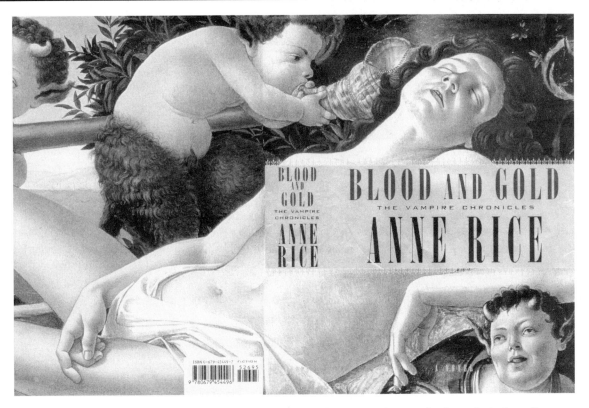

Dust jacket for Rice's 2001 novel, in which the mentor of several of the vampire characters from her earlier books recalls his life from ancient Egypt to the present (Richland County Public Library)

that Rice's fans would enjoy the book. Rice, in better health than she had been in years as a result of gastric bypass surgery earlier in 2003, promoted the book through television, radio, and a national book tour. By 10 November a second printing of the book had been ordered. *Blood Canticle* appeared on *The New York Times* best-seller list for five weeks, just as *Blackwood Farm* had a year before.

Anne Rice has touched readers for years with her best-selling novels, and she has drawn attention from the academic community. More than one hundred million copies of Rice's books have been sold worldwide. They have been transformed into audio books, e-books, and a comic-book form known as graphic novels. *The Feast of All Saints* became a two-part *Showtime* television miniseries (with teleplay by John Wilder) in 2001, and a critically panned movie version of *The Queen of the Damned* (with screenplay by Scott Abbott and Michael Petroni, and starring Stuart Townsend as Lestat) was released in 2002. That year NBC purchased rights for a television miniseries based on *The Witching Hour, Lasher,* and *Taltos,* and in 2003 Warner Bros. Entertainment announced that it had hired Elton John and Bernie Taupin to create a Broadway musical based on three of Rice's novels about Lestat. Both projects have been slated for 2005.

In 1994 Twayne Publishers produced a monograph, *Anne Rice,* offering scholarly criticism of Rice's work. Author Bette B. Roberts states, "To date her novels have demonstrated the continuing vitality of the Gothic as a means of probing serious human concerns while appealing to the imagination." Hoppenstand and Browne point out that Rice's work was drawing more scholarly attention at the national Popular Culture Association conference meetings in the mid 1990s than that of any other popular horror-fiction writer. More than twenty-five doctoral dissertations and masters theses as well as more than fifty articles in scholarly journals are further evidence of the academic community's interest in Rice's work.

On 9 December 2002 Stan Rice died of a brain tumor. As Anne Rice informed her readers of her husband's death that night, she expressed the hope that whatever pain she suffered would help her be more sensitive to others, and she offered support to struggling writers. Speaking on her fan phone line about future plans, she stated, "My direction will be so strange that many may abandon me, but who knows? . . . Let me be your cultural bandit forever."

Interviews:
Bob Summer, "Anne Rice," *Publishers Weekly,* 234 (28 October 1988): 59–60;

Mikal Gilmore, "The Devil and Anne Rice," *Rolling Stone* (13–27 July 1995): 92–103, 122–123;

Michael Riley, *Conversations with Anne Rice* (New York: Ballantine, 1996);

A Visit with Anne Rice, videotape, Corbitt Design, 1997;

Melinda L. Shelton, "From Garden to Jungle," *Lambda Book Report,* 9 (October 2000): 6–10;

Linton Weeks, "The Writers Related by Blood; Anne Rice and Her Son Know Death Up Close. And They Live to Tell the Tale," *Washington Post,* 20 October 2000, p. C1;

Francine Russo, "Heading Home: A Best-Selling Novelist Reflects on the Pull and Power of Her Southern Roots and Loves," *Time,* 158 (22 October 2001): G12.

Biography:

Katherine Ramsland, *Prism of the Night: A Biography of Anne Rice* (New York: Dutton, 1991).

References:

AnneRice.com: The Official Site <http://www.annerice.com/>;

Linda Badley, *Writing Horror and the Body: The Fiction of Stephen King, Clive Barker, and Anne Rice,* Contributions to the Study of Popular Culture, no. 51 (Westport, Conn.: Greenwood Press, 1996);

George Beahm, ed., *The Unauthorized Anne Rice Companion* (Kansas City, Mo.: Andrews & McMeel, 1996);

Joy Dickinson, *Haunted City: An Unauthorized Guide to the Magical, Magnificent New Orleans of Anne Rice* (Secaucus, N.J.: Carol Publishing Group, 1998);

Gary Hoppenstand and Ray B. Browne, eds., *The Gothic World of Anne Rice* (Bowling Green, Ohio: Bowling Green State University Popular Press, 1996);

James R. Keller, *Anne Rice and Sexual Politics: The Early Novels* (Jefferson, N.C.: McFarland, 2000);

Katherine Ramsland, *The Roquelaure Reader: A Companion to Anne Rice's Erotica* (New York: Plume, 1996);

Ramsland, *The Vampire Companion: The Official Guide to Anne Rice's The Vampire Chronicles* (New York: Ballantine, 1993);

Ramsland, *The Witches' Companion: The Official Guide to Anne Rice's Lives of the Mayfair Witches* (New York: Ballantine, 1994);

Bette B. Roberts, *Anne Rice* (New York: Twayne, 1994);

Jennifer Smith, *Anne Rice: A Critical Companion,* Critical Companions to Popular Contemporary Writers (Westport, Conn.: Greenwood Press, 1996).

Christopher Rice

(11 March 1978 –)

Nathan G. Tipton
University of Memphis

BOOKS: *A Density of Souls* (New York: Hyperion/Talk Miramax, 2000; London: Pan, 2002);

The Snow Garden (New York: Hyperion/Talk Miramax, 2002; London: Pan, 2003).

Christopher Rice's literary debut, *A Density of Souls* (2000), was overshadowed by derisive criticism and accusations of nepotism stemming from his family ties: his father is the artist, poet, and writing professor Stan Rice, and his mother is best-selling horror writer Anne Rice. However, by successfully incorporating complex social issues of homophobia, incest, and rape within the framework of an intriguing murder mystery, Rice has overcome skeptical reviewers and readers alike. In the process, he has earned a measure of literary respect and popular success on the basis of both *A Density of Souls* and its follow-up novel, *The Snow Garden* (2002).

Christopher Travis Rice was born on 11 March 1978 in Berkeley, California. He never knew his sister, Michele, who died of leukemia in 1972 at the age of six; and until Rice himself reached the age of six, his parents withheld information from him about Michele. Rice later remarked that he was profoundly affected by this willful omission, but he used his parents' reasoning creatively in order to explore secrets and the justifications for keeping them.

Rice grew up in the Castro District of San Francisco and, at age ten, moved with his family to New Orleans, Louisiana. The move proved difficult for him. In a 2000 interview with *Advocate* columnist David Bahr, Rice stated, "I went from a school in San Francisco where we called our lesbian teachers by their first names to this uptown, private elementary school where we all had to go to chapel in the morning." In 1996 Rice graduated from Isidore Newman School and attended Brown University in Providence, Rhode Island, where he became involved in theater. After completing one year at Brown, Rice enrolled in the Tisch School of Arts at New York University to study

Christopher Rice (photograph © Steve Read; from the dust jacket for A Density of Souls, *2000; Richland County Public Library)*

film, but he dropped out after one semester to move to Los Angeles.

While at Brown, Rice had begun writing screenplays, and he continued his screenwriting in both New York and Los Angeles. His screenplays, though, brought him little success. He said that although his mother's name helped him get meetings with people who would otherwise throw scripts in the trash, nothing developed, and no jobs were ever forthcoming. In December 1998 Rice received a phone call from New Orleans informing him that his mother had fallen into a diabetic coma, compelling him to return home. Living in New Orleans for the duration of his mother's recovery, Rice began writing the first incarnations of *A Density of Souls*. He has described the origins of the novel alternately to interviewer Brian Perrin as "this short story that just grew and grew and grew" or to Bahr as the "merging [of] five screenplays into one literary page-turner." Nevertheless, after three months, Rice had completed a 320-page manuscript that was in dire need of revisions, but as he has remarked, "there was a story to it."

Rice showed the draft to his father, who recognized its potential and predicted, "This is going to change your life." The elder Rice also encouraged him to continue with revisions. However, he waited until he completed his revisions before showing it to his mother, who further buoyed his optimism by sending it to Lynn Nesbit, her agent. Nesbit agreed to represent the novel and brought it to the attention of five publishers, of whom two were interested immediately.

Heralded by a fifty-thousand-copy first printing and a twenty-two-city book tour, *A Density of Souls* appeared in August 2000 to enthusiastic reviews from *Booklist, Publishers Weekly,* and *USA Today.* Reviewers recognized Rice's talents as a new novelist, noting particularly his realistic depictions of the teenage characters' painful psyches. *Publishers Weekly* (7 August 2000) called it an "intriguing, complex story, a hard-nosed, lyrical, teenage take on Peyton Place" and noted, "Rice is sensitive to the emotional undercurrents that compel teenagers to both mask and wallow in their intense feeling." Most reviewers, however, offered more mixed notices. Jennifer Reese, in a muted appraisal for *The New York Times Book Review* (10 September 2000), concluded that while the novel offers "bold, ambitious, and wildly campy plotting," it nevertheless "takes itself far too seriously to be fun: It's scarily sincere and ultimately preposterous." Kimberly Shearer Palmer, in *The Washington Post* (28 August 2000), derided it as "more depressing than twisting your ankle and getting dumped on the same night," although she noted that the novel successfully redeemed itself by taking on the hallmarks of a cleverly planned mystery.

Amazon.com editor Jane Adams, echoing many other reviewers, faulted the book for reading "like a roman à clef" and stated, "Rice might have been wiser to tell someone else's story rather than his own." Adams's recognition of the roman à clef style cannot be overlooked or ignored. In his interview with Ron Hogan, Rice acknowledged, "I did physically model the major character after myself: I gave him blonde hair, I made him tall, I gave him blue eyes. And he is gay." However, while *A Density of Souls* is autobiographical in tone, it is certainly not a memoir. The hero, Stephen

Conlin, is a sensitive New Orleans high-school student who, as a result of his quiet demeanor and overtly stereotypical homosexual appearance, becomes the victim of repeated homophobic cruelty from his antagonist, football player Brandon Charbonnet.

Brandon and Stephen had been childhood friends, along with cheerleader Meredith Ducote and second-string football quarterback Greg Darby. Indiscreet youthful homosexual encounters involving Greg and Stephen, however, affected the group's dynamics profoundly. On separate occasions, Meredith and Brandon discovered Greg and Stephen's furtive couplings, but while their respective reactions of disgust and rage were markedly different, Meredith and Brandon share a collective sense of betrayal. Although the characters grow and mature, this betrayal alters their friendship, even as they are still bound together by the unspoken secrets.

While Rice sidesteps the direct suggestion that Brandon is a repressed homosexual, nevertheless there are clear implications that he is emotionally conflicted and morally enraged by his feelings for and about Greg and Stephen. Secure in the knowledge that Greg is a football player and thus presumably incapable of harboring overt homosexual desires, Brandon surmises that Stephen has unilaterally played the role of seducer. In so doing, Brandon is able to overlook Greg's complicity in the "relationship" and focus his wrath squarely on Stephen. Greg, however, is not so easily dissuaded because, in fact, his own conflicted desires are painfully real. At an out-of-town football championship game, Greg's younger brother, Alex, is killed in a freak car accident, and in his grief Greg views Alex's death as a form of divine retribution. Through his "sins of the flesh" Greg knows that he has flouted divine and natural law, and, like Brandon, Greg sees Stephen as a demonic, unnatural tempter.

The dramatic climax of the novel overtly illustrates the struggle of good versus evil, God and Satan, religious imagery and iconography. Accompanied by Hurricane Brandy, an apocalyptic storm bearing down on New Orleans, Brandon kidnaps Stephen and takes him to the bell tower of a nearby Catholic elementary school. At the height of the hurricane, Brandon brings his vengeful religious fury to the fore: "Wanna know what God does, Stevie? God owns the devil. And when he made the world, he took a big handful of evil and threw it down on the earth. It's everywhere, only it tries to bury itself. In people. It's in you, Stevie. I've known that all my life, and you know it too." Ultimately, the hurricane winds sweep Brandon out of the tower portico, leaving Stephen clinging precariously, arms outstretched on the tower supports in direct reference to a crucifixion, injured, but still alive.

Throughout *A Density of Souls* Rice uses religious symbolism and secrecy to enhance characterization and to underscore the themes of the novel. Apocalyptic images become more prominent and integral as the novel progresses, where they reflect the characters' actions and resulting consequences. Each character in the novel has a secret, and Rice structures the climactic events around the revelation of these secrets and on the motivations behind keeping them intact. The novel is both poignant and exciting, despite the somewhat unsettling ending, because it alters significantly the concrete distinctions of good and evil, righteousness and right.

In Rice's second novel, *The Snow Garden,* these themes of secrecy, righteousness, sexual torment, and apocalyptic consequences are once again deployed. Based loosely on Rice's year at Brown University, *The Snow Garden* is a murder mystery that received decidedly mixed reviews. In a positive assessment for *Booklist* (15 November 2001), reviewer Kristine Huntley called the novel "an enthralling narrative that is certain to be as popular as his first book." Joe E. Jeffreys, in *The Advocate* (19 February 2002), compared Rice's writing to a combination of Stephen King and Edmund White and remarked that *The Snow Garden* "offers finely nuanced character studies as its pages whiz by to its chilling conclusion." Other reviewers, though, found fault with the wooden characters and convoluted story lines. Rebecca House Stankowski noted in *Library Journal* (December 2001), "Rice tries to imbue this pretty much plotless novel with an aura of foreboding, but it just ends up being tiresome." *Publishers Weekly* (5 November 2001) observed that, while the novel could have been a "decent gay-themed mystery," it nonetheless came off as muddled.

The Snow Garden is a far more dark and confusing novel than its predecessor. Its characters are all amoral, and precisely because of this universal amorality, Rice pays little attention to character depth or development. As in *A Density of Souls,* everyone in *The Snow Garden* has a secret that threatens to be revealed. The ostensible hero, Randall Stone, is a Gucci-clad, world-weary, homosexual college freshman, or so he seems. At Atherton University, appearances are always deceiving, and Rice depicts a collegiate atmosphere of continual reinvention, not merely from Randall but from the entire campus community. This same lack of fixity, however, makes Rice's characters seem hollow and slimly drawn.

In lieu of fixed identities, what binds everyone together at Atherton is, instead, an air of pansexual mystery and secrecy. Randall's best friend, Kathryn, finds at college an escape from her dark sexual secrets back home in San Francisco. Jesse, Randall's bisexual

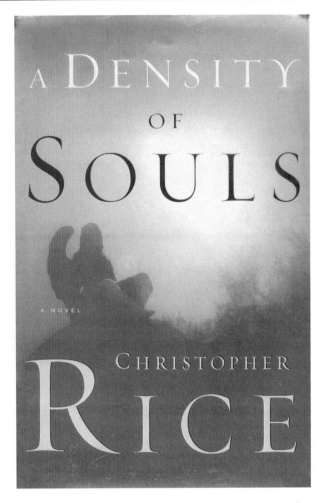

Dust jacket for Rice's literary debut, a semi-autobiographical novel about a New Orleans high-school student who is abused by a homophobic football player

roommate, preys on supposedly innocent students by getting them to reveal their innermost sexual urges and then acting on these newly uncloseted desires. Randall also seduces married art-history professor Eric Eberman, and they soon become enmeshed in a faculty-student sexual imbroglio that threatens to ruin Eberman's academic career.

Compounding matters, Eberman's influential book on the Hieronymus Bosch triptych *The Garden of Earthly Delights* also serves as the impetus for the creation of a cult-like band of quasi-religious adherents who, following Bosch's work, seek to purify themselves bodily and spiritually through uninhibited sexual release achieved by mixing wine and prescription painkillers. Kathryn almost gets caught up in this group but escapes and alerts Eberman, who views the group's wild, orgiastic revels as a corruption of his "pure" utopian ideals. Subsequently, in order to demonstrate to the group that he knows of their perversion, as well as

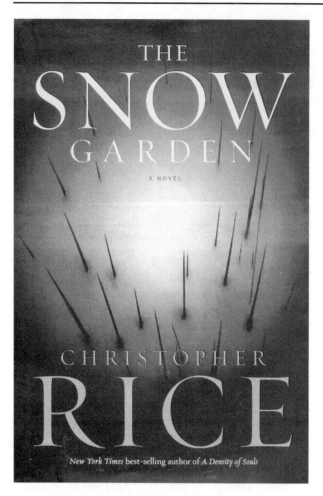

*Dust jacket for Rice's 2002 novel, about sexual perversity,
religious cultism, and murder on a college campus
(Richland County Public Library)*

to punish them for their straying. The professor doses the cult's wine bottles with a powerful narcotic drug. He succeeds in sedating all the group members save one, Eberman's protégé and de facto cult leader Mitchell Seaver. Mitchell kills Eberman and, in the process, destroys both the cult progenitor and the cult headquarters. Coincidentally, at the same time Eberman and his cult are extinguished, Randall, the proximate cause of Eberman's troubles, also disappears.

Alongside thematic similarities, *The Snow Garden* shares with *A Density of Souls* an apocalyptic climax that combines both natural and supernatural elements. Rice once again reminds readers that secrets revealed lead invariably to destructive consequences. Readers learn that Randall is not only a male prostitute but is also, in fact, the "kept boy" of Michael Price, Atherton benefactor and Eberman's first homosexual lover. Price, however, miscalculates Randall's level of affection for Eberman (itself one of Randall's most closely guarded

secrets) and, when Price reveals his delight at Eberman's demise, Randall retaliates and kills him.

Although in *A Density of Souls* Rice relied heavily on positive and, in fact, almost redemptive portrayals of homosexuals, *The Snow Garden* offers a far more tempered and muted view. While Randall, Jesse, and Tim Mathis, an investigative reporter and Randall's former boyfriend, are ultimately redeemed, nevertheless their characters are shaded with a persistent, melancholic ennui. Price, who appears through most of the novel as a gay exemplar, becomes instead the pre-eminent villain. Rice, remarking on this novelistic attitudinal change toward homosexuals, stated, "I think young gay men right now are in a state of flux and transition. And I think too many of them to go unmentioned are leading pretty lousy lives and treating each other pretty horribly. I see young gay men whose value systems seem highly questionable to me." Although Rice has always affirmed his distaste for overt political activism, this remark, along with his revisionist characterizations, indicates that he may be moving toward a more actively vocal role in gay community politics and relations.

Although *Kirkus Reviews* (1 December 2001) concluded that *The Snow Garden* was a "callow novel about adolescents for adolescents," Rice's works are generally considered as viable additions to both gay and mainstream fiction. Rice appeared surprised, however, at the initial attention he received for *A Density of Souls*. In an *Advocate* interview with gay horror writer Clive Barker, Rice stated, "I didn't think it would sell the way it did, because it was so gay. I didn't think it would get mainstream attention." That *A Density of Souls* was an almost "can't-miss" proposition, combining Rice's talent with his familial connections, makes his statement to Barker somewhat disingenuous.

However, as Rice noted to Hogan, "even the major bad reviews have been on the basis of the story itself. You know, they say things like it's excessive, it's over the top, it's got too many points of view. They don't just dismiss it as a product of nepotism." It seems unlikely, though, that he will be able to extricate himself completely from his mother's literary shadow. Indeed, reviewers and interviewers alike have wasted little time noting the family connection. *Publishers Weekly* (7 August 2000) observed in an "FYI" about *A Density of Souls,* "The author is the son of novelist Anne Rice and poet Stan Rice, which no doubt is why the name 'Rice' dominates the book's jacket." This constant questioning of Rice's talent and credentials has, in fact, been an ongoing source of contention for Rice. Speaking with Barker, Rice remarked, "the question that really makes me really just turn red is, 'Are you still around because of who your mother is?' My response to that is, 'If that's all I had going for me, *A Density of Souls* would have evaporated within 10 minutes.'" By the publication of *The Snow Garden,* this authorial anxiety had become so pervasive that Rice seemingly internalized it, making him see every negative review as a critical reflection on his family connections.

Rice told Barker about a significant piece of literary advice he received from his father (before Stan Rice died in 2002): "There was an awful review of *The Snow Garden* recently, and my father read it and he said, 'Cut this out and put it on your wall and look at it and say, "This is who I'm fighting."'" Even before *The Snow Garden* some reviewers were consciously distancing themselves from drawing comparisons between Rice and his mother. In an interesting and undoubtedly deliberate elision for *Booklist* (July 2000), Huntley noted of *A Density of Souls,* "That the author's parents are both writers (father Stan is a poet) will generate interest in this novel, but its originality and merits stand on their own." The influences of family aside, however, Rice's talent for crafting entertaining and complex novels has made itself evident.

Interviews:

David Bahr, "A Chip Off the Old Blockbuster," *Advocate* (29 August 2000): 38–41;

Tony Buchsbaum, "January Interview: Christopher Rice," *January Magazine* (October 2000) <http://www.januarymagazine.com/profiles/crice.html>;

Brian Perrin, "A Density of Talent," *Lambda Book Report,* 9 (October 2000): 10–14;

Jeff Walsh, "Christopher Rice Makes a Name for Himself with Amazing First Novel," *Oasis Magazine* (5 December 2000) <http://www.alternet.org/print.html?StoryID=10178>;

Ron Hogan, "Christopher Rice," *Beatrice.com* (December 2000) <http://www.beatrice.com/interviews/rice>;

Clive Barker and Christopher Rice, "Dark Lords," *Advocate* (19 February 2002): 61–64.

Reference:

Katherine Ramsland, *Prism of the Night: A Biography of Anne Rice* (New York: Dutton, 1991).

Anita Shreve

(1946 –   )

Heather Salter
Northwestern State University

BOOKS: *Dr. Balter's Child Sense: Understanding and Handling the Common Problems of Infancy and Early Childhood,* by Shreve and Lawrence Balter (New York: Poseidon Press, 1985);

Working Woman: A Guide to Fitness and Health, by Shreve and Patricia Lone (St. Louis: Mosby, 1986);

Remaking Motherhood: How Working Mothers Are Shaping Our Children's Future (New York: Viking, 1987);

Who's in Control?: Dr. Balter's Guide to Discipline without Combat, by Shreve and Balter (New York: Poseidon Press, 1988);

Women Together, Women Alone: The Legacy of the Consciousness-Raising Movement (New York: Viking, 1989);

Eden Close (San Diego: Harcourt Brace Jovanovich, 1989; London: Macdonald, 1990);

Strange Fits of Passion (San Diego: Harcourt Brace Jovanovich, 1991; London: Macdonald, 1992);

Where or When (New York: Harcourt Brace, 1993; London: Little, Brown, 1993);

Resistance (Boston: Little, Brown, 1995; London: Little, Brown, 1995);

The Weight of Water (Boston: Little, Brown, 1997; London: Little, Brown, 1997);

The Pilot's Wife (Boston: Little, Brown, 1998; London: Little, Brown, 1999);

Fortune's Rocks (Boston: Little, Brown, 2000; London: Little, Brown, 2000);

The Last Time They Met (Boston: Little, Brown, 2001; London: Little, Brown, 2001);

Sea Glass (Boston: Little, Brown, 2002; London: Little, Brown, 2002);

All He Ever Wanted (Boston: Little, Brown, 2003; London: Little, Brown, 2003).

PRODUCED SCRIPT: *The Pilot's Wife,* screenplay by Shreve and Christine Berardo, television, CBS, 14 April 2002.

Anita Shreve's background in journalism and experience in sociological studies have influenced her style of writing and the subject matter of her novels. Shreve's

Anita Shreve (photograph by Norman Jean Roy; from the dust jacket for Fortune's Rocks, *2000; Richland County Public Library)*

nonfiction work focuses on women's issues such as child care, health, and career. Shreve has also examined sociological and psychological concerns, such as the effects that working and single mothers have on their children. In her novels Shreve portrays psychological struggles within the minds of her characters and explores the adversities and complexities of relationships between men and women. She sets her novels mostly in New England and Europe in the midst of political and social turmoil and often focuses on human emotion rather than action and suspense. Critics praise Shreve for her well-researched material and attention to detail.

Anita Shreve was born in Dedham, Massachusetts, in 1946. Few specific details of Shreve's personal life are available; Shreve is protective of her privacy. After graduating from high school, Shreve majored in English at Tufts University in Medford, Massachusetts. She began writing short stories while teaching at Hingham High School in Massachusetts, earning the O. Henry Award in 1976 for "Past the Island Drifting," published in *Forum* (Winter 1975). After leaving her position as a high-school teacher and before becoming a novelist, Shreve worked as a writer for *US, Quest,* and *Newsweek* in Nairobi, Kenya, for three years. When she returned to the United States, she worked as an editor for *US* and as a writer for *Newsweek* special issues.

While caring for her children (she has a daughter and a son), Shreve worked for nearly ten years as a freelance writer and submitted articles to various periodicals, including *Seventeen* and *The New York Times*. In 1987 and 1988 she used the advance from a nonfiction book, *Women Together, Women Alone: The Legacy of the Consciousness-Raising Movement* (1989) to help subsidize the writing of her first novel, *Eden Close* (1989), published in the same week as the nonfiction volume. Since then, Shreve has taught two semesters of writing at Amherst College in Massachusetts, and in 1998 she received both the PEN/L. L. Winship Award and the New England Book Award in Fiction. Around 1998 Shreve was married at a summer camp in North Andover, a special retreat that she visited every summer as a child. (The marriage was her second). She currently resides in western Massachusetts with her husband and children.

In her first novel, *Eden Close,* Shreve tells the story of the title character through the point of view of her former neighbor, Andrew, a successful advertising executive who has just returned home to attend his mother's funeral. Before Andrew left for college many years ago, his friend Eden was raped and blinded. Eden's blindness forced her to stay behind while Andrew pursued a college degree. Andrew stays in town for a while after the funeral and discovers that he still has strong feelings for Eden. He searches for Eden's attacker and seeks answers to the problems in his own life. Rather than focusing on the suspenseful events in the novel, Shreve emphasizes the feelings of the characters, the significance of childhood memories, and the harsh realities of life.

Shreve's detailed descriptions, character development, and deep revelations are strong components of the novel, according to reviewers. Carolyn Banks in *The New York Times* (3 September 1989) said that the insights in the novel are "keen" and that Shreve's prose is "measured" and "haunting." However, reviewers have called attention to problems with the plot and res-

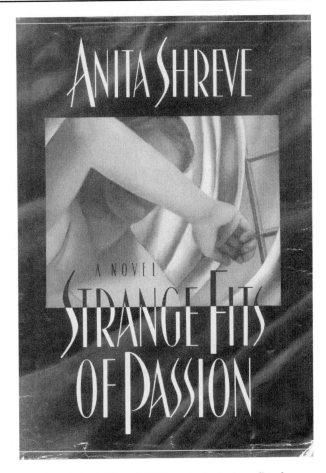

Dust jacket for Shreve's 1991 novel, about a journalist who gains wealth and fame by writing about a woman who killed her abusive husband (Richland County Public Library)

olution. Michiko Kakutani in *The New York Times* (25 August 1989) claimed that the events in the novel seem "unlikely" and "slickly contrived" but also admitted that the novel does have some redeeming qualities. Kakutani said that Shreve's characters are "highly vivid, sympathetic people" and was impressed with Shreve's ability to "delineate their relationship over time." Susan Dooley in *The Washington Post* (24 August 1989) criticized the happy ending of the novel and claimed that it seemed false. In spite of the mixed reviews, most critics agreed that the character development is the strongest element of the book.

Shreve continued the theme of violence against women and explored the theme of ethics in journalism in her second novel, *Strange Fits of Passion* (1991). The novel tells a story of domestic abuse through reporter Helen Scofield's notes and through the prison letters of Maureen English. As the novel begins, Scofield, who has become rich and famous from her article on the murder of Maureen's husband, visits Maureen's daughter and gives her the journal and notes that she used to write her

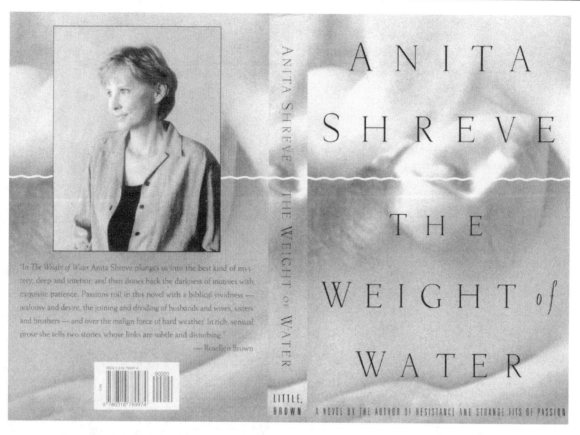

Dust jacket for Shreve's 1997 novel, in which a reporter investigates a century-old double murder on an island off the New Hampshire coast (Richland County Public Library)

article twenty years before. The novel follows Maureen's fate and chronicles the events leading up to her husband's murder. Maureen and her husband, Harrold, were once successful journalists. Shortly after their marriage, he became abusive. Finally his drunken rages become so intense that Maureen flees to Maine, taking her daughter with her. Harrold eventually discovers Maureen's whereabouts and is murdered when he tries to pursue her. A jury convicts Maureen of murder and sends her to prison. Maureen tells Scofield her story, and Scofield uses Maureen's anguish and personal tragedy for her own gain. Scofield's character is the stereotypical journalist who distorts the facts and who is only interested in selling a story. Although they considered *Strange Fits of Passion* a bit dull at times, critics praised the novel for portraying the stigma of domestic violence and for conveying gripping messages. Don O'Briant in the *Atlanta Journal-Constitution* (5 May 1991) called the novel "troubling" and "powerful" and claimed that the strength of the novel lies in the creation of multiple points of view and Maureen's "chilling" first-person accounts. On the other hand, Irene Wanner in *The Seattle Times* (7 July 1991) asserted, "We feel no pain or terror, we never see or hear Harrold's rages. Instead, Shreve chooses to offer

a flat, anaesthetized narrative, utterly undermining her compelling subject."

Where or When (1993) is about an adulterous love affair between Charles and Sian, who first met when they were both thirteen, at a Catholic summer camp. Thirty-one years after their last meeting as teenagers, Charles sees Sian's picture in a newspaper, writes to her, and begins their affair through letters. Relying on alternating points of view to reveal the inner secrets of the characters, Shreve opens with Sian's first-person point of view and then shifts to a third-person account of Charles's life. Through letters, Charles and Sian relive memories of their short teenage obsession with each other, revive their love, and move toward a catastrophic reunion. Timing and undying love are key elements of the novel. Some critics said that *Where or When* fails to produce original themes and three-dimensional characters; however, they praised Shreve for her understanding of the painful complexities of forbidden love and for her ability to create anticipation through the use of flashbacks. Joyce Slater in *The St. Petersburg Times* (6 June 1993) commented that the reason the novel reaches powerful levels of intimacy is because Shreve "captures well the ambivalence, guilt and obsession that are part and parcel of an extramarital affair." In spite of these keen insights, Shreve failed to create a satisfactory ending, according to some critics. Wanner in *The Seattle Times* (4 July 1993) said that Shreve's "competent prose self-destructs" when Sian's and Charles's spouses discover the affair. Wanner claimed, "Her last 20 pages—lame language, repetition, rhetorical questions, summarized action, distanced emotion—prove disappointing." Thus, some critics suggested that Shreve was unable to sustain the anticipation that she created in the first chapters of the novel.

Resistance (1995), Shreve's first historical novel, is set in Nazi-occupied Belgium during World War II and tells the story of Belgian villagers and of the wounded American pilot Ted Brice, who falls in love with Claire Daussois, a married woman. As activists in the Resistance movement, Claire and her husband hide refugees in an attic room until they can safely cross the French border. When Ted's plane crashes, a young village boy takes him to Claire's house, and the two fall in love while she nurses his wounds. Because of their circumstances and Claire's unhappy marriage, Ted and Claire's love grows stronger and more hopeless during a fierce German attack after a Belgian uprising in the village. While addressing the nightmare of this German attack and the horrors of war, Shreve explores courage, loyalty, passion, and despair in the hearts and minds of her characters. Critics praised Shreve for her portrayal of the complications of an impossible love affair and the chaos of a brutal war. Danielle Roter in *The Los Angeles Times* (7 May 1995) said, "The writer's respect for her characters (even the ignoble ones) is striking, as is the meticulous attention to detail." Nancy McAllister in *The Columbus Dispatch* (30 April 1995) commented: "In beautiful unpretentious language the author embarks on a complex journey exploring the human spirit." A 2003 movie version, starring Julia Ormond and Bill Paxton, was written by director Todd Komarnicki.

The Weight of Water (1997) is an expanded version of Shreve's short story "Murder at Smuttynose." Published in *The Cimarron Review* in 1975, the story is based on an actual nineteenth-century double murder. Authorities convicted a man for the murder, but Maren Hontvedt, the only survivor of the attack, remained a suspect for more than a century before and after her own death. The main character of the novel, Jean, a photojournalist, travels on an assignment to the scene of the crime, the Isle of Shoals off the coast of New Hampshire. Jean's husband, Thomas, and their daughter, as well as Thomas's brother and girlfriend, travel with Jean in their houseboat to unravel the century-old mystery. During the voyage, Jean notices a romance developing between her husband and his brother's girlfriend, Adaline. Putting her own problem to the side for a while, Jean finds a major clue in solving the double murder while sifting through archival material

in Portsmouth. Taking the box of material back to the boat, Jean finds Maren's own accounts of the murders and the events leading up to them. The novel also traces Maren's unbearable life at Smuttynose, her unhappy marriage, and her incestuous love for her brother. Shreve combines the themes of marital distress and jealousy in the lives of both Jean and Maren.

Amy Waldman in *The Milwaukee Journal Sentinel* (16 February 1997) praised the strong plot: "The total effect is the literary equivalent of a whirlpool, sucking the reader so slowly into an emotional vortex that when she reveals her last, brilliantly devastating surprise, the effect is as shocking as the discovery of a sudden undertow." Yet, other critics found the novel lacking in character development. Dooley in *The Washington Post* (23 January 1997) admitted that the novel was suspenseful and interesting but that "there is nothing about the character of these two women, who lived a hundred years apart, that would lead us to expect either of them to behave as they do." Dooley's main arguments were that the characters' actions were unrealistic and that the climax of the story was faulty and failed to reach a satisfying resolution. In 1998, however, *The Weight of Water* was short-listed for the Orange Prize, a prestigious British literary award given to novels written by women. A movie version, with screenplay by Alice Arlen and Christopher Kyle and starring Sean Penn, Catherine McCormack, and Elizabeth Hurley, was released in 2000.

Shreve's next novel, *The Pilot's Wife* (1998), is also set in New Hampshire. A union representative travels to Kathryn Lyons's home near Elly Falls, New Hampshire, to inform her that her husband, a commercial pilot, has died in a plane crash in Ireland. He explains that investigators believe the crash to be suicide. Conducting her own investigation, Kathryn becomes suspicious of her late husband's fidelity. Traveling to London to confirm her fears, she encounters his mistress and discovers his involvement in the Troubles in Ireland. *The Pilot's Wife* addresses inner anguish, secrets, betrayals, and methods of survival as a distraught widow comes to terms with her husband's death and infidelity. Although some critics claimed that the book lacked a central focus, it received mostly good reviews. Lucinda Ballantyne in *The Boston Globe* (10 May 1998) explained that the major problem in the novel was that the themes were underdeveloped and confusing and that Shreve's purpose was unclear. Oliver Burkmen in *The Observer* (21 November 1999) admitted that he found the novel to be intriguing and enjoyed Shreve's unconventional writing style. He claimed that Shreve turned what could have been an overdone melodrama into a gripping analysis of "how even the closest bonds never permit us to know another person entirely." Other critics praised the suspenseful plot, sympathetic characters, and original prose. The novel was a selection

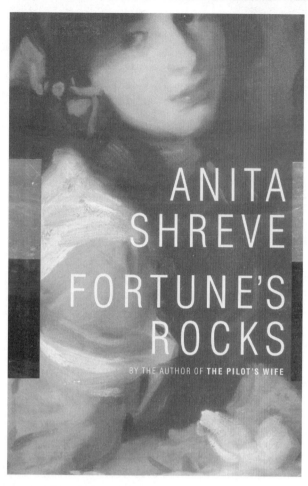

Dust jacket for Shreve's 2000 novel, set in nineteenth-century New Hampshire, about a fifteen-year-old who becomes an unwed mother as the result of an affair with a married man three times her age (Richland County Public Library)

of Oprah Winfrey's book club, and Shreve was a coproducer of the 2002 television-movie version starring Christine Lahti, John Heard, and Campbell Scott, for which Shreve wrote the screenplay with Christine Berardo.

Fortune's Rocks (2000) is set in the same house as *The Pilot's Wife* a century earlier, when Fortune's Rocks, New Hampshire, was a retreat for wealthy Bostonians. The novel follows the struggles of fifteen-year-old Olympia Biddeford, who spends her summers in the beach house where Kathryn Lyons will one day live. Olympia's downfall begins when she has a passionate affair with her father's friend, John Haskell, a doctor and married man three times Olympia's age. After Haskell's wife and Olympia's parents discover the short-lived affair, Olympia and her disgraced parents return to Boston. After Olympia gives birth to Haskell's baby, her father gives the child to an orphanage and later sends Olympia to a women's seminary in western Massachusetts. Olympia

struggles to find her child and repair her life, and later finds solace in helping other unwed mothers. Critics agreed that *Fortune's Rocks* resembles the works of Edith Wharton and Henry James, but that the novel is overloaded with unimportant and often contradicting symbolism. Suzanne Rhodenbaugh in *The St. Louis Post-Dispatch* (19 December 1999) said, "Shreve is heavy on the symbolism and a sense of the portentous, but toward no apparent purpose other than a kind of verbal drum roll." However, the novel did possess some redeeming qualities. Gail Caldwell in *The Boston Globe* (19 December 1999) stated that Shreve's "attention to the opposing social milieus of the summer rich and the mill workers, a tension that will figure in Olympia's plight, has done her story a world of good, opening it up beyond a romance cum morality tale to greater narrative sweep."

Shreve continues the theme of obsessive love affairs in her next novel, *The Last Time They Met* (2001). The story is about the love affair between poets Linda Fallon and Thomas Janes, Jean's husband from *The Weight of Water*. The novel is told in reverse chronological order and is divided into three sections: "Fifty-two," "Twenty-six," and "Seventeen," referring to Linda's age at the times she encounters Thomas. At the beginning of the novel, they find each other at a literary festival in Toronto where both are guest speakers. The novel then recounts their affair in Kenya twenty-six years earlier, when they are married to other people. Their spouses discover the affair. The last section takes place in Boston and tells the beginning of the lovers' lifelong passion. In an interview with Robert Allen Papinchak in *The Writer* (November 2001), Shreve discussed the major theme of the novel: "The area of love is a wonderful place in which to place characters. It's something extraordinary that happens to ordinary people. It's often as well a terrific testing ground for moral character."

In spite of its universal theme, the novel received mixed reviews. Some critics praised Shreve's innovative way of using reverse chronological order, and others found the organization of the novel to be unsatisfactory. Moreover, Ruth Watts in *TLS: The Times Literary Supplement* (9 February 2002) asserted that the plot is "hampered by a clumsy conceit revealed only on the final page." Monique Polak in *The Gazette* (18 August 2001) stated, "In spite of its melodrama and unrealistic premise, *The Last Time They Met* is redeemed by some clever dialogue and an unflinching portrayal of marital infidelity." A reviewer for *Publishers Weekly* commented that this novel may be Shreve's "most mature to date."

Sea Glass (2002) is set in the same house as *The Pilot's Wife* and *Fortune's Rocks*. In "The Origins of *Sea Glass*," a 2002 essay on her publisher's website <http://www.twbookmark.com/authorslounge/articles/2002/february/article14386.html>, Shreve explains her fascination with the real-life model, a house in Maine; she points out, "A house with any kind of age will have dozens of stories to tell. I suppose if a novelist could live long enough, one could base an entire oeuvre on the lives that weave in and out of an antique house." This novel tells the story of the 1929 resident of the house, newlywed Honora Beecher, and the ways in which her life becomes entangled with three other residents of Elly Falls and Fortune's Rocks. When Honora's husband, Sexton, loses his sales job around the same time that the 1929 stock market crashes, he begins to work in one of the mills in town and becomes involved in a union strike. The other main characters of the novel are McDermott, a twenty-year-old loom fixer who falls in love with Honora; Alphonse, an eleven-year-old mill worker; and Vivian Burton, a spoiled but good-hearted socialite. The novel presents the viewpoints of each principal character as they head toward a violent confrontation. The themes of the novel are loyalty, betrayal, responsibility, and dishonor.

Sea Glass received good reviews for its interesting look into domestic lives in New England during the onset of the Great Depression. However, reviewers also criticized Shreve for creating stereotypical characters and for providing suffocating social interpretations. Cynthia Smith in the *Atlanta Journal-Constitution* (5 May 2002) remarked, "As with any of Shreve's novels, this book is gripping. Yet, Shreve's heavy-handed political commentary detracts from the plot's trajectory." Janet Maslin in *The New York Times* (8 April 2002) said, "As with many stories that build momentum into the discovery of how separate plot elements will align, *Sea Glass* does a better job of building suspense than of coaxing it toward a denouement."

The narrator of Shreve's next novel, *All He Ever Wanted* (2003), is Nicholas Van Tassel, who tells the story of his doomed marriage while on a train trip from New Hampshire to Florida in 1933. Van Tassel, an English professor at Thrupp College, recounts his first meeting with his future wife, Etna, in 1899, when they both escaped a hotel fire in New Hampshire. Van Tassel fell passionately in love with Etna, who agreed to marry him even though she was in love with Samuel Asher, a Jew who is the brother of Van Tassel's academic rival. In addition to his relationship with Etna, Van Tassel also tells about his attempts to bring down Samuel's brother Phillip. He even convinced his daughter to falsely accuse Phillip of molesting her. Some of the themes addressed in the novel are anti-Semitism, chauvinism, and independence. While critics admitted that Shreve addresses important feminist topics in *All He Ever Wanted,* reviewers found problems with her unreliable narrator. Judy Budz in *The Boston Globe* (11 May 2003) called Van Tassel's narration "pedantically boring." Jocelyn McClurg in *USA Today*

Dust jacket for Shreve's 2002 novel, set in the same New Hampshire house as Fortune's Rocks *and* The Pilot's Wife *(1998) but in a different era, in which the characters face the onset of the Great Depression (Richland County Public Library)*

(15 April 2003) claimed, "With such an unattractive narrator, *All He Ever Wanted* is a bumpy ride, not unlike Van Tassel's train trip to Florida"; yet, McClurg also admitted, "Even when Shreve isn't at the top of her game, there's something addictive about her literary tales of lust and love."

Critics agree that Shreve creates psychological suspense while delicately and sympathetically addressing disturbing subject matter and portraying a deep understanding of love, infidelity, disloyalty, courage, and brutality. Her witty discourse, historical accuracy, and realistic details have contributed to her ranking among noteworthy twenty-first-century novelists.

Interviews:

Robert Allen Papinchak, "Testing the Water," *Writer* (November 2001): 26–29;

Sue Fox, "Anita Shreve: A Fortune Found in the Seas of Love," *Independent* (30 March 2002) <http://enjoy ment.independent.co.uk/books/interviews/story.jsp? story=279865>.

Omar Tyree
(15 April 1969 –)

Carol E. Henderson
University of Delaware

BOOKS: *Colored, On White Campus: The Education of a Racial World* (Wilmington, Del.: MARS Productions, 1992); republished as *BattleZone: The Struggle to Survive the American Institution* (Wilmington, Del.: MARS Productions, 1994);

Flyy Girl (Wilmington, Del.: MARS Productions, 1993);

Capital City: The Chronicles of a D.C. Underworld (Wilmington, Del.: MARS Productions, 1994); revised and republished as *The Underground,* as The Urban Griot (Charlotte, N.C.: MARS Productions, 2001);

A Do Right Man (New York: Simon & Schuster, 1997);

Single Mom (New York: Simon & Schuster, 1998);

Sweet St. Louis: An Urban Love Story (New York: Simon & Schuster, 1999);

For the Love of Money (New York: Simon & Schuster, 2000);

Just Say No! (New York: Simon & Schuster, 2001);

Leslie (New York: Simon & Schuster, 2002);

Diary of a Groupie (New York: Simon & Schuster, 2003);

One Crazy-A** Night, as The Urban Griot (Charlotte, N.C.: MARS Productions, 2003);

College Boy, as The Urban Griot (New York: Pocket Books, 2003).

RECORDING: *Rising Up!* as The Urban Griot, Nu Millennium, 2003.

OTHER: "Meet the New Invisible Man: The Young Black Male Nobody Knows," *Washington Post,* 18 July 1993, p. C5;

"From White to Black Campus," in *Testimony: Young African Americans on Self-Discovery and Black Identity,* edited by Natasha Tarpley (Boston: Beacon, 1995), pp. 129–132;

"Reflections on Success," *Black Collegian Online* (2001) <http://www.black-collegian.com/issues/30thAnn/reflectotyree2001-30th.shtml>.

Omar Tyree brings a double perspective to the craft of writing–that of his own upbringing in one of

Omar Tyree (photograph by Daniel B. McNeill; from the dust jacket for Single Mom, *1998; Bruccoli Clark Layman Archives)*

the most prominent urban American centers, and that of years of watching young African American men self-destruct from the pressures of the street. These experiences provided fertile ground for his imagination and influenced his literary career, which began in the 1990s. The weight of his observations from his personal perspective prompted him to write *Flyy Girl* (1993), his best-selling novel about a young black woman coming of age in Philadelphia during the materialistic 1980s. In *Capital City: The Chronicles of a D.C. Underworld* (1994) Tyree merges both cultural perspectives into a fully developed aesthetic vision that establishes his distinct position in the African American literary renaissance genre he terms Urban American Life Novels. These novels offer readers a mature, serious, and purposeful meditation on those issues that plague America's inner cities. Tyree distinguishes Urban American Life Novels from those novels written by authors such as Terry McMillan, whose writings he characterizes as "relationship books"—books that continuously explore bedroom issues of African American men and women. Urban American Life Novels offer a more complex rendering of social issues, not what Tyree has called a "watered-down" synopsis of African American life that does not take into consideration the various experiences African American people share in the struggle for human equality in this new millennium.

Omar Rashad Tyree was born in Philadelphia, Pennsylvania, on 15 April 1969. The second of five children, Tyree was raised by his mother, Renee McLaurin Alston, until she remarried when he was nine. Tyree's stepfather, a physically imposing figure, had a major influence on Tyree's life. Tyree credits him with "showing the way to manhood, sometimes forcefully when he had to"; the alternative, as Tyree had witnessed with other young men in his life, might have been "the young black man's new rite of passage: jail." Tyree's mother had a similar impact on his life. The oldest of eight children, she graduated third in her high-school class. In her freshman year at Temple University, she received an academic scholarship to the School of Pharmacy. During this time, Tyree was born. Three years later, after completing her studies at Temple, Alston was awarded a bachelor's degree and was one of only four African Americans to graduate in her class of 1973.

Tyree's academic life followed a similar path of excellence. He graduated from Central High School in 1987 and enrolled at the University of Pittsburgh (Pitt) as one of thirty minority students admitted under a challenge grant scholarship program in the fall of 1987. He also became a member of Pitt's Big East track team. In the spring of 1988 the Phi Eta Sigma freshman honor society recognized Tyree for his academic achievements in science and math after he earned a grade point average of 3.58 the previous semester. As a result, he was awarded a $3,400 tuition scholarship to study pharmacy. While at Pitt, Tyree also discovered his talent for writing. After earning an A in his freshman English course in 1988, Tyree was one of only a few freshmen allowed to enroll in a creative-writing course. Later that same year his journal, "The Diary of a Freshman," was published as part of the minority counseling news pamphlet. In 1989 Tyree transferred to Howard University after experiencing some "distasteful" incidents of racism at Pitt and changed his major from pharmacy to journalism. During his senior year at Howard, he became the first student to have a featured column published in the award-winning school newspaper, *The Hilltop*, and in December 1991 Tyree graduated cum laude with a degree in print journalism.

Following the completion of his undergraduate studies, Tyree was hired as a reporter and assistant editor at *The Capital Spotlight*, a weekly newspaper in Washington, D.C. He later served as chief reporter for another weekly newspaper, *News Dimensions*, while freelancing for *Washington View* magazine. Sometime during the early part of 1992, Tyree decided to write and publish books. After relocating to Delaware, he formed his own publishing company, MARS Productions, with the financial backing of family and friends. In October 1992 he self-published his first novel, *Colored, On White Campus: The Education of a Racial World*, a fictional account loosely based on his own struggles as a student at Pitt. In 1994, Tyree revised and subsequently republished this novel as *BattleZone: The Struggle to Survive the American Institution*. The novel describes protagonist Troy Potter's psychological and emotional journey through the hierarchy of academic culture as he strives to find his purpose in life while attending a predominantly white university. Potter's multiple experiences with racism underscore the larger concerns of societal racism embedded in the educational system. The "battlezone," as Tyree adeptly points out, is the psyche of young Potter as he earnestly tries to reconcile the schism that exists between his own blackness and the pervasive whiteness of the university student body. *Colored, On White Campus* went largely unnoticed by critics and readers, even with its repackaging; however, its sales financed his next novel, *Flyy Girl*.

Tracy Ellison, the protagonist of *Flyy Girl*, is materialistically driven and self-centered—a self-described "flyy girl"—willing to use her looks, her wit, and her biting attitude to gain acceptance from her peers. Her middle-class upbringing in Germantown, one of Philadelphia's most comfortable and scenic black neighborhoods, affords Tracy the privilege of being raised with luxuries such as private lawns, patios, driveways, and trees. Tracy's father, Dave Ellison, "a deep cocoa-brown and hazel-eyed" man, is a pharmacist. Her mother, Patti, is described as a "light skinned" and "curvaceous" dietitian for a local nursing home. The Ellisons' professional careers make for a volatile relationship as Dave's responsibilities cause him to spend long hours away from home. This tension, exacerbated by the lack of

Dust jacket for Tyree's breakthrough novel, about a black businesswoman whose two sons' fathers want to become involved in their lives (Bruccoli Clark Layman Archives)

enrolls in college with the hope of learning how to be a true black woman who respects and loves herself.

Flyy Girl is distinct from novels such as Ntozake Shange's *Sassafrass, Cypress & Indigo* (1982) or memoirs such as Nathan McCall's *Makes Me Wanna Holler* (1994) in its narrative focus on the decadent period of the 1980s. The lure of the fast-lane lifestyle that many surrendered to during this era makes this novel as much a critique of American excess as it is a poignant portrayal of the perils of the street. Tyree's decision to make Tracy a product of a two-parent, middle-class family allows the reader to gain significant insight into the idealized image of black suburban life. Some of Tyree's detractors, however, consider this novel an "unremarkable" coming-of-age story. In particular, one critic from *Publishers Weekly* (26 August 1996) determined that while "Tyree captures black language as it is spoken among peers . . . the narrative flow is often disrupted by too many italics and slang-defining asides, and by a rocky imbalance between neutral narration and vernacular." The reviewer added, "The conversation of youngsters caught in a highly pressured sexual atmosphere, test-driving their sexuality long before they're old enough for a license, is profane and vivid." Tyree's direct, and all too real, portrayals of young teenagers makes *Flyy Girl* a favorite among young readers. To date, this novel has sold some two hundred thousand copies; this total includes sales from the first publication by MARS Productions and its 1996 republication by Simon and Schuster.

In 1993, while sketching the characters for his next novel, Tyree began to reassess his vision of urban literature and its connection to black male identity. He revisited the works of such literary giants as Richard Wright, Chester Himes, and Iceberg Slim. These reflections led him to write *Capital City*. Reminiscent of Wright's "The Man Who Lived Underground" (1944) and Ralph Ellison's *Invisible Man* (1952), Tyree's novel explores the aura of the underground, a domain that functions within and beneath mainstream America. Its inhabitants, overlooked and underseen by dominant culture, are marginalized, and in most cases disenfranchised from America's economic and social order. Intense, political, and action-packed, *Capital City* presents an uncompromising account of the fate of many young African American men who reside in this underworld. These individuals must make difficult decisions about their lives and the directions they will take. For some, the journey will end in a hail of bullets or in the penitentiary. For others, death will only touch their lives for a moment, yet they will be irrevocably changed by it. Characters such as Butterman (Jeffrey Kirkland Jr.), Wes (Raymond West), and Shank (Darnell Hall) are men whose investments in the capital city

passion and intimacy shared by Dave and Patti, causes the couple to separate for a period of time. Disenchanted with her parents' unstable relationship, Tracy turns to the street for love and security. Her parents eventually resolve their differences, each recommitting to the marriage and the raising of their two children, Tracy and Jason (who was conceived during one of their reconciliations and born while they were living in separate residences).

Tracy's maturation process, however, anchors this novel. By the time her parents reconcile, she has evolved into young womanhood, losing her virginity at the age of thirteen to a rough but sensitive street thug named Victor Hinson. Tracy's growing dependence on sex and material possessions leads her to associate with known felons and drug dealers. By the end of the novel, Victor has been arrested and is serving time in a nearby prison. During his incarceration, Tracy rethinks her careless sexual behavior and dangerous association with abusive men. Always a good student, Tracy

drug culture pay immediate dividends of fast cars and pretty women but, in the long run, deprive them of security and peace of mind. Tyree's investigation into this volatile yet sizable culture underscores the irony of such a community existing in the shadow of the nation's capital. The reader is left to consider the contradictions of the American Dream, the promise of freedom, and the ability to pursue happiness unencumbered by poverty or prejudice.

With limited resources and word of mouth as his only form of promotion, Tyree sold twenty-five thousand copies of his self-published books at various venues up and down the East Coast. The success of his venture attracted the attention of Simon and Schuster in August 1995. He negotiated a two-book contract with them in September of that same year, which included the republication of *Flyy Girl* in hardcover in October 1996 as well as the initial publication of Tyree's next novel, *A Do Right Man,* in October 1997. In *A Do Right Man* Tyree's observations of black manhood move from the street to the boardroom. Bobby Dallas, the central character, is a budding radio talk-show host who struggles with his love life and his career. He is a sensitive man, willing to admit his fears, anxieties, and uncertainties about his future. Dallas's mother is an educator, a hard woman who pushes him because she knows her son's potential, and his father is a quiet man who provides humor in moments of familial unrest, encouraging Dallas to follow his dreams. *A Do Right Man* also offers a full spectrum of characters and types, from professional basketball player Gary Mitchell, whose sexual escapades mask his insecurity about his marginal status within the NBA, to Frank Watts, an "average Joe" in the radio business who befriends Dallas and educates him about the treacherous nature of the career upon which he is about to embark.

According to Norwood Holland of *Metroconnection* (26 November 1999), Tyree's characterizations in *A Do Right Man* are "believable, wholesome, intelligent and admirable in every way." Holland suggested that Tyree's assessment of the black male struggle is comparable to writers such as Charles Chesnutt and Himes. Despite such reviews, *A Do Right Man* was not a commercial success. The novel went largely unnoticed by many mainstream literary critics, but like his earlier publications, it solidified his standing among his followers. Tyree's invisibility within mainstream literary circles changed, however, with the publication of *Single Mom* (1998), a novel that became a national best-seller.

Single Mom charts the life of a self-made businesswoman, Denise Stewart, who finds herself increasingly involved with each of her sons' fathers. Walter Perry Jr. seeks custody of his twelve-year-old son with Denise after he attends the Million Man March in Washington,

D.C. Denise's older son, Little Jay, is a promising basketball player. At fifteen, he is already six feet, five inches tall, and his father, J.D., hopes that his son will avoid the pitfalls of urban life that cost him two and half years in the Indiana State Correctional Facility for armed robbery. J.D. himself had been a basketball player, but bad grades and Denise's subsequent pregnancy during his senior year in high school thwarted his chances of attending a Division I college on a basketball scholarship. Disillusioned, he started hanging out with the "Gangster Disciples," a crew whose membership included J.D.'s older brother, Marcus, and his younger brother, Juan. J.D.'s incarceration and the deaths of his two brothers have caused him to rethink his life and the choices he has made concerning his future and his family.

Single Mom is, at its center, a social commentary on the state of affairs of the black family. In a 1998 article titled "What Happened to the Patriarch in Black Families" and posted on his website, <http://www.omartyree. com>, Tyree contemplates the disintegration of the nuclear black families. He writes:

> In five consecutive years of my youth, I viewed three of my young male cousins at their wakes, and helplessly watched three more who were sent to juvenile detention centers. None of them had strong or stable father figures in their lives like I had, and all of this activity went down before I was old enough to decisively influence the situation as an older cousin.

Tyree's need to disrupt the cycle of what he calls "the pathology of another young black male without a father figure" supports his premise that black literature should be more than just entertainment. It should bring to the forefront of American literature new, multidimensional characters whose life experiences serve as contemporary examples of shared human existence.

In 1999 Tyree published *Sweet St. Louis: An Urban Love Story.* Tyree's intent, as evident from the subtitle, is to focus on those social factors that can negatively or positively impact a developing love connection. The narrative aligns itself (in tenor at least) with those novels Tyree termed "relationship books," concerned only with the bedroom issues of African American men and women. Nonetheless, the charm of *Sweet St. Louis* rests on the idea not only that a "playa" can be tamed but also that love can be found with an unassuming mechanic (even in the age of the buppie), and, furthermore, this love can flourish in the chaos of American urban centers.

Tyree's persistence in presenting three-dimensional portraits of his characters, of creating a diverse and vibrant "underworld" that counters the often homogenous view of this culture within America's larger social

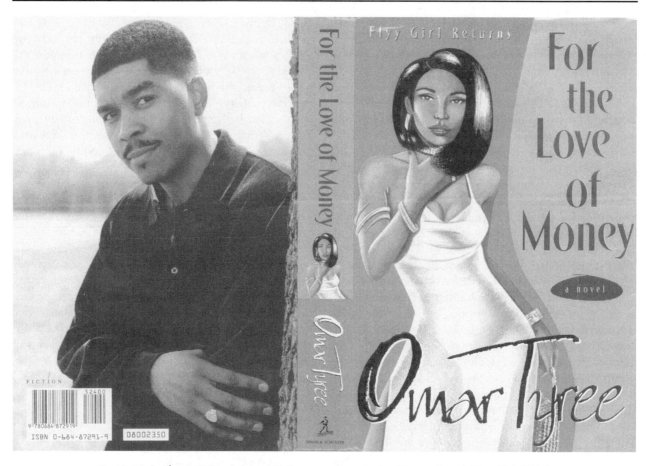

Dust jacket for Tyree's 2000 novel, in which the wayward protagonist of his second novel, Flyy Girl *(1993),
has become a successful author, screenwriter, and actress (Bruccoli Clark Layman Archives)*

context, was rewarded in March 2001 when he was presented with an NAACP Image Award for outstanding literary work in fiction for his August 2000 release, *For the Love of Money*. This sequel to *Flyy Girl* revisits the life of Tracy Ellison Grant, now twenty-eight and a successful author (of the book *Flyy Girl*), screenwriter, and rising movie actress. Tracy faces some of the same issues in her adult life that she faced in *Flyy Girl,* namely how to maintain self-love despite the seductions of a materialistic culture. *For the Love of Money* became Tyree's first *New York Times* best-seller.

In August 2001 Tyree published *Just Say No!,* a contemporary novel that investigates the youthful indulgences of the music industry. Set in Charlotte, North Carolina (where Tyree had moved sometime between 1999 and 2000), the novel follows the careers of two childhood friends: Darin Harmon, a popular athlete, and John Williams, an emerging rhythm and blues singer. The book charts the progress of their individual journeys as it exposes the pitfalls of stardom and the lure of fame, sex, and drugs.

With *Leslie* (2002) Tyree enters into a new literary genre: urban horror. Set in New Orleans, *Leslie* follows the college career of Leslie Beaudet, an exotic and intelligent Haitian coed whose beauty and cultural dabblings into voodoo and other religious practices create interesting subplots of murder, envy, drugs, and intrigue. Tyree's next novel, *The Diary of A Groupie* (2003), builds on many of these themes as the narrative centers on the sexual exploits of twenty-six-year-old Tabitha Knight, whose relations with super-rich celebrity boyfriends give her ample material for her journal which, to date, spans thirteen volumes. When a private investigator, Sylvia Green, asks Tabitha to get close to a famous actor suspected of having sex with underage women, Tabitha must make a decision between her current lifestyle and her emerging "moral" consciousness. Moreover, Tabitha's life, and the lives of her foster sisters Janet, Patrice, and Marisol may be in danger, as some of her former lovers fear exposure (and loss of privacy) if Tabitha's diary becomes public.

Reviews are mixed concerning Tyree's later novels. Some readers felt that he had strayed from those earlier thematic concerns that made his first few novels distinctive. Tyree returns to his origins, however, in *College Boy* (2003), one of the novels he began publishing under the pseudonym The Urban Griot. As he explains on his website for this persona, <http://www.theurbangriot.com>, The Urban Griot is "here to investigate what brothers are feeling. . . . I'm coming with hardcore, fast-moving, plot-driven stories that males can take to naturally." In *College Boy* Tyree reexamines the life of Troy Potter, a young African American basketball player from inner-city Philadelphia whose talents on the court earn him a scholarship to a predominantly white college. Potter's cultural adjustments anchor this book as he contemplates not only his role as a basketball player but also what it means to be a black man in white America. Tyree reconsiders his earlier explorations of W. E. B. Du Bois's "double consciousness" as he intuitively expresses the fears, frustrations, and challenges faced by many African American college students, especially those who carry the double burden of athletic prowess.

Tyree has also kept busy with projects such as an Urban Griot album titled *Rising Up!* (2003), plans for his own record label, and a screenplay about the music industry, "Move the Crowd," which he is working to get produced. He is trying to get *Flyy Girl* made into a movie as well, and a third Tracy Ellison Grant book is slated for 2005.

By the time he signed his third two-book contract with Simon and Schuster, Tyree had solidified his place within the African American literary tradition. With the success of his novels, Tyree has demonstrated that he is willing to delve into such controversial issues as absentee fathers, single parenthood, and the search for good black men. His roles as publisher, lecturer, performance poet, playwright, and now recording artist have made him a popular favorite among colleges, high schools, and civic organizations. He shares a home in Charlotte with his wife, Karintha, and their two sons, Ameer and Canoy, and he remains passionate about educating black people about themselves and the world around them. His unflinching view of the emotional and spiritual turmoil that so readily encompasses the urban community places Tyree in the literary lineage of Ellison and Wright, as he documents the interaction between black men and women and their struggles to form meaningful personal relationships in spite of the disheartening prospects of life in urban America.

Rebecca Wells

(1952 –   )

Susie Scifres Kuilan
Louisiana State University

BOOKS: *Little Altars Everywhere* (Seattle: Broken Moon
    Press, 1992; London: Pan, 1998);
Divine Secrets of the Ya-Ya Sisterhood (New York: Harper-
    Collins, 1996; London: Pan, 1998).

PLAY PRODUCTIONS: *Splittin' Hairs,* Seattle, Seattle
    Repertory Theater, 1982;
Gloria Duplex, Seattle, Empty Space Theater, April 1987.

RECORDINGS: *Divine Secrets of the Ya-Ya Sisterhood,*
    abridged, read by Wells, New York, HarperAu-
    dio, 1998;
Little Altars Everywhere, abridged, read by Wells, New
    York, HarperCollins, 1999.

Rebecca Wells's novels *Little Altars Everywhere*
(1992) and *Divine Secrets of the Ya-Ya Sisterhood* (1996) are
set in central Louisiana. Each novel reflects important
issues of life in the Bayou State by showing the influence
of family and region on the search for individual identity.
The phenomenal sales of these novels are noteworthy
when one realizes that her books were not destined to be
best-sellers. Initially, neither *Little Altars Everywhere* nor
Divine Secrets of the Ya-Ya Sisterhood was reviewed by any
major publication and did not appear on any best-seller
list. Wells also made none of the traditional national
appearances, such as the morning television shows on
the major networks, but word of mouth eventually generated the sales that are reflected today: *Divine Secrets of
the Ya-Ya Sisterhood* has sold more than three million copies, and *Little Altars Everywhere* has sold more than one
million copies. Wells's importance must also be considered in view of critics' comparisons to other writers, most
notably the word-of-mouth success story of Jill Conner
Browne's *The Sweet Potato Queens' Book of Love* (1999).

Despite Wells's reticence to discuss her family,
critics have learned some basic information about her
early life. Wells was born in 1952 in Rapides, Louisiana. She was raised in central Louisiana, where her
father was a self-employed businessman running a plantation owned by his family since 1795. From an early

*Rebecca Wells (photograph © Susan Rothschild; from the dust jacket
for* Divine Secrets of the Ya-Ya Sisterhood, *1996;
Richland County Public Library)*

age, Wells was a voracious reader, storyteller, and performer, and as a child she produced plays using friends
and relatives as fellow cast members. She attended
Catholic schools, and after high school she attended
Louisiana State University, where she received a B.A.
in English in 1970. Following college graduation, Wells
traveled the country extensively and studied with Allen
Ginsberg at the Naropa Institute in Boulder, Colorado.
Wells's childhood acting experiences eventually led to a
career as an actress, playwright, and novelist. To pursue acting, she moved to New York City and studied
with Maurine Holbert-Hogaboom, who taught the
Stanislavsky method. This method of acting stresses the
importance of learning a role by acquiring the internal
characteristics of the character rather than just the

external movements. During Wells's time in New York City, she performed in several Off-Broadway productions. Wells later acknowledged Holbert-Hogaboom in *Divine Secret of the Ya-Ya Sisterhood,* calling the drama instructor her mentor.

In 1982 Wells went to Seattle to begin a chapter of Performing Artists for Nuclear Disarmament (PAND) and to perform in various productions. She loved the Pacific Northwest, eventually moving to the area permanently. Wells married Tom Schworer, a photographer, and the couple lives on an island across the Puget Sound from Seattle. Since settling in Washington, Wells has written, produced, and starred in *Splittin' Hairs* and *Gloria Duplex*–both of which won local awards. She has also written scripts for ABC and CBS, but these have not been produced. When not writing, Wells performs readings from her novels around the country.

Wells's first book, *Little Altars Everywhere,* was published in Seattle by Broken Moon Press to mixed reviews in 1992. Despite a small initial print run of five thousand, *Little Altars Everywhere* won the Western States Book Award in fiction in 1992 as well as praise from best-selling Southern novelist Pat Conroy, who called it "a splendid first novel." Some reviews of *Little Altars Everywhere* attempted to relegate the novel to the young-adult shelves, and a critic for *Publishers Weekly* (29 June 1992) suggested that the dialect and slang were superficial and the narrators seemed contrived. *Little Altars Everywhere* focuses on a dysfunctional family, and as the *Library Journal* (1 November 1999) review points out, it tackles such issues as "loss of innocence, the traditional roles of women in the South, and the plight of farmers." These themes, in addition to the exploration of family and community, have made this book popular with reading groups. This popularity led HarperCollins to create a reading discussion guide that focuses on these and other issues such as religion, humor, racism, acceptance, and healing.

Little Altars Everywhere begins with protagonist Sidda, a successful New York director, relating a dream that she has of a happy childhood memory, which initially leaves her feeling warm and good upon awakening. She tells the reader, "I still want my mother to come to me and take me in her arms." Following this prologue, portions of the story are narrated by Sidda; her father, Big Shep; her brothers, Baylor and Little Shep; her mother, Viviane (Vivi); and her sister, Lulu. In the first part of the book, these multiple narrative voices generally depict humorous childhood memories from the 1960s with only glimpses of the pain caused by living with two alcoholic parents. The family's recollections focus on Vivi and each narrator's stormy and dramatic relationship with her. Despite Vivi's drama,

the Walker family connections are strong, and as Big Shep says, "this one night with my family in the bed with me is like living on a safe island. It's the least lonely I've been in my whole life." Through various escapades related by the different narrators, Vivi takes on the Girl Scouts, a sheriff opposed to skinny-dipping, and the Catholic Church. When the narration moves into the present in part two of the book, however, Willetta and Chaney, the African American couple who work for the Walkers, join the other narrators from an objective point of view that provides an insider's knowledge of a climactic episode from the past:

> I done heard them chilren screamin fore my eye even seen what was goin on. All four of my babies lined up against the wall of that brick house and every one of them buck naked. Miz Vivi out there with a belt, whuppin them like horses. And them just standin against the red brick. Yellin and cryin and screamin, but not even trying to get away from her.

The stories told in the present focus on Sidda and the other Walker children, showing them either trying to forget this episode and other similar ones or trying to analyze such episodes. The narratives of Vivi's adult children show that they are neither able to forget nor to provide perspective on the alternating periods of loving "snuggling" and abuse.

Divine Secrets of the Ya-Ya Sisterhood begins with Sidda breaking the rules by discussing family secrets with a reporter. The story becomes front-page news, causing her mother to disown her. The remainder of the book portrays Sidda's search for answers about herself and her relationship with her mother. The impact of the past on the present becomes more apparent as Sidda peruses her mother's scrapbook, which contains memorabilia from Vivi's childhood and traces her relationships with a group of friends known as the Ya-Yas. Sidda's reading of the scrapbook eventually leads her to an acceptance of herself and her relationship with her mother. Sidda returns to Louisiana to reunite with Vivi; this reconciliation is possible because Sidda finally discovers that she and her mother are "good enough" and that perfection is not required in their relationship.

A review for *Publishers Weekly* (8 April 1996) claimed that *Divine Secrets of the Ya-Ya Sisterhood,* like its predecessor, suffered from "superficial characterization and forced colloquialisms" and that "this novel attempts to wed a folksy home-spun tale to a soul-searching examination of conscience. But while Wells's ambition is admirable and her talent undeniable, she never quite makes this difficult marriage work." On the other hand, Donna Seaman in *Booklist* (1 June 1996) described *Divine Secrets of the Ya-Ya Sisterhood* as a wacky, "wonderfully irreverent look at life" and the Ya-Yas as a "gang of

Dust jacket for Wells's 1996 novel, in which a theater director returns to Louisiana to reconcile with her alcoholic mother after reading a scrapbook about the mother's circle of lifelong friends (Richland County Public Library)

merry, smart, brave, poignant, and unforgettable goddesses." This goddess theme is expanded by Lori Rowlett, who argues in a 2001 essay that "Although religious themes and allusions appear frequently in the works of Southern writers, Rebecca Wells gives religion a fresh twist which is uniquely Louisianian." Other religious issues in the novel include the contrast between personal values and spirituality and the legalism of church rules. Wells attaches significance to religious imagery by beginning and ending *Divine Secrets of the Ya-Ya Sisterhood* with "The Holy Lady." To Sidda, the Holy Lady is the divine woman in the moon who watches over her earthly children and loves them without judgment. At the beginning of the novel, the Holy Lady allows Sidda to know "there has never been a time when she has not been loved," and at the end the Holy Lady looks upon her "imperfect children" and smiles, giving credence to Sidda's realization that being "good enough" does not require perfection and that sometimes she may

break the rules without losing everything. The idea of breaking society's rules, and the conflict between these rules and the Ya-Yas' personal values, is discussed by Patricia Gantt in her 2001 analysis.

Divine Secrets of the Ya-Ya Sisterhood and its predecessor have proven popular with reading groups and initially sparked the creation of many national Ya-Ya groups. The Ya-Ya clubs use the novel as a sort of club operating manual. Wells says in an interview with Rebecca Bain that "What I'm finding is that somehow the books seem to bring out girl groups. And I use the word girl lovingly. . . . Because when we tap into that girl part of us that usually got knocked out of us at about puberty, it's contacting a lot of power, a lot of humor, and a lot of solidarity." *Divine Secrets of the Ya-Ya Sisterhood* shows that the bonds between women can last a lifetime and withstand many obstacles, and in this transient world, this bond represents the type of closeness that many women desire.

The Internet has helped link these various clubs together with an official website endorsed by Harper-Collins <http://www.ya-ya.com/welcome.htm>. This website includes information about Wells, her books, and Ya-Ya groups around the country. Wells occasionally visits the site to post a letter directed to her "dahlins." At one point, a national Ya-Ya convention was in the planning stages. This widespread interest led Bette Midler's All-Girl Productions to purchase the movie rights to *Divine Secrets of the Ya-Ya Sisterhood,* and the movie (adapted by Mark Andrus, with screenplay by director Callie Khouri) was distributed by Warner Brothers in 2002 and starred Ellen Burstyn, Ashley Judd, and Sandra Bullock.

In the first long letter that she wrote on the Internet site, titled "Ya-Ya Notes from Cane Country," Wells discusses the creation around the country of Ya-Ya clubs by the women who identify with Vivi and her band of friends. Other Ya-Ya groups were formed by women who identify with Sidda's lack of close female bonds and seek the type of friendships that the Ya-Yas have. While Wells envies much of what Vivi and her friends had in terms of the seemingly carefree life, she also says that the culture they grew up in "did its damnedest to trim their spirits and curtail their dreams." In discussing the fact that men can be Ya-Yas, Wells also says, "Without a doubt, men and women express their intimacy in different ways, but we all ache for community; we all ache to not feel so alone." The theme of community and belonging is prevalent in both novels, which could account for the broad appeal the works have for both men and women.

Although readers note similarities between Wells's life and her novels, she denies writing autobiographical fiction. In an interview for *Contemporary Authors* Wells says, "I grew up in the fertile world of storytelling, filled with flamboyance, flirting, futility, and fear. My work, though, is a result of my imagination dancing a kind of psycho-spiritual tango with my own history, and the final harvest is fiction, not memoir." In another letter on the official Ya-Ya website Wells says, "I know y'all all understand that my books are fiction; not autobiography. And while I certainly use the locale, food, music, scents, and dialect SHAMELESSLY in my work, Alexandria isn't Thornton, and my family isn't the Walker clan."

Readers and reviewers alike have noticed other similarities between Wells and her protagonist, Sidda. Like Sidda, Wells generally writes in seclusion, jealously guarding her time. After an extended tour in support of her books, Wells admits in an August letter on the website that she longs for some uninterrupted time for "the simple hard sometimes delirious pleasure of writing," because "I'm not so good at writing on the road." Wells continues to write, and several articles published in 1998 and 1999 stated that she was working on a third novel that is based on her play *Splittin' Hairs*. According to these earlier reports, the Ya-Yas play a minor role in the new novel. *Splittin' Hairs* is set in Thornton, but the main character is a hairdresser who travels in different circles than the plantation-owning Walkers and their friends. Wells has been quoted as saying that her fourth novel will probably be a Ya-Ya book representing a return to the characters that made her so popular.

Wells spends a large portion of her writing time in the South, and in one of her on-line letters she reports that she is working in Louisiana on a new novel. She quips, "The South is a grand, glorious, rich, fertile, depraved, erotic place–I love it!" In her interview, Bain comments that Wells "is living proof that you can take a girl out of the South, but you can't take the South out of the girl." While Wells may have nostalgic feelings for the South, in both novels, Sidda has more mixed feelings. In *Little Altars Everywhere* Sidda says, "I don't go back to Louisiana very often. It makes me too sad. I get an emotional hangover for months afterward." In *Divine Secrets of the Ya-Ya Sisterhood* Sidda displays the same attitude and only returns to Louisiana at the end of the novel in an effort to heal her relationships with her mother, herself, and her fiancé.

Although Wells loves the South and has been compared to such notable Southern writers as Conroy, Ellen Gilchrist, Fannie Flagg, Mary McCarthy, and Anne Rivers Siddons, she does not like being labeled a Southern writer. Despite Wells's many attempts to reject the label, however, she realizes the hold that the South has on her. In the interview with Bain, Wells says, "While I've spent a good part of my life learning to drop that southern accent and to really become a voice that was not identified with the South, in fact my writing has always gone back to the South and now I find that I want to go back to the South."

Rebecca Wells may not have intended to write pure Southern novels, but her books, with their emphasis on community and family, have a definite Southern flavor. Her novels portray the distinctive brand of Southernness in Louisiana, using one family's story. Both novels end with acceptance and healing, and both involve Sidda going home to Louisiana and accepting her mother and her motherland for what they are.

Interview:

Rebecca Bain, "Women Everywhere Embrace the Ya-Ya Sisterhood of Rebecca Wells," *BookPage* (October 1997) <http://www.bookpage.com/9710bp/first person2.html>.

References:

"Divine Write," *People Weekly* (5 October 1998): 87;

Patricia Gantt, "'Against Regulations': Southern Women in the Fiction of Rebecca Wells," in *Songs of the New South: Writing Contemporary Louisiana,* edited by Suzanne Disheroon-Green and Lisa Abney (Westport, Conn.: Greenwood Press, 2001), pp. 163–171;

Shana McNally, "You'd Know If You're a Ya-Ya," *South Coast Massachusetts Standard-Time* (18 April 1999) <http://www.s-t.com/daily/04-99/04-18-99/ e07li181.htm>;

Lori Rowlett, "Lady of the Earth and Moon: Goddess Imagery and the Ya-Yas," in *Songs of the New South: Writing Contemporary Louisiana,* edited by Disheroon-Green and Abney (Westport, Conn.: Greenwood Press, 2001), pp. 115–122;

Mary Ann Wilson, "Living on the Edge in Rebecca Wells's *Little Altars Everywhere,*" in *Songs of the New South: Writing Contemporary Louisiana,* edited by Disheroon-Green and Abney (Westport, Conn.: Greenwood Press, 2001), pp. 3–9.

Michael Lee West

(15 October 1953 –   )

Lisa Abney
Northwestern State University

BOOKS: *Crazy Ladies* (Atlanta: Longstreet Press, 1990);
She Flew the Coop: A Novel Concerning Life, Death, Sex, and Recipes in Limoges, Louisiana (New York: HarperCollins, 1994);
American Pie (New York: HarperCollins, 1996);
Consuming Passions: A Food-Obsessed Life (New York: HarperCollins, 1999);
Mad Girls in Love (New York: HarperCollins, forthcoming 2004).

RECORDING: *Crazy Ladies,* abridged, read by West, New York, HarperAudio, 1999.

Beginning with her novel *Crazy Ladies* (1990), Michael Lee West has developed characters whose voices echo not only those of her family but also that of the South as a whole. Witty anecdotes drawn from the stories of her family members have become fodder for her fiction, and her retelling confirms their humor and power as folk narratives. West's work illustrates the growth of a third wave of writers from the South since the Southern Renaissance, and her novels demonstrate the abilities of these authors to depict universal themes and experiences in regional locales.

West's family was upper middle class, and she grew up during the period of post–World War II prosperity. She was born Michael Lee Helton in Lake Providence, Louisiana, on 15 October 1953. Her father, Ralph Helton, was a store manager who for many years worked for a chain of stores called Morgan and Lindsay. Later he bought a Ben Franklin store in Cookeville, Tennessee, and that is where Michael Lee was raised from around the age of eight. Her mother, Ary Jean, encouraged and supported Michael Lee's reading habit. The Heltons were fanatical readers who rarely bought books but instead frequented their local library. West's love of reading was fueled when she was confined to bed for an extended period after she was diagnosed with histoplasmosis, which her doctor believed she contracted while on a Girl Scout trip to Mammoth Cave. During her illness, she was given a

Michael Lee West (photograph © 1996 Bill Cramer; from the dust jacket for American Pie, *1996; Richland County Public Library)*

set of Louisa May Alcott's *Little Women* (1868–1869) and *Little Men* (1871), which became prized possessions. After she read these and many other children's books, West's selections included Margaret Mitchell's *Gone with the Wind* (1936), *Intern* by "Dr. X" (1965), and later, Jacqueline Susann's *Valley of the Dolls* (1966). As West grew older, her reading habit continued, and she was a serious student. In a 2002 personal interview she said of her high-school years, "I wasn't a cheerleader or anything like that. I worked in my father's dime store and had a tidy little babysitting 'career' on the side." West graduated from Cookeville High School in 1971 and shortly thereafter began her college coursework. She was married for a short time in the 1970s and gave birth to her oldest son, Trey.

In 1978 she married Willard Mahlon West, a medical doctor, with whom she has a son, Tyler. West completed her B.S. in nursing at East Tennessee State University in 1981 and worked as a nurse for several years. During the late 1970s and early 1980s, West began to read the works of Flannery O'Connor, William Faulkner, and Eudora Welty, and one day she read a short story in *Redbook* magazine by Lee Smith. West became intrigued with Smith's writing and quickly read all of her novels. In 1982 West met Smith at a writers' workshop in Nashville. West recalled: "She read my short story in class and made me believe that it was possible for a little nurse (and soccer mom) who had NOT read the classics to become a writer. And it happened!" Smith's confidence in West encouraged her, and by 1990, West had brought her first novel, *Crazy Ladies*, to publication. She described the process of writing *Crazy Ladies* in stolen moments:

> I wrote the novel in a tiny room while my youngest child built Lego cities around my feet. Late in the evening, while drifting off to sleep, characters would suddenly start spouting off bits of dialogue, or whole scenes would expand. Careful not to wake my sleeping husband, I would creep into the bathroom and sit on the tile floor, propped against the tub. I had no notion of universal appeal. I just wrote frantically, as if someone might snatch my pen at any second.

West continues to live in Tennessee with her husband, family, and a vast array of dogs and cats; she balances her family's needs and a rigorous writing schedule.

West's works mirror the traditions, lives, and cultures of a diverse group of Southern residents. Set in Louisiana and Tennessee, her novels accurately portray the social stratification of the region through characters who hail from a variety of classes and from both African American and Anglo races. Her works generally include themes of social class, love, forgiveness, hypocrisy, alienation, the quest for one's place in the world, the roles of women in society, the importance of community, and traditional ways in contrast to contemporary ways, particularly in terms of food.

West's debut novel, *Crazy Ladies,* chronicles the Hamilton family through three generations. West credits the inception of *Crazy Ladies* to a dream that she had one night:

> I was standing in my grandmother's kitchen, watching her make biscuits, and a gruff-looking man pushed through the screen door. My granny picked up her

Dust jacket for West's 1990 debut novel, which chronicles the lives of three generations of a Southern family—based on the author's own—in which the women are stronger and more resilient than the men (Richland County Public Library)

shotgun, took aim, and pulled the trigger. Together (in the dream, of course!) we buried him in the backyard, beneath the honeysuckle vines. I woke up with my heart racing, and it took a few minutes to realize it was just a dream. But I kept thinking how awful it would be to have a secret—literally buried in the backyard. And how terrifying to know that it could be discovered, that you would spend the rest of your days guarding it from the world. I immediately reached for my legal pad and wrote 30 pages. This became the opening chapter to *Crazy Ladies*.

Crazy Ladies provides a realistic portrayal of small-town life in the South from the 1930s to 1980s. Characters who face difficult challenges from the Depression, World War II, and the Vietnam War provide depth and realism to West's fiction. In this novel, which is bleak at times, West establishes a theme that appears in many of her works: the importance of a closely knit female community. The males in this novel do not appear to be able to withstand the tough times that the

Dust jacket for West's novel in which three Southern sisters seek comfort from their grandmother after one is injured in an automobile accident (Richland County Public Library)

trademark—hypocrisy, familial love, and class relations—emerge strongly in this initial novel.

Critical response to the book was positive. A reviewer from *Publishers Weekly* (13 July 1990) stated: "The characters in West's promising first novel are richly eccentric and they exist in a colorfully evoked setting." Ellen Pall of *The Washington Post* (7 October 1990) called the work "a wonderful first novel" and continued, "In fact, I can't think of enough nice things to say about *Crazy Ladies*. The voices are sharp, wry, and utterly convincing." Carolyn See, in a review for *The Los Angeles Times* (24 September 1990), called the book "a splendid new take on the South."

West's follow-up novel, *She Flew the Coop: A Novel Concerning Life, Death, Sex, and Recipes in Limoges, Louisiana,* appeared in 1994. This novel depicts the suburban world of 1950s-era Limoges, loosely modeled on West's birthplace, Lake Providence. The novel opens with Vangie Nepper, an upper-middle-class, overweight housewife, discovering that her pregnant teenage daughter, Olive, has attempted to kill herself by drinking rose poison in a soft drink. Vangie's husband, Henry, a pharmacist, has been carrying on an affair with trashy store clerk DeeDee Robichaux, who is married to a paraplegic. Vangie endures the death of Olive (who succumbs to the poison after lingering several days), the disintegration of her marriage, the death of her estranged husband, and the emergence of her self-reliance. Along the way, she is assisted by her housekeeper, Sophie—whose husband, Burr, causes as much trouble for Sophie as Henry does for Vangie—and by her Yankee sister-in-law, widow Edith, who begins a relationship with funeral-home owner Cab Beaulieu. The novel includes other interesting minor characters such as Cordy King and DeeDee's Aunt Butter. The tale, like that of *Crazy Ladies,* focuses upon the reliance of women upon each other as they share triumphs and tragedies. An additional bonus in the novel comes in the form of interspersed recipes that correlate with the story line.

Critics gave *She Flew the Coop* positive reviews. Fran Handman, in *The New York Times* (10 July 1994), called the novel "a funny, irreverent story." Dick Roraback, in a *Los Angeles Times* review (16 October 1994), asserted: "Only a book conceived and executed as well as this one can carry the rhythms and pauses, the smells and tastes and languor and the very continuity of a Southern town and its people, at once flawed and gracious. Well worth a detour." Joan Mooney, in a *Washington Post* review (3 July 1994), wrote:

> The women are the most interesting characters, but West is good at getting into the minds of the men, too. Her shifting point of view makes it impossible to find

family endures: Charles Hamilton, his grandson Mack, and his son-in-law, Hart Jones, die or become walking wounded. Mack and Charles emotionally (and to some extent physically) remove themselves from their families. The female characters, however, survive intact and learn to rely upon one another, though they are not without their own problems. Dorothy maintains her belief that she is unloved by her mother, while her sister, Clancy Jane, who is lovable but also emotionally fragile, struggles to survive. Clancy Jane's daughter, Violet, and Dorothy's daughter, Bitsy, form an uneasy alliance, but they grow closer as the novel progresses. The women need one another, yet their allegiances are changeable, and as in reality, their relationships are often complex and difficult—filled with both love and jealousy. The themes that have come to be West's

clear villains (with a couple of exceptions, like the preacher) and adds a complexity that is generally missing from small town gossip.

In general, the novel was praised for its intricate plot and nonstereotypical Southern characters.

After the success of her first two books, West continued to write, and in 1996 she produced *American Pie*. This novel again features a collection of strong women and the bonds between them. In this work, three sisters—Fredrika (Freddie), Eleanor, and Jo-Nell McBroom—converge upon their grandmother Minerva when all three end up needing a stabilizing force in their lives following Jo-Nell's injury in a car accident. Eleanor, almost an agoraphobic, maintains a scrapbook of grisly tragedies, while Freddie wrestles with the difficult choice of leaving her biologist husband. Jo-Nell, the rowdy youngest sister, possesses a less-than-sterling moral reputation. The sisters fight physical injury, emotional difficulties, and mental illness as they rally around Jo-Nell after her near-fatal crash. The reunion brings the four women together physically, but many wounds exist for all of them, and the accident provides them the opportunity to make amends, heal, and unknowingly prepare for Minerva's death at the end of the novel. The sisters undergo several epiphanies about their lives, and their ultimate realization is that they need one another in order to survive and to gain a sense of self.

As with West's other novels, critics expressed positive opinions about *American Pie*. Joanne Wilkinson, a *Booklist* reviewer (August 1996), stated: "West's brash, funny novel is immensely appealing, and it is both a paean to and a send-up of family bonds." A reviewer from *Publishers Weekly* (1 July 1996) wrote: "Freddie, Eleanor and Jo-Nell McBroom may be the most satisfying trio of offcenter Southern sisters since [Beth Henley's] *Crimes of the Heart*." Bettye Dew, in a review for the *St. Louis Post-Dispatch* (27 October 1996), asserted that "West, herself, is a master of control. She stirs up a commotion, then manages it deftly, with a comic touch that owes a debt to Eudora Welty." While most reviewers praised West's creative plot and characters, a critic for *Kirkus Reviews* (15 July 1996) said that "Southern

gothic and soap-opera hype collide exuberantly in West's vivid if hokey third novel."

In her next publication, *Consuming Passions: A Food-Obsessed Life* (1999), West expanded her writing style and gathered a collection of recipes around which she wrote chapter-length essays. Filled with the humor exemplified by her novels, this book pleases both cooks and general readers. The chapters focus on family stories, reminiscences, and traditions relating to food in the South; "Funeral Food," for example, documents the Southern commitment to burial traditions and the cultural practices incorporated into funeral wakes and visitations.

Consuming Passions met with few reviews, but those that did appear praised its innovation and humor. A *Publishers Weekly* (15 March 1999) reviewer described it as "not a cookbook in the strictest sense, but the humorous narrative is laced with recipes." The reviewer continued, "West manages to portray Southern charm without falling back on stereotypes, and meanwhile stylishly explaining the mystical, eternal link between family and food." Macia Langhenry of the *Atlanta Journal-Constitution* (15 July 1999) said of *Consuming Passions*: "Categorizing this book is not nearly as easy as reading it. Nonfiction, it is memoir with embellishments."

West's next novel, *Mad Girls in Love* (forthcoming 2004), is a sequel to *Crazy Ladies*. Michael Lee West's work, while regional in its settings, continues to transcend the South in the development of themes and characterizations.

References:

Lisa Abney, "Food and Foodways in Michael Lee West's *She Flew the Coop: A Novel Concerning Life, Death, Sex, and Recipes in Limoges, Louisiana*," in *Songs of the New South: Writing Contemporary Louisiana*, edited by Suzanne Disheroon-Green and Abney (Westport, Conn.: Greenwood Press, 2001), pp. 11–18;

"Michael Lee West '81: 2000 Outstanding Alumna," *ETSU Alumni* <http://www.etsu.edu/alumni/00Award_West.htm>.

James Wilcox
(4 April 1949 –   )

Anne K. Jones

and

Lisa Abney
Northwestern State University

BOOKS: *Modern Baptists* (Garden City, N.Y.: Dial, 1983; London: Secker & Warburg, 1984);

North Gladiola (New York: Harper & Row, 1985; London: Alison, 1985);

Miss Undine's Living Room (New York: Harper & Row, 1987; London: Secker & Warburg, 1987);

Sort of Rich (New York: Harper & Row, 1989; London: Secker & Warburg, 1990);

Polite Sex (New York: HarperCollins, 1991; London: Fourth Estate, 1996);

Guest of a Sinner (New York: HarperCollins, 1993);

Plain and Normal (Boston: Little, Brown, 1998; London: Fourth Estate, 1998);

Heavenly Days (New York: Viking, 2003).

James Wilcox has published eight novels, most of which focus upon life in the South–particularly life in Louisiana. Wilcox depicts the confusions, displacements, and juxtapositions of the absurd found in the everyday, which serve as major elements of his writing. Wilcox's ordinary characters are often comic and inept but also poignant, because Wilcox possesses a certain amount of affection for them. His ability to create characters that are well developed and realistic has been the aspect of his writing most frequently acclaimed. His work most often presents themes such as alienation, community, and the quest for self.

James Peter Wilcox was born on 4 April 1949 and was raised in Hammond, Louisiana, but he spent many years living in New York City. His father, James Henry Wilcox, emigrated from England as a child, and he met and married Wilcox's mother, Marie Wiza, in Milwaukee. Wilcox's father was a Methodist, and his mother was a Polish Roman Catholic, which is the faith in which the children were raised. This religious upbringing has imbued Wilcox's work with a strongly spiritual character. Wilcox's Catholicism also caused

James Wilcox (photograph by Thomas Cooper; from the dust jacket for Sort of Rich, *1989; Richland County Public Library)*

him a certain amount of anxiety as a child about the state of his father's salvation. Wilcox is the third child of five and the first son; he has three sisters and a younger brother.

Music brought Wilcox's parents to the South and to Louisiana. His father and mother met while both worked in a Milwaukee orchestra, where she played oboe and he played French horn. Later, his father became a music professor at Southeastern Louisiana

College (now Southeastern Louisiana University). Wilcox was trained in piano and cello and remembers his childhood as being filled with music. He also experienced many special opportunities, such as working for a music festival in Vermont and sitting in on a master class with Pablo Casals. Wilcox's father hoped that Wilcox would also be a musician, but his younger brother, a violinist who teaches at Youngstown University, became one instead. Wilcox drifted away from music when he went to Yale University to study creative writing under Robert Penn Warren. Wilcox's musical background, however, has not gone untapped, for the theoretical ideas behind music and ideas about musical form appear in his literary work. Wilcox uses recurring themes and motifs as a composer would in constructing a symphony. This manner of writing can be seen particularly in his first novel, *Modern Baptists* (1983), in which he layers many themes and plots over one another and ties them together at the end of the novel.

Wilcox completed his B.A. at Yale in 1971, and during the 1970s he worked in New York City as an editor at Random House and later at Doubleday. His salary was meager, but he gained a wealth of experience; he worked on James A. Michener's best-selling *Centennial* (1974) and early works of Cormac McCarthy. By 1978 he felt the time was right to make a career change. Encouraged to write by fellow editors Toni Morrison and Jacqueline Kennedy Onassis, Wilcox began what later became *Modern Baptists*. Once he wrote this first novel, he quit the publishing business and became a full-time writer. His income, however, remained barely enough to support himself. A profile of Wilcox by James B. Stewart in *The New Yorker* (1994) presented the author as a struggling artist living in near poverty and volunteering at a soup kitchen. Times, however, have improved for Wilcox, who currently serves as the director of creative writing at Louisiana State University. His stories have appeared in *The New Yorker, Avenue,* and *Louisiana Literature*. Wilcox was awarded a Guggenheim Fellowship, and his novel *Plain and Normal* (1998) was listed a "Notable Book of 1998" by *The New York Times Book Review*.

Several of Wilcox's early novels depict life in the small, fictional Louisiana town of Tula Springs. The main character of *Modern Baptists,* Carl Bobby Pickens, is a middle-aged, overweight assistant manager of the Sonny Boy Bargain Store. The novel opens with Pickens preparing for the return of his ungrateful half brother, Francis Xavier (F.X.), from prison. Additionally, he is worried because he thinks he has melanoma—information that he is reluctant, at first, to share with F.X. During the course of the novel, Pickens loses his job at the Sonny Boy Bargain Store, has an unfulfilling

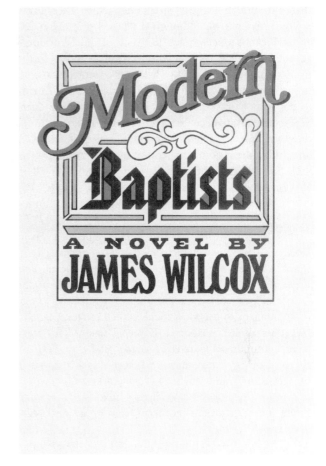

Dust jacket for Wilcox's first book (1983), a comic novel set in the fictional town of Tula Springs, Louisiana, in which the overweight, middle-aged protagonist fails at work and at love while his half brother, a former convict, enters into an affair with a feminist lawyer (Richland County Public Library)

sexual encounter with his coworker Burma, and develops an obsessive crush on the trashy (but in his eyes, glamorous) Toinette Quaid. Toward the end of the book, Burma's boyfriend Emmet and Pickens have an altercation that results in Pickens's getting a black eye from Miss Mina, the owner of the local gas station where the fight occurs. Meanwhile, Pickens has failed at a job at Donna Lee Keely's law office; Keely is a liberal and liberated woman who maintains the notion that she can change the backward ways of Tula Springs. She has an affair with F.X. and tries to help him rejoin society after his incarceration. The novel concludes with F.X. reaching out to his brother and inviting him to join in the Christmas Eve celebrations at the Keely family home.

Throughout the novel, Pickens is full of good intentions and has an essentially moral character, but he is equally inept and makes a series of bad decisions that put him in difficult situations, which then grow beyond his control. Although the novel primarily concerns Pickens's search for both social and emotional acceptability, Wilcox shifts the focus of the novel to the minor characters through Pickens's interactions with them, from his awkward sexual encounters with Burma to his poor work ethic at Donna Lee Keely's law firm. These characters become selectively more significant as they struggle to assert their emotional independence and fulfill their desire for community in rural Louisiana. Such minor characters are at the heart of all of Wilcox's novels and create his hallmark comedy.

Modern Baptists has been acclaimed for its humor and realistic characters. Ann Fisher, writing for *Library Journal* (1 June 1983), asserted that "The story rolls along well and vividly depicts life in Tula Springs, Louisiana." Noted writer Anne Tyler, in *The New York Times Book Review* (31 July 1983), commented on the "sense of particularity—a granting of a full measure of individualism to the most incidental character, place or fact—that makes 'Modern Baptists' seem startlingly alive, exuberantly overcrowded." *Modern Baptists* received praise from critics, and there was a resurgence of interest in it and Wilcox's other works after the *New Yorker* profile appeared. Wilcox's next Tula Springs novel shared a similar reception from critics and readers alike.

North Gladiola (1985) is Wilcox's first novel with a female protagonist. This novel also draws on Wilcox's knowledge of music and stringed instruments, because the protagonist, Ethyl Mae Coco, is an aspiring performer who has organized the Tula Springs Pro Arts Quartet. The quartet is rife with resentment and has a way of growing and shrinking that is similar to Ethyl Mae's own family situation. She is the mother of six, but has only one child who remains in town; the rest have tried to get as far from their mother as possible. Ethyl Mae's life reaches a crisis when she discovers that fifty-year-old Korean graduate student Duk Soo, who is the cellist for the quartet, has fallen in love with her; concurrently, Ethyl Mae is suspected of killing her neighbor's Chihuahua. Unlike *Modern Baptists,* this novel deals not only with moral issues but with spiritual issues as well. Ethyl Mae finally finds help for her crises through her confession to a Samoan Catholic priest. Again, Wilcox creates a set of minor characters who serve to reinforce the themes and the difficulties in the lives of his protagonists.

Writing for the *National Review* (23 August 1985) about *North Gladiola,* J. O. Tate noted: "Wilcox's fiction rests on a technique of surreal transcription, on effects of historical montage and acoustical collage. The author's voice, collapsing one thing with another in the accordionlike squeeze of consumer culture, imposes a style, asserts a vision." The interesting characters drew praise from Lisa Zeidner of *The New York Times Book Review* (30 June 1985); she observed, "The half-snide, half-sincere delight the reader feels in meeting these characters again bodes well for the town as material for sequels." Michael Esposito wrote in *Library Journal* (1 April 1985): "There is plenty here to satisfy both casual and thoughtful readers."

In Wilcox's third Tula Springs novel, *Miss Undine's Living Room* (1987), middle-aged Olive Mackie is a consummate social climber and wanna-be, but she lacks the tools to succeed. Her efforts to attain status in her community are continually thwarted by an endless cycle of emotional and financial strains, which she views as beyond her control: the underemployment of her husband; the high-priced tuition for her only child, Felix; and the responsibility of caring for her elderly uncle L.D. The primary crisis of the novel becomes the resolution of the mystery surrounding the death of her uncle's attendant, Mr. Versey. During the course of the story, a series of love affairs spark and ebb as the characters stumble through their lives.

Upon its publication, reviewers lauded the creativity of the novel and its characters. Michiko Kakutani wrote in *The New York Times Book Review* (12 August 1987): "*Miss Undine's Living Room* is not without its pleasures: Mr. Wilcox has lost neither his gift for slapstick nor his instinct for finding and describing the incongruities of modern life." Sybil Steinberg, in a *Publishers Weekly* review (26 June 1987), called the characters "a motley collection of southern folk stumbling through the vicissitudes of life who manage to survive and even taste a bit of grace." Walter Kendrick, writing for the *Village Voice* (25 August 1987), praised the book: "Each time out, Wilcox gets better—subtler, more complex, closer to the fusion of the pathos and joy that makes for the highest comedy."

Wilcox's next novel, *Sort of Rich* (1989), also garnered high praise for characterization and plot. *Sort of Rich* provides a pivotal link between the Tula Springs novels and the subsequent ones set in New York City. Gretchen Peabody Aiken-Lewes is a former resident of New York and came to Tula Springs when she married Southern businessman Frank Dambar. The small-town values of Tula Springs and the eccentric characters who surround her husband come into constant conflict with Gretchen's New York ways. Frank's sudden death leaves Gretchen stranded within a community from which she feels alienated. Wilcox is particularly concerned with exploring Gretchen's Northern and outsider perspective on Tula Springs, and his New York novels typically include a character with a Southern perspective. He considers the impact of cultural homogenization on both the Northern and Southern perspectives and uses his characters to comment on this phenomenon. Wilcox, however, illustrates the differences between North and South despite the homogenization of cultures. In this work Wilcox also explores the idea that psychological and spiritual conflicts are closely related.

Sort of Rich has drawn the most critical attention of all of Wilcox's works, and these reviews have primarily been positive. A *Time* (19 June 1989) review called the novel "an exceedingly well-crafted tale of blind spots and self-delusions, alternately hilarious and sobering, in which dogs are seen as cats, friends as foes, strangers as lovers." Chilton Williamson Jr.'s lengthy article in the *National Review* (2 June 1989) praised Wilcox: "there is as well a spiritual quality to everything I have read by this writer: a thing that is rarely discernible in contemporary fiction and that, deftly infused by Wilcox's light touch, amounts merely (!) to a quiet insistence upon the moral nature of man." Fellow Southern writer Jill McCorkle noted in *The New York Times Book Review* (28 May 1989): "Mr. Wilcox employs the zany eye for comic detail that has become a trademark of his fiction and makes his characters wholly original."

Sort of Rich serves as a bridge to Wilcox's next three books, which are all set in New York. *Polite Sex* (1991) sports a far younger female protagonist, Emily Brix, than Wilcox's other novels have, and it also covers a much larger time frame and features Wilcox's most experimental and postmodern narrative style. The novel focuses upon Emily and her friend Clara Tilman, who at one time was the girlfriend of F.X. from *Modern Baptists*. Both girls hail from Tula Springs originally, but they have moved to New York in the hopes of landing acting careers. *Polite Sex* tracks their lives from the 1970s through the late 1990s, alternating between the perspectives of Clara and Emily and moving ahead and back in time. Emily is an intelligent and talented actor and writer, while Clara is beautiful but not particularly bright. Clara gains both career and personal success, while Emily deals with one crisis after another, including the loss of her husband to the priesthood and a child given up for adoption. This novel does not focus on the origins of Wilcox's characters but uses their origins as a way to help create their sense of disenfranchisement. Wilcox also explores the "necessity of struggling to accept the lot life deals," as Hugh Ruppersburg terms it in his 1997 article about Wilcox.

Polite Sex drew mixed reviews from critics. Elinor Lipman, writing for *The New York Times Book Review* (14 July 1991), lauded *Polite Sex* as "engaging . . . Emily's perfect seriousness invites the irreverent nudge of his [Wilcox's] elbow, the nip of his sly social satire, and earns *Polite Sex* our complicitous smiles." Jonathan Probber, in a *Washington Post* review (17 June 1991),

Dust jacket for Wilcox's 1985 novel, about a Tula Springs musician whose problems with her string quartet, her family, and her neighbor are resolved with the help of a Samoan Catholic priest (Richland County Public Library)

asserted: "Those in search of a novel with both teeth and charm would do well to get *Polite Sex,* the latest of James Wilcox's studies of the people of imaginary Tula Springs." He praised Wilcox's creation of voices and realistic characters. Steinberg, however, in *Publishers Weekly* (26 April 1991) faulted the novel for its "jolting last-minute revelation" that "comes too late; in its proper place in the narrative it might have given this tale the poignancy and credibility it never quite achieves."

Wilcox's next book, *Guest of a Sinner* (1993), is his only novel not to have at least one character from Tula Springs, but Wilcox maintains a tentative connection to the South through the protagonist's father, who lives in Tallahassee, Florida. Southern origins, however, do not play a central role in the book. Middle-aged protagonist Eric Thorsen is a modestly talented pianist who makes his living by giving lessons to underprivileged children.

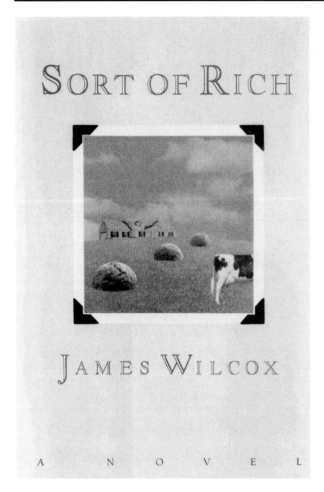

Dust jacket for Wilcox's 1989 novel, about a New York City woman who suffers culture shock when she moves to Tula Springs (Richland County Public Library)

He earns additional money by playing gigs as an accompanist. Eric tries to maintain some distance from human interaction, but he finds himself constantly thrust into situations that force him to interact, mostly because of his good looks. Wanda Skopinski is a love-struck secretary who has a crush on Eric. They meet in church and then embark upon a series of adventures involving the pursuit of a rent-controlled apartment. Eric, through many humorous and interesting plot twists, learns to adjust to his life and accept the things he cannot change. He even finds a meaningful relationship. This novel, more than Wilcox's other works, ends on an optimistic note.

Guest of a Sinner has been praised for its intricate plot, interesting characters, and well-timed humor. A critic for *Kirkus Reviews* (1 February 1993) expressed relief that "after the surprisingly inert *Polite Sex*," Wilcox has produced "a convivial romp through contemporary Manhattan—a comedy of errors with all sorts of

sexual quandaries, not a few downright crazy characters, and a spiritual dimension to top it all off." An anonymous *Time* reviewer (26 April 1993) called the novel "a funny, rambling chronicle of half a dozen people in New York City whom any sociologist would label misfits." A reviewer for *Publishers Weekly* (22 February 1993) called *Guest of a Sinner* "an endearing tale of ordinary, bumbling New Yorkers as they deal with the fascinations and annoyances of both the big city and their loved ones."

In Wilcox's next novel, *Plain and Normal,* middle-aged Severinus Lloyd Norris faces his long-repressed homosexuality, revealed by his former wife when she wanted a divorce in order to marry another man. Lloyd and his former wife are both originally from Tula Springs and live in the suburban area of Yonkers, New York. Lloyd, who is the most plain and normal character in the book, must deal with the reactions of coworkers and potential boyfriends as well as his spastic colon. Once again, the author creates minor characters similar to those found in *Modern Baptists* who serve to advance the plot and to create complex sidebar narratives, but he also explores new territory, adding elaborate plot twists and subduing the farcical qualities found in his earlier works. According to Wilcox, *Plain and Normal* was one of his hardest novels to write; it took him nearly five years to finish it.

Critics gave *Plain and Normal* mixed reviews. Peter Szatmary stated in the *Houston Chronicle* (24 November 1998) that *Plain and Normal* is "a gentle inversion of stereotypes" amounting to "a minor comedy of gay manners that doesn't ACT UP, much less act out." Szatmary accused Wilcox of falling in love with his characters but conceded that in the end it is a book that has "bittersweet fun with people's misreading of each other and desire for love and friendship." Robert Plunket in *The Advocate* (29 September 1998) noted that Lloyd's situation as a newly outed gay man stumbling toward romance is "portrayed in such a rueful and hilarious way that *Plain and Normal* instantly becomes a classic on the subject." A *Publishers Weekly* review (6 July 1998) stated: "While Wilcox's humor is affectionate, the cast of supporting characters are almost uniformly self-centered, obtuse, manipulative and devious. . . . In the end, this novel is a comedy of errors that tickles the funnybone but fails to tug at the heartstrings in the way that Wilcox's fans have come to expect."

Wilcox's eighth novel, *Heavenly Days* (2003), returns readers to Tula Springs with a new set of protagonists. Lou, short for Dr. Louise Jones, is a former college professor who has made a substantial career change. She works as a receptionist at WaistWatch, a Christian weight-loss and makeover center. Her husband, Don, an executive who for many years has maintained an opulent and expensive lifestyle, recently lost his job and has decided to move to his parents' house, which is empty since they have moved to Arizona. During the course of the novel, however, Lou comes to realize that her worldview is vastly askew and that her husband is an obsessive-compulsive lowlife. Lou undergoes an array of epiphanies, all of which provide humor and pathos. Lou, Don, and Grady (Lou's best friend) lead readers through several plot twists as Wilcox addresses the issues of religion, politics, race, and the suburbanization of rural Louisiana. Tula Springs becomes the setting for religious zealots, political fanatics, and a wide array of various kinds of agitators.

Critics praised this return to Wilcox's strengths. Mary McCay, for the New Orleans *Times-Picayune* (21 September 2003), asserted: "Wilcox has a sympathetic understanding of the foibles of his characters, but he does not let them wallow in self pity. His sense of the absurd tempers his moral message and creates a world of characters who are both funny and still desperately human." She added, "*Heavenly Days* realizes all of Wilcox's earlier promise." Janet Maslin wrote in *The New York Times* (11 September 2003): "The amount of quirkiness that piles up in *Heavenly Days* would ordinarily be smothering. But Wilcox manages a peculiar balancing act, offsetting a nerve-jangling array of cute gambits with such outlandish flourishes that a reader would follow him anywhere." Another reviewer in *The New York Times* (5 October 2003) called Wilcox's work "A delicious novel, balanced between hilarity and pathos." The novel also was listed as a "Notable Book of 2003" by *The New York Times Book Review*.

From *Modern Baptists* to *Heavenly Days,* James Wilcox has become identifiable as a comedic writer with a great deal of compassion for his hapless characters. His protagonists, who are sometimes flawed in their moral character, struggle to lead decent lives. A deep sense of spirituality exists in his works, but salvation comes not from God but from the necessary interconnectedness of humanity.

Interview:

John Lowe, "An Interview with James Wilcox," *Mississippi Quarterly,* 52, no. 4 (1999): 617–653.

References:

Hugh Ruppersburg, "James Wilcox: The Normality of Madness," in *Southern Writers at Century's End,* edited by Jeffrey J. Folks and James A. Perkins (Lexington: University Press of Kentucky, 1997), pp. 32–43;

James B. Stewart, "Moby Dick in Manhattan," *New Yorker,* 70, no. 4 (1994): 46–61.

Books for Further Reading

Amiran, Eyal, and John Unsworth. *Essays in Postmodern Culture*. New York: Oxford University Press, 1994.

Baldick, Chris. *Criticism and Literary Theory: 1890 to the Present*. New York: Longman, 1996.

Beardslee, Karen E. *Literary Legacies, Folklore Foundations: Selfhood and Cultural Tradition in Nineteenth and Twentieth-Century American Literature*. Knoxville: University of Tennessee Press, 2001.

Bernstein, Cynthia Goldin. *The Text and Beyond: Essays in Literary Linguistics*. Tuscaloosa: University of Alabama Press, 1994.

Berry, J. Bill, ed. *Home Ground: Southern Autobiography*. Columbia: University of Missouri Press, 1991.

Berry, ed. *Located Lives: Place and Idea in Southern Autobiography*. Athens: University of Georgia Press, 1990.

Billington, Monroe Lee, and Roger D. Hardaway. *African Americans on the Western Frontier*. Niwot, Colo.: University Press of Colorado, 1998.

Birkerts, Sven. *The Gutenberg Elegies*. New York: Fawcett Columbia, 1994.

Bonner, Thomas, Jr., and Robert E. Skinner. *Above Ground: Stories about Life and Death by New Southern Writers*. New Orleans: Xavier Review Press, 1993.

Butler, Judith. *Gender Trouble: Feminism and the Subversion of Identity*. New York: Routledge, 1990.

Calinescu, Mark. *Five Faces of Modernity: Modernism, Avant-Garde, Decadence, Kitsch, Postmodernism*. Durham, N.C.: Duke University Press, 1990.

Chafe, Wallace. *Discourse, Consciousness, and Time*. Chicago: University of Chicago Press, 1994.

Cobb, James C. *Redefining Southern Culture: Mind and Identity in the Modern South*. Athens: University of Georgia Press, 1999.

Cohen, Josh. *Spectacular Allegories: Postmodern American Writing and the Politics of Seeing*. Sterling, Va.: Pluto Press, 1998.

Dynes, Wayne R., and Stephan Donaldson. *Homosexual Themes in Literary Studies*. New York: Garland, 1992.

Eagleton, Terry. *The Illusions of Postmodernism*. Oxford: Blackwell, 1996.

Edson, Linda. *Reading Relationally: Postmodern Perspectives on Literature and Art*. Ann Arbor: University of Michigan Press, 2001.

Flora, Joseph M., and Robert Bain, eds. *Contemporary Fiction Writers of the South: A Bio-Bibliographical Sourcebook*. Westport, Conn.: Greenwood Press, 1993.

Folks, Jeffrey J. *From Richard Wright to Toni Morrison: Ethics in Modern and Postmodern American Narrative*. New York: Peter Lang, 2001.

Foster, Hal, ed. *The Anti-Aesthetic: Essays on Postmodern Culture*. New York: New Press, 2002.

Gallagher, Susan VanZanten, ed. *Postcolonial Literature and the Biblical Call for Justice*. Jackson: University Press of Mississippi, 1994.

Geyh, Paula, ed. *Postmodern American Fiction: A Norton Anthology*. New York: Norton, 1997.

Green, Suzanne Disheroon, and Lisa Abney, eds. *Songs of the New South: Writing Contemporary Louisiana*. Westport, Conn.: Greenwood Press, 2001.

Green and Abney, eds. *Songs of the Reconstructing South: Building Literary Louisiana, 1865–1945*. Westport, Conn.: Greenwood Press, 2002.

Guinn, Matthew. *After Southern Modernism: Fiction of the Contemporary South*. Jackson: University Press of Mississippi, 2000.

Harper, Phillip Brian. *Framing the Margins: The Social Logic of Postmodern Culture*. New York: Oxford University Press, 1994.

Hatch, Mary Jo. *Organization Theory: Modern, Symbolic, and Postmodern Perspectives*. Oxford: Oxford University Press, 1997.

Hedges, Elaine, and Shelley Fisher Fishkin. *Listening to Silences: New Essays in Feminist Criticism*. New York: Oxford University Press, 1994.

Herr, Cheryl Temple. *Critical Regionalism and Cultural Studies: From Ireland to the Midwest*. Gainesville: University of Florida Press, 1996.

Hobson, Fred. *The Southern Writer in the Postmodern World*. Athens: University of Georgia Press, 1991.

Holman, David M. *A Certain Slant of Light: Regionalism and the Form of Southern and Midwestern Fiction*. Baton Rouge: Louisiana State University Press, 1995.

Hooks, Bell. *Yearning: Race, Gender, and Cultural Politics*. Boston: South End Press, 1990.

Jagger, Alison, and Susan R. Bordo. *Gender/Body/Knowledge: Feminist Reconstructions of Being and Knowing*. New Brunswick: Rutgers University Press, 1990.

Johnstone, Barbara. *Stories, Community, and Place: Narratives from Middle America*. Bloomington: Indiana University Press, 1990.

Jordan, Shirley M. *Broken Silences: Interviews with Black and White Women Writers*. New Brunswick: Rutgers University Press, 1993.

Jurca, Catherine. *White Diaspora: The Suburb and the Twentieth-Century American Novel*. Princeton: Princeton University Press, 2001.

Kaplan, Caren. *Questions of Travel: Postmodern Discourses of Displacement*. Durham, N.C.: Duke University Press, 1996.

Kearney, Richard, and Alan Sanders. *The Wake of Imagination: Toward a Postmodern Culture*. London: Routledge, 1998.

Kershner, R. B. *The Twentieth Century Novel: An Introduction.* Boston: Bedford Books / Basingstoke, U.K.: Macmillan, 1997.

Koppelman, Susan. *Women in the Trees: U.S. Women's Short Stories About Battering and Resistance, 1839–1994.* Boston: Beacon, 1996.

Kuehl, John. *Alternate Worlds: A Study of Postmodern Antirealistic American Fiction.* New York: New York University Press, 1991.

Landow, George P. *Hypertext: The Convergence of Contemporary Critical Theory and Technology.* Baltimore: Johns Hopkins University Press, 1992.

Landow, ed. *Hypertext Theory.* Baltimore: Johns Hopkins University Press, 1994.

Lanser, Susan Sniader. *Fictions of Authority: Women Writers and Narrative Voice.* Ithaca, N.Y.: Cornell University Press, 1992.

Ledbetter, Mark. *Victims and the Postmodern Narrative, or, Doing Violence to the Body: An Ethic of Reading and Writing.* Basingstoke, U.K.: Macmillan / New York: St. Martin's Press, 1996.

McCaffery, Larry, ed. *Postmodern Fiction: A Bio-Bibliographical Guide.* Westport, Conn.: Greenwood Press, 1998.

McCaffery, ed. *Storming the Reality Studio: A Casebook of Cyberpunk and Postmodern Science Fiction.* Durham, N.C.: Duke University Press, 1992.

McCracken, Ellen. *New Latina Narrative: The Feminine Space of Postmodern Ethnicity.* Tucson: University of Arizona Press, 1999.

Moraru, Christian. *Rewriting: Postmodern Narrative and Culture Critique in the Age of Cloning.* New York: State University of New York Press, 2001.

Parker, Peter. *A Reader's Guide to the Twentieth-Century Novel.* New York: Oxford University Press, 1995.

Punter, David. *Writing in the 21st Century: An Introduction to Postmodern Literature.* Oxford: Blackwell, 2002.

Ruland, Richard, and Malcolm Bradbury. *From Puritanism to Postmodernism: A History of American Literature.* New York: Penguin, 1991.

Schor, Naomi, and Elizabeth Weed. *The Essential Difference.* Bloomington: Indiana University Press, 1994.

Schwartz, Felice. *Breaking with Tradition: Women and Work: The New Facts of Life.* New York: Warner, 1992.

Sedgwick, Eve Kosofsky. *The Epistemology of the Closet.* Berkeley: University of California Press, 1990.

Sedgwick. *Tendencies.* Durham, N.C.: Duke University Press, 1993.

Shiloh, Ilana. *Paul Auster and Postmodern Quest: On the Road to Nowhere.* New York: Peter Lang, 2002.

Showalter, Elaine. *Hystories: Hysterical Epidemics and Modern Media.* New York: Columbia University Press, 1997.

Showalter. *Sexual Anarchy: Gender and Culture at the Fin de Siècle.* New York: Penguin, 1990.

Simpson, David. *The Academic Postmodern and the Rule of Literature: A Report on Half-Knowledge.* Chicago: University of Chicago Press, 1995.

Slethaug, Gordon E. *The Play of the Double in Postmodern American Fiction.* Carbondale: Southern Illinois University Press, 1993.

Smarr, Janet Levarie. *Historical Criticism and the Challenge of Theory.* Chicago: University of Illinois Press, 1993.

Storey, John, ed. *What is Cultural Studies? A Reader.* New York: Arnold, 1997.

Varsava, Jerry A. *Contingent Meanings: Postmodern Fiction, Mimesis and the Reader.* Tallahassee: Florida State University Press, 1990.

Walsh, William J. *Speak So I Shall Know Thee: Interviews with Southern Writers.* Jefferson, N.C.: McFarland Publishers, 1990.

Watkins, James, ed. *Southern Selves: From Mark Twain and Eudora Welty to Maya Angelou and Kaye Gibbons.* New York: Vintage, 1998.

Weinstein, Arnold. *Nobody's Home: Speech, Self, and Place in American Fiction from Hawthorne to DeLillo.* New York: Oxford University Press, 1993.

Wolf, Margery. *A Thrice-Told Tale: Feminism, Postmodernism, and Ethnographic Responsibility.* Stanford: Stanford University Press, 1992.

Contributors

Lisa Abney . . . . *Northwestern State University*

Austin Booth . . . . *SUNY Buffalo*

Keith E. Byerman . . . . *Indiana State University*

Jean W. Cash . . . . *James Madison University*

Laurie Champion . . . . *San Diego State University, Imperial Valley*

J. Elizabeth Clark . . . . *LaGuardia Community College*

Kate Cochran . . . . *Northern Kentucky University*

J. Rocky Colavito . . . . *Northwestern State University*

Cecelia Conway . . . .*Appalachian State University*

Suzanne Disheroon-Green . . . . *Northwestern State University*

Barbara Ewell . . . . *Northwestern State University*

Susan Farrell . . . . *College of Charleston*

Roy C. Flannagan . . . . *South Carolina Governor's School for Science and Mathematics*

Jeffery K. Guin . . . . *Provencal, Louisiana*

Joan Wylie Hall . . . . *University of Mississippi*

Roxanne Harde . . . . *Queen's University*

Carol E. Henderson . . . . *University of Delaware*

Anne K. Jones . . . . *Natchitoches, Louisiana*

Paul Christian Jones . . . . *Ohio University*

Eileen A. Joy . . . . *Southern Illinois University–Edwardsville*

Julie Kane . . . . *Northwestern State University*

Persis M. Karim . . . . *San José State University*

Susie Scifres Kuilan . . . . *Louisiana State University*

Suzanne Leonard . . . . *University of Wisconsin–Milwaukee*

Lisa A. Kirkpatrick Lundy . . . . *University of North Texas*

D. Mesher . . . . *San José State University*

Betsy Bryan Miguez . . . . *University of Louisiana at Lafayette*

Robin Miller . . . . *Pineville, Louisiana*

Ashley Minton . . . . *Pineville, Louisiana*

Michael R. Molino . . . . *Southern Illinois University*

Jeffrey F. L. Partridge . . . . *Central Connecticut State University*

Lori Rowlett . . . . *University of Wisconsin–Eau Claire*

Heather Salter . . . . *Northwestern State University*

Joseph Schaub . . . .*Newberry College*

Stephen Spencer . . . . *Wilmington College*

Robert D. Sturr . . . . *Kent State University, Stark Campus*

Nathan G. Tipton . . . . *University of Memphis*

Jennifer Vance . . . . *Hoover, Alabama*

Cumulative Index

Dictionary of Literary Biography, Volumes 1-292
Dictionary of Literary Biography Yearbook, 1980-2002
Dictionary of Literary Biography Documentary Series, Volumes 1-19
Concise Dictionary of American Literary Biography, Volumes 1-7
Concise Dictionary of British Literary Biography, Volumes 1-8
Concise Dictionary of World Literary Biography, Volumes 1-4

Cumulative Index

DLB before number: *Dictionary of Literary Biography,* Volumes 1-292
Y before number: *Dictionary of Literary Biography Yearbook,* 1980-2002
DS before number: *Dictionary of Literary Biography Documentary Series,* Volumes 1-19
CDALB before number: *Concise Dictionary of American Literary Biography,* Volumes 1-7
CDBLB before number: *Concise Dictionary of British Literary Biography,* Volumes 1-8
CDWLB before number: *Concise Dictionary of World Literary Biography,* Volumes 1-4

B

G

H

K

L

MacLaverty, Bernard 1942- DLB-267

MacLean, Alistair 1922-1987 . . . . .DLB-276

MacLean, Katherine Anne 1925- DLB-8

Maclean, Norman 1902-1990 . . . . .DLB-206

MacLeish, Archibald 1892-1982
. . . . . . DLB-4, 7, 45; Y-82; DS-15; CDALB-7

MacLennan, Hugh 1907-1990 . . . . .DLB-68

MacLeod, Alistair 1936- DLB-60

Macleod, Fiona (see Sharp, William)

Macleod, Norman 1906-1985 . . . . .DLB-4

Mac Low, Jackson 1922- DLB-193

Macmillan and Company DLB-106

The Macmillan Company DLB-49

Macmillan's English Men of Letters,
First Series (1878-1892) DLB-144

MacNamara, Brinsley 1890-1963 . . . . . . .DLB-10

MacNeice, Louis 1907-1963 . . . . .DLB-10, 20

Macphail, Andrew 1864-1938 . . . . .DLB-92

Macpherson, James 1736-1796 . . . . .DLB-109

Macpherson, Jay 1931- DLB-53

Macpherson, Jeanie 1884-1946 . . . . .DLB-44

Macrae Smith Company DLB-46

MacRaye, Lucy Betty (see Webling, Lucy)

John Macrone [publishing house] DLB-106

MacShane, Frank 1927-1999 . . . . .DLB-111

Macy-Masius DLB-46

Madden, David 1933- DLB-6

Madden, Sir Frederic 1801-1873 . . . . . . .DLB-184

Maddow, Ben 1909-1992 . . . . .DLB-44

Maddux, Rachel 1912-1983 . . . . . .DLB-234; Y-93

Madgett, Naomi Long 1923- DLB-76

Madhubuti, Haki R. 1942- DLB-5, 41; DS-8

Madison, James 1751-1836 . . . . .DLB-37

Madsen, Svend Åge 1939- DLB-214

Madrigal, Alfonso Fernández de (El Tostado)
ca. 1405-1455 . . . . .DLB-286

Maeterlinck, Maurice 1862-1949 . . . . . . .DLB-192

Mafūz, Najīb 1911- Y-88

Nobel Lecture 1988 . . . . Y-88

The Little Magazines of the
New Formalism DLB-282

Magee, David 1905-1977 . . . . .DLB-187

Maginn, William 1794-1842 . . . . . .DLB-110, 159

Magoffin, Susan Shelby 1827-1855 . . . . . .DLB-239

Mahan, Alfred Thayer 1840-1914 . . . . . . .DLB-47

Maheux-Forcier, Louise 1929- DLB-60

Mahin, John Lee 1902-1984 . . . . .DLB-44

Mahon, Derek 1941- DLB-40

Maikov, Apollon Nikolaevich
1821-1897 .DLB-277

Maikov, Vasilii Ivanovich 1728-1778 . . . . .DLB-150

Mailer, Norman 1923-
. . . . . . DLB-2, 16, 28, 185, 278; Y-80, 83, 97;
DS-3; CDALB-6

Tribute to Isaac Bashevis Singer Y-91

Tribute to Meyer Levin Y-81

Maillart, Ella 1903-1997 . . . . .DLB-195

Maillet, Adrienne 1885-1963 . . . . .DLB-68

Maillet, Antonine 1929- DLB-60

Maillu, David G. 1939- DLB-157

Maimonides, Moses 1138-1204 . . . . .DLB-115

Main Selections of the Book-of-the-Month
Club, 1926-1945 . . . . .DLB-9

Mainwaring, Daniel 1902-1977 . . . . .DLB-44

Mair, Charles 1838-1927 . . . . .DLB-99

Mair, John circa 1467-1550 . . . . .DLB-281

Maironis, Jonas 1862-1932 . . DLB-220; CDWLB-4

Mais, Roger 1905-1955 . . . . .DLB-125; CDWLB-3

Maitland, Sara 1950- DLB-271

Major, Andre 1942- DLB-60

Major, Charles 1856-1913 . . . . .DLB-202

Major, Clarence 1936- DLB-33

Major, Kevin 1949- DLB-60

Major Books DLB-46

Makanin, Vladimir Semenovich
1937- DLB-285

Makarenko, Anton Semenovich
1888-1939 .DLB-272

Makemie, Francis circa 1658-1708 . . . . . . .DLB-24

The Making of Americans Contract Y-98

Maksimović, Desanka
1898-1993 . . . . DLB-147; CDWLB-4

Malamud, Bernard 1914-1986
. . . . DLB-2, 28, 152; Y-80, 86; CDALB-1

Bernard Malamud Archive at the
Harry Ransom Humanities
Research Center Y-00

Mălăncioiu, Ileana 1940- DLB-232

Malaparte, Curzio
(Kurt Erich Suckert) 1898-1957 . . . . .DLB-264

Malerba, Luigi 1927- DLB-196

Malet, Lucas 1852-1931 . . . . .DLB-153

Mallarmé, Stéphane 1842-1898 . . . . .DLB-217

Malleson, Lucy Beatrice (see Gilbert, Anthony)

Mallet-Joris, Françoise (Françoise Lilar)
1930- DLB-83

Mallock, W. H. 1849-1923 . . . . .DLB-18, 57

"Every Man His Own Poet; or,
The Inspired Singer's Recipe
Book" (1877) DLB-35

"Le Style c'est l'homme" (1892) DLB-57

Memoirs of Life and Literature (1920),
[excerpt] .DLB-57

Malone, Dumas 1892-1986 . . . . .DLB-17

Malone, Edmond 1741-1812 . . . . .DLB-142

Malory, Sir Thomas
circa 1400-1410 - 1471 . . . .DLB-146; CDBLB-1

Malouf, David 1934- DLB-289

Malpede, Karen 1945- DLB-249

Malraux, André 1901-1976 . . . . .DLB-72

Malthus, Thomas Robert
1766-1834 . . . . DLB-107, 158

Maltz, Albert 1908-1985 . . . . .DLB-102

Malzberg, Barry N. 1939- DLB-8

Mamet, David 1947- DLB-7

Mamin, Dmitrii Narkisovich 1852-1912 . .DLB-238

Manaka, Matsemela 1956- DLB-157

Manchester University Press DLB-112

Mandel, Eli 1922-1992 . . . . .DLB-53

Mandeville, Bernard 1670-1733 . . . . .DLB-101

Mandeville, Sir John
mid fourteenth century DLB-146

Mandiargues, André Pieyre de
1909-1991 . . . . .DLB-83

Manea, Norman 1936- DLB-232

Manfred, Frederick 1912-1994 . . . DLB-6, 212, 227

Manfredi, Gianfranco 1948- DLB-196

Mangan, Sherry 1904-1961 . . . . .DLB-4

Manganelli, Giorgio 1922-1990 . . . . .DLB-196

Manilius fl. first century A.D. DLB-211

Mankiewicz, Herman 1897-1953 . . . . . . .DLB-26

Mankiewicz, Joseph L. 1909-1993 . . . . . . .DLB-44

Mankowitz, Wolf 1924-1998 . . . . .DLB-15

Manley, Delarivière 1672?-1724 . . . . .DLB-39, 80

Preface to *The Secret History, of Queen
Zarah, and the Zarazians* (1705) DLB-39

Mann, Abby 1927- DLB-44

Mann, Charles 1929-1998 . . . . Y-98

Mann, Emily 1952- DLB-266

Mann, Heinrich 1871-1950 . . . . DLB-66, 118

Mann, Horace 1796-1859 . . . . .DLB-1, 235

Mann, Klaus 1906-1949 . . . . .DLB-56

Mann, Mary Peabody 1806-1887 . . . . . . .DLB-239

Mann, Thomas 1875-1955 . . . .DLB-66; CDWLB-2

Mann, William D'Alton 1839-1920 . . . . . .DLB-137

Mannin, Ethel 1900-1984 . . . . .DLB-191, 195

Manning, Emily (see Australie)

Manning, Frederic 1882-1935 . . . . .DLB-260

Manning, Laurence 1899-1972 . . . . .DLB-251

Manning, Marie 1873?-1945 . . . . .DLB-29

Manning and Loring DLB-49

Mannyng, Robert flourished 1303-1338 . .DLB-146

Mano, D. Keith 1942- DLB-6

Manor Books DLB-46

Manrique, Gómez 1412?-1490 . . . . .DLB-286

Manrique, Jorge ca. 1440-1479 . . . . .DLB-286

Mansfield, Katherine 1888-1923 . . . . . . .DLB-162

Mantel, Hilary 1952- DLB-271

Manuel, Niklaus circa 1484-1530 . . . . . . .DLB-179

Manzini, Gianna 1896-1974 . . . . .DLB-177

Mapanje, Jack 1944- DLB-157

Maraini, Dacia 1936- DLB-196

March, William (William Edward Campbell)
1893-1954 . . . . .DLB-9, 86

Marchand, Leslie A. 1900-1999 . . . . .DLB-103

Marchant, Bessie 1862-1941 . . . . .DLB-160

Marchant, Tony 1959- DLB-245

Marchenko, Anastasiia Iakovlevna
1830-1880 .DLB-238

Marchessault, Jovette 1938- DLB-60

Marcinkevičius, Justinas 1930- DLB-232

Cumulative Index

ISBN 0-7876-6829-X

90000